KW-051-138

PERCEPTION
AND
ARTISTIC STYLE

ADVANCES IN PSYCHOLOGY

73

Editors:

G. E. STELMACH

P. A. VROON

NORTH-HOLLAND
AMSTERDAM • NEW YORK • OXFORD • TOKYO

PERCEPTION AND ARTISTIC STYLE

D.M. PARKER
University of Aberdeen
Scotland

J.B. DERĘGOWSKI
University of Aberdeen
Scotland

1990

NORTH-HOLLAND
AMSTERDAM • NEW YORK • OXFORD • TOKYO

NORTH-HOLLAND
ELSEVIER SCIENCE PUBLISHERS B.V.
Sara Burgerhartstraat 25
P.O. Box 211, 1000 AE Amsterdam, The Netherlands

Distributors for the United States and Canada:
ELSEVIER SCIENCE PUBLISHING COMPANY, INC.
655 Avenue of the Americas
New York, N.Y. 10010, U.S.A.

Library of Congress Cataloging-in-Publication Data

Parker, D. M.
Perception and artistic style / D.M. Parker, J.B. Deręgowski.
p. cm. -- (Advances in psychology ; 73)
Includes bibliographical references and indexes.
ISBN 0-444-88702-4
1. Art--Psychology. 2. Visual perception. I. Title.
II. Series: Advances in psychology (Amsterdam, Netherlands) ; 73.
N71.P27 1990
701'.15--dc20 90-14154
CIP

ISBN: 0 444 88702 4

Printed in The Netherlands

PREFACE

The ideas in this book owe a great deal to Władysław Strzemiński's *Teoria Widzenia* (Theory of Vision). In discussing his ideas we have been led into many interesting avenues and our ideas about the processes of making and viewing pictures have been changed. This work, which took Strzemiński's views as its starting point, sets out an approach to the influence that purely visual factors may exert in the process of picture making and deliberately avoids issues of symbolism and iconography; the latter area in particular has been explored in a wealth of texts by art historians over the last fifty years. We are concerned with pictures as a record of the artist's *visual* experience and how this might be interpreted by the viewer. How perceptual processes influence the creation and viewing of pictures are our major concern.

The range of the book is then extensive but of course it comments on only one aspect of painting. If this statement appears self-contradictory the reader should reflect on the enormous range of socio-cultural and psychological factors which impinge on a work of art's production; perhaps it would then become apparent why a work may be extensive but cover only a fraction of a possible area of study.

The preliminary draft of this book was prepared during the second author's Fellowship of the Netherlands Institute for Advanced Studies in Humanities and Social Sciences in Wassenaar. Thanks are therefore due to the Institute and in particular to two members of its staff - Miss Dinny Young, the librarian, who ensured a continual and rapid flow of books and publications and whose interest in the slow progress being made was most encouraging; and to Sra. P. van Breda who translated Italian and Spanish texts and typed the first version. The opinions of other Fellows at the Institute extended from that of Professor Albert Dunning who thought the book "the most idiosyncratic project of the year" and provided an excellent dinner, to that of Professor Jan Strelau, who thought that "there may be something in it" and extended an invitation to visit the University of Warsaw; this in turn enabled consultation of various Polish publications location of which would not however been possible without the kindness of Mrs L. Rosak. Also in the Netherlands, but outwith the Institute, Dr. J.A.F. de Rijk, read a first draft and encouraged its further progress. Pieter Huybers and Gerrit van der Ende of the Delft University of Technology provided the computer simulations of the pinhole camera photographs which we used in Chapter 6 and which we gratefully acknowledge.

In Aberdeen, Drs Dziurawiec and N.E. Wetherick kindly read and commented on the draft, and Dr R. Lishman gladly shared his expertise in computing which in particular allowed us to gain an interesting insight into Wolfflin's idea of a linear-painterly dimension in art. Miss Helen Cable, Miss Elaine Duncan and Miss Ann Wiggins prepared the various versions of the manuscript enduring repeated changes which required reformatting of the text. Mr Peter Bates worked tirelessly on the many drawings and figures which are included in this book and we owe him a particular debt of gratitude. Mr Alex Jaffrey prepared many of the photographic plates. We were particularly fortunate to have such talented and flexible technical assistance available to us. At various times Dr R. H. Logie gave willing assistance when problems arose with formatting the final version of the text. Of course we are indepted to all the technical staff of the Department who enabled the new empirical work, reported at various points in the book, to be carried out. Particular thanks in the regard are due to Mr Eddie Stephen who led the technical support team in what were very difficult circumstances for the Department and the University.

We are indebted to Professor Santiago Sebastian of the University of Valencia for providing us with a copy of Figure 4.9, to Dr Franco Mezzena for Figures 6.4 and 6.5, to Mr S.M. Deręgowski for the mathematical deduction given in the notes and to Mrs E. Deręgowska who assisted with the proof reading of the manuscript.

Since the funds for the journey to Poland, were provided by the Scottish Carnegie Foundation the book has in the course of its development become an international enterprise. And so it should be.

Yet, an apology is also in order: work on this volume inevitably retarded other work; it is hoped that M.M. Kurdelebele will accept this as the only reason for the second author's tardiness concerning the joint study of Bushman Art, and Dr Laurent Mottron will wait a little longer for the first author's contribution to the study of perceptual processes in idiot-savants.

CONTENTS

Figure 1.1 J. van Eyck. "The marriage of Giovanni Arnolfini and Giovanna Cenami". (Reproduced by courtesy of the Trustees, The National Gallery).

Chapter I

The Naive And The Sophisticated Eye

Artists produce their work in particular places at particular times. Consequently it is inevitable that cultural context will influence their choice of subject, its mode of representation and the nature and range of symbol, allegory and allusion within the picture. If one examines carefully the picture shown in Figure 1.1, Jan van Eyck's portrait of Giovani Arnolfini and his wife Giovanna de Cenami, it soon becomes apparent that one is dealing with more than a fifteenth century snapshot. The painting shows in detail the interior of a room in which a man and woman stand. The mood is formal, almost austere and the gestures give the appearance of having being carefully arranged to convey to the viewer something of significance. In the centre of the picture the hands of the man and woman are joined and the man's right hand is raised to indicate that some kind of solemn and legally significant statement is being made. Peering closely at the picture we can distinguish rings on the woman's left hand. The bed on the right, the single candle burning in the elaborate chandelier despite the fact that the events are taking place in daylight, and the presence of the little dog (a late medieval symbol of fidelity) all reinforce the view that one is reading a carefully constructed pictorial document which indeed has been formally attested "Johannes de Eyck fuit hic 1434" (above mirror centre). The picture in fact bears witness to a legal marriage[1].

Turning from the iconological aspects, which have only been sampled superficially above, it is clear that at the purely visual level the painting is a feast. Each object and texture in the room has been explored carefully and rendered in a pleasing harmony of tone and colour. A sense of space has been evoked by effective (but inconsistent) use of linear perspective and by the curved mirror which both intensifies the sense of depth and allows the witnesses to the ceremony to make their appearance. In studying the picture it becomes obvious that in order to provoke the humanistic and religious echoes which the artist desires, he must negotiate the particular paths which the visual mechanism allows. We can distinguish the specific devices the artist used to instigate the viewer's perceptions, his style, from the thematic content of the picture. Style and content can be seen to be independent of each other and viewers may be moved by either, even though in the greatest works the two aspects harmonise and complement each other. In reviewing the course of art's history it is clear that at certain times thematic and other times stylistic aspects of art have attained primacy. In medieval religious art the symbolic and allegorical aspects could charm the cognoscenti while the concrete features of the images could instil simple devotion in the intellectually pedestrian. In modernist works however it is frequently the purely visual aspects of the painting which captivate the viewer.

Visual works of art must then be approached with care since different artists and different ages developed their own conventions and had different aims. It is impossible to formulate general rules that would allow any work of art regardless of the time or place of inception to be read like a page of print. Some works, such as those of the seventeenth century master Nicolas Poussin, are frequently deeply intellectual, while in others such as those of the modernist Victor Vasarely (Chapter IX) the purely visual element is primary. Despite these reservations there are certain aspects of visual art which can profitably be explored regardless of the historical or social constraints under which it occurred. This is because the immediate origins of pictorial art lie in the visual process itself and so it is this medium which contributes substantially to the range of stylistic variation which has been found in picturemaking. An examination of some of the intrinsic characteristics of the eye (eye used here as a shorthand for the entire visual perceptual system), leads to an enhanced appreciation of some of the limitations and subtleties of painting.

The word style, as used in pictorial art, refers to all those aspects of painting which allow particular works to be assigned to a time and place and, ultimately, a particular hand. Thus it can include the content of a painting, the objects, the people, the kind of landscape as well as the way the picture space is represented, the use of colour and the way in which the paint is applied. The term includes then many dimensions which allows it to be linked to a range of adjectives which confer a varying degree of precision, for example 15th century Flemish style, High Cubist Style, American Primitive Style, Baroque style etc, as well as to specific artists, for example, in the style of Raphael or even a critical grouping of techniques, for example "linear" or "painterly". An examination of all these dimensions is obviously outside the scope of any book, but in any case we are concerned only with the contribution of visual perception to the generation and viewing of pictorial art. Because of this we can only contribute to elucidating a single dimension of artistic style. We have chosen to confine our discussion largely to the examination of what are broadly the spatial properties of painting; the way in which space and object are represented and how these reveal the sensitivity of artists to the vagaries of the system which realises their art. Our view is essentially ahistorical. To illustrate our thesis paintings and drawings have been chosen because they embody particular stylistic features. This is not to deny that works of art can be grouped into schools, and that these schools mutually influence each other. However we would argue that an alternative grouping is possible where painters could be arrayed according to the visual characteristics they employed and such an arrangement would be as valid as any historical or geographical arrangement. For example Japanese artists of the 19th century became as obsessed by linear perspective as Italian Rennaissance artists were. Despite this theoretical independence, artistic style does not appear to have shown itself to be randomly associated with the progression of history. When one looks at the broad sweep of western painting from medieval to modern times one is struck by one glaring trend. Medieval art used a restricted range of depth cues and was, in modern pictorial terms, rather flat. Even with a restricted field of view, such as looking at the picture through a cardboard tube (simply a device which enhances perception of pictorial depth), one is never in any doubt that one is looking at a two dimensional surface. With the discovery of the rules of perspective and the incorporation of other cues indicative of distance (discussed at length in Chapter 2), the paintings of the high Renaissance presented the viewer with a surface "through" which one views a scene. Indeed, during the later Baroque period the incorporation of trompe l'oeil devices in picture to perceptually "break" the surface of the canvas and further involve the viewer in the scene was a frequent occurrence used among others by Caravaggio and Rembrandt. Familiar as we are with high quality images in the late 20th century we should not blind ourselves to the evocative power of these Renaissance works. This tendency to express ideas or simply charm the eye by giving the pictorial surface a veneer of reality persisted broadly for three hundred years. But consciousness of the medium itself appears gradually to have asserted itself and the interplay of the painter, the picture surface and the viewer became increasingly the object of artistic concern. Probably as early as 1800, with the impact of the revolutionary images of Turner, the tide had already turned and an increasing analysis of the medium and its perception by the viewer began. Just as Quattrocento painters turned to the scientific analysis of spatial projection to aid their expression, so increasingly during the nineteenth century artists capitalised on the experimental analysis of vision to achieve innovative styles. With contemporary paintings it is sometimes difficult to tell whether one is confronting a work of art or whether one has inadvertently strayed into the laboratory of a visual scientist.

This view, however simplistic, does enable one to see a thread which has run through artistic endeavour over the last five hundred years. Inevitably the characteristics of the eye have been of concern to visual artists. The thesis that one of the essential features of artistic style consists of the particular characteristics of the eye's mechanisms that the painter chooses to explore is however an idea that has not been extensively examined although, as will become clear in the course of this text, it has been implicit in the work of a number of commentators. A source of this idea was the work of W. Strzemiński, whose *Teoria Widzenia*[2] (Theory of Vision) proposed the notion of the importance of the eye's mechanisms in artistic style and pictorial perception which is developed here. Traces of his argument are used in attempts to relate various characteristics of the eye to art, but his idea that the usage of these characteristics and hence artistic styles followed an organised historical sequence is not entertained. This is because his historical thesis, which is based on Marxist-Leninist principles, appears to be entirely, disingenuous and indeed, as we have already indicated, the approach favoured here is essentially ahistorical.

Our concern then will be the eye and its relation to observable variations in artistic style. As already intimated we will take the eye to include the perceptual system, in its neural and cognitive aspects, associated with the process of seeing. Having said this however we must make a further decision as to what theoretical view of the eye we wish to adopt. Broadly speaking there are two opposing theories of how we come to perceive our visual world veridically. One view regards the eye as providing sensations from which the brain and/or mind constructs a representation of the world, usually by associating patterns of sensation with each other so that eventually we see the world more or less as it really is. Thus to borrow a phrase from the philosopher/psychologist William James the infant is initially conscious only of a "big, booming, buzzing confusion". The brain/mind through a process of learning imposes order on this chaos and in doing so achieves a mature harmony between the individual and environment. In this view the process of seeing is really a matter of "sophisticated sensation", but it is a view which we reject!

The alternative position takes as its starting point an evolutionary view of human vision. Non-human species have at their disposal systems for seeing, hearing, feeling etc. which are appropriate to enable them to survive in a dangerous world. Not only can the new-born wildebeest run within a short time of birth but it is capable of detecting and staying close to its mother. The honey bee does not need to learn to use the sun or the plane of polarisation of light to navigate successfully through its environment. This skill is part of its natural endowment. In an analogous way human infants have the kind of mechanism for seeing that is attuned, not to the detection of simple sensory qualities like light or dark or vague distributions of luminance, but rather to the detection of faces, objects, people etc. The system is not fully developed at birth but it is already, at the neonatal stage, attuned to the world rather than to sensory qualities. Neonates may thus turn their eyes in the direction of sounds or even in some circumstances imitate the facial gestures of adults. The world is evidently less confusing for them than it is to certain sophisticated philosophers since these infants are really "naive perceivers".

It is this latter view of the eye we have adopted here, not only because it accords with the balance of evidence but because it nicely coincides with everyday experience. So powerful is our immediate awareness of our visual environment that it is often difficult to explain to the new student of perception the problems faced by our visual system in providing us with our stable extended world. The very difficulties found by pictorial artists in developing perspective representation of their chosen scenes, which sometimes involved prolonged training and sometimes opticomechanical aids (such as those used by Dürer and Vermeer), attests to problems of overcoming what the eye perceives in order to arrive at an approximation of what the retina senses. This tension between what is sensed and what is perceived has been one acutely felt by many artists since they are by natural endowment "naive perceivers" and, by training, "sophisticated sensors". In the ensuing pages we endeavour to explore some of the consequences of this tension.

Our remarks about the perceptual abilities of the newly born might suggest that we incline towards a perceptual theory similar to that associated with Gibson[3] or perhaps with one of his precursors. Our view of the Gibsonian theory will therefore be briefly examined. Gibson maintains that information about the surrounding world consists of the invariants which the observer can derive from the environment, and which convey directly what the environment is like. These invariants tell the observer about the surfaces of the forms which he encounters, their mutual relationships and their relationships to him. His is a theory concerned with an active animal which explores the environment using all his senses, and which therefore has little time for such analytic studies of perception as have traditionally been practised in the psychological laboratories and which yielded many of the concepts discussed in the next chapter.

Our view is however that an analysis which extends beyond Gibson's general theory and which is specifically concerned with perceptual mechanisms is essential not only for a proper understanding of perceptual processes, but also to allow us to unravel those operations on which successful pictorial representation ultimately depends. In addition there are two problems specifically concerned with the perception of pictures which make it necessary to take a wider perspective than that adopted by Gibson. First, pictures which are recognised by the viewer as representing aspects of the visual world provide two mutually contradictory types of invariants, one indicating the flatness of their surfaces and another showing that they represent objects which are not flat. Second, the invariants pertaining to the objects depicted in pictures do not form a homogeneous category. Gibsonian invariants are essentially spatial and connected with the "affordances" which a particular object provides (such as this is edible, this can be sat upon). It is difficult therefore to apply this notion to pictorial figures which although labelled correctly by perceivers are not seen as having volume, because they contain only a sample of the perceptual properties which solid objects provide.

It is easy to create a picture that, although it portrays a readily recognisable three-dimensional object, contains no direct perceptual cues as to the object's solidity, and is generally seen as flat. Such is the case with stick and silhouette drawings. These pictures are termed epitomic. They fail to evoke an experience of three dimensional space and therefore lack the basic ingredient of reality. They cannot be mistaken for objects because they do not depict specific objects, but abstractions of objects and they are of necessity representational in nature.

Epitomic pictures differ fundamentally from eidolic[4] pictures, which have a readily apprehensible spatial quality, providing the viewer with a strong impression of spatial depth. However, they do not necessarily represent any known object. Perception of eidolicity guarantees neither correctness nor viability of the percept, indeed, a figure may be seen as wrong because of its eidolic quality, as is the case with the well known Escher pictures showing impossible buildings and waterfalls defying the laws of gravity.

The distinction between epitomic and eidolic pictures divides the category which Gibson thought homogeneous, since he postulated that all pictures, including those of stick-figures, are displays of invariants which are nameless and formless and are derived from observation of depicted objects[5]. A picture, according to him, is a surface which furnishes an optic array of invariants to the observer. It is a product of an art of depiction which is arrived at by the fortuitous discovery that certain scribbles yield invariants that coincide with invariants derived from real objects. However, this does not seem to be the case. Gibson maintains that since the times of Cro-Magnon man drawings have been found in all cultures. Indeed one would expect it to be so if his outlined theory of the origin of drawings were true. Unfortunately for the theory this is not so, as anthropological data show. Fortes describes drawings obtained from a population which he studied in the 1930's and which knew no pictorial art. When he requested the Tallensi (of the then Gold Coast, now Ghana) to draw, they did so, initially, scribbling on paper, but when enjoined to draw something they abandoned their scribbles and set purposefully to the task, making epitomic, stick-like drawings. There was no suggestion in their behaviour of stumbling accidentally on such drawings and of experiencing a chance discovery of a complex of invariants similar to those which could be derived from objects in their environment. Their act of drawing was a deliberate act and their first figures are deliberate reflections of their intentions. They did not regard their primarily epitomic stick figures as duplicates of depicted objects. This observation may agree with another of Gibson's tenets, that a picture does not create an illusion of reality. But even this support for his view is illusory, for one would not expect an epitomic picture to create an illusion, and there is ample evidence showing that pictures incorporating both eidolic and epitomic cues can be mistaken for depicted objects[6]. Further, and very cogent, evidence for the ability of pictures to evoke an illusion of reality is provided by animal studies; surely when an ape, whose visual system is as sophisticated as humans, makes an attempt to pick up a pictorially depicted insect it is because she has mistaken it for a morsel and has been deceived by the two-dimensional representation.

This distinction between these two types of drawing has certain implications for the use of Piagetian[7] analogies to explain development in art, such as those put forward by Gablik and by Blatt. The essential idea here is that the development of artistic sophistication with cultural changes depends on the same psychological factors which are involved in cognitive growth from infancy to adulthood. Both these authors concern themselves primarily with the changes in eidolic aspects of depiction. However it could be said that the epitomic aspects, because they involve more generalised images, are closer to the abilities of abstraction with which Piaget was concerned. The Piagetian analogy can also be questioned because Piaget's theory deals with the entire cognitive development of an individual whereas the analogy, used by Gablik and Blatt concerns art only and ignores the fact that very complex notions in other areas of human endeavour flourished at levels incompatible with that of art. For example the philosophical, theological and indeed scientific ideas which flourished during the Ancient and Medieval period, can hardly be described as "pre-operational" in nature, yet they were contemporaneous with works of art judged to display "topological relations" and thus characteristic of the "pre-operational stage" in Piagetian theory. General theories of perception or of cognitive development do not appear to provide particularly useful insights into the nature of artistic endeavour.

The two conceptually distinct characteristics of drawings which have been introduced above, the epitomic and eidolic, although seldom found in their pure form, as most drawings present a blend of both, are psychologically important, as is the relationship between them within any picture. It may well be that the epitomic figures, which were so spontaneously drawn by pictorially unsophisticated Tallensi, have particular psychological and historical significance[8]. These figures were an element of the earliest cave decorations and paralleled closely the visually more striking and therefore more generally admired eidolic pictures. Both "pin" and "silhouette" representations are to be found in the Altamira and in the Lascaux caves, and are characteristic of later palaeolithic Iberian and North African art where they are used to depict the daily activities of people such as hunting or honey gathering; and because they involve interactions among portrayed figures, they are imbued with a greater symbolic value than those eidolic pictures which merely portray single animals[6].

It is apparent then that pictorial representations may vary considerably in their visual sophistication from skeletal scratching to richly textured images evocative of a particular place and a specific time. Realisation of this fact makes it obvious that the act of pictorial depiction can sample an enormous range of possible devices in which epitomic and eidolic aspects can be emphasised or blended. It would be difficult, if not impossible, for any one perceptual theory to encompass the range of pictorial representations which are possible. Thus the Gibsonian view would emphasise invariants in the optical array which the artist chances upon, while the Gestalt approach would stress the organism's preference for well-structured forms.

Our view is more eclectic. Perception is a complex process which can be viewed as being designed to ensure the harmony of the human species and its environment. It is supported by physiological and cognitive mechanisms which we do not have to be aware of to ensure their operation. Nevertheless these mechanisms have been of interest not only to visual scientists but to those who have striven to capture aspects of the visual world or to project their ideas by evoking visual echoes. Painters and draughtsmen in developing their skills and exploring their medium of expression have inevitably encountered many of the distortions and illusions by which the viewer's perceptions are manipulated. Their obsession with a particular medium has led them to study its vicissitudes closely. Consequently it is not surprising that they have manipulated perceptual mechanisms unknown to the ordinary "naive perceiver". Many of these would be considered "unnatural" or "ecologically invalid" by Gibsonians since they would be seen as deriving from the two-dimensional view limited "frame" that the artist has chosen. We, on the other hand, regard them as perfectly natural attempts to exploit the possible range of visual experience which an artist may encounter and may wish to introduce to the viewer.

As a final preparation before commencing our exploration of the influence of visual perception on artistic style perhaps we should consider the schematic structure of our visual system (see

Figure 1.2). When we examine a visual scene two inverted images of the scene, which are slightly disparate, are projected on to the retinas of our eyes. These retinal images are in one sense ideal constructions since our eyes are always in motion and hence an optical image which is stationary over time is not provided. But in a very real sense these retinal images form a basis for our perception of the world. A great deal of information can be obtained in a single instantaneous glance. If the reader doubts this, all that is required to support this statement is to take a photographic flashgun into a dark room and fire it once. In this brief illumination (less than a thousandth of a second) colour, pattern and depth will be seen and yet all of this information must be derived from a single static glance at the scene. The importance of the retinal image for the visual scientist is that the majority of our knowledge of the visual world must be obtained via it, so it must transmit a rich informational array to support the richness of our visual experience. For some artists the retinal image has provided a conceptual basis for our visual experience. Some of its properties may be mimicked in the perspective projection, or the tonal gradation, or the degree of definition of the various regions of the picture which appears on the canvas. By viewing the canvas the spectator may capture something of the idealised "glance" that the artist has selected.

However, we as perceivers are not designed to examine retinal images; rather the retinal images are there to provide the basis of our visual world. We are not normally conscious of the distortions in the optical projections or the limitations in detail provided by the retina over much of the field of view. We are aware of spatial extent, relative sizes, surface textures, properties, etc. of real objects and their position in the external world. A book lying on the table in front of us is perceived as a rectangular object of a certain size and colour rather than a trapezium projecting a number of wavelengths. Nor does it appear to change dramatically in size as we move our head towards or away from it. We can, particularly if we close one eye, become aware that there are projective changes which occur with changes in our position, although we would be likely seriously to underestimate their extent. The information we pick up via our eyes provides us with the support we require to maintain a stable visual world. As we have said before, this stable extended property of the visual world is so immediate that we require time and training to detect part of its basis in the distorted views our eyes can obtain.

The ability of the higher processes in our visual systems to recover the visual structure of the external world is obviously based on their sensitivity to the properties of the optical projection, both static and dynamic. Some of the static properties, which can be used in painting, are discussed in Chapter 2. Through an analysis of the information in the optical projection the visual system constructs a view-specific representation of the external world. This representation has the distortions inherent in the retinal image removed and, within it, objects have been subjected to constancy scaling. For example, even though one person may be standing twice as far away from me as another, one at say two metres and the other at four metres, the more distant person does not appear to be half the height of the nearer one despite the fact that in the retinal image this is so. Thus we have available to us a representation of the world which is specific to our current viewpoint. This representation is visually speaking extremely rich; colour, texture, depth and pattern are all available. However it is limited by what we can actually see rather than what we know. We see the front of a person who stands immediately facing us; a book lying before us on the table has three sides visible. The view-specific representation is as its name implies just view-specific, limited by the particular stance of the observer at a moment in time, even though the observer may know more about the visual world than is currently visible to them.

Obviously what is currently visible forms only a part of what we know about the visual world. We know the person who stands before us has a back as well as a front and the book lying on the table has six sides even though only three are currently visible. What we know then goes beyond what we see.

If we choose we can verify our knowledge by walking around the person or picking up the book. If we decide to make a drawing of a person that includes both a frontal and profile view, as a cubist artist might, clearly we are going beyond what is possible in immediate visual experience. Either we would draw one profile and then walk around the person and draw the other, creating the two views in whatever way we choose on the paper or else we would have to remember the features of the other side of the face and reproduce them in our drawing. In either case we would have stepped outside the view-specific constraints in order to attain the image we desired.

It is evident when we look at the tranformation of the optically based information which occurs in our visual systems that the range of representational devices available to visual artists are very wide indeed. The artist may strive to produce a picture which despite its two dimensional structure will contain information leading to the impression of depth. In order to do this successfully some basic properties of the optical projection must be incorporated into the painting (the artist must be sensitive to the properties of A in Figure 1.2). Alternatively the artist may ignore the rules of optics (through ignorance or deliberate choice) and paint a representation that reflects his immediate view-specific experience. Such a picture will have a spatial construction very different from the other but will not provide any problems of recognition for the viewer (the artist will work at level B of Figure 1.2). However the artist is quite free to ignore both optical constraints and view-specific constraints and

build the picture from several different views or even incorporate information from visual memory (the artist will work at level C of Figure 1.2) [9].

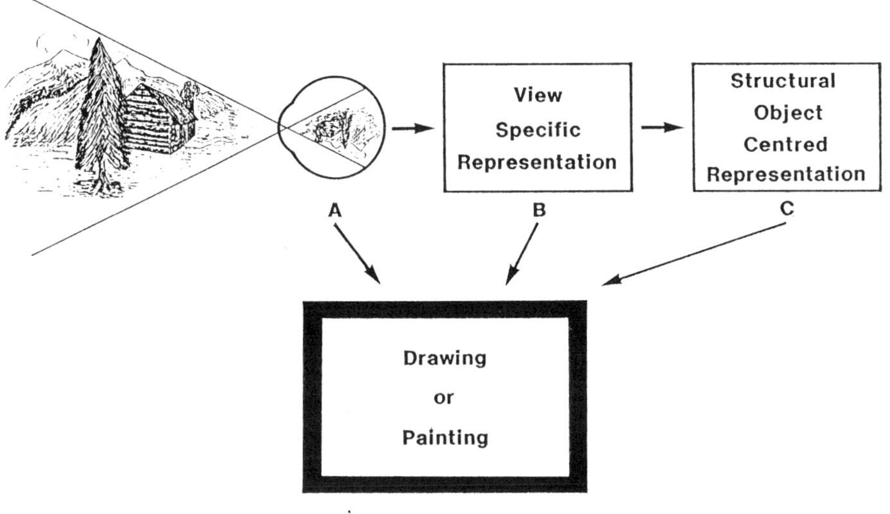

Figure 1.2 When choosing how to render a scene artists may be guided by a) the optical projection onto the retina, b) the view of the scene which they are immediately aware of and which incorporates a re-scaled awareness of the real dimensions of visual space, e.g. things do not really get smaller as they get further away or c) their knowledge of the structure of the objects in the scene, e.g. the cabin has a back door which the artist may incorporate in a unfolded "cubist" drawing. Any or all of these levels of access to visual input may be incorporated in a painting.

The following chapters explore the implications of this view of the relationship between visual perception and painting. While this view may appear simplistic, in fact when examined in detail it can help to elucidate a wide range of stylistic features. Of course it can only elucidate the purely visual aspect of painting so the choice of subject, gesture, iconographic and symbolic features must remain mainly the province of the art historian. However it is our belief that consciousness of the influence of perceptual mechanisms in picture construction enhances our understanding of painting and increases the pleasure of the viewer. It may even lead to readers viewing pictures in a manner quite different to that which obtained previously.

Chapter II

Counterfeits Made To Beguile

The presence of peculiarities or distortions in the paintings of certain artists has been frequently remarked on, and on occasion suggestions made that they may be the consequence of visual abnormalities from which the artists suffered[1]. Thus, for example, the elongated figures charactistic of El Greco's paintings are explained by postulating that an eye defect, from which El Greco suffered, made him see real figures as thinner and longer than they appear to other men, and he drew them as he saw them. An analogous explanation has also been advanced to account for the very tall, very slim and very nude Venuses from Lucas Cranach's workshop. This, obviously cannot be right because abnormal vision would affect not only the artist's perception of models but also their own drawings. Hence to match the models the pictures would have to have exactly the same proportions, and so an anomaly of the eye could not affect the work of art any more than the length of a man's stride can affect the relative magnitude of two distances which he has paced out. Of course, if the anomaly of vision were such as to affect only the model but not its representation or only the representation but not the model (unlikely occurrences, and equivalent in our analogy to the use of two different paces for the two distances paced) then the postulated explanation might be valid.

One may be tempted to extrapolate from the dubious "theory of the defective eye" in these cases, and draw a conclusion that "all those characteristics of depictions commonly referred to as 'style' are also completely independent of the perceptual attributes of the eye". Bearing in mind the caveats which were introduced earlier concerning the word style this proposition implicitly elevates the notion of style into higher cognitive realms making it much more a matter of reflection and speculation than of mere seeing. This, we argue, is doing the eye an injustice and is contrary to the established tenet of efficient reasoning that the simplest satisfactory explanation is the best. As was argued in the previous chapter, this is not to claim that the eye is the dominant influence in all aspects of style, but rather to argue that its contribution has been greatly undervalued, and that the nature of its contribution differs from style to style. Perceptual mechanisms are, we would argue, involved directly in the structuring of artistic styles. Such a statement is probably of more interest to psychologists than to art critics and art historians who, generally, show little interest in the perceptual mechanisms. Most of them tacitly assume, and in this they agree with the majority of psychologists, that perceptual mechanisms do not vary greatly between cultural groups. However, our contention is not that the variety of styles rests upon differences of the eye, but that it is a result of the different ways in which the eye's capabilities are used. This postulate should be of interest to students of art in general. For if relatively simple mechanisms can be shown to influence artistic style then, given the universality of such mechanisms, in those cases where cultural contagion and spontaneous parallelism of creation are about equal contestants in explaining similarity of styles, the scales would swing in favour of parallelism.

We begin our examination of perceptual mechanisms by considering those pictorial cues which are so routinely mentioned in texts on the psychology of perception that they may well be called classical. Those who are familiar with those basic perceptual cues responsible for the perception of visual space can briefly scan the following pages since much of the material will be well known to them. In presenting each of these cues we shall usually show it in a simplified form typically used in psychological experiments on perception. We shall consider the kind of visual apparatus that each cue implies; working, as it were, from the cue inwards in an attempt to answer the question: "Given that this cue works and assuming that we know nothing of the structure of the eye, what is the simplest mechanism that would permit its correct use ?"

It is important at this point to remind ourselves of the distinction, discussed in the previous chapter, between two kinds of pictures, *epitomic* and *eidolic*. Epitomic pictures are those which convey the nature of the depicted object without directly *visually* conveying that the object has three dimensions, as is the case with for example a pin-figure of a man. We do not *see* such a figure as solid although we immediately label it 'man' and know that one of the essential physical characteristics of men is their extension in space. Eidolic pictures on the other hand evoke the perception of space. Most pictures embody in various measures both the element of epitomy and eidolicity; they are recognisable as depicting objects (a house, a river, a man), and also portray at least some of their spatial attributes so that these objects are *seen* as existing in space, not only *known* to be three-dimensional. Our prime concern in this chapter is the examination of these eidolic elements in pictures.

A note of caution is warranted here: although listed under separate headings, the various cues which we discuss are not mutually exclusive. That is to say, it is possible to create a cue which falls into two or more categories. It is possible, for example, to draw a pattern which would embody both a *density gradient* and *linear perspective*. In fact ultimately the cues of density and linear perspective can be seen as variants of a single cue namely that projected size is directly proportional to distance.

Such an overlap of the categories used does not however deny their essential usefulness for taxonomical purposes.

Aerial Perspective

This cue[2] derives from the simple fact that given sources of light of equal power, those further away will appear dimmer because light coming from them has to penetrate a thicker layer of air in its journey to the eye. More often than not the sources are not themselves emitters of light, such as stars or lighthouses, but simply reflect light falling upon them; but this does not affect the argument, since the information about the origin of illumination is seldom available to the eye and its only source of information is the light itself.

In painting, the cue is easily utilised by portraying more dimly, as if obfuscated by the aerial veil, those parts of the composition which are intended to be seen as being further away from the viewer. Since the extent of obfuscation can be infinitely graduated, the protrayed pictorial depth can be subdivided very finely. Objects can be made to appear further or nearer depending on the clarity with which they are portrayed and the artist can use several scales within the same picture by indicating that the depicted aerial medium is not homogeneous, that, for example, some parts of the scene are behind clouds of smoke or wisps of mist, and others simply further away in clear air.

As it is part of daily experience that distant hills are seen less distinctly than those closer by, and a burning cigarette grows brighter as a smoker approaches the observer, the percepts derived from the experience of movement through one's environment and from visual experience are concordant. The viewer can walk to those distant hills. He can hear, he can smell, and he can eventually touch the approaching smoker.

Strictly speaking,in order to perceive this cue the eye has to fulfil only one requirement; it must be able to discriminate between various intensitites of illumination in different regions of the visual field. This is a very modest demand indeed which is met by anatomically much simpler eyes than those of man. However this cue exercises itself through its relative effect on other forms; hills, foliage, buildings are increasingly veiled with distance and so its ability to enhance the sense of space is only appreciated when it is used in the appropriate context.

Overlap or Interposition

We have just seen that inhomogeneities of the medium in which objects are placed introduce discontinuities in visual stimulation which can be exploited by an artist. The extreme case of such inhomogeneity is overlap[3], which occurs when an object partly obscures another object thus conveying unambiguously that the obscured object is further away from the viewer. An interpretation of the cue, when encountered, relies necessarily either on knowledge or, more generally, on a perceptual assumption of the shape of the overlapped object.

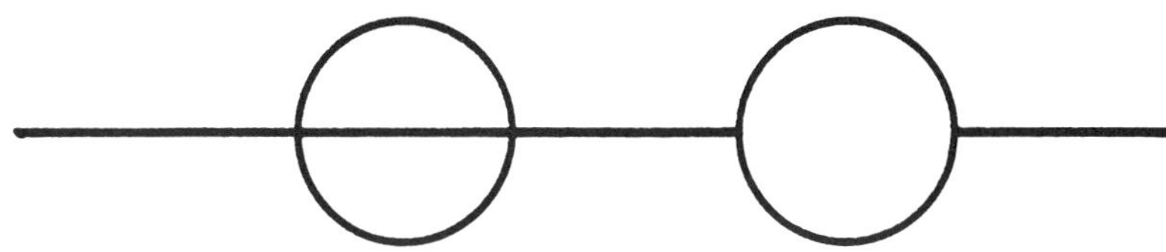

Figure 2.1 The two circles are equal but the circle on the right seems smaller, probably because the visual system assumes that it lies *in front* of the horizontal line and there fore nearer to the viewer than the left hand circle which lies *behind* the line. Based on Coren and Girgus (1975).

The cue is directly translatable into paintings. The artist merely paints the "nearer" figure so that it partly covers the figure which is intended to be seen as being further away. The restriction implicit in the desired familiarity of the further figure is not really severe because perceptual hypotheses, based on similarity of the visible part of the occluded object to some familiar object as well as on the geometrical shape of the depictions, are readily generated.

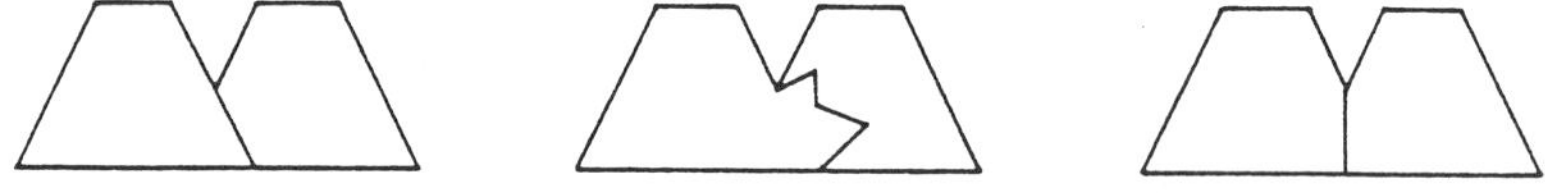

Figure 2.2 Three simple figures. In the first two the eye readily assumes that they consist of an "overlapped" triangle, in the first case by another triangle and in the second by an irregular figure. In the third case the "overlap" is not normally seen.

The surprising strength of the hypotheses is clearly shown by such abstract figures as those forming the illusion shown below (Figure 2.1). · In both figures the circle is of exactly the same size, yet it seems larger in the left hand figure where the horizontal line crosses its surface, than in the right hand figure where the two short radial segments touch the circumference. It seems that even in such an abstract configuration an assumption is made that the line is continuous in both cases and that, therefore, it passes in front of a disc in the one case and behind the disc in the other case. Thus the disc which is behind the line must be further away and so be objectively larger. Other less startling but simpler demonstrations of the effect are illustrated in the next figure (Figure 2.2). Only in the case of the third of these drawings is the eye unwilling to see an overlap. The first figure is more readily perceived as two trapezia than as a trapezium in contact with a quadrilateral or a trapezium overlapping some other of the infinity of possible figures. The second is more readily seen as a trapezium overlapped by a somewhat imperfect trapezium than any configuration not involving an overlap. The third figure is composed of two quadrilaterals symmetrically arranged and evokes no notion of overlap.

Unlike aerial perspective, the overlap cue does not offer a fine gradation of possibilities. The objects which are overlapped are simply behind the overlapping objects; how far behind cannot be shown although the cue can be used in a cascade where several objects overlap in turn. Just as in aerial perspective the overlap cue is readily confirmed in another modality. We have to reach further than a book to get a pencil which is partly visible from behind a book, we have to walk further than the gate to reach a house which we see behind the gate.

The cue demands however more complex assumptions about the nature of the eye than does aerial perspective. The eye must be sensitive to much more than mere differences in local intensity. It must either be able to recognize the shapes of the objects from which the light is reflected or must make intelligent references about them.

Shadow

When light falls upon an uneven surface it creates shadows[4] in those recesses which it does not reach whilst illuminating the protuberances.

This phenomenon can be readily exploited by an artist and it effectively conveys the unevenness of the depicted object, provided that the viewer makes a correct assumption about the direction from which light was falling upon the model; if he does not, then he may erroneously treat the picture as if it were a negative of itself, regarding the protuberance as recesses and recesses as protuberances. There is, not surprisingly, a general tendency to assume that light falls from above and to treat depictions accordingly; however not all depictions are equally dependent on such an assumption. Those categories of objects, it seems, with which the observer is likely to be very familiar, such as human faces, resist such transformation and are seen as undistorted whatever the direction from which the light might have fallen when they were photographed (Figure 2.3).

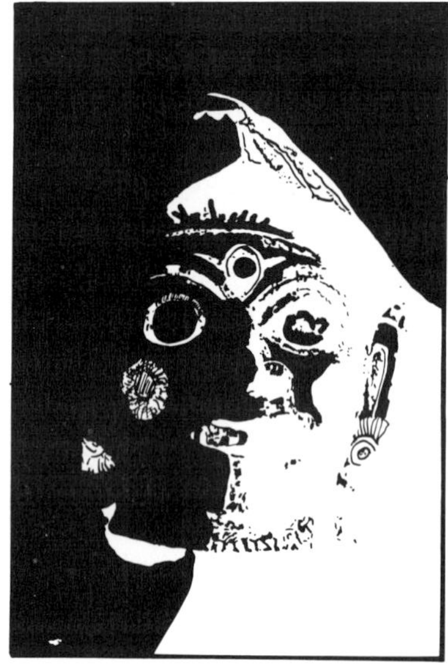

Figure 2.3 Oriac Masks. Photographed under two different conditions of illumination, from above on the left and from below on the right.

The cue has a parallel in tactile experience, because surfaces which reflect light unevenly can be felt to be uneven. Only a very simple eye is needed to perceive the differences in illumination. On the other hand the assembly into one cohesive whole of a figure made of patches of darkness and light is a complex perceptual process and this task does indeed constitute the basis of a standard psychological test (Street, 1931). Reduced to its simplest form, the task is that of distinguishing between the figure and its background.

Familiarity and Relative Size

Recognition of a silhouette, or of an outline, as representing an object is evidence of pictorial perception but it does not in itself constitute perception of pictorial space; however, a combination of two or more of such images may evoke perception of space. A drawing of a figure of a man next to a figure of a house, the man being much larger than the house, leads to a perception of the man as nearer to a viewer than the house, unless the house is taken to be a doll's house.

There are two aspects to this cue: knowledge of the depicted objects and the ability to infer depth from the relative sizes of figures which are, generally, much smaller than the objects which they represent. The latter effect is of immediate interest, and is perceptually related to the phenomenon of size constancy which is described below.

Elevation

A row of street lights when seen on a dark night can be misperceived as a row of lights gradually decreasing in height with distance, and a row of car headlights on the same level street can be misperceived as a row of lights which ascend with distance from the bystander. Differences in elevation thus imply differences in distance from the observer. The cue is ambiguous unless the observer is aware of the direction of his line of sight, and can make a deduction about the inclination of the surface he is looking at with respect to his line of sight. The simple rule which the above example suggests, that points further away from the line of sight are closer to the observer, is not, as the diagram below shows, always valid. It is valid for an observer looking straight ahead along a corridor (Figure 2.4A), but not, for example, when he chances to look down because the situation then changes (Figure 2.4B).

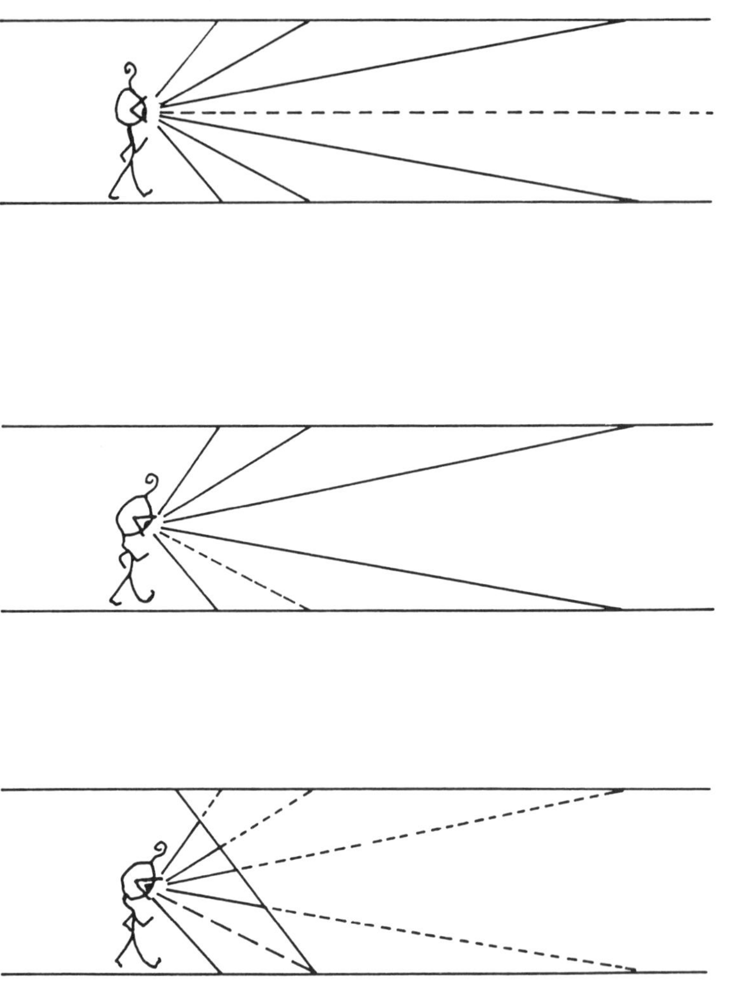

Figure 2.4 In the top part of the illustration the observer looks straight down the corridor. The greater the angular deviation of a point from the line of sight the closer this point is to him. If the observer looks down (middle part of illustration) the same rule applies for points below, but not above, his line of sight. In the third case (bottom) the manikin walks towards an unusual slanting surface. This restores the case to that obtaining in the top diagram.

The cue is readily incorporated in pictures, but it is not interpretable on its own because an artist cannot use it to control the direction of the viewer's gaze, although he can do this, and often does, by the use of other cues.

There is a general tendency, however, related to experience of the natural environment, to regard those figures which are higher up as being further away. This cue derives no comforting support from the viewer's tactile experience. Things do not feel higher up as one stretches one's hand across the desk-top. Nor does one feel, while walking along a level corridor, that one is walking uphill.

Possibly the simplest assumption which need be made about the structure of the eye to explain perception of this cue, is that the eye is sensitive to the relative spatial position of light sources in the visual field i.e. takes into account the angle of incident light.

Texture gradient

The same object, say a finger, held in front of an eye so that it completely obscures a distant cat will only obscure an elephant either if that animal is at about a tenfold distance or if the finger is brought much closer to the eye. Such "real world" observations suggest that painting of a series of patterns decreasing in size might induce the perception of pictorial depth. This is indeed so. The elements involved need not be geometrically identical. The effect is evoked readily by pebbles and by grains of sand on a beach, as well as their depictions.

The cue might be thought of as belonging to the same category as Aerial Perspective because it obeys the general rule that the weaker (dimmer, smaller) the signal the further away its source. The retinal area stimulated by objectively equally sized elements decreases linearly with distance and the eye's sensitivity to this size gradient enables it to be used as a cue for depth. It is a powerful cue. It is found in an elementary form in Baldwin's illusion (Figure 2.5A) and in its more usual form in Figure 2.5B. The horizontal lines in both figures are equal but are not seen as such. The line joining the pair of larger squares is seen as shorter, presumably because the squares are regarded as really equal, hence the larger squares must be closer to the observer.

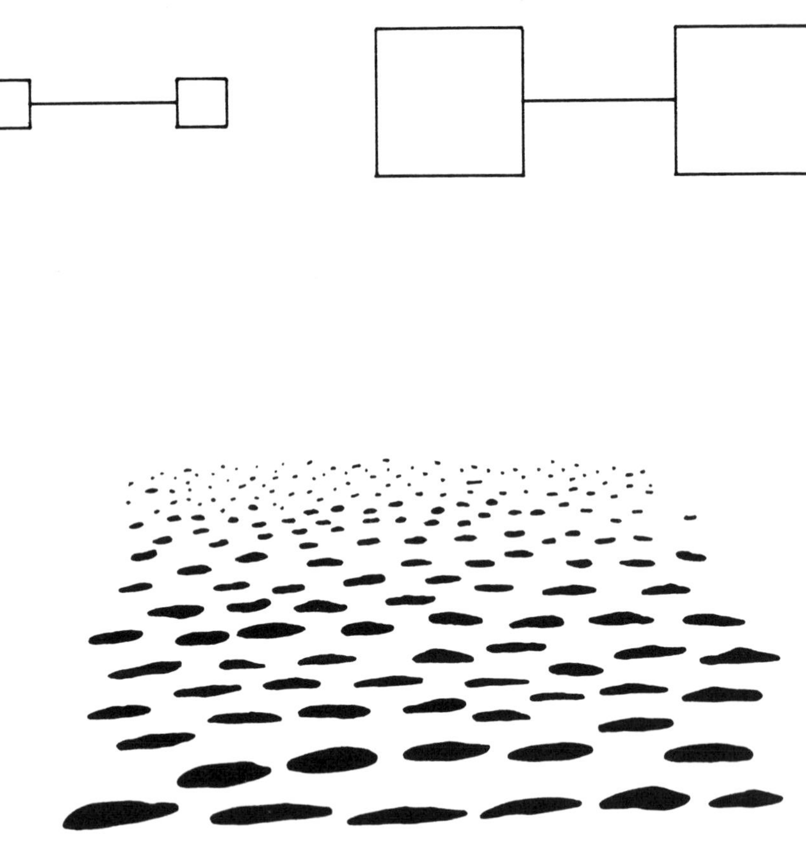

Figure 2.5 A- Baldwin's illusion. Of the two equal horizontal lines which that bounded by the larger squares appears to be shorter. B- a conventional texture gradient.

Linear convergence (Linear perspective)

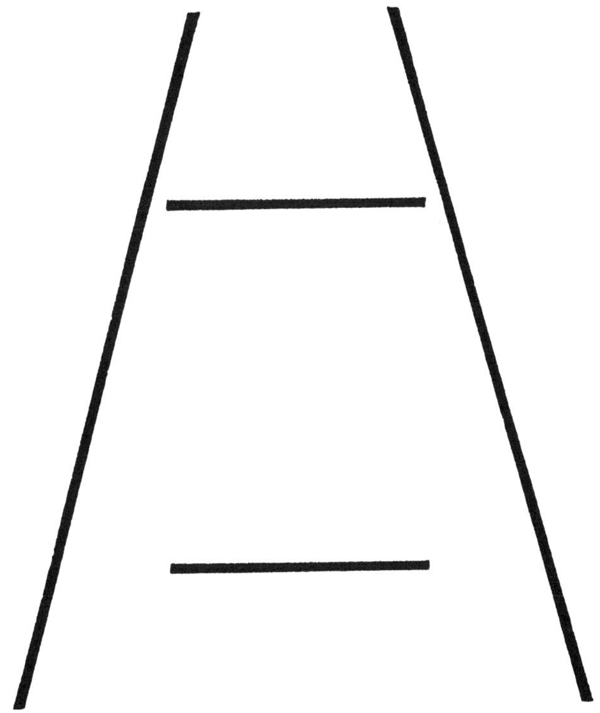

Figure 2.6 The Ponzo figure. This is one of the best known of the perceptual illusions. The two objectively equal horizontal lines appear unequal, the upper line seeming longer than the lower.

This cue is probably the most widely discussed of pictorial devices although, as we have said, it has ultimately the same origin as that of the texture gradient. If the gradient, of our example above, consisted not of pebbles but of, say, railway sleepers, and on a drawing the ends of the sleepers were to be jointed, the lines joining them would converge with the implied distance. The cue is potent and can readily be shown to be effective even in the case of such an abstract figure as the Ponzo illusion (Figure 2.6).

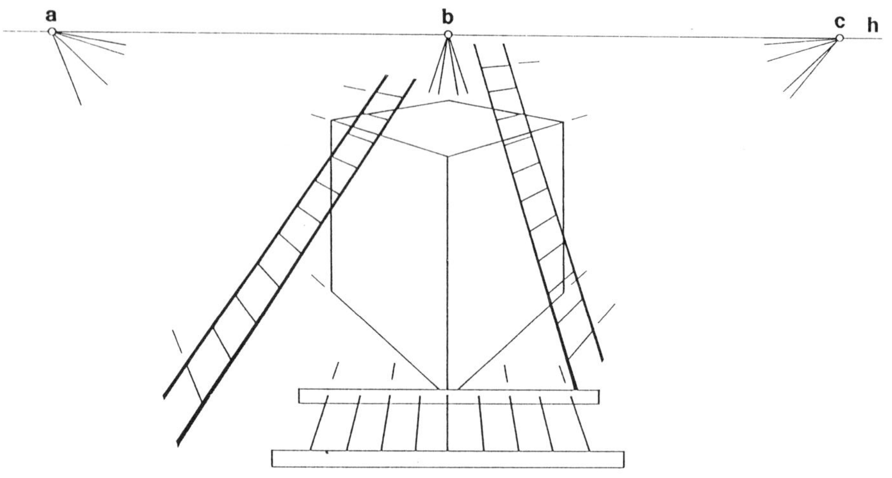

Figure 2.7 The vanishing points of the extensions of various contours in a perspective drawing.

The assumptions which this cue demands about the structure of the eye are exactly the same as those called for by the use of the density/texture gradient. As the placement of the point (or points) of convergence within a picture is the distinguishing feature of various schemes of perspective drawing, it needs to be considered carefully. To do so the reader should imagine a long, straight ladder. The rungs of the ladder are equispaced between two parallel side-pieces. The ladder can be put in any orientation and in every position the rung closest to the eye will support the largest angle at the eye and the rung furthest away the smallest. Similarly the inter-rung spacings will support decreasingly smaller angles as their distance from the eye increases (Figure 2.7). The rectangular spaces between the pairs of rungs will therefore form a row of quadrilaterals decreasing in size with distance, and, in the case of an infinitely long ladder, vanishing at the vanishing point. This is the principle of convergence. Depicted convergence is affected however by the shape of the surface on which the picture is painted. One can think of this surface as a membrane interposed between the portrayed object (in our case the ladder) and the eye. In most cases the surface is flat. This ensures that the ladder is painted as having both straight side-pieces and rungs. The location of the point of convergence of the ladder depends on its position in space. If it is laid on a level ground and stretches away from the observer this point lies at the horizon directly in front of the eye. If the ladder now is turned so that one of its side-pieces remains on the ground and the rungs are vertical the point of convergence will be unchanged. (This is an instance of the "simplest" perspective wherein the dominant elements are either vertical or stretch away from of the viewer.)

If on the other hand the ladder remains flat on the ground but is put at an angle to the observer it will appear to converge at a different point on the horizon. If now the ladder is set in a non-horizontal plane the point of convergence will no longer fall on the horizon but will lie somewhere else in space. In fact, given that the ladder can be placed in a theoretically infinite number of orientations with respect to the observer, the vanishing point can occupy any position in the picture (Figure 2.7).

When the pictorial surface is not flat then the rectilinearity of straight elements is not necessarily preserved, and straight lines may be replaced by curves, the distance between which, as measured in the surface, may decrease, remain constant or even increase with distance, depending on the shape of the surface.

The last two cues (texture gradient and linear convergence) fix the notional eye in space relative to the depicted scene, and imply that there is only one point from whence the picture containing such cues can be viewed to be correctly perceived. This apparently very restrictive conclusion is in practice, as we shall see, greatly attenuated by the flexibility of the eye. Before moving on to consider other mechanisms it may be as well to clear up a misunderstanding which haunts some writings on linear perspective.

It is an established fact that the eye moves continually in short rapid shifts know as saccades, which occur several times each second and which the observer does not perceive. Therefore the projected image changes its position even though the eye, as far as the observer is aware, looks with a steely gaze upon the scene. It is also established that when a complicated optical apparatus is used to compensate for these movements so that the projection of the scene falls upon the same part of the retina, then after a few seconds, the image fades, and the observer can no longer see the scene (Ditchburn, 1973). The perceptual stability of the visual world occurs then despite the restlessness of the organ system which senses its structure.

This phenomenon has been taken by some to constitute a sufficient ground for questioning the organismic origins of linear perspective. The argument arises out of a misunderstanding of the ideal requirements for correct perception of pictures drawn in perspective. These are that such a picture should be viewed monocularly, with the centre of rotation of the eye fixed at the unique and critical point of the picture's construction, its centre of projection. This requirement does not preclude saccadic movements. Indeed it does not preclude other movements, but a shift to peripheral vision from central vision would affect the clarity with which the object is seen and even introduce distortions which derive from the eye's intrinsic mechanisms; these aspects are discussed at length in Chapter 7. A remark that one could as well measure the fidelity of drawing "in terms of rays directed at a closed eye" (Goodman, 1969) seems therefore merely a mischievous jest, and the more so because the effects of *complete* immobilization are independent of whether the observer is looking at a real scene or a picture. The critics of perspective would therefore have to argue that one cannot look intently for more than a few seconds at any object. One only hopes that they never have to wait at traffic lights.

Constancies

The great effectiveness of the cues just described might give the reader an impression that in their absence no pictorial depth can be perceived. This is not so. A simple hexagon, such as shown below (Figure 2.8), is seen by many (but it often has to be looked at for some time before the percept emerges) as a lattice cube which spontaneously turns inside out.

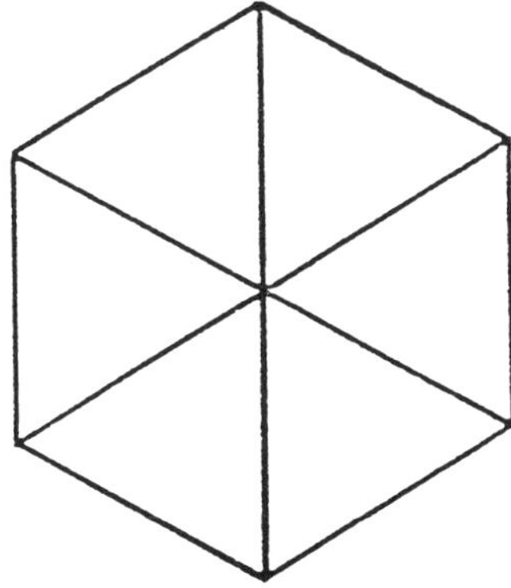

Figure 2.8 There is a tendency to see this simple hexagon as a cube after some time has been spent looking at it.

Since the cube "reverses", its front appearing now above and now below its back face, the only cue which could be put forward to explain perceived depth is obviously ineffective here. In either of the two possible settings *all* the faces of the cube are seen as square. This tendency to see squares in place of rhombi is an instance of perceptual constancy and is related to the device of foreshortening in art.

The term *constancy*[5] is used to describe the perception of stability and unchangeability of the environment. This stability is greater than considerations of the characteristics of the projection which objects cast upon the eye would suggest. Thus the fact that a person walking away from the observer does not appear to decrease in size, although his projection does so, is said to be a demonstration of *size constancy,* and the fact that a page of a book when turned does not appear to change shape, although its projection does so, is said to be a demonstration of *shape constancy.* Analogously other terms such as *brightness constancy* (that is the tendency for an object to retain the same brightness in spite of the changes of intensity in illumination) and *colour constancy* (the tendency for the colour of objects to remain unchanged in spite of changes in the wavelength of light falling upon them) are used.

In the "real world" size constancy is not, as the above examples might imply, perfect. It breaks down gradually and we see objects, as the distance increases, not quite as small as the mathematical calculation based on their distances would lead us to expect, but smaller than we would expect under conditions of perfect constancy. A compromise percept thus emerges. As the distance increases further, this compromise is abandoned and objects are seen so small as to look toylike. The most commonly quoted experience of this type is that of passengers looking down through an aeroplane window on the houses below them.

One of the major influences on perceived size is the comparison between the object seen and other objects on the field of view. This is one of the factors responsible for the Moon Illusion. The moon is seen as much smaller when it is well above the horizon in the void of the sky than when it is near the horizon. This apparent difference is not, however, confirmed by photography. The moon whenever photographed, high above or on the horizon, appears to be of the same size. The explanation of the illusion lies, in part, in the presence of other features in the field of view when the moon is above the horizon; the trees, the buildings and the expanse of the earth all provide cues about the great distance of the moon and thereby perceptually expand it. A view of the earth from an aeroplane is, as far as the cues are concerned, similar to the view of the elevated moon. There are practically no cues to indicate how high the aeroplane is over the earth, and although various features, the house, the swimming-pools, the cars and the trains are all properly scaled down relative to each other they are all about equidistant and the constancy mechanism does not correct for their distance to the observer.

Scaling of features is also found in pictures, but looking at pictures is somewhat different to looking at the objects which they portray. When looking at a picture we really look *into* it as well as *at* it. That is, we are aware of the fact that it is a picture. This *subsidiary awareness* is capable of influencing the perception of pictorial space (see Chapter 3). Does constancy ensure that a book is seen as a book and a horse is seen as a horse from whatever angle they are viewed or depicted?

Gestalt psychologists cogently argue that the transformations of the book and a horse are not analogous, but their arguments do not seem to be generally understood. Even Arnheim's oft repeated admonition that "the percept will correspond to the shape of a foreshortened physical object when, and only when, this shape happens to be the simplest figure possible under the circumstances", has not dissuaded Goodman, a philosopher, from putting forward a contrary thesis. He claims that a theory of perspective drawing has become a integral part of visual understanding or of our "visual sense" to such an extent that it affects our seeing. This implies that constancy is a derivative of experience of the theory of drawing and should affect both the square and the horse alike.

But experimental evidence of the Gestalt school runs contrary to such a view. Consider, it says, a pure shape without any depth cues attached; not a view of a plate or a wheel or a penny but a simple ellipse (Figure 2.9). This shape may exist, as it were, of its own right or it may be a projection of some other shape. Given simple linear transformations, such as may be brought about by casting shadows, and an ellipse could be a projection of a circle or of another ellipse. It belongs to a large family of ellipses ranging from an ellipse so thin that it is a straight line to that where axes are equal and which is therefore a circle. Arnheim's rule when adapted to our ellipse would run as follows: the ellipse is likely to be regarded as a portrayal of a circle and not of another ellipse, although, of course, mathematically it is an equally legitimate portrayal of either.

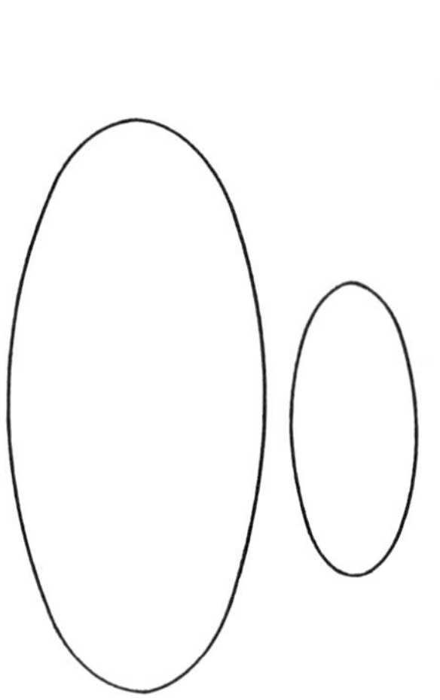

Figure 2.9 Drawing of ellipses without (left) and with (right) information which aids shape constancy.

The proof of the pudding is in the eating. When a person is shown an ellipse and later asked either to draw it or find a matching figure does he respond by drawing (or choosing) an identical ellipse or a circle? The answer is neither. He choose an ellipse intermediate between the original stimulus and the circle. This choice has been traditionally described in psychology as a drift towards constancy (away from the original stimulus and towards the circle); it could also be described as a drift in the opposite direction by arguing as follows. Since the observer on viewing the original ellipse sees it as representing a circle his response shows a drift from the circle towards its elliptic representation. It is doubtful whether such re-labelling of a choice, which Thouless in his seminal work on constancies regarded as a compromise, clarifies the issue. It certainly runs contrary to the terminology which the extension of our observations suggests, because when the same ellipse is shown in the context of other cues (such as a density gradient) which stress that it is a representation of a circle, the responses made fall closer to the circle. A statement that increased stress on circularity increases the drift towards the circle seems to have, prima facie, satisfying consistency.

Typical Views

There is a general rule that a depiction is most efficacious when the artist concentrates on those aspects which have the greatest information value, that is those aspects which show features at the instant at which they undergo most rapid change. Thus the simplest and most effective way of depicting a square of a certain size using but four dots is to place them in the position of the four corners, that is those points at which the straight line of the side suddenly makes a right-angled turn, and not by placing them in some other mathematically equally unique positions, say, midpoints of sides. In the case of depiction of animals, the profile is simply a line constructed of points which denote a position of the very rapid change of curvature on the animals' bodies, as shown in Figure 2.10 below. The same, the figure suggests, applies also to portrayal of human heads in profile, but even a superficial survey will show that a large number of human heads are drawn *en face* so that an explanation has to be offered for this deviation from the suggested rule. This happens most probably because it is much easier to communicate emotional state by showing a face in full. The matter is therefore more complex in the case of portrayals of people as their fellows are generally more interested in their emotions than in those of animals.

Figure 2.10 The figure on the left shows a profile drawing of an animal which provides the line of maximum information content. The figure on the right provides less information about the animal's structure but may be visually more interesting.

It is difficult for an artist to abandon the lines of maximum information and to use *foreshortening* (simply another term for linear perspective). Foreshortening may affect the entire depicted model when it is drawn from an "unusual" stance, as that of the corpse in Rembrandt's *Dr. Tulpe's Anatomy Lesson* (Figure 2.11), or it may affect different parts of the figure differently thus conveying effectively the model's movement. This was clearly attempted in the figure of Death (Figure 2.12) in a French manuscript which also shows the difficulties experienced by the artist, who, in despair, drew two parts of a horse, the forequarters in profile and the hindquarters in the back view. Joining these two disparate components would have constituted a major problem, which the artist evaded by judicious placement of the rider.

Because the experimental evidence shows that the constancy drift in pictures is also towards the more regular forms, it suggests that pictorial depth is more difficult for an artist to create than for a viewer to grasp. The artist depicting a circle as an ellipse has to go *against* the tendency towards "constancy"; the viewer seeing an ellipse as a portrayal of a circle has merely to allow himself to drift in the direction constancy dictates. This may account for pictures found in a variety of cultures in which wheels of chariots, carriages and carts are shown as perfect circles although the orientation of the bodies of the vehicles to which they are attached suggests that they should be ellipses. In the early Greek attempts at portraying wheels, found on the Attic amphorae, they appear initially as straight lines and later as approximations to the ellipses, made up of two arcs of a circle intersecting at rather a sharp angle at the lowest and the highest points. The amphorae on which such foreshortened views of wheels are found also show foreshortened views of horses. In this they differ from earlier amphorae which combined the frontal views of quadrigae with pseudo-foreshortened views of the horses similar to the medieval figure just discussed. But although such coincidence of foreshortenings of wheels and horses may reflect a general change in the skills of the artist, it is unlikely to result from the operation of the same mechanism. For whilst it seems plausible that there may be neural mechanisms responsible for perceptual constancies of simple shapes such as circles and squares, or that past experience ensures that transformations of such shapes are remembered, it is unlikely that these facilitating effects could also apply directly to such complex shapes as animals.

The pictorial cues hitherto considered are imitative in nature. They try to present the eye with the same stimulation as would be supplied by depicted objects, thus creating an illusion of depth. The picture's surface is in these circumstances immaterial, but it is important that no hint of the surface *qua* surface should be minimised if the perfect but fragile illusion is to prevail. If the surface is too obvious, it will contradict the depth cues and may decrease their effectiveness. A surface which is most self-effacing is spherical. When a picture is painted on the inner surface of a sphere and the eye placed in its centre the effects of the uniform density gradient which a surface of itself may have is nullified. In practice, however, such surfaces are seldom used, although when used, the percpetual effects are very powerful and paradoxically, as we shall see, very unstable. Generally, the artist has to be satisfied with a flat surface, and, by combining all the devices at his disposal, try to combat its *perceptual* flatness. The degree of his success depends not only on his skill but also on the subject matter depicted. The distortions resulting from the observer's awareness of the picture's surface are certain to be more noticeable in a traditional perspective drawing of a row of columns supporting a Grecian portico than such a drawing of a row of dancing satyrs whose real shape is not likely to be known to the observer. These distortions, it must be stressed, occur because of the observer's knowledge of the picture's surface although the pictorial depth cues projected to his eye are *identical* with those which would be provided by the portrayed models themselves, and they are of crucial importance. They provide, it seems to us, a satisfactory explanation of certain characteristics of non-western artistic styles. We shall return to them.

Figure 2.11 (Opposite) Rembrandt van Rijn. "The Anatomy Lesson". Note the fine gradations of foreshortening used. This contrasts strongly with the technique of the author of figure 2.12. (Reproduced by courtesy of the Mauritshuis, The Hague).

Figure 2.12 An example of pseudo-foreshortening. The horse is made of two parts; the forequarters which are travelling west and the hindquarters which are on their way north. Mors (death) is so seated as to conceal the unfortunate mismatch.

However skilfully the cues just described are used to depict an object its representation is always seen within the greater context of the surrounding pictorial space. The extent of this space is defined not only by the depth cues embodied in other elements of the picture but also by the somewhat prosaic element of the picture's frame. The perceived distance of the depicted objects from the observer is therefore dependent on the extent of the frame. A solitary manikin, for example, so drawn that it just fills a small frame, is seen as much smaller and more distant when placed within a much expanded background bounded by a larger frame[6]. This effect, just like other pictorial spatial effects described, may be either concordant with or contrary to such effects as the artist might have incorporated in the picture. Thus a perspective view of a cube showing very little convergence and therefore implying that it is at a great distance may seem nearer to the viewer when it fills the entire picture than another drawing of a cube in which accentuated convergence stresses its proximity but which is drawn in the middle of a large expanse of space.

The slow convergence of the edges of Cézanne's table (See Figure 7.8) suggests that it is far away from the viewer. This suggestion is however contradicted by the extent to which it fills the pictorial space. It fills it entirely and impresses upon the observer its closeness. Thus a "non-pictorial" cue of the boundary between the pictorial and real spaces affects perception of the picture. Nor is it a solitary instance of interaction between perception of real and pictorial spaces, for as we shall see in the following chapter the perception of the picture's surface, qua surface, has great influence on what we see in the picture.

In this chapter we have discussed a number of cues to space perception which can be readily incorporated into pictures to provide an illusion of space and depth and it should be noted they are all effective with monocular viewing. If all of these cues are used consistently then a compelling illusion can be created. However not all of these pictorial devices need be used. Any subset of the available range will add something to the picture. In Renaissance painting the full range of cues was frequently incorporated, while in Medieval European and pre-nineteenth century Japanese art a restricted set of depth cues, principally those of interposition and height in the visual field, were used. Thus space can be depicted in different ways, and, without doubt the greater the number of cues which are consistently included in the picture the more convincing it will appear. In saying this however one is ignoring the artist's intention. Any painter is free to use whichever cues he chooses (assuming that he is knowledgeable and skilful enough to manipulate them) and those which are selected will depend on a variety of cultural and personal determinants.

Figure 3.1 A. Pozzo, "Allegory of the missionary work of the Jesuit order", Saint Ignazio, Rome.

Chapter III

Why Two Eyes Are Better Than One

The fact that we have two eyes, rather than one, introduces a factor into pictorial perception which demands consideration. Inter-ocular disparities enable the observer to judge distances, particularly within the person's immediate action space. Disparities arise from the fact that we have two eyes which see two slightly different images of the field of view. Furthermore, these disparities between the projected images on the retinae of the eyes give rise to a qualitatively unique experience, stereopsis; a sensory quality which is as remarkable as colour. A second, but less sensitive, binocular cue to the distance of objects, particularly over near distances, is convergence. This is the extent to which the eyes turn inwards as objects get closer to the observer. However stereoscopic depth discrimination works over a very wide range, from close inspection of objects up to distances of 400 to 500 metres. Its effectiveness is limited mainly by the acuity of the retina and, as we shall see below, the power of other possibly conflicting, depth cues.

Binocular disparities could inform viewers that they are indeed looking at a picture by constantly reminding them that they are looking at a flat surface, although monocular cues suggest otherwise[1]. For this reason binocular cues might be thought the major obstacle to veridical pictorial perception. This, as Pirenne has demonstrated, is not so.

In architectural painting (quadratura) the painted ceiling of the church of St. Ignazio in Rome offers a startling demonstration of the power and limitations of linear perspective. It was decorated by Fra Andrea Pozzo[2], a man greatly interested in perspective and an author of a treatise on the subject, *Perspectiva Pictorum et Architectorum,* which describes how the ceiling was painted. This was done as follows: The entire church ceiling is divided structurally into three distinct parts, the hemicylindrical nave, the flat circular middle transept and curved ceiling above the altar. Pozzo treated these segments separately, decorating each with a different design based on a different point of view. The method used was however the same. Decoration of the largest of these segments, the ceiling of the nave, shows St. Ignazio being received in heaven. It contains numerous figures of angels in flowing robes as well as, and this is important, a depiction of an upward extension of the fabric of the building. The impression created is that of a much taller roofless building which extends into the heavens in which angels fly.

As the initial step in preparation of the picture architectural drawings of the intended "extension" of the building were prepared. These were used to make a drawing showing what the decorated ceiling would look like when viewed from the floor below. It was drawn in strict linear perspective, assuming that the distance from the point of view was at about the eye level in the centre of the nave. Such a drawing could be made into a transparency. This, when placed above a source of light occupying the position of the hypothetical eye, would project upon the ceiling its own image ready for copying. Such a device was, however, not available to Pozzo, who solved the problem thus: he superimposed a grid of lines upon the drawing, and suspended under the vault a geometrically similar grid made of twine, so that it spanned horizontally between its lower edges. He then transferred the co-ordinates of the intersections of this net to the curved surface of the ceiling above by stretching thin cords from the point of the hypothetical eye to the ceiling so that they touched on the way the nodes of his net. Projection of each node was thus found and marked on the ceiling, and when these marks were joined, projection of the entire grid was created such that, to the eye in the hypothetical-eye position looking upwards, the net suspended below coincided with it perfectly. The next step was relatively simple, it was to transfer from the original drawing, cell by cell, the intended design, taking into account that on the surface of the ceiling the original square cells were now transformed into less regular figures. This method of architectural painting became widely used and can be found in many European countries (Figure 3.1).

The technique used by Pozzo accords well with that illustrated in Dürer's famous woodcuts showing a *Method of drawing a portrait* (Figure 3.2). The only adaptation made is that of reversal of the positions of the projecting model and the surface upon which it is being projected. In Dürer's drawing this surface is interposed between the model and the artist's eye, which is kept in a fixed position by an annulus through which the artist has to look. In Pozzo's case the model (the architectural drawing) was placed between the projection surface and the eye; as a result the projected drawing was larger than the model whereas in Dürer's case it was smaller.

Pirenne describes that when one stands in Pozzo's church at the spot which Pozzo has considerately marked on the floor, so that one's eyes are at the place of the hypothetical eye, and looks upwards, the entire scene in the painting seems real, and the depicted architectural elements are seen as natural extensions of the church's structure. A great trompe l'oeil takes place. But, and this is of great significance, movement away from the spot does not affect this illusion of depth but deforms the perceived space so that the impression one gets is that the whole structure becomes unstable.

Figure 3.2 Dürer, "Method of drawing a portrait".

Pirenne supposed that this is so because the binocular cues and the cue of accommodation which normally would provide information about the change in the position of the surface of the painting as seen by the observer are not effective as the ceiling is beyond their range of competence. The painting is therefore treated as if it were a real object; the changing projections, which the movement of the observer brings about, being interpreted as changes in the structure. However similar distortions of depicted space occur in paintings within the range of binocular vision although the effects are not so dramatic[3].

We know that the ceiling of St. Ignazio is well within the range of stereoscopic vision and under normal circumstances a viewer would have no difficulty in perceiving it correctly. However the painted surface provides powerful monocular perspective cues which override the stereoscopic cue and allow the illusion of a space ascending above the ceiling to be created. The painted architectural features which extend from the real features of the body of the church help to reinforce the illusion when the viewer is in the correct position. However as the viewer moves the architectural features of the church are perceived appropriately but their painted extensions now look inappropriate and the perceptual distortions are emphasised. It is the absence of a real three-dimensional setting for normal paintings which has probably been responsible for the belief that systematic distortions do not occur when we view paintings. In fact substantial distortions do occur (Figure 3.3) but the absence of a real world reference (for example in the case of St. Ignazio the contrast between the real columns in St. Ignazio and the painted columns) enables them to escape the attention of the unobservant.

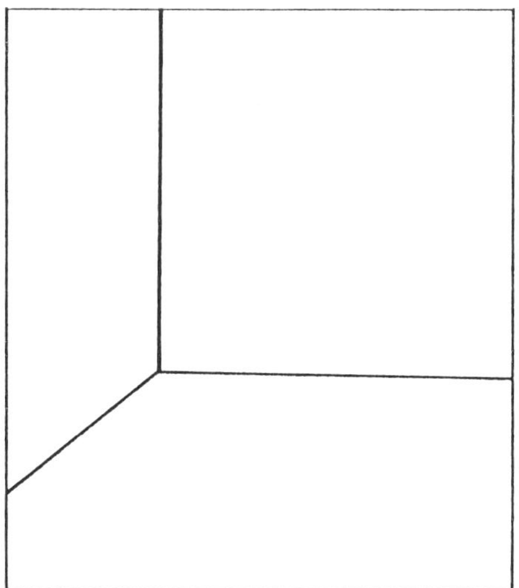

Figure 3.3 The drawing reproduces the three major axes from Vermeer's "The Music Lesson", see figure 7.1. The side-wall floor joint (diagonal line) appears to change orientation depending on whether the picture is placed to the left or right of the observer.

Byzantine church paintings, just as Pozzo's ceiling, rely for the power of their aesthetic effect on the minimising of subsidiary awareness. They are deliberately placed within churches outwith the effective range of cues to surface texture, above the heads of the beholders. "Well-meaning but misguided photographers" are said to be responsible for the currency of the notion that the Byzantine figures of the Pancreator and his attendants should be seen as unnaturally elongated. They have foisted this notion on gullible viewers by taking photographs from positions not normally accessible to the faithful, who can look at the figures only from below and therefore see them foreshortened. "Unlike Renaissance artists", Weale (1976) observes, "who imitated, those of the Byzantine and Romanesque eras compensated for the visual effects: they knew the reality and if the weakness of the human frame distorted it, they were at hand to render assistance and restore the status quo".

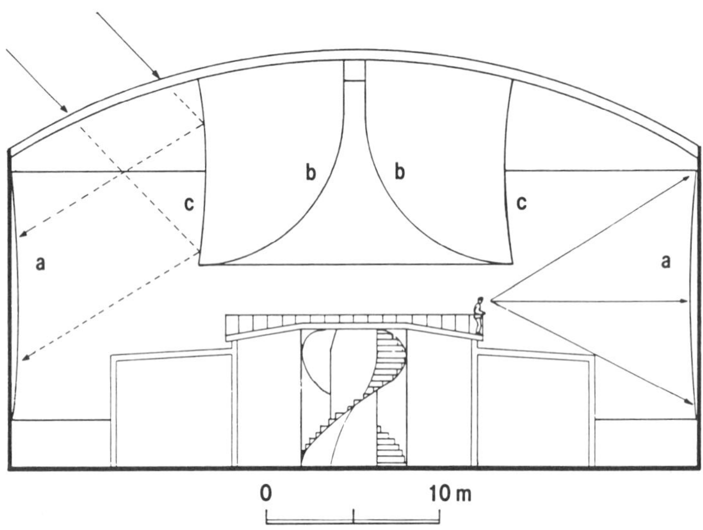

Figure 3.4 A vertical section through a typical panorama gallery.

The same optical principles and therefore the same effects as those associated with the Pozzo ceiling are also embodied in panoramas[4]. Panoramas are pictures painted on huge canvases and hung in special galleries. A sketch showing a section through such a gallery is shown in Figure 3.4. The building is cylindrical and has a spiral staircase entwined about its axis. This leads to an annular platform elevated at about half the height of the external wall, which is lined with the canvas which surrounds the platform completely. On entering the building, the viewer is led through a confusing subterranean passage via the corkscrew of a staircase onto a poorly illuminated platform to face the well illuminated canvas so painted that when viewed radially it projects into his eye a geometrically correct pattern. The space between the canvas and the platform is used to reinforce the illusion which this pattern evokes. It serves to display real objects which merge into the picture. Thus for example sand, scattered with such objects as may be found on the foreshore, may be spread in the foreground to merge with painted dunes, or a real fence may be continued as a painted fence on the canvas. All these effects combine to create an overwhelming illusion which completely envelops the observer within the pictorial space. In consequence, just as in the case of Pozzo's ceiling, the perceived scene changes with changes of the observer's line of sight. Notably any marked deviation of the line of sight from radiality violates the intentions of the artist and changes perceived shapes; for example, a cottage which when viewed radially has an appearance shown in Figure 3.5-a, will when the gaze is turned to the left look like the cottage shown in Figure 3.5-b and when the gaze is turned to the right like the cottage shown in Figure 3.5-c.

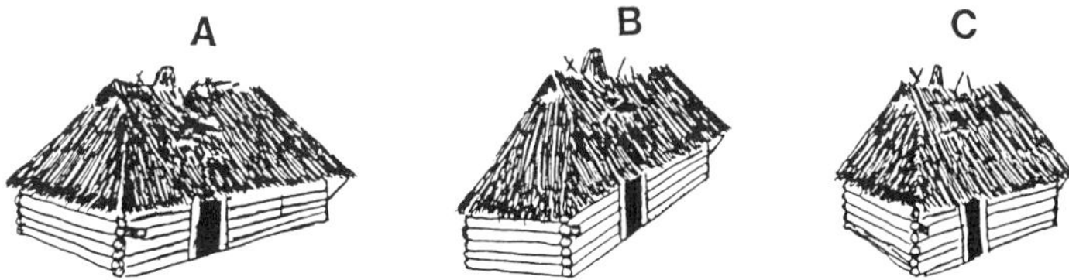

Figure 3.5 Perceived shape of a panoramic picture of a building, as seen from different stances. See text for further details.

Such dramatic changes are not experienced when looking at paintings even if they contain strong perspective cues. When viewing such a painting a considerable departure from the point which the eye should theoretically occupy can be made without the viewer noticing any deformation of the painting except in the rather special case of eyes or a pointing arm, whose case will be discussed below. Indeed, as Pirenne points out, if the viewer was especially sensitive to such deformations and pictures seen from different angles appeared to differ substantially, then passport photography would have only very limited use. It would also be impossible for two architects to look at the same drawings and discuss the merits of a design, as their percepts, just as the percepts of two men looking at Pozzo's ceiling from different stances, would be entirely different.

The *subsidiary awareness*[5] of the picture's two-dimensionality and of its position in space offers means whereby such perceptual distortions can be controlled, by bringing the observer, as it were, closer to the focal point than he physically occupies and enhancing the agreement between cues perceived from different stances. In essence the observer treats the picture as a window through which a section of the world is seen and as they look from different angles the depicted space changes. Consider Vermeer's *The Music Lesson* (Figure 7.1). If the viewer holds the picture immediately in front of him an approximately correct perspective projection of a room is seen. If the viewer sees the picture from the extreme right or extreme left noticeable distortion of the position of the left side wall occurs. If one had been looking through a window at a real scene and then walked to the left and turned and look through the window again, the left hand wall should no longer be visible. If it is visible then the angle of the "window" with respect to the room must be different to that previously obtaining. In looking at the Vermeer picture, or any other perspective projection, the observer automatically makes this correction. And so the binocular cues which show that the picture is flat paradoxically help the viewers to make better use of the monocular cues which convey pictorial depth, and hence help them to make better use of pictures.

This corrective power of *subsidiary awareness* is not, however, limitless, and when the viewer moves far away from the ideal stance, so that monocular cues no longer approximate to the organised pattern which they were intended to provide, pictorial depth is no longer perceived and the picture is seen merely as a mottled plane. Even before the total disintegration of the percept, changes can often be observed. In the case of pictures, with strong perspective cues such as Vermeer's *The Music Lesson* such changes take the form of systematic transformations of the percept as the observer walks past the picture. A notable exception of this rule is provided by the anamorphoses[6]; those rare pictures deliberately painted so that they have to be viewed from an unusual stance, generally at a very sharp angle, or with the assistance of an optical aid such as a curved mirror or a special lens. In the latter case the light reflected by the picture is transformed in such a manner that when it reaches the observer's eye it has the same pattern as that which would be derived from the depicted object or from an "ordinary" picture. The simpler type, which does not involve an optical aid but which requires that the picture be viewed from a rather unusual position, generally monocularly, offers another, and complementary, aspect of the perceptual game involving binocular and monocular cues.

The apparent movements of various elements of Pozzo's ceiling and perspective paintings appear to be akin to the more commonly observed movement of eyes which "follow" moving observers from portraits[7]. This phenomenon was known to the ancients. Ptolemy remarks upon it in his optics, and indeed it might be that it was in some part responsible for the relatively slow development of the foreshortening of eyes in the faces drawn in profile. Some portraits, most typically Egyptian, show the eyes in frontal view, although the faces are in profile. They are in a stiff formal style. Their eyes which follow the observer, although not with the persistence of pairs of eyes found in later portraits, are the only features which are imbued with life. Foreshortening of the eyes drains such figures of life entirely.

Figure 3.6A "The Nativity", illustration from J. de Voragine, *The Golden Legend,* W. Caxton, Westminister 1487, Aberdeen University Library.

Speculations about the reasons for the perceived movement suggest two causes. First, there is an empirically demonstrable tendency for observers to look the painted figures in the eyes. This explains why the phenomenon is so readily noticed rather than how it occurs. Second, there are the characteristics of depictions themselves. As seen from the front, the eyes do not fill great depth and lend themselves easily to the trompe l'oeil treatment. When eyes are painted looking straight ahead, so that they truly "look" at the viewer when he squarely faces the picture, then they present central irises flanked by two, about equal, white triangles, just as the eyes of a real person would. However, if a person continued staring ahead and the viewer walked to the side of him, the size of the visible triangles would change, those further away from the viewer becoming relatively smaller. This change is clearly limited in a picture. Here movement leaves the ratio of the two triangles much less disturbed than in a real life encounter and this relative stability of the stimulus is taken as indicating that the eyes are still looking at the beholder; that they have followed him.

Figure 3.6B Indian border painting, late 16th or early 17th century, from Jahangin's Album.

Such following movements, however, are not confined to the eyes, but are also, albeit less strikingly, made by other depicted elements which are unambiguously orthogonal to the plane of the picture, such as an outstretched arm or a straight receding road. These features, just like the eyes, change in width but not in general appearance when viewed at an angle. Both the arm and the road look narrower but continue to point at the viewer. There is then a family of phenomena which are linked to the observers' compensation for the angle of view, a process of compensation which results in the perceptual rearrangement of elements within the picture.

Just as binocular vision is involved indirectly in the effects we have just discussed it is probably also a contributor to "inverted perspective", an artistic phenomenon with which it has been particularly problematic to deal. This effect masquerades under various names such as "inverse perspective", "anti-perspective", "oriental perspective", but its essential, unchanging characteristic is that parallel lines diverge as they recede into pictorial depth. One can treat this phenomenon as a random error of draughtsmanship or accept it as a puzzle demanding an explanation. It occurs spontaneously in drawings made by children and illiterates, was common in pre-Renaissance painting (Figure 3.6A) and is still to be found in some oriental art (Figure 3.6B) and indeed occasionally in modern western works of art (Figure 3.6C). Its appearance under such a variety of circumstances suggests that it has a firm organismic basis. It is, as its names clearly declared it to be, the antithesis of linear perspective.

Its origins have been speculated upon[8] by many and several explanations proposed; the desire to show more of the object than is warranted by correct linear projection; the experience that the width of the field of view closer to the eye is less than that of the field at a further distance; the lack of skill of draughtsmen in handling of foreshortening and, finally, in the actual experience of such distortion under certain circumstances resulting from binocular vision.

Figure 3.6C P. Picasso, " Sitting woman with a fish hat". (Reproduced with permission of the Stedelijk Museum, Amsterdam). The woman's face is a collage of two *typical views* and her chair violates the rule of perspective convergence.

The case for the first of the postulated origins simply rests on the fact that representation of a cube in a manner shown in Figure 3.7A enables an artist to show both side faces as well as the frontal face and thus to tell us more about the solid; and what is true for the cube is also true for a table, a cupboard, a tomb and other similar shapes. However, the device was also used when the artist was not particularly concerned with showing the three faces. It could be argued that this was due to contagion. This *might* be so, but the case for the postulated reason is nevertheless weakened by this "unnecessary" use. Nor is this use always helpful in providing the opportunity to show more of the depicted scene, for whilst it makes protrayal of additional external surfaces possible its consistent use makes it impossible to draw, say, three internal walls, a floor and a ceiling of a room. The reader is invited to convince himself that this is so by sketching in inverse perspective a view down a long empty corridor. For these interior scenes convergent perspective offers the same advantages as the divergent does for exterior views. Nevertheless it is apparent that the artist in Figure 3.6A has shown at least two views of the nativity scene. The monk or friar (who probably represents St. Joseph) on the left of the picture is rather awkwardly drawn; the torso and head imply an almost rear view while the right leg and foot imply a side view. The window at the top right appears to show the inner surfaces of both vertical sides and the left gable of the stable is shown enface in contrast to the side view of the extended roof. This incorporation of two views may help to explain why the two ends of the crib should both be visible and acceptable to the artist. These two views however do not explain why the picture has clear evidence of reverse perspective and so other explanations must be considered.

The second suggestion is exemplified as follows: consider an observer standing near the edge of a football pitch and looking across it. In this position he will see two boundary lines painted on the grass, one at his feet and the other parallel to it on the other side of the field. Our observer will, therefore, see a shorter segment of the first line than of the second line.

This is necessarily so because his angle of vision admits a lesser extent of the near than of the far environment. The frontal projection of the two segments will therefore have the form of a shorter line below a parallel longer line. Connecting of the ends of these lines will yield a trapezium diverging "away" from the observer. This argument contains an implicit notion that the shape of the observer's visual field is in some manner influencing his perception and depiction of objects within it. This certainly was the case with one of Bartel's architectural students. This competent draughtsman confessed that whenever he was required to draw a perspective view of a parallelogram, he had to resist a spontaneous inclination to draw parallel lines as converging towards the bottom of the picture since a mischievous argument suggested itself to him that the light rays converge at the eye, and therefore must be further apart at greater distance.

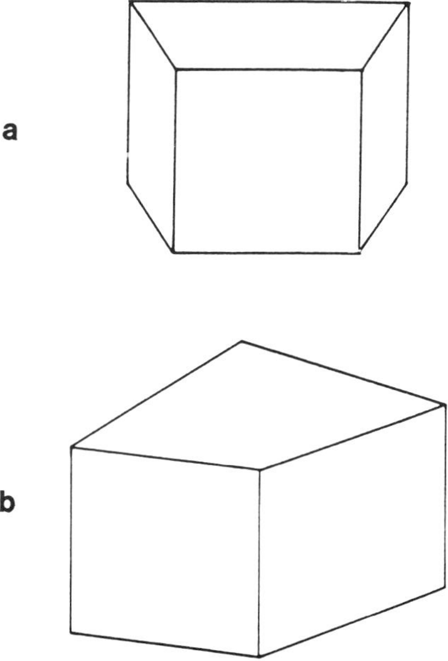

Figure 3.7 A- shows a cube drawn in the manner which enables the artist to show four of its faces. This facility may be responsible for this style of drawing. B- another kind of distorted cube. Compare it with the chair on which Picasso's "Woman with a fish hat" is seated (figure 3.6C).

The third suggestion refers to a draughtsman's inability to resist the drift towards the true shape and away from the shape of the projection. This causes him to draw the visible side of a cube (see Figure 3.7) as more squarish than it should be whilst the top edge of the invisible face is drawn at a more or less correct angle with the inevitable consequence of divergence. One would expect therefore a more skilled draughtsman to be less prone to this error, and one would not expect such an error to become a characteristic of an artistic style. But it is characteristic of oriental art, and this weakens the argument.

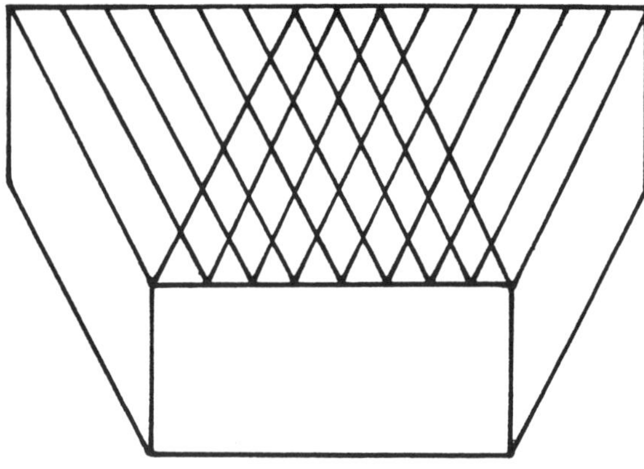

Figure 3.8 Inverse perspective as seen by most observers in the experiment. Occasionally when one eye takes over entirely only one of the two overlapping elements is seen and the divergence vanishes.

The fourth suggestion can best be expounded by means of two demonstrations: the first demonstration concerns binocular vision. Take a matchbox, and mark on its top surface in the middle of the edge abutting the "drawer" two points, one at each end. Place the box in front of you on the table at about 40 cm. from the eyes so that the two marks are in line with your nose. Fixate on the mark nearest to you. The edge at the further mark will now appear (contrary to the rules of perspective) longer than the corresponding nearer edge. If you close one of your eyes the phenomenon will vanish. The phenomenon is due to binocular vision, which in the case of the further edge furnishes the observer with two overlapping images (as shown in Figure 3.8) which, when combined, exaggerate the width, but which also occasionally fade, one at a time, so that even with both eyes open the box is seen as "convergent" just as it is seen monocularly.

Figure 3.9 Look at the centre of the figure from the distance indicated by the straight line below it. Note that the pattern looks regular.

The second demonstration indicating the experience of seeing diverging lines as parallel derives from Helmholtz's observations on monocular vision. He notes that pairs of divergent hyperbolae when viewed from a carefully chosen point appear to be parallel straight lines, suggesting that geometric divergence may in certain circumstances be used to evoke the perception of parallelity. This effect can be readily experienced by looking with one eye directly downwards on the centre of Figure 3.9, keeping the eye the appropriate distance above the point. The divergent lines of the figure will then be seen as parallel[9].

To what extent these four postulated factors and experiences arising from the perception of after-images contribute to the establishment of inverse perspective is a matter of speculation, but in the present context the last factor is most important because it demonstrates most directly that inverse perspective probably has a real perceptual origin.

The fact that correct drawing of a perspective view has so often given rise to problems is attested by the development of optico-mechanical devices to guide the draughtsman such as those shown in Figure 3.2. It is interesting to note that it is when the draughtsman overcomes the tendencies insinuated by their naive appraisal of the visual scene that the representation is judged to be superior. Thus tracing the projections of the camera obscura was seen as a major advance in artistic representation; the picture being structured according to straightforward optical principles led to admiration of its "reality". Surely a strong argument against the view that perspective is merely a convention!

Under natural conditions the eye works by sampling the environment and evaluating the samples in order for us to perceive a stable extended world. A picture can be seen as just a portion of the environment in which an artist can place a selection of cues in any manner he wishes and thus bias the eye's samples and, in consequence, the viewer's perception. The cues which he provides rely for their evocative effectiveness on their similarity to the "natural" cues available from the environment. Not all environmental cues can be included in a picture and hence even in the most realistic painting the choice of samples provided is less than that available from nature. On some occasions it approximates to nature's range but does not fill it. On the other hand as we have seen, a picture provides subsidiary cues which are not available in the scene portrayed but which are crucial to the picture's utility. However, the cues chosen within the picture mimic natural cues, and in part, determine the style in which a picture is made.

But an artist can go further than merely mimicking of the environment. He can cross Dürer's projection screen and seek a more intimate contact with the object by mimicking the eye's reactions and so make a picture which not only includes information provided by the environment but which also includes a sample of the eye's very response. This addition extends further the range of available "styles", for there are several responses of the eye which can be chosen for combination with a variety of environmental cues. These devices and their use in art are discussed extensively in chapter 7.

Further extension of the range of stylistic possibilities arises because the eye does not respond only to those cues which are in exactly the same form as the "natural" cues, but shows considerable tolerance for approximations and will treat as good coins those which are clearly counterfeit. What a viewer makes of the furnished cues depends on his sensitivity and knowledge. His mundane experience tells him that not all elements, not all the cues which he perceives, should be given equal weight; that some of them need be attenuated relative to others in order to make sense of the stimulus. It is not necessary for observers to rely on the same cues to the same extent to arrive at the same answer, any more than it is necessary for the same physical acts to be performed to arrive at the same outcome. Thus for example, the manner of hand-knitting used in Jutland differs radically from that used in Scotland, but the same garments having identical characteristics can be made in both ways.

Similarly observers may sample different cues from the environment and yet arrive at the same conclusion about which objects are present and, which is more important here, different samples of cues (i.e. which can lead to different artistic styles) can be used to depict the same object. The acceptability of imperfect representations which systematically deviate from the cues obtainable "naturally" is particularly important because it makes the introduction of techniques for creation of such approximations worthwhile. Such techniques, as is the case with central linear perspective, can form a guide to pictorial composition, and provided that they are not allowed to dominate the creative process, but merely to serve it, prove extremely useful.

The main purpose of this chapter was to draw the reader's attention to the important notion of *subsidiary awareness*. Binocular cues can be overcome to enhance an effect (as in Pozzo's painting) or they can be utilised to "remind" the viewer that a picture is being viewed and so certain allowances must be made. We have shown that when the paradox which paintings present, of visually being both flat *and* three-dimensional, is clearly resolved in favour of unquestionable three-dimensionality and subsidiary awareness is lost, then the viewer finds himself in a perceptually pliable world and the representational utility of the painting is circumscribed by the demands of a restricted viewing position. The distortions in most painting which occur with changes in viewing position are still there but usually pass unnoticed probably because viewers only attend to the structure of a picture when looking from a fairly central position.

The paradox can also be resolved in just the opposite manner by abandoning all the claims to visual three-dimensionality. This can be done by creating an epitomic picture (see Chapter 1) which conveys clearly what is depicted but embodies no monocular depth cues. A pin-man is such a figure. Viewing such a drawing at an extremely shallow angle does not affect greatly the resulting percept. This is also true of other more complex but flat pictures such as van der Leck's *Musicians* (Figure 3.10). Seen at a very sharp angle from a side, so sharp that the *subsidiary awareness* of the picture's surface does not offer sufficient compensation, the two musicians are seen as somewhat slimmer than they "really are" and their dog seems somewhat shorter, but the picture remains essentially unchanged.

Figure 3.10 Bart van der Leck, "The musicians", a meaningful picture with no pictorial depth. (Reproduced with permission of Rijksmuseum Kröller-Müller, Otterlo, Holland).

CHAPTER IV

The Limits Of Perspective

The perceptual mechanisms of vision are flexible and, daily experience shows, quite capable of handling visual cues which are incomplete or which are in some other manner obscure. It does get tricked at times, it may for example mistake a short narrowing passage for a much longer one having parallel walls. Such "tricks" have indeed been used by architects. In the overwhelming majority of cases, however, the eye is not tricked and errors do not occur; if they did our chances of survival would be greatly reduced.

The ability to extract correct visual information rests on continuous sampling of the environment by observers who look at different times on different features of their surroundings. These glances allow their visual systems to provide them with material for rapid and unconscious construction of a rich perceptual synthesis of the visual environment. An artist does not, in this respect, differ from other people, but he has an additional task, that of representing certain aspects of the visual world. In doing this he can choose to acknowledge the existence of samples from which his notion of the world was derived or he may choose to present the stable world as he immediately perceives it i.e. he may incorporate aspects of the retinal projection or alternatively portray the scene embodying a "naive" rendering of object proportion. The "acknowledgements" can take, as we shall see, many forms and these generally convey spatial rather than temporal aspects of experience. Only in the relatively rare pictures which represent orderly, repetitive or similar rhythmic movement is representation of temporal aspects possible and has occasionally been attempted; Chwistek has done so, for example in his painting of a duel between swordsmen (Figure 4.1A) as have several futurist painters like Giacomo Balla whose painting of a dog on a leash (Figure 4.1B) captures the rhythmic repetition of the movements[1]

Figure 4.1A L. Chwistek, "A Duel". In this and the succeeding picture by Balla the rhythm of the movements is emphasised.

In the great majority of works of art in which perceptual samples (and often the more sensory aspects of the perceptual process) are made explicit, the temporal aspects are purely incidental and spatial aspects predominate. Since the representation of the "samples" does not imply reproduction of actual samples but rather reproduction of the experience of sampling, the artist has at his disposal a useful technique for accentuating selected facets of his observation. This is exemplified by Mondrian's *Composition* (Figure 4.2). In the *Composition* the centre of the picture is clearest. Both the black horizontal and vertical lines, so characteristic of Mondrian's paintings, are most distinct there and the colours of the little blocks are purest. Away from the centre the lines fade and the colours become more diluted, with pink dominating the top, and darker blue the bottom margin of the picture.

Figure 4.1B G. Balla "Dynamism of a dog on a leash", 1912. Reproduced by permission of the Albright-Knox Art Gallery, Buffalo, New York. Bequest of A. Conger Goodyear; a gift of George F. Goodyear.

Although the *Composition* is not a descriptive work of art it incorporates a device derived from daily experience and presents a pattern as it would be seen in a single glance, the beholders eye looking at its very centre, while surrounding regions are less distinctly perceived. When we look at a particular point of visual space the clarity of our vision degrades progressively as we move away from the line of light and Mondrian's picture captures this aspect of the visual process. This degrading of clarity happens because the retina itself can only resolve fine grain optical information close to the line of light (see Chapter 7 for a much fuller account of this effect).

Figure 4.2 P. Modrian, "Composition", 1913. Reproduced with permission of the Rijkmuseum Kröller-Müller, Otterlo, Holland. Note the fading from centre to edge of the painting.

An even gentler hint of the positions theoretically occupied by the artist's eye can be found in those paintings in which depictions of parallel lines have more than one point of convergence. Jan van Eyck's *Portrait of Giovanni Arnolfini and his Wife* (Figure 1.1) is such a picture. When, as shown in the diagram (Figure 4.3), the joints of the floor are extended, these are found to converge at a point lying on the vertical axis of the picture at the height of the couple's hands. When the joints of the ceiling are extended, they converge at a point on the same vertical line but at the level of Arnolfini's nose. Furthermore extensions of the top and bottom of the left hand window and of the edge of the cupboard immediately below it all converge at yet another point in the right-hand half of the painting close to Donna Arnolfini's arm. In the "real world" all these lines, forming three disparate sets, were parallel orthogonals to the projection plane and should therefore, if the rules of linear perspective are obeyed, converge at one point. Since there are at least three points of convergence, the notional artist's eye must have occupied at least three distinct positions. The beholder's eye does not readily notice this lack of unity and the painting seems to be well composed. Thus the beholder's eye can compensate for, or has sufficient tolerance of, the movements of the artist's eye and a coherent perceptual experience may be derived. However close inspection leaves one with a feeling that the spatial composition of the picture is not quite right. The reasons for this will now be examined.

Although perception is generally veridical, it is not inevitably so. To assume that it always is, is tantamount to accepting the eye as the final arbiter and adopting the crude "eye is like a camera" analogy, which, although in some respects helpful, is also misguided.

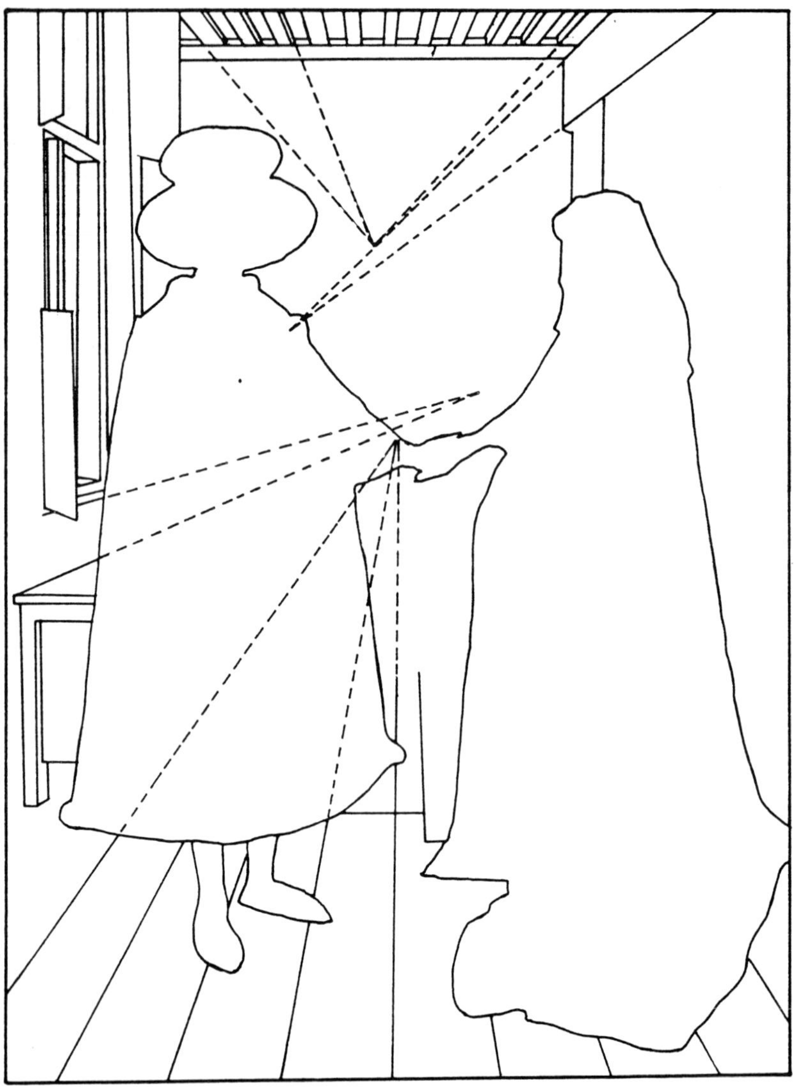

Figure 4.3 The diagram shows the inconsistencies in perspective in the van Eyck portrait shown in figure 1.1. One would expect them to be readily noticeable but in fact they are not.

A variety of simple geometric configurations known as *Visual Illusions*[2] show the dangers of such a simplification. Two of these are reproduced below. They were chosen because both of them can easily be reproduced by the reader in the "real world". The first figure (Figure 4.4) is called the horizontal-vertical illusion. Its striking characteristic is that it evokes overestimation of the upright line relative to the horizontal line. The same effect is evoked by two equal pencils identically arranged, whether laid out flat on the page or held so that one of them is vertical. The second figure consisting of four lines is the Ponzo illusion which was introduced earlier (Figure 2.6). Again, an appropriate arrangement of the two pencils at an angle corresponding to that of the two longer lines and two paper-clips in position of the shorter lines which the reader can construct for himself will convince him that the phenomenon can be found in the "real world" and is not confined to drawings.

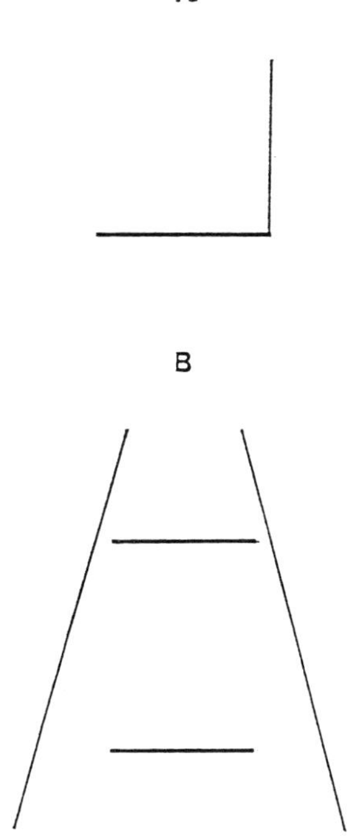

Figure 4.4 A- the horizontal vertical illusion. B- the Ponzo illusion.

Even more cogent evidence against the eye-is-like-a-camera analogy is provided by the eye's capacity to summarise a series of retinal images, or a continuously transforming image, none of which shows a complete object and each of which is seen at a different time, into a percept of a complete object[3]. This happens, for example, when one views a picture through a shield with a narrow slit sliding over its surface so that only a small part of the surface is visible at any time. If the slit is moved fairly quickly one has the clear impression of seeing the object at once as a complete pattern.

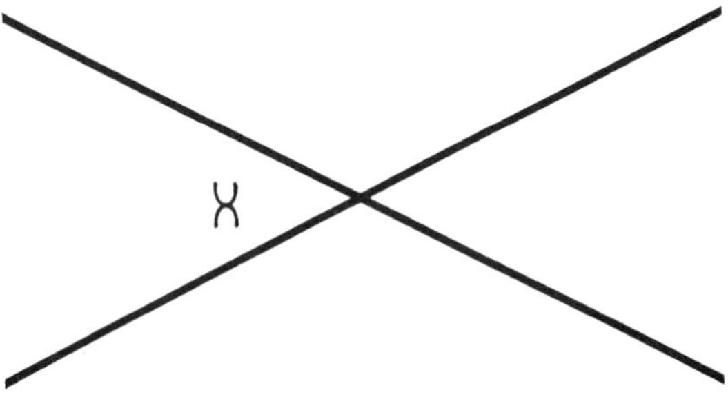

Figure 4.5 Fixation of the point marked X within the St. Andrew's cross apparently expands the angles opposite. The perceived angles within the figure are thus affected by the direction of gaze.

Other phenomena which are of special interest in the present context because they question the absolute validity of the rules of linear perspective are those concerning the perception of angles. The rules of perspective imply that when the same rate of convergence is used to depict a floor and a ceiling of a corridor or a room, these should be seen as receding at the same rate. The experimental evidence contradicts this. A pair of converging lines is seen by most as converging more rapidly when their point of intersection is below them than when it is above them. The reader can experience this by viewing the Ponzo figure in its normal orientation and upside down. Perceived angles are also affected by the direction of gaze; this too is contrary to the rules of perspective. Thus, when the St. Andrew's cross, shown in Figure 4.5, is viewed with eyes fixed at

X the angle opposite is seen as expanded relative to the angle containing X. Analogous changes are noted when the point of fixation is placed in the other three fields; in each case there is an apparent expansion of the field opposite.

Another instance in which the retinal projection is not an entirely reliable guide to the percept and which, as we shall see, is of crucial importance to an understanding of the alternative ways of representing pictorial depth, was that investigated by ten Doesschate.

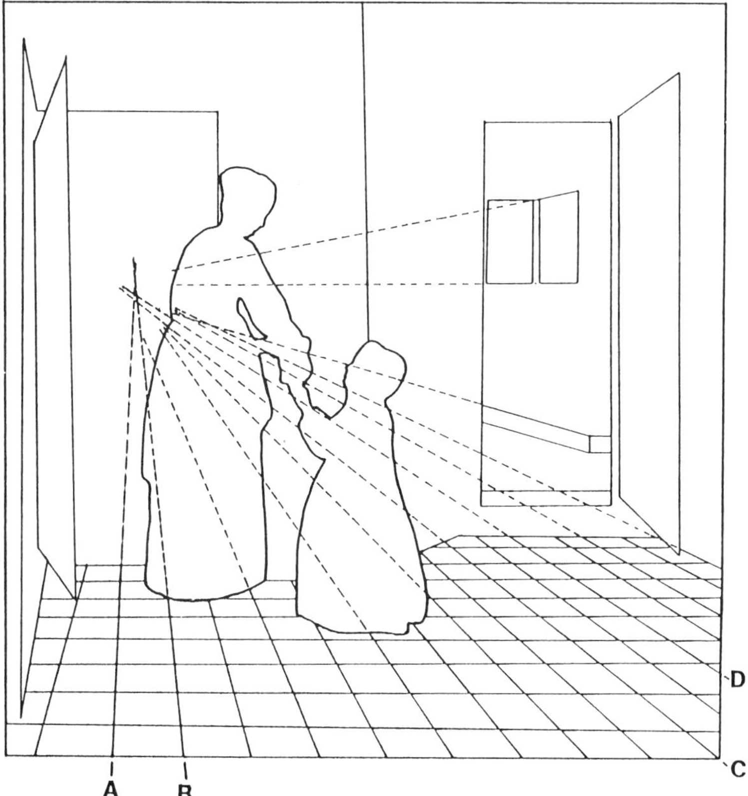

Figure 4.6 Drawing after P. de Hooch "The Pantry". The floor tiles on the right hand side have been drawn using the same point of convergence as the rest of the floor, yet viewers do not generally perceive this. Lines A and B are seen as converging to the left of the point of convergence of C and D.

The essence of linear perspective[4], as described previously, is that all lines in a picture which represent parallel elements perpendicular to the observer's frontal plane converge to a central vanishing point. Thus the joints of the tiled floor of Pieter de Hooch's *Pantry* (Figure 4.6) either run parallel to the horizontal edges of the picture or converge to a point just behind the back of the young woman. Convergence of the joints lying in the left hand side of the picture, below the vanishing point, and therefore also below the point occupied by the hypothetical eye, is particularly convincing. Viewers shown the picture and asked to show where the joints A and B converge indicate the true point with considerable accuracy. Such accuracy is not noted when the same observers are asked to indicate where joints C and D converge. The point chosen in response to this request falls to the right of the true point of convergence. Similar effects can be noted in "real life". An observer standing on the pavement of a long straight road sees the two edges of the pavement converging into the distance in front of him. The edges of the parallel pavement or the other side of the roadway, although also appearing to converge with distance, do not seem to do so at a sufficient rate to reach the same focus but appear to intersect at a point further away from the observer. These observations are confirmed by ten Doesschate's investigations showing that recognition of parallelism is not tantamount to recognition of a single point of convergence. Observers placed in a darkened room at the ends of two parallel fluorescent tubes and on the line equidistant from both of them described them as parallel and indicated where they thought that the tubes, if extended, would appear to converge. When a third tube was placed in parallel with the other two, observers, remaining in the same position, reported it to be parallel but they did not see it as tending towards the same point as the other two. To create this impression the third tube had to be set at an angle relative to the others so as to introduce real spatial convergence. A rule which these observations suggest is that the degree of apparent convergence decreases with the distance of the parallels from the observer's line of sight.

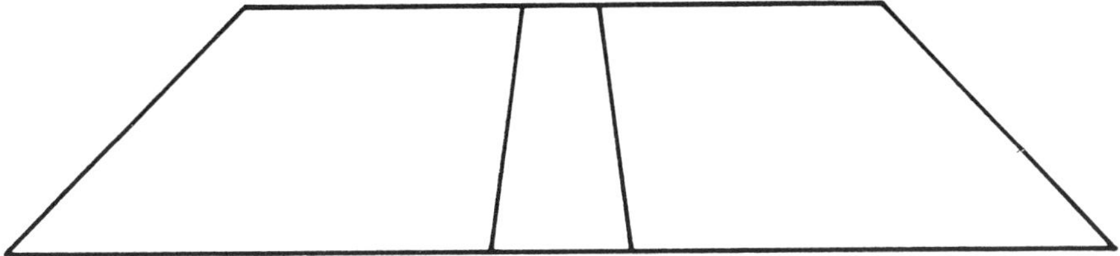

Figure 4.7 Where is the point of convergence of the two outer sloping line? Where is the point of convergence of the two inner sloping lines? Generally the former is reported as being closer to the figure than the latter. In fact they are coincident.

A similar effect can readily be demonstrated on a diagram (Figure 4.7). Unprejudiced observers when asked to indicate the point of convergence of (i) the two sloping lines within the figure, (ii) the two sloping sides of the figures' edges, tend to show the latter as being nearer to the body of the figure than the former. In fact all four lines have a common point of convergence, and could therefore according to the rules of linear perspective be taken to represent, say, an outline of a rectangular floor with a narrow central carpet.

The observations obtained by means of fluorescent tubes and by means of a simple diagram are concordant. In the former case parallel lines do not appear to converge to one point; those at the greater lateral distances appear to converge more reluctantly and meet at more distant points. In the latter case convergent lines are not seen as such; those at greater lateral distances converging more rapidly and meeting "in front" of the more central lines. Both cases demonstrate therefore that a perspective drawing having a single point of convergence for a set of parallel, laterally spaced lines is but an approximation to a perceptually correct drawing. The former case shows that a single point of convergence is not seen in nature under such circumstances; the latter that when a single point of convergence is used in making a drawing the drawing seems imperfect.

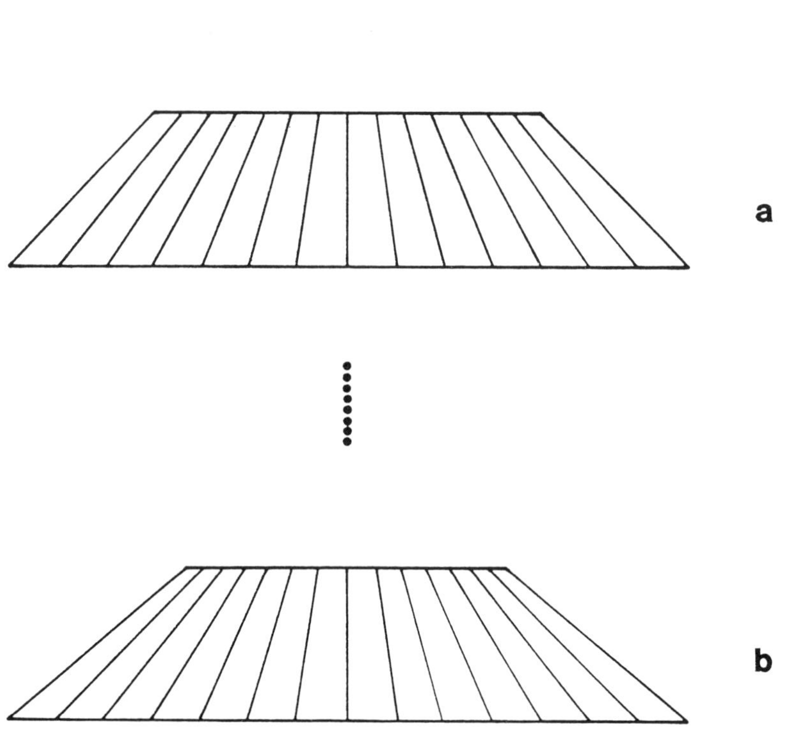

Figure 4.8 Two ways of conveying a receding surface; (a) true (b) false convergence. Figure (b) is seen by many as superior in conveying pictorial depth although, as shown by the dots, the point of convergence for each pair of lines is different.

These observations argue that for reasons which are not as yet clear, linear perspective does not satisfactorily convey parallelism of lines orthogonal to the picture's surface, and that a superior depiction of a surface can be achieved by increasing convergence of the outer lines, that is to say that Figure 4.8B conveys an impression of such a surface better than Figure 4.8A. There are however technical difficulties with the use of this modified representation. There is no system of draughtsmanship which can readily be applied. When drawing strictly in perspective an artist has but to select a point on the surface in order to represent the projected position of the eye, and all lines radiating from it will represent orthogonals; no such unfailing guide can be offered to an artist who wishes to allow for different rates of convergence.

To summarise what we have said so far: (i) Parallel lines overhead appear to converge less than equivalent lines below the line of sight; (ii) laterally placed parallel lines appear to converge less rapidly than more centrally placed parallel lines. If a painter noted these perceptual peculiarities and tried to correct for them so that what appeared to be a uniform pattern of convergence was presented to the viewer then a picture very like the Van Eyck portrait (Figure 1.1) would be produced. It is as if Van Eyck has offered us his version of a subjective perspective system. Unfortunately he has over corrected, particularly with the wall and the bed so that the over rapid convergence of the contours of these has opened up the room making it more like a stage set than the interior of a room. However the picture has to be carefully examined before this distortion is really appreciated. Most viewers find the spatial arrangement acceptable.

One device occasionally employed to give an impression of depth is substitution of two sets of parallel lines for convergent lines; the lines to the left of the central line of the surface sloping towards the right and those to the right sloping towards the left. The effect is not entirely convincing since the differential rates of convergence are not thereby achieved;

moreover the confluence of the two sets of lines often presents difficulties, as shown in the floor pattern of all early Spanish illustrations in the *Libro del Consultado del Mar* (Figure 4.9). The miniaturist who painted the king of Valencia being petitioned by his subjects (Christians on the right, Moors on the left) solved the problems of depiction of the floor and of the royal canopy in two different ways. The floor is painted using two sets of parallel lines which converge forming a series of inverted V shapes, but the canopy, surprisingly, is rendered in accordance with rules approximating to those of perspective.

Figure 4.9 A drawing from a miniature in the *Libro Consulado del Mar*. The figure shows two ways of conveying pictorial depth. The stripes of the canopy converge (albeit not to a single point). The stripes on the floor run in parallel forming a series of inverted "V"s.

When a painting shows a relatively unconstrained view, a well defined zone of convergence rather than a single point may, however, provide an elegant solution, as demonstrated by Van Gogh's *View of Saintes-Maires* (Figure 4.10).

Figure 4.10 Drawing from V. van Gogh's "View of Saintes Maries". Rows of plants do not converge to a single point but to a restricted region.

Representation of interiors in which the floor and the walls and the ceiling are all expected to converge is more difficult. Two stratagems are available and commonly used by artists: concealment and distraction.

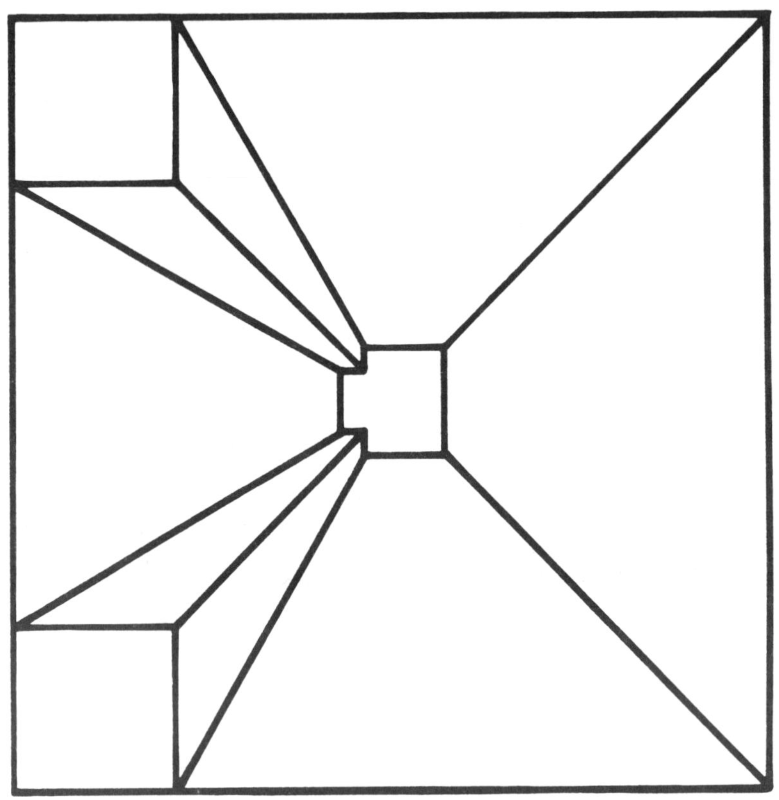

Figure 4.11 The left hand side of the figure shows how an apparently too rapid rate of convergence of the joints of the wall with the ceiling and the floor can be concealed by an artist. The right hand side shows the unconcealed joints.

Figure 4.11 shows a windowless cell drawn in accordance with the rules of linear perspective by an artist whose eye looked constantly at the middle point of the back wall. One would expect the drawing to suffer from the same defect of an unacceptably rapid rate of convergence as the drawing of the floor just considered and indeed it does. The effect can however be easily reduced by the introduction of two "boxes" which conceal the offending joints between the walls, the floor and the ceiling. Such a device has been repeatedly and very successfully used by painters, for example by Pieter de Hooch both in his *Pantry* and in his *Linen Cupboard* (Figure 4.6 and Figure 4.12), where the left side of the picture is filled with a massive piece of furniture.

Figure 4.12 P. de Hooch, "The Linen Cupboard". (Reproduced by permission of Rijksmuseum-Stichting, Amsterdam, Holland).

In both pictures there is an open door on the right, which effectively breaks the space and which in the case of *The*

Linen Cupboard enables the artist to abandon the dominant point of convergence by introducing the diamond pattern of floor tiles leading to a sunny street. The subterfuge is not normally noticed. Such ruses are also found in other well known pictures. In Vermeer's *The Music Lesson,* for example, the right hand wall is not visible and the point of convergence is so placed that only a very short segment of the joint between the left-hand wall and the ceiling appears in the picture. The extent of the floor joint is somewhat larger, but it is submerged in darkness, and the diamond pattern of the floor provides no strong linear cues.

In Jan van Eyck's *Arnolfini and his Wife* (Figure 1.1) a similar device is used to avoid the clash which would be created by lines drawn to different points of convergence from the edges of the left-hand wall and of the ceiling and those of the left-hand wall and the floor. The use of such tricks by that assumed puritan of perspective, Saenredam, will be discussed in the next chapter at some length.

Further and equally cogent evidence against the notion that simple linear perspective furnishes a perfect representation of the world is provided by a series of experiments conducted by Kazimierz Bartel[5] The experiments were concerned with the perceived location of objects in real and pictorial space.

In the first experiment students were seated so that on their right-hand side they had a receding wall as shown in Figure 4.13. A thin long black pole was attached to the wall in the distant corner, and identical poles were equispaced along its length. Each student was required to draw the six poles on a sheet of paper showing a perspective outline of the wall. These drawings were analysed. A geometrical construction was used to derive the ratios of true distances which, assuming that the drawings made obeyed the rules of perspective, were represented by each student. In the second experiment students seated in the same position and looking at the wall on which only the nearest and the furthest poles were displayed, instructed an assistant to place the remaining four poles so that all six poles appeared equispaced. The spacings obtained were recorded. In the third experiment of the series, the students were again required to draw in the poles within the outline, but on this occasion the spacing of the poles was that experimentally determined in the second experiment i.e. the placings they themselves had determined. As in the first experiment the ratios of the represented distances were determined.

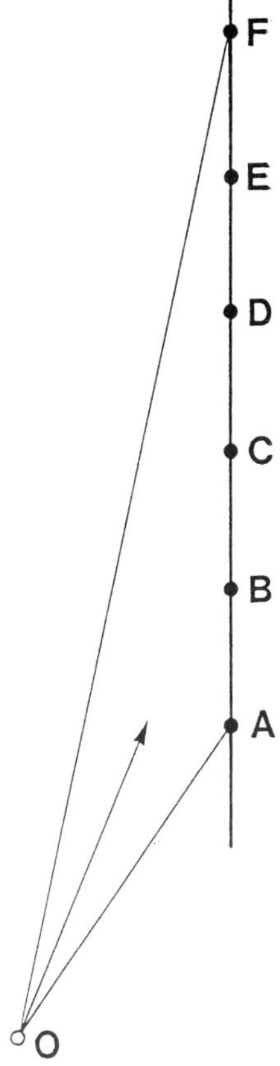

Figure 4.13 Experimental arrangements in Bartel's study. In the first experiment students were required to indicate, on an outline provided, the positions of poles A - F. In the second experiment they had to place poles B - E in appropriate positions. In the final experiment they prepared another drawing of six poles spaced in accordance with their own placings in the second experiment. O = observer's position.

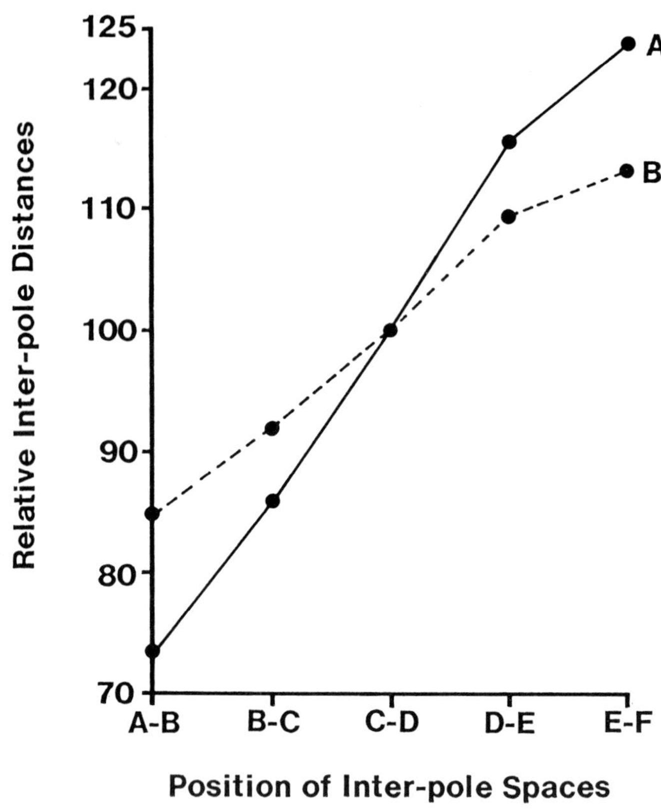

Figure 4.14 Graphical representation of Bartel's experimental results. The graph shows the relative size of the spacings resulting from (a) placing the poles in a perspective drawing (the first experiment) and (b) placing the poles B to E between poles A to F on the wall of the experimental room (second experiment). If the spacings had been correct both functions would have been horizontal.

Figure 4.14 shows spacings obtained in two of Bartel's experiments. It shows clearly that whether drawing the poles or locating them in real space the students increasingly exaggerated the spatial intervals as the distance from the point of observation increased. Instead of using equal intervals they used progressively longer intervals for the spaces further away. In no condition were the rules of perspective strictly observed.

Furthermore responses made in the third experiment, in which an arrangement perceived as equispaced had to be drawn, the progressive increase in the length of intervals was even further accentuated showing that the extent of deviation from correct perspective spacing was affected by the act of drawing. The effect observed in real space had, it seems, to be strengthened further when represented in pictorial space.

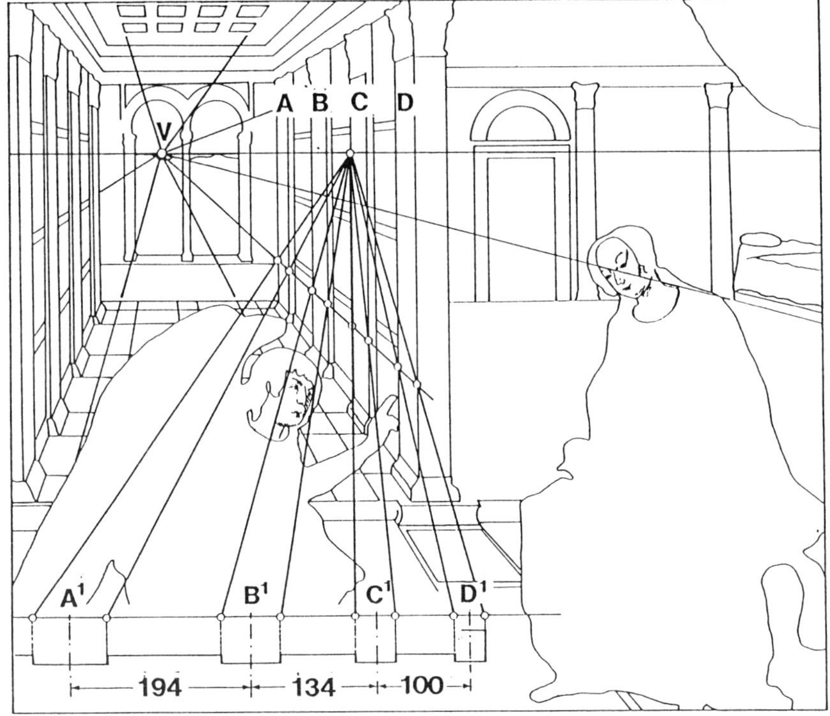

Figure 4.15 P. Pollaiuolo, "Annunciation". The diagram shows the spacings of the depicted columns using the reconstruction method of Bartel (1947).

All three experiments involved the representation of, or perception of, real space and it is possible that when a draughtsman has to deal with pictorial space only, as when painting from imagination, the effect will not be observed. Bartel checked this by presenting students with a true perspective drawing of a road with two telephone poles and requesting them to insert in it four intermediate telephone poles. The ratios of true distances were again derived. It was apparent that they showed the same pattern as the ratios derived from truly spatial observations. A further experiment confirmed that these ratios were preferred to "correct" ratios. The similarity of the elements used here to those forming density gradients is readily apparent, and since perspective and density gradient cues are formally related, the implications of these observations are unlikely to be confined to linear perspective.

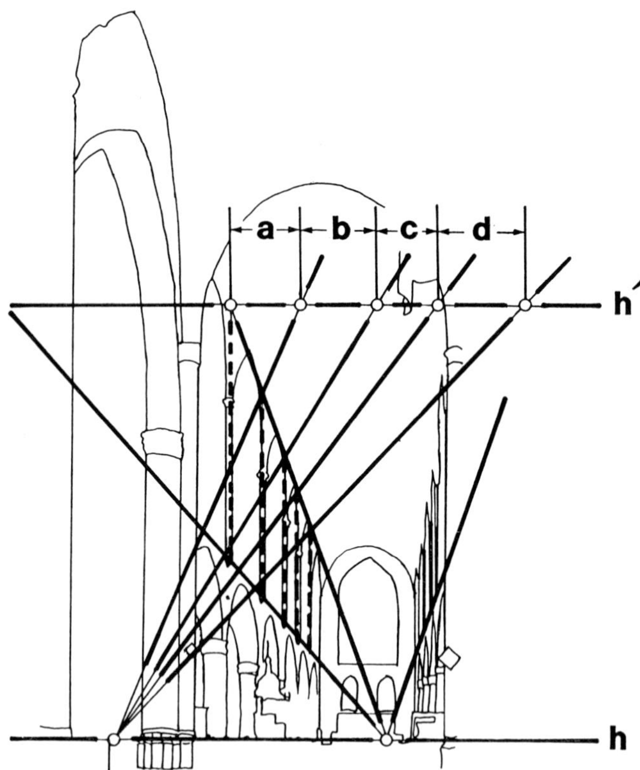

Figure 4.16 Diagram of the arrangement of columns in P. Saenredam's, "Interior of St. Bavo's Church called the 'Groote Kerk' at Haarlem".

Do the deviations from "correct" perspective which we have discussed prevail in recognised works of art? Indeed they do. Figure 4.15 is a reproduction of a painting by Piero Pollaiuolo. This figure shows the spacing which the apparently equispaced columns would really have. Application of the same technique to Saenredam's picture of the *Groote Kerk* (Figure 4.16) shows that this supposedly meticulous architectual painter did not remain true to the tenets of simple linear perspective. The geometric construction used here and in the experiments described above is given in the notes[5] The reader may wish to apply it to pictures of his own choosing.

The obvious question to which these violations of linear perspective, as well as those successful attempts to conceal its imperfections, give rise is: To what extent is linear perspective purely a matter of convention? A final answer to this will have to wait until the final chapter, although we have already hinted at our view in the previous chapter and we discuss this issue again in Chapter 6.

Chapter V

Views Typical And Otherwise

We have discussed at some length the difficulties of extrapolation of an imaginary point of convergence of three luminous tubes *known* to be parallel and *seen* as being parallel and the difficulties of extrapolation of a common point of convergence of four short lines drawn, in accordance with the rules of perspective, to represent parallel lines. We have concluded that these difficulties are probably related. This failure to extrapolate the point of convergence, when this is feasible, contrasts with observers' responses to certain drawings in which convergence is seen, although it is not there. Thus the majority of observers find Figure 5.1 a perfectly acceptable representation of a truncated pyramid: a solid having two horizontal triangular faces (the base and the top) and three sloping trapezoidal sides. This impression is often so strong that a suggestion that the solid drawn could not possibly exist - that it is an *impossible*[1] truncated pyramid - is rejected, and even the explanation that, as its edges do not converge to a single point, it must be such, is questioned on the grounds that one is demonstrating this on a *drawing* of a solid, and not on the solid itself. Even the argument that, given the single stance from which the solid is drawn, the projection of its notional apex can only be a single point and not three separate points, as shown in the figure, does not always meet with ready acceptance. The depicted solid *becomes* possible when the notion that it has a triangular base is abandoned, but such interpretations are not normally put forward by those who argue that the figure is possible.

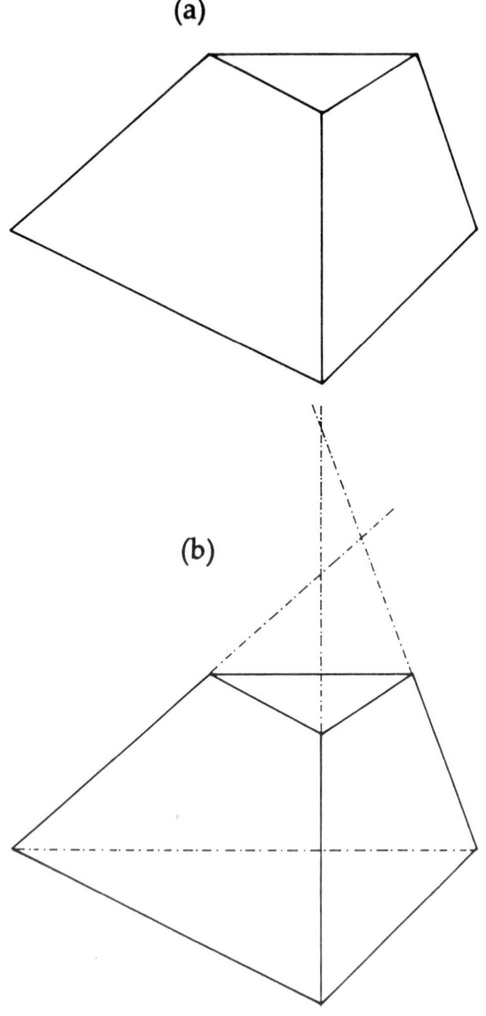

Figure 5.1 An impossible pyramid (a) is shown and the impossibility clearly demonstrated in (b).

These observations on the perception of convergence contrast with those made earlier when discussing simple linear perspective. In perceiving a depicted solid, convergence of the edges is accepted both when the depicted edges converge and when they do not do so. In the case of perspective drawings true convergence may be perceived as divergence and three divergent lines may convey parallelity better than three convergent lines. It has long been known to psychologists that physical space and psychological space are not completely isomorphic. All the examples discussed above indicate that the representation of visual space need not conform with the rules which govern an accurate two-dimensional projection of three-dimensional space in order to be found perfectly acceptable by observers. It may be asked whether there is a corollary to these observations, namely whether there are instances where true two-dimensional projections of objects are rejected by the observer as unacceptable. It is to this question that we shall now turn our attention.

A cube so placed that two of its faces are parallel to the projection plane and directly in front of the eye will project as a square, so that a square is a legitimate representation of a cube, and artists seeking to represent a cube sometimes, albeit rarely, simply draw a square. Strictly and geometrically speaking, all projections of a cube are unique, in the sense that at no point is the projection identical with that at some other point. The same mathematical equations cater for all the projections, but the values of the co-ordinates yielded for each projection are different. The perceptual mechanism does not, however, operate in such a simple way. It copes with the environment by categorising and it breaks up such geometrically cohesive categories into perceptual categories, a fact which can be easily verified by presenting an observer with a set of projections and asking him to sort them into different groups. When such a sorting task is performed the square is categorised as the odd figure, and its representative status is often not recognised. It is stripped of the authority to represent a cube and reduced to the rank of a plane figure. To retain the status of representing a cube, it has to occur in a context, either the situational context of a person drawing a square when presented with a cube, which is of little interest to us at the present, or a pictorial context which shows, generally by inclusion of other features, that the square is really intended to represent a cube.

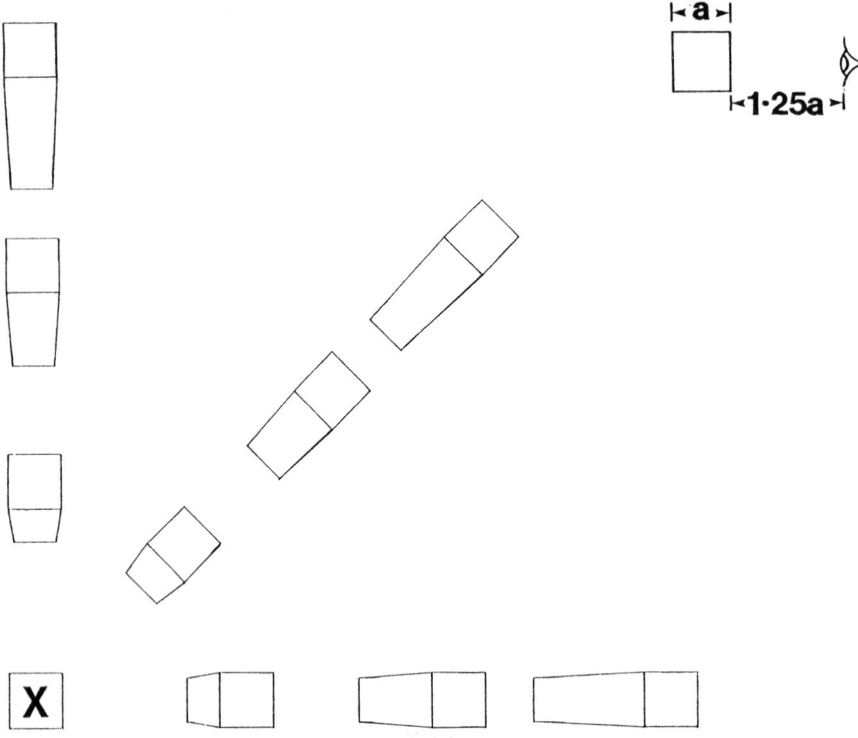

Figure 5.2A A quadrant from a ring of coplanar cubes; computer simulation of a pinhole camera photograph. The eye is assumed to be 1.25 units from the cube marked X and normal to the face of that cube. A unit = length of the edge of the cube. Note the enlargement of the projections of the side faces of the cubes.

This observation poses two questions, which must be answered with regard to any figure which is intended to represent a solid. These are:

1. Does the figure evoke the notion of the solid it is intended to represent?

2. Does the figure correspond to a projection of the solid present to an eye?

Obviously, in the case just discussed, the answer to the first of these questions is *no* and to the second it is *yes*. Let us now examine some other projections of the cube in search of those which appear to satisfy the first of the two criteria.

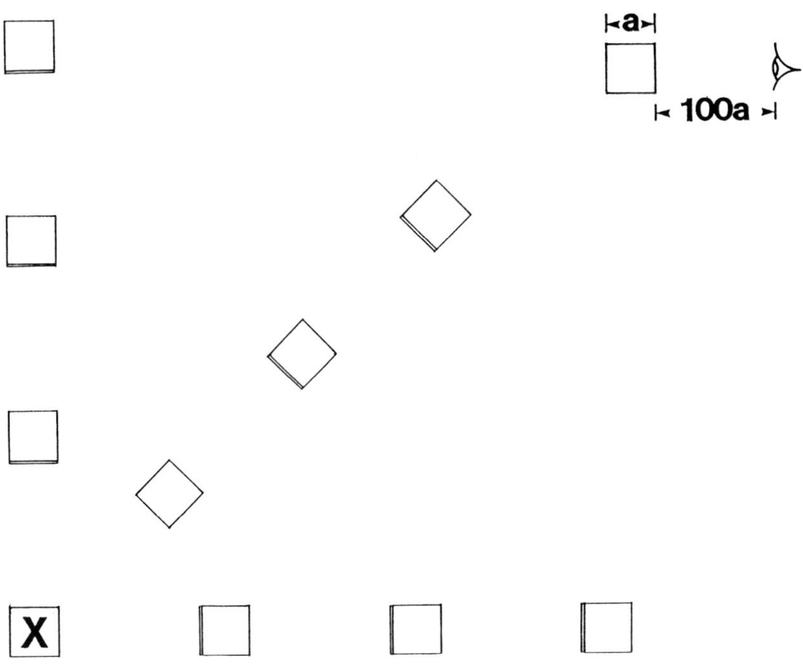

Figure 5.2B The same quadrant as in (A) but viewed from a distance 100 units from the face of the cube marked X.

Let our hypothetical Cyclop's eye remain fixed and let the cube be moved sideways or up, or down, or in any other direction but always so that its frontal face remains in the same transverse plane. Projections of the frontal face from these new positions remain entirely unchanged. They are all identical squares. Likewise sets of parallel lines which are also parallel to the projection surface would *not,* when drawn in perspective, converge. A point which has puzzled many and which was eloquently dealt with by Ruskin in 1838 (or rather by Kata Phusin, as he signed his article) when endeavouring to explain the principles of projection to a certain Mr. Parsey.

"Let Mr. Parsey look out of *his* window and I will look out of mine. It is within 3 feet of me and beyond it, at a distance of about fifty yards, rises one of the most noble buildings of Oxford, to the height of about 72 feet .... the perpendicular lines of the window frame fall precisely on those of the distant building. I try then again and again .... there is not an angle between them which a mite could measure; ..." This eminently sound argument based on empirical evidence might have convinced Mr. Parsey but unfortunately it failed to take root, for recently suggestions have been made that in perfect perspective drawings such lines should converge and therefore that perfectly rectangular tall buildings should be drawn as tapering upwards.

Let us consider further the transformation of the projection of our cube as it slides in a plane parallel to the projection plane. As the cube moves the side faces of the cube nearer to the observer will become visible, and so will either its top or its bottom depending on whether it is placed below the observer's line of sight or above it. Further, its receding edges will converge with the apparent depth. The rate of convergence will vary both with the distance which the cube has been displaced from the observer's line of sight and its distance from the observer. Figure 5.2A shows the unique square projection when the line of sight is normal to the face of the cube in the lower left corner of the figure and three sets of other projections forming a quadrant derived from three surrounding rings. These projections are obtained when the eye is positioned very close to the surface of the cube, just more than the diagonal distance across the cube's face. Figure 5.2B shows another projection of the same quadrant obtained with the hypothetical eye placed at 80 times this distance. The drawing obtained with the more distant point shows that convergence of the receding edges is not noticeable; placing the eye at intermediate distances would of course produce an intermediate projection (Figure 5.2C).

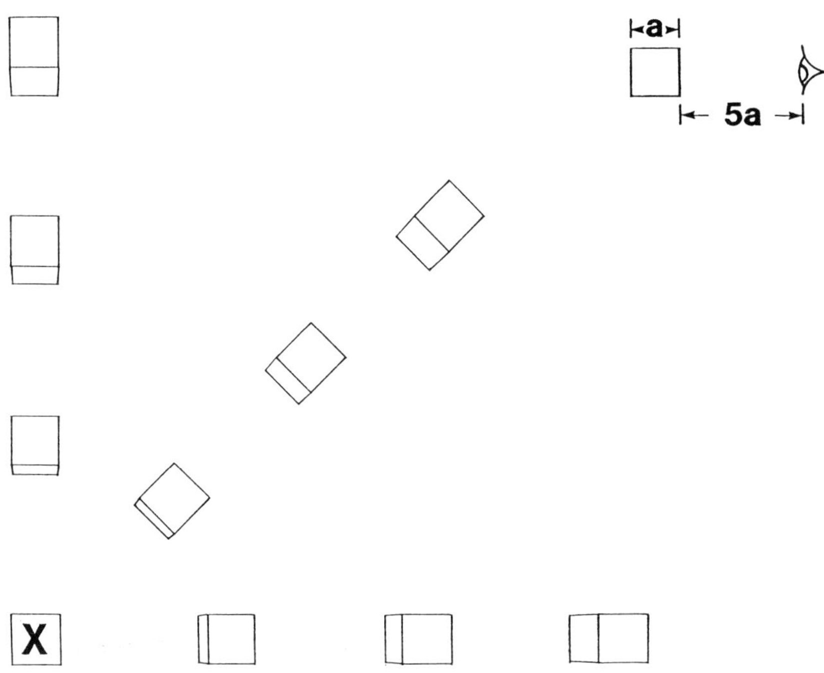

Figure 5.2C The same quadrant as that shown in (A) and (B) viewed from a distance of 5 units.

Replacement of our array of cubes by an array of squat cylinders, and subject to an analogous transformation, yields projections shown in Figure 5.3A and B. The distortions in the projections of the circular faces of the cylinders are particularly noticable in Figure 5.3A where the viewing position is very close to the cylinders but it is still apparent in Figure 5.3B where the viewing distance has been increased by a factor of 4.

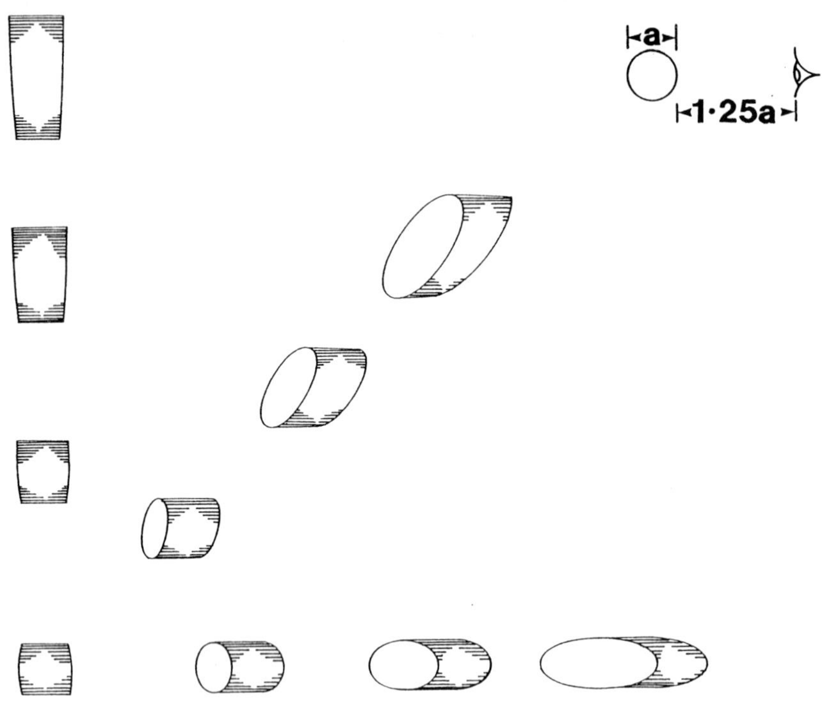

Figure 5.3A A ring of coplanar cylinders; computer simulation of a pinhole camera photograph. The eye is assumed to 1.25 units from the bottom left cylinder. Diameter of cylinder = 1 unit.

It must be reiterated here that all the figures presented show patterns which are projected into the eye, looking at the "real world", at a cube or a cylinder under the conditions described. This is readily demonstrated by placement of a screen with a pinhole in front of the eye. This procedure, as Pirenne reports, leads to the perception of such figures as undistorted solids. However, such pinhole screens also restrict the field of view so that the grossest "distortions" are not seen by the observer, and consequently their perception cannot be investigated with this technique. It is therefore possible to argue, and ten Doesschate's experiments suggest this, that the eye may not recognise as correct, figures drawn with strict adherence to the rules of perspective and falling outwith the central zone of vision.

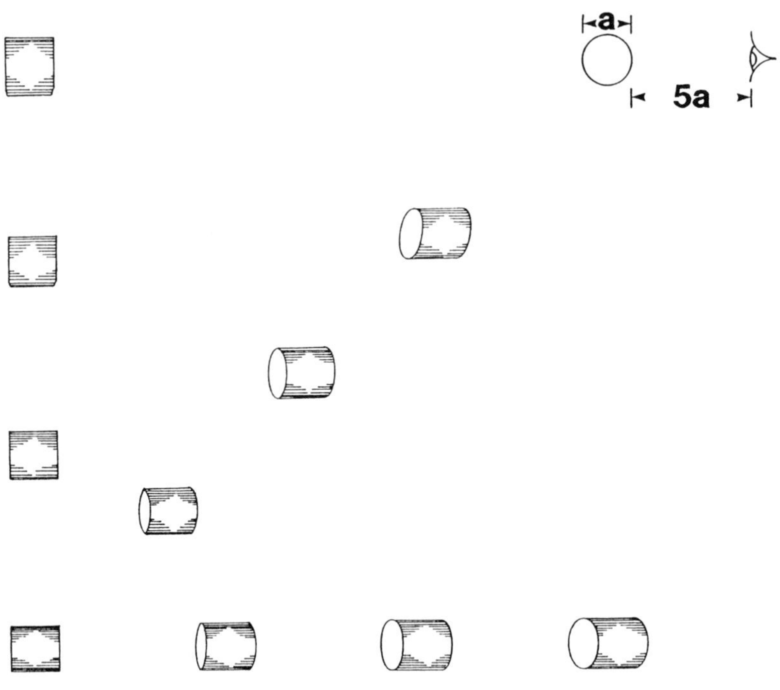

Figure 5.3B The same quadrant as that shown in (A) viewed from a distance of 5 units. The distortion is less marked than in (A) but is still present.

This correctness and equivalence of seemingly grossly distorted figures form the cornerstone of our argument that certain stylistic "distortions" are perfectly legitimate records of visual experience, provided the viewer attends carefully to the shape of objects seen in the peripheral field of view. It must be admitted that not many viewers do this but the same thing cannot be said of artists who have frequently given due attention to the appearance of objects.

Let us consider again various projections of a cube. The projections of the lateral zone assume characteristics similar to those of traditional Oriental paintings, such as those shown below, the only difference being that the scarcely noticeable convergence of receding lines is absent in Oriental art (Figure 5.4). It is therefore arguable that paintings done in this style are not purely ideoplastic, that is to say, they do not reflect knowledge about the objects which their authors have and which is a distillation of previous experience nor do they constitute global and general impressions of the figures. Instead, they are based on and sustained by the direct perceptual experiences of the artist. These experiences are shared by all draughtsmen, but exploited by those drawing in this particular idiom.

Figure 5.4 Note the lack of convergence and the lack of size reduction in the figures with distance in this Japanese view of a bath house (Itcho, "Baths").

A western draughtsman wishing to convey his impression of a cube would not generally choose the same projection as the Chinese artist who selects from the field laterally displaced from the line of light. Nor would he choose the very central projection, which, as we have seen, is a square. He is more likely to choose one of the figures from an intermediate ring made of figures which show the frontal face as a square, but which also show two other convergent faces. It is the type of perspective found in Renaissance pictures, for example in the depiction of the splendidly inlaid Linen Cupboard in Pieter de Hooch's picture (Figure 4.12).

The draughtsmen of the two cultures rely on different projections to represent the solid, but the Chinese projection differs from that of the Renaissance by its lack of linear convergence.

Because these choices made by the two cultural groups are about equally rational, and derive from visual experience, neither choice can be thought of as conventional, in the sense that the style chosen is itself a convention. They are conventional only in the sense that the choices made have been widely accepted. This essential naturalness of both artistic styles explains why it is possible for the practitioner of either of them, as well as for the person consistently exposed to one of them, to see his style as right and the other as wrong. This might explain the following story told by Yoshio Markino. "When I got a book of the drawing lessons at my ('European') grammar school there was a drawing of a square box in the correct perspective. My father saw it and said, 'What? This box is surely not square, it seems to me very much crooked'. About nine years later he was looking at the same book and he called me and said, 'How strange it is! You know I used to think this square box looked crooked, but now I see this is perfectly right'". This is not, we argue, a story of a sudden discovery of the true way and abandonment of error, but simply a designation of another equally natural manner of representation as an appropriate one for the purposes of depiction, almost certainly as a consequence of frequent exposure to it.

Consider now the depictions of "solids of revolution", the cylinders and the spheres, and their embodiments in such common objects as pots, bottles or columns. Some artists, including Cézanne and van Gogh, have drawn "distorted" utensils and these distortions are such as to suggest that the drawings are records of projections from the peripheral visual field (see Chapter 7). There are only a few artists who have chosen to use these marginal projections to depict the 'solids of revolution'. These forms are not generally characteristic of the western nor of the Chinese styles. In both these schools of art the central projection has been adopted as the proper representation of such bodies. The practitioners of both idioms thus withdrew to the image found at the line of sight, and both schools treat the "solids of revolution" in a manner inconsistent with their treatment of solids bounded by planes. Had each school been consistent then, both of them would be representing spheres by ellipses, but the ellipses would be relatively slimmer in oriental pictures.

This inconsistency between portrayals of two types of solids probably has its origins in the desire to depict the contour of maximal information content: that very contour which is responsible for the popularity of profiles of animals and men. A cube has definite ridges at the edges, where its surface undergoes a rapid change of direction and which therefore defines its shape precisely. A cylinder has no such ridges on its curved surface, but only at the ends; and a sphere has no such ridges at all.

A draughtsman has to detect the contours of maximal information and to transfer them onto a flat surface in such a manner that they evoke sensations identical with, or, at least closely resembling, those evoked by the model. Both the "Renaissance" and the "Oriental" depictions of cubes, and their derivatives, satisfy these criteria, albeit in slightly different ways. Both of them reject the central projection, which, being a square, does not display as many contours as the more peripheral projections. In the case of the sphere, on the other hand, both schools adopt the central projection as characteristic of the solid. They do so because the more peripheral projections do not, in this case, add any further contours, and hence they are, iconographically speaking, of little help. Examination of Figure 5.5 shows the distortion inherent in the peripheral projection of a sphere. Indeed an artist who, by following strictly the rules of perspective for the picture as a whole, accidentally stumbles upon the seemingly distorted projections of spheres or cylinders is likely to find them an embarrassment, as for example Pieter Saenredam did (Figure 7.1). It appears then that the choice of projection in Western and Oriental painting cannot be described as arbitrary. A range of possible correct projections of objects are available and in some instances different traditions have selected different subsets and in other instances the same subsets from this range.

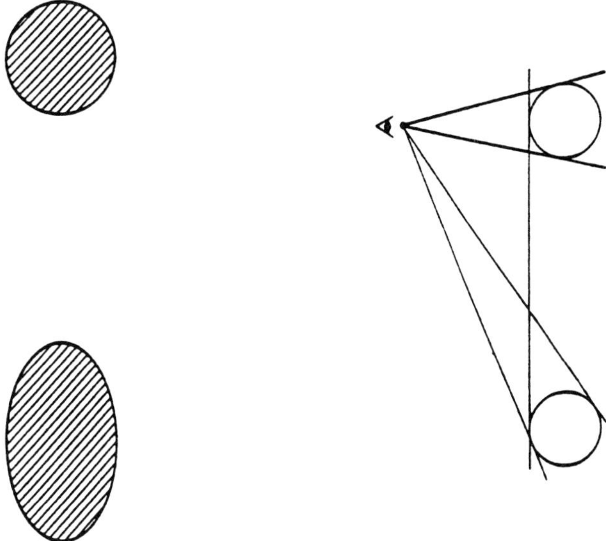

Figure 5.5 Projection of a sphere in central and peripheral vision. Note the elliptical peripheral view which echoes the peripheral projections described in figure 5.3.

Figure 6.1 J. M. W. Turner, "Rain, Steam and Speed - the Great Western Railway". (Reproduced with permission of the Trustees, The National Gallery, London).

Chapter VI

Communalities Of Distortions

Both an oriental and a western draughtsman, when drawing a sphere, use entirely different strategies than those used by them when drawing a cube. They draw a circle, choosing a unique central projection to represent the solid. A caricature of the sphere, which embodies its quintessential characteristic is thus adopted and is universally recognised as the appropriate representation in the case of spheroidal bodies. For this reason, as will be discussed at length in the next chapter, Cézanne's and van Gogh's pots, glasses and bottles seem to many western observers as misshapen as do "oriental" representations of cubes; these painters do not avoid the use of peripheral projections even though a representation of a peripherally seen object is in this case perceived as odd. One suspects that this is so even among those who regard peripheral views as an important source of artistic inspiration, claiming that it softens edges, modifies colours and accentuates radial and tangential lines and leads to linear distortions in the peripheral field which are artistically as important as those of clear and undistorted central vision. Turner's *Rain, steam and speed* (Figure 6.1) is put forward as a great work of art embodying the desired balance between the two kinds of vision. This is contrasted with paintings having much detail which, as a consequence, tend to prove "tiresome on prolonged acquaintance, as perhaps do too strong flavours, too sharp odours and too violent emotions."

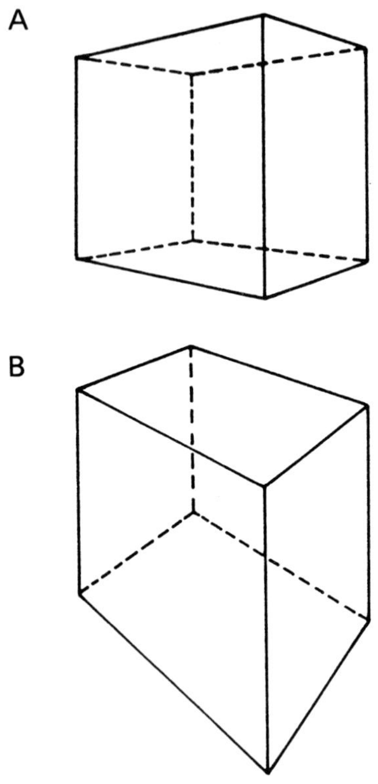

Figure 6.2 Projection of cubes laterally displaced from the line of sight. The figure represents true projections of peripherally viewed cubes which when looked at directly appear to be distorted. A- a lateral displacement of a cube. B- a cube displaced laterally and downwards.

The apparent distortion of peripherally seen objects when correctly represented, and also of the "oriental cubes", implies both that the "three-dimensional" element of the figures is apprehended and, that the drawings fail to match the beholder's expectations; the depicted objects look "crooked". In the case of familiar objects these expectations may originate from the experience of repeated exposure. This explanation is less plausible in the case of figures such as Figure 6.2. Here the perceptual unease which the figure elicits is probably due to its ambiguity. When seen in the far periphery of the visual field the figure is a correct projection of a cube. The natural tendency is, however, to regard it centrally, whereupon it presents itself as a projection of a non-rectangular solid. Central non-rectangularity and peripheral rectangularity are thus the horns of a dilemma and the cause of perceptual unease.

Depth cues found in traditional representational pictures, which grace many of our art galleries, are generally stronger than those found in an isolated figure. There are more of them and they generally affect several depicted items in the picture and are thus echoed and mutually reinforced. The extent to which such an interaction prevails depends upon the cohesiveness of the picture. Pictures such as those of Pieter de Hooch or of Pieter Saenredam have strong overall cohesiveness resulting from the combination of pictorial depth cues examined in the second chapter. Such cues lock every depicted object in place, leaving few perceptual ambiguities to puzzle the viewer. Thus by binding the depicted objects together, they also specify the position of the hypothetical painter's eye and, hence, the ideal position of the viewer's eye.

Even in these superfically consistent pictures, however, one can often find imperfections in adherence to a single point of view. Figures of men which should be subject to distortions similar to those of Saenredam's columns, are not so painted, but are portrayed as if they all were on the line of sight. Other violations of depth cues also pass unnoticed. One such violation in Jan van Eyck's portrait of Arnolfini and his wife (see Chapter 4) eludes most beholders.

There are pictures in which spatial inconsistencies are readily apparent. This is so, to the western eye, in many oriental works. There, typically, more distant figures seem too large for the position in pictorial space which they occupy (Figure 6.3).

Do such "inconsistencies" arise because the individual cues are a matter of convention?

Figure 6.3 Persian miniature. A western observer would expect much greater variation in size with elevation in the picture. 15th century copy by Bihzad from *Buston* Ms.

It has sometimes been suggested, as we have already remarked, that linear perspective is a pure convention, and the failures on the part of observers to interpret perspective correctly in simple geometric drawings under laboratory conditions and in some pictures appear to support this view. So do the difficulties which perspective was shown to create for architectural painters and others and the"legitimacy" of inverse perspective. Indeed, if perspective is an invention, perhaps a very convenient invention, but an invention nonetheless, then it should properly be excluded from further consideration as irrelevant to our discussion. However, it might be that by so doing we would be overhasty. It is better to re-examine the evidence.

Little can be said in favour of the argument, claimed to be based on Einstein's theory of relativity[1], that linear perspective is wrong because "space is curved" or because "light does not travel in straight lines". But since this argument will not die, in spite of the fact that it should have done so long ago, we shall quote Pirenne's well-grounded verdict:

> "As far as the geometric astronomy of the solar system is concerned - with the exception of the movements of the planet Mercury - Einstein's theory of relativity is hardly of any practical significance. Its practical importance in architecture, surveying and navigation, is nil."

And it can therefore be safely said that it is also nil as far as the validity of linear perspective is concerned. Pirenne continues:

> "If a contemporary artist did straight lines as curves as a result of his study of Relativity Theory, this could only be either because he had misunderstood the theory, or because, for some reason or other, he was wilfully misapplying it."

With this notion peacefully laid to rest, let us now turn to other, subtler, arguments of the conventionalists, choosing Goodman[2] as their spokesman. The misunderstanding of the nature of the restrictions placed upon the eye in circumstances designed to induce perception of the depicted space as real (monocular vision with the eye placed at the focal point of a picture) has already been dealt with, but it seems desirable to examine the essence of the objection which this misapprehension concealed. The essence is that the conditions specified for observation of the picture are highly abnormal. Goodman finds the argument that by appropriate "stage managing" one can "wring out of the picture drawn in perspective light rays that match those we can wring out of the object presented" both odd and futile, as far as fidelity of perspective is concerned.

This statement neatly exposes the gap between an experimental student of vision (and indeed any empirical scientist), on the one hand, and a detached theoretician on the other. The fact is that in empirical science approximations matter and furthermore the perceptual system thrives on approximations. If it did not, if every decision taken by man and beast had to depend on the presence of all the symptomatic cues, not only would medical practice cease but so would crossing of roads, ingestion of food and, indeed, the very business of living. The experimental approach dictates a continuum of approximations requiring different quantities of "stage management", if they are not to be mistaken for the "real things". The less "stage management" they need, the better they approximate to the "real thing"; or, to put it in a different way, the more cues the picture incorporates, the more likely it is to succeed in creating an illusion of real visual space. It so happens that linear perspective is one of the cues which strengthen the illusory effect and, therefore, makes the picture more "life-like".

The argument that people from certain cultures have difficulty in dealing with pictures may, perhaps, prove weightier. After all, if the Hairy Ainu, who lack, or rather lacked, contact with pictorial cultures, respond as described below by Landor[3], then surely learning must be involved.

"For instance, while I was sketching, Benry and his friend ... sat ... by my side and when my sketch was finished I showed it to them. 'Pirika, Pirika! Nishpa!' ('Very pretty, very pretty sir!') Benry exclaimed with perfect self-assurance; but when I asked him what he thought the sketch represented, he cut me short by saying that I had done the picture and I ought to know what it was meant for; he did not. His friend agreed with him. When my work was done we walked back ... From their conversation and gestures I caught that it seemed incomprehensible to them that I should sit in front of an Ainu and ... to use their expression ... 'make all sorts of signs on a wooden panel".

There is no reason for doubting Landor's veracity. There are similar anecdotes from other, previously, remote populations. The question, however, is, what does his evidence demonstrate. More careful experimentation indeed reveals that there are populations some of whose members have difficulties with perceiving pictures - but there is no evidence that they have difficulty with perceiving perspective, since that factor was not specifically investigated. On the other hand, carefully collected evidence from a large number of very disparate cultural groups suggests that the effect of perspective convergence, as embodied in a version of the Ponzo figure, and therefore in a very abstract form, is universal, although there are intergroup differences[4]. The problem with the interpretation of data obtained by means of more complex stimuli under less well controlled conditions lies in the confounding of many variables so that the root cause is impossible to trace. When, as we have described, a Me'en nomad from Ethiopia, for example, on being given a drawing, sniffs it and listens carefully to the sound it makes when crumpled, does he not see the picture? Or does he regard the surface pattern on the piece of material - the paper - which has just been handed to him and with which he is unfamiliar, as the attribute least worthy of his immediate attention?

Intercultural comparisons, therefore, cannot be said to question the basic assumption of our argument, that since the beginning of Art the eye has remained virtually unchanged. This assumption does not deny that perceptual abilities may vary within any population. Nor does it deny that there probably have always been, just as there nowadays are, differences between populations in their perceptual abilities[5]. Evidence shows, for example, that there is little difference on certain simple perceptual tasks between Scots and Eskimos but there are considerable divergences between these two groups and the Temne of Sierra Leone[6]. Since the three groups differ in their genetic stock, in the environment they inhabit, and in their cultures, it is impossible to apportion the influence of each of these factors in determining the differences; nor is such an allocation of causation important under the present circumstances. But it is important to note that there is no evidence of the existence of populations incapable of accepting simple pictorial representations as meaningful after a short and deliberate introduction to them. There are to be found, on the other hand, considerable and surprising disparities in the development of pictorial art between often neighbouring societies. Thus the nomadic, hunting and gathering groups, such as the Bushmen of Southern Africa, are often far more skilful in creating pictures than their cattle herding, and hence "more advanced" Bantu neighbours.

Our argument is not that all men are equally able, nor that they were equally able when the first figures were drawn, but simply that the task of drawing was performed with the help of the same perceptual mechanisms, having the same weaknesses and strengths as those of modern man, although the expertise with which these mechanisms were used and the motor skills which were employed in the execution of the pictures might have been different. Unfortunately, one cannot separate the perceptual abilities and draughtsmanshp in the case of those distant populations whose art we know only from the artefacts which they have left behind. When a picture or a bone engraving is in some manner imperfect it is impossible to attribute with certainty the reason for this. If, however, such an artefact is satisfactory, it must then be accepted that neither perceptual nor motor skills were deficient.

Regrettably, ancient artefacts are not easy to analyse[7] Detection of pictorial cues depends on the perceived relationships amongst various depicted items *and* on the perceiver's willingness to assume that particular cues have been used. Overlap is probably the least ambiguous of the cues. It clearly occurs in several palaeolithic engravings, where an animal is shown obscuring another. This issue is much more muddled when perspective is concerned.

Figure 6.4 Paleolithic art from Palermo; diagram of the parietal engraving.

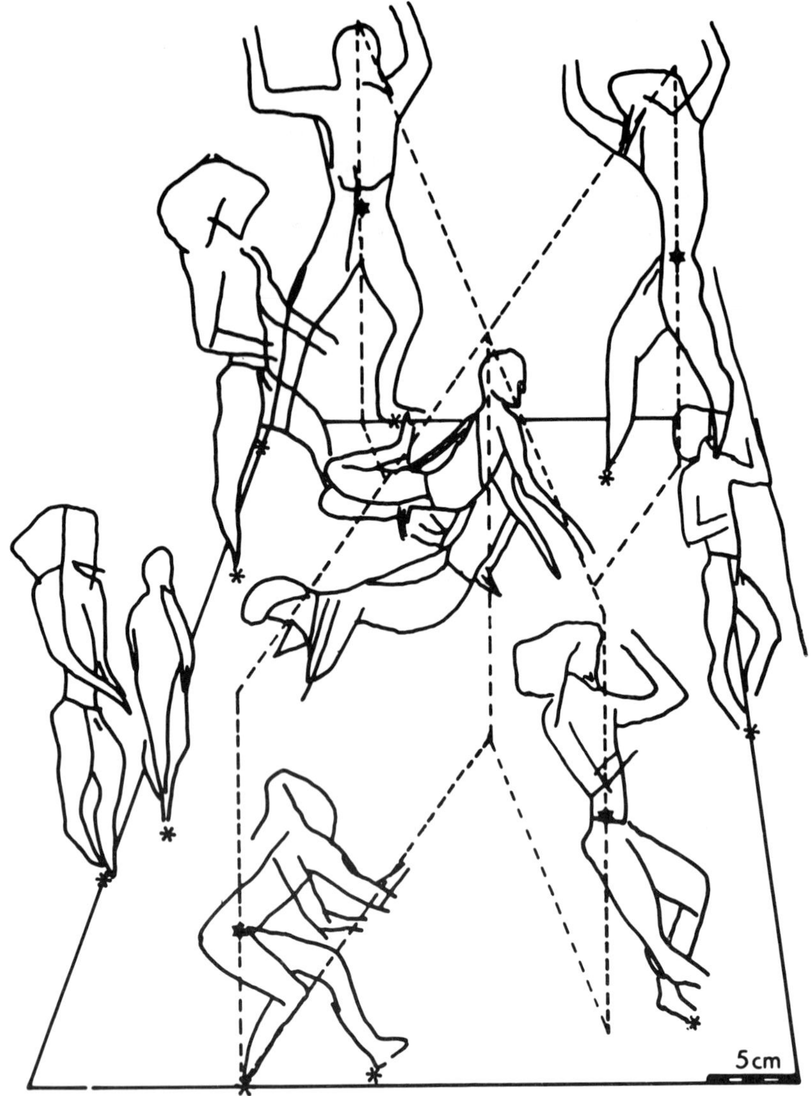

Figure 6.5 Analysis of part of the parietal engraving shown in figure 6.4 suggested by Mezzena.

Analysis of a parietal engraving found in a cave near Palermo[8] shows, it has been suggested, that the principles of perspective were known to Italian palaeolithic artists. The diagrams (Figures 6.4 & 6.5) show the main elements of the engraving and, superimposed upon them, two notional vertical planes and a horizontal plane suggested by an archeologist. The two vertical planes link, crosswise in pairs, the nearer and the more distant figures. The two more distant figures are said to be throwers who have just launched the two prone figures (said to be those of boys or young men) towards their corresponding catchers at the bottom of the picture. The entire picture is therefore reminiscent of the central ring in *Children's Games* by Pieter Breughel the Elder, as shown in the sketch (Figure 6.6).

Figure 6.6 Diagram based on P. Breughel's picture "Children's Games", showing, it is suggested, a similarity to figure 6.5.

Whether such an interpretation of the ancient engraving is acceptable to a viewer depends, in no small measure, on his willingness to accept that perspective could have been used and his willingness to ignore serious violations of the rules of linear or natural perspective within the drawing.

Figure 6.7 Bone engraving. Does this picture represent movement?

Similarly judgement needs also to be exercised when interpreting another engraving, a well known piece of palaeolithic art, shown in Figure 6.7. It shows splendidly horned reindeer at each end. They frame a series of delicately sketched horns which decrease in size from the two extremities towards the middle. It has been argued that the engraving shows a herd of reindeer whose main body, indicated only by horns, is far away from the viewer, and thus that it too is evidence for an early use of perspective. But it has also been suggested that the artist did not intend to show perspective, but merely to sketch in the central part of the herd quickly and so showed only the animals' horns. It could also be claimed perhaps a trifle more extravagantly, that a movement or just a single reindeer is portrayed here by the two extreme figures showing the initial and the final positions of the animal, and the intermediate dashes merely showing that the animal has moved. On the evidence available a confident conclusion is not possible.

There are other equally ancient engravings which may depict movement by recording the positions which a part of a body occupied at various times. The engraving of the Charging/Expiring Mammoth shown in Figure 6.8 belongs to this group. The head of the animal is surrounded by lines showing its alternative positions. It is arguable however whether these positions are intended to show movement of the head of a charging mammoth, or whether they are tracings of positions which the animal's head occupied as it jerked in the throes of death[9]. It can be argued that the artist began to draw the dying animal, then its head jerked to another position forcing the draughtsman to abandon the original outline and to begin again. Before he could finish his drawing this happened again. Only on the third attempt did the artist succeed.

The differences between the two explanations is important, as it implies no movement but merely a spatial coincidence of three independently made sketches. This explanation is supported by the observation that the positions and other characteristics of the limbs of many of the animals drawn in the quartenary caves are such as to suggest that they represent dead animals. This inclines towards acceptance of the latter explanation. However in assessing the plausibility of these explanations it should be remembered that those drawings are in fairly inacessible places where the opportunity to draw large animals directly from life (or in death) would not have been possible. In the case of the reindeer, however, the very extent of this displacement makes a similar explanation unlikely.

The absence of a definite framework delimiting individual pictures and frequent instances of painting of one object on top of another, so that the "nearer" figure appears to be transparent in those places where it overlaps the "further" figure, often make it difficult to interpret palaeolithic pictures. There is, however, a group of artefacts left by nomadic hunter-gatherers, whose material culture was simple, which shows considerable spatial sophistication. These are the shallow engravings depicting local animals found in South Africa[10]. They are attributed to the Bushmen.

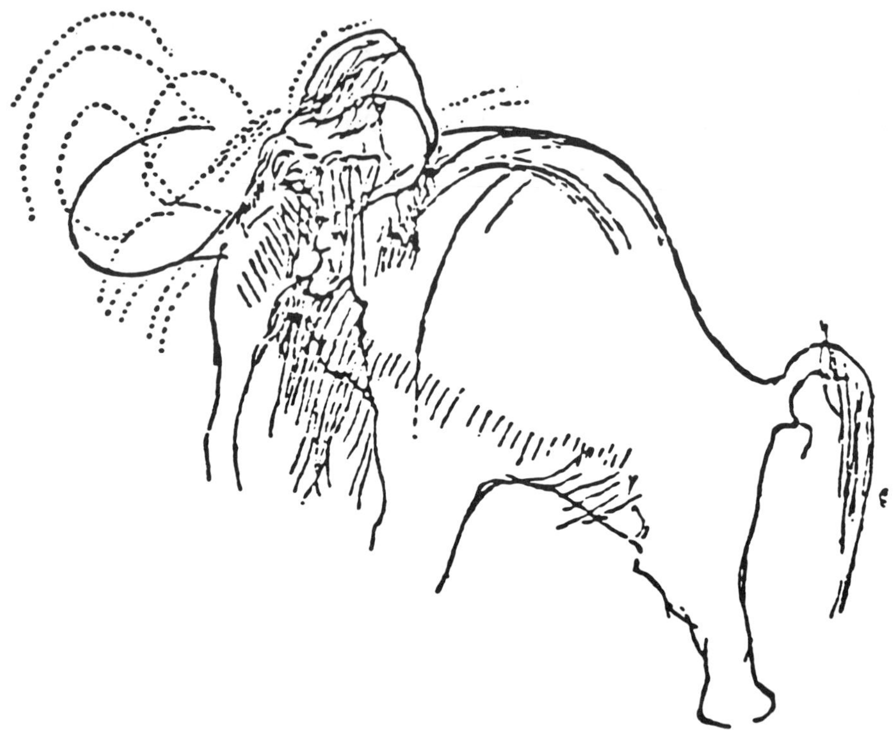

Figure 6.8 Expiring (?) mammoth. Has the animal moved whilst being sketched? If so was it because it was charging or because it was dying or do the alternative positions of the head and trunk represent different attempts by the same or different artists?

The feature of interest to us is the way in which heads and horns of animals are shown. The heads are in profile, thus acknowledging it as a typical view, just as the vast majority of artists has done throughout the history of Art. But, in this view horns present a problem, for if they are also shown strictly in the side view, and therefore coincide, the animal appears to have only one horn. There is, of course, the Egyptian or "Cubist" solution of showing the horns in a frontal view mounted upon a profile head, which results in a twisted view. The Bushman artists avoided these pitfalls and developed a method as simple as it is effective. They engraved the "further" horn slightly out of line with the "nearer" horn and introduced a sliver of space between the animal's head and the more distant horn, just large enough to create the illusion of depth, thus avoiding configurations that would suggest that the animal had a crumpled horn or that the animal had only one horn. A fine sense of perceptual balance indeed (Figure 6.9).

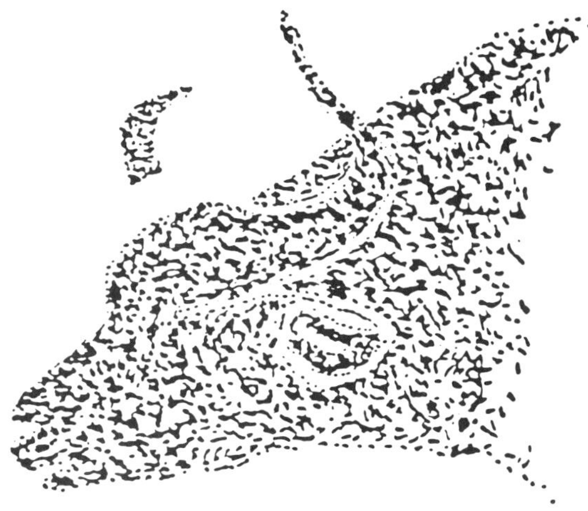

Figure 6.9 Bushman engraving (petroglyph) from South Africa. Note the detached horn.

When a particular depth cue is absent, the failure is more likely to lie with the artist as a maker rather than with the artist as perceiver. A simple experiment carried out on children suggests that this is so. The children were shown a drawing of a cube. They readily recognised that the drawing represented a cube. When asked to copy it they did so correctly. But when they were merely allowed to look at a drawing for a time and then required to draw it from memory, they made errors similar to those made by other children when drawing a cube from the solid model. This congruence of errors not only shows that the drawing was correctly perceived, but it also shows that the major difficulty was not that of seeing the intended relationships in the picture but that of translating from space onto surface. The difficulty is that of utilising and transforming visual information and not of simple perception.

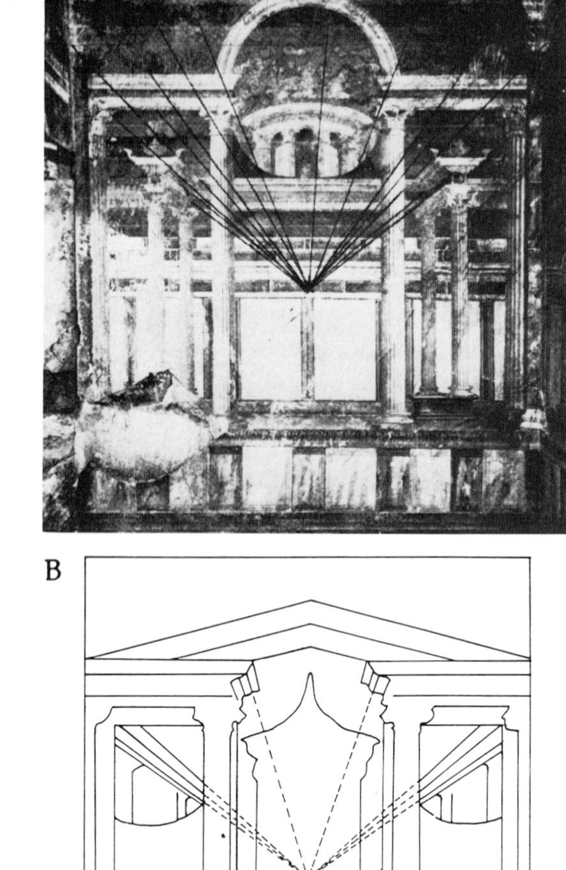

Figure 6.10 A- Beyen's photograph together with B- an outline sketch showing convergence.

Figure 6.11 Master of the Rebel Angels, "Fall of the Rebel Angels". (Reproduced by courtesy of the Louvre, Paris). Linear convergence is clearly indicated in the upper part of the picture. From 14th century Sienna and therefore unusual in showing perspective.

It follows that whilst the nature of some of the early forms of art is such that it makes it difficult to decide with certainty which of the available pictorial depth cues were used, it clearly gives no reason for supposing that the *perceptual* skills of those populations whose works we have inherited were, in their essence, less developed or inferior to those of modern man.

One must distinguish sharply between the depiction of an object on its own and that of several objects interrelated by an activity or by a layout dictated by aesthetic considerations. The second kind of relationship will not be considered here, but the first kind will. First, however, we shall have to make the following rather obvious, but nonetheless important point. An artist usually draws one object at a time. His attention is concentrated on the object that he is drawing. This concentration on the task in hand, to the exclusion of the planning of more general relationships between elements of a drawing, is seen as its most poignant in pictures made by young children, who occasionally draw hybrid figures made up of assorted elements, such as horses with dog's tails, or made of elements whose mutual spatial relationship is erroneous, because they have not planned the drawing as a whole and because they sometimes change their minds in the course of drawing as to what they intend to depict. Even though an artist may plan a work carefully he will usually attend to particular elements in the picture for concentrated periods.

The concentration on a single item at a time implies that pictorial cues are more likely to be used consistently with reference to single items than with reference to all the items forming a picture. Perspective convergence may therefore appear as it indeed often does, in isolated items without being consistently used for all items, or even most of the items in the picture, a point already made with respect to van Eyck's portrait.

This is acceptable to the eye which, whilst sampling, does not embrace the entire field of view at once but shifts from one point within it to another guided by peripheral vision. The relationship that guides it on its way is tripartite, involving the primary link between the object viewed at the particular time and the observer and, in the light of this, evaluation of peripheral cues for the most useful item to which the gaze should next be directed. Once the choice is made, the gaze is quickly transferred and a new link between the observer and the scene is established. Throughout the process of looking at the scene, therefore, a series of links between the observer and various items of the scenery is forged. The links among the items of scenery, unless chosen for special attention, are very much a secondary factor and as such are less readily noticed; and indeed, when recorded are sometimes thought disruptive rather than helpful to pictorial comprehension. Thus the shadows and the reflections which the dishes on Claesz's table (*Still life* ,Figure 9.1) cast upon each other unify the picture but are of little importance as far as individual items are concerned. Indeed they are not characteristic of those items, and are entirely dependent on the environment in which the items find themselves.

Perspective convergence cannot be readily conveyed in the case of isolated non-rectangular items whose precise form is unknown to the beholder. This is particularly so with irregular shapes such as trees, human figures or mountains. Since such natural phenomena are encountered in a wide range of shapes, only when the portrayals become so unusual that they approach the borders of human experience (as they seem to do in some El Greco paintings) is their veracity questioned and, even then, new and wider limits of tolerance can often be set by reclassifying the picture as representing not an individual object, but rather a type of object in the manner in which a stick-man represents a man. Consideration of such pictures would, however, take us to an entirely different kind of representation than that with which we are now concerned.

If we accept, and we have the authority of no lesser man than Delacroix to do so, that perceptually speaking foreshortening is essentially the same as perspective, then we certainly have records of perspective in palaeolithic times. We have records of its use in Ancient Greece and in the first century B.C. in the mural paintings of Pompeii, Rome and Boscoreale[11]. The importance of these Roman paintings was brought to general attention by a Dutch archeologist, Beyen (Figure 6.10)[12]. Since they present fairly elaborate depictions of buildings with easily traceable central convergence, and since they seem to be by the hand of inferior craftsmen, they are thought to be distant descendants of Greek paintings made specially for scenographic purposes, which are referred to in literature in Greek drama but of which no examples survive. Later in Byzantine art perspective, even in the form of foreshortening, was little used[13]. However, isolated instances of perspective can still be found, sometimes in an inverted form, generally in portrayals of buildings. Similarly, during the post-classical and medieval periods in the West, pespective was not thought important, although careful scrutiny of contemporary works shows it was occasionally used. It is present, for example, in the fourteenth century Sienese painting of the *Fall of the Rebel Angels*[14] (Figure 6.11).

Thus throughout the history of art, before its official birthday (in the 15th century), instances of perspective can be found. It was always, it seems, present but at times neither wanted nor sought for.

The fact that a style shuns linear perspective does not mean that its propagators desire that their works look flat, nor that they avoid it entirely. In the classical Chinese artistic tradition there is no convergence of the receding edges of rectangular solids. The sides of parallelopipeds are drawn as either rectangles or parallelograms. Yet the authoritative manual of Chinese paintings, *The Mustard Seed Garden Manual of Painting*[15] from 1679, lists *Six Qualities* which a painter must master, and one of these is 'on the flatness of the picture plane to achieve depth and space' and this is augmented by two of *The Twelve Things to Avoid,* the second of which is "far and near not clearly distinguished" and the seventh "stones and rocks with one face". This clearly shows concern for an effective illusory space.

Indeed, examples of illustration given in the manual expound how, by skilful use of cues other than linear convergence, a very effective illusion of depth can be evoked. More importantly, some illustrations in this very manual show clear instances of foreshortening and some even show definite perspective convergence with distance. It is so in the case of a drawing of a wooden footbridge, "that may be drawn over churning waters since it is built on rocks in the water" (Figure 6.12). The Ancient Egyptian, mainly ideographic, style which avoids perspective and foreshortening also, on occasion, relaxes its strict rules about appropriate poses. It would appear, therefore, that a plausible argument can be made for a much wider distribution of perspective, especially in the form of foreshortening in pictorial art than would at first appear.

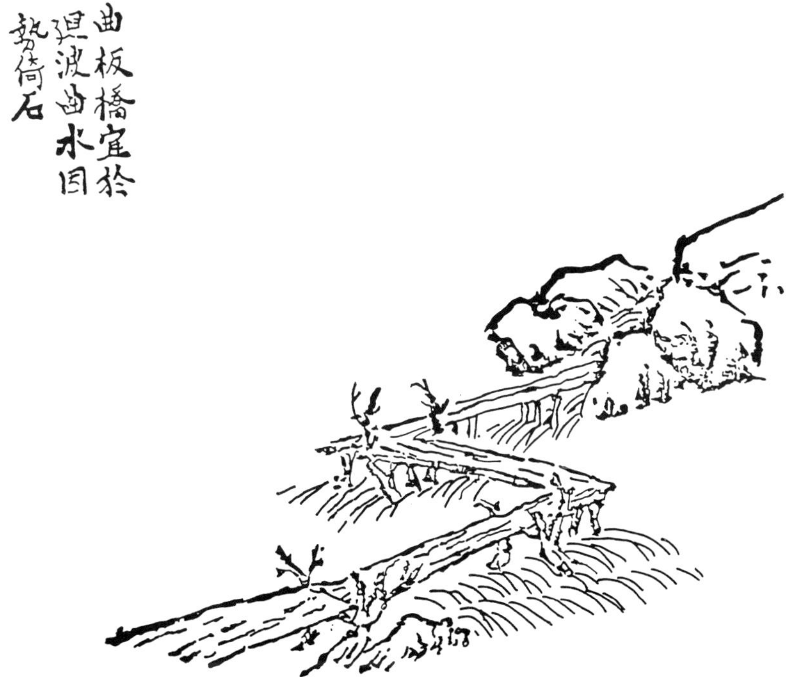

Figure 6.12 Drawing from the *Mustard Seed Garden*, explaining how to draw a stream.

Of the other arguments which are advanced against the "naturalness" of perspective, that concerning the fact that a picture is perceived correctly even from a different stance than the one from which strictly speaking it should be viewed, and that concerning the considerable tolerance of contradictions within pictures which the eye has to exercise, have been dealt with extensively in the preceding chapters. Both arguments are vitiated by the simple facts that the phenomena referred to are largely a function of their falling in the artists' peripheral visual field and, above all, that the perceptual mechanism is, indeed must be, flexible.

There are thus, so far, no grounds for accepting the Conventionalist thesis, and one would be happy to dismiss it entirely if it were not for the inverse perspective - the phenomenon that won't go away. It has been shown that inverse perspective has a legitimate foundation in the optical system. Its dismissal would be contrary to all the evidence presented. Moreover, since isometric projection, in which receding parallel lines neither converge nor diverge with pictorial depth, but remain parallel, lies on the boundary between the "normal" and the "inverse" types of perspective, it too should be given consideration, especially as it is common in oriental art. But if the entire continuum from convergence to divergence is thus admitted, the rules governing choice within it may be thought arbitrary and the percept of perspective thereby reduced to the nebulous statement: "Depictions of parallel lines, in order to convey an impression of depth, should either converge, remain parallel or diverge". Scarcely a helpful guide and certainly not a rule.

The reality is more complex. The two mutually contradictory "real life" experiences, that of "normal" and that of "inverse" perspective, can furnish, it is true, the basis for two contradictory versions of perspective in pictures, and these experiences are accessible to all. The result of the choice is not, however, arbitrary but is determined by the accessibility of the two experiences, both equally "natural" and spontaneous, but not both equally available. It will be recalled that very specific instructions had to be followed in the experiment in which a matchbox was used to elicit a divergent percept, and that even so the percept was unstable, now and then one of the eyes gaining absolute dominance in the binocular rivalry, so that the box was seen as converging with the distance. No such conditions need to be abided by to ensure perception of apparent convergence. With one eye closed it is experienced over the entire depth of the visible field, and keeping both eyes open only introduces a slight element of confusion in the very close proximity of the observer. So although there is an organismic basis for both kinds of perspective, the chances of selecting the divergent type as representative of one's experience of depth are small, and the chance of it reaching the status of the chosen manner of drawing is, in view of the contrary choice made by the majority of draughtsmen, even smaller.

Hence both convergent and divergent perspectives are natural discoveries, but the latter is much handicapped relative to the former in the competition for the status of the culturally accepted way of drawing and to be strictly accurate should only be used over a range of close distances where the presence of a double image induces the distortion.

The use of parallelograms to depict rectangles, that is the avoidance of linear convergence, is perhaps most convincingly explained as follows. It presents a compromise solution which removes such conflict as might arise in the eye of a perceiver favouring convergent perspective when confronted with divergent perspective, and such a conflict which might arise in the eye of his counterpart, having the opposite inclination, and indeed in the eye of the viewer who is unable to make up his mind which type of perspective is right. Moreover, and much more importantly, it offers a formal and simple rule which can be used by draughtsmen so that the fickleness of their senses is kept in check by their intellects. In some cultures in which rules are kept in great esteem this solution may indeed be thought preferable for this rather than for purely perceptual reasons.

Furthermore because parallel projection in effect rescales space in the direction of constancy it has some intrinsic psychological appeal. It is also more in accord with what one "perceives" about near and far rather than with what one "senses", i.e. the artist is influenced chiefly by level B as shown in Figure 1.2.

Thus, the evidence shows that cues conveying perspective are encountered daily in the "real" world. They are therefore natural. An unsophisticated viewer need not however be aware of them, any more than an unsophisticated eater need be aware of the effect of various substances on his tastebuds. The use of cues in pictures to create illusory effects is a result of a discovery, not an invention, of an effective means of *drawing* in perspective in the form of rules and constructions which yield convincing approximations to an optical projection. Various draughtsman's aids; frames, grids and other complicated paraphernalia, are inventions made to satisfy the need for efficacious construction. Perspective and the means of creating pictures in perspective, ought not to be confused. Nor should the mathematical formulations, which can elegantly and precisely describe the relationships between the phenomenon and invented tools, becloud the issue.

Gombrich is therefore right to contend in his urbane and highly erudite review that: "One cannot insist enough that the art of perspective aims at a correct equation: It wants the image to appear like the object and the object like the image." To do so entirely effectively it should apply to all the items within a picture and has to do so in such a manner that the whole pictorial space is treated as a single unit. This, and not its applications to isolated items, became the fascination, and in Ucello's case almost an obsession[12], at the time of its blossoming in the fifteenth century, which is sometimes thought to be the time of its origin. But it would be wrong, as we have seen, to claim that in the fifteenth century the concept of unified perspective was first mooted. It is true, however, that that era has left us a large volume of evidence of preoccupation with the topic, of attempts to develop mechanical aids and geometrical techniques of drawing correctly in perspective, and indeed of pictures so executed.

In order to avoid inconsistencies within a picture, pictorial cues, including perspective, have to be used in a coherent manner. Thus once the point of convergence is established, the relative sizes of objects at various distances are also established: so is their pictorial elevation and overlap. Even the density gradient and its close relation, aerial perspective, derive hints as to their proper disposition within a picture, and foreshortening is automatically taken care of. The cues which evade this control by the central perspective are those involving additional factors, which cannot be caught in the network of the geometric construction lines connecting the eye with various items of the environment. Light and its accompanying shadows belong to this group, and so do all those cues which spring from the attributes of the beholder; his notions of relative size obviously influence the use made of familiar size cues, and attributes of his eye affect those cues which we called *intrinsic*, which will be discussed in the following Chapter 7.

The case for "naturalness" of other pictorial depth cues is simpler than in the case of perspective but, again, convincing evidence for it can be found only in those styles in which the intended composition can be recognised. Pictorial elevation, for example, is common in Ancient Egyptian, in Chinese and in Bushman art, as is the overlap of the figures.

The subtler cue of aerial perspective requires a fine control of the media and above all a different approach to painting, for it calls for an introduction of an effect whose only purpose is to convey to the viewer the relationship among depicted objects. The artist is thus obliged to obscure to some extent the features of that object in which he is particularly interested in order to create the impression of space. Such differential obfuscation is scarcely possible without precise control of techniques and probably unwanted in any group where the representations of space itself has not become a specific issue.

Chapter VII

Cues Intrinsic To The Eye

Although the cues considered in previous chapters do imply certain characteristics of the eye, one need not assume any particular structure of the eye in order to understand how these cues work[1]. They work, as we have said, by providing the eye with stimulation ideally identical with, but generally only approximating to, that which the eye would derive from looking at the real scene. "Consequently", as Pirenne[2] points out,"since painting and objects do affect the eye in the same way, they will look the same to the observer, independently of the structure and functioning of the eye, the properties of the brain and the nervous system, and the psychological characteristics of the spectator". This argument is, in essence, the same as that which we have earlier advanced against any notion that "distortions" in El Greco's paintings were a consequence of an ocular defect. There are however characteristics of painting and, hence, characteristics of artistic styles which cannot be understood without reference to the structure of the eye. To these we shall now turn.

One of the repeated assumptions in our discussion of the imitative pictorial cues was that the eye views the entire surface of a picture in the same uniformly dispassionate manner[3]. This in fact is not so; the line of most acute vision moves over the surface of the picture in the manner of a pond skater skimming on the surface of a pond[4]. It stops in one place, then darts to another, then perhaps to the third or perhaps back to the first point. These movements are not random but are influenced by the features of the picture, and if the eye were looking not at a picture but at a real scene they would involve major changes in the eye, since each stop would be associated not only with a different location of the eye's central zone of clearest vision, but often with changed accommodation (focus) and convergence for the different distances of objects from the observer.

At least four vectors influence the wanderings of the eye over the picture: the relative brightness (contrast) of the elements, the significance of various elements to the narrative aspects of the pictorial composition, the geometric nature of the patterns, and pictorial depth cues. Thus in a depiction of a small figure of a hunter in a forest, the canopy and undergrowth of which provide rich density gradients converging at the horizon, the eye repeatedly inspects the figure of the hunter and repeatedly scans the horizon. In more complex pictures and maps, it tends to scan the areas of uncertainty which contain clues as to the nature of the portrayal. Informationally barren areas, such as large optically homogeneous expanses, and elements having simple and readily predictable characteristics, merit few glances. Students of art are right when they say that the perspective cues in pictures "lead" the eye. The figure below is an example of classical perspective as used by Vermeer (Figure 7.1). It has a single point of convergence, as shown in the sketch. The eye is repeatedly led to this point from all its exploratory forays. If a picture were drawn, contrary to the notion of a stationary eye but in agreement with the notion of a roving eye, such as to incorporate several points of convergence, the eye would be led to them and their relationship in the picture would in some measure dictate the manner of visual exploration.

Figure 7.1 Diagram after Johannes Vermeer, "The Music Lesson". The perfect perspective convergence is indicated in the the diagram. Had the painter adhered to *all* aspects of perspective, however, he would have drawn the jug on the extreme left as *distorted* as is the case with the utensils in Cézanne's *Still Life with Fruit Basket* (figure 7.8).

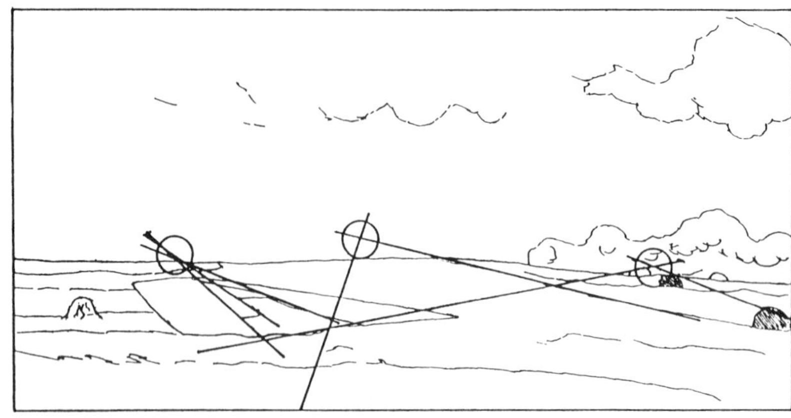

Figure 7.2 Vincent van Gogh, "Field under a Blue Sky". (Reproduced with permission of the Stedelijk Museum, Amsterdam). The diagram shows the three focal points on the horizon (after Strzemiński, 1974).

Van Gogh uses multiple points of convergence in this way in his *Field under the Blue Sky* (Figure 7.2). As the accompanying sketche shows, the artist has put in the picture three points of convergence, all of which fall on the horizon. One of them bisects it and the others bisect the resulting halves. The entire horizon of the picture is thus divided into four, about equal, segments. The horizon itself is marked by transition from the flatly receding density gradient of the field to that of the sky above. The density gradient of the field creates a strong impression of pictorial depth, the three focal points of the horizon stretch it sideways and in combination provide the impression of vastness of the open fields under the expanse of the sky.

But a variety of points of convergence can be chosen for other reasons than the desire to convey the extent of space. In his *Le Crau Seen from Mountmajor* (Figure 7.3), Van Gogh used a number of points, some of which are on the horizon, with the same purpose as those of the *Fields under the Blue Sky*, but some other points are used to show the folds of the land mass. In Van Gogh's *Night Cafe* (Figure 7.4), too, several focal points are to be found. The principal one, which is formed by the convergence of the joints of the floor-boards, the extension of the joint between the ceiling and dominant wall and the top of the panelling on this wall, as well as by corresponding features of the other receding wall, occurs at the back of the portrayed space near the heads of the two customers seated on the left. The others, which are less powerfully marked, occur, as shown in the diagrams, near the right hand edge of the picture. At the two seated figures there are two foci, and yet another weak focus falls near the clock.

Use of multiple points of convergence reflects the painter's veracity. It is certainly correct to say that Van Gogh's picture represents the artist's experience of the depicted scene somewhat more correctly than does Vermeer's picture, since Van Gogh acknowledges that the painter's eye moved whilst looking at the scene. But this is only a *token* acknowledgement, and a skilfully selected token at that, because it is improbable that the painter's eye rested on only those points which are indicated in the picture.

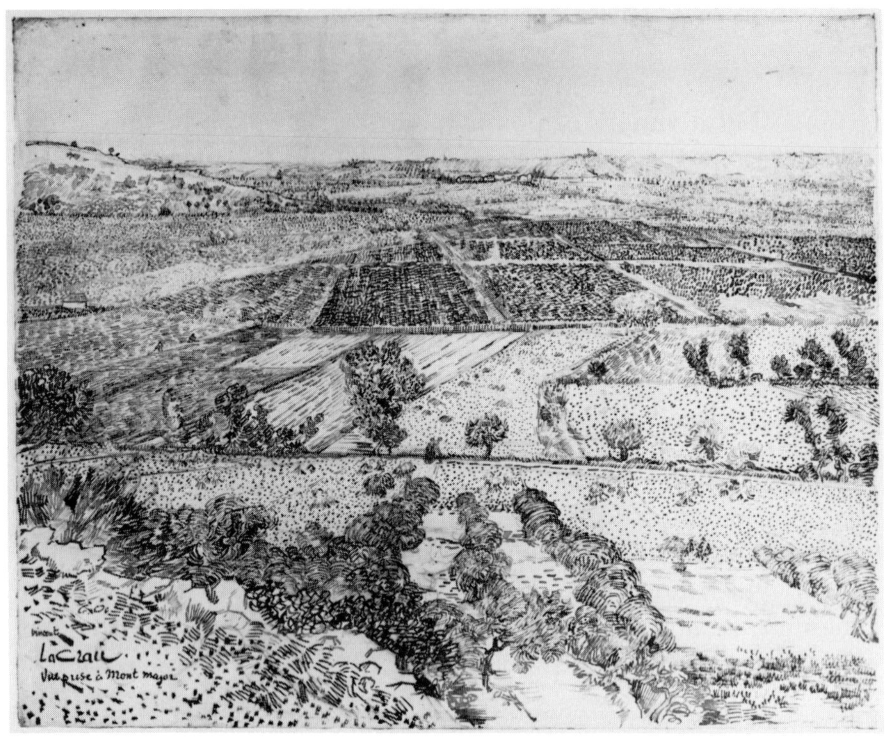

Figure 7.3A Vincent van Gogh, "Le Crau". (Reproduced by courtesy of the Stedelijk Museum, Amsterdam).

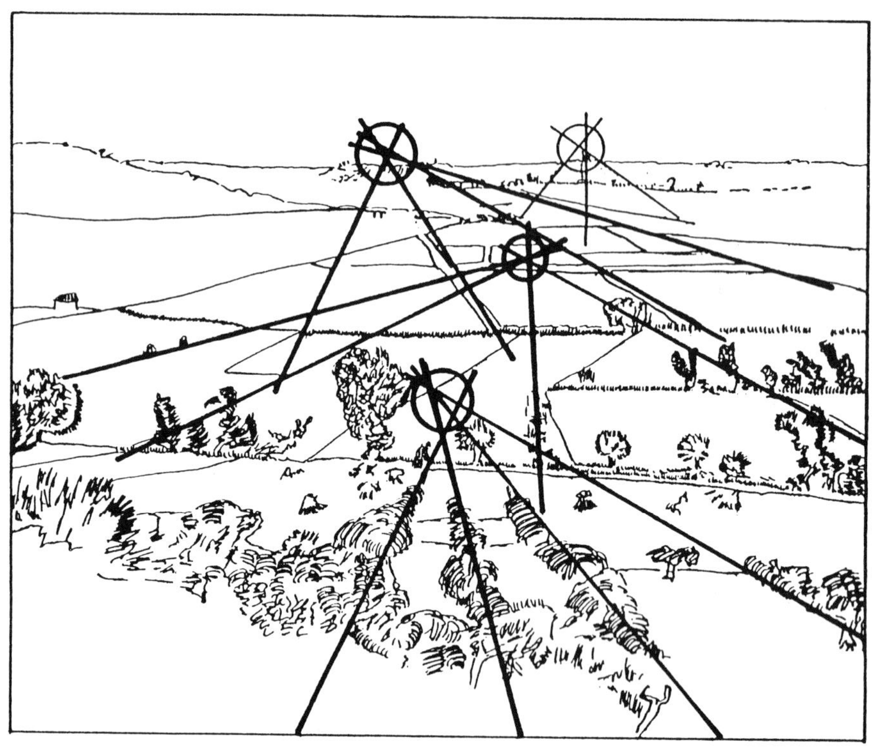

Figure 7.3B Focal points implicit in van Gogh's *Le Crau* are shown in this diagram.

In the examples discussed above the implication that the artist's eye had rested on different locations in the scene was derived from consideration of the pattern of convergence of contours in the paintings. However, as we will see, this is not the only source of evidence about the fixation pattern of the artist's eye.

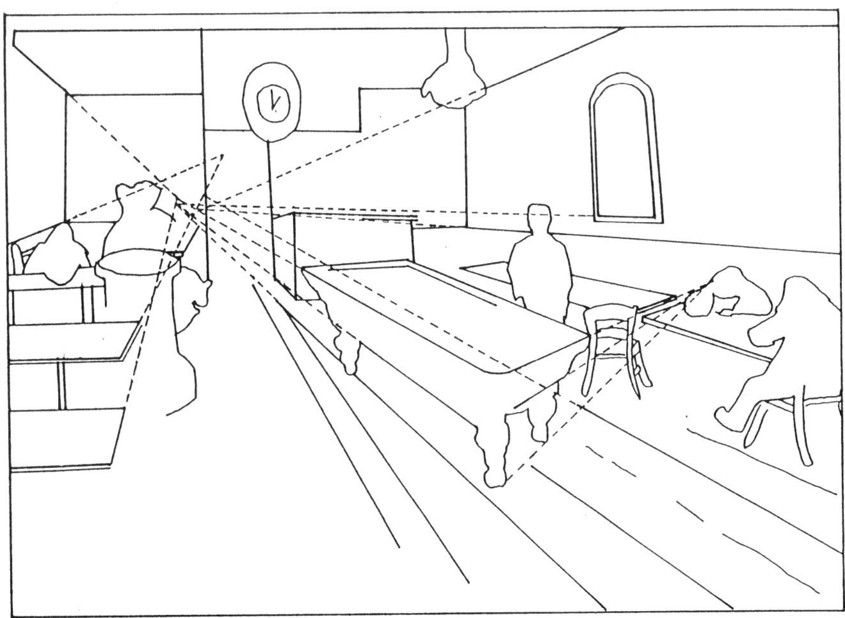

Figure 7.4 Diagram derived from van Gogh's "The Night Cafe" (after Strzemiński, 1974). Points of convergence of horizontal contours are shown. All horizontal parallels should, if the rules of linear perspective are observed, converge on the horizon.

When scanning a real scene the eye would not only sweep but it would also focus so that objects which were, at that particular time, under scrutiny would be seen clearly and both those nearer and those further away would be rendered indistinct. This would not differentiate amongst the three glances cast on the horizon simply because they are on the horizon, but it would make a substantial difference to glances cast at nearer objects. A picture which has a single focal point

can therefore be thought a depiction of a single glance. But a picture which presents a clear view of objects stretching over a large proportion of its depth cannot be such a sample because it lacks a definite focal plane in which objects were seen more clearly than elsewhere. It must therefore be a reconstruction of a series of samples. Vermeer's *The Music Lesson* belongs to such an anachronistic kind, it consists of a sample taken with the eye in one position, in combination with depiction of a very clear view of the scene, which could only be obtained in the course of a series of glances at different focal planes (or result from the painter making a detailed copy of a projected, focussed image).

Since the structure of the eye is such that within the plane at which it is focussed it sees more distinctly those areas closest to the line of sight[5], there is yet one more factor to be considered. The combined effect of depth of focussing and differential acuity results in a zone of clear vision. Objects which are laterally displaced from this zone are unclear because of the retina's differential acuity and objects nearer or further than this zone are unclear because they are out of focus. Objects found within that area will be seen clearly, all the other objects will be more or less blurred. Renoir's *The Little Cafe* (Figure 7.5) acknowledges these ocular characteristics. The most clearly visible person is the young man in a top hat. A young woman in the foreground, who is clearly seated closer to the viewer, is blurred. Her companion, who is closer to the plane containing the young man but away from the axis, is markedly more blurred as are the other guests, who although closer to the axis are at a greater depth. The latter are scarcely discernible. Thus, in this picture both the depth of field of the optical apparatus of the eye and the declining acuity of the retina from central (visual axis) to periphery are acknowledged. By using these devices the artist has not created a picture which gives the impression of a textbook illustration; the painting remains a balanced work of art.

Figure 7.5 P. A. Renoir, "Little Cafe". (Reproduced with the permission of the Rijksmuseum Kröller-Müller, Otterlo, Holland).

This device of selective enhancement of the detail of a picture is not uncommon in painting and certainly not confined to the French impressionists. Figure 7.6 shows another example,

a group portrait of a dinner party by the Scottish artist Alfred Edward Emslie.

Figure 7.6 After Alfred Edward Emslie, "Dinner at Haddo" 1884.

In this picture the hostess, the Marchioness of Aberdeen, is seated with her back to the painter and immediately to her right is the the prime minister Gladstone who is shown in less detail than the guest to the left of the hostess, the Earl of Roseberry. Again the guest whose face is shown between the arms of the candelabrum is depicted in rather more detail than those on either side. In the latter instance perhaps the effort to capture the appearance of this guest as his head moved behind the candelabrum led to the artist paying more attention to him than to his immediate neighbours and this fact revealed itself in the greater detail included. Incidentally this picture does not have a single vanishing point and may echo the shifts in the painter's stance as he tried to catch the features of the guests, who were likely to have been rather more active than those sitting for a normal portrait.

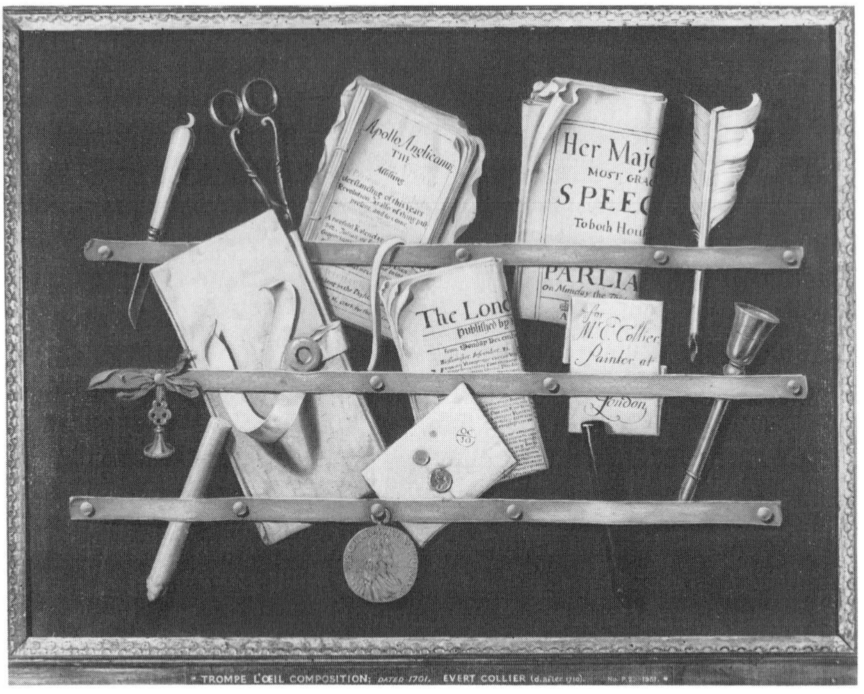

Figure 7.7 Edward Collier, "Trompe l'Oeil with Writing Materials". (Reproduced with permission of the Victoria and Albert Museum, London).

We have argued when contrasting Vermeer's *The Music Lesson* with Van Gogh's *Field* that the former picture could be described as a product of many samples taken with the eye in a single setting. Further we analysed several pictures whose multiplicity of points of convergence declared them to be combinations of samples which differed both in terms of the setting of the line of sight and of the depth of the field. Before proceeding with examinations of even more intricate ways of sampling, we must note that paintings corresponding closely to a truly unitary sampling scheme are also to be found and belong to that distinct group known as *trompe l'oeil*[6]. These pictures

(Figure 7.7) generally portray such a small depth that it could easily have been accommodated in a single focussing of the eye, and their width of field is typically so restricted that it could well have been grasped in a single glance, provided the picture is viewed at a reasonable distance. The themes of such paintings are often arrangements of inert, thin objects such as letters, newspapers, keys, leaves and feathers.

Figure 7.8A After P. A. Renoir, "Les Grands Boulevards"

When an artist combines intrinsic cues derived from the movement of the eye and differential focussing, an entirely new effect results, as shown by Renoir's *Les Grands Boulevards* (Figure 7.8A).

Figure 7.8B Diagram to show areas of lucidity in the Renoir picture shown in figure 7.8A.

The tall building on the right conveys a strong cue of linear perspective, suggesting that the artist's eye rested somewhere above the second carriage travelling along the boulevard (see diagram Figure 7.8B). But the distribution of obfuscation is not concordant with linear perspective. There are areas of notable lucidity. These are small lacunae in the hazy obfuscated field. One such area centres on the two men standing on the pavement presumably engrossed in a conversation and the region that runs across from these to the leaning man on the left of the picture. Another, on a lady, who is accompanied by two children and passes closely by; as the area is small, only one of the children, the girl on the left, falls within it. Both these sets of figures are clearly at a greater pictorial depth (as suggested by the imitative cues of perspective and elevation) than is the solitary newspaper reader at the extreme left, who is as distinctly portrayed. Further lacunae of lucidity are found on the right hand edge of the picture. The elements which they accentuate are the striped window blind of the corner shop and the rectangular window just above it, and the foliage of the tree hiding the house above the rectangular window. Since the foliage hides the house it is clearly in front of it. Thus we have in close proximity *in the plane of the picture* an aerially unoccluded upper portion of the house and aerially unoccluded foliage in front of it. The foliage is much closer to the viewer than the house, hence another set of contradictions. There is yet another area of clearly portrayed foliage, it is in the middle of the upper margin of the picture. The sixth pocket of lucidity encloses the horse and the equipage. The gradual merging of this element in the surrounding hazy brushwork is noteworthy. The horse's head is portrayed quite distinctly and forms the centre of this area of the painting, the horse's body less clearly so, the driver is even less so, and the passengers of the carriage are scarcely discernible. The remainder of the picture is rendered in relatively vague brushwork presenting a backdrop from which these islands of clarity emerge.

The overall impression is therefore that the artist's eye rested on several points of the scene and at different depths, and at each point the painter depicted the region which he inspected and testified to the fact that the sharpness of his vision declined away from the point of fixation. These tell-tale traces of the wanderings of the eye are however no more likely to be true representations of the artist's exploration of the scene than the points of convergence in van Gogh's *Night Cafe*, which we have just discussed, were the representations of the movement of his eyes. They too are a sample of the artist's experiences selected by him for presentation to the viewer.

The artist's choice is not likely to be random, but its determinants can only be speculated upon. One could surmise for example, that the relative differences in clearness with which various parts of the equipage are represented are due to the difference in the movements which they execute. The horse, which moves vigorously, pulling forward and nodding its head, is shown more clearly; the driver, who sways a little perched on his elevated seat, less so, whilst the two passengers snug inside the carriage remain almost still and are almost indistinct. The movement of the equipage, it can be hypothesised, drew the artist's attention to it, and the artist transferred this impression onto canvas. This might well have been so. If so, different explanations, not involving movement, need to be put forward for the other areas of lucidity in the picture. The reader may wish to speculate about them. And, if so, it should also be noted that the argument that the horse's head in Renoir's picture is clearly portrayed because its movement attracted the artist's attention to it is paradoxical because movement should, as every photographer will say and as every Futurist will confirm, blur the image. Indeed Futurists depicted moving objects by multiple images which are themselves *not* directly related to perception or sensation but have instead arisen partly from the application of knowledge of cinematography to painting. Two pictorial styles can thus arise from the same phenomenon, depending upon whether one regards movement as responsible for drawing attention to the moving object, or whether one regards portrayal of the movement itself as of importance.

We have considered three manifestations of the properties of the eye, and their reflection in styles of painting: the fact that the eye moves, the fact that it adjusts itself to the distance of the object at which it is looking by focussing, and the fact that it is not equally sensitive over its entire field of view because its acuity decreases with distance from the central line of sight. Incorporation of these cues in works of art has been illustrated using three pictures which portrayed wide open scenes. It may be instructive therefore to consider a picture which does not fall into this category, but which not only has some of the already discussed attributes but also shows some characteristics, hitherto not remarked upon[7].

Figure 7.9A P. Cézanne, "Still Life with Fruit Basket". (Reproduced by courtesy of the Louvre, Paris).

Consider Cézanne's rather untidy *Still Life with Fruit Basket (*Figure 7.9A). The features which strike a casual viewer most when looking at the table are the distorted shapes of various utensils. One can perhaps accept the distortion of the basket laden with fruit; baskets may lose their shape with use, and Cézanne might have painted an *old* basket; but the lopsidedness of the tureen and the jug and the asymmetry of the large spheroidal pot are more difficult to explain . Even more so, though not so readily noticeable, is the discontinuity of the front edge of the table itself. The edge is much lower at the left side of the picture than it is at the right (see Figure 7.9B). The discontinuity escapes the viewer's attention because a crumpled serviette covers most of the central part of the table where the two visible segments of the edge, had they been continued, would have failed to meet; a device similar to that used by the creator of *Death* (Figure 2.12). Furthermore, the abundance of colourful fruit and dishes on Cézanne's table distracts the eye upwards away from the edge.

Figure 7.9B This diagram, after Strzemiński, reveals the distortions shown in 7.9A.

To explain these strange transmogrifications of the shapes of commonplace utensils we need to consider two unrelated phenomena, one inherent in the geometry of linear perspective and the other in the intrinsic characteristics of the eye. We have already described the former by considering the changes of a projected shape of a body moving in a plane parallel to the pictorial plane (Chapter 5, Figures 5.2 & 5.3). The problems which these "distortions" presented to draughtsmen have been known for a considerable time. We shall discuss them again presently. The difficulty of a perceptually convincing depiction of solid objects in accordance with the rules of linear perspective was one of the preoccupations of Leonardo da Vinci. When such objects are laterally displaced from the line of sight their depictions, although obeying all the rules of perspective, appear impossibly distorted. Resulting distortions are especially noticeable in the case of rows of columns and of spherical objects (Figure 5.3), probably because columns are generally uniform and because it is difficult to imagine a sphere projecting any other shape than a circle, and yet correctly projected shapes of spheres are often clearly elliptical. In the case of cubes placed with their faces parallel to the surface of projection the distortions take the form of gradual elongation of the visible side faces, eventually to grotesque proportions (Figure 5.2). It should also be stressed that equal displacements in any direction from the line of sight affect projections equally (see Figures 5.2 & 5.3).

This entirely legitimate, as far as the rules of perspective are concerned, transformation has provided generations of architectural draughtsmen with an irritant, especially potent whenever they attempted to draw a projection of a portico supported by a row of columns[8]. In their drawing they find that the projections of the columns grow thicker as they lie further from the assumed visual axis. If the depicted row of columns is parallel to the plane of the projection, such thickening spreads symmetrically sideways. This problem has been examined in detail in Chapter 4 and the reader will probably already have concluded that Cézanne's bizarre images derive from a similar source.

Artists have dealt with the problem in a variety of ways. The simplest way is not to draw shapes (such as a sphere) in positions where they could be subject to such unacceptable transformations. Taken to extreme this would argue for avoiding such recalcitrant shapes altogether. This may explain why Leonardo da Vinci, who was so well aware of the problem, left no artistic drawings of a sphere at all. A less radical method is to ignore the injunction of perspective and to draw falsely circular projections of spheres, whenever these occur, away from the line of sight, as Raphael has done in his *School of Athens*, or to fill these areas remote from the line of sight with depictions of objects whose "distortions" cannot be readily noticed, or simply to moderate such "distortions" or to banish them entirely, thus introducing into the picture disparate perspectives, often not merely implying that the eye has moved but that the painter has walked parallel to the canvas when painting those elements which would otherwise appear distorted. A truly ingenious method of dealing with the problem was used by Saenredam, a Dutch painter and an architectural draughtsman of 17th century, who in his *Interior of S. Bavo* (Figure 7.10) adheres to the rules of perspective, but cunningly paints only portions of the two side columns, which would, if painted in full, appear grossly distended.

Figure 7.10A A sketch of Saenredam's picture, "St Bavo's Church".

Perceptual distortions of an entirely separate origin, namely the intrinsic characteristics of the eye, can be readily experienced by means of a simple demonstration suggested by Helmholtz. Stand so that a brightly painted door is at either your left or your right and can just be seen peripherally with the single opened eye. Note the size of the door and then turn your head and look at it directly. This change from peripheral to central vision will result in a change of shape of the door. It will appear both lower and broader. Alternatively place a sheet of paper on the floor and look horizontally over it so that it is in your peripheral vision. Note the size of the sheet and then look at it directly. This too will lead to apparent change in shape; the sheet will shrink laterally on transfer of the line of vision.

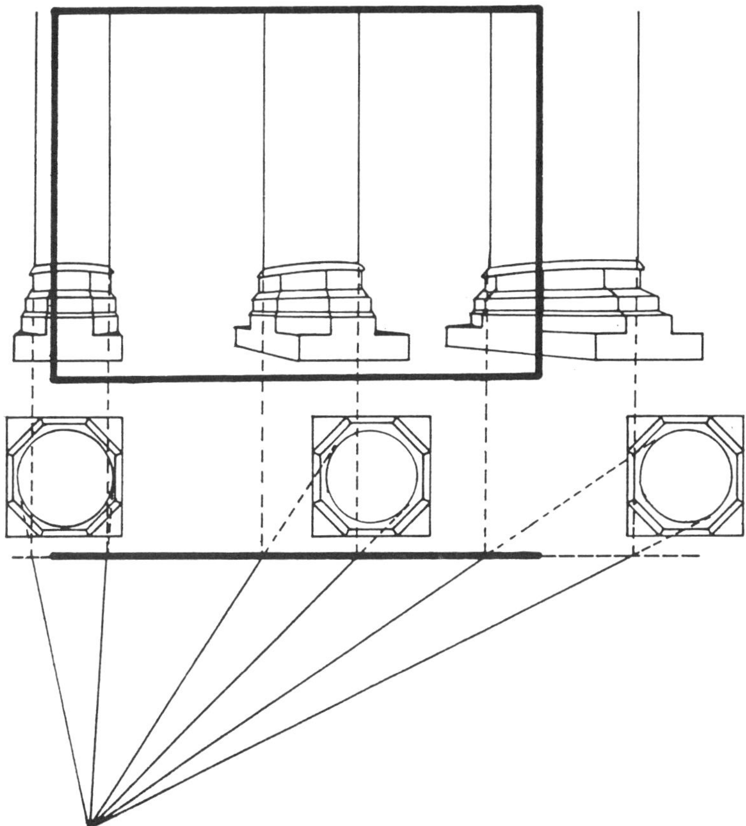

Figure 7.10B This sketch shows the effect of a judicious choice of limits in the boundary of the painting of St Bavo's church. The distortion of the column on the right would have been obvious if included in the picture.

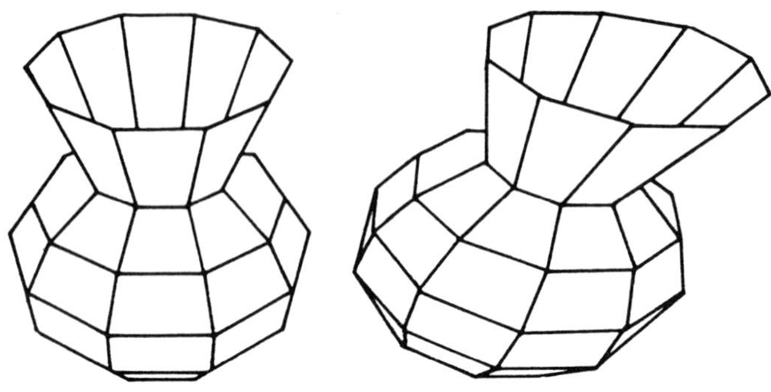

Figure 7.11 Two computer drawings of a vase obeying the principles of linear perspective. Note the distortion.

Both considerations of linear perpective and of peripheral vision argue for distortion, but the nature of the distortion is not the same in both cases. Perspective projection onto a pictorial plane may differentially enlarge, and hence distort, those element of the representation which convey depth (see Chapter 5 Figures 5.2 & 5.3). These perspective distortions can only be understood by visualising a pictorial plane cutting through a bundle of projective rays. Peripheral vision, on the other hand, completely disturbs the perception of elements lying on the periphery of the field of view and furthermore the distortions are readily and directly experienced. It is probable therefore that the latter type of perceptual experience is at the root of the distortions favoured by some artists.

The "distortions" in question depend on the angle subtended at the eye by the scene being viewed: the closer the object and the larger the angle the more noticeable the "distortion" of the objects on Cézanne's table. The projection is very close to the viewer and one would therefore expect gross distortions. It is a small and rather overburdened table, yet it almost fills the picture. There is no indication of a unique line of sight and the shapes of the three utensils, the tureen, the pot and the jug, are such as to question the possibility of their having been drawn on the assumption of a single line of sight (if this were so the distortions would be mutually compatible, which they are not).

Consider the tureen. One would expect the knob on its lid to be placed centrally. Therefore a vertical line drawn through the knob should divide the picture of the tureen into two parts and their mutual superimposition should clearly show any disparity between them. Such a disparity is clearly apparent in the diagram (Figure 7.9B). In the case of this tureen, and in the case of the jug and pot, areas of striking contrast of colour and light are to be found near their "smaller" sides. Thus, in the case of the tureen, this area lies to the left just above the table where it overlaps the dark background; in the case of the large pot, to the left of the opening. If a plausible assumption is made that it is the artist's intention that the eye should be attracted to these areas of contrast (and indeed, studies of eye movement show this happens) then analysis suggests that the "deformations" are embodiments of three glances each at a different angle. A picture of two vases drawn by computer, strictly in accordance with the conventions of linear perspective, confirms this interpretation and shows the nature of such distortions clearly (Figure 7.11). It must be stressed again, at a risk of labouring the point, that if these "distortions" derive from considerations of perspective then they truly represent the pattern of light at the pictorial plane; and the picture must have involved at least three separate viewing positions. A pinhole photograph of such a "distorted" element of the picture and a photograph of the depicted scene taken with a properly positioned camera would not be distinguishable. Under these circumstances they are therefore not distortions at all but correct views of the depicted objects[9]. However it is not certain that Cézanne based his "distortions" on a true optical projection. It is in our view more likely that they were based on his own experience of peripheral viewing of objects, which we discussed earlier in the context of Helmholtz's demonstrations.

There are then two sources of apparent distortion which might influence a painter's style, the extent to which an object falls in the periphery of the field of view (its distance from the optical axis) and the angle of regard of the painter's eye with respect to the surface being viewed. The discontinuities in Cézanne's table are probably due to changes of the direction of gaze; if the left-hand side of the table was viewed with a more steeply inclined eye than was the right-hand side the discontinuity would be explained. When this is taken account of and the reason for the apparent distortions is recognised, much of the "untidiness" of the *Table* is explained, but the *Table* does not thereby become less interesting. The distortions of the crockery, on the other hand, are probably due to the use of peripheral views.

A perspicacious reader would have noticed the similarities of some of the "distorted" shapes obtained in the diagrams assuming frontal projection to those obtained assuming an oblique plane (Figure 5.2 & 5.3). Could not, therefore, the shape of Cézanne's[10] crockery be described in terms of *combination* of non-central vision and obliquity? After all a change of visual angle has been postulated in explaining the distortion of the table itself. Yes, it could, and our insistence that it was due to the peripheral nature of view can be defended solely by invoking the economy of causes. The transformation of the table involved, as we have seen, the matching of two incompatible views. Other transformations resulting from obliquity would require further complex explanations, whereas the explanation in terms of non-central vision only does not call for them.

Figure 7.12A V. van Gogh, "Countryside near Arles". (Reproduced by kind permission of der Bayer Staatgemäldesammlungen, Munich).

All the intrinsic cues hitherto considered concern the responses of the eye to the immediate environment. None of them involves physiological changes in the eye which result from an earlier experience, influencing later perception. That such effects occur is suggested by such common experiences as the difficulty with finding a cinema seat on entering the theatre from a brightly illuminated foyer or the inability to see clearly the road ahead because one has been dazzled by headlights of a car which has passed sometime ago. These are overwhelming effects. One would expect similar effects incorporated in pictures to be of a much more muted and subtle kind, but to rest upon essentially the same principle of the influence of immediate past experience on present perception.

Figure 7.12B The diagram shows where after-images would play an important role in viewing this picture (after Strzemiński).

The eye when moving from one area of a picture to another may not do so unencumbered but carry with it a trace of impressions made by the patterns just left behind. These impressions which are affected by both the colour and the shape of the stimuli are known as after-images and fade with time[13]. The after-images of shapes do not dissolve gently and uniformly but as time passes they disintegrate, various parts disappearing completely, then occasionally re-emerging to form a new pattern. Thus, an after-image of the letter B, may disintegrate to become "P", then perhaps "b" or "I". Strong after-images, such as are commonly used in psychological investigations, appear to be affected by pictorial depth cues. Observers report that after-images appear to be smaller when projected at the divergent end of a figure consisting of two mutually inclined lines (such as those of the Ponzo illusion, (see Figure 2.6) than they do when shifted towards the convergent end of the same figure. They appear to abide by the expectancies derivable from linear convergence in so far as this affects perceived distance.

If these effects are also present with much weaker after-images, such as may arise in the course of normal picture viewing, then they have important consequences for our perception of pictures. The presence of an after-image would presumably foster recognition for geometrically similar features in a picture. The important assumption here is that the eye moves in such a manner as mechanically to overlap the template created by the after-effect with the new stimulus, and hence exploit the relevant similarity. Thus in the case of van Gogh's *Countryside near Arles* (Figure 7.12A) the after-images may reinforce the rhythm created by the clouds above, and the trees, the ricks of beans and the boundary between the field and the meadow below (Figure 7.12B). The same effect, it could be argued, is to be found in Roger van der Weyden's *The Descent from the Cross* (Figure 7.13) in which depictions of hands, a foot and a skull form a chain of high contrast areas which produce after-images and link the skull of Adam with the torn palms of the Saviour through the hands of the Virgin eventually leading to the eyes of the man standing on the right of the cross. The after-image in effect sets up a visual echo which continues to resonate in the eye as it moves down the picture.

The putative influence of after-images on the perception of similarity of elements in receding gradients, for example linear convergence, leads to some interesting transformations. When objectively equal elements are placed at, pictorially, small and large distances then an eye movement from "near" to "far" will result in the after-image appearing as larger than the element and the movement from "far" to "near" will result in the after-image looking smaller than the element. Thus, in neither case will there be a congruency between the after-image and the element on which it rests. When the "near" element is larger than the "far" element (as would normally be the case when a horizontal pavement leading away from the observer is drawn) then the movement from "far" to "near" would result in a decrease in the perceived size of the after-image and therefore in an increased contrast with the elements depicted as being nearer. A movement in the opposite direction from "near" to "far" would also enlarge the contrast between the after-image and the element with which it is being compared. The very opposite of this effect would be observed in the case of reversed perspective when, that is, the near elements are drawn smaller than the "far" elements. Here movement in either direction would result in increasing similarity between the elements and after-images.

Figure 7.13.A R. van Weyden, "Descent from the Cross". (Reproduced by courtesy of the Prado, Madrid).

The phenomenon of after-images could therefore be suggested as one of the factors contributing to the acceptance of the "reversed perspective" which is common in certain styles of painting, and which we have considered earlier. This suggestion is tentative because after-images evoked by stimuli of low intensity are very ephemeral.

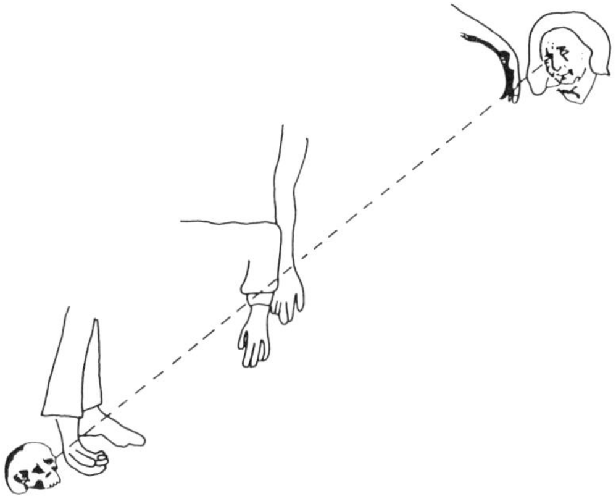

Figure 7.13B Diagram shows where high contrast elements may evoke after-images and emphasise the composition of the picture shown in figure 7.13A.

There are two further visually intrinsic pictorial cues which ought to be considered. The first of these, which is particularly favoured by the Op Artists, is that of subjective contours[14] and is discussed in the following chapter. Such contours enable an artist to induce in a viewer a percept of overlap and pictorial depth without depicting it in the usual manner by painting the overlapping and overlapped areas in immediate contact.

Thus three indented black figures and three inequality signs, arranged as shown below, convey to the majority of viewers a surprising effect of an equilateral triangle (Figure 7.14). This triangle has clearly visible edges spanning between its vertices which coincide with the indentations in the three black figures, and the surface of which appears to be brighter than that of the surrounding paper. Moreover the triangle appears to float above the page and other parts of the pattern. This depth effect is so strong that when two *equal* rings are drawn, one on the triangle and one near it, the former, since it seems to be nearer, is seen as the smaller of the two in agreement with the principle of perspective.

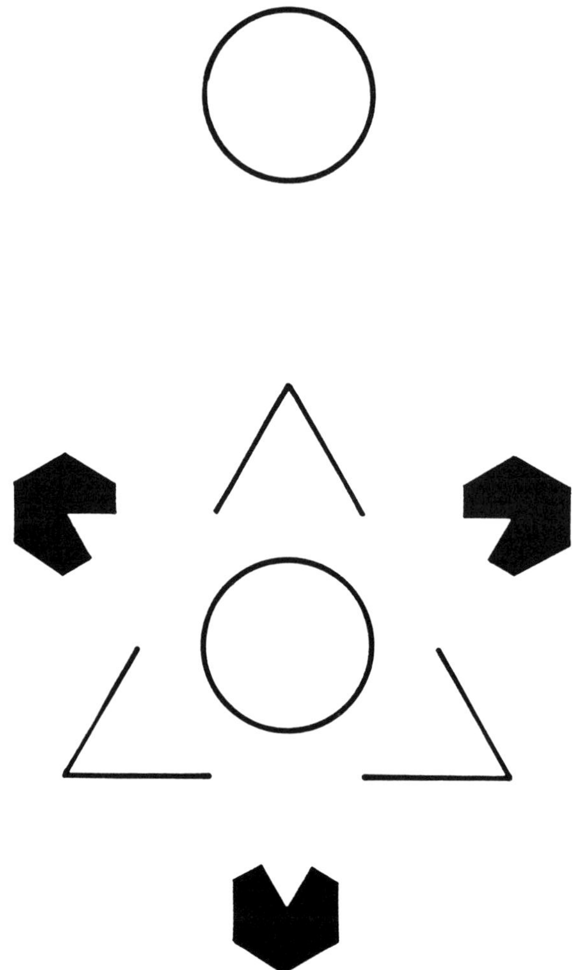

Figure 7.14 Subjective contours. The ghostly triangle affects the perception of size. The black ring drawn within the triangle seems to float above the surface and appears smaller than the physically equal ring drawn above.

The second intrinsic cue, which unlike the preceding ones has a venerable place in the recorded history of art, is associated with the spontaneous tendency of the eye to increase contrast between neighbouring areas of uniform colour. Thus when uniform stripes of different shades of greyness are laid side by side, as in Figure 7.15, the eye does not see them as such. Instead a lighter band is seen running parallel to the boundary within each lighter stripe of each pair and is accompanied by an illusory darker band within the darker neighbour[15]. The boundary is thus accentuated and the entire arrangement of flat uniform grey stripes is seen as a set of scalloped grooves.

Figure 7.15 Mach's Bands. All bands are of uniform shade but differ in greyness. A darker strip is perceived within each band at its boudary with its lighter neighbour and a lighter strip bounds its edge with its darker neighbour.

Such augmentation of contrasts is spontaneous but it can also be imitated by painting the bands of lighter and darker colour;

thus rendering real what is normally illusory and strengthening the effect with which Leonardo da Vinci was familiar and which can be found in pictures by Mantegna and Carpaccio. Canaletto too has frequently resorted to this device in creating townscapes notable for clear delineation of architectonic elements, and the same device was used much later by Seurat. Weale, a man of science, and the author of an exhilarating romp through the history of Western art, reprimands the latter for so doing. "It is one thing for a photographic realist like Canaletto to paint what the retina really manages better on its own, and another for Seurat to do likewise. It is as though, aware of the physiological basis of impressionism, he tried to retrieve the balance by adding the sharpening effect of the Mach bands" (as the phenomenon is called).

The basis of all the intrinsic effects described in this Chapter is to be found in the monocular field of view. Like linear perspective and the classic pictorial depth cues, such as aerial perspective and interposition, painting and drawing, of necessity, have derived their most powerful influences from monocular vision. Painters have rarely capitalised directly on the existence of stereoscopic depth in exploring visual space.

Chapter VIII

Art Via Illusion

It was noted in Chapter 1 that the awareness of the intrinsic mechanisms of the eye and their relation to artistic representation became increasingly evident during the nineteenth century. Van Gogh, Renoir, Cézanne and others incorporated into their paintings what might be described as a selective history of their exploration of a visual scene; one or a number of locations on which their eye rested and which had a particular point of focus, or a limited number of glances from the same or a few different viewpoints. This technique can be seen to confer a new set of freedoms and constraints on picture making. The subject(s) of interest in the picture need no longer be central or artificially enhanced with highlights. Nor need the artist resort to gesture or geometric arrangement of figure or objects to lead the eye to a particular point. The significance of any part of the picture can for instance be delineated purely by detail and so the viewer's eye discovers in a subtle manner the artist's visual accent as it searches the canvas. In this way an intrinsic aspect of the eye's sampling techniques, which had been largely ignored by previous painters, was elevated to a central stylistic feature.

When we move into the twentieth century the multiplicity of stylistic variations provides a confusing array from which to select examples for our exploration. Of course not all stylistic features in painting can be ascribed an origin in the artists' awareness of specific aspects of the eye's mechanisms. It might appear, for example that the Futurists would be prime examples of painters who concerned themselves with perceptual devices. Their manner of depicting speed and motion however had its origin not in the eye but in the mechanics of movie photography. The Cubists could have provided a fertile area of inquiry; especially their use of unusual geometric and atmospheric perspective and deliberate generation of internal visual conflict. However there is one group of modernists who have carried the process of capitalising on the eye's mechanisms further than any other and because of our thesis this makes them of special interest. These are the Op artists.

Op Art[1], an abbreviation of optical art, is a product of the post-war period and was probably most in the public gaze during the 1960's. Despite the fact that Op artists have frequently exhibited with Kinetic artists, the two styles are formally distinct. Op Art relies exclusively on the viewer to generate the visual effects which arise from the perception of the objectively static surface of the picture, while in Kinetic art movement of the work itself combines with the viewers perceptions to produce new and perhaps less predictable visual effects. Of course the title Op art is, in so far as it derives from optical art, misleading. As is the case with most of the so called optical illusions, few of the effects capitalise on the truly optical properties of the visual system. Rather they involve visual mechanisms which are located in the retina-brain pathways and structures, the truly neural part of the visual apparatus. It should also be noted that the techniques and devices employed by this artistic school have been evident in the work of earlier artists, among them Birolli, Delauney, Kandinsky and Kupka. Other contemporary artists, such as Maurits Escher, frequently employed techniques which are hallmarks of the Op movement. However, the systematic use and deliberate amplification of specific effects in the Op school marks it for treatment as a distinct group.

Figure 8.1 After "Ondhu" by Victor Vasarely.

If we examine a picture similar to Victor Vasarely's Ondhu, (Figure 8.1) a number of interesting effects can be experienced. The abstract theme of the picture is the contrast of straight line and curve, and this is expressed in a number of ways particularly by the careful use of ambiguity. The large dark disk at the top of the picture contrasts strongly with the light ellipse to its right. This ellipse may represent the circular lid of the cylinder to its left which has been flipped sideways and so is seen in perspective view. On the other hand this ellipse may in fact be part of a solid form which includes the crescent on its right so forming an ovoid shape. No matter how carefully we explore the picture the exact relationships of the structures at the top of the picture are not resolved and we continue to generate hypotheses about their nature. The dark and light squares at the bottom of the picture also have an ambiguous status since they are both related to adjacent lines which imply visual depth but in an inconsistent manner. The high contrast of the black disk and square and the white ellipse and square are great enough to produce visible persistence if the viewers fixate part of the picture for a few seconds and then move their eyes. Brief duration after-images such as this are frequently evoked in Op art. Figure 8.2 shows how this device may easily be employed to generate contrasting images.

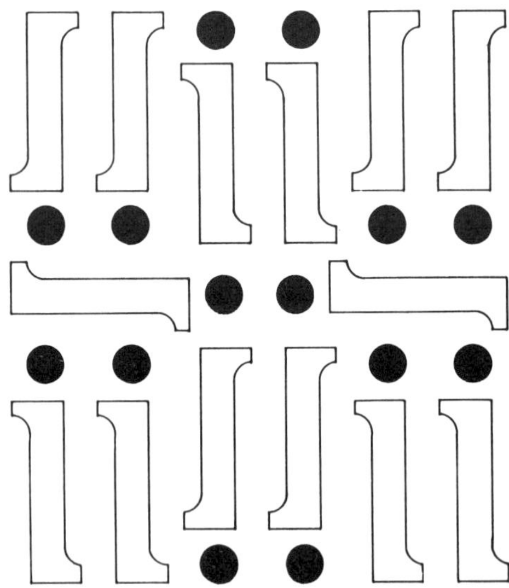

Figure 8.2 Bright Is. Look steadily at the centre of one of the spots for 20 - 30 seconds. Note the appearance of after-images.

Turning from the devices employed in the top and bottom sections of the picture to the central area it is evident that the theme of straight and curved is continued and the depth ambiguity is also maintained. The surface into which the square and circular shape are inscribed is composed of a set of straight horizontal lines. As one moves up the picture the spacing of these lines becomes closer, implying a surface receding in depth. However this depth cue is only partly complied with since if one looks at a true texture gradient shown in Figure 8.3 then it is evident that not only does the spacing of the elements change but also their size diminishes with apparent distance.

Figure 8.3 A texture gradient of squares. Note how they convey the impression of a receding plane.

This is necessary in order to comply with the basic rule of linear perspective that more distant locations support smaller visual angles. In the Vasarely picture however the fact that line thickness does not systematically decrease as we move further up the picture renders the depth effect insecure and we are aware of this instability as we view the picture.

Figure 8.4 Nicholas Wade, "About Turn".

Set in this surface of horizontal lines are a square and a circular shape. The square on the left is produced by offsetting a number of horizontal lines by a small amount. By doing so two vertical illusory contours[2] are evoked (see Figure 7.2, Chapter 7) and the more carefully one inspects the junction of these offsets the more sure one is of seeing them as continuous contours despite the intellectual certainty that they do not exist as continuous edges. The resulting square shape is indeterminately located above or below the surrounding surface. The hemisphere which has been delineated with a series of curved lines to the right of the square is also ambivalent. At one moment it is a concave surface, at another convex. In the case of these shapes, square and hemisphere, the equivocal relative depth locations of the surfaces comprising the picture is maintained and the two shapes change their apparent depth independently of each other.

This rapid and incomplete exploration of the picture shows how Vasarely has exploited a number of elementary mechanisms which are part of the eye's intrinsic repertoire. These perceptual components which have been utilised in the picture may be listed as visual persistence, perspective, illusory contours and texture or density gradient. In most cases these perceptual components have been evoked by using a minimum of information so that the eye must both work to provide the necessary perceptions of depth and shape together with their interrelations and also manufacture the alternatives that arise from the picture's ambiguity. To a greater extent than has been the case in works of art by other schools the picture only completes itself in the presence of the viewer and this completion is itself a dynamic process. Thus all artists use line, edge or gradient of shade to suggest an object or scene that the viewers must themselves perceive on the basis of the cues provided. In the case of Op Art the viewer's eye must often construct the contour itself because only the minimum of information to evoke the percept is provided. No matter how long the viewer regards the picture the devices ennumerated above continue to assert themselves. Knowledge of the mechanisms involved does not help as the eye has been effectively ensnared by the very devices it uses to construct our perception of a visual scene.

If we turn to paintings by other artists of the Op school, notably the British artist Bridget Riley, we encounter a further set of devices which have been frequently exploited in this movement. Paintings, such as *Fall* (1963) or *Crest* (1964), are composed of black wavy lines running from top to bottom on a white background (or vice versa!). These and other paintings by this school are illustrated and discussed in a number of books (Barrett, 1970; 1971; Compton, 1967; Lucie-Smith, 1975). For illustration purposes we will describe a picture by Nicholas Wade (Figure 8.4) which uses devices very similar to those employed by Riley. In looking at the picture one gains an impression of shimmering movement. The clarity of the individual lines waxes and wanes especially in the region connecting the crests and troughs, where their fading forms horizontal fuzzy bands which contrast with the top to bottom flow of the picture. The curves in the lines form a series of crests or troughs, whose spacing varies as one moves down the picture. The horizontal crests/troughs create strong impressions of depth, which like the depth effects in Vasarely's picture are ambivalent, sometimes appearing to rise from the surface, sometimes seeming to recede. Again one is aware of being in a state of dynamic interaction with the picture. If one analyses one's experiences carefully then inconsistencies are evident. There is no systematic perception of alternating crests and troughs as one goes up or down the picture. A band of curves may appear as troughs on one side of the picture and as a crest on the other. Where this is repeated neighbouring bands may appear to shear from each other in depth. This is because there is nothing in the curvature cue which indicates its direction and so fairly local visual mechanisms work independently and prevent a unified, consistent view of the picture's relationships emerging. The continuous movement in the picture exerts a hypnotic effect in the viewer which allows the eyes focussing to drift, which in turn intensifies the perceptual effects described above.

The explanations of the effects found in this picture are fairly straightforward. The ambiguity of the curvature cue in providing a basis for the perception of depth has already been discussed. The shimmering movement is probably engendered by two aspects of the eye's normal behaviour. It has been noted on several occasions in previous chapters that despite our impression of stability in our visual world our eyes are extremely active, moving from point to point as we survey a scene. Superimposed on these fixation movements are other movements, eye tremor, which is extremely fast, and also slow drifts. We are usually unaware of these effects because our visual system is designed to cope with them. A second phenomenon we should note is the presence of small changes in the curvature of the lens within the eye as the visual system strives to maintain as sharp an image as possible. These small changes in accommodation, as the mechanism for bringing patterns into focus within the eye is called, are not uniform across the surface of the lens and so minor transient astigmatism is produced, whose axis also fluctuates over time. The inherent instability of the retinal image can be readily appreciated when one examines a regular pattern such as that shown in Figure 8.5. If one looks steadily at the centre of this pattern shimmer and instability are soon experienced. Shadowy fluctuations are particularly marked towards the centre where the line spacing is closest and where minor changes in image sharpness are likely to have the most obvious effect. This latter sensation is also very evident in the Wade picture.

Figure 8.5 An adaptation of McKay's pattern. Look steadily at the centre of the pattern and note the shimmering and shadowy fluctuations of the lines.

The experiences seen with this type of pattern can be abolished by forming an after-image of the pattern on the retina using a transparency of it together with an electronic flashgun. The after-image is not influenced by changes in accommodation or eye movements and so it is perceived as a stable pattern. Of the two mechanisms, minor rapid eye movements and fluctuations in accommodation, which we have discussed, experimental investigations make it quite clear that it is variable accommodation which is by far the most significant contributor to the observed effects. It should also be noted that this is the only Op Art effect we have discussed which is genuinely optical in nature[3].

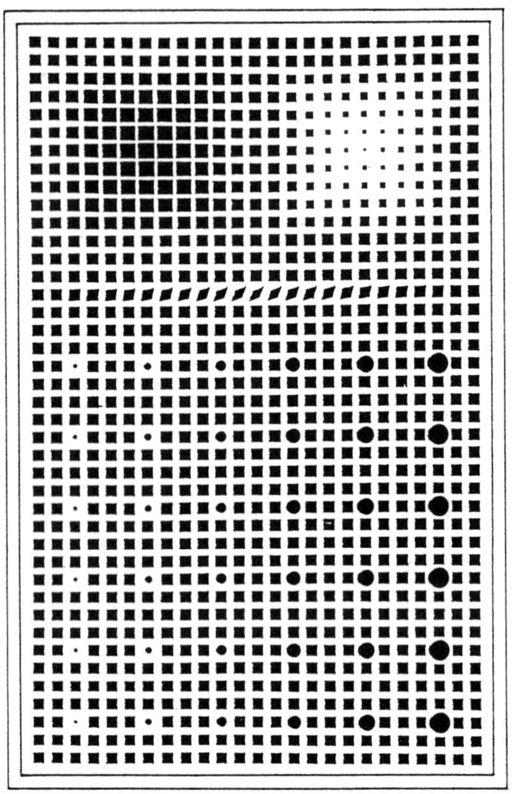

Figure 8.6 After "Supernovae" by Victor Vasarely.

The third painting we shall consider here is an adaptation of *Supernovae* by Victor Vasarely (figure 8.6). This work is obviously a series of variations on the theme of the square; the presence of the 36 circular shapes only serves to emphasise the presence of the thousand or so small squares of which the picture is composed. The vast majority of the squares are of the same size and are spaced at regular intervals. Both the regularity and the alterations in size or shape of these basic pictorial elements allow the artist to introduce a series of illusory effects which give the picture its vibrancy.

In the upper region of the picture two contrasting areas of dark and light are formed by the enlargement and diminution respectively of the square elements. The dark area on the left appears to bulge forward from the picture surface; the large, more crowded squares at the centre of this region appearing nearer to the viewer than the surrounding smaller elements. In contrast the lighter area on the right is isolated from its surroundings by the converse process; the squares are made progressively smaller as they approach the centre of this region leading to an impression that they lie behind the picture surface. These differences in apparent depth are not startling to the viewer since, as with the majority of Vasarely's effects, they are minimally evoked by the cue of relative size i.e. surfaces which are nearer to you normally project larger images than those which are further away. By manipulating the size of the square elements the artist has produced two quite distinct effects. The first effect is due simply to the alteration in the perceived brightness of these regions, which has the effect of drawing the eye to explore them. The second is the impression of contrasting depth between each of these regions and their surrounding elements and between the regions themselves.

Moving down the picture, the next perturbation in the square elements which we encounter is the progressive transformation of squares to diamond and back to squares as we move across the picture. Once again the eye is drawn to this region of the picture because the distortions of the squares produce a greater proportion of white and this brightness difference acts as a lure for the eye. The distortions of the square shape are interpreted by the majority of viewers as an alteration in the orientation of the square in depth; as if each of the squares has been simply rotated about a diagonal axis running from its top left to its bottom right. Once again a minimal distortion can produce an impression that the picture has real depth.

In the lower half of the picture (approximately) the regular square elements are interrupted by a number of discs which have the effect of grouping the squares into regular arrays. These spontaneous perceptual groupings occur despite the differences in the size of the discs, although most viewers find the grouping effect stronger on the right of the picture where the discs forming the corners of the group are the largest. This spontaneous grouping in which the rows and columns of squares joining the discs appear to have an added emphasis is again an arrangement which is added to the picture by the viewer's perceptual system. These boundary squares are not emphasised in any way by the artist except in so far as they can be perceived as members of a group. The variation in the strengths of this grouping tendency across the surface of the picture adds to the dynamism of the viewer's experience.

We have left until last any mention of the illusion which pervades the picture. Grey spots are visible at the intersections of the grid formed by the squares and their background. These spots are optimally visible at a fixed distance from the picture (the viewer may experiment by holding Fig. 8.6 at various distances from the eye). In fact peering closely at these intersections results in the spots vanishing from the area we are examining, although we may still be aware of their presence in the surrounding region. The only area in which this is not true is in the dark region in the upper left of the picture, where the finer white intersections allow one to see the spots even at the centre of the point of fixation. These illusory spots, known eponymously as the Hermann grid illusion[4], have been the subject of intermittent study over the last hundred years and are now believed to be directly attributable to a feature of the neural organisation of the retina. Some aspects of this illusion already alluded to above indicate that it is very closely bound up with the acuity structure of the eye. To see the spots in central vision one must have a fine grid while to see the spots in peripheral vision one must have a coarse grid; in other words, to evoke the illusion optimally the grid size must be related to the sensitivity pattern of the retinal region on which it is imaged. The presence of this evanescent effect in the stark black and white picture field gives the work much of its immediate vibrancy.

Consideration of these pictures, which employ techniques typical of the Op movement, makes it apparent that this group mastered certain important aspects of the processes which mediate normal perception as well as certain incidental consequences of the visual process (e.g. after-images) and have exploited them in order to involve the viewer in a visual dialogue with the pictures. Texture gradients, line and curve, contour completion, perspective, interposition and stereoscopic depth combine in perception under natural conditions to produce a scene in which the various cues are congruent with each other. In Op art, however, these cues are stripped of their normal context and concordance. The viewer is denied the support of familiar objects, typical people or places and so the stability of the cues is lost and their effects become indeterminate. Surfaces change their orientation or alter their apparent depth with respect to the picture's surface. Lines that are known to be fixed appear to wave and shimmer. In stark contrast to the artistic endeavours of Renaissance painters, where eye and mind are totally engaged in the picture, in viewing Op art works the mind is hardly involved in the main interaction between painting and perceiver. These pictures contain neither symbol nor allegory and the absence of any familiar anthropological or geographical reference render them effectively culture free. Despite the fact that a title such as Supernovae may lead to speculation about connections between the painting and cosmological phenomena, such links are tenuous and in the authors' view largely irrelevant. The majority of works produced by this school could be appreciated by individuals from any cultural background and as such could have some claim to be an approximation to a universal art. Our perceptions of these art works may be passively experienced or we may if we choose speculate about relationships between the painting's effects which continue to work independently of our hypotheses. Despite the fact that the artist has carefully minimised the cues the viewer is provided with, in order to preserve ambivalence and generate a dynamic visual experience, the art itself is not minimal; on the contrary it is visually rich. There is no doubt however that it has become so securely interlocked with the mechanisms of the eye that style and theme have become unified.

Chapter IX

Art And Reality

We began our review by pointing out that in discussing a painting it was possible, in most circumstances, to make a distinction between the thematic content of the picture and the particular style by which the artist realised his theme. Of course this division is easily made in some circumstances and is difficult in others. It is probably useful to imagine pictorial representations varying from Egyptian hieroglyphics at one extreme, where the visual element was purely a code to deliver the linguistic message, to the works of the Op artists at the other, where the visual effect is the major goal of the artist. This is not to say that skill or aesthetic evocation play no part in mainly symbolic representations, as is attested by the pride of some calligraphers in their work, but the functional balance of the work in certain instances is shifted to one extreme or the other. For the great majority of pictorial works this separation of content and style could be made reasonably easily and it then became possible to address the question of purely visual factors as determinants of artistic style. The specific issue we chose to examine was how far variations in artistic style could be explained by assuming that artists have differentially capitalised on particular visual mechanisms and that it is the specific sample of such mechanisms which they have exploited that constitutes the essence of their style. This idea may initially strike one as being too crude but in the course of exploring its implications it proved both subtle and robust.

In following this idea we discussed how particular cues which furnished information about our visual environment were seized on and utilised in picture making. The fact that the artist utilises some of the same mechanisms to evoke a response from the viewer that the natural environment elicits in the perceiver leads us to reject the notion that pictorial devices are mere conventions. The fact that no artist uses all possible mechanisms in a picture and different schools and traditions utilise different samples may mean that certain forms of depiction become conventional but, nevertheless, they may reflect the valid elicitation of natural visual mechanisms. Even the apparently aberrant reverse perspective may be shown to have a basis in a viewer's experience under specific conditions. It is also clear that the consequences of adopting particular stylistic mechanisms, such as linear perspective, were not always followed through even when the devices were most in vogue. Peripheral projections of spheres or columns were eschewed if they clashed with the artist's aesthetic sense even during the high Renaissance. Later artists, such as Claesz (Figure 9.1), felt free to render a still life in which the utensils were portrayed in free caricature rather than in the apparent distortion of true linear projection. Such instances exemplify what we were referring to in our introductory chapter when we spoke of the tension between what is perceived and what is sensed. Claesz presumably believed that what was normally perceived by a viewer, that is symmetrical plates and baskets, was a better representation of the world than Cézanne's table. As we have seen however Cézanne's table is in many senses a truer representation of what is sensed, although, in the final analysis neither representation can be said to be correct. Cézanne's and Claesz's representation of objects are both legitimate renderings of objects on the visual route from the sensory to the conceptual (see Chapter 1).

All this inevitably brings us to the question of what is real or considered as real in pictures. The idea we have been following, that different aspects of the eye's mechanisms are revealed in the artistic styles of different artists, does not allow adjudication. This is because it does not specify that the use of any particular combination of sensory or perceptual processes is a better reflection of reality than any other. Rather it draws our attention to a range of equally valid mechanisms and invites us to consider their contribution to the composition which confronts us. Thus the single vanishing point of a Canaletto landscape, with its implication of the single stationary impassive eye, contrasts with the multiple vanishing points of a van Gogh, with its implication of a restless exploring eye. Obviously when we use the word real to describe a work by either artist we are enmeshed in ambiguity and it is to this ambiguity that we must now turn.

Figure 9.1 P. Claesz, "Still Life with Turkey Pie". (Reproduced with permission of the Rijksmuseum Stichting, Amsterdam). Compare the forms of the utensils with those of Cézanne's "Still Life with Fruit Basket", figure 7.8A.

When a picture evokes in the eye a percept which is sufficiently close to that evoked by the depicted object it is said to be *realistic*. The term *realism* has, when so used, an absolute value. It is however possible to use the term subjectively by insisting that a realistic picture should convey correctly the *visual* experiences of the artist. All the artist's visual experiences are material which may be included in such a picture, not just those which are known to be shared with other viewers of the depicted objects. Such a notion of realism embraces the earlier definition and is broader, since it insists the realistic work of art is that which matches the self-awareness of the eye i.e. knowledge of the artist concerning what it means to "see" something. It follows then that when this self-awareness changes, so does the notion of realism. This usage is, of course, radically different from that currently in vogue, wherein realistic is meant to be the polar opposite of abstract; so that it might be said that the utensils of Claesz's table (Figure 9.1) are more realistic than those of Cézanne's (Figure 7.8A). Strzemiński [1], whose work inspired these speculations, would deny this, saying that to those whose eye's self-awareness matches that of Cézanne, Cézanne's table and all the things upon it are realistic, and, in contrast, Claesz's table lacks realism as it does not present truthfully the painter's real experiences. (It does so, of course, for those who share Claesz's level of awareness.)

There are therefore, in this view, no realistic or non-realistic styles[2], but there are styles which differ because their creators had consciously used various attributes of their visual systems, and in painting acknowledged this fact. A failure to see a picture as realistic, in terms of this taxonomy, is tantamount to seeing it as a picture which is wrong, in the sense that it does not evoke the full, or a satisfactory sample of the experience of viewing the object, i.e. not necessarily only of the physical appearance of the object itself, but also perhaps the changes in the eye associated with looking at the object.

In viewing pictures, then, we have to be aware of the objects as depicted and of the numerous ways in which an object could have been evoked. A case can be made for an extension of the concept of differentiated awareness in perception of pictures so as to embrace the information "behind the picture's surfaces", such as the depth cues described in the second chapter. Those features which need to be clearly apprehended for correct interpretation of a picture could be said to call for primary awareness; those which help the eye to decide on the true nature of the former, for "secondary awareness". Consider again a picture showing a wheel at an angle. The projected shape is an ellipse, a primal stimulus which, because of the shape constancy, is a potential circle; as is the case with every ellipse: a circle trying to get out, but it needs help. This can be furnished by, say, an appropriate density gradient. The gradient *per se* is unimportant. Its only function is that of a perceptual midwife who ensures that the correct shape is apprehended. The analogy of its role with that of the picture's surface is obvious; it is just as secondary to perception of the correct shape as the picture's surface is to perception of correct relationships within pictorial space.

The concepts of primal, by which we mean the minimum "skeletal" characteristics necessary to convey recognition of an object or feature, and secondary characteristics, by which we mean shading, texture, colour etc., may prove useful in describing styles of art. It could be said that whereas such styles as exemplified by De Hooch's art rely greatly on subsidiary characteristics, those exemplified by Ancient Egyptian art and Cubist art rely more on the primal ones and are essentially naive in nature since they make little use of the secondary mechanisms[3]. Secondary characteristics, one should note, by embracing pictorial depth cues, texture, colour etc., implicate various perceptual mechanisms, some of which we have discussed. These distinctions affect only imitative cues. Intrinsic cues, discussed in Chapter 7, do not relate directly to the depicted world, but inform the beholder how the artist viewed the world and, therefore, only very indirectly convey information about the world.

We have repeatedly stressed that the eye will accept approximations to the real and that such approximations are the rule in pictures. The simplest and the most common of such approximations, which we have not discussed here since we have explicitly excluded considerations of colour, is that inherent in representing the "real world" in monochrome. We have concerned ourselves largely with approximations to the geometric attributes of the "real world". The geometry of external stimuli can be approximated to by the pigment distribution on the painting's surface, which simply ensures that the flux of light reflected by the picture and entering the eye is approximately the same as the flux of light which would be reflected from the depicted objects. This type of approximation is inherent in the use of imitative cues. Looked at from the opposite end of the perceptual process, an approximation can be regarded as a stimulus which exploits the measure of tolerance inherent in the perceptual system, which is prepared to regard stimuli that are not quite correct imitations as fascimilies. This tolerance ensures, for example, that in spite of the absence of linear convergence the hexagon, shown in Figure 2.8 in the second chapter, is seen as a cube, and that most people do not notice the inconsistencies in perspective in the double portrait of *Arnolfini and his Wife* (Figure 1.1) Although these two examples concern linear convergence, examples involving other cues can easily be found. Indeed, a list of works entirely free from such trickery, if compiled, would be very short indeed.

This tolerance of the eye is particularly important because it allows an artist to use mechanical aids and standardised procedures. The use of Dürer's frame (Figure 2.2) and of similar devices, which were very popular at one time, facilitates correct reproduction of the projected image but also, as ten Doesschate's studies show, relies upon such leniency. The extrapolation from Saenredam's painting (Figure 7.12) clearly shows how close to the limits of tolerance the painter has approached.

The tolerance which we have so far discussed concerns the eye's ability to accept as good cues, those which are really counterfeit in the sense that they do not correspond with any correct projection of real objects. But it extends further than that. It is not necessary in "real life" for observers to rely on the same percept. A familiar coffee pot will be recognised as such in spite of changes of illumination, orientation and setting. Different perceptual mechanisms responding to different cues can lead to correct recognition of an object, just as different muscular movements can be used to achieve the same end. This tolerance of the perceptual mechanisms in real life conditions is normally referred to as perceptual constancy but it appears that similar processes can obtain even under the more constraining conditions of looking at pictures. Hence, as already indicated, different combinations of cues can be used in pictures to elicit a particular percept, although the resulting style and, consequently, the aesthetic attributes of the picture will be affected by the choice of cues.

But the artist need not confine himself by using imitative cues to mere mimicking of the visible world. He can penetrate Dürer's projection screen and seek a more intimate contact with the eye by simulating its very actions, and making a picture which not only includes information provided by the environment, but also information descriptive of the eye's response to the environment, thus extending further the spectrum of styles. Any visual experience which can be encoded in a pictorial form can become a characteristic of an artistic style and, conversely, an explanation of the visual aspects of any artistic style can be sought in visual experience or experiences, there being often several possible but not equally plausible explanations. An interesting instance of such an explanation is the putative use of non-Euclidean space by van Gogh. This rests on the following empirical finding.

Figure 9.2 V. van Gogh, "Bedroom in Arles". (Reproduced with permission of the Rijksmuseum Stichting, Amsterdam).

When an observer is placed in total darkness and required to judge the positions of faint points of light, his judgements show that he does not perceive spatial relationships in the same manner as he does normally. Enforced reliance on only the binocular cues creates a different, non-homogeneous, visual space[4]. This space has three distinct zones: that near to the observer, wherein objects bulge forward, that far away from him, wherein they cave in against the spherical bound of the space, and an intermediate, transitory zone. This experience, it is suggested, although not generally consciously savoured, may be accessible to some visually sensitive people who can, therefore, exploit it in their art. Van Gogh's *Bedroom in Arles* (Figure 9.2) is said to show that van Gogh did indeed do so. So too, it is said, does the sketch of the *Fountain in the Garden of St. Remy Asylum* (Figure 9.3). Two characteristics of the *Fountain* are claimed to support the thesis: the near part of its basin is distended and protrudes forward markedly, indeed even the very surface of the water bulges forward. These are the traits of the "near" zone of the space. But the most striking characteristic of the Fountain is surely its gross asymmetry about the vertical line passing through its spout. In this vertical asymmetry it is similar to the dishes on Cézanne's *Kitchen Table* and Van Gogh's containers in the *Absinthe Glass and Carafe* (Figure 9.4). These "distortions" are however explicable in terms of the effects of peripheral vision, which were already called upon to explain the shape of utensils of Cézanne's *Still Life with Fruit Basket.* There are thus at least two competing explanations of the origin of the Fountain's shape, of which that invoking peripheral vision, being simpler, is perhaps the more acceptable. It should be pointed out that sensitivity to the distortions apparent in optical projections may occur in the drawing of idiot savants and autistic children and adults, when no formal artistic training has been given. To propose a similar origin of distortions in Van Gogh's paintings should not be seen as psychologically outlandish.

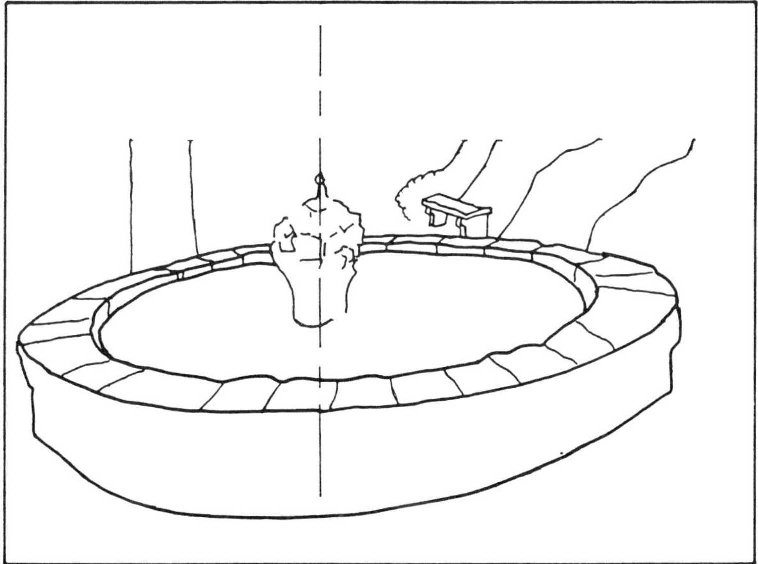

Figure 9.3 Diagram after V. van Gogh, "Fountain in the Garden of St. Remy Asylum". Note the asymmetry of the fountain's basin.

To sum up, then, the artist has at his disposal means to stimulate various perceptual mechanisms inherent in the beholder's eye. Some of these are triggered by those cues which are present in the light reaching the eye and which would therefore be recorded by any light sensitive device, such as a photographic camera, but others arise out of the structure of the eye itself and its method of gathering information and are not directly related to the laws of optics. It is also argued that the artist need not use all the available cues and therefore need not involve all the perceptual mechanisms in order to convey his intended impression to the beholder. Indeed, by selectively attenuating the cues and omitting some of these entirely he can create a large range of aesthetic devices with which to refine his message, without at the same time losing the representational value of his picture. Alternatively, as in the case with the Op artists, any attempt at representation is abandoned and the painter tries to evoke a dynamic experience utilising a specific blend of visual mechanisms.

The reasons for the choice of a particular style by an artist are difficult to specify as they are so extremely complex. An artist's actions, just as those of any other person, are influenced by three vectors. These can be briefly and crudely defined as: (i) his reference group, (ii) his paymasters, and (iii) his individual characteristics. These vectors determine the question which the visual artist attempts to answer in his work. In his profound but little known essay on *Plurality of Reality* Chwistek (1960), a logician and an artist, identified four possible questions of different complexity. The simplest question is What are things like? In answering it the artist is trying to convey the properties of objects as they are, not the properties as he sees them, nor those which it seems to him that the objects may have. Chwistek associates this question with the popular notion of reality and calls the style of painting to which it leads primitivist. In our scheme of representation (Figure 1.2) this would approximate to level B, view-centred representations, but with the added restriction that a particular "typical" view which best represents the object is selected. A more complex question, concerning the relationship among objects and the light and the observer, is tackled by artists accepting the physicist's rather than the popular notion of reality. In paintings made in answer to this question the involvement of the artist is expressly acknowledged, for example the stance which he occupied in relation to the depicted objects is traceable from the work. In our scheme this would approximate to level A, the optical. The impressionist school which tries to answer the questions: *What is seen at a given moment?* fosters even deeper involvement of the artist in his work and is associated with the psychologist's reality. This in our classification scheme would approximate to a special subset of the information available at level A. Finally when the question becomes *Which of the impressions experienced by the artist constitute the basic elements of reality?* the reality represented in the works of art is that of visionaries, says Chwistek. This does not really match up with a particular level in our scheme but it would encompass aspects of level C, the structural of level of representation, but also perhaps more expressionist aspects which we have not considered. Of course Chwistek's view of artistic style confines itself to commenting on art which can loosely be described as representational and would ignore truly abstract works. Also given the time at which it was written this article cannot be criticised for not incorporating modern knowledge of the perceptual process.

Discussion of the largely psycho-social vectors which shape the four realities is beyond the scope of this book, devoted as it is to discussion of the perceptual processes which are used differently by different schools. But, perceptually speaking, the artist's development of a technique is dependent on his own eye and the changes in it, whilst the existence of schools of art is evidence of stability and hence of lack of such changes.

Figure 9.4 Vincent van Gogh, "Absinthe". (Reproduced with permission of the Rijksmuseum Stichting, Amsterdam). The distortions are similar to those in Cézanne's "Still Life with Fruit Basket", figure 7.8A.

Our key notion is that the eye offers a variety of mechanisms only some of which need be triggered for the perceiver to recognise a depiction. Since a large number of choices is available the number of resulting combinations is large and each combination when consistently employed defines a style. Clearly some of the combinations may entail elements which are mutually reinforcing (for example density gradients and linear convergence both of which affect perception of pictorial depth); and some of which are not (for example, familiarity with the depicted object and the indication of the position of the artist's central cone of vision).

When mutually reinforcing cues are gradually accumulated over a span of time the resulting historical interpretation is that of a steady and systematic change in artistic style. Indeed sometimes this notion of advancement is expressly claimed by critics and experienced by artists. It was experienced by the pioneers of the linear convergence in its early days. Their deliberate search for a method to achieve a satisfactory rendering of perspective must have provided them with a feeling of achievement and indeed of progress when the self-set goal was approached.

From a historical stance likewise, steady movement towards more realistic representation, say, may appear as preordained progress governed by laws which are independent of culture at large and derive from visual tradition alone. Such a grand view was held by Wolfflin. This idealistic theory is however not supported by empirical evidence since a posteriori organisation of historical trends is not acceptable as a predictor of the future trends, nor does his theory attempt to explicitly to relate the observed changes to the workings of the perceptual system. Therefore although historically appealing it is not psychologically satisfying. Even psychological factors apart such an approach is difficult to embrace as the following considerations show.

The notion of progress implies not only that there is a systematic change but that this change results in improvement, which can be assessed by comparing conditions at the moment with those which prevailed previously and bearing in mind the desired direction of change. This progress can be likened to a journey towards a distant beacon and its assessment to comparisons of measurements of the distances from the beacon at various times, their decrease signifying progress. Clearly, it is difficult to argue that such progress in art is demonstrable because it is difficult to define to the satisfaction of all reasonable men the nature of the beacon, as there is no unanimously agreed goal for art.

The more restricted definition of progress relies on more down to earth criteria. If at some time in the history of art, painters strive to express some notion to their satisfaction (for example to paint a dewdrop on foliage) and make several public attempts to achieve it, and then an artist paints a picture which corresponds more closely than any of the preceding attempts to the desired goal (say, his dewdrop looks more life-like) such an artist can be said to have progressed, and not only he himself but also his colleagues and members of the public will agree with this; after all he has done better than before. This view of progress is inherent in the Classical Greek anecdote about Zeuxis, whose painting of grapes fooled the birds and Parrhasius, whose painting of a curtain fooled Zeuxis. The difference between this notion of progress and that dismissed above is, of course, in the nature of the goal. The former goal is undefinable in terms of the current experience, the latter goal, derived as it is from immediate experience, is clearly definable and leads to an observable step on the path of history. There is however no way of knowing whether this step shortens the distance from the ill-defined (and perhaps illusory) beacon. It is advisable therefore to confine our considerations to the notion involving immediate goals, regarding it not as synonymous with *progress* but rather as synonymous with orderly change.

Therefore the questions can be: (1) is there evidence of orderly change in the history of art? and (2) how do the speculations on the origin of artistic styles examined in this book relate to such evidence?

The first question and therefore also the second could be dismissed by adducing Hagen's[5] (1985) essay boldly entitled "There is no development in art", if that essay fulfilled the promise of its title. Sadly it fails to do so for the simple reason that the evidence examined therein is not relevant to the issue. This evidence derives from two sources: characteristics of works of art from various cultural groups, and developmental studies of drawing.

When considering works of art Hagen uses a compilation of very broadly defined artistic styles, each of the styles being assessed on two criteria: the nature of projection used (four systems of projection are described but only three of them are used by the author[6]), and the number of points of view used by the artist (two categories are used; single and multiple points of view). It is readily demonstrable that such a simple index cannot possibly provide an adequate description of different styles. Spanish monks of the eleventh century have designed manuscript illustrations incorporating "cubist" views of angels and beasts which in the terms of the index in question are precisely equivalent to some paintings of Picasso and therefore presumably could be said to sustain the claim of "no development in art". Since however not even a viewer of most meagre artistic sophistication would regard the pictures painted by the monks and those painted by Picasso as stylistically identical the validity of the measure is put to question, and the entire schema collapses. While Picasso and the eleventh century monks converged in this stylistic element other aspects of their work are so disparate that the overall impression is of an entirely different style. Another less specific and perhaps more telling argument against the schema is that one cannot expect artistic trends to be continuous from culture to culture amongst cultures which did have contact with each other. It is true that the Bushmen[7] and the Ancient Egyptians shared the same continent but there is no evidence that the two cultures have even been in contact and therefore no reason to suppose that the Bushmen would reap any benefits of the Egyptian artistic experience or vice versa. Clearly evidence for systematic change or lack thereof can only be obtained from societies which enabled one generation of artists to learn from another.

Examination of developmental stages in drawing and the observation that even some relatively sophisticated adults remain deficient in skills of drawing likewise cannot be said to provide relevant evidence[8]. Art is a cultural activity. It extends beyond an individual and an individual's ability to produce works of art, or even reasonable representations of objects, has little bearing on his ability to appreciate works of art created by the more gifted who carry the torch and pass it from generation to generation. Indeed an even more fundamental handicap is that the inability to appreciate particular styles by an individual or a group of individuals does not of itself threaten its survival. These fatal weaknesses in Hagen's argument oblige us to consider the relationship of our thesis to the notion of orderly change in art.

The grand theories of artistic change were proposed by Wolfflin and Panofsky[9] the founders of the history of art as an academic discipline. Both of these theorists accept that the eye undergoes acculturation as a result of experience. This in itself does not contradict our thesis, as we are ready to admit that cultural pressures decide which visual mechanisms are used by both the artist and the viewer. We would however remain agnostic as to the sequence in which various characteristics of the eye are exploited, as the chronological sequence is not dictated by them. Indeed the very presence of these visual idiosyncrasies while allowing an "orderly" change also enables deviant perception and deviant art, and poses problems for theories of development in art such as those of Gablik and Blatt[10]. Gablik has proposed that changes in art should be seen as stages of development corresponding to stages in the Piagetian developmental schema. An idea similar in its essence to an earlier conceptualisation of Wolfflin, who maintained that changes in art were a function of laws independent of other considerations. In Wolfflin's[11] notion styles having certain characteristics (such as being *linear*) inevitably develop into styles which have polarly opposite attributes (such as being *painterly*), as the change from Renaissance to Baroque shows. All notions of mysterious ill-defined powers which, guided by unchanging laws, drive the development of art on some predestined course seem to us questionable for the reasons expounded by Sir Karl Popper, the gist of which is that the very concept of unchallengeable law is unscientific. Provision of analogies (such as those derived from Piaget's theory) does not remove this difficulty but merely confounds the issue by nefariously enforcing a framework derivative from an unrelated discipline, which calls for classification of works of art and inevitably obliges the classifier to admit that some works do not fit the schema being either grossly "retarded" or "far in advance" of the works thought appropriate at that stage or period. Our view is that such works are not deviant anomalies but, as far as their style is concerned, show artists' reliance on more diverse characteristics of the eye than do those prized by their colleagues.

The problem which this leaves unexplained is that of defining the reasons that the majority of artists following a certain dominant style and for their deviant minority. Our notion of a choice of perceptual mechanism merely shows that differences in style are, from a perceptual point of view, both possible and legitimate. It does not indicate why they should arise, but arise they do. When they do arise the artistic eye, one presumes, becomes even less innocent than it was before.

The notion of the possibility of perfect innocence of the eye viewing a picture was questioned by Panofsky whose iconological analysis of the marriage portrait of Giovanni Arnolfini and Jeanne de Cename provided material for the introductory paragraphs of this book. According to him the entire cultural experience shapes our visual ability. A thorough examination of this view (as well as of a narrower view that experience of art is the primary factor in moulding the eye's characteristics) falls outside the bounds of the terrain which we have set out to explore. Nevertheless since it bears on one specific issue which is central to our discussion, that of perception and depiction of space and of the use of perspective, we shall examine it with reference to this particular problem. According to Panofsky, paintings which embody perspective do not represent space as we really see it but they do represent it in the way other paintings represent it. This is contrary to our thesis that perspective paintings are usually legitimate as they present the viewer with *some* of the information which the depicted objects would provide him with and that their veracity derives from their compatibility with certain characteristics of the visual system and is therefore not purely an outcome of experience.

It is true that there are certain cultural groups which show a relatively high degree of shape constancy (i.e. they report that circular objects viewed at an angle are relatively less elliptical) and which produce paintings in which likewise objects are depicted as less elliptical than they would be in western art. An argument can therefore be made that the pictures which they produce reflect the characteristics of their visual system.

But, as in all egg-chicken-egg controversies, it is possible to turn the entire argument upside down and claim that observed differences in constancy derive not from characteristics of the perceptual system but rather from exposure to styles of art in which constancies are exploited[12]. A person who picks an ellipse as a correct representation of the shape of a plate placed on a table in front of him, does not respond by indicating what he sees but by indicating what shape would be used by a draughtsman skilled in the art of perspective to portray what he, the observer, sees. Thus the observer shows himself to be a sophisticated perceiver, having abilities which can only be acquired by learning about perspective through deliberate instruction, repeated exposure to appropriate pictures, or careful analysis of their own experience. Art, this interpretation proposes, modifies vision.

A demonstration, therefore, that cultures in which less ellipsoidal discs are chosen as the representations of the pictorial plate also boast of works of art which show rather weak perspective cues (as is the case with traditional Indian miniatures) can have two mutually contradictory interpretations: one claiming that the art has been affected by the predisposition prevalent in the population at large; the other, claiming just the opposite.

The choice of a shape by a highly acculturated person from a culture in which perspective is used in art can be interpreted differently depending whether it is seen as conscious and deliberate or subconscious. The former instance does not so much reflect the observer's perceptual process as his knowledge of convention. He picks his response, just as he would pick his words, in such a way as to ensure that the experimenter understands him correctly. No connection is postulated between the chosen shape and the shape of the object other than that arising from a convention learned from experience of works of art. Such a conscious effect is dubious, as the following simple demonstration shows. An ellipse made of wire is rotated slowly about its longer and vertical axis in front of an observer. It projects into his eye a shape which ranges from a straight line (which appears twice in the course of every rotation) through ellipses of increasing degrees of obesity to the true frontal projection of the ellipse as it really is. It never projects a circle. Yet observers consistently report that they see it, for a part of its traverse, as a slowly rotating circle. The explanation that observers choose to refer to the figure as a circle cannot be explained by a desire to tell the experimenter what figure he would have to draw in order to depict the rotating object, but conveys an immediate perceptual experience. The ellipse appears, probably for reasons reflecting fundamental neurological processes, to be a true representative of a circle.

An observer who displays perfect constancy when looking at the now proverbial plate in spite of instructions to indicate a shape as it *appears* to him and persists in saying that it looks circular is, in our view, simply lacking in perceptual skills. He uses the visual cues present to derive the most "naive" of interpretations, and is unaware that another interpretation is possible. He acts rather like a person who is presented with the sentence "He sat working at a table" and asked for the meaning of the word "table" answers that it is a piece of furniture, unaware that the sentence could also describe a statistician at work in an armchair, or of Epharim the Palmist at work earning his living seated on a sofa.

There is of course a fundamental difference between the linguistic example employed in the above and the visual example; a difference which cannot be overemphasised. Whereas the word "table" *per se* does not perceptually contain the meanings which it can express and these meanings have to be linked to the sound by learning (the reader has probably just learned of the use of "table" as meaning "hand" by the palmists) this is not so in the case of a visual stimulus. An inclined disc does provide information which can be interpreted in two different ways depending on the mental set adopted by the perceiver, and both a circle and an ellipse lie on the same perceptual as well as mathematical continuum. Therefore the view that the connection between a circle and an ellipse as a means of representing a circle is purely fortuitous seems to us untenable. So by implication seems the extension of the claim that perspective is an arbitrary culturally and historically conditioned phenomenon, as Panofsky, one of the great art historians, has advocated.

It may be, we contend, that the decision which an individual makes to employ perspective in his drawings or to recognise perspective as a correct way of representing spatial arrangements is historically and culturally conditioned to the extent that the current social usage encourages development of certain motor and perceptual skills.

However, these skills rest on the foundation of perceptual mechanisms which offer a limited range of possibilities not all of which are exploited by every culture or every aritistic style; nor is any individual living in a particular cultural milieu obliged to accept the culturally sanctioned usage. By rejecting it he may himself become a cultural reject but he may also become a great innovator. Perspective therefore is an instance of putting one set of such possibilities to good use. It is an efficacious mode of representation because, as we have seen, it has a consistent manner in which it uses various visual cues for describing the scene and because it has a firm psychological foundation.

Since we have argued that the eye as far as its potential is concerned has not changed in the course of the history of art, evidence for use by artists of all techniques should be obtainable throughout history. All techniques would not be used equally at all times, for at any time there will be an accepted selection of techniques to which the influential subscribe, involving a particular blend of perceptual characteristics, while at its edge there are likely to be found (products of bold experimentation and of blissful ignorance) other, *not* accepted techniques. Some of the latter are the precursors of new techniques and therefore of new styles, but others do not achieve such status and remain like eddies at the edge of the main current. Perceptual analysis of accepted styles does not therefore provide a true picture of the artistic capacities of a population. To obtain such an assessment the eddies as well as the main stream need to be examined, and it is our contention that when this is done, at any period, it will be discovered that a much fuller range of cues has been used than examination of the mainstream would lead us to expect.

It follows that since perceptual skills do not appear to vary greatly among the art-creating populations, the artistic winds of change are those of skills of depiction and artistic fashion and not those due to changes in basic perceptual abilities. The generative clouds which they bring may encourage new perceptual skills, but such skills rely on the new uses made of the ever-present perceptual mechanisms of the human visual system.

New rules of depiction and new fashions emerge, and the timid and the intimidated obey them; the adventurous agree with Blake:

"The errors of wise men make your rule,
Rather than the perfections of a fool."

NOTES

General Note

Discussion of pictorial perception will be found in Gombrich's (1962) erudite *Art and Illusion,* Arnheim's (1954) gestaltist *Art and Visual Perception,* and his other words (1966, 1969, 1986), Bartel's *Perspektywa Malarska* (1928/1958) is the most thorough examination of perspective, intended for achitects but a great general interest as it presents systematic geometrical analysis of numerous works of art. A more readily accessible slimmer volume on the same topic is by Dubery and Willats (1983). Ten Doesschate (1964), terse and rather inaccesible volume contains a wealth of ideas about vision and pictorial perception unequalled by any other publication. Gregory, Gombrich and Blakemore (1973), Gombrich, Hochberg and Black (1972), Pirenne (1970), Deręgowski (1984) all deal with Art and Perception. The number of books on perception is very large; Gregory (1966), Gregory (1970), Frisby (1979), Hochberg (1978 and 1979) Humphreys & Bruce (1989) are all recent and useful, whilst Kennedy (1974) is devoted exclusively to perception of pictures. White (1957) examines the problem of pictorial space in historical perspective and Deręgowski (1989) does this in the context of cultural variation.

Chapter 1 - The Naive and the Sophisticated Eye

1. *Van Eyck's Portrait.*

A detailed examination of the picture will be found in "Jan van Eyck's Arnolfini Portrait" by Erwin Panofsky, (1934/1970).

2. *Strzeminski's Theory.*

The origin of Strzemiński's theory is discussed in Przyboś's introduction to Strzemiński's (1974) posthumous book. There seems little doubt that Strzeminski introduced the Marxist element into his thesis in part, at least, in order to ensure continued employment at the Łódź Art School. The subterfudge proved ineffective. He was accused of "formalism" a grave if ill defined crime, in the eyes of the communist party, and discharged. The book, which is unfinished is based on his lectures on the history of art.

3. *Gibson's Theory and Art.*

See Gibson (1966, 1979) and for a recent analysis of the Gibsonian approach to painting, Steer (1989).

4. *Classification of Pictures.*

For a general examination of the epitomic/eidolic distinction which has implications for Gablik's (1976) and Blatt's (1984) views see Deręgowski (1984).

5. *Gibson's Theory and Representation.*

It is sometimes suggested that a Gibsonian invariance can be found in the fact that in a drawing done in linear perspective depictions of all equal objects drawn as resting on the same horizontal plane are divided in identical ratios by the line of the horizon. For example all telephone poles along a receding road are so divided. However the essence of this geometrical effect is not confined to the horizon but applies to any straight line passing the centre of perspective and corresponding planes, and more importantly the centre of perspective does not exist outside the world of pictures as ten Doesschate (1964) has shown; it is not to be found in spatial vision. It is found in pictures because it furnishes very convenient means for constructing convincing facsimiles of the real world. These issues are discussed in Chapter 4, "The limits of perspective".

6. *Mistaking Pictures for Reality.*

Experiments by Smith and Smith (1961) in which observers were required to aim at depicted features indicate how effectively people may be misled by a two-dimensional photograph of a scene.

7. *Piaget's Theory of Development.*

Piaget's theory of intellectual development in children has been very influential. He proposed that cognitive development from neonate to adulthood involved major qualitative changes, from the sensory-motor stage in infancy, to the stage of formal operations in adulthood. There is a wealth of literature on this topic but an excellent introduction is provided by Boyle (1969). However, the application of this theory to the explanation of stylistic differences in the art of adults can be charitably described as dubious.

8. *Marr's Theory of Vision.*

This mode of "bare bones" representation is interestingly enough of particular relevance to the recent Marr and Nishihara theory of visual representation of objects (Marr 1982, Marr & Nishihara, 1978). The theory is essentially concerned with computer modelling of perception, and as such would not interest us if it were not for the nature of the basic elements from which it constructs representations of objects. The basic units are solids of revolution, generalised cylinders which are defined by two parameters, the length of their axes of rotation and the shape of the curves which are rotated. An object is described as an assembly of different cylinders. A man can, for example, be described as consisting of one big cylinder forming the trunk, four narrow and relatively long cylinders forming the limbs, and a short, small cylinder forming the head. The axes of these cylinders form a spatial network determining their relative positions. These axes on their own, it must be noted, also provide a representation of a man. Indeed they form the classical epitomic pin-figures.

When non-circular cylinders have to be used, as for example in descriptions of the shape of a bottle of Chianti, the curve which has to be rotated about the axis is that which would be used in drawing a silhouette of the bottle, and the silhouette is as we have seen another typically epitomic representation of an object.

Thus this computing theory derives its descriptions of objects essentially from the elements of their epitomic and therefore less life-like portrayals; echoes of the most primitive of representations may be found in the most sophisticated computer models!.

9. *Levels of Representation in Works of Art.*

The ideas developed in this book bear some relationship to a theory of stylistic variations recently and independently proposed by Wade (1990). Wade argues that artists' work can be better understood if we can appreciate the kind of "image" they are trying to produce e.g. whether they are working at the level of the "retinal image", the "visual image" the "mental image" or the "graphical image" etc. Furthermore he proposes that artistic styles have developed in the reverse sequence to perceptual imaging - working from the mental to the optical. While we share his starting point, we believe that this view is too simple since at any one level e.g. the optical, a variety of stylistic variations is apparent. Furthermore any ideas of development of style must be seen in a broader cultural context that post-Rennaissance western art and when this is done it becomes more difficult to see stylistic change as following a defined sequence. It is clear for instance that classical Greek and Roman wall-paintings show an appreciation of optical constraints that were forgotten until their re-emergence in the Rennaissance. However, Wade's work should prove of particular interest to those interested in perceptual influences on styles in art.

Chapter 2 - Counterfeits Made to Beguile

1. *Distorted Pictures*

The argument, as presented here, assumes simple matching between an object and its depiction, but this may not always take place. An object may be seen under different physical conditions (for example, at a greater distance in different light) and therefore look different than it would appear if it occupied the very spot that the canvas occupies. An object, too, might be painted from memory, and physical conditions of the artist may be different at the time of perception and at the time of reproduction. Trevor-Roper (1957, 1970) provides a very readable and richly illustrated review of the problems of opthalmology and art. Arguments about El Greco's astigmatism are reviewed in Marquez (1929).

2. *Aerial Perspective*

This embodies the phenomenon of perception of transparency, which substantiates the distinction between the purely physical concept of light and the psychological concept of light as a medium of information about the environment. Bishop Berkeley (1709) in his Essay was concerned with the former when he wrote "It is agreed that the *distance* of itself and immediately, cannot be seen. For distance being a line directed end-wise to the eye, projects only one point in the fund of the eye, which point remains invariably the same whether the distance be longer or shorter". Since we can see both the window pane and through the window pane, this psychologically speaking is not so. Gibson (1975) takes perception of transparency to be one of three telling arguments against Berkeley (the other two are: perception or recession of a surface, and perception of occlusion of one surface by another). For further discussion of transparency see Metelli (1976).

Cast shadow can be thought of as a form of transparency, since it overlaps but does not occlude the object upon which it falls. Yonas (1979) discusses the use of attached cast shadows in indicating the character of the depicted objects.

See also under note 4 below.

3. *Overlap*

The effect of an overlap of one figure by another can be strengthened by increasing the contrast between the figures, for example by using different colours for them, or by accentuating their outlines. The latter method has often been used by Cézanne. The same artist also resorted to darkening the region of the overlapped figure in the neighbourhood of the line of overlap, an equally efficacious device (Carpenter, 1951). The latter method can be thought of as relying on the eye's assumption that the overlapping figure casts a shadow upon the overlapped figure. The fact that such a "shadow" may be incompatible with the direction of light, as indicated by general illumination in the picture, is not an insurmountable obstacle, as the eye is quite tolerant of inconsistencies. For a psychological discussion of the role of boundary lines in pictures, see Kennedy (1974).

4. *Perception of Shadows*

For illustration of the effect using casts of a man's face, see Gregory (1973), which also contains a very useful discussion of perceptual hypotheses. The mask shown in Figure 4 comes from Orissa, India.

5. *Shape Constancy*

The hexagon (Figure 2.8) is, of course, only an approximation to a perspective projection of a cube since a true projection by converging rays would entail a degree of convergence of receding elements.

Kanizsa (1975) argues that the perception of the hexagon as a cube, although explicable in terms of figural goodness, may be affected by some other factors, as the effect can also be observed in the case of irregular figures, "which are not much more regular when seen as three dimensional". Welford (1968) would argue that, indeed, this very slightness of the difference in regularity between the two versions makes the translation perceptually uneconomical. (See also Hochberg & Brooks (1960) and Deręgowski (1976).)

Langdon (1951) observed that when all the pictorial depth cues are removed, shape constancy no longer prevails, but when a luminous hoop used in such an investigation is rotated the phenomenon of constancy re-emerges, although there is no apparent reason for the shape be seen as rotating rather than being squeezed in and out.

6. *Effects of a Frame on Spatial Perception*

Kraft & Green (1989) have investigated this effect in viewers' perceptions of photographs.

Chapter 3 - Why Two Eyes are Better Than One

1. *Stereoscopic Disparities*

For a general examination of stereoscopic perception see Julesz (1971) and for a discussion of the range and limitations of binocular acuity Southall (1961) and Ogle (1961). The relationship between stereoscopic disparity and the perception of the Müller-Lyer, Poggendorff and Zolner illusions was investigated by Gregory and Harris (1975). The investigation showed that the illusory effects vanished when the stereoscopic and perspective cues agreed. This contrasts with cases of such a marked dissonance between the stereoscopic information and perspective that changes in stereoscopic information alone cannot eliminate illusory effects. This happened, Gregory argues, in the Georgeson and Blakemore (1973) investigation of the Müller-Lyer illusion.

This question of the relationship between stereoscopic and monocular cues to depth is a particularly important one for those interested in the perception of pictures. Under normal circumstances when looking at a solid extended visual world monocular and stereoscopic cues are in agreement with each other. The availability of stereoscopic information enhances our perception of depth and indeed up to approximately 2 metres allows accurate absolute judgements of the distance of objects (Wallach and Zuckerman 1963, Morrison and Whiteside 1984). However it is also quite clear that the availability of conflicting information in the visual array does not negate the experience of depth. We have already indicated (Chapter 2 note 5) that the perception of a cube in depth is readily perceived from a hexagonal figure (Figure 2.8). This would be impossible if stereoscopic cues indicative of a flat surface overrode the possible perception of a cube in depth. The perception of a cube emerges despite the fact that the perspective cues to depth are not present in this picture and it is within the range of most accurate absolute depth judgements i.e. below two metres. Indeed if clear stereoscopic depth cues are held constant in a true stereo version of the Necker cube it continues to change in apparent depth (reverse) in direct conflict with those stereo cues [Julesz, 1971].

It has been known for some time (Wheatstone 1852) that stereo information does not survive contradictory monocular cues. Experiments by Stevens and Brookes (1988) systematically explored viewers' perceptions when stereo and monocular cues were placed in conflict. Monocular cues dominated. Given this experimental evidence it is hardly surprising that viewers perceive depth when placed before flat surfaces which contain rich monocular cues to depth, even when the surfaces are within the range where the visual system is capable of making very accurate absolute depth judgements. There is no need for Pirenne to suggest then that Pozzo's ceiling is particularly effective because it minimises binocular cues. It would probably work even if flagrantly conflicting and powerful stereo cues were available.

2. *The Work of Fra Andrea Pozzo*

For description of Pozzo's work see Pirenne (1970), and for photographs of the St. Ignazio ceiling Pirenne (1967a, 1970).

3. *Viewing Stance and Spatial Perception in Pictures*

Deręgowski and Parker (1988) investigated perceptual distortion in the Vermeer masterpiece "The Music Lesson" (also known as "A Lady at the Virginals with a Gentleman"). Viewers showed systematic distortion of the spatial proportions of the depicted room as their angle of view changed. As the viewing distance varied between four and two metres there was never any doubt by subjects that they were viewing a projected slide.

When in identical circumstances an arrangement of two obliques was presented to a moving observer the angle between the lines did not seem to him to change but the figure seemed to rotate in a whole so that he saw himself as being co-planar with the bisector of the rotating angle. The phenomenon observed in the Vermeer picture is therefore intimately connected with the obliquity of the "moving line". Investigations presenting isolated oblique lines confirm this. Unlike vertical and horizontal line in the plane of a picture which appears not to be affected by the observers' movement the oblique lines are inherently unstable and are readily affected. The rotation of the bisector observed here is clearly perceptually related to apparent movement of portrayed eyes. Wallach (1976) points out that perception of changes in a picture drawn in perspective as one walks past it (see also Goldstein, 1979), involves that same perceptual mechanism which ensures that real world objects remain perceptually stable as one walks past them.

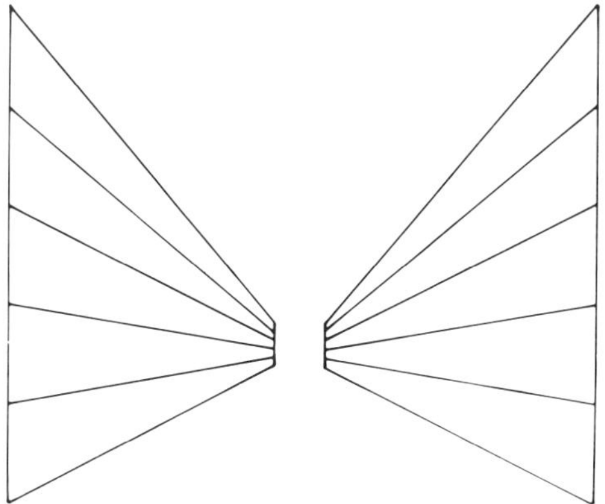

Figure N1 A diagram after Jerison (1967). See below for explanation.

An interesting demonstration of this is discussed by Jerison (1967) on whose description the diagram reproduced below is based. When this figure is placed in front of the viewer both elements are seen as equal. When it is moved say, 50 c.m. to his right the left element is seen. This argues against the notion that perspective is a pure convention as does the Deręgowski and Parker (1988) study of apparent transformations of Vermeer's "The Music Lesson". Fascinating percepts can be evoked by rotating a picture in front of a beholder . When arrangements of simple geometrical figures embodying various pictorial depth cues are used these are seen to oscillate in the manner of Ames' window (described Ittleson, (1952); see Gregory (1970) or any other recent text on psychology of perception). This happens, for example, when the Ponzo figure (Figure 2.6) is used as a rotating pattern (see Cannestrari, 1975).

4. *Panoramas*

The first man to conceive and execute a panorama was Robert Barber (1739-1806). It was exhibited in Edinburgh in 1788 and showed a battle scene. Throughout the eighteen hundreds panorama grew in popularity and reached its zenith at the turn of the century. They were painted in special workshops often using aids not unlike those developed by Pozzo, and occasionally with two artists being simultaneously involved, one of them taking the physical position of a viewer and guiding the other in painting. The themes used were those obviously suitable for such presentations and included views of famous towns, seascapes and landscapes, the latter often enlivened by battle scenes. These pictures were transported from town to town and exhibited in specially constructed buildings. Our description of a typical panorama is based on Bartel (1958). The cottage in Figure 3.5 is taken from Panorama Racławicka originally at Lwów now at Wrocław.

This panorama is painted on canvas measuring 120m x 15m and is therefore of about average size. It is a joint work of several artists of whom J. Styka and W. Kossak made the most significant contributions working on the painting from its inception till its completion. The picture represents the battle of Racławice, 1974, between Polish and Russian troops. Steinborn (1985) presents the historical background of the depicted event as well as of the picture itself.

5. *Subsidiary awareness*

The concept is introduced and discussed by Polanyi (1962), who cites an experiment by Buytendijk (1930) who reported that a rat learning a maze explores all turns and corners, but once familiar with it it merely uses these features as signposts. This change is analogous to the contrast between behaviour of the nomadic Me'en who on their first encounter with a picture sniffed it, nibbled it, and even crumpled it to hear what sound it would make - but paid no attention to the pattern (Deręgowski, Muldrow and Muldrow, 1972), and the behaviour of an experienced perceiver who use the information about the physical attributes of the picture's surface merely to compensate for his position in space. For a discussion of the skills involved in pictorial perception see Serpell and Deręgowski (1980) and Deręgowski (1989a). In a later paper Polanyi (1970) discusses at length the role of subsidiary awareness within the context of Art (painting, drama, poetry) and cogently argues that it is the blending of the incompatibles, such as the subsidiary awareness (but awareness nevertheless) of pictures' surfaces and awareness of the pattern of paint that determines that pictures are seen for what they are and neither as real things nor as meaningless patterns. When no subsidiary awareness of the surface is present the stimulus is either a real object or, if this awareness has been removed by trickery (as in Pozzo's ceiling), an illusion. When both the surface and the pattern fall within the domain of the focal awareness the stimulus can sometimes be seen as a meaningless pattern. ("The assembling of pieces expected naturally together produces either a perception or an illusion, while the integration of artistic elements designed to be incompatible produces transnatural things like paintings, plays and poetry" Polanyi, 1970.) It is important to note that the two elementary types of awareness evoked by pictures are not of equal perceptual status, as is made clear in our discussion in Note 1 above; it follows that definition of a picture as a 'pattern on a flat surface', is misguiding because it appears to give equal weight to the two physical elements, ignoring their psychological weighting. Both Ames (1925) and Schlosberg (1941) have observed that viewing of pictures through a reduction screen (as small opening) monocularly enhances the perception of depth. Polanyi's terminology differs from that of Gombrich. To the former there can be no illusion in a painting which evokes subsidiary awareness, to the latter the strength of illusion is determined by the extent to which a painting can be mistaken for reality.

6. *Anamorphoses*

One of the best known of these is the double portrait by Holbein the Younger *The Ambassadors*. A correct percept of the central smudge can be had by viewing the picture at a sharp angle (see Deregowski, 1984); but it can also be had, more comfortably, as Samuel (1963) has ingeniously demonstrated, by viewing the picture through a glass tube held parallel to the pictures surface and inclined about 24° to the vertical. (This supports Bartel's (1958) earlier suggestion that the element was painted with the help of a concave cylindrical mirror). In the former case different information reaches the eye from the picture than would reach it if it viewed the painting squarely. In the latter case the information from the square view of the picture is optically transformed before it reaches the eye. Another noteworthy feature of this picture is as Bartel (1958) points out, the geometrically imperfect portrayal of the pattern on the floor.

7. *Apparent movement of eyes*

Gombrich (1962), who has left no stone unturned in the history of art, presents a bibliographic guide. Ten Doesschate (1964) suggests that the phenomenon may be due to the moving observer seeing, as he moves, essentially the same configuration of two white triangles and the central circular iris which form the depicted eye. These do not change although their shapes are foreshortened, whereas in a real eye the relative magnitudes of the elements change markedly with the observer's movement. Hence in the former case an unchanging eye follows the observer but in the latter it does not. Diagrams illustrating the two effects are shown below (Figure N.2). The importance of eyes as signalling devices, and hence their use not only in communication but also for defence (See Hinton, 1973), is well documented. Wollaston (1824) argued that the perceived direction of the gaze depended on the perceived direction of the head. His pictures were realistic, however, and this relationship may not hold for other pictures.

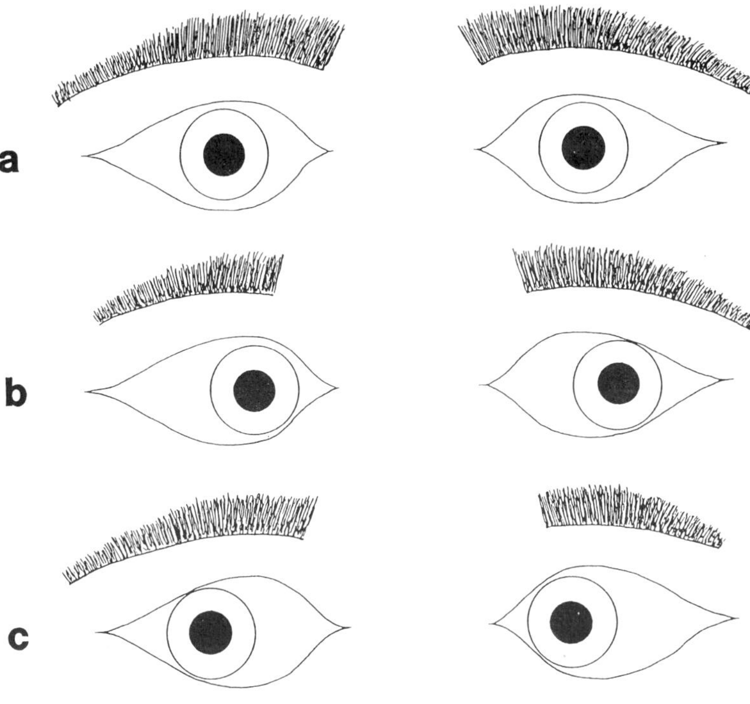

Figure N2 This diagram shows (a) the type of eye pattern which evokes the perception of eyes tracking the viewer. (b) The type of pattern which would be seen by the observer standing to the left or to the right (c) of a real pair of eyes which continued to look straight ahead.

This apparent movement is clearly similar to that observed in the Vermeer picture and described above (Note 3). However, the causes of the phenomenon are clearly different as no obliques are involved here. It seems likely that the essential symmetry of the pattern is the root cause, the eye appearing about the same from whatever position it is seen, as explained in the diagram below. Since as shown the changes of position merely result in the depicted eye changing in width the position of the pupil relative to the eye remaining constant, the direction of gaze is therefore perceived as remaining fixed on the viewer. The argument just advanced is essentially that of ten Doesschate.

8. *Divergent Perspective*

For recent discussions of this topic, see Arnheim (1954), ten Doesschate (1964), Wyburn et al. (1967), Pickford (1972) and Zajac (1961), from whom the "matchbox" experiment is taken. Pickford also notes that Divergent Perspective may be due to "a very much exaggerated index of phenomenal regression, found indeed in some persons, although very rarely, from whom receding objects actually seem to become larger instead of smaller."

A simple experiment shows that perception of receding parallel lines as divergent is not confined to the very restricted conditions of Zajac's matchbox investigation. Parallel lines of point lights were placed on the floor of a laboratory and subjects were required to adjust a moving arm so that it appeared to them to be parallel with each of the rows in turn (see Figure N.3). The adjustments made show that some of the subjects saw some of the parallel lines as diverging. This was more frequent with the laterally displaced pairs of lines, and appeared to increase progressively with lateral displacement. This argues that the tendency to see and therefore to depict parallel lines as divergent is for some subjects quite natural.

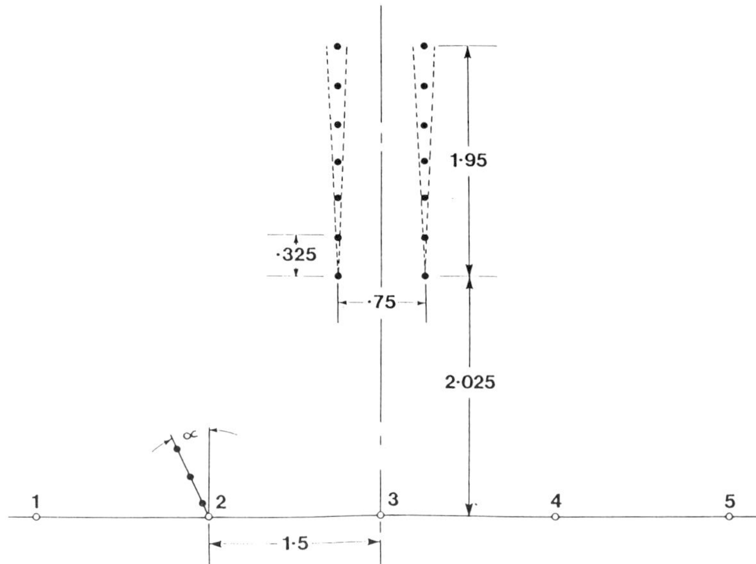

Figure N3 The experimental arrangement used to measure observers' perception of the orientation of lines. The numbers 1 - 5 represent the observers' positions with respect to the illuminated rows of lights. The angle "alpha", shown at 2, was measured when the observer set a moveable arm so that it appeared to him to be parallel to a row of lights. All dimensions shown are in metres.

Gombrich (1972) with extreme patience takes Goodman (1969) to task for his ill considered claim that linear convergence is a convention. Gibson (1979) also disagrees with Goodman, as does Colney (1985). Incidentally, Saenredam's *De Groote Kerk at Haarlem* shows an example of convergence upwards from the line of view; the central column is thinner at the top than it is at the base. This might be taken as a hint from the artist that the viewer should conceive of his line of sight as elevated above the horizontal plane, as it often would be when viewing an impressive ecclesiastical edifice; it might be an instance of "gilding the lily" by introduction of perspective cues where they are not optically appropriate in order to accentuate the height of the building; it might also be an error. The last of these explanations is unlikely since the painter was a skilled architectural draughtsman.

It has been suggested (Humphrey, 1971) that inverse perspective may be a result of misapprehension of parallel perspective which, in turn, is the consequence of the desire to draw equal lengths as equal. However, in all the instances adduced as evidence the figures are in fact not parallelograms, but classical embodiments of inverse perspective trapezoids. The argument therefore lacks force; on the contrary, the very frequency of trapezoids used to depict rectangles argues that they are unlikely to be mere lapses. It is true that a parallelogram on its own is often seen as if it were a trapezium with its upper (and therefore "further") edge slightly longer, but there seems to be no reason why this illusion should be exaggerated rather than attenuated by the artists. Humphrey's notion was later taken up by Moray and Moray (1981), who demonstrate that there is a tendency to overestimate the length of a side of a parallelogram (forming on a drawing, a face of a truncated wedge), which, because it is higher up, is seen as being further away. Again, whereas there are reasons (ease of drawing, and dimensional correspondence) for drawing a parallelogram where, according to perspective convergence and according to the evidence of the sense of sight, a trapezoid should be drawn, it is difficult to see why "copyists" would go against the evidence of their own eyes. One would think that they would either adhere to the rule, or be swayed by such evidence, as people generally are, in shape-constancy experiments.

N. Boretz (1979), an artist and an art teacher, notes in her charming paper that many of her students after having "laughingly hooted at inverse perspective" drew inverse perspective.

Topper and Simpson (1981) investigated the perception of pictorial depth in four works of art involving different perspective cues, using Gregory's Pandora's Box (Gregory, 1974). Their findings were that depth was perceived in all the pictures independently of whether perspective convergence was present or absent, and whether it was evoked by normal or inverse perspective. But since the other depth cues were not controlled these findings do not show the influence of convergence alone, and no conclusion can be drawn about the relative efficacy of the two types of convergence.

There is a similarity between the restricted span within which inverse perspective is acceptable to the perceptual system and the restricted span within which the pointillist technique of painting works. There is a very brief and interesting article on the latter topic by Weale (1972). Jameson and Hurvich (1976) examine some of the phenomena relevant to the thesis put forward by Weale to explain the failure of pointillism. See also Non-Euclidean space and Van Gogh; Notes on Ch. 7.

9. See Helmholtz (1901/1962), Chapter 28, *The Monocular Field of Vision.*

Chapter 4 - The Limits of Perspective

1. *Movement*

For a recent discussion of depicted movement, see Ward (1979) and Vitz and Glimcher (1984).

2. *Illusions*

Coren (1978) and Robinson (1972) provide concise compendia of studies of illusions. A comparison of responses to illusions of seventeen populations (ranging from Anakole to Zulu) was carried out by Segall *et al* (1966). For more recent reviews of cross-cultural studies see Deręgowski (1980b). For the relationship between illusions and constancies, see S. Coren and J. S. Girgus in Epstein (1977).

3. *Anorthoscopic Perception*

This perceptual effect sometimes called anorthoscopic perception, is discussed in Robinson (1972) and again by Morgan, Findlay and Watt (1982). It is clear that the image is not simply painted on the retina and read out from a normal extended representation since the effect occurs even if the eye tracks the slit in such a way that successively derived contours overlie each other.

4. *Perspective*

There are many books on perspective. Apart from those listed in the "general" section, the following may prove of interest: Richter (1937), White (1957), Edgerton (1976), Oxford Companion to Art (Osborne, 1981), and Goodman (1969). For Markino's anecdote, see Markino (1912). See also ten Doesschate and Kylstra (1955 and 1956). Lack of consistent perspective convergence in some works of art is eruditely discussed by Finkelstein (1979).

The tolerance of the eye is also responsible for acceptance as correct of those inconsistent representations of perspective which, ironically, occasionally occur in modern textbooks of psychology and are sometimes used in experimental investigations. Gillan's (1981) note draws attention to these occurrences.

Gillan's paper is however, in error in implying that *Albertian* perspective is "true" or "correct".

It is noteworthy that some severely autistic children draw in perspective and do so much earlier in their lives than unhandicapped children (Selfe, 1983, 1985). A discussion of perspective destroying illusions will be found in Gregory (1979).

5. *Bartel's method of restitution*

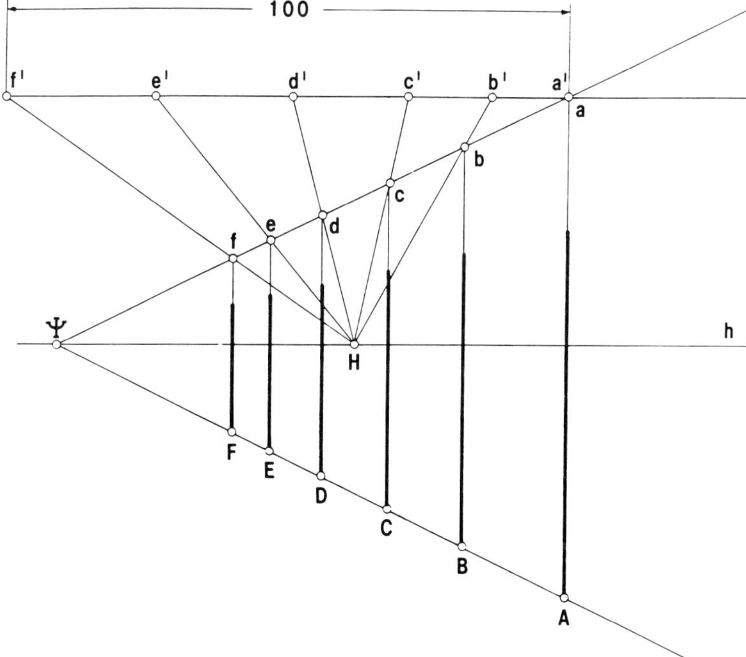

Figure N4 Bartel's method of restitution.

Geometric restitution of the ratios of the depicted elements provides means whereby the extent to which the artist adhered to the rules of perspective can be assessed. The resistution is easy to carry out. It is described and illustrated below.

Procedure (see diagram)

A) If need be, by extending converging lines intended to represented horizontal elements determine a vanishing point (not necessarily the central vanishing point) C and the horizon line *h*.

B) From C draw a line *a* passing through the elements whose spacing is of interest (or these elements extended) marking the points of intersection E1, E2, E3, E4.

C) Draw an artibrarily placed line *b* parallel to *h*.

D) From any convenient point D or h draw a set of rays passing through E1, E2, E3, E4 ... and intersecting *b* at B1, B2, B3, B4....

The ratio of the distances B1-B2: B2-B3: B3-B4.... is the same as the ratio of the true distances between the depicted elements if the picture is drawn in accordance with the rules of perspective. For perspective depictions of equispaced items, therefore, all these distances would be equal. If the ratios decrease the items are either increasingly more closely spaced with distance or the artist has exaggerated the perspective effect. If, on the other hand the ratios increase then either the spacing increases as the artist has adopted "divergent" perspective.

This method of restitution was applied to Saenredam's *Interior of St. Bavo's Church* and yielded the results shown on Figure 4.16. Clearly the painter has not followed the rules of perspective when spacing his portrayals of equal spaced columns. (He was not alone in violating these rules for aesthetic purposes;

his contemporary Gerrit Berckheyde's painting *The Interior of the Groote Kerk, Haarlem.* When subjected to Bartel's restitution it shows similar distortions. (Figure N.5 below). Pictures can of course be further analysed given information about actual size of the depicted objects. Such an analysis when applied to the Saenredam picture (Kemp 1984) shows further 'violations' of the rules of perspective.

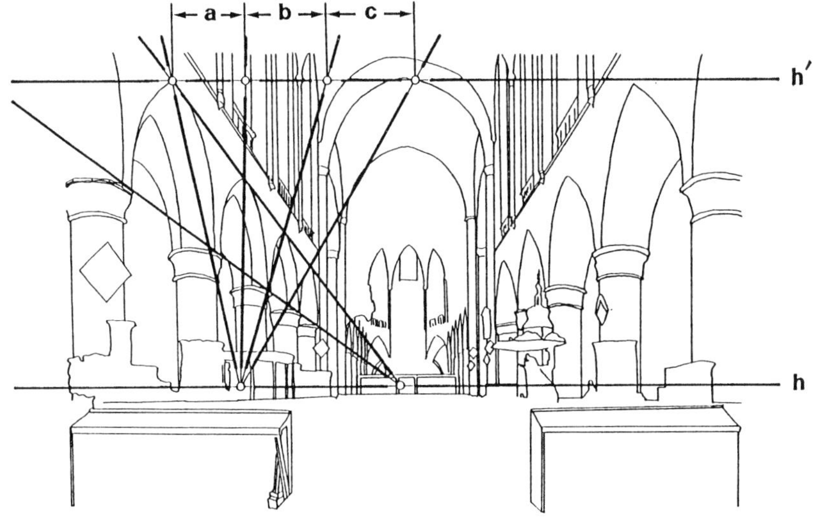

Figure N5 Berkheyde's interior of "Groote Kerk, Haarlem", subjected to Bartel's method of restitution.

It should be noted that the notion that convergence of parallel lines is the essence of perspective and that provided that it is adhered to when drawing a picture then that picture will be seen in perspective, is very widespread. The frontispiece from Cusack's tutorial handbook (Armstrong 1893, brought to our attention by Freeman 1989 (Figure N.6) does indeed have this attribute. It can easily be demonstrated, using Bartel's method, that the chimney pots on the right-hand-side of the street are not correctly spaced, if they are intended to represent chimney pots which are equispaced in reality. The restitution shows the probable deficiencies in the picture clearly and emphasises how common violations of correct perspective are.

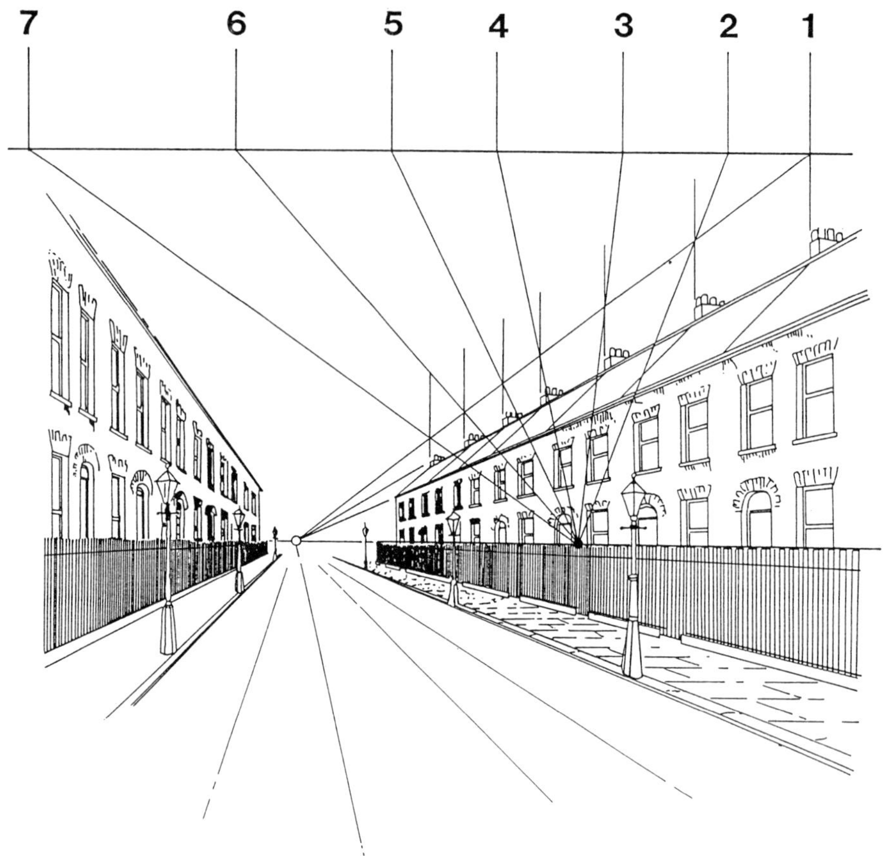

Figure N6 Frontispiece form Cusack's tutorial

For further discussion of Bartel's method see Deręgowski (1989b).

Bartel (1958) offers this and other geometrical constructions for analysing various aspects of depiction and applies them to a large number of works of art obtaining some very interesting results. A brief discussion of the essence of the construction used by Bartel and described above will also be found in Kolbuszewski (1953).

Chapter 5 - Views Typical and Otherwise

1. *Impossible Figures*

Draper (1978), examines the "impossible figures" belonging to the Penrose's (or, as it should really be called, Reutersvard's - see Kulpa, 1983) triangle family.

Chapter 6 - Communalities of Distortion.

1. *Relativity and Perspective*

For Pirenne's opinion about the invocation of Einstein's theory, see Pirenne (1959).

2. *Conventionalism and Perspective*

Goodman (1969) puts forth the Conventionalist notion of perspective and is criticised by Gombrich (1972). It is evident from the evidence we have presented in this book there is little to be said in favour of Goodman's views.

3. *Culture and Pictorial Perception*

Observations in a pictureless culture are those of Landor (1883). For other relevant reports see Deręgowski et al. (1972) and Deręgowski (1980b, 1989a).

4. *Cross-cultural Studies of Illusions*

Segall et al.'s (1966) study compared 26 samples of adults and children, drawn from a wide range of cultures, on a rather weak version of the Ponzo illusion. Only one, Bété children, showed a *negative* effect. All others (including Bété adults) showed a positive effect. (Bété live on the Ivory Coast).

5. *Cross-cultural Studies of Space Perception*

Serpell and Deręgowski (1978) discuss pictorial perception as a skill. A difference of skills between populations, or indeed absence of certain skills within certain populations, does not imply a difference in or absence of the physio-psychological means needed to exercise such skills. Perkins (1972) and Perkins and Deręgowski (1982) investigated perception of drawings of simple solids. For a recent examination of cross-cultural studies of pictorial space see Deręgowski (1989a).

The study of the Me'en is reported in Deręgowski, Muldrow and Muldrow (1972).

6. *Cross-cultural Studies of Vision*

Berry (1966) in an extensive study compared Scots, Eskimos and Temne on a variety of perceptual tasks.

7. *Paleolithic and Primitive Art and Representation*

Ucko and Rosenfeldt (1967) present a compact review of paleolithic cave art; see also Graziosi (1960), Florczak (1972) and Guinea (1979). For a recent noteworthy discussion on the psychological significance of paleolithic art see Halverson (1987), who advances the idea that paleolithic art reflects early stages of cognitive development in which forms are abstracted for re-presentation.

There are different forms of abstraction which serve different purposes. Deręgowski (1989) proposed a taxonomy of representations applicable to all pictures some of which convey depth immediately (eidolic pictures) and some do so indirectly (epitomic pictures). Furthermore essentially different abstractions are obtained when an artist attends to an outline of the object than when he attends to the axes of its constituent parts. A version of the taxonomy taken from Deręgowski (1989a) is presented below (Figure N.7). The table it is argued suggests that pin figures differ in the very essence of abstraction from outline figures. The former are more abstract, less isiosyncratic and their meaning is less easily confounded by subperfect reproduction and they are easier to draw. They are therefore a bridge between pictures and abstracted concepts such as "a man" or "a cow" whereas the latter being idiosyncratic express ideas such as "the man" or "the brown cow".

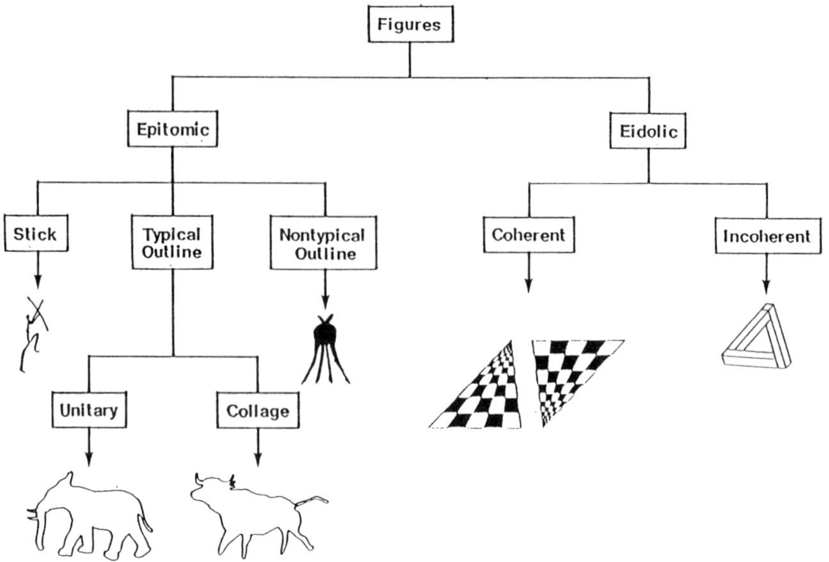

Figure N7 A taxonomy of simple figures. All simple figures can be divided into *epitomic*, in which depth is not represented but which still represents solid objects, and *eidolic* in which depth/solidity is represented. Epitomic figures can be outlines, shadow figures or "stick" figures.

The notion of a typical view of a solid, which is defined by extending Attneave's (1954) notion about the distribution of information in plane figures, has been used by Deręgowski (1989) to explain certain pictorial "distortions" such as those of the Kakadu crocodile (Figure N.8) whose head, body and tail do not seem to be co-planar. When a solid is viewed the amount of information present at any point on its surface is proportional to the rate of change of curvature at that point. Thus, for example in the case of an egg the largest amount of information is present at the pointed end. The efficiency of an outline in representing an object depends on the total informational value of the surface points through which it passes. The larger the relative value of this outline the more effective, for recognition purposes it is. A longtitudinal outline of an egg, for example, which provides an oval shape is a better representation than a transverse outline, which produces a circle. Thus given a simple object, the most cogent outline can be obtained by placing the draughtsman's eye in a position where the line of vision is perpendicular to an imaginary plane, which passes through the model so that the outline traced upon it has the largest informational value. This is achieved by so placing the plane that it passes through the maximum possible points of concentration of information on the object's surface.

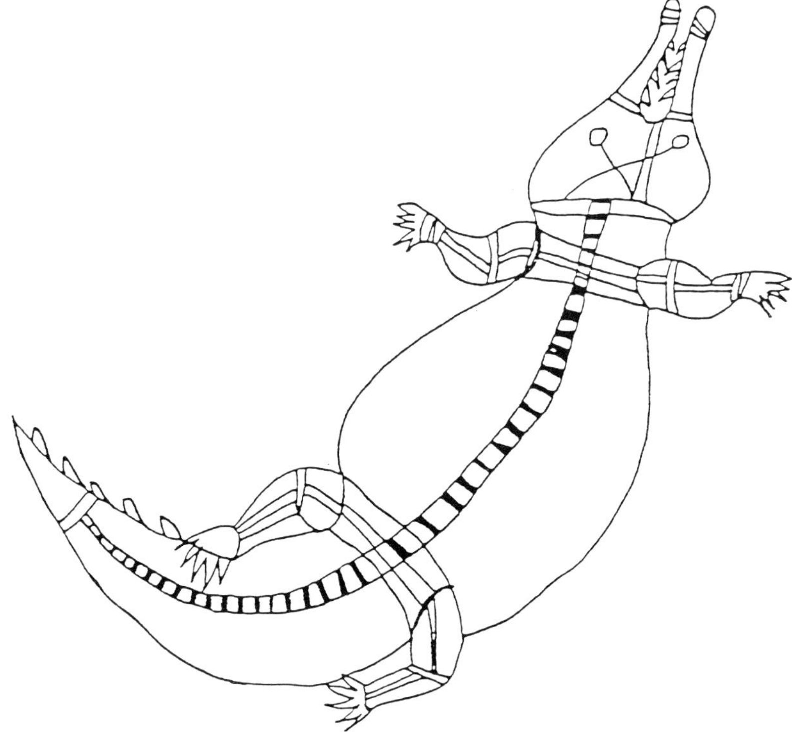

Figure N8 The Kakadu crocodile. Note the changes in the assumed position of the viewer which would be required to make the depiction of the head, body and tail independently valid.

It seems reasonable to expect that an observer who has seen an object from many points of view, when asked to draw its outline will draw the most representative outline even if his present point of view does not furnish it. Indeed, there is empirical evidence that one of the difficulties which young children have with drawing is that of abandonning typical outlines. Indeed they may utilise typical representations of different parts of a complex object and combine them in the same manner as the "master of the Kakadu crocodile" (Dziurawiec and Deręgowski 1990).

8. *Palermo Parietal Engraving*

Described and analysed by Mezzena (1976).

9. *Quarternary Art from Live Models?*

Leason, P. A. (1939, 1956) examines Quarternary art and argues that many of the animals represented were drawn from dead models. This, incidentally, may also explain why contemporaneous portrayals of men are infrequent. Ucko and Rosenfeldt do not accept Leason's interpretation although they accept the similarities of the depicted animals to dead animals, and claim that Leason looked at the paintings with the eye of modern man. However they do not indicate how one knows that one is in a correct frame of mind when looking at these paintings.

10. *Art of the Bushman*

For the most recent review of South African rock art and a guide to further reading, see Lewis-Williams (1983).

11. *Perspective in the Ancient World*

A brief review of the history of perspective in the ancient world is given by Levy (1943), who refers to the presence of foreshortening from cave art onwards, although often it is only "occasional", and thinks that the "Skenography" of Agatharchus (5th cent. B.C.), which is known only from second hand literary sources, did not incorporate a vanishing point although it did include convergence. To what extent this opinion would have been affected by knowledge of the work of Beyen (1938), is uncertain, but the available descriptions of Agatharchus' ideas are really too vague to enable one to decide whether single point convergence was known to the Ancient Greeks, as the following shows:

> "Agatharchus ... first applied 'skenography' to stage scenery, and wrote about it ... Democritus and Anaxagoras wrote on the same topic in order to show how if a fixed centre is taken then taking account of the point of sight and natural divergence of rays. Lines must fall according to a natural law, so that from an uncertain object uncertain images may be given the appearance of buildings in the scenery of the stage and what is figured upon vertical and plane surfaces can seem to recede in one part and project in another" (Vitruvius, BK7, preface; 1 cent B. C.).

Equally ambivalent evidence can be found in the seventh chapter of Ptolemy's *Geography*, which shows that Ptolemy knew that an oblique view of a circle is a result of the rules of perspective. This does not mean, however, that this knowledge was generally available to the artists of Greece although evidence from recent archaeological excavations of the Macedonian Greek area would suggest it was. Edgerton (1976) maintains that Ptolemy's book brought the notion of perspective to Florence. (For a translation of a commentary on Ch. 7 of Ptolemy's Geography, see Neugebauer, 1959). Delacroix (1932) wrote on the 13 Jan. 1857: "Raccourcis, Qu'il y en a toujours, meme dans une figure toute droite, les bras pendants. L'art des raccourcis ou de la perspective et de le dessin sont tout un!"

12. H. R. Beyen had a chair at the University of Leiden. The Department of Archaeology of that University had kindly provided the authors with photographs which appeared in Beyen's (1939) paper.

13. *Byzantine Art*

For discussion of Byzantine Art, see Demus (1948), (1970).

14. Noted by Weale (1976).

15. *Chinese Painting*

See Sze (1957). For an attempted evaluation of the perception of perspective cues in oriental and western subjects see Binnie-Dawson and Choi (1982).

16. *Ucello and Perspective*

Ucello's infatuation is reported by Vasari (1550). There are many translations of his *Lives of the most excellent Painters, Sculptors and Architects.*

Chapter 7 - Cues Intrinsic to the Eye

1. *Intrinsic Cues*

The importance of these cues in pictorial perception is advanced by Strzemiński's (1974). Various aspects of his analysis are reflected in this volume, however, his main thesis that the awareness of the visual processes changed in the course of time and determined the development of art, is not embraced here. On the contrary, it is argued that awareness of these mechanisms and their use in styles of painting are independent processes. Picasso was well aware of conventional perspective cues but did not choose to use them slavishly in his painting.

2. *Painting as a Normal Optical Input to Vision*

The quotation comes from Pirenne (1959) and its good sense may be appreciated by comparing it with the outcome of the experiments of Smith and Smith (1961), see Chapter 1 Note 6 . Reports of Pirenne's observations, which are crucial to the present thesis, will be found in Pirenne (1967b) and, in an expanded form, in Pirenne (1970). See also Pirenne (1963) and Pirenne (1967a).

3. *Retinal Image*

This implies that the eye can be treated as a sophisticated camera whose main task is to acquire an "image" or "reproduction" of the scene. Some writers on this topic appear to be infatuated with the concept of the *Retinal Image.* Ames, Proctor and Ames (1923) went so far as to suggest that a picture, in order to be pleasing, should reproduce the impression made by nature and should therefore be distorted in the manner in which the retinal projection, owing to the curvature of the retina is distorted. The precise extent of distortion is the deviation of the retinal picture laid flat on a surface from a picture which would obtain if the retina were flat. There is an inherent weakness in the argument put forward; it presumes that the retina "knows" that it is curved. The reasons for the suggestion appear to be rather tenuous, especially so when it is recalled that the retinal projection is merely a stage in the passage of the information through the organism; a stage at which *some* of the information being transmitted is in a form open to visual observation. In addition there is the rather obvious fact that the real world is not curved but the distortion is introduced by the optical system of the eye. Therefore to paint a picture which is distorted would be to produce an optical input which was unlike natural stimulation which would rather defeat the purpose of the exercise. This is not however the entire story. Some information passing through the other eye, which forms the basis of the binocular cues, adds to what can be obtained from one retinal image, nor is the retina constituted of undifferentiated cells with equal "transmission rights" for passage of information nor are the eyes immobile.

A further interesting suggestion made by Ames et al. is that of creation of paintings which present collages of two monocular views. Such figures are commonly found in texts on vision, but there the two views are printed in different colours (generally green and red) and have to be viewed through special spectacles. Ames et al. suggests that the figures should not differ in colour and that they should be viewed normally. The photographs which they reproduce to advance their thesis are not, however, convincing.

4. *Eye Movements*

The pioneering study of eye movements in which pictures served as stimuli was carried out by Buswell (1935). Studies of eye movements in reading, which are technically considerably easier, have been undertaken earlier. See Yarbus (1967) for the woodland scene described. Mackworth and Morand (1967) deal with the relation of the eye movements to selection of information. Molnar (1968) investigated eye movements, evoked by simple pictorial patterns. He concluded that eye-fixations are a good measure of attention, and suggested that in *Dr. Tulpe's*

Anatomy Lesson (Figure 2.11) a definite order of scanning will be found with the eye moving repeatedly between the faces of individual students and the dissected arm.

A paper by Rock and Halper (1969) examines several interesting studies of "form perception without a retinal image", where the perception of shape takes place as an observer tracks a relatively slowly moving point of light.

The important distinction between the real physical eye movements and the movement of the mind's eye is made by Finkelstein (1979) who analyses changes of percepts which occur without any eye movement. Hayashi (1977) considers the role the movement of the mind's eye on perception of pictures in general. Kennedy (1976) examines the effect of shifts in attention on apparent brightness of surfaces.

5. *Acuity and the Shape of Pictures*

Recognition of this phenomenon, the high acuity of the retina at the fovea and fall off in sensitivity with distance from the line of sight, in the nineteenth century caused a debate about the proper shape of pictures in which Ruskin engaged with vigour. He argued that although the natural shape of the picture would be a circle, such a shape would impose unwelcome restrictions on artistic creativity notably on disposition of the verticals and the horizontals within the painting, for example he felt that a circular frame would inevitably place the horizon on the horizontal diameter and this "would take away all power form the artist". Movements of the eye when looking at landscapes led him to consider an ellipse as the potentially optimal shape and this in turn to suggest the traditional rectangular frame as an approximation to ellipse. He calculated the desirable proportions of the frame, which should be viewed at such a distance, that the picture supports at the eye an angle of about 60 degrees. Clearly in this conception little room was left for the eye to exercise its flexibility and the artist was left with no opportunity of acknowledging some of its hidden characteristics.

6. *Trompe l'oeil*

For a variety of illustrations of this phenomenon, see Dars (1979). Ten Doesschate (1951) investigated the merging of painted and real depths.

7. *Distortion of Projected Shapes*

This discussion owes much to Pirenne (see references above - note 2). The evidence for Leonardo da Vinci's avoidance of spheres is that of La Gournerie (1859), cited by Pirenne (1970). As all sections of a sphere are circles, the lines extending to the eye from the surface of a sphere inevitably form a cone which when sectioned can yield an ellipse, a hyperbola or a parabola. The shape projected by a sphere on the pictorial surface is determined by the relationship between the sphere and an imaginary plane parallel to the picture plane and containing the eye. When this plane and the sphere do not meet (the most common occurence) the sphere projects as an ellipse (or as a special case of the ellipse: a circle). When the plane intersects the sphere, the sphere projects a hyperbola (for example the horizon of the sea photographed from a tall building projects a hyperbola). In the intermediate case, when the plane just touches the sphere, the projected curve is a parabola. For a reproduction of Raphael's *School of Athens*, see Osborne's (1981) *Oxford Companion of Art.* For discussion of Saenredam's technique, see Carter (1967), Liedke (1971) Dubery and Willats (1983) and Kemp (1984).

Haber (1979) agrees with Pirenne that compensation is an important element of pictorial perception. He disagrees, however, about the psychological antecendents of compensation.

8. *Projection Surfaces*

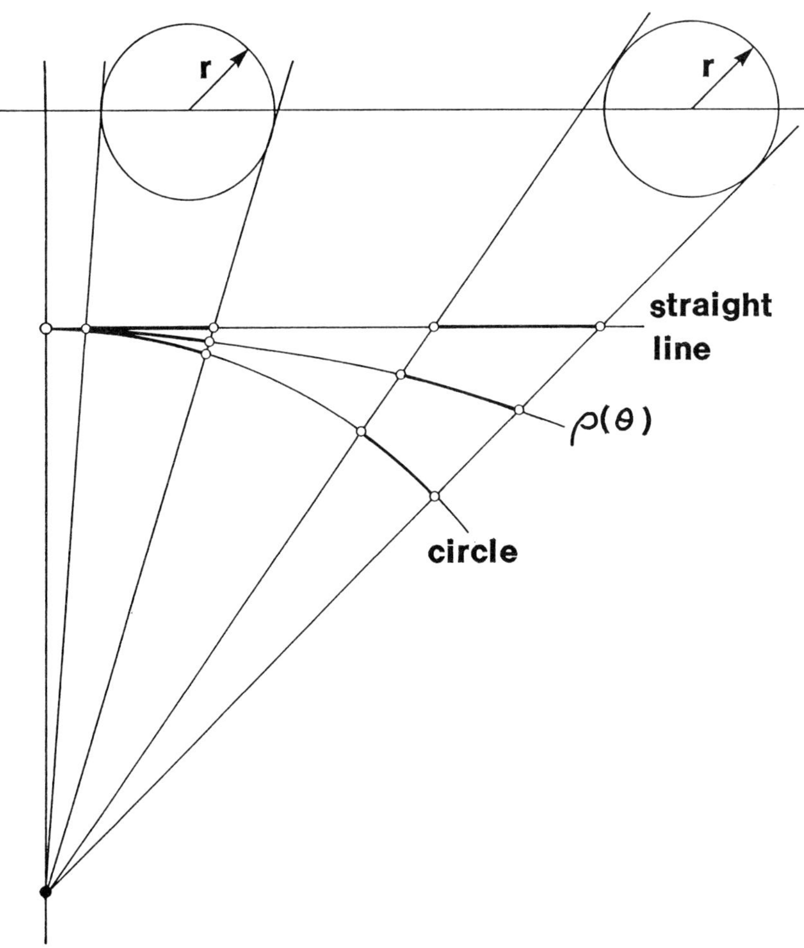

Figure N.9 Projections of two cylinders at two lateral displacement on to i) a flat surface (straight line), ii) a cylindrical surface (circle) and iii) a special curved surface whose construction is explained in the text.

The projection of a row of columns onto a pictorial plane results in the lateral distention of the columns away from the line of sight. Replacement of the plane by a cylinder, centred on the eye, leads to the expected decrease in width of the side columns, but also to non-linear decrease in their height, so that lines which have a horizontal component (only vertical lines do not have it) become distorted. Most notably horizontal lines bow out (See Dubery & Willats, 1982). It is of course possible to construct a projection surface, intermediate between a plane and a cylinder, so shaped that all the projections on it would be of equal width. The mathematical equation for such a curved surface seen from above and expressed in polar form is:

$$\left(\frac{d\rho}{d\theta}\right)^2 + \rho = \frac{c^2}{\cos^2\theta}$$

where $\rho(\theta)$ is the curve in question.

Clearly as lateral displacement increases projections onto the straight line increase in size, those onto the circle decrease, while those onto the curve remain constant (figure N.9).

9. *Pictorial Space*

For methods of determining the effects of change of the point of view on pictorial space, see Bartel (1958) or Faber and Rosinski (1978).

For discussion of peripheral views in Art see Mills (1936).

10. *Cézanne*

For an insightful analysis by an artist of Cézanne's *Still life with a fruit basket* and of many other of his paintings, see Loran (1943), who presents juxtapositions of photographs of the scenes painted by Cézanne with reproductions of his pictures.

11. *Persistence of Vision*

The studies of persistence of vision have a long and curious history beginning with Aristotle's (see Aristotle 1975) observations on after-images in his treatise *On Dreams*. He links them to the waterfall illusion (the discovery of this which is, sometimes erroneously attributed to Addams (1834) see Dember, 1964). The after images, according to Aristotle, are always present but are too weak to influence perception when the intellect is at work; but in sleep when the powers of judgement fade the images reassert themselves in dreams. "... influence remains in the sense organs ... not only whilst they perceive but also when they have stopped to do so ... for example when we turn from sunlight to darkness we see nothing because the excitation of our eyes caused by the light is still within them. Also, after looking for a long time at a colour ... any object to which we transfer our eye looks of that colour. Further, when after looking at a bright object, we close our eyes ... it seems to be still there ... and fades gradually. The same endurance of vision can be observed when after looking at moving objects e.g., rivers, especially those flowing rapidly stationary objects seem to move." Plateau (1877) points out that Aristotle makes an error in saying that the after-image of a red stimulus will be red and not, as it really is, green. This error has in turn been repeated by Ptolemy, Alhazen and Kepler, all of whom it appears placed greater reliance on the authority of the ancient sage than on their own sensory experience.

An investigation of the influence of pictorial background on after-images was carried out by Frank (1923). Her subjects who projected after-images onto a perspective drawing of a tunnel reported that these seemed larger when projected onto the convergent (and therefore apparently further) part of the figure than when projected onto the divergent (and therefore apparently nearer) part. For a resume of this experiment see Koffka (1935). This work has been further advanced by Sonoda (1961).

12. *Illusory Contours*

"Illusory contours" have been examined by Coren (1972) and Kennedy (1978a, b and 1979).

13. *Mach's bands*

Weale (1976 and 1979) discusses their places in art. Information about the psycho-physiological aspects of the phenomenon will be found in Pirenne (1967), Fiorentini (1972) and Frisby (1979). Relevant observations by Leonardo da Vinci will be found in Perdetti (1965; carta 32). Leonardo also points out that an outline of a vertical pole appears very dark when the background is white and much brighter when the background is dark, even though in each case the light which descends onto the pole is equally brilliant.

Chapter 8 Art Via Illusion

1. *Op Art*

Reviews of the perceptual effects exploited by Op-artists may be found in Wade (1978 and 1982).

2. *Illusory Colours*

These are discussed with fascinating examples provided in Kanizsa (1976, 1979). See also the references under Note 12 Chapter 7.

3. *Movement and Blurring*

A detailed analysis of these effects will be found in Wade (1978) pages 31-35.

4. *Hermann Grid Illusion*

First described by L. Hermann in 1870 there is now considerable evidence that this illusion is explained by the neural organisation of the retina. The relation between certain perceptual effects (including Hermann's grid) and visual neurophysiology is discussed by Jung (1973).

Chapter 9. Art and Reality

1. For the Mustard Seed Garden Manual of Painting (1679), see Mai-Mai Sze (1957). Strzemiński's notion of realism is rather different than those generally held. He maintains that perception of a style as realistic depends on accummulation of cultural experience. Pictures which may be seen as realistic in one time may not be seen as such in another. The bounds of realism are set by the level of "development of visual awareness determined by the history" (historycznie uwarunkowany rozwój). The changes in awareness are not associated with any changes in the optical structure of the eye.

2. *Realism*

For a recent philosophical discussion of realism and the divergence between the views of Gombrich and those of Gibson see Topper (1983). For a philosophical discussion of the theories of pictorial representation see Conley (1985).

3. *Culture and Style*

The demonstration of recurrence of the same pictorial usages at various times in the history of Art does not deny, as has been said, the thesis that cultural values affect the selection of these usages. Examination of the relationship beetween modern art and modern science has recently been carried out by Vitz and Glimcher (1984); it covers the entire spectrum of visual perception and concerns sculpture as well as painting. An earlier study by Vitz (1979) covers similar ground, whilst studies by Teuber (1974, 1976) show how two artists, M.C. Escher and Paul Klee, derived their inspiration directly from psychological writings (mainly those of the Gestalt school). Discussion of the use of the figure/ground ambiguity by Salvador Dali will be found in Fisher (1967).

Wartofsky (1979) embraces views contrary to those expressed here. In his opinion human vision is a cultural and a historical product, the plasticity of the visual system being so great that a biological account of its evolution (whether phylo- or onto-genetical) is inadequate for explaining it. This implies a much deeper involvement of the social determinants of perception than that put forward in the present thesis. The present thesis is that social factors influence the choice as to which of the attributes of the perceptual mechanism artists will exploit in any historical period, but does not hold that the mechanisms themselves are in their essence affected by the artistic practice of the day.

4. *Binocular Vision*

For analysis of binocular vision see Luneberg (1947). The suggestion that related experiences are responsible for the style of some of van Gogh's work was put forward by Heelan (1972). In his latest book Heelan (1983) endeavours to put these observations in a broader philosophical context. Our inclination to question it rests on two points: (1) The mathematical description of the binocular space and the picture in question do not match well. But it may be that the notion of non-Euclidean (Reimannian) space is used rather loosely by some of the advocates of this interpretation. (2) Acquisition of such a notion of space based on binocular vision would require (i) perceptual suppression of monocular cues for the time during which the notion is being acquired, for such cues would hinder its distillation and (ii) reimposition of these cues onto the newly acquired notion in order to paint. This seems a very complex process. It also ignores the weakness of binocular cues in the presence of conflicting monocular cues which was discussed in Chapter 3 Note 1. Fisher's (1968, 1969) suggestion that the *Bedroom at Arles* shows unmistakable traces of extreme excitement resulting from the artist's ill health, although falling outwith the scope of this book, ought to be mentioned. A recent selection of papers on the art of the psychiatrically disturbed will be found in Jakab (1968, 1969). Anastasi and Folley's (1941) work is still a useful guide here. Pickford (1967) provides a more recent evaluation. A briefer discussion of the topic is that by Trevor-Roper (1970).

5. See Hagen (1985) and also (1986).

6. *Hagen's Systems of Projection.*

Three rather than four systems are used presumably because Hagen wrongly thinks that the systems which she calls *Orthogonal* and *Similarity* yield gemoetrically similar projections. Indeed she claims that this is so for single objects. This, as shown in the diagram below is not true. (Figure N. 10). If this were true then the distortions due to lateral displacement which we have discussed at length in Chapter 4 simply would not arise.

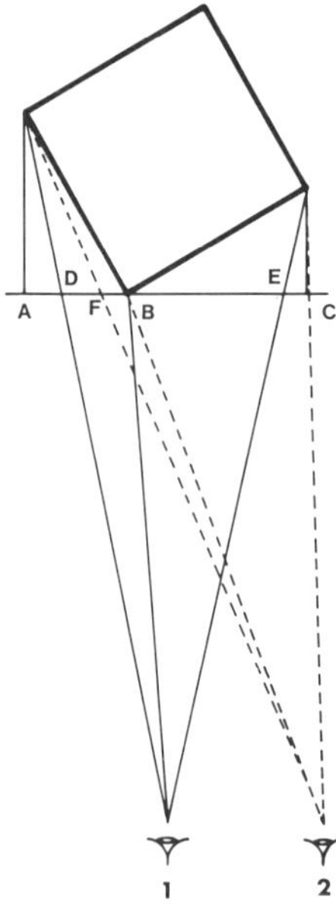

Figure N.10 As the point of view changes from 1 to 2 the projection of the left hand face of the cube deceases from DB to FB, and that of the right hand face increases from BE to BC. However, the orthogonal projection on the plane running from A through B and C remains the same.

The adjective orthogonal in orthogonal projection describes the relationship between the direction of the projection lines and the projection plane. It bears no implications as to the orientation of the model relative to the plane. Therefore an object can be portrayed orthogonally on a plane placed anywhere in space, provided that there exists a set of normal projection lines from the object to the plane. Hence a bird's eye view as well as a worm's eye view of a house can be so drawn as indeed can all the views obtainable on earth's surface. These views, obviously, do not contain the same amounts of information about the nature of the depicted objects and it seems misguided to equate them with canonical views as is sometimes done, (Hagen, 1985, 1986).

7. *Dating of Bushman Art.*

Bushman Art is in the compilation provided placed firmly as flourishing in 1000 A.D. This seems somewhat arbitrary since according to Woodehouse (1978) South African Rock art (which is somewhat loosely described as Bushman Art) flourished between about 2700 B.C. and the last century. This timespan entirely envelops the timespan of the Ancient Egyptian Art. For extensive discussions of Bushmen and their art see Cooke (1969), Woodehouse, (1979), Tobias (1978), Lewis-Williams (1981) and Pager (1972). Pager's meticulous treatise of paintings in the Ndedema Gorge contains some excellent reproductions.

8. *Drawing Skills of Adults.*

Observations of sophisticated adults inability to draw pictures has been examined by Cameron (1938). The problem is partly that of lack of skill in *drawing* and partly that of interpretation of instructions. When asked to draw they may decide to create either primarily epitomic or primarily eidolic images. Epitomic images are easier to create. It is much easier to draw a pin-man than to draw a trompe l'oeil figure of a man, and since both convey the meaning 'man' equally effectively, the former is likely to be drawn when the request "Draw a man" is made.

Hence epitomic drawings incorporating symbolic or conventional elements such as arrows to show directions are often made, as Cameron (1938) has observed, and serve the purpose of communication admirably. However the purpose of art is greater than that of showing for which sex a particular facility is intended, and such drawings, made under these circumstances do not inform us about the development of artistic styles.

9. *Aculturation of Vision.*

Panofsky's extensive and very influential work on the relationship between culture and art is reviewed by Holly (1984) who in discussing his essay on perspective (Panofsky, 1927) points out that similar ideas have been recently put forward by Wartofsky (1972, 1980) one of the few philosophers of science who appears to have read the relevant psychological literature.

10. Gablik's (1976) treatise presents in essence the same argument as does Blatt (1984) in his much more detailed work which comprehensively reviews theories of Western art. See also Note 4, Chapter 1.

11. *The Linear and the Painterly.*

See Wolfflin (1899,1952) and 1956). Wolfflin's idea of a linear-painterly dimension in artistic style is interesting and may have more scientific weight than he, or later critics, have realised. However, he probably misplaced the end point of the scale on which he was positioning paintings. Wolfflin (1956) argued that there was what amounts to a paradigm shift in the way in which painters rendered their subjects between the sixteenth and seventeenth century. The importance of clearly defined line in a composition was downgraded and the distribution of regions of light and shade emphasised.

Wolfflin saw this as a movement from the representation of the plastic, tangible qualities of the painter's subjects to a purely visual dimension. This contrast can be clearly been in comparisons of the work of Dürer and Bronzini (linear) on the one hand and Rembrandt and Velasquez (painterly) on the other. However, movement from the linear to the painterly can also be seen in the contrasts between the younger and older Rembrandt and Titian.

Whether this linear - painterly dimension can be accurately described as a transition from a more plactic to a more visual rendering of the subjects strikes us as doubtful because it ignores the richness of purely visual experience. If one examines Figure N.11A which shows a computer digitised picture of a human face, we can see a representation which would be characterised as linear in Wolfflin's terminology; strong line with rigid separation of subject and background. Figure N.11B and N.11C show the same portrait which has been moved two steps along the linear - painterly dimension.

The softening of the edges and the less rigid separation of subject and background with emphasis more firmly placed on the distribution of light and shade has been achieved by digitally filtering Figure N.10a to remove fine detail (high spatial frequencies). But we can also remove the broad distribution of regions of light and dark (low spatial frequencies) and produce versions of the portrait which are decidely more linear than N.10a. This has been done in two steps in N.10d and N.10e. Here line is emphasised when the coarse visual information in the scene is removed.

The normal portrait (N.11A) includes then both fine detail (line) and coarse information (light and shade) and falls in the middle of the extremes seen in N.11E and N.11C. In the same way painters like Dürer, Bronzino and the younger Rembrandt can be seen as falling midway along the linear-painterly dimension since they incorporate within their works the *full* spatial range.

Figure N.11A A digitised portrait with full (includes low, medium and high spatial frequencies) spatial bandwidth.

Figure N.11B Some of the fine detail (high spatial frequencies) have been removed from the portrait resulting in softening of the edges.

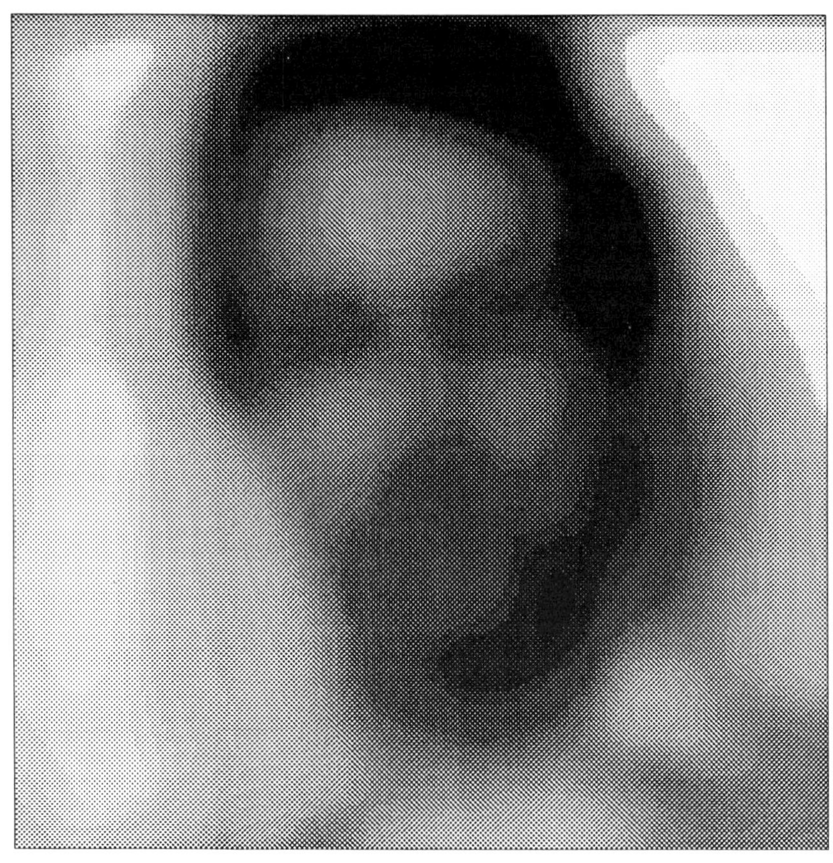

Figure N.11C Even more of the finer information has been removed from the portrait leaving one which falls at a relatively extreme position on the linear - painterly dimension, towards the painterly pole.

Figure N.11D Removal of some of the coarse information (low spatial frequencies) from the portrait shown in figure N.11A.

Figure N.11E Removal of a substantial amount of the coarse information from the portrait shown in figure N.11A. This picture would fall at a relatively extreme position on the linear - painterly dimension, towards the linear pole.

The true end of the linear dimension can be seen in line drawings, although paintings can also be seen to be towards the linear end of this dimension e.g. Cézanne's "Still Life with Fruit Basket" (Figure 7.8a) or Bart van der Lech's "The Musician's" (Figure 3.9).

The points made above indicate that one can easily derive a quantitative description of a pictorial dimension that is very close to Wolfflin's linear-painterly one. For those interested in this area of visual perception further information may be found in Ginsburg (1980), Olzak and Thomas (1986), and Parker, Lishman and Hughes (1990).

12. Cultural differences in constancy.

Cultural differences in constancies are discussed in Deręgowski (1980). The opposing views of the source of such differences presented are those of Thouless (1932), who thought that Indians see differently and therefore draw differently, and Piotrowski (1935), who thought that Indian art affects the perception of Indians.

References

Addams, R. (1834). "An account of a peculiar optical phenomenon seen after having looked at a moving body". *Philosophical Magazine,* 3 (5), 373. (Reprinted in Dember, 1964)

Allen, F. (1926). "The persistence of vision". *American Journal of Physiological Optics, 7,* 439 - 57.

Ames, A., Proctor, C. A. and Ames, B. (1923). "Vision and the Technique of Art". *Proceedings of American Academy of Arts and Sciences, 58,* 3 - 47.

Ames, A. (1925). "The illusions of depth from single pictures". *Journal of the Optical Society of America, 10,* 137 - 148.

Anastasi, A. & Folley, J. P. (1941). "A survey of the literature on artistic behaviour in the abnormal II. Approaches and inter-relationships". *Annals of the New York Academy of Sciences, 42,* 1 - 71.

Aristotle (1975). *Parva Naturalia: On Dreams.* Hett, W.H. (Trans), Goold, G. P. (Ed). The Loeb Classical Library: Vol. 8 Harvard University and Heinemann, London.

Armstrong, C. (1893). *Cusack's Model Drawing.* City of London School of Art.

Arnheim, R. (1954). *Art and Visual Perception.* University of California Press, Berkeley.

Arnheim, R. (1966). *Towards a Psychology of Art.* University of California Press, Berkeley.

Arnheim, R. (1969). *Visual Thinking.* University of California Press, Berkeley.

Arnheim, R. (1986) *New Essays on the Psychology of Art.* University of California Press, Los Angeles.

Attneave, F. (1954). "Some informational aspects of visual perceptions". *Psychological Review, 61,* 183-193.

Barrett, C. (1970). *Op Art.* Studio Vista, London.

Barrett, C. (1971). *An Introduction to Optical Art.* Studio Vista, London.

Bartel, K. (1928/1958). *Perspektywa Malarska.* Książnica-Atlas, Lwów/Państwowe Wydawnictwo Naukowe, Warszawa.

Berkeley, G. (1709). *An Essay towards a New Theory of Vision.* Dublin.

Berry, J. (1966). "Temne and Eskimo perceptual skills". *International Journal of Psychology, 1,* 207 - 227.

Beyen, H. G. (1938). *Die Pompejanische Wanddekoration vom zweiten bis zum vierten Stil.* Band I., Marinus Nishoff, Haag.

Beyen, H. G. (1939). "Die antike Zentralperspektive". *Jahrbuch des Deutschen Arch‥ologischen Instituts, 54,* 47 - 72.

Binnie-Dawson, J. L. M. and Choi, P., P-C. (1982). "A study of perceptual and cultural cues in Chinese and Western paintings". *Psychologia, 25,* 18 - 31.

Blatt, S. J. (1984) *Continuity and Change in Art: the Development of Modes of Representation.* Lawrence Erlbaum Associates, Hillsdale, New Jersey.

Boretz, N. (1979). "The reality underlying abstraction". *In* Nodine, C.F. and Fisher, D.F. (Eds.) *Perception and Pictorial Representation.* Praeger, New York.

Bothwell, D. R. (1976). *Beyond Aesthetics,* Thames and Hudson, London.

Boyle, D. G. (1969). *A Student's Guide to Piaget.* Pergamon Press, Oxford.

Buswell, G. T. (1935). *How People look at Pictures. A Study of the Psychology of Perception in Art.* University of Chicago Press, Chicago.

Buytendijk, F. J. J. (1930). "Zeilgerichtetes Verhalten der Ratten in einen freien Situation". *Archives Nederlandises de Physiologie de l'Homme et des Animaux, 15,* 402 - 412.

Cameron, N. (1938). "Functional immaturity of the symbolisation of scientifically trained adults". *Journal of Psychology, 6,* 161-175.

Cannestrari, R. (1975). "A further study on the pehenomenon of the 'rotating trapezoidal window'" *In* D'Arcais, G. G. F. (Ed.) *Studies in Perception'* Martello-Guinti, Milan.

Carpenter, J. M. (1951). "Cézanne and Tradition". *Art Bulletin, 33,* 174 - 186.

Carter, A. R. (1967). "The uses of perspective in Saenredam". *Burlington Magazine, 109,* 594 - 5.

Chwistek, L. (1961). *Pisma filozoficzne i logiczne.* Państwowe Wydawnictwo Naukowe, Warszawa. Originally published in 1924 in *Przegląd Współczesny*

Colney, B. G. (1985). *Theories of Pictorial Representation: Goodman's Relativism and Similarity Theory,* Ph.D. Thesis, University of Minnesota.

Compton, M. (1967). *Optical and Kinetic Art.* Tate Gallery, London.

Cooke, C. K. (1969). *Rock Art of Southern Africa.* Books of Africa, Cape Town.

Coren, S. (1972). "Subjective contours and apparent depth". *Psychological Review, 79,* 359 - 367.

Coren, S. (1978). *Seeing is Deceiving: The Psychology of Visual Illusions.* Halsted Press, New York.

Coren, S. and Girgus, J. S. (1975). "A size illusion based on a minimal interposition cue". *Perception, 4,* 251 - 254.

Coren, S. and Girgus, J. S. (1977). "Illusions and constancies" *In* Epstein, W. (Ed.) *Stability and Constancy in Visual Perception: Mechanisms and Processes.* J. Wiley, New York.

Dars, C. (1979). *Images of Deception: The Art of Trompe l'oeil.* Phaidon Press, Oxford.

Delacroix, E. (1932). *Journal de Eugene Delacroix, Vol. 3,* Librarie Plou, Paris.

Dember, W. N. (1964) *Visual Perception : The Nineteenth Century.* J. Wiley, New York.

Demus, O. (1948). *Byzantine Mosaic Decoration: Aspects of Monumental Art in Byzantium.* Kegan Paul, Trench, Trubner, London.

Demus, O. (1970). *Byzantine Art and the West.* Weidenfeld and Nicholson, London.

Deręgowski, J. B. (1976). "'Principle of Economy' and perception of pictorial depth: A cross-cultural comparison". *International Journal of Psychology, 11,* 15 - 22.

Deręgowski, J. B. (1980). "Perception". *In* Trandis, H. and Lonner, W. (Eds.) *Handbook of Cross-Cultural Psychology,* vol. 3, Aldison and Wesley: New York.

Deręgowski, J. B. (1980b). *Illusions, Patterns and Pictures.* Academic Press, London.

Deręgowski, J. B. (1984). *Distortion in Art: The Eye and the Mind.* Routledge and Kegan-Paul, London.

Deręgowski, J. B. (1989a). "Real space and represented space: Cross-cultural perspectives". *The Behavioral and Brain Sciences, 12,* 51-119.

Deręgowski, J. B. (1989b). "Geometric reconstruction of perspective: Bartel's method". *Perception, 18,* 595-600.

Deręgowski, J. B., Muldrow, E. S. & Muldrow, W. F. (1972). "Pictorial recognition in a remote Ethiopian population". *Perception, 1,* 417 - 425.

Deręgowski, J. B. & Parker, D. M. (1988). "On the changing perspective illusion within Vermeer's 'The Music Lesson'". *Perception, 17,* 13-21.

Ditchburn, R. W. (1973). *Eye Movements and Visual Perception.* Clarendon Press, Oxford.

Draper, S. W. (1978). "The Penrose triangle and the family of related figures". *Perception, 7,* 283 - 296.

Dubery, F. and Willats, J. (1983). *Perspective and Other Drawing Systems.* The Herbert Press, London.

Dziurawiec, S. & Deręgowski, J. B. (1990). "Twisted perspective in young children's drawings." *British Journal of Developmental Psychology.* In Press.

Edgerton, S. Y. (1976). *The Renaissance Rediscovery of Linear Perspective.* Harper and Row, New York.

Epstein, W. (Ed.) (1977). *Stability and Constancy in Visual Perception: Mechanisms and Processes.* J. Wiley, New York.

Faber, J. and Rosinski, R. R. (1978). "Geometric transformations of pictured space". *Perception, 7,* 269 - 282.

Finkelstein, L. (1979). "On the unpicturelikeness of our seeing". In Nodine, C. F. and Fisher, D. F. (Eds.) *Perception and Pictorial Representation.* Praeger, New York .

Fiorentini, A. (1972) "Mach band phenomena". *In* Jameson, D. & Murvich, L. M. (Eds.) *Handbook of Sensory Physiology Visual Psychophysics (Vol. VII/4),* Springer Verlag, New York.

Fisher, G. H. (1967). "Ambiguous figure treatments in the art of Salvador Dali". *Perception and Psychophysics, 2,* 328 - 330.

Fischer, R. (1968). "Space-time co-ordinates of excited and tranquilized states". *In* Jakab, I. (Ed.) *Psychiatry and Art.* Karger, Basel.

Fischer, R. (1969). "On creative, psychotic and ecstatic states". *In* Jakab, I. (Ed.) *Art Interpretation and Art Therapy.* Karger, Basel.

Florczak, Z. (1972) *Sztuka łamie milczenie.* Wydawnictwo Literackie Kraków, Kraków.

Frank, H. (1923). Uber die Beeinflussung von Nachbilden druck de Gestalteigenschaften der Projektionflasche. *Psychologische Forschung, 4,* 33 - 37.

Freeman, N. H. (1989). A computational approach to picture production and consumption is needed right here. *Behavioral and Brain Sciences, 12,* 81-84.

Frisby, J. P. (1979). *Seeing.* Oxford University Press, Oxford.

Gablik, S. (1976). *Progress in Art.* Thames & Hudson, London.

Georgeson, M. A. and Blakemore, C. (1973). "Apparent depth and the Muller-Lyer Illusion". *Perception, 2,* 225 - 234.

Gibson, J. J. (1966). *The Senses Considered as Perceptual Systems.* Houghton Mifflin, New York.

Gibson, J. J. (1975). "Three kinds of distance that can be seen or, how Bishop Berkeley went wrong". *In* Glores D'Arcais, G. B. (Ed.) *Studies in Perception,* Martello Guinti, Milan.

Gibson, J. J. (1979). *The Ecological Approach to Visual Perception.* Houghton Mifflin, New York.

Gillan, B. (1981). "False perspectives". *Perception, 10,* 313 - 318.

Goldstein, E. B. (1979). "Rotation of objects in pictures viewed at an angle: Evidence for different properties of two types of pictorial space". *Journal of Experimental Psychology - Human Perception, 5,* 78 - 87.

Goldstein, E. B. (1984). *Sensation and Perception.* Wadworth Pub. Co., Belmont, California.

Gombrich, E. H. (1962). *Art and Illusion.* Phaidon Press, London.

Gombrich, E. H., Hochberg, J. and Black, M. (1972). *Art, Perception and Reality.* Johns Hopkins University Press, Baltimore.

Gombrich, E. H. (1972). "The 'what' and the 'how' of perspective representation and the phenomenal world". *In* Rudner, R. and Scheffer, I. (Eds.) *Logic and Art.* Bobbs-Merrill, Indianapolis.

Goodman, N. (1969). *Languages of Art.* Oxford University Press, Oxford.

Gournerie, J., de la (1859). *Traite de Perspective Lineaire.* Dolmant et Dunod, Paris.

Graziosi, P. (1960). *Palaeolithic Art.* Faber, London.

Gregory, R. L. (1966). *Eye and Brain.* Weidenfeld and Nicolson, London.

Gregory, R. L. (1970). *The Intelligent Eye.* Weidenfeld and Nicholson, London.

Gregory, R. L. (1970). *The Intelligent Eye.* Weidenfeld and Nicholson, London.

Gregory, R. L. (1973). "*The confounded eye*". *In* Gregory, R. L., Gombrich, E. H. and Blakemore, C. (Eds.) *Illusion in Nature and Art.* Duckworth, London.

Gregory, R. L. (1979). "Space in Pictures". *In* Nodine, C. F. and Fisher, D. F. (Eds.) *Perception and Pictorial Representation* Praeger, New York.

Gregory, R. L., Gombrich, E. H. and Blakemore, C. (Eds.) (1973). *Illusion in Nature and Art.* Duckworth, London.

Gregory, R. L. and Harris, J. P. (1975). "Illusion destruction by appropriate scaling". *Perception, 4,* 203 - 220.

Guinea, M. A. G. (1979). *Altamira.* Silex, Madrid.

Haber, R. N. (1979). "Perceiving the layout of space in pictures: A perspective theory based on Leonardo da Vinci". *In*: Nodine, C. F. and Fisher, D. F. (Eds.) *Perception and Pictorial Representation.* Praeger, New York.

Hagen, M. A. (1985). "There is no development in art". *In* Freeman, N. H. & Cox, M. V. (Eds.) *Visual Order.* Cambridge University Press, Cambridge.

Hagen, M. A. (1986). "*Varieties of Realism: Geometries of Representational Art*". Cambridge University Press, Cambridge.

Halverson, J. (1987). "Art for art's sake". *Current Anthropology, 28,* 68-89.

Hayashi, M. (1977). "On the compositions of Imakimono scrolls". *Hiroshima Forum for Psychology, 4,* 3 - 7.

Heelan, P. (1972). "Toward new analysis of pictorial space by Vincent van Gogh". *Art Bulletin, 54,* 478 - 492.

Heelan, P. A. C. (1983). *Space-Perception and the Philosophy of Science.* University of California Press, Berkeley.

Helmholtz, H. (1910/1962). *Physiological Optics,* vol. III. Dover, New York.

Hinton, H. W. (1973). "Natural Deception". *In* Gregory, R. L., Gombrich, E. H. and Blakemore, C. (Eds.) *Illusion in Nature and Art.* Duckworth, London.

Hochberg, J. (1978). *Perception.* Prentice Hall, New York.

Hochberg, J. (1979). "Some things that paintings are not". *In* Nodine, C. F. and Fisher, D. F. (Eds.) *Perception and Pictorial Representation,* Praeger, New York.

Hochberg, J. R. and Brooks, V. (1960). "The Psychophysics of form; reversible perspective drawings of spatial objects". *American Journal of Psychology, 73,* 337 - 354.

Holly, M. A. (1984). *Panofsky and the Foundations of Art History.* Cornell University Press, Ithaca.

Humphrey, N. K. (1971). "Contrast illusion in perspective". *Nature,* 232, 91 - 93.

Humphreys, G. W. and Bruce, V. (1989). *Visual Cognition: Computational, Experimental and Neuropsychological Perspectives.* Lawrence Erlbaum, London.

Ittelson, W. H. (1952). *The Ames demonstrations.* Princeton University Press, Princeton.

Jakab, I. (Ed.) (1968). *Psychiatry and Art.* Karger, Basel.

Jakab, I. (Ed.) (1969). *Art Interpretation and Art Therapy.* Karger, Basel.

Jameson, D. and Hurvich, L. M. (1976). "From contrast to assimilation." *In* Henle, M. (Ed.) *Vision and Artifact.* Springer, New York.

Jerison, H. J. (1967) "Apparent motion of a vista: an illusion of perspective". *American Journal of Psychology, 80,* 448-453.

Julesz, B. (1971). *Foundations of Cyclopean Perception.* University of Chicago Press, Chicago.

Jung, R. (1973). "Visual perception and neuropsychology" *In* Jung, R. (Ed.) *Handbook of Sensory Physiology,* volume VII/3 *Central Processing of Visual Information Part A.* Springer, Berlin.

Kanizsa, G. (1975). "The role of regularity in perceptual organisation". *In* Flores D'Arcais, G. B. (Ed.) *Studies in Perception.* Martello Guinti, Milan.

Kanizsa, G. (1976). "Subjective contours". *Scientific American, 234,* 48-52.

Kanizsa, G. (1979). *Organisation in Vision.* Praeger, New York.

Kemp, M. (1984). "Construction and cunning : The perspective of the Edinburgh Saenredam". *In Dutch Church Painters: Saenredam's "Great Church of Haarlem" in context.* National Gallery of Scotland, Edinburgh.

Kennedy, J. M. (1974). *The Psychology of Picture Perception.* Jossey-Bass, San Francisco.

Kennedy, J. M. (1978a). "Illusory contours and the ends of lines". *Perception, 7,* 605 - 607.

Kennedy, J. M. (1978b). "Illusory contours not due to completion". *Perception, 7,* 187 - 189.

Kennedy, J. M. (1979). "Subjective contours, contrast and assimilation". *In* Nodine, C. F. and Fisher D. F. (Eds.) *Perception and Pictorial Representation.* Praeger, New York.

Koffka, K. (1935). *Principles of Gestalt Psychology.* Harcourt, Brace, New York.

Kolbuszewski, J. (1953). "The significance of perspective in painting". *Journal of Royal Society of Arts, 101,* 375-378.

Kraft, R. N. & Green, J. S. (1989). "Distance perception as a function of photographic area of view". *Perception & Psychophysics, 45,* 459-466.

Kulpa, Z. (1983). "Are impossible figures possible?" *Signal Processing, 5,* 201 - 220.

Landor, A. H. S. (1883). *Alone with the Hairy Ainu or 3800 Miles on a Pack Saddle in Yezo and a Cruise to the Kurile Islands.* John Murray, London.

Langdon, J. (1951). "The perception of a changing shape". *Quarterly Journal of Experimental Psychology, 3,* 157 - 165.

Leason, P. A. (1939). "A new view of the Western European group of quarternary cave art". *Proceedings of the Prehistoric Society,* N.S.5, 51 - 66.

Leason, P. A. (1956). "Obvious facts of quarternary cave art". *Medical and Biological Illustration,* 209 - 214.

Levy, G. R. (1943). "The Greek discovery of perspective; its influence on Renaissance and modern art". *Journal Royal Society British Archeology,* 51 - 57.

Lewis-Williams, J.D. (1981). *Believing and Seeing: Symbolic Meanings in Southern San Rock Paintings.* Academic Press, London.

Lewis-Williams, J. D. (Ed.) (1983). *New Approaches to Southern African Rock Art.* South African Archaeological Society, Cape Town.

Liedke, W. A. (1971). "Saenredam's space". *Oud Holland, 86,* 116 - 141.

Loran, E. (1943). *Cézanne's Composition. Analysis of his Form with Diagrams and Photographs of his Motifs.* University of California, Berkeley.

Lucie-Smith, E. (1975). *Movements in Art since 1945.* Thames and Hudson, London.

Luneberg, R. K. (1947). *Mathematical Analysis of Binocular Vision.* Princeton University Press, Princeton.

Mackworth, N. H. and Morand, A. J. (1967). "The gaze selects informative details within pictures". *Perception and Psychophysics, 2,* 547 - 552.

Markino, Y. (1972). *When I was a Child,* Constable, London.

Marquez, M. (1929). "El nundo exterior, la imagen retiniana y la funcion visual, con motivo del pretendido astigmatismo del Greco". *Revista Espanola de Medicina y Cirugia,* 12, 264 - 273.

Marr, D. (1982). *Vision.* W. H. Freeman & Co., San Francisco.

Marr, D. & Nishihara, M. K. (1978). "Representation and recognition of the spatial organisation of three-dimensional shapes". *Proceedings of the Royal Society of London, Series B, 200,* 269-294.

Metelli, F. (1976). "What does 'more transparent' mean? A paradox". *In* Henle, M. (Ed.) *Vision and Artefact.* Springer, New York.

Mezzena, F. (1976). "Nuova interpretazione delle incisioni parietali paleolitiche della grotta Addaura a Palermo". *Rivista di Scienze Preistoriche, 31,* 61-85.

Mills, L. (1936). "Peripheral vision in art". *Archives of Opthalmology* (Chicago), *16,* 208 - 219.

Molnar, F. (1968). "Une recherche experimentale sur le role des mouvements oculaires dans le perception de la composition picturale". *In* Aler, J. (Ed.) *Proceedings of the Fifth International Congress of Aesthetics,* Amsterdam (1964). Mouton, The Hague.

Moray, G. and Moray, N. (1981). "A note on the basis of reversed perspective". *Perception, 10,* 703 - 705.

Morgan, H. J., Findlay, J. M. and Watt, R. J. (1982). "Aperture viewing: A review and a synthesis". *Quarterly Journal of Experimental Psychology, 34A,* 211-233.

Morrison, J. D. and Whiteside, T. C. D. (1984). "Binocular cues in the perception of distance of a point source of light". *Perception, 13,* 555-566.

Neugebauer, O. (1959). "Ptolemy's Geography, Book 7, Chapters 6 and 7". *Isis, 50,* 22 - 9.

Nodine, C. F. and Fisher, D. F. (Eds.) (1979). *Perception and Pictorial Representation.* Praeger, New York.

Ogle, K. N. (1961). "Spatial localisation through binocular vision". *In* Davson, H. (Ed.) *The Eye.* Volume 4, *Visual Optics and the Optical Space Sense.* Academic Press, London.

Olzak, L. A. and Thomas, J. P. (1986). "Seeing spatial patterns". *In* Boff, K. R., Kaufman, L. and Thomas, J. P. (Eds.) *Handbook of Perception and Human Performance. Volume 1. Sensory Processes and Perception.* Wiley, New York.

Osborne, H. (Ed.) (1981). *Oxford Companion to Art.* Oxford University Press, Oxford.

Pager, H. (1972). *Ndedema.* International Scholarly Book Services, Portland.

Panofsky, E. (1934). "Jan van Eyck's Arnolfini Portrait". *Burlington Magazine,* 64; 117-124. (also in Gilbert, C. (Ed.) 1970, *Renaissance.*)

Panofsky, E. (1927). "Die Perspective als 'symbolische Form'". *Vortrage der Bibliothek Wartburg,* Leipzig.

Parker, D. M., Lishman, J. R. and Hughes, J. "Temporal integration of Spatially Filtered Visual Images". In Preparation.

Pedretti, C. (1965). *Leonardo da Vinci: On Painting, A lost Book.* University of California Press, Berkeley.

Perkins, D. N. (1972). "Perception of parallelepipeds". *Perception and Psychophysics, 12,* 396 - 400.

Perkins, O. N. and Deręgowski, J. B. (1982). "A cross-cultural comparison of the use of a Gestalt perceptual strategy". *Perception, 11*, 279 - 286.

Pickford, R. W. (1967). *Studies in Psychiatric Art.* Thomas, Springfield.

Pickford, R. W. (1972). *Psychology and Visual Aesthetics.* Hutchinson, London.

Pickford, R. W. (1976). "Defective Vision and Art". *In* Bothwell, D.R. (Ed.) *Beyond Aesthetics.* Thames and Hudson, London.

Piotrowski, Z. (1935). "Racial differences in linear perspectives". *Journal of Social Psychology, 8*, 479 - 485.

Pirenne, M. H. (1959). "A review of Decio Gioseffi's Perspectiva Artificialis". *The Art Bulletin, 41*, 213 - 217.

Pirenne, M. H. (1963). "Les lois de l'optique et la liberté de l'artiste". *Journal de Psychologie Normale et Pathologique, 60*, 151 - 166.

Pirenne, M. H. (1967a). *Vision and the Eye.* Chapman Hall, London.

Pirenne, M. H. (1967b). "On perspective and perception of pictures". *Physiology, 192*, 7 - 9.

Pirenne, M. H. (1970). *Optics, Painting and Photography.* Cambridge University Press, Cambridge.

Plateau, J. (1877). "Bibliographie analitique des principaux phénomènes subjectifs de la vision, depuis les temps anciens jusqu'a la fin du XVIIIe siecle suivie d'une bibliographie simple pour la partie ecoulee du siècle actuel". *Academie Royale de Belgique, 42.* Bruxelles.

Polanyi, M. (1962). *Personal Knowledge: Towards Post-critical Philosophy.* Routledge and Kegan Paul, London.

Polanyi, M. (1970). "What is painting?" *The British Journal of Aesthetics, 10,* 225 - 236.

Richter, G. M. A. (1937). "Perspective, ancient, mediaeval and renaissance". *Scritti in onore di Bartomeo Nogara.* Citta del Vaticano.

Robinson, J. O. (1972). *The Psychology of Visual Illusion.* Hutchinson , London.

Rock, I. & Halper, F. (1969). "Form perception without a retinal image". *American Journal of Psychology, 82,* 425 - 440.

Samuel, E. R. (1963). "Death in the glass ... new view of Holbein's 'Ambassadors'". *Burlington Magazine, 105,* 436 - 441.

Schlosberg, H. (1941). "Stereoscopic depth from single pictures". *American Journal of Psychology, 54,* 601 - 605.

Segall, M. H., Campbell, D. T. and Herskovits, M. J. (1966). *The Influence of Culture on Visual Perception.* Bobbs-Merill, Indianapolis.

Selfe, L. (1983). *Normal and Anomalous Representational Drawing Ability in Children.* Academic Press, London.

Selfe, L. (1985). "Anomalous drawing development: some clinical studies". *In* Freeman, N.H. and Cox, M.V. (Eds.) *Visual Order.* Cambridge University Press, Cambridge.

Serpell, R. and Deręgowski, J. B. (1980). "The skill of pictorial perception: an interpretation of cross-cultural evidence". *International Journal of Psychology, 15,* 145 - 180.

Smith, P. C. & Smith, O. W. (1961). "Ball throwing responses to photographically displayed targets". *Journal of Experimental Psyhology, 62,* 223-233.

Sonoda, G. (1961). "Perceptual constancies observed in plane pictures". *Kyushu Psychological Studies, 2,* (4), 20 - 29.

Southall, J. P. C. (1961). *Introduction to Physiological Optics.* Dover Publications Inc., New York.

Steer, J. (1989). "Art history and direct perception: a general view". *Art History, 12,* 93-108.

Steinborn, B. (1985). *W kręgu panoramy raclawickiej* Ossolineum, Wrocław.

Stevens, K. A. and Brookes, A. (1988). "Integrating stereopsis with monocular interpretations of planar surfaces". *Vision Research, 28,* 371-386.

Street, R. F. (1931). "A Gestalt Completion Test". *Contributions to Education, No. 481.* Bureau of Publication, Teachers College, Columbia University, New York.

Strzemiński, W. (1974). *Teoria Widzenia.* Wydawnictwo Literackie, Kraków.

Sze, M. M. (1957). *The Tai Painting.* New York.

ten Doesschate, G. (1951). "On imaginary space and paintings". *Opthamologica, 122,* 46 - 50.

ten Doesschate, G. (1964). *Perspective, Fundamentals, Controversials, History.* B. De Graaf, Nieuwkoop.

ten Doesschate, G. and Kylstra, J. (1955). "The perception of parallels". *Aeromedica, 4,* 115 - 119.

Teuber, M. L. (1974). "Sources of ambiguity in the prints of Mauritius C. Escher". *Scientific American, 231,* 90 - 104.

Teuber, M. L. (1976). "Blue Night by Paul Klee". *In* Henle, M. (Ed.) *Vision and Artifact.* Springer, New York.

Thouless, R. H. (1932). "A racial difference in perception". *Journal of Social Psychology, 4,* 330 - 339.

Tobias, P. R. (1978). (Ed.) *The Bushmen.* Human & Roussean, Cape Town.

Tongue, M. H. (1909). *Bushmen Paintings.* Clarendon Press, Oxford.

Topper, D. R. (1983). "Art in the realist ontology of J. J. Gibson". *Synthese, 54,* 71 - 83.

Topper, D. R. & Simpson W. A., (1981) "Depth Perception in Linear and Inverse Perspective Pictures". *Perception, 10,* 305 - 312.

Trevor-Roper, P. D. (1975). "The influence of eye disease on pictorial art". *Proceedings of the Royal Society of Medicine, 54,* 721 - 744.

Trevor-Roper, P. D. (1970). *The World through Blunted Sight.* Thames and Hudson, London.

Ucko, P. J. and Rosenfeldt, A. (1967). *Paleolithic Cave Art.* Weidenfeld and Nicolson, London.

Vasari, G. (1550, many subsequent editions). *Lives of most excellent Painters, Sculptors and Architects.*

Vitz, P. C. (1979). "Visual science and Modernist art: Historical parallels". *In* Nodine, C. F. and Fisher, D. F. Eds. *Perception and Pictorial Representation.* Praeger, New York.

Vitz, P. C. and Glimcher, A. B. (1984). *Modern Art and Modern Science, The Parallel Analysis of Vision.* Praeger, New York.

Wade, N. J. (1978). "Op art and visual perception". *Perception, 7,* 21 - 46.

Wade, N. (1982). *The Art and Science of Visual Illusions.* Routledge and Kegan Paul, London.

Wade, N. (1990). *Visual Allusions: Pictures of Perception.* Lawrence Erlbaum, London.

Wallach, H. (1976). "The apparent rotation of pictorial scenes". *In* Henle, M. (Ed.) *Vision and Artifact.* Springer, New York.

Wallach, H. and Zuckerman, C. (1963). "The constancy of stereoscopic depth". *American Journal of Psychology, 76,* 404-412.

Ward, J. L. (1979). "A piece of action. Moving figures in still pictures". *In* Nodine, C. F. and Fisher, D. F. (Eds.) *Perception and Pictorial Representation.* Praeger, New York.

Wartofsky, M. W. (1972). "Pictures, representation and the understanding". *In* Rudner, R. and Scheffer, I. (Eds.) *Logic in Art.* Bobbs-Merrill, Indianapolis.

Wartofsky, M. W. (1979). "Picturing and representing". *In* Nodine C. F. and Fisher, D. F. (Eds.) *Perception and Pictorial Representation.* Praeger, New York.

Wartofsky, M. W. (1980). "Visual scenarios: The role of representation in visual perception". *In* Hagen M. A. (Ed.) *The Perception of Pictures, Vol. II.* Academic Press, New York.

Weale, R. A. (1972). "The death of pointilism". *The Listener, 85,* 273 - 74.

Weale, R. A. (1976). "Trompe l'oeil to rompe l'oeil: Vision and art". *In* Bothwell, D. R. (Ed.) *Beyond Aesthetics.* Thames and Hudson, London.

Weale, R. A. (1979). "Discoverers of Mach bands". *Investigative Opthalmology and Visual Science, 18,* 652 - 654.

Welford, A. T. (1968). *Fundamental of Skills.* Methuen, London.

Wheatstone, C. (1852). "On some remarkable, and hitherto unobserved phenomena of binocular vision". *Philosophical Magazine Series, 4,* 504-523.

White, J. (1956). *Perspective in Ancient Drawing and Painting.* Society for Promotion of Hellenic Studies, London.

White, J. (1957). *Birth and Rebirth of Pictorial Space.* Faber, London.

With, A. (1968). "Patologia oculare e arti figurativi". *Atti de la fondazione Giorgio Ronchi, 23,* 445 - 466.

Wolfflin, H. (1899/1952) *Classic Art.* Phaidon Press, London.

Wolfflin, H. (1956) *Principles of Art History : The Problem of the Development of Style in Later Art.* Dover, New York.

Woodehouse, M. C. (1978). *Rock Art.* Prunnell, Cape Town.

Woodehouse, M. C. (1979). *The Bushman Art of Southern Africa.* Prunell, Cape Town.

Wollaston, W. H. (1824). "On apparent direction of the eyes in a portrait". *Philosophical Transactions of the Royal Society,* London, 247 - 259.

Wyburn, G. M., Pickford, R. W. and Hirst, R. J. (1967). *Human Senses and Perception.* Oliver and Boyd, Edinburgh.

Yarbus, A. L. (1967). *Eye Movements in Vision.* Plenum Press, New York.

Yonas, A. (1979). "Attached and cast shadows". *In* Nodine C. F. and Fisher, D. F. (Eds). *Perception and Pictorial Representation.* Praeger, New York.

Zajac, J. L. (1961). "Studies in perspective". *British Journal of Psychology, 52,* 333 - 340.

Author Index

Subject Index

Deuxième édition revue et augmentée

ISBN : 2-200-21576-2

Armand Colin Éditeur, 103, boulevard Saint-Michel - 75240 Paris Cedex 05

Charles-Robert Ageron

La décolonisation française

DU MÊME AUTEUR

Les Algériens musulmans et la France (1871-1919), 2 vol., 1298 p., Paris, 1968, P.U.F., (Publications de la Faculté des Lettres de Paris-Sorbonne t. 44 et 45).

Politiques coloniales au Maghreb, Paris, 1973, P.U.F., 291 p.

L'Anticolonialisme en France de 1871 à 1914, Paris, 1973, P.U.F.

France coloniale ou parti colonial? Paris, 1978, P.U.F., 302 p.

Histoire de l'Algérie contemporaine (1871-1954), tome II : *De l'insurrection de 1871 au déclenchement de la guerre de libération*, 643 p., P.U.F., 1979.

«L'Algérie algérienne» de Napoléon III à De Gaulle, 264 p., Paris, Sindbad, 1980.

Histoire de la France coloniale, t. II (1914-1990), pp. 309-570, Armand Colin, 1990.

Modern Algeria, C. Hurst & Company, London, 1991.

Histoire de l'Algérie contemporaine (1830-1994), «Que sais-je?», 128 p., P.U.F., 1994.

Introduction

Le mot décolonisation, qui signifie actuellement le processus par lequel une colonie devient indépendante ou la cessation pour un pays de l'état de colonie, n'est couramment employé en français que depuis 1952. Il l'avait été pourtant dès 1836 sous la plume d'un journaliste du *Mémorial bordelais*, Henri Fonfrède, dans un manifeste intitulé « Décolonisation d'Alger », qui invitait le gouvernement à abandonner la Régence d'Alger. Le mot et ses dérivés (décolonisés, décolonisateur) eurent un certain succès puisqu'ils figurent dans un dictionnaire des néologismes, *L'enrichissement de la langue française* (1845), dû à J.B. Richard de Radonvilliers. Ces mots nouveaux tombèrent ensuite dans l'oubli pendant la période des conquêtes coloniales. Même les économistes libéraux qui inventèrent l'expression péjorative de colonialisme en 1898, ne pensèrent pas à les utiliser. Ce fut, semble-t-il, un « anticolonialiste » marxiste Manabendra Nath Roy qui le premier le relança dans son livre *The Future of Indian politics* (Londres, 1927). Au vrai il désignait sous le nom de *decolonization* une politique : l'ensemble des concessions faites par les classes dirigeantes anglaises à la « bourgeoisie nationale » indienne pour permettre au capitalisme britannique de poursuivre son action. Cette théorie, qui sera plus tard reprise sous le nom de néocolonialisme, fut alors condamnée par les doctrinaires marxistes puisque Lénine avait seulement justifié une alliance tactique du prolétariat avec la « bourgeoisie révolutionnaire ». Quoi qu'il en soit, le mot de décolonisation utilisé désormais en allemand (*die Entkolonisierung*) et en anglais (*Decolonization*) servit à désigner, aussi bien la libération des colonies de peuplement européen dans les Amériques de 1778 à 1825 que celle que revendiquaient par exemple les nationalistes des Indes britanniques. On remarquera enfin que décolonisation acquit en Europe un droit d'usage au moment où les mots de colonies et coloniaux commençaient à être remplacés par ceux de « territoires d'Outre-Mer » (et ce jusque dans la constitution néerlandaise de 1922 ou en France dans le nom de l'École coloniale devenue École de la France d'Outre-Mer en 1931).

La décolonisation française est tout entière postérieure à la Deuxième Guerre mondiale. Elle ne s'explique pourtant pas seulement comme la conséquence directe et immédiate de ce conflit. S'il est de tradition de placer la période d'apogée de l'Empire colonial français en 1931, on montrera que les forces de dissociation de ce vaste empire étaient à l'œuvre, au moins depuis le premier conflit mondial. Les premiers signes avant-coureurs du « réveil » des peuples colonisés apparaissent même dès les premières années du XXe siècle (1908 en Indochine). Les insurrections locales des années 1914 à 1918 (en AOF et en Algérie notamment), la guerre du Rif ou celle des Druzes peuvent aussi s'analyser comme les prodromes des guerres d'indépendance nationales des peuples colonisés. Quant à l'action des forces de dissociation extérieures, américaines et soviétiques, elle est également sensible dès les années 1918 à 1920 au moment où la Société des Nations avec l'institution des mandats coloniaux accréditait, un peu malgré elle, l'idée d'un droit de regard international sur la gestion des colonies.

En France, pourtant, l'opinion ralliée à l'idée coloniale ne fut guère sensible aux premiers craquements de l'Empire et la bonne conscience l'emporta facilement, malgré le réveil de l'anticolonialisme d'extrême gauche. Pour les Français, l'ensemble de leurs possessions (colonies, protectorats, mandats de la S.D.N.) apparaissait désormais comme constituant un empire, le 2ᵉ du monde après celui des Britanniques. On parlait même, à la veille de la Deuxième Guerre mondiale, de «l'Empire», un empire colonial de 12 356 636 km^2 peuplé d'environ 67 800 000 habitants; mais pour certains l'Empire c'était «la France de 110 millions d'habitants», la «Grande France». Qui aurait osé envisager la décolonisation de cet Empire dont les Français attendaient surtout qu'il assurât la défense d'une France menacée?

Décolonisation de l'Afrique française

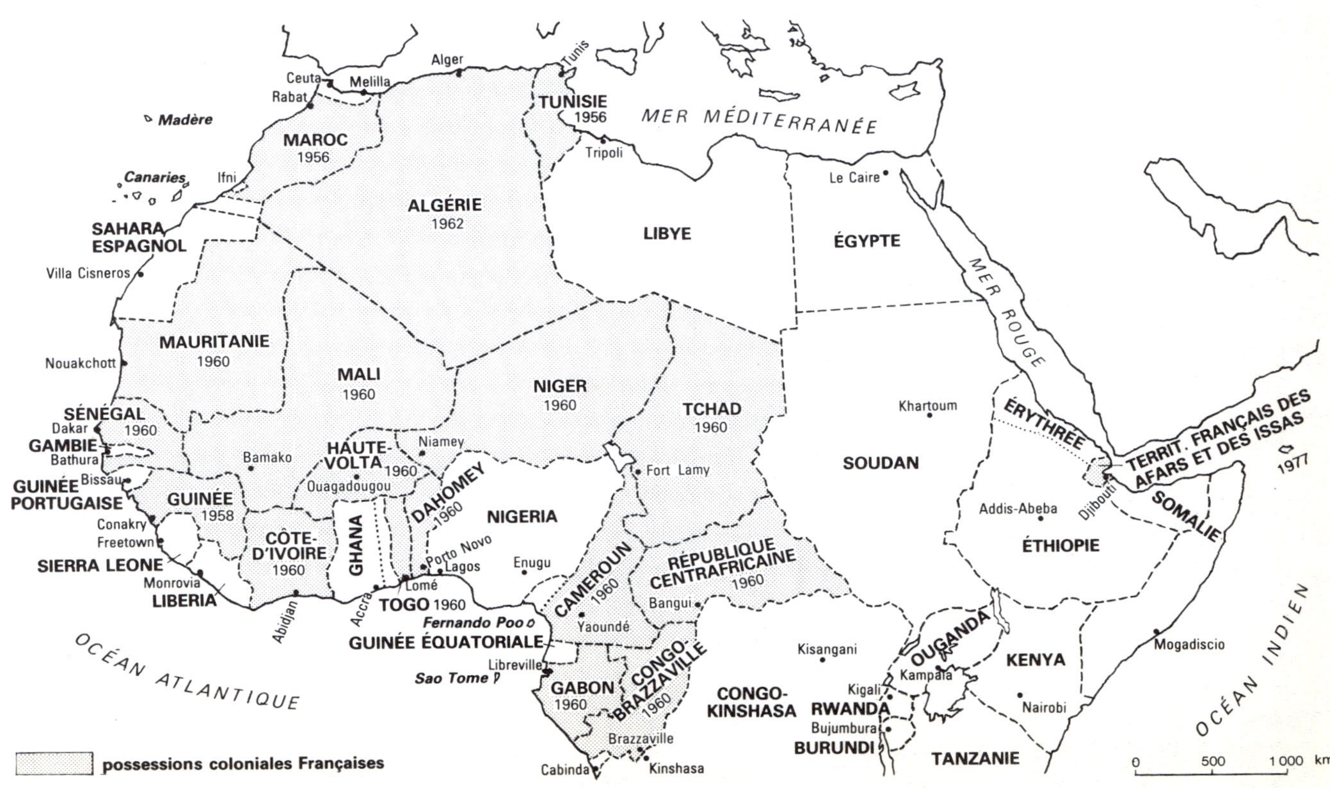

1 Les prodromes de la décolonisation française

L'INFLUENCE DE WILSON ET LE RÔLE DE LA SOCIÉTÉ DES NATIONS

LE WILSONISME

Les prises de position anticoloniales du président américain Woodrow Wilson à l'issue de la Première Guerre mondiale devaient faire lever bien des espoirs chez les peuples colonisés. Ce professeur de droit, presbytérien idéaliste et fervent démocrate, affirmait dans ses discours du 27 mai 1916 et du 22 janvier 1917, «qu'aucun peuple ne peut être contraint de vivre sous une souveraineté qu'il répudie». Il croyait à la nécessité d'accorder à chaque peuple, quel que fût son développement, le droit de déterminer seul son destin, de s'administrer et de se gouverner librement. Son hostilité radicale aux pratiques de l'impérialisme et aux régimes de domination coloniale explique qu'il étendait aux peuples colonisés le principe de l'autodétermination (*self-determination*) jusque-là conçu pour les seules populations européennes. C'est pourtant avec une rare précaution de langage qu'il énonça le 5e des XIV points de son programme de paix, le 9 janvier 1918. Il y préconisait : «Un arrangement librement débattu dans un esprit large et absolument impartial de toutes les revendications coloniales, fondé sur la stricte observance du principe que dans le règlement des questions de souveraineté, les intérêts des populations concernées pèseront d'un poids égal aux revendications équitables du gouvernement dont le titre sera à définir». En clair, les exigences de territoires coloniaux formulées par les vainqueurs ne devaient pas avoir plus d'importance que les intérêts des peuples colonisés. Cela revenait à suggérer, avec prudence, que ces peuples devraient avoir droit à s'exprimer, voire à s'autodéterminer. C'est ainsi, du moins, que ce 5e point fut compris et interprété.

Wilson ne put faire prédominer ses idées à la conférence de la Paix en 1919 face aux revendications coloniales formulées par les Alliés. L'Allemagne dut céder ses colonies et ses zones d'influence économique aux puissances victorieuses, sans que les intérêts et les vœux des populations de ces territoires aient été recueillis et pris en compte. Du moins, Wilson fit-il accepter à la conférence de la Paix, le principe nouveau des mandats coloniaux de la Société des Nations.

Est-ce à dire que les théories wilsoniennes restèrent inconnues des colonisés? Tout au contraire, ces idées, et spécialement le principe de *self-determination*, furent immédiatement connus et salués outre-mer. Même dans les colonies françaises, politiquement moins évoluées que les colonies britanniques, on perçoit les échos du wilsonisme. Dès avril 1918, la *Revue du Maghreb*, animée à Lausanne par des Tunisiens exilés, proclame ce droit à l'autodétermination : «un référendum des populations déterminera leur sort futur». Ces mêmes personnages adressèrent au président américain et au «congrès de la Paix» un mémoire qui affirmait : «Le peuple algéro-tunisien revendique son indépendance complète. Il en appelle à la conscience universelle pour lui (faire?) reconnaître son droit à disposer librement de son sort, et saisit de ses revendications légitimes le congrès de la Paix pour remanier la carte du monde et formuler des principes nouveaux pour la garantie des droits de l'homme et des peuples». En avril 1919, le nouveau «parti tunisien» adressa de Tunis au président Wilson une pétition tendant à faire bénéficier les Tunisiens de l'application de ces principes.

D'Indochine, où des troubles révolutionnaires localisés n'avaient pas cessé de 1916 jusqu'en 1919, ne parvinrent que peu de voix. Pourtant le futur Hô Chi Minh adressait, au début de 1919, une requête écrite exposant les revendications du peuple annamite «en attendant que le principe des nationalités passe du domaine de l'idéal à celui de la réalité, par la reconnaissance effective du droit sacré pour les peuples de disposer d'eux-mêmes».

Plus surprenante fut la démarche de certains Jeunes Algériens qui se disaient ralliés à une politique d'assimilation. L'un d'entre eux, un descendant d'Abd-el-Kader, le capitaine Khaled n'hésita pas à faire remettre au président Wilson, le 23 mai 1919, une requête dans laquelle il disait notamment : «Nous venons, au nom de nos compatriotes, faire appel aux nobles sentiments de l'honorable Président de la Libre Amérique. Nous demandons l'envoi de délégués choisis librement par nous pour décider de notre sort futur, sous l'égide de la *Société des Nations*. Vos quatorze conditions de paix mondiale acceptées par les Alliés et les Puissances centrales doivent servir de base à l'affranchissement de tous les petits peuples opprimés, sans distinction de race ni de religion.» On a récemment prétendu que l'émir Khaled, petit-fils d'Abd-el-Kader, ne mesurait pas la portée indépendantiste de sa revendication. Mais les Français et les Algériens, qui la connurent à l'époque, ne doutèrent pas que «fasciné par les principes wilsoniens» l'émir ait rédigé une requête «en faveur de l'indépendance». Aussi bien, éclairée sur ses intentions, l'Administration française n'eut de cesse de le contraindre à l'exil.

En Syrie, les nationalistes et le chérif Housayn réussirent à convaincre le président Wilson du droit des Arabes à constituer un royaume indépendant. À leur demande, Wilson persuada le conseil des Quatre de la nécessité d'envoyer une commission d'enquête composée de deux professeurs américains : H.C. King et C.R. Crane. Celle-ci se prononça pour la création de cet État arabe. Mais Wilson étant tombé malade, le rapport de cette commission américaine n'eut aucune influence sur le sort de la Syrie.

Les idées wilsoniennes avaient, en revanche, imposé la création d'une association de nations, fondée sur le droit des peuples à disposer d'eux-mêmes, la Société des Nations. Or la SDN allait se voir chargée de régler une partie des questions coloniales par le système des mandats.

LA SOCIÉTÉ DES NATIONS ET LES MANDATS

Il est assez singulier qu'on trouve l'origine des mandats dans un livre qui a eu l'étonnant privilège d'inspirer, à la fois, Lénine et Wilson : *Imperialism, a study* (1902) dû à un libéral anglais J. Hobson. Cet économiste pensait que l'administration des colonies, ces contrées sous-développées, ne pouvait pas être abandonnée à des nations impérialistes. Cette «mission sacrée» devait être dénationalisée et internationalisée. Un organisme international représentatif de la civilisation confierait cette tâche par mandats à des tuteurs conscients de leurs responsabilités. Ainsi serait mis fin aux guerres impérialistes et à l'exploitation des indigènes. Cette doctrine, plusieurs fois précisée par J. Hobson, enthousiasma les milieux pacifistes et le *Labour Party*. Elle séduisit aussi le président Wilson, tandis que Lénine n'en retint que les dénonciations de l'impérialisme.

Lors de la conférence de la Paix, Wilson expliqua que les colonies allemandes occupées par les armées alliées et les territoires non turcs de l'Empire ottoman devraient être confiés à l'administration d'un organisme international, la SDN. Devant le refus des Français et des Britanniques soutenus par leurs dominions, Wilson se rallia à la solution pratique suggérée, pour l'Europe, par le général sud-africain Smuts, dans un petit livre *The League of Nations* : la SDN chargerait un État particulier d'agir en son nom et pour son compte suivant les prescriptions d'une charte spéciale.

Le pacte de la SDN, du 25 avril 1919, qui proclamait la mission sacrée de la civilisation envers les peuples non encore capables de se diriger eux-mêmes, déclarait : «La meilleure méthode de réaliser pratiquement ce principe est de confier la tutelle de ces peuples aux nations développées qui, en raison de leurs ressources, de leur expérience et de leur position géographique, sont le mieux à même d'accepter cette responsabilité. Elles exerceraient cette tutelle en qualité de mandataires et au nom de la SDN.»

On distingua trois types de mandats :

les mandats A pour les communautés détachées de l'Empire ottoman furent remis à la France (Syrie et Liban) et à la Grande-Bretagne (Palestine, Transjordanie, Iraq). Ces mandats provisoires n'étaient valables que jusqu'à ce que ces communautés fussent capables de s'administrer et de se gouverner elles-mêmes;

les mandats B concernant les ex-colonies allemandes d'Afrique furent attribués à la France (Cameroun, Togo), à la Belgique (Ruanda, Burundi) et à la Grande-Bretagne (Cameroun du Nord-Ouest, Togo occidental et Tanganyka);

les mandats C appliqués aux territoires vides ou arriérés du Sud-Ouest africain (confiés à l'Union sud-africaine), aux territoires du Pacifique et aux archipels au Nord de l'Équateur (remis au Japon), aux îles du Sud-Pacifique et à la Nouvelle-Guinée orientale (accordées à l'Australie), à l'île de Samoa occidentale (remise à la Nouvelle-Zélande).

Dans tous les cas, le mandataire devait envoyer au conseil de la SDN, assisté d'une commission permanente des Mandats, un rapport annuel concernant les territoires dont il avait la charge. La Commission donnerait au Conseil son avis sur toutes les questions relatives à l'exécution des mandats.

Ce système du mandat, tenu par les Alliés comme un expédient propre à les sortir d'une impasse fâcheuse, était une institution juridiquement boiteuse : les traités de paix n'allaient pas attribuer les colonies allemandes ou les territoires arabes à la SDN, mais aux Alliés. Les Allemands y virent une «annexion pure et simple conformément à la répartition décidée par les principales puissances». Les Américains n'acceptèrent ce système que comme une mesure transitoire, susceptible d'être étendue dans l'avenir à tous les territoires dépendants et se montrèrent réticents vis-à-vis des attributions à la France du Togo et du Cameroun. Le gouvernement français ayant décidé de placer ces territoires sous l'autorité de commissaires français en 1921, les États-Unis protestèrent. Ils n'acceptèrent une reconnaissance implicite qu'après avoir obtenu la garantie de la liberté commerciale, le 13 février 1923.

La Commission permanente composée de dix membres, dont la majorité appartenait à des pays non mandataires, ne devait pas avoir un rôle décisif. Néanmoins, elle pouvait recevoir des pétitions indigènes et citer devant elle les hauts-commissaires des puissances mandataires; elle formulait des recommandations, voire des condamnations. La France ne fut nullement ménagée; la Commission la blâma pour la manière dont furent construites certaines voies ferrées du Cameroun avec 8000 travailleurs requis. Le SMOTIG (Service de la main-d'œuvre obligatoire pour les travaux d'intérêt général) instauré à Madagascar fut critiqué indirectement et l'affaire soumise au Bureau international du travail.

La Commission veilla à ce que la France n'étendît pas sa politique assimilationniste, en accordant par exemple à certains Togolais la nationalité française. Elle ne cessa de protester lorsque, pour des raisons d'économie budgétaire, le petit Togo fut, à partir de 1934 administré par des fonctionnaires coloniaux du Dahomey voisin.

L'inefficacité était certes le lot habituel des recommandations de la Commission genevoise, puisqu'elles étaient dépourvues de sanctions. Pourtant en élaborant les conditions requises pour la fin des mandats, en exigeant des futurs États indépendants la protection des minorités de race, de langue ou de religion et le respect de la liberté de conscience, la Commission posait des principes utiles. Elle fut considérée par les Syriens et les Camerounais comme une instance d'appel. Aussi longtemps que la SDN fut respectée, c'est-à-dire jusque vers 1930, les débats de Genève éveillèrent la curiosité internationale. En provoquant l'intervention des opinions publiques, ils ont eu incontestablement une influence sur la gestion des mandats et plus largement sur celle des colonies.

L'ACTION ANTICOLONIALE DU COMMUNISME DE 1919 À 1939

LA IIIe INTERNATIONALE CONTRE LA COLONISATION

Marx et Engels, malgré leurs critiques contre les politiques coloniales anglaise et française, n'ont jamais condamné le principe de l'expansion coloniale, dans la mesure du moins où celle-ci s'était révélée comme «un instrument inconscient de l'histoire». En détruisant les vieilles sociétés non européennes et en posant les fondements matériels de la société occidentale dans le monde, la colonisation facilitait les progrès du capitalisme et de la civilisation.

Pourtant, les partis socialistes d'inspiration marxiste n'en condamnèrent pas moins, avant 1914, les violences de la conquête et de la domination coloniale, ce qu'ils appelaient le colonialisme. Bien rares étaient les socialistes qui imaginaient l'émancipation des peuples colonisés et leur droit à disposer d'eux-mêmes. En général, les théoriciens professaient que la révolution sociale qu'accomplirait le prolétariat européen libérerait l'humanité tout entière.

Cette espérance messianique fut d'abord fermement réaffirmée par l'Internationale communiste ou IIIe Internationale. Fondée le 2 mars 1919, elle expliquait dès le 5 mars que «les ouvriers et les paysans des colonies ou semi-colonies européennes ne pourront jouir d'une existence indépendante que le jour où les ouvriers d'Angleterre et de France prendraient le pouvoir». Mais ayant mesuré la force révolutionnaire que constituaient dans l'empire tzariste, «cette prison des peuples», les revendications des populations opprimées par le peuple grand-russe, Lénine leur avait promis «le droit effectif de disposer d'elles-mêmes». Devant l'échec des partis ouvriers européens, Lénine pensa que la Révolution devait partir des peuples colonisés. Il eut l'idée de lier leur potentiel révolutionnaire à l'action du prolétariat organisé par les bolcheviks et lança dès lors les mots d'ordre selon lesquels «le prolétariat de la nation dominante doit revendiquer la liberté de séparation politique pour les colonies et les peuples opprimés par sa nation.»

Ainsi, d'une tactique révolutionnaire propre à la situation russe, Lénine fit une stratégie valable pour l'ensemble des nations coloniales. Demander l'indépendance des colonies, c'était avant tout une stratégie à long terme, destinée à tuer le monde capitaliste avancé. Lénine estimait notamment que l'Europe ne pourrait survivre à la perte de ses dominations coloniales, terres d'exploitation et marchés exclusifs; privée de ses pilotis coloniaux, l'Europe capitaliste s'effondrerait, les ouvriers dépossédés des bénéfices indirects de la plus-value coloniale s'appauvriraient et se révolteraient.

L'Internationale communiste approuva en juillet 1920 ces nouvelles *Thèses sur les questions nationale et coloniale* : «La suppression par la révolution prolétarienne de la puissance coloniale de l'Europe renversera le capitalisme européen. La révolution prolétarienne et la révolution des colonies doivent concourir dans une certaine mesure à l'issue victorieuse.» En conséquence, parmi les 21 conditions fixées pour l'admission à la IIIe Internationale, la condition n° 8 précisa avec netteté : «Tout parti appartenant à la Troisième Internationale a pour devoir de dévoiler impitoyablement les "prouesses" de "ses" impérialistes aux colonies; de soutenir, non en paroles mais en fait, tout mouvement d'émancipation dans les colonies, d'exiger l'expulsion des colonies des impérialistes de la métropole, de nourrir au cœur des travailleurs du pays des sentiments véritablement fraternels vis-à-vis de la population laborieuse des colonies et des nationalités opprimées et d'entretenir parmi les troupes de la métropole une agitation continue contre toute oppression des peuples coloniaux.»

L'Internationale fixa également la tactique à suivre : les partis communistes devaient combattre aux colonies le mouvement bourgeois démocratique nationaliste, même s'il demandait l'indépendance politique; ils devaient également lutter contre les missionnaires chrétiens, contre l'islam et le panislamisme, contre le panasiatisme. Certes la Révolution dans les colonies ne pouvait pas être, dans son premier stade, une révolution communiste, mais la direction du mouvement révolutionnaire devait appartenir aux communistes. Cette tactique devait être modulée par l'exécutif du *Komintern*, qui autorisa ou non des relations temporaires avec les «démocrates-bourgeois» des colonies, en fondant ses analyses sur la situation d'un petit nombre de pays : l'Inde, la Chine, l'Égypte. Mais le *Komintern* lança aussi des appels retentissants, par exemple«pour la libération de l'Algérie et de la Tunisie», le 20 mai 1922. Cet appel de l'Internationale fut d'ailleurs considéré comme une erreur par les communistes français d'Afrique du Nord. Ceux-ci assurèrent qu'«un soulèvement victorieux des masses musulmanes d'Algérie qui ne serait pas postérieur à un soulèvement victorieux des masses prolétariennes de la métropole amènerait fatalement en Algérie un retour vers un régime voisin de la féodalité», et dénoncèrent la bourgeoisie musulmane «support du nationalisme héréditaire profondément enraciné». L'Internationale choquée exigea l'exclusion de ces «esclavagistes coloniaux» d'Algérie, ces «survivances social-impérialistes».

Un autre appel «contre l'impérialisme français et pour l'indépendance de la Syrie» fut formulé le 11 mai 1924 par l'Internationale sans soulever beaucoup d'écho en France. Précisément, au 5e Congrès de l'Internationale en juin 1924, un délégué «indochinois» Nguyên Ai Quôc, le futur Hô Chi Minh, bien que membre du parti communiste français, s'en prit avec vivacité à son parti qui négligeait la propagande révolutionnaire aux colonies et ne comprenait rien à la stratégie léniniste. Le délégué soviétique D. Manuilsky partageait son opinion et donna le mot d'ordre suivant : «La France doit lâcher ses colonies», ce qui fut traduit en français : «La France devrait reconnaître publiquement le droit de ses colonies à faire sécession.» Les communistes français s'y attachèrent, dans les années suivantes, sans d'ailleurs donner satisfaction aux exigences du *Komintern* (cf. le texte «L'anticolonialisme des communistes», p. 19).

C'est ainsi qu'au 6e Congrès de l'Internationale en août 1928, il fut notamment prescrit au P.C.F. d'intensifier sa propagande dans les troupes coloniales et auprès des travailleurs coloniaux résidant en France. On lui réclamait simultanément un appui plus résolu au mouvement révolutionnaire dans les colonies et aux peuples insurgés, car «les pays coloniaux étaient devenus le secteur faible du front impérialiste». Accessoirement le Congrès discuta du problème de la «décolonisation». S'interrogeant sur le fait de savoir si un développement économique et l'apparition d'une bourgeoisie indigène pouvaient entraîner une émancipation progressive des peuples colonisés, le Congrès conclut que cette hypothèse était illusoire et que la révolution prolétarienne restait indispensable. C'est pourquoi l'Internationale, tirant surtout la conclusion de l'échec du parti communiste chinois, ordonna de renoncer à la tactique d'alliance avec les bourgeoisies nationales. Les communistes devaient dénoncer «le national-réformisme» des bourgeoisies coloniales et attaquer furieusement «les gredins de la IIe Internationale», c'est-à-dire les socialistes. Moscou resta fidèle à cette tactique sectaire jusqu'en 1934.

Au 7e Congrès, en 1935, l'Internationale communiste, eu égard à la situation internationale et à la menace hitlérienne, décida de changer de ligne politique et de recourir à la tactique du Front populaire. Il fallait, en Europe, tendre la main à tous les démocrates radicaux ou socialistes et sur le plan colonial à tous les réformistes de la «bourgeoisie conciliatrice», de manière à constituer «le Front populaire anti-impérialiste». Derrière le jargon des formules, il fallait surtout comprendre que la lutte prioritaire des partis communistes n'était plus dirigée contre le colonialisme, mais contre le fascisme.

Dès lors, les mots d'ordre d'indépendance des colonies, d'expulsion des impérialistes et de libération nationale s'amenuisèrent. Pour les colonisés, le droit au divorce subsistait, mais il ne signifiait pas l'obligation de divorcer (cf. le texte de Maurice Thorez du 25 décembre 1937, p. 21). La France du Front populaire retrouvait désormais une mission de progrès et de civilisation et les peuples coloniaux avaient donc un intérêt à rester unis au peuple de France «dans une union libre, confiante et fraternelle». Cette nouvelle ligne, qui se mit lentement en place, troubla beaucoup de communistes chez les peuples colonisés, qui y virent un retour à l'idéologie coloniale; mais elle devait être interrompue pendant la période du rapprochement germano-soviétique. Ces volte-face de la stratégie politique du *Komintern* ne furent pas toutes, il est vrai, ressenties par les contemporains. Elles ne doivent surtout pas entraîner une sous-estimation de la continuité de la propagande anticoloniale du *Komintern*. Celui-ci disposait d'une imposante organisation, d'un appareil de presse considérable et d'instructeurs spécialisés. Certes la mise en œuvre des mots d'ordre dans les colonies françaises relevaient du P.C.F., et les organisations communistes coloniales n'étaient considérées que comme des sections du parti français.

Cependant l'Internationale faisait aussi agir diverses organisations satellites. Ainsi l'agitation parmi les travailleurs coloniaux installés en France fut d'abord confiée à *l'Union inter-coloniale, Association des originaires de toutes les colonies*, puis à divers groupements spécialisés comme *l'Étoile nord-africaine* ou *La Ligue de défense de la race nègre*. Pour développer la propagande anticoloniale auprès de l'opinion européenne fut constituée *La Ligue anti-impérialiste*. À la suite de son congrès international de Bruxelles en 1927, elle donna naissance à une Ligue française «contre l'impérialisme et l'oppression coloniale», qui établit des relations directes avec certaines colonies : l'Algérie et Madagascar, ainsi qu'avec la Syrie. Elle se montra fort active, organisant en 1931 une contre-Exposition coloniale, l'Exposition anti-impérialiste. Elle changea de nom et de programme en 1935 en devenant *l'Association pour la défense et l'émancipation des peuples colonisés*.

Bien d'autres organisations communistes tels le *Secours ouvrier international*, ou *Secours rouge international*, *l'Internationale syndicale rouge*, *l'Internationale des travailleurs de l'enseignement*, *l'Internationale communiste des jeunes*, intervinrent aussi à l'occasion dans les questions coloniales françaises. Mais les activités essentielles, notamment l'édition des journaux communistes spécialisés et des bulletins de propagande anticoloniale, étaient assurés par le P.C.F.

L'ACTION DU COMMUNISME DANS LES COLONIES FRANÇAISES DE 1919 À 1939

De sa fondation jusqu'à la fin de l'année 1935, l'Internationale communiste ou *Komintern* demeura fidèle à sa condamnation absolue du système colonial et de «l'impérialisme». Pour elle les colonies ne paraissaient exister que comme terrains de «luttes anti-impérialistes»; d'où le soutien presque inconditionnel qu'elle entendait apporter aux nationalistes qui osaient s'affirmer dans les pays colonisés. Il semble que la situation des colonies françaises ait particulièrement retenu l'attention du *Komintern* et de la section française de l'Internationale communiste : le parti communiste ou S.F.I.C.

Ce parti, tout en s'adressant surtout aux prolétaires français, dut appuyer les «nationalistes» en Afrique du Nord; il tenta même de présenter comme tels tous les critiques du régime français et de les rallier à ses idées. C'est ainsi qu'après avoir longtemps attaqué le principal opposant politique algérien, l'émir Khaled, qu'il traitait de féodal ou de bourgeois, le P.C.F. tenta de le récupérer lorsqu'il se fut exilé d'Algérie. Il lui organisa des conférences publiques à Paris, le célébra dans sa presse comme un champion du nationalisme algérien et le présenta même à des élections locales en Algérie, alors qu'il y était inéligible. L'émir Khaled devint aussi le président d'honneur de la première *Étoile nord-africaine* fondée à Paris en 1926 à l'instigation des communistes. Et l'Étoile reprit pour titre de son journal *l'Ikdam nord-africain* celui de l'hebdomadaire disparu de Khaled.

Les communistes soutinrent de la même manière les nationalistes tunisiens du *Destour*; ils participèrent à la fondation en 1924 de la C.G.T.T. (confédération générale du travail tunisienne), déclenchèrent des grèves et manifestations politiques. Le parti communiste tunisien fut l'objet de poursuites et trois de ses dirigeants furent condamnés. Pour le P.C.F. «la France n'avait qu'un droit en Tunisie, celui de s'en aller!».

Vis-à-vis de Ben 'Abd-el-Krîm les communistes hésitèrent. Au début, le *Komintern* ne le soutint pas, car il croyait que le mouvement rifain était fomenté contre l'Espagne par la France. Avec les succès et les progrès de la République du Rif, leur point de vue changea. Dès le 24 septembre 1924 le comité directeur du P.C.F. adressait un télégramme de félicitations à Ben 'Abd-el-Krîm, qui se terminait ainsi : «Vive l'indépendance du Maroc!» C'est alors que les communistes proclamèrent publiquement, par la voix de Jacques Doriot, leur doctrine anticolonialiste : «Vous avez dans vos colonies 54 millions d'hommes que vous opprimez et que vous exploitez de la façon la plus odieuse. Je dis au nom du parti communiste tout entier, que ces peuples ont droit à leur indépendance et qu'ils ont le droit de la conquérir par les armes» (Chambre des députés, 2e séance du 23 août 1924). Et Jacques Doriot de préciser à la Chambre le 23 juin 1925 : «Dès qu'ils arriveront au pouvoir, les communistes dirigeront leur dictature contre la bourgeoisie; ils proclameront l'indépendance complète des colonies et ils laisseront aux indigènes de la Tunisie, de l'Algérie, du Maroc, de Madagascar et d'ailleurs le droit de se donner la forme gouvernementale qui leur convient».

Dès que les hostilités furent ouvertes, en avril 1925, les communistes se mobilisèrent contre la guerre du Rif. Leurs mots d'ordre s'appelaient : «Paix immédiate avec le Rif»; «Fraternisation des soldats français et rifains»; «Évacuation immédiate du Maroc». Dans l'histoire du P.C.F., cette campagne, soutenue par des manifestations, des réunions publiques et des grèves, fut tenue pour exemplaire. À l'époque, les Soviétiques félicitèrent les communistes français de leur lutte courageuse et efficace, avant de mesurer que le P.C.F. voyait ses effectifs diminuer et son audience baisser. Peut-être est-ce la raison pour laquelle, malgré les appels des communistes syriens, le P.C.F. se borna à un soutien de principe aux insurgés de la guerre des Druzes?

Il devait se montrer un peu plus actif entre 1929 et 1931 pour soutenir «les luttes du peuple indochinois contre la domination cruelle de l'impérialisme français». Il fit l'éloge des insurgés de Yên-Bay (février 1930), les saluant comme «les héroïques représentants d'une grande révolution anti-impérialiste et agraire», ce qu'ils n'étaient pas. Mais en présentant l'action de patriotes annamites, même sans contact avec les groupes communistes, comme une manifestation du bolchevisme, ils firent surtout le jeu de ceux qui voyaient, à tort, «la main de Moscou» derrière tous les mouvements nationalistes et toutes les manifestations paysannes. En Indochine s'unifia cependant un parti communiste indochinois, reconnu en 1931 comme section nationale de l'Internationale communiste. Mais les cadres en furent décimés par une vive répression menée par la Sûreté indochinoise.

Dans les années 1928-1935 les communistes français ou indigènes s'attaquaient, sans cesse, non seulement aux féodaux et aux bourgeoisies réactionnaires, mais aussi à ceux qu'ils appelaient, par exemple en Algérie, les «national-réformistes». Ils les accusaient de collaborer avec l'administration coloniale. À les en croire, les Destouriens de Tunisie avaient même cessé d'être un parti national-réformiste et s'étaient «transformés en agence de l'impérialisme». Il en allait de même pour la fédération des élus musulmans d'Algérie qu'ils croyaient manœuvrée par des organisations libérales comme le *Comité d'action franco-musulman* ou par des socialistes aimablement qualifiés de «social-fascistes» ou de «gredins de la IIe Internationale». En attaquant de plus l'Islam et les *'ulamâ'* (savants musulmans), les communistes se virent dénoncés par les hommes de religion, qui stigmatisaient «le communisme maudit». Aussi le parti communiste avait-il presque disparu en Tunisie et ne comprenait-il en Algérie qu'un dixième d'adhérents musulmans.

Les communistes se bornèrent, en ce qui concernait les colonies françaises d'Afrique noire, à faire passer des manifestes et des journaux dont certains étaient édités par des Africains résidant en France, tels *la Dépêche africaine, la Race nègre, le Cri des nègres*, journaux épisodiques, ou *l'Ouvrier nègre*, organe de l'Internationale syndicale rouge. Quant au *Comité de défense de la race nègre*, ce n'était qu'une squelettique organisation dépendant de la Commission coloniale du P.C.F., au même titre que *la Ligue de défense de la race nègre* et que *l'Union des travailleurs nègres*, qui lui succédèrent. De 1935 à 1939 les «communistes nègres» privés de ressources furent condamnés au silence.

Après le tournant stratégique de 1935, le parti communiste français appliqua fidèlement la nouvelle ligne du *Komintern*. Puisqu'il fallait désormais se rapprocher des organisations et des personnalités nationalistes-réformistes, les communistes firent partout des ouvertures à ceux qu'ils assimilaient la veille à des «traîtres». Au nom du Front populaire, ils prêchèrent l'union indispensable entre «travailleurs indigènes et européens». Le nouveau parti communiste algérien rejoignit les élus et les *'ulamâ'* dans le *Congrès musulman*. Après avoir dénoncé le projet Viollette, d'esprit assimilationniste, les communistes en vantèrent les vertus démocratiques car, en accordant le droit de vote à quelque 20000 Algériens, il serait un premier pas vers le suffrage universel et l'éligibilité pour tous. La revendication indépendantiste fut progressivement gommée : «toute tentative en ce sens étant vouée à un échec certain jusqu'au jour où la France serait dirigée par un pouvoir communiste» (G. Monmousseau au 2e congrès du P.C.A.).

Face à la résurgence de la violence de la part des nationalistes tunisiens et marocains, en 1937 et 1938, les communistes répondaient désormais : «Il ne saurait y avoir de salut pour les peuples coloniaux, hors de l'union indispensable avec la démocratie française.» Ils condamnaient même les nationalistes musulmans du parti du peuple algérien en se proclamant internationalistes. Mais eux-mêmes en arrivaient à retrouver l'idéal assimilationniste français. Maurice Thorez vint à Alger affirmer que la nation algérienne de l'avenir intégrerait Arabes, Berbères, Juifs et colons français ou étrangers et se constituerait «dans le mélange de vingt races».

À Madagascar, des noyaux communistes furent mis en place à partir de 1930. En septembre 1936 fut fondé un *parti communiste de la région de Madagascar*, le P.C.R.M., qui fonctionna jusqu'à la fin de 1938. L'hérérogénéité de sa composition sociale et de sa direction ne lui permit pas d'avoir une ligne politique cohérente, mais il révéla des leaders comme Ralaimongo et Ravoahangy; ce dernier continua à défendre la thèse indépendantiste et fut ensuite, en 1960, ministre de la première République malgache.

En Indochine le parti communiste était un parti autochtone sur lequel l'influence du P.C.F. était faible. Il dépendait directement de l'Internationale et suivait, avec nuances, ses directives. Devenu parti légal en juin 1936 en Cochinchine, le P.C. indochinois tenta de mettre sur pied un Front commun démocratique «contre le fascisme japonais» et de préparer un congrès ouvert aux nationalistes. Cela provoqua leur rupture avec les trotskystes de Saigon. Cependant vis-à-vis du Front populaire qu'il déclarait souenir, le P.C.I. se montra plus réservé, refusant toute collaboration franco-annamite. Malgré d'incontestables progrès, le P.C.I. devait être détruit par la police française en 1939, à l'exclusion des dirigeants clandestins.

Si l'action du communisme international à destination des colonies françaises ne se relâcha pas dans toute la période de l'entre-deux-guerres, on ne saurait pourtant dire que le Parti communiste français apporta un intérêt primordial à la question coloniale. Sauf pendant la guerre du Rif, sa lutte contre le colonialisme demeura secondaire et se borna à une propagande abstraite, souvent inefficace. C'est pourquoi sans doute les nationalistes révolutionnaires des pays coloniaux, tentés par le communisme, ne tardèrent pas à reprocher au P.C.F. son aide conditionnelle et son attitude versatile. Celle-ci, il est vrai, lui était imposée par les diktats du *Komintern*, conformes aux seuls intérêts de l'URSS.

L'ANTICOLONIALISME DES COMMUNISTES EN 1929

Notre position fondamentale consiste à protester non seulement contre les annexions présentes et futures, mais également contre les annexions passées. Nous considérons comme parfaitement légitime que les peuples opprimés veuillent réviser ces annexions [...].

Ce mot d'ordre du droit des peuples à disposer d'eux-mêmes ne peut non plus être séparé de la signification qu'il prend dans l'époque actuelle. Aussi il n'est pas seulement une protestation contre les annexions, il est encore un mot d'ordre de ralliement servant à soulever le monde colonial contre l'impérialisme [...]. Nous cherchons à unir deux forces anti-impérialistes qui luttent actuellement pour la transformation du monde. Ces deux forces sont : le prolétariat révolutionnaire luttant dans les pays capitalistes pour le renversement de la bourgeoisie et l'ayant déjà renversée en URSS, et les peuples coloniaux luttant pour leur libération du joug impérialiste. La conjonction de ces deux forces doit, selon nous, changer le monde et substituer le socialisme au capitalisme.

Les peuples opprimés coloniaux ou demi-coloniaux sont une masse formidable. Sur 1 850 000 000 hommes que compte le monde, 1 250 millions sont dominés par les pays impérialistes. Sur ce nombre il n'en est guère qui ne luttent pour l'indépendance [...]. Certains ont déjà fait appel de leur sort à l'Histoire, les armes à la main, comme la Chine, le Maroc, la Syrie, l'Indonésie, la Corée. D'autres s'en sont tenus à des mouvements primaires de non-coopération, de non-participation, mouvements d'ailleurs en pleine transformation à cause de l'entrée en lutte des ouvriers vers les solutions plus radicales, comme les Indes, l'Égypte, la Tunisie. D'autres enfin élèvent, sous des formes différentes, des protestations plus ou moins énergiques, comme les Philippines, l'Indochine, l'Algérie. La forme varie, mais rares sont les colonies ou demi-colonies qui n'ont pas agi contre la domination étrangère. La guerre a produit un ébranlement profond de la domination impérialiste. La longévité de la révolution russe stimule tous ces mouvements.

Or c'est en vue de cette situation internationale originale que nous insistons tout particulièrement sur la question de l'indépendance des colonies [...]. Dans la mesure où ce milliard d'hommes lutte contre les pays capitalistes, les affaiblit, détruit un peu ou beaucoup de leur puissance dominatrice, il aide objectivement et sans contestation possible la lutte de la classe ouvrière pour le socialisme.

Les colonies ne peuvent pas espérer passer par un stade capitaliste indépendant car leur développement économique est toujours conditionné par l'impérialisme qui n'a pas en vue de faire des colonies des pays économiquement indépendants, mais bien d'user d'elles comme force d'appoint pour sa propre industrie [...]. L'exemple de l'Indochine est caractéristique à cet égard : on y assiste à un véritable pillage des ressources minérales de ce pays. Aucune idée chez les colonisateurs de développer économiquement l'Indochine. Une seule considération agit sur eux : extraire le charbon pour l'exporter.

Laisser les colonies sous la domination capitaliste, ce n'est pas favoriser leur évolution en pays capitalistes indépendants, c'est les vouer à être éternellement des annexes, des pays d'appoint pour les pays capitalistes devenus de plus en plus parasitaires.

Ainsi notre opposition à la colonisation, la proclamation du droit immédiat à l'indépendance des colonies n'apparaissent plus seulement comme commandées par l'intérêt des classes ouvrières européenne et américaine, mais aussi par l'intérêt historique des peuples coloniaux eux-mêmes.

Source : Jacques Doriot, *Les Colonies et le communisme*, Paris, 1929.

N.B. L'auteur était alors le principal animateur de la Commission coloniale du Parti communiste français. Il ne sera exclu que le 26 juin 1938.

LE PARTI COMMUNISTE ET LES PROBLÈMES COLONIAUX

(extrait du rapport de Maurice Thorez, secrétaire général du P.C.F. le 25 décembre 1937)

La revendication fondamentale de notre parti communiste concernant les peuples coloniaux reste la libre disposition, le droit à l'indépendance.

Rappelant une formule de Lénine, nous avons déjà dit aux camarades tunisiens, qui nous ont approuvés, que le droit au divorce ne signifiait pas l'obligation de divorcer. Si la question décisive du moment, c'est la lutte victorieuse contre le fascisme, l'intérêt des peuples coloniaux est dans leur union avec la France et non dans une attitude qui pourrait favoriser les entreprises du fascisme et placer par exemple l'Algérie, la Tunisie et le Maroc sous le joug de Mussolini, ou faire de l'Indochine une base d'opération pour le Japon militariste.

Créer les conditions de cette union libre confiante et fraternelle des peuples coloniaux avec notre peuple n'est-ce pas, là encore, travailler à remplir la mission de la France à travers le monde?

L'APPARITION DES NATIONALISMES DANS LES COLONIES ET LES TERRITOIRES DE SOUVERAINETÉ FRANÇAISE

LE NATIONALISME ARABE DANS LES ÉTATS DU LEVANT

Le nationalisme arabe est né au début du XXe siècle contre la domination ottomane et s'est affirmé dans divers clubs d'officiers et mouvements de jeunes. Bien loin d'être alors opposé à la France, il recherchait au contraire son appui. Il était particulièrement actif dans la bourgeoisie éclairée de Damas et de Beyrouth, ce qui explique que les diverses sociétés arabes de Paris aient suggéré à la France, peu avant 1914, d'intervenir en Syrie. Du côté français, à la suite des campagnes du *Comité de l'Asie française*, les gouvernements entendirent profiter de l'effondrement de l'Empire ottoman pour installer la France au Levant.

Aux termes des accords consécutifs aux traités de 1920 (conférence de San Remo, avril 1920; traité de Sèvres le 10 août 1920), la France reçut des Alliés un mandat sur la Syrie et le Liban. Ce mandat lui fut officiellement accordé par la Société des Nations le 24 juillet 1922. Il devait prendre fin du jour où ces États seraient aptes à se diriger eux-mêmes.

La France se présenta comme le mandataire désiré du Liban chrétien, qui demandait effectivement un protecteur. Mais elle fut mal accueillie en Syrie où les nationalistes arabes réclamaient l'indépendance. Pour lutter contre ce nationalisme, la France crut devoir jouer la politique des minorités : elle divisa le pays en entités politiques séparées, créant un État alaouite, un État druze à côté de l'État syrien. Simultanément, la France agrandit le Liban traditionnel avec des territoires syriens pour constituer le Grand Liban. Or les nationalistes arabes considéraient le Liban comme la façade maritime de la Syrie. Leur sentiment national syrien exaspéré les poussa dès lors à réclamer non seulement l'indépendance, mais l'unité.

C'est pour réaliser ce double objectif que la Syrie s'insurgea en 1925 et 1926, car ce que les Français appelèrent la guerre des Druzes fut en fait celle de tous les Syriens. Les armées françaises réprimèrent cette révolte sans réussir à éteindre le nationalisme syrien. Celui-ci, battu sur le terrain militaire, transporta la lutte sur le terrain de la non-coopération. Et lorsqu'en 1933 un gouvernement syrien modéré accepta de signer un traité d'alliance franco-syrien, les nationalistes le contraignirent à se retirer. Le traité fut déclaré caduc, parce qu'il reconnaissait l'autonomie des Druzes et des Alaouites.

Au début de 1936, les nationalistes déclenchèrent une vaste agitation qui contraignit la France à reprendre la négociation du traité. Le gouvernement français ayant reconnu le principe de l'unité syrienne, les nationalistes acceptèrent de venir négocier à Paris. Un traité franco-syrien fut signé le 9 septembre 1936, qui prévoyait la fin du mandat pour 1939 et le «maintien de troupes françaises au djebel Druze et aux Alaouites pour une durée de cinq années». La France renonçait en revanche au remboursement prévu par la SDN des dépenses engagées pendant le mandat «pour l'organisation de l'administration, le développement des ressources locales et l'exécution des travaux publics» soit 4743 millions de francs.

Un traité franco-libanais semblable fut signé à Beyrouth le 13 novembre 1936 : il prévoyait également l'indépendance totale après une période transitoire de trois ans et l'admission de la République libanaise à la SDN. Les négociateurs syriens furent portés en triomphe à leur retour; le gouvernement syrien organisa aussitôt des élections qui furent un succès éclatant pour le Bloc nationaliste.

En France, les partisans du régime mandataire (sociétés concessionnaires et fonctionnaires civils et militaires) dénoncèrent les dangers de ces traités et le gouvernement Léon Blum n'osa pas les faire venir à ratification. La classe politique protestait : «Allons-nous perdre la Syrie et le Liban à la veille d'une guerre mondiale où ces régimes pourraient servir de bases stratégiques?» Dès lors les gouvernements français successifs renoncèrent à faire ratifier ces traités. Le gouvernement syrien essaya bien de forcer la main à la France, notamment en créant des ambassadeurs, mais ses décisions furent annulées par le haut-commissaire de France. Le gouvernement syrien démissionna et le 8 juillet 1939 le président de la République syrienne se démit de ses fonctions. Au Liban, les clans étaient si antagonistes et les partis si nombreux que la puissance mandataire eut moins de peine à gouverner. Au total la France avait en

1939 réussi à tenir en échec le nationalisme arabe en aggravant le régime du mandat, mais elle s'était attiré la haine vigilante des nationalistes, plus sensibles à leur humiliation qu'aux progrès matériels de leurs pays.

LE NATIONALISME TUNISIEN

Les Tunisiens épris de modernisation et de progrès — ceux que les Français qualifièrent de Jeunes-Tunisiens par référence aux Jeunes-Turcs — s'étaient fait connaître sur le plan politique depuis les années 1905 à 1907. En 1908 le journal hebdomadaire de ce parti exprimait le désir que la Tunisie fût dotée à nouveau, comme en 1861, d'une constitution libérale (en arabe *Dustûr*) abolie en fait par le Protectorat. D'où le nom que devait prendre, le 15 juin 1920, le premier parti nationaliste : le parti libéral constitutionnel ou *Destour*. L'un de ses leaders 'Abd-el-Azîz Ta'albi avait fait connaître les vœux de ces patriotes tunisiens en publiant à Paris, sous l'anonymat, un ouvrage qui fit date, *la Tunisie martyre - Ses revendications*. Le but poursuivi par Ta'albi et ses amis n'était pas différent de celui des Tunisiens qui s'étaient exprimés dans l'exil : l'indépendance de la Tunisie (cf. encadré : Aux origines du nationalisme tunisien).

Le Destour réclamait un régime constitutionnel : une assemblée élue par les seuls Tunisiens avec un gouvernement responsable devant celle-ci. En 1922 les destouriens adoucirent leur programme et eurent l'habileté de faire reprendre leurs revendications par le bey régnant : Mohammed en-Nacer. Celui-ci, en conflit avec le résident, lui présenta un programme en dix-huit points qui reprenait toutes les demandes du Destour. À la veille de la visite du président de la République à Tunis, le bey fut mis en demeure de se désavouer et de destituer son Premier ministre (5 avril 1922). Après cette capitulation, et pendant une vingtaine d'années, aucun souverain tunisien n'osa s'associer au mouvement national.

Cependant, les Destouriens s'efforcèrent de continuer leur agitation, de concert avec les communistes qui multipliaient les grèves politiques. Ils s'associèrent ainsi à la création de la C.G.T.T. (Confédération générale des travailleurs tunisiens). Les «décrets scélérats» du résident général en 1926 eurent raison de leur activisme et le Destour stagna jusqu'en 1933. Quelques mesures maladroites concernant les naturalisés firent alors craindre aux Tunisiens que la France ne veuille appliquer une politique d'assimilation, contre laquelle le Congrès musulman de Jérusalem avait demandé «une lutte à outrance». L'agitation politique reprit et s'accentua dans le climat de crise économique et sociale. Le résident Manceron usa de mesures répressives : suspension de journaux, dissolution du parti destourien (31 mai 1933) mais ne réussit pas à ramener le calme. Son successeur, Peyrouton, n'hésita pas à négocier avec certains dirigeants du Destour. Mais les plus jeunes, dont Me Habib Bourguiba et le Dr Materi, dénoncèrent leur trahison et commencèrent à constituer un parti : l'Action de la jeunesse tunisienne.

Le 2 mai 1934, des Destouriens dissidents créèrent, sous le nom de Néo-Destour, un parti plus populaire et plus violent. L'essentiel de son programme, outre son opposition au Vieux-Destour, consistait dans «la lutte en vue d'obtenir l'indépendance de la Tunisie en s'opposant à l'impérialisme français et

AUX ORIGINES DU NATIONALISME TUNISIEN

En 1917 fut publiée à Lausanne une brochure intitulée *Tunisie et Algérie - Protestation contre le despotisme français*, par le cheikh Salah Cherif, ex-professeur à l'Université Zitouna de Tunis et le cheikh Ismayl Safaihi, ancien qadi en Tunisie. On y pouvait lire en conclusion :

« Le peuple n'a jamais renoncé à sa liberté, à son indépendance, ni à se réunir avec le Calife pour lequel son cœur a conservé des racines profondes d'amour et de vénération. Les patriotes travaillent en secret à la libération de leur pays. Aujourd'hui, le moment est venu pour le peuple de demander justice contre ses oppresseurs, de réclamer son droit à la vie, à la liberté, à l'indépendance [...]. Les Tunisiens et les Algériens n'ont jamais accepté volontairement la tyrannie à laquelle ils sont soumis et ils sont prêts à défendre leur cause à la première occasion [...]. Ils veulent leur indépendance. »

Signature : Le Comité pour l'indépendance de la Tunisie et de l'Algérie

à la colonisation responsable de la misère dans laquelle est plongé le pays ». Les deux partis nationalistes rivalisèrent dès lors dans l'action politique. Le Vieux-Destour conservateur et xénophobe s'orienta vers les milieux traditionalistes et religieux, jouant la carte de l'arabisme. Le Néo-Destour, s'inspirant des techniques du fascisme italien, tentait de mobiliser les classes populaires, en créant des jeunesses en uniforme et en multipliant les cortèges revendicatifs. Il invitait au boycott des produits français et au refus de l'impôt. Devant ses succès, le résident Peyrouton revint à la manière forte : les principaux dirigeants du Néo-Destour furent envoyés en résidence forcée dans les territoires militaires du Sud. Ils étaient 54 internés en octobre 1934 et, malgré quelques libérations, ils étaient à nouveau une soixantaine en 1935. Paris jugea que « le satrape Peyrouton » avait échoué et en mars 1936 il fut muté à Rabat.

Son successeur, A. Guillon, libéra les internés et fit amnistier les étudiants condamnés. Avec lui commença ce que les nationalistes appelèrent « la première expérience franco-tunisienne ». Cette phase de rapprochement fut rendue possible par le secrétaire d'État aux affaires étrangères Viénot, qui définit publiquement une politique réformatrice. Bourguiba déclara faire confiance à la France et promit une collaboration loyale. Cette politique acheminerait, pensait-il, la Tunisie vers l'indépendance. Mais de cette politique les Français de Tunisie — que les nationalistes appelaient depuis 1906 les « prépondérants » — ne voulaient pas et le firent savoir de manière provocante. Bientôt des conflits sociaux limités entraînèrent des incidents sanglants et la mort de quinze ouvriers.

Le climat politique se détériora encore plus après la démission du gouvernement Léon Blum et le retour en Tunisie du vieux leader destourien Ta'albi. La guerre des deux Destours se ralluma. Bourguiba, ayant assez vite triomphé de Ta'albi, crut pouvoir faire céder le gouvernement français. Le Néo-Destour, dont les quelque 400 cellules irradiaient tout le pays, était devenu un État dans l'État. Ne pouvant admettre une centrale syndicale indépendante, il tenta même de s'emparer de la C.G.T.T., mais provoqua la réunification des syndiqués autour de la C.G.T. Le résident Guillon, effrayé par le ton révolutionnaire du Néo-Destour, fit arrêter plusieurs leaders dont le parti exigea la mise en liberté par des manifestations et des grèves. Le 9 avril 1938 une émeute spontanée secoua la ville de Tunis. L'état de siège fut proclamé, les chefs du Néo-Destour arrêtés. Le gouvernement procéda à la dissolution du parti : vingt leaders furent inculpés de complot, mais leur procès n'eut jamais lieu.

Malgré le retour au calme en 1939, tous les observateurs français notaient les progrès du nationalisme tunisien. En vingt années celui-ci s'était transformé : alors qu'il ne touchait en 1919 qu'une faible partie de l'élite citadine, il était devenu un mouvement populaire puissant jusque dans les campagnes et les petites villes.

LE NATIONALISME MAROCAIN

Les origines sociales et culturelles du nationalisme marocain sont en vérité antérieures au Protectorat, mais l'établissement de celui-ci hâta le processus de maturation du sentiment national et d'une idéologie nationaliste. Les résistances populaires armées à l'occupation française qui se poursuivirent jusqu'au début des années 1930 y contribuèrent largement : c'est seulement en 1933 que le Haut Atlas central et le djebel Sarhro furent «pacifiés».

Mais la guerre du Rif qui se poursuivit de 1921 à 1926 fut plus qu'un épisode de résistance tribale. Déclenchée par un chef féodal, Mohammed ben'Abd-el-Krîm, elle prit figure d'une lutte nationale contre les impérialismes espagnols et français. En créant une République confédérée des tribus du Rif, Ben'Abd-el-Krîm apparut comme un leader moderniste et nationaliste, même s'il n'hésita pas à faire appel aux peuples musulmans du monde entier pour soutenir sa cause : l'indépendance du Rif. Après sa reddition, il devint le symbole de l'indépendance marocaine et du patriotisme persécuté par les «colonialistes».

Une partie de la jeunesse marocaine se prit alors à rêver d'un Maroc politiquement rénové en lutte contre la volonté française d'établir une administration directe, tandis que d'autres développaient plutôt leurs espérances au sein d'un mouvement de réforme de l'islam. Pourtant, dès 1927, l'unité était réalisée entre ces deux tendances. Et c'est d'un seul élan que les Jeunes-Marocains s'affirmèrent brusquement en profitant d'une erreur politique grave de la Résidence : le *dahîr* (décret) berbère du 16 mai 1930.

L'Administration française avait en effet obligé le jeune sultan Sidi Mohammed ben Youssef à apposer son sceau sur un *dahîr* révolutionnaire qui prétendait organiser en pays berbère une justice différente de la justice coranique. Pour les infractions criminelles, seuls les tribunaux français devenaient compétents, aux dépens du Haut Tribunal chérifien. Avec ce *dahîr* s'affirmait la volonté du résident Lucien Saint de renforcer au Maroc une politique de division qui opposerait le monde rural berbère aux cités et à la culture arabo-musulmane. Cette «politique berbère» avait déjà été appliquée avec plus ou moins de continuité en Algérie au XIXe siècle; elle avait été esquissée au Maroc depuis 1914 dans la même perspective : *divide ut imperes*. S'y ajouta la volonté de certains ecclésiastiques catholiques de travailler à la conversion des Berbères : ils les croyaient à tort des musulmans superficiels qu'il serait possible de christianiser et de franciser pour peu qu'on les tînt à l'écart des musulmans arabes.

Les Marocains ainsi provoqués, puisqu'on contestait au sultan sa souveraineté sur les 700000 Berbères des tribus classées et qu'on semblait donner toute leur liberté à ceux qu'ils appelaient «les évangélisateurs», réagirent avec une rare efficacité. Dès le mois de juin 1930, les mosquées retentirent de la prière de détresse de l'islam : le *Latîf* (l'appel au «Sauveur») et les Jeunes Marocains politisés entraînèrent la population dans un mouvement de protestation. Celui-ci gagna même tout le monde musulman et les pétitions affluèrent à Paris contre «la politique de désislamisation de la France». La Résidence fut contrainte de différer l'application du *dahîr* berbère avant de l'aménager et de le retirer *de facto*.

Enhardis par ce succès inattendu, les Jeunes Marocains révélèrent alors leurs revendications politiques. Ils créèrent des revues et des journaux comme la revue *Maghreb* imprimée à Paris à partir de juillet 1932, en collaboration avec certains hommes politiques français tels Robert Jean-Longuet et Gaston Bergery, comme *l'Action du peuple*, hebdomadaire de langue française créé à Fès le 4 août 1933, ou *La Volonté du peuple*. Les Jeunes Marocains renforcés par les associations d'étudiants et d'anciens élèves des collèges musulmans affirmaient leur nationalisme en toutes occasions et notamment en célébrant, avec la nouvelle Fête du trône, la souveraineté de Sidi Mohammed, «le Sultan des jeunes», bientôt honoré du titre nouveau de Roi (*Al-Malik*).

Les leaders Jeunes Marocains, Hassan Ouazzani, Balafrej, 'Allal al-Fasî, Ben'Abdeljalil, El-Yazidi regroupés dans le *Comité d'Action Marocaine* (*C.A.M.*) publièrent le 1er décembre 1934 un long document de 134 pages : *le Plan de réformes marocaines*. Sur le plan politique étaient demandées : l'application stricte du traité de Protectorat et la suppression de toute administration directe; l'unité administrative et judiciaire pour tout le Maroc; la participation des Marocains à l'exercice du pouvoir dans les différentes branches de l'administration; la séparation des pouvoirs cumulés par les pachas et les qaïds; la création de municipalités élues, de conseils de circonscription, de Chambres économiques et d'un Conseil national formé de représentants marocains, musulmans et israélites. Le programme de réformes signé par dix nationalistes s'étendait au domaine économique et social, à l'enseignement qui devait être modernisé et ouvert à tous les Marocains. Ce plan, qui ne réclamait pas ouvertement l'indépendance et reconnaissait le Protectorat, était patronné par quinze personnalités politiques françaises qui l'avaient jugé sérieux et réaliste. Il ne fut pourtant pas retenu par les services de la Résidence, ni par ceux du Quai d'Orsay. Le C.A.M. jugea alors nécessaire de susciter un vaste mouvement d'opinion au Maroc et en France en profitant du Front populaire. Devant l'échec, il organisa des manifestations de rues au Maroc, en novembre 1936, provoquant répression et arrestations. Le Secrétaire Général du C.A.M., Ouazzani, qui n'avait pas été consulté sur le plan de bataille, se sépara de son parti dirigé par 'Allal al-Fasî. Ce dernier voulait un mouvement populaire appuyé sur les masses musulmanes. Son activisme inquiéta la Résidence et provoqua la dissolution du C.A.M. le 18 mars 1937, 'Allal al-Fasî répliqua en fondant aussitôt un «parti national pour la réalisation des réformes», cependant que Mohamed Hassan Ouazzani créait de son côté le mouvement nationaliste (*Al-Harakat al-qawmiya*) (cf. le texte «Le nationalisme des Jeunes Marocains», p. 26).

Avec la crise économique et politique, les revendications nationalistes trouvaient un public plus nombreux et plus violent. En septembre et octobre 1937 éclatèrent dans diverses villes, notamment à Meknès et à Fès, des émeutes

LE NATIONALISME DES JEUNES MAROCAINS DÉFINI PAR MOHAMED HASSAN OUAZZANI

Notre nationalisme

Nous, Jeunes Marocains, qui sommes animés d'un souffle purement patriotique, avons une mission à remplir pour le salut de notre chère patrie.

Nous avons déjà établi un *Plan de réformes*, posant ainsi les bases d'une action utile et fixant notre but. Dès lors toute notre pensée, tous nos efforts, toute notre énergie ont convergé vers ce but.

[...] À ceux qui croient encore que le peuple marocain est condamné à être éternellement exploité et asservi, à ceux-là nous opposerons un front d'action, de courage, de patriotisme. Notre action se fait et se fera de plus en plus sentir et nous ne nous déclarerons satisfaits que le jour où tous les Marocains, sans distinction de race ni de religion, recouvreront la plénitude de leurs droits.

[...] Nous sommes donc fiers de notre mouvement national. Nous savons que dans nos veines circule un sang noble, celui des Arabes et des Berbères qui ont formé un grand peuple, dont l'action a contribué pour une grande partie à éclairer et à guider l'Europe dans sa progression vers la civilisation moderne. Nous nous rappelons encore l'éclatante civilisation musulmane qui, pendant que l'Europe était plongée dans les ténèbres de l'ignorance et dans l'anarchie, illuminait tout l'Orient et l'Occident depuis Baghdad jusqu'à Cordoue. Nous nous rappelons encore que pendant l'épanouissement de la civilisation arabe, les peuples d'Europe vivaient sous la tyrannie de la féodalité et le despotisme de la monarchie et que les universités arabes de l'Andalousie étaient les seules sources où l'on pouvait puiser toutes les sciences.

Nous savons aussi que notre peuple arabo-berbère, que l'Europe méprise aujourd'hui, a été pendant plusieurs siècles le maître incontesté d'une grande partie du monde et que c'est grâce à lui que s'est transmise et perpétuée la civilisation gréco-latine qu'on glorifie tant aujourd'hui. Nous savons enfin, et c'est là la cause profonde de notre mouvement, que le Maroc a de tout temps joui de sa pleine liberté et de son entière indépendance et que, pendant longtemps, l'autorité de ses souverains s'étendait jusqu'en Tripolitaine et au Sud même de la France, la Gaule de jadis.

Quant à nous, Jeunes-Marocains, héritiers de cette glorieuse civilisation et dignes continuateurs de ces nobles et vaillantes générations, nous ne voulons pas faillir à la mission qui nous est léguée par nos ancêtres. C'est pourquoi nous ferons revivre leur prestige et briller leur gloire.

Source : *L'Action du peuple*, n° 48, 15 juillet 1937.

populaires qui firent des morts et des blessés; l'agitation gagna même certains bourgs ruraux (Khemisset - Kenitra). La Résidence fit arrêter plusieurs leaders nationalistes, dont 'Allal al-Fasî, et occuper Fès par l'armée. 'Allal al-Fasî fut condamné au bannissement et transporté au Gabon où il devait rester six ans. La plupart des chefs nationalistes furent assignés à résidence : Ouazzani fut exilé jusqu'en mai 1946. Le mouvement nationaliste ainsi décapité, la fièvre politique tomba, au moins provisoirement. Le général Noguès, qui passait pour libéral, s'était décidé à agir avec brutalité, persuadé à tort que le nationalisme marocain, encouragé par Moscou, était pénétré d'influences orientales venues de Syrie et d'Égypte. Mais il agit ensuite avec habileté.

Les partis nationalistes divisés, aussi bien en zone espagnole que dans le Protectorat français, réduisirent leur activité, tandis que le général Noguès s'efforçait, non sans un certain succès, d'attirer à lui quelques leaders modérés.

LA NAISSANCE DU NATIONALISME EN ALGÉRIE

Jusqu'au début du XXe siècle, les populations algériennes se sentaient seulement rattachées à la communauté musulmane et ne se résignaient pas à la domination coloniale. C'est seulement peu avant la Première Guerre mondiale, que s'affirmèrent les Jeunes Algériens laïcisés et francisés. Pour échapper à la sujétion coloniale, ils demandaient à entrer dans la patrie française à égalité avec les Européens et les juifs d'Algérie. Pourtant, quelques-uns de ces Algériens refusaient l'assimilation et l'abandon de leurs ancêtres. Ils se choisirent comme leader le capitaine Khaled, parce qu'il était l'un des petits-fils de l'Émir Abd el-Kader. Comme on l'a vu, l'émir Khaled, sans oser réclamer publiquement l'indépendance, demanda secrètement au président Wilson, que des Algériens musulmans puissent venir discuter de la situation de leur patrie à la Société des Nations. Sa démarche fut à peine connue, mais aux yeux des masses le combat politique de l'émir, dans les années 1918 à 1923, annonçait le réveil du patriotisme islamique. Les Jeunes Algériens politisés de *la Fédération des élus indigènes* ne demandaient pourtant que leur entrée dans la cité française, par l'extension de leurs droits politiques. Seuls une poignée d'Algériens, endoctrinés par les communistes, rêvaient d'une République socialiste soviétique d'Algérie et d'une révolution sociale.

Les leaders Jeunes Algériens, presque tous des bourgeois libéraux, comme le Dr Benthami, le Dr Bendjelloul ou le pharmacien Ferhat Abbas ne revendiquaient qu'au nom de l'élite. Pour être entendus du Parlement français, ils entendaient y avoir leurs représentants et ne désespéraient pas d'obtenir la citoyenneté que de nombreux démocrates métropolitains leur promettaient. Mais l'opposition résolue des Français d'Algérie et des partis conservateurs de la métropole devait interdire même le modeste projet de loi Blum-Viollette, déposé en décembre 1936. Après cet échec, les Jeunes Algériens assimilationnistes perdirent leur prestige et leur audience au profit des hommes de religion, dits '*ulamâ*' réformistes (*muçlihin*) parce qu'ils étaient partisans d'une réforme religieuse (*Içlah*).

Le cheikh 'Abdelhamîd Ben Bâdîs, que ses fidèles appelèrent « l'imâm du siècle », s'efforça avec ses compagnons et associés de travailler au relèvement moral et religieux de ses frères, mais aussi sur le plan politique de faire reconnaître la nationalité algérienne. En avril 1936, il proclamait que la nation algérienne, que les Jeunes Algériens disaient n'avoir pas rencontrée dans l'histoire, existait en réalité depuis fort longtemps : « La nation algérienne s'est formée et existe comme se sont formées et existent toutes les nations de la terre. Cette nation a son histoire illustrée d'innombrables hauts-faits; elle a son unité religieuse et linguistique; elle a sa culture propre, ses traditions, ses mœurs avec ce qu'elles comportent de bon et de mauvais comme il en est de toutes les nations. Nous disons ensuite que cette nation algérienne n'est pas la France; il n'est pas possible qu'elle soit la France. Elle ne veut pas devenir la France, et même si elle le désirait elle ne le pourrait pas... Elle ne veut point d'assimilation». Cette doctrine enseignée dans les écoles libres des réformistes et dans un grand nombre de cercles politico-religieux, diffusée grâce à une presse combative, eut un succès inattendu, notamment auprès de la jeunesse. Le mouvement scout musulman y puisa son ardeur patriotique. Les clubs sportifs, les troupes théâtrales travaillèrent à cette renaissance des valeurs arabo-islamiques. Partout s'imposait le nouveau credo de Ben Bâdîs : «l'Islam est ma religion — l'arabe est ma langue — l'Algérie est mon pays.»

Pourtant un mouvement nationaliste révolutionnaire développait lui aussi, surtout parmi les travailleurs immigrés temporaires, une autre forme de patriotisme. L'organisation communiste qui s'efforçait de les encadrer politiquement et syndicalement fut bientôt concurrencée par *l'Étoile nord-africaine*. Ce petit parti, créé par le P.C.F. en 1926, s'émancipa de la tutelle communiste dès 1928-1929. *L'Étoile* multipliait dans sa presse les références à l'arabisme culturel et tenait un discours plus nationaliste que marxiste. Son principal animateur Messali Hadj proclamait : «les Algériens désirent l'indépendance et non la tutelle communiste.» Bien que dissoute en 1929, et réduite à une demi-clandestinité, *l'Étoile* continuait sa propagande nationaliste et révolutionnaire auprès des ouvriers algériens, s'intitulant fièrement islamo-nationaliste. Son journal *El Ouma* (pour *Al-Umma* : la communauté musulmane) réaffirmait en 1933 : «Ma tâche est de combattre l'impérialisme français, mon idéal est l'émancipation du Maghreb et son indépendance.» Nord-africaine, *l'Étoile*, surtout peuplée d'Algériens, donnait naturellement la priorité à l'Algérie. Elle réclamait le retrait des troupes d'occupation, la formation d'une armée nationale, et d'une Assemblée constituante élue au suffrage universel. Elle se dota d'un drapeau vert et blanc, frappé de l'étoile et du croissant islamiques, qui est devenu le drapeau national.

Peu après que Messali fut venu au cours d'une brève tournée allumer la flamme du nationalisme révolutionnaire en Algérie, l'Étoile nord-africaine fut à nouveau dissoute par le gouvernement Léon Blum. Messali riposta en constituant un nouveau mouvement, en mars 1937, le *parti du peuple algérien* (P.P.A.) dont le programme était un peu adouci : «Ni assimilation ni séparation, mais émancipation». Malgré les arrestations de ses leaders, le P.P.A. se développa des deux côtés de la Méditerranée. Le nationalisme révolutionnaire né en France et longtemps contenu dans l'Hexagone avait franchi l'obstacle. Le P.P.A. avait réussi là où la savante stratégie du *Komintern* avait échoué. En quelques années, il allait devenir le premier parti musulman par les effectifs. Il fut interdit en septembre 1939.

LES PROGRÈS DU NATIONALISME EN INDOCHINE

Les peuples d'Indochine, surtout les Vietnamiens qu'on appelait alors des Annamites, n'eurent pas à découvrir le nationalisme après 1919. La tradition patriotique, forgée à l'époque de la domination chinoise, s'était renforcée dans les résistances des lettrés et des paysans à la conquête française. Avant comme après la Première Guerre mondiale, ni les élites ni les populations villageoises n'étaient résignées au Protectorat français qui d'ailleurs évoluait vers l'administration directe.

Les rares nationalistes francophiles qui avaient espéré que la France victorieuse les associerait à la gestion de leur pays furent déçus par la timidité des réformes administratives consenties par la France entre 1920 et 1926. Même la création en 1928 du *Grand Conseil des intérêts économiques et financiers de l'Indochine* (composé de 28 délégués français et de 23 indochinois) n'amorça aucune libéralisation du régime. Certains éléments de la bourgeoisie, qui avaient tiré profit de la prospérité économique des années 1920, mesurèrent avec colère que leur dépendance politique était toujours aussi étroite. Dans ces conditions, les nationalistes annamites multiplièrent les partis politiques ou associations revendicatives. Ils agirent d'abord en Cochinchine dont le statut de colonie française permettait paradoxalement un peu plus de liberté d'expression. Là les *Jeunes Annamites* revendiquaient des droits politiques comme prélude à l'affranchissement. Telle fut aussi l'action du *parti constitutionnaliste* fondé en 1923 par un «retour de France» Bui-Quang-Chieu : il remit au gouverneur général Varenne ses *Cahiers de vœux annamites*. Hors de Cochinchine s'agitait aussi la *Ligue pour la restauration du Viêt-nam* fondée dès 1912 par Phan-Bôi-Châu : ce lettré patriote monarchiste devint peu à peu un républicain révolutionnaire.

On a déjà évoqué les organisations communistes apparues à partir de 1925 dont la *Ligue révolutionnaire de la jeunesse vietnamienne* fondée par Nguyên-Ai-Quôc. Auteur d'un *Procès de la colonisation française* (1924), devenu le chef de la section Extrême-Orient du *Komintern*, Nguyên-Ai-Quôc parvint en 1930 à souder les trois factions communistes rivales et à faire reconnaître par Moscou en 1931 le nouveau parti communiste indochinois. Les objectifs essentiels de celui-ci formulés en dix points (cf. encadré : «le *programme d'action du PCI*») s'inspiraient des résolutions du VIe Congrès de l'Internationale.

Le parti le plus important depuis 1927, le V.N.Q.D.D. (Viêt-nam Quôc Dân Dang), le parti national vietnamien, avait un programme fort simple : «1) chasser les Français, ces maîtres cruels, du territoire du Viêt-nam; 2) former un gouvernement républicain vietnamien sincèrement démocratique». Il tenta en 1930 de provoquer un soulèvement militaire, mais seule, le 10 février, la garnison de Yên-Bay s'insurgea en massacrant ses officiers français. Le mouvement fut facilement écrasé par quelques avions et le parti anéanti dans les années suivantes. De mai 1930 à septembre 1931, le parti communiste réussit à prendre la direction des «marches de la faim» des paysans du Nord-Annam victimes de la famine. Les communistes les poussèrent à attaquer les centres administratifs provinciaux et à déclencher une révolution sociale contre les possédants et les notables. Les autorités françaises dénoncèrent les procédés de «la Terreur rouge en Annam», les assassinats inutiles et atroces, cependant que l'Internationale célébrait les «soviets du Nghê-Tinh». Les communistes tentèrent en France d'alerter l'opinion sur l'ampleur de la répression et y réussirent avec le succès du livre d'Andrée Viollis : *SOS Indochine* (1939) préfacé par André Malraux.

Après l'échec de ces tentatives révolutionnaires, les nationalistes modérés retrouvèrent leur influence. Le jeune souverain d'Annam, Bao Daî, annonça en 1932 une politique de réformes sur les conseils d'un intellectuel confucéen de grande valeur, Pham-Quynh. Il nomma à la tête de la commission des

PROGRAMME D'ACTION DU PARTI COMMUNISTE INDOCHINOIS (IN APPEL LANCÉ PAR HÔ CHI MINH, LE 18 FÉVRIER 1930)

1. Renverser l'impérialisme français, la féodalité et la bourgeoisie réactionnaire du Viêt-nam;

2. Conquérir l'indépendance complète de l'Indochine;

3. Former le gouvernement des ouvriers, paysans et soldats;

4. Confisquer les banques et autres entreprises impérialistes et les placer sous le contrôle du gouvernement des ouvriers, des paysans et des soldats;

5. Confisquer toutes les plantations et autres propriétés des impérialistes et des bourgeois réactionnaires vietnamiens, pour les distribuer aux paysans pauvres;

6. Appliquer la journée de travail de 8 heures;

7. Abolir les emprunts forcés, la capitation et les taxes iniques qui frappent les pauvres;

8. Réaliser les libertés démocratiques pour les masses;

9. Dispenser l'éducation à tous;

10. Réaliser l'égalité entre l'homme et la femme.

Source : Hô Chi Minh, Ecrits 1921-1960, pp. 36-38.

(Un nouveau programme d'action en dix points assez largement différent, termine les *Thèses politiques d'octobre 1930.* Il n'y est plus question de « bourgeoisie réactionnaire », ni de soldats dans le gouvernement; la distribution des terres s'étend aux « paysans moyens », mais la propriété revient désormais au « gouvernement des ouvriers et des paysans ». Le point 7 disparaît et un point 8 apparaît qui réclame la « mise sur pied d'une armée des ouvriers et des paysans ». Le point 9 est effacé. Un nouveau point 10 affirme « soutenir l'Union soviétique, s'allier au prolétariat mondial, au mouvement révolutionnaire dans les colonies et semi-colonies ».)

Réformes un jeune mandarin réputé Ngô-Dinh-Diêm. Mais celui-ci démissionna en 1933 et Bao Daî écœuré se réfugia dans l'abstention.

L'avènement du Front populaire suscita pourtant, comme dans toutes les colonies françaises, une vague de confiance et d'espoir, notamment parce qu'il décréta une amnistie assez générale. La stratégie du parti communiste indochinois était alors de mener campagne en vue de réaliser un front démocratique indochinois. Celui-ci travailla à la formation d'un vaste mouvement d'union, au programme modéré, qui devait s'appeler *le Congrès indochinois.* Mais le Front populaire indochinois ne put pas se réaliser, ni le Congrès indochinois être réuni; le ministre des Colonies l'interdit. Communistes et trotskystes qui s'étaient alliés en Cochinchine s'opposèrent à nouveau et se combattirent. L'administration coloniale, rendue plus libre par la rupture du Front populaire en France, en profita pour réagir contre les progrès des révolutionnaires vietnamiens. En juillet 1937, il y eut une première vague d'arrestations. En septembre 1939, les leaders trotskystes furent presque tous arrêtés ainsi qu'un certain nombre de communistes du P.C.I., les chefs ayant plongé dans la clandestinité.

La période 1936-1939 fut marquée par un brusque éveil de la vie politique en Indochine. Bien que de nouvelles forces politiques se soient révélées, comme le parti démocrate ou le mouvement caodaïste qui développa un véritable État religieux dans l'État, la période fut surtout favorable au parti communiste indochinois. Non seulement il créa des organisations, des syndicats, des mutuelles, mais il noyauta de vieilles associations nationalistes et persuada la jeunesse que l'avenir national du Viêt-nam passait par une révolution sociale.

LES FRANÇAIS FACE AUX PROBLÈMES COLONIAUX DE 1919 À 1939

Face au succès du wilsonisme, à la propagande anti-impérialiste du *Komintern* et devant l'apparition ou les progrès des nationalismes coloniaux, que furent les attitudes et les politiques de la France ? La République, qui tirait gloire d'avoir édifié le deuxième empire colonial mondial derrière l'Empire britannique, ne pouvait, semble-t-il, rester sans réaction, ni sans projets. Avec le recul de l'histoire, on s'attendrait soit à un renforcement des structures d'un Empire émietté, à un développement en France de la conscience impériale et à la construction d'une économie d'Empire, soit à une redéfinition du principe de la colonisation qui, travaillant pour le progrès des populations sujettes, saurait les associer ou les intégrer sur un pied d'égalité à la République. En fait, la réalité historique de l'évolution des colonies françaises ne répond pas à ces solutions, même si telles ou telles d'entre elles furent parfois formulées. La IIIe République, dans les années 1919-1939, n'a su, face à l'extension de la contestation des colonisés, ni définir ni appliquer une politique adaptée aux temps nouveaux. La crise politique intérieure et l'ampleur de la crise économique n'ont sans doute pas permis à des gouvernements faibles et souvent éphémères de concevoir une politique coloniale de quelque envergure : les colonies sont restées administrées selon les errements antérieurs. Les fonctionnaires coloniaux ont mené le plus souvent un combat retardateur sans imagination, parfois un effort de modernisation sans moyens. Mais la responsabilité essentielle ne devrait-elle pas être attribuée au peuple français, qui dans l'ensemble ne s'intéressa guère aux questions coloniales ou à l'avenir de l'Empire ?

LA CONSCIENCE COLONIALE DES FRANÇAIS

À la fin de la Première Guerre mondiale, on put croire, selon un slogan répandu par le parti colonial, que « les Français avaient découvert l'immensité, les richesses et l'avenir illimité de notre vaste Empire d'outre-mer ». L'apport militaire et économique fourni par les colonies à la métropole avait été une heureuse révélation pour l'opinion jusque-là sceptique quant aux avantages de l'expansion coloniale. De 500000 à 600000 soldats coloniaux, dont 300000 Nord-Africains, et peut-être 200000 travailleurs requis, dont 140000 Nord-Africains, étaient venus, disait-on, « secourir la Mère-Patrie »;

de 66000 à 71000 hommes, suivant les sources, étaient «morts pour la France»; et 5 millions de tonnes de produits coloniaux avaient soutenu la consommation et la production.

Dès lors certains hommes politiques, et pas seulement ceux qui appartenaient aux groupes parlementaires du parti colonial, parlaient de constituer un «bloc France-Colonies», une «Plus Grande France» de 100 millions d'habitants. Des associations populaires comme *la Ligue maritime et coloniale* — qui devait rassembler environ 100000 adhérents en 1930 — des sociétés puissantes et riches comme *l'Union coloniale*, firent un effort de propagande en ce sens. Mais dans l'ensemble la population française y fut insensible. Un ministre des Colonies imaginatif, Albert Sarraut, proposa en vain, dès avril 1921, un ambitieux programme de travaux publics et de mise en valeur des colonies; mais le coût de l'opération, de l'ordre de 3 milliards et demi, parut prohibitif aux parlementaires plus soucieux de reconstruire la France que d'équiper les colonies. D'aucuns, parmi eux, parlaient même en 1924 et 1925 de vendre des colonies pour désendetter la France.

Aussi bien une partie de la gauche française — communistes et socialistes essentiellement — ne cachait pas «son hostilité fondamentale au colonialisme, forme la plus redoutable de l'impérialisme» (Léon Blum). Bien qu'adversaires des solutions simplistes des communistes, les socialistes estimaient, dans leurs congrès de 1926 et 1927, que les buts à assigner à la politique coloniale, c'étaient l'indépendance et l'évacuation aussi promptes que possible des colonies ou l'internationalisation de certaines, sous le contrôle de la SDN. Ce discours trouvait une audience certaine dans les milieux d'enseignants (cf. le texte p. 34). Les partis politiques modérés tenaient à l'occasion un tout autre langage, mais se refusaient, malgré la prospérité revenue, à des investissements publics dans les colonies.

Le parti colonial se lança alors dans une nouvelle et longue campagne de propagande : pendant cinq ans, de 1927 à 1931, de la création des Semaines coloniales à l'Exposition coloniale internationale de Vincennes, des publicistes multiplièrent les films, les conférences et les ouvrages à la gloire de l'Empire. Les fêtes du centenaire de l'Algérie de 1930 et l'Exposition coloniale de 1931 obtinrent un succès réel auprès du public, mais ces festivités ne devaient pas transformer les mentalités. Tel fut d'ailleurs l'avis du maréchal Lyautey : «Ce fut un succès inespéré», déclarait-il le 14 novembre 1931, mais il ajouta en 1932 que «l'Exposition n'avait en rien modifié la mentalité des cerveaux adultes ni ceux des gens en place qui n'étaient pas par avance convaincus». Tout au contraire, se développa dans les esprits un «malaise colonial», né peut-être de la révélation de certains abus coloniaux et de la violence de l'agitation révolutionnaire, notamment dans l'Annam. D'influents journalistes interrogeaient : «Faudra-t-il évacuer l'Indochine ?» et des hommes politiques demandaient publiquement : «l'Algérie [française] vivra-t-elle ?» Simultanément l'anticolonialisme retrouvait une certaine vigueur; de grands écrivains, comme André Gide ou André Malraux, venaient relayer l'action de Romain Rolland ou de Félicien Challaye. Leurs livres, leurs articles de presse développaient chez beaucoup d'intellectuels de gauche une mauvaise conscience qui n'épargnait pas certains chrétiens. Aussi bien le Vatican croyait que l'ère coloniale prendrait fin «dans quarante ans» et y préparait déjà les ordres missionnaires.

Tandis que l'ampleur de la crise économique obligeait la France à aider indirectement les producteurs des colonies, l'idée d'autarcie impériale faisait son apparition. Mais cette transformation souhaitée par les milieux coloniaux, était défavorable aux intérêts des paysans français concurrencés par les produits venus d'outre-mer (riz, blés et vins notamment). Les exportateurs de nombreux articles industriels souffraient des mesures de rétorsion décidées par certains États, victimes de la préférence accordée par la France aux productions de ses colonies (sucres, cafés, cacaos). Bref, la propagande coloniale ne faiblissait peut-être pas, mais son audience diminuait de 1932 à 1936. La célébration en 1935 du tricentenaire des Antilles françaises et celle du quarantenaire de la conquête de Madagascar passèrent à peu près totalement inaperçues.

Ce fut seulement avec la montée des périls extérieurs que se fit jour l'idée opposée : l'Empire permettrait seul à la France d'équilibrer le dynamisme et l'expansionnisme des États fascistes : «Le salut est dans l'Empire, la France doit jouer sa carte coloniale [...], l'Empire rétablira notre destin quoi qu'il arrive.» À nouveau le potentiel colonial apparaissait comme le fondement essentiel de la sécurité de la France, le suprême recours en cas de guerre européenne. Certains hommes politiques n'hésitèrent pas en 1939 à annoncer l'arrivée de 2 millions de soldats coloniaux qui seraient «les boucliers de la France».

Depuis 1934 la jeune droite proclamait : «Ou la France sera impériale et coloniale ou elle devra renoncer à sa place au rang des grandes nations». Le nouveau *parti social français* (P.S.F.) du colonel de la Rocque invoquait : «la République impériale française» et le *parti populaire français* avait lancé dès 1936 le mot d'ordre : «Faisons l'Empire de 104 (*sic*) millions de Français.» Il devait préciser ensuite qu'il refusait l'assimilation des peuples conquis.

Mais si l'Empire devait être le salut de la France, encore fallait-il veiller au salut de l'Empire. Il fallait dire non aux revendications coloniales du IIIe Reich, car Hitler réclamait, violemment depuis 1936, la restitution des ex-colonies allemandes «volées en 1919 par la France et l'Angleterre».

Du coup les pacifistes se découvrirent anticoloniaux : ils ne voulaient pas plus mourir pour le Cameroun ou le Togo que pour la défense de la Tchécoslovaquie. Un organe pacifiste, le *Canard enchaîné*, appelait de ses vœux le 5 octobre 1938 une seconde conférence de Munich pour résoudre heureusement la question des ex-colonies allemandes. À cette date, une majorité absolue de Français interrogés par sondage, était prête à «donner des colonies à l'Allemagne», soit 59 % contre 33 % d'un avis opposé. Ils étaient en revanche très opposés à faire droit aux «prétentions italiennes sur la Tunisie, la Corse et la Côte des Somalis.» En février 1939, malgré un retournement de l'opinion en faveur de l'intangibilité de l'Empire, on comptait encore 44 % de Français qui préféraient céder des territoires coloniaux plutôt que d'avoir à les défendre, 40 % acceptant au contraire de se battre. Mais 53 % (contre 44 % d'avis contraires) estimaient «aussi pénible de devoir céder un morceau de notre empire colonial qu'un morceau du territoire de la France».

Est-ce à dire que les Français aient enfin accédé à ce que l'on appelait la conscience impériale? La courte majorité révélée par ce sondage était trop faible pour qu'on puisse assurer que les Français avaient pris conscience de l'existence virtuelle d'une communauté impériale et des responsabilités

CONTRE « UN CERTAIN COLONIALISME INTEMPÉRANT »

Au nom de ses collègues de la Régionale de Montpellier, Jean-Rémy Palanque, dans le *Bulletin de la Société des Professeurs d'histoire*, écrivait en janvier 1928 : « La nature a-t-elle vraiment fait de notre "Empire" le prolongement de notre sol natal? Il y a, nous semble-t-il, quelque exagération à présenter les colonies comme des parties intégrantes de notre France [...]. Peut-on prétendre qu'il y a une "plus grande France" : 100 millions de Français, dont une bonne moitié de Noirs et de Jaunes? On n'a pas le droit, me semble-t-il, d'aller jusque-là. De bons Français, patriotes autant que d'autres, ont pu accepter le traité du 4 novembre 1911 où nous cédions une partie du Congo, en échange d'autres avantages; d'autres ont pu envisager l'éventualité d'une vente de certains territoires, tout cela sans parler de trahisons, ni créer le mythe d'Alsaces-Lorraines tropicales.

Beaucoup enfin s'orientent, de nos jours, vers des conceptions nouvelles de la colonisation, dont les territoires sous mandat, avec contrôle de la SDN, peuvent donner une idée; l'on peut imaginer des États asiatiques rendus à l'indépendance politique, moyennant une alliance diplomatique et des traités de commerce nous assurant de larges avantages pour nos achats de matières premières par exemple. Ce jour-là, dira-t-on encore que ces royaumes souverains d'une civilisation originale intéressante, respectable font partie de la chair de notre patrie? L'enseignement imprégné de telles idées ne risque-t-il pas de fausser l'esprit de nos élèves, de provoquer chez eux quand ils seront devenus citoyens, des sentiments de révolte en présence d'évoluons raisonnables, bienfaisantes au total pour tous et capables d'éviter les révolutions sanglantes, les arrachements brutaux et néfastes que les événements pourraient nous imposer? On voit jusqu'où peut nous entraîner le colonialisme. »

qu'elle impliquait. Une forte minorité restait probablement sceptique ou réservée vis-à-vis de cet Empire dans lequel beaucoup ne voyaient toujours qu'« un slogan à la mode ».

RÉFLEXIONS ET PROPHÉTIES SUR L'AVENIR DES COLONIES FRANÇAISES

Si les Français de l'entre-deux-guerres n'ont donc pas partagé les espérances ou les alarmes des coloniaux, il reste qu'un petit nombre d'hommes, plus ou moins influents, réfléchirent avec intelligence sur l'avenir des colonies. On privilégiera ici, à titre d'exemples, ceux d'entre eux qui surent formuler de justes diagnostics et ceux qui anticipèrent l'idée de décolonisation.

Albert Sarraut, qui fut sept fois ministre des Colonies, deux fois président du Conseil, apparaît aujourd'hui comme le ministre de la Parole coloniale, plus que comme un homme d'action. Du moins exprima-t-il avec bonheur les principes d'une politique éclairée. À deux reprises de 1912 à 1919, il avait été gouverneur général de l'Indochine et s'y montra notamment soucieux de développer l'instruction populaire et la justice française. À son départ définitif, le 27 avril 1919, il confia aux notables annamites réunis à la Pagode de

Confucius le sens de sa politique et sa volonté de voir créer une «charte indochinoise» : «Par l'instruction, je veux vous grandir [...]. Je veux vous mettre à même d'arriver là où vous serez dignes d'atteindre [...]. De cette œuvre d'éducation sortiront un jour les droits du citoyen indigène qui permettront aux meilleurs d'entre vous de partager, avec nous, les responsabilités de l'action et de l'administration du pays [...]. Il faut augmenter la représentation indigène dans les assemblées locales déjà existantes, créer la représentation indigène de ces assemblées là où elle n'existe pas encore et élargir le corps électoral indigène qui désignera ses représentants [...]. Chaque pays de l'Union indochinoise devra avoir, outre des assemblées provinciales, une assemblée locale composée de représentants de tous les intérêts et de toutes les provinces [...]. Au-dessus de ces assemblées locales, une assemblée plus haute, comparable au Conseil supérieur du gouvernement actuel, mais bien plus importante, plus nombreuse [...] pourvue d'attributions plus larges et mieux définies, siégera en sessions régulières pour délibérer sur les budgets et sur toutes les grandes questions qui concernent la vie générale de la colonie. À côté des représentants élus de la population française, les représentants des pays indigènes participeront à ces délibérations en nombre plus étendu qu'aujourd'hui, et seront désignés par un suffrage plus large exprimant plus exactement les vœux et les sentiments de nos sujets et protégés. La collaboration indigène sera ainsi en réalité plus certaine et plus vivante.»

En 1921, ministre des Colonies, il définissait ce que devait être une authentique politique d'association : «À son effort civilisateur, la France veut à la mesure de leur capacité associer ses protégés, les appeler progressivement à la gestion de leur pays, les habiliter par l'éducation à cette collaboration et, partageant avec eux les responsabilités comme les bénéfices, hausser leur conscience peu à peu éveillée et transformée jusqu'au sentiment lucide de leurs devoirs, des obligations qu'ils contractent envers nous pour l'accroissement, la garde et la commune défense d'un patrimoine solidaire.»

Dans son livre, *La Mise en valeur des colonies françaises* (1922), Sarraut s'interrogeait sur l'évolution des colonies, et affirmait d'abord les vertus d'une certaine autonomie administrative : «Les colonies ne doivent pas vivre et exister que pour la métropole. Elles ont droit à une vie personnelle [...]. Le lien qui les unit à la métropole est moins de vassalité que de solidarité, car c'est le lien de la famille nationale.» Et songeant sans doute à l'Indochine, il écrivait que certaines grandes colonies ou bien évolueraient à la manière britannique vers la forme des Dominions, ou bien dans la liberté d'un *self-government* intégral, elles reprendraient toute leur indépendance. Mais, même s'il devait en être ainsi, «ce ne serait point une raison d'attiédir dès à présent, l'ardeur des hauts devoirs que nous trace notre mission tutélaire, vis-à-vis des pays dont l'avenir nous est confié [...]. Ne serait-ce donc rien que d'avoir modelé, dans le limon obscur des humanités attardées, le visage lumineux et frémissant de nations nouvelles? Serait-ce donc aussi un faible avantage que d'avoir créé outre-mer des États ou des sociétés où persisteraient, élargissant leur influence chaque jour, la langue, la tradition, les leçons, le souvenir, l'âme même de la France. Et ne serait-ce point encore pour la mère-patrie le meilleur des résultats [...] que d'avoir ainsi noué avec ses enfants adultes, par les liens durables de la gratitude et de l'intérêt, des rapports économiques et

MARÉCHAL LYAUTEY

(extraits de la Directive du 18 novembre 1920)

Il faut regarder bien en face la situation du monde en général et spécialement la situation du monde musulman et ne pas se laisser devancer par les événements. Ce n'est pas impunément qu'ont été lancées, à travers le monde, les formules du droit des peuples à disposer d'eux-mêmes et les idées d'émancipation et d'évolution dans le sens révolutionnaire. Il faut bien se garder de croire que les Marocains échappent ou échapperont longtemps à ce mouvement général. Si, pendant des siècles, la xénophobie du Maghreb[1], son esprit d'indépendance jalouse ont établi une cloison étanche entre lui et le reste du monde et l'ont maintenu figé dans une forme théocratique immuable, ces temps sont passés...

[...] Mais ce dont il faut être persuadé c'est que des temps nouveaux se lèvent et menacent.

Le succès des bolchevistes en Crimée, leur approche de Constantinople, du Levant, le contrecoup qui va s'en produire en Islam, les proclamations d'indépendance en Égypte, en Tripolitaine sont des événements mondiaux qui vont créer demain une situation nouvelle. Il ne faut pas se laisser surprendre. La Tunisie et l'Algérie sont déjà profondément remuées. Il serait inexcusable de s'endormir au Maroc et d'imaginer qu'on pourra longtemps éviter le contrecoup de tels événements. Le meilleur palliatif est d'y donner le plus tôt possible à l'élite marocaine les moyens d'évoluer dans sa norme, en donnant à temps satisfaction à ses aspirations inévitables, en remplissant auprès d'elle dans toute son ampleur le rôle d'un tuteur, d'un grand frère bienfaisant auquel elle ait intérêt à rester liée et en bénéficiant ainsi d'avoir affaire ici non pas à de la poussière, mais à une nation dont l'émancipation se fera sous notre tutelle, sous notre direction à notre profit et alors que ce serait une si périlleuse illusion d'imaginer que nous la tiendrons indéfiniment en mains avec notre mince et fragile pellicule d'occupation.

Source : *Lyautey l'Africain : Textes et lettres*, t. IV, 1919-1925, pp. 24 sq.

1. Nom arabe du Maroc : Maghreb al-Aqsa.

politiques dont la métropole resterait la bénéficiaire privilégiée, sans supporter les charges ou les responsabilités d'autrefois. »

Cette belle page sereine, Sarraut la reprit sans y changer un mot dans un livre publié en 1931, *Grandeur et servitude coloniales*. L'accélération de l'histoire avait brusquement actualisé ces lignes qu'on dirait écrites pour le bon usage de la décolonisation. Car Sarraut ne s'y méprenait pas : « l'heure était venue des ressacs, des chocs en retour de la civilisation, l'heure de la contre-offensive des énergies qu'elle a éveillées ». Dès lors, ce libéral inquiet se mua en conservateur : Sarraut ne voulut plus prôner que la résistance à l'évolution des colonisés en constituant une Sainte-Alliance des peuples colonisateurs européens.

L'un des leaders du parti colonial, le député radical Léon Archimbaud, n'avait pas plus hésité dans son livre *La Plus Grande France* (1928) à condamner l'absence d'une politique coloniale. «Nulle part, avouait-il, les indigènes de nos colonies n'ont une part sérieuse dans le gouvernement de leur pays. Parler dans ces conditions d'association ou de collaboration, ce n'est qu'une mauvaise plaisanterie [...].» Certes un peu partout des conseils consultatifs ont été créés, mais leur rôle est généralement de pure façade : la majorité des indigènes est nommée par le gouvernement local [...]. Une telle parodie de représentation populaire n'est pas digne de la France. Lui aussi pensait que «l'autonomie de nos possessions (devait) être le but plus ou moins lointain de notre politique coloniale. Indigènes et colons français doivent un jour s'administrer eux-mêmes. C'est inéluctable et c'est aussi souhaitable».

Un autre colonial, Gaston Caussé, ne voyait à la même date d'autre solution au *«Problème colonial français»* qu'une évolution vers l'autonomie : face aux propagandes nationalistes et pour «éviter des événements chargés de tragiques inconnues», il fallait laisser l'Indochine, le Maroc et même l'Algérie devenir des Dominions.

Mais l'utopie anticipatrice d'un colonial aussi prestigieux que Lyautey mériterait d'être plus connue : certains historiens ne seraient pas loin de voir aussi en lui un prophète lucide de la décolonisation. Défenseur acharné du principe du protectorat, «résolu à se porter garant de l'autorité religieuse et politique du sultan traditionnel du Maroc», Lyautey ne cessa de mettre en garde les Français contre leur penchant à l'administration directe. Il les exhortait aussi à témoigner une véritable considération à la personnalité morale des peuples colonisés. Mais en 1920, il allait plus loin en expliquant : «Voici le moment de donner un sérieux coup de barre au point de vue de la politique indigène et de la participation de l'élément musulman aux affaires publiques. Il faut regarder bien en face la situation du monde en général, et spécialement la situation du monde musulman et ne pas se laisser devancer par les événements. Ce n'est pas impunément qu'ont été lancées à travers le monde les formules du droit des peuples à disposer d'eux-mêmes et les idées d'émancipation et d'évolution dans le sens révolutionnaire.

[...] Le meilleur palliatif est de donner le plus tôt possible à l'élite marocaine les moyens d'évoluer dans sa norme, en donnant à temps satisfaction à ses aspirations inévitables, en remplissant auprès d'elle, dans toute son ampleur, le rôle d'un tuteur, d'un grand frère bienfaisant auquel elle ait intérêt à rester liée et en bénéficiant ainsi d'avoir à faire ici non pas à de la poussière, mais à une nation dont l'émancipation se fera sous notre tutelle, sous notre direction, à notre profit, et alors que ce serait une si périlleuse illusion d'imaginer que nous la tiendrions indéfiniment en mains avec notre mince et fragile pellicule d'occupation.»

En 1925, peu avant de quitter son commandement au Maroc, Lyautey saluait en termes politiques l'aurore des temps nouveaux au Maghreb et indiquait ce que devait être l'attitude de la France :

«Il est à prévoir et je le crois comme une vérité historique, que dans un temps plus ou moins lointain, l'Afrique du Nord évoluée, civilisée, vivant de sa vie autonome, se détachera de la métropole. Il faut qu'à ce moment là — et ce doit être le but suprême de notre politique — cette séparation se fasse sans douleur et que les regards des indigènes continuent de se tourner avec affection vers la France.»

DÉCLARATION DU MARÉCHAL LYAUTEY FAITE À RABAT AU CONSEIL DE POLITIQUE INDIGÈNE, LE 14 AVRIL 1925

Il est à prévoir, et je le crois comme une vérité historique que, dans un temps plus ou moins lointain, l'Afrique du Nord, évoluée, civilisée, vivant de sa vie autonome, se détachera de la métropole. Il faut qu'à ce moment-là — et ce doit être le suprême but de notre politique — cette séparation se fasse sans douleur et que les regards des indigènes continuent toujours à se tourner avec affection vers la France. Il ne faut pas que les peuples africains se retournent contre elle. À ces fins, il faut dès aujourd'hui nous faire aimer d'eux...

[...] Je n'ai pas cessé d'espérer créer entre ce peuple [marocain] et nous un état d'âme, une amitié, une satisfaction intime qui font qu'il restera avec nous le plus longtemps possible. Mais qui auront pour résultat final, que si les événements le détachent politiquement de nous, toutes ses sympathies resteront françaises. C'est la pensée avec laquelle je vis, qui me porte, qui est une directive essentielle : je veux nous faire aimer de ce peuple.

Source : Georges Spillman, *Du protectorat à l'indépendance*, Plon, 1967, pp. 26-27.

En 1931, Lyautey confiait à ses amis que «le monde asiatique allant comme il allait, la France ne pourrait conserver longtemps encore ses possessions, à commencer par l'Indochine, dans cet énorme continent surpeuplé trop grand pour nous, trop loin de nous.»

De moindres personnalités coloniales se déclarèrent partisans d'une politique libérale qui fonderait sur des assises morales la possession des territoires d'outre-mer. Elles ne cessèrent de suggérer des réformes politiques, montrant la nécessité de reconnaître aux colonies au moins des droits de citoyenneté locale. Celle-ci d'abord réservée aux élites serait progressivement étendue à la masse au fur et à mesure de son éducation.

Mais une vive opposition se fit toujours sentir chez les colons, qui par préjugé racial n'acceptaient pas d'être confrontés avec des colonisés devenus leurs égaux. Presque tous ils affirmaient que «les indigènes n'ont nul besoin d'une extension de leurs droits.» Pour eux, comme pour beaucoup d'administrateurs et de coloniaux métropolitains, les indigènes ne connaissaient que la force et il suffisait d'appliquer, à ceux qui revendiquaient, les rigueurs de la loi.

Devant ce front du statu quo échouèrent les quelques gouverneurs qui furent aussi des hommes de progrès, tels Alexandre Varenne en Indochine ou Maurice Viollette en Algérie. Ce dernier, parce qu'il s'interrogeait avec angoisse sur l'avenir de l'Afrique française (*l'Algérie vivra-t-elle ?* ainsi titrait-il en 1931 un gros livre) ne cessa de 1925 à 1936 de dire aux Français d'Algérie la nécessité d'accorder des droits politiques à l'élite algérienne :

«Les Musulmans quand ils protestent contre les abus qu'ils constatent, vous vous indignez. Quand ils applaudissent, vous suspectez et quand ils se taisent, vous redoutez. Il y va du sort du pays. Ces hommes vous disent : "Nous n'avons pas de patrie; nous voulons la patrie française". Si vous refusez, craignez qu'ils ne s'en créent bientôt une autre.» (mars 1935)

C'était avouer que l'égalité était à ses yeux le seul moyen de combattre le nationalisme. Devenu ministre dans le gouvernement du Front populaire, Maurice Viollette déposa un projet de loi qui envisageait d'admettre environ 20000 Algériens musulmans au bénéfice de la citoyenneté française. Ce projet modeste suscita l'opposition résolue de la majorité des Français d'Algérie. Une série de délégations d'élus se succéda à Paris en 1937 et 1938 et vint ameuter l'opinion contre ce projet qui aurait menacé la souveraineté française. Bientôt, le projet de loi Blum-Viollette apparut impossible à tous les hommes politiques français. En mars 1938 lorsque le ministre de l'Intérieur, A. Sarraut, eut fait savoir sa volonté de voir néanmoins aboutir le projet, les maires d'Algérie démissionnèrent, les députés français d'Algérie invitèrent leurs mandants à se mettre en état d'alerte contre cette «provocation à l'adresse de l'Algérie française.» Finalement, le gouvernement Daladier, pas plus que les gouvernements de Front populaire, n'osa imposer le projet par décret-loi, cependant que la Chambre refusait de s'en saisir.

Viollette fut un Cassandre incompris, lui qui dès 1931 avait prévenu : «Si la jeunesse algérienne se dressait en protestataire contre la situation injuste qui lui serait faite, j'affirme qu'avant vingt ans, nous connaîtrions en Afrique du Nord les pires difficultés.»

Certains hommes politiques français, généralement des non-conformistes, n'hésitèrent pas à titre personnel, à se prononcer pour que la France fît droit aux revendications nationalistes et reconstruisît son empire sur le modèle d'un Commonwealth. Mais leurs prises de position, celles du député Varenne en faveur de la constitution «d'États associés» ou celles d'un André Philip par exemple, ne trouvèrent nul écho en dehors des congrès de la S.F.I.O. ou d'une presse militante. L'ex-radical Gaston Bergery, fondateur du Frontisme, se fit même le porte-parole des nationalistes coloniaux, comme Robert Jean-Longuet l'était pour les nationalistes marocains. Cependant, G. Bergery allait plus loin en suggérant par exemple de regrouper les États du Levant et ceux du Maghreb dans un système méditerranéen de sécurité collective, à forme fédérale. Plus généralement, jusqu'en 1936, il était favorable à une évolution des colonies vers un système fédéral sous direction française. Toutefois, après un voyage en A.E.F., il se rallia au mythe impérial traditionnel.

Pourtant l'opinion assimilait ces non-conformistes aux anticolonialistes doctrinaires des milieux communistes ou des chapelles surréalistes, trotskystes et anarchistes, celles-ci dépourvues de toute audience en France.

Même parmi les coloniaux, il s'en trouva toujours pour penser et pour écrire que l'empire colonial de la France était une charge trop lourde. Le mirage de l'Empire n'éblouissait pas tous ceux qui savaient les difficultés politiques d'une domination et le caractère inéluctable d'une décolonisation. L'un de ces prophètes méconnus, le Dr Auguste Vallet, adjurait dès 1925 dans *Un nouvel aperçu du problème colonial* le peuple français de procéder, au moins, à un repli stratégique. Comme l'avait écrit Onésime Reclus dans un livre célèbre *Lâchons l'Asie, prenons l'Afrique*, A. Vallet conseillait de se débarrasser de toutes les colonies d'Asie et d'Amérique et de se concentrer, sans trop d'illusions, sur l'Afrique : «Toute colonie, quelle qu'elle soit, a été occupée par la force. Elle se libérera par la force aussitôt qu'elle en aura les moyens matériels.» D'où son slogan : «Vendons, vendons nos colonies!» En 1931, l'amiral Castex répétait que la France ne devait conserver de son

Empire que le bloc africain : « Qui nous débarrassera de l'Indochine ? [...] La défense de l'Indochine contre les Japonais est une chimère absolue. » Et l'amiral d'ajouter qu'il fallait nous dégager « au plus tôt » de la Syrie et du Liban en leur accordant l'indépendance qu'ils réclament.

Que ces francs-tireurs soient restés inconnus ou aient été tenus à l'écart ne peut faire oublier que des intellectuels célèbres ne tenaient pas un autre langage, tels André Gide ou André Malraux, et que certains d'entre eux prétendaient à une action politique. C'est ainsi que quelques figures de proue de l'anticolonialisme parisien : Félicien Challaye, Romain Rolland, René Maran, Andrée Viollis, constituèrent en 1937 un Rassemblement colonial de nuance Front populaire, qui se révéla vite peu efficient. De son côté Daniel Guérin, avec Marceau Pivert, leader de la tendance Gauche révolutionnaire au sein de la S.F.I.O., finit par mettre sur pied un *Parti socialiste ouvrier et paysan* (P.S.O.P.) qui se déclarait dans sa charte constitutive « solidaire des travailleurs indigènes qui luttent en tant que peuple pour le droit à disposer d'eux-mêmes, sans qu'aucune limite puisse être assignée à ce droit. » Il crut pouvoir créer un *Centre de liaison anti-impérialiste*, mais celui-ci fut interdit fin avril 1939.

Aussi bien ces anticolonialistes n'envisageaient-ils, en général, aucune évolution politique raisonnée et progressive de l'outre-mer français en dehors des indépendances. On fera pourtant exception pour un projet de transformation de l'Empire colonial en une Fédération de peuples associés, dont le député P.-Olivier Lapie se fit le champion en 1939. L'idée n'était pas neuve, puisqu'elle avait été présentée dès 1899 par Emile Démaret, un ancien professeur de l'Alliance française, dans un livre intitulé : *Organisation coloniale et Fédération : une fédération de la France et de ses colonies.* Mais relancée en 1939, elle devait inspirer de nouveaux projets pendant et après la Deuxième Guerre mondiale.

Rétrospectivement l'historien s'explique mal l'échec des tentatives de réforme, voir le non-aboutissement des grandes commissions d'enquête. Les commissions parlementaires qui se succédèrent dans les colonies de 1935 à 1937 : la commission Steeg, la commission Guernut, la commission Lagrosillière par exemple ou la Conférence des gouverneurs généraux, réunie à Paris en 1936, formulèrent toutes de justes remarques, des vœux justifiés, des propositions opportunes. Si les conclusions de tous ces rapports ne purent servir de base à des réformes concrètes, la faute en revint peut-être à l'intervention de personnalités guidées par des préoccupations d'intérêts privés, mais plus probablement à l'impuissance globale du système politique. Alors que tous les spécialistes s'étaient prononcés depuis 1920 pour la création d'un fonds d'équipement colonial et la mise en application d'un programme de mise en valeur, le Fonds prévu en 1937 fut rejeté par le Sénat pour des raisons politiciennes. Quant aux réformes politiques et sociales annoncées par le gouvernement de Front populaire, bien peu connurent un début de réalisation (amnistie partielle aux prisonniers politiques indigènes, suppression du bagne en Guyane, octroi du droit syndical en A.O.F. et aux Européens du Maroc, atténuation du régime des prestations, suppression du travail forcé interdit par la convention de Genève de 1931, Code du travail indigène en Indochine). Mais la politique de répression (dissolution de l'Étoile nord-africaine, du Comité d'Action marocaine) souligna l'échec des réformes politiques. Dès lors fallait-il s'étonner de la montée des forces révolutionnaires? «Bouder aux réformes, c'est sourire aux révolutions», dit un proverbe français.

LES PROBLÈMES ÉCONOMIQUES DE L'EMPIRE

Peu de domaines plus que les questions économiques ont donné lieu à autant de débats et de simplifications polémiques dont se sont nourris les doctrinaires coloniaux ou anticoloniaux. Il paraît nécessaire d'en dire quelques mots pour expliquer au moins les réactions passionnées des colonisés et les arguments de certains décolonisateurs.

Pour les défenseurs de la colonisation, les colonies étaient source de puissance économique et de justes profits; encore fallait-il les intégrer dans l'économie française. «La mise en pratique de la solidarité impériale est absolument conforme à l'intérêt national qui se confond avec l'ensemble des intérêts particuliers», répétait un des porte-parole des grandes sociétés coloniales. Pour le parti colonial dans son ensemble, les colonies étaient devenues, dans les années 1920, le premier partenaire commercial et le premier actif financier de la France; cela suffisait à en mesurer la valeur. Aussi bien l'exportation des capitaux privés vers l'outre-mer était-elle régulièrement croissante jusqu'en 1929 parce que les placements coloniaux assuraient sécurité et rentabilité. Ainsi les colonies se développaient-elles tout en enrichissant la métropole : la mise en valeur s'effectuait progressivement au profit de tous, colonisés et sociétés françaises, exportateurs et rentiers français.

Les anticolonialistes dont les colonisés acceptèrent ou renforcèrent plus tard le discours, affirmaient que la métropole pratiquait toujours le «pacte colonial» comme au temps du mercantilisme («tout pour la métropole, tout par elle»); elle pillait les richesses naturelles, utilisait la force du travail des populations, sans développer l'infrastructure ou l'équipement industriel des régions attardées. Le marché colonial ne servait qu'à écouler au prix fort, objets fabriqués et produits agricoles, souvent invendables ailleurs. Pendant la crise des années trente, la France privée de débouchés et de clients, se repliait sur l'Empire, dont l'exploitation accrue permit seule la sauvegarde du capitalisme métropolitain.

Or les réalités de l'économie et des échanges France-colonies sont fort différentes. Certes les exportations vers l'Empire dépassaient à partir de 1928 celles de 1913, mais pour peu d'années et les exportations intéressaient surtout les branches traditionnelles de l'industrie, en voie de déclin. Certes l'Empire devenait un fournisseur essentiel, mais pour certaines matières premières de seconde importance : il ravitaillait la France en cacao, café, bananes, mais ne lui apportait que 2 % du coton, 8 % des laines consommés par l'industrie française. Le resserrement des liens commerciaux entre la France et les colonies, la création progressive d'un bloc protectionniste baptisé *l'Unité économique de la France totale* ne furent pas bénéfiques pour l'économie française. Imposé d'ailleurs aux milieux d'affaires les plus dynamiques le renforcement des protections douanières entre 1928 et 1933 asphyxia la production française, dont le quart était exporté avant la crise.

La tendance à faire vivre la France et ses colonies en autarcie profita au contraire à certaines colonies, celles surtout qui étaient le plus étroitement liées à la France. Elle se trouvèrent en partie protégées contre la dépression mondiale, puisque le marché français leur ouvrait des débouchés assurés et, grâce à des mesures de soutien et des primes, des prix nettement plus élevés que ceux du marché mondial. La préférence impériale obligeait la France à importer de ses colonies une part croissante de sa consommation, par exemple 56,1 % du cacao en 1929, 83,7 % en 1936 et 88,4 % en 1938 ; pour le café les pourcentages étaient de 3,7 % en 1929, 17,2 % en 1936 et 42,7 % en 1938 ; pour le caoutchouc les chiffres respectifs atteignaient 9,3 % en 1929, 19 % en 1936, 25,1 % en 1938. Or ces produits étaient achetés par la métropole en moyenne deux fois plus cher qu'au cours mondial. Le prix moyen du quintal de marchandises coloniales atteignait 168 F en 1938, celui du quintal fourni par l'étranger, 84 F. Les matières premières utilisées par l'industrie coûtaient 113 F le quintal quand elles venaient des colonies, 64 F quand elles venaient de l'étranger.

En francs constants, le montant des ventes de matières premières coloniales doubla de 1928 à 1938. Inversement, les exportations françaises vers les colonies diminuaient de 35 % pendant la même période. Calculées en milliards de francs–1928, ces exportations qui avaient atteint 4,8 milliards en 1913 et 9,7 en 1929, régressaient à 4,7 milliards en 1936 et 3,6 en 1938. L'autarcie impériale jouait en faveur des colonies, au détriment de la métropole.

Les exportations de produits alimentaires français dans les colonies étaient tombées à l'indice 58 en 1938 pour un indice 100 en 1930. En revanche, les importations des produits alimentaires coloniaux se situaient à l'indice 119 en 1938. Concrètement, cela se traduisait par l'augmentation de la production des cultures spéculatives dans l'outre-mer et l'aggravation de la crise agricole en France : les paysans français durement concurrencés par l'importation de céréales et de vins coloniaux protestaient, mais seuls les puissants betteraviers parvinrent à se faire entendre.

La crise, qui augmentait les déficits de la balance commerciale France-colonies aux dépens de la métropole, privait certes les colonies du flot antérieur des investissements privés. Mais les gouvernements coloniaux furent autorisés à partir de 1930 à emprunter largement et à des taux faibles sur le marché français. Alors que de 1920 à 1929 les emprunts publics des colonies ne dépassèrent pas 676 millions de F-or, ils atteignaient 5 fois plus dans les années 1930. Or ces emprunts obligataires, qui totalisèrent 3 388,9 millions de F-or de 1930 à 1939, furent souscrits par les épargnants français pour une rémunération modique, 4 à 5 %. Ils serviront à des fins diverses, mais toutes utiles : grands travaux d'hydraulique agricole (en Indochine), équipements portuaires et routiers (en Afrique noire), mais on les utilisa aussi pour réaliser des équilibres budgétaires souvent nécessaires. L'investissement public substitué à l'investissement privé déficient avait certes des inconvénients, essentiellement le poids accru de la dette. Un quart du budget général de l'A.O.F. y était consacré en 1939 et le cinquième de celui de l'Indochine. Mais il avait l'avantage d'éviter le recours aux finances locales et à la fiscalité immédiate. Ainsi s'efforçait-on d'équiper les colonies et de maintenir le niveau de consommation des colonies, fût-il très bas.

La crise n'en affecta pas moins douloureusement les campagnes, surtout en Indochine et au Maghreb. La paysannerie pauvre déjà victime d'une surpopulation galopante souffrit considérablement. Le chômage paysan en

Indochine, peuplée désormais de 23 millions d'habitants, était tel que dans le delta du Tonkin sur quatre paysans, un seul eût été nécessaire, et en Cochinchine, un sur deux. Or chaque année la population s'accroissait de 180000 habitants. La paupérisation des petits fellahs maghrébins se traduisit jusque dans la statistique foncière : les petits propriétaires qui représentaient 70 % du nombre des propriétaires musulmans algériens en 1930, virent leur nombre ramené à 65,3 % du total en 1939. Simultanément, la grande propriété coloniale augmenta. Partout les paysans endettés et expropriés affluaient dans les villes. Cette offre de travail surabondante eut surtout pour effet de déprimer les salaires. Cette révolution sociale qui déracinait des ruraux traditionalistes allait être lourde de conséquences : des sous-prolétaires s'entassaient dans des bidonvilles et formaient un milieu social explosif.

La solution, qui aurait consisté à développer une industrie de main-d'œuvre, était certes proposée par quelques personnalités du monde des affaires; peut-être aurait-elle été profitable à l'Indochine. Mais outre le fait qu'elle était difficile à susciter pendant une crise de surproduction, elle ne pouvait que «concurrencer l'industrie métropolitaine et y accroître le chômage», comme l'expliqua le ministre des Colonies Marius Moutet. Pourtant dans certaines zones où les capitaux privés continuaient à s'investir, au Maroc par exemple, l'industrialisation avait démarré très vite. Elle continuait à se développer sur la lancée antérieure en Indochine; ailleurs elle était presque inexistante, sauf dans le domaine des Travaux publics.

Dans ces conditions, il paraît difficile comme le faisaient alors les théoriciens marxistes, d'incriminer le seul capitalisme métropolitain responsable de «la grande misère des indigènes». Certes les sociétés installées aux colonies furent longtemps de «bonnes affaires» pour leurs actionnaires, puisqu'elles réalisèrent longtemps des taux de profit, en moyenne supérieurs aux taux métropolitains. Mais on sait aujourd'hui qu'aucun système économique n'eût été de toute manière capable de transformer en quelques années l'économie de territoires dépourvus de sources d'énergie et souvent surpeuplés. Et l'on a pu calculer que dans diverses colonies, les années 1920-1929 tout au moins, furent marquées par une forte croissance économique.

Évaluations ou recensements de la population de la France d'outre-mer en 1936

	Superficie en km²	Européens et assimilés		Populations indigènes en milliers	Population totale en milliers
		Français	Étrangers		
AFRIQUE					
Algérie	2 204 864	835 209	134 043	6 248	7 235
Tunisie	155 830	108 068	105 137	2 395	2 608
Maroc	398 627	177 049	59 553	6 059	6 296
A.O.F.	4 701 575	97 657 (a)	7 650	14 597	14 702
Togo	56 500	336	91	738	739
Cameroun	422 000	1 761	563	3 759	3 798
A.E.F.	2 487 000	3 856	893	3 418	3 423
Madagascar	592 000	25 255	14 343	3 759	3 798
et dépendances	350 000				
Réunion	2 511	203 319	5 539		209
Côte française des Somalis	21 700	923	958	44	46
TOTAL	11 392 807	1 471 433	328 770	39 597	41 397
ASIE					
Indochine	740 400	41 285	975	22 988	23 030
Kouang-Tchéou-Wan	842	266	4	206	206
Établissements de l'Inde	513	190 000		270	299
États du Levant	200 000	11 000		3 000	3 217
TOTAL	941 355	242 551	979	26 464	26 752
AMÉRIQUE					
St-Pierre-et-Miquelon	240	3 969	206		4
Guadeloupe et dépendances	1 780	303 000			304
Martinique	1 106	245 565	1 147		247
Guyane et Inini	91 000	27 000	6 000	4	37
TOTAL	94 126	579 534	7 353	4	592
OCÉANIE					
Nouvelle-Calédonie et dépendances	18 653	15 472	1 912	36	53
Ets français de l'Océanie	3 998	25 779	721	17	44
Nouvelles-Hébrides Condominium franco-britannique	12 000	861	259	49	50
TOTAL	34 651	42 112	2 892	102	197

(a) dont 80 509 Africains citoyens français.

Total Afrique + Asie + Amérique + Océanie : superficie (km²) 12 462 939

Populations européennes et assimilées	2 335 630	Français
	339 994	Étrangers
Population totale	68 938 000	

2 *Les conséquences de la Deuxième Guerre mondiale dans l'évolution de l'outre-mer français*

LE RÔLE DES FORCES EXTÉRIEURES

LA POLITIQUE ANTICOLONIALISTE DU PRÉSIDENT ROOSEVELT

Conscients de leur origine coloniale et de leur réussite lorsqu'ils furent devenus une fédération d'États indépendants, les Américains accentuèrent, pendant la Deuxième Guerre mondiale, leur prédication anticoloniale. Pour eux l'indépendance était le but final, inévitable et moral que devaient atteindre toutes les colonies.

Le président Roosevelt, connu comme le fidèle disciple du président Wilson, partageait ses opinions anticolonialistes. Pour ces démocrates convaincus les impérialismes coloniaux mettaient en jeu la paix du monde et les dominations coloniales interdisaient l'avènement d'un monde libre. D'ailleurs, tous les peuples «dépendants», colonies ou protectorats, avaient droit comme les colonies anglaises d'Amérique à être libérés du joug européen. La mission des États-Unis était de les y aider.

C'est ainsi que le président Roosevelt ne cessa de répéter que la charte de l'Atlantique (12 août 1941), et spécialement son point 3, étaient pleinement applicables à tous les peuples coloniaux. Son secrétaire d'État, Cordell Hull, fit le 23 juillet 1942 une importante déclaration où il affirmait que l'adhésion à la charte de l'Atlantique impliquait l'obligation d'accepter le droit des peuples coloniaux à se gouverner librement : «Cela a été notre but dans le passé, et restera notre but dans l'avenir d'user pleinement de notre influence pour aider tous les peuples à reconquérir leur liberté.»

Au mois de mars 1943, le département d'État proposa une «Déclaration des Nations unies sur l'indépendance nationale» qui prévoyait que toutes les puissances coloniales prendraient l'engagement d'amener progressivement leurs colonies à l'indépendance, en fixant même des dates pour celle-ci. L'avenir des territoires coloniaux revêt, disait-elle, un caractère international et ne concerne pas seulement les puissances coloniales.

Ce projet, accepté par F.D. Roosevelt, mais jugé trop modéré par le vice-président Wallace et par d'autres leaders, républicains, comme Wendell Wilkie dans son livre *One World*, ou démocrates comme Sumner Welles dans

Time for Decision, se heurta au refus des Britanniques et aux réserves d'autres Départements américains, ceux de la Guerre et de la Marine. F.D. Roosevelt n'en restait pas moins décidé à imposer dans l'après-guerre un système de *trusteeship* international. Celui-ci consistait à placer les territoires de peuples dépendants sous une tutelle, remise à des *trustees* (fidéi-commis) chargés «d'aider ces peuples à se développer au point de vue matériel et culturel, à se préparer eux-mêmes aux devoirs et aux obligations qu'entraîne l'autonomie et à parvenir aussi à l'indépendance.» Ce système correspondait certes à l'idéal français du protectorat réformateur et au principe du mandat de la SDN, mais il devait être international et soumis soit à la juridiction de la future Organisation des Nations unies, soit à celle d'un Conseil de grandes Puissances. L'idéalisme américain n'ignorait donc pas la place à réserver aux intérêts politiques et stratégiques de ces dernières.

Les préoccupations économiques et commerciales n'étaient pas non plus absentes de ces projets. Comme la plupart des experts économiques et des hommes d'affaires américains, F.D. Roosevelt entendait aussi faire triompher le principe de la «porte ouverte» dans le commerce international et supprimer les pratiques protectionnistes chères, en particulier, au colonisateur français.

Quand, le 23 octobre 1944, le président Roosevelt reconnut enfin le gouvernement provisoire de la République française, dirigé par le général de Gaulle, cela pouvait signifier aussi qu'il renonçait à ses projets de *trusteeship* sur l'empire colonial français. En fait, il demandait cependant un peu plus tard, que les Français promettent solennellement que l'indépendance serait un des buts de leur politique en Indochine et qu'ils ne fermeraient pas la porte de leurs colonies au commerce américain. Dans une conférence de presse, tenue deux mois avant sa mort, il revenait même à son idée d'un Conseil international qui dirigerait l'Indochine.

Le cas de l'Indochine lui paraissait, en effet, le plus clair, celui qui appelait une solution d'urgence. En aucun cas, répéta-t-il souvent, l'Indochine, lorsqu'elle sera libérée de l'occupation japonaise, ne devra être replacée sous l'autorité française. Roosevelt, qui n'avait jamais visité l'Indochine, imaginait la domination de la France comme ayant livré ce pays au pillage et à l'exploitation la plus éhontée : «La France a possédé l'Indochine depuis près de cent ans (*sic*). Or ce peuple de 30 (*sic*) millions d'habitants (23 en 1939) vit aujourd'hui beaucoup plus mal qu'au début de l'occupation [...]. Les habitants de l'Indochine ont finalement droit à un sort sensiblement meilleur» (Mémorandum pour le secrétaire d'État Hull).

Quand son représentant à Alger, Robert Murphy, eut signé avec le général Giraud un accord militaire et économique, qui prévoyait expressément la garantie américaine du retour à la France de l'ensemble de son Empire, Roosevelt lui écrivit : «Jamais vous n'auriez dû faire cela. Je n'ai nullement l'intention de rendre l'Indochine à la France.» Et aux chefs d'État-Major, il déclara : «Murphy a outrepassé ses droits en garantissant l'intégrité des possessions coloniales françaises. Je ne veux pas m'engager sur leur retour à la France. Il n'est pas question de lui rendre l'Indochine.» Lors de son entretien au Caire avec le général Tchang Kai-chek, le chef de la Chine nationaliste, le 23 novembre 1943, il lui confia : «L'Indochine doit devenir indépendante», cependant qu'il précisa au Premier ministre turc Ismet Inönü qu'il avait décidé de placer ce pays sous *trusteeship* international. Lors de la conférence de Téhéran, il affirma que «les habitants de l'Indochine vivaient plus mal qu'à l'époque où ils n'étaient que des sauvages» et qu'il fallait liquider le système colonial français. La Nouvelle-Calédonie, notamment, devait être placée sous *trusteeship* et, plus encore, l'Indochine. Mais Roosevelt hésitait pourtant sur la forme de la tutelle : il proposa plus tard un conseil de trois commissaires : un Américain, un Chinois et un Anglais, puis fin février 1945, un Conseil de tuteurs internationaux comprenant «un Chinois, un Russe, un Français, un ou deux Indochinois et peut-être un Philippin ou un Américain». Ce rêve tenace d'internationalisation se situait à un moment où la Conférence de Yalta (4-11 février), avait finalement décidé que le *trusteeship* ne s'appliquerait qu'aux territoires déjà sous mandat de la SDN ou détachés des États ennemis et à ceux qui y seraient volontairement placés.

Lorsque Roosevelt fut surpris par la mort le 12 avril 1945, il n'avait pas encore arrêté de mesures précises concernant l'avenir politique de l'Indochine. Il avait seulement donné l'ordre aux services secrets américains d'aider la résistance intérieure aux Japonais, mais il entendait par là la seule résistance des communistes vietnamiens de Hô Chi Minh, à l'exclusion de la résistance française.

LES ÉTATS-UNIS ET LE MAGHREB (1942-1944)

Les U.S.A. furent aussi contraints, dès novembre 1940, de s'intéresser à l'Afrique du Nord. En prévision de leur entrée en guerre et de la possibilité d'utiliser cette région comme base d'attaque contre les pays de l'Axe, ils y envoyèrent aux fins d'information une nuée d'agents et de diplomates. Ils acceptèrent même de l'aider économiquement (accord Murphy-Weygand du 26 février 1941). Cette pénétration facilita le débarquement anglo-américain de novembre 1942 : bientôt en mai 1943, quelque 300000 soldats américains se trouvaient en Afrique du Nord.

En principe l'Administration américaine s'était engagée à respecter le statu quo colonial. Robert Murphy l'avait assuré par écrit le 2 novembre 1942 : la restauration de la France dans toutes ses possessions d'outre-mer est l'un des buts de guerre des Nations unies. Les accords Clark-Darlan du 22 novembre et Eisenhower-Darlan-Boisson du 7 décembre 1942 l'avaient confirmé : les États-Unis n'étaient intervenus en Afrique que pour libérer la France et «réaliser la restauration intégrale de l'Empire français».

Bien que certains historiens américains affirment que «les Américains ne seraient pas restés assez longtemps pour exercer une quelconque influence sur le cours des événements», le général Juin a pu écrire : «Il est de notoriété publique que les agents diplomatiques américains se sont toujours faits en Afrique du Nord les avocats des nationalistes les plus intransigeants.» On pourrait citer notamment le consul général américain Hooken A. Doolittle, dont une rue de Tunis porte aujourd'hui le nom. Ce diplomate activiste avait, dès février 1942, proposé à son gouvernement de réaliser un coup d'État, pour renverser le ministère Lakhoua, complètement inféodé aux autorités françaises. Il soutint ensuite aussi bien le chef du Vieux-Destour, Ta'albi, que les Néo-Destouriens adversaires de l'Axe, et spécialement Habib Bourguiba. Les fonctionnaires français n'ignoraient rien de ses activités et l'amiral Esteva notait avec agacement, en septembre 1942, «l'insistance des protagonistes de l'indépendance tunisienne à être en relations avec les États-Unis». Le consul américain intervint publiquement en 1943, pour défendre les nationalistes et empêcher la déposition de Moncef Bey, mais vainement. Il réussit en revanche, à soustraire Bourguiba aux poursuites judiciaires.

Mais les Français de l'époque, exaspérés par le comportement du consul américain, ignoraient que Doolittle agissait de sa propre initiative et qu'il en était réduit à dénoncer son supérieur Robert Murphy, pour «son appui souvent inconditionnel aux thèses colonialistes». Celui-ci tira argument des demandes françaises pour faire rappeler Doolittle en juillet 1943. Roosevelt, qui tint à le recevoir, lui aurait dit que son engagement auprès des nationalistes arabes était seulement prématuré. Doolittle, ayant été ensuite nommé au Caire, on lui attribua la responsabilité de la fuite de Bourguiba en Égypte. Douze vice-consuls extraordinaires agirent ainsi, quoique plus discrètement, en Afrique du Nord, confondant la révolution antivichyssoise qu'ils avaient été chargés d'allumer avant novembre 1942 et l'agitation anticoloniale.

Au Maroc ce fut le président Roosevelt qui joua en personne les agents provocateurs, faisant briller aux yeux du sultan la possibilité d'échapper au Protectorat français. Lors de la conférence d'Anfa-Casablanca en janvier 1943, Roosevelt fit comprendre au sultan Sidi Mohammed, puis à quelques membres de son entourage, que les États-Unis appuieraient le Maroc dans ce but et que les capitaux américains s'y investiraient largement. Le grand vizir expliqua alors à Harry Hopkins, le conseiller intime de Roosevelt, les desiderata du Maroc : un plébiscite pour proclamer l'indépendance, la garantie américaine pour l'assurer et le refus de tout privilège accordé aux Juifs. Or Roosevelt n'était pas favorable à l'indépendance immédiate et il songeait à une tutelle internationale. Il fit seulement savoir que l'application d'un *numerus clausus* appliqué aux Juifs était légitime pour limiter leur influence. Roosevelt laissa ignorer aux Marocains qu'il envisageait un protectorat international provisoire confié à trois *trustees* : un Français, un Anglais et un Américain. Pourtant, des revues américaines comme *Victory* ou *The Arab World* célébraient «le nationalisme contre l'impérialisme français au Maroc», avant de dire «la nécessité impérieuse d'un protectorat américain». Une partie de la presse américaine reprenant les suggestions du célèbre *columnist*, Walter Lippman, fixait comme l'un des buts de guerre essentiels «la reconnaissance par les U.S.A., en temps opportun, du droit d'autonomie régionale pour les musulmans d'Afrique du Nord.» Ses agents de l'O.S.S. (*Office of Strategic Services*) dont le célèbre Walter Cline, exerçaient leur propagande dans les villes du Maroc, promettant l'aide économique, la formation technique et jusqu'à la création d'une université américaine. Dans ces conditions, les nationalistes marocains se sentirent assez forts pour lancer, le 11 janvier 1944, une déclaration d'indépendance. Ils escomptaient une vive pression américaine en leur faveur, mais furent déçus.

Il en alla de même en Algérie où la présence américaine et des rumeurs incontrôlées firent croire aux nationalistes qu'ils pourraient compter sur une aide américaine. Dès le 20 décembre 1942, ils avaient adressé un *Message des représentants des Musulmans algériens aux autorités responsables*, comme si la souveraineté française avait déjà disparu. Le *Manifeste du peuple algérien* (10 février 1943), rédigé par Ferhat Abbas, fut-il inspiré par Robert

Murphy, représentant personnel du président Roosevelt? Les résistants français l'ont affirmé, mais leur accusation ne repose sur aucun début de preuve. R. Murphy ne fit jamais de promesses de libération aux Algériens et ne rencontra F. Abbas qu'une seule fois. Quant aux propos de ce dernier, selon lesquels il aurait été reçu par le président Roosevelt en rade d'Alger, et que lui aurait été promise la formation d'un gouvernement sous sa direction, ils relèvent de l'affabulation.

On ne saurait pourtant négliger le fait que les Américains répandirent à profusion en Algérie des milliers d'exemplaires de la charte de l'Atlantique et qu'ils ne démentirent jamais les nouvelles selon lesquelles la conférence de San Francisco allait obliger la France à renoncer à sa souveraineté en Algérie et à ses protectorats marocain et tunisien. Dans un rapport rédigé par le *State Department* le 28 mai 1948, celui-ci reconnut que «la propagande de guerre des U.S.A. fut en partie responsable du récent sursaut du nationalisme en Afrique du Nord et du présent malaise dans cette zone.» Vis-à-vis de l'Afrique sub-saharienne, au contraire, les États-Unis se montrèrent pendant l'immédiat après-guerre aussi indifférents que l'étaient alors les Soviétiques.

LE RÔLE DE L'U.R.S.S. ET DU COMMUNISME INTERNATIONAL (1939-1945)

L'U.R.S.S., en principe favorable à l'indépendance de tous les peuples colonisés, ne put jouer qu'un rôle effacé à l'extérieur de ses frontières pendant la Deuxième Guerre mondiale. Vue sous l'angle français, elle parut même assez indifférente aux questions coloniales qui, sauf pour l'Indochine, relevaient de l'action du Parti communiste français.

Pendant la période de rapprochement avec l'Allemagne hitlérienne (septembre 1939 à juin 1941), le *Komintern* se montra cependant violemment hostile à «l'impérialisme français». Sa propagande contre les colonialistes français manqua toutefois d'efficacité. Ce fut seulement en Cochinchine que les communistes osèrent déclencher une insurrection, rapidement étouffée en quinze jours (22 novembre - 6 décembre 1940); elle avait pour but de constituer un gouvernement populaire de la République démocratique indochinoise.

Après juillet 1941, le *Komintern* cessa d'attaquer l'impérialisme français dans la mesure où la France libre devint peu à peu une alliée de l'U.R.S.S. Bientôt la dissolution tactique du *Komintern* obligea les communistes à une certaine réserve. Mais ces revirements imposés aux partis communistes coloniaux et au P.C.F. ne changeaient rien au jugement que les dirigeants soviétiques portaient sur la France et l'avenir de ses colonies. Lors de la Conférence de Téhéran (28 novembre - 2 décembre 1943), Staline affirma nettement que la France, «cette nation si perfide ne devait pas retrouver l'Indochine ni son empire colonial». Il le répéta à la Conférence de Yalta en février 1945 : «Je ne vois pas pourquoi les Alliés devraient suer du sang pour rendre l'Indochine à la France [...]. Ce qui se passe au Liban démontre que notre premier devoir est de donner l'indépendance aux peuples des anciens empires coloniaux [...]. Il ne faut pas rendre aux Français leurs colonies. Ce serait de la folie de leur laisser des points stratégiques importants.»

Presque abandonnés à eux-mêmes, les partis communistes coloniaux, devenus clandestins depuis septembre 1939, n'en continuèrent pas moins à agir. En Algérie, par exemple, le premier numéro de la *Lutte sociale*, illégal, réclamait à nouveau en novembre 1940 «l'indépendance de l'Algérie pour constituer dans notre pays un gouvernement démocratique algérien». Le journal poursuivit dans cette voie jusqu'au moment de l'invasion de l'U.R.S.S. Intervint alors un virage total de la ligne des partis communistes : c'était le retour à la tactique du Front populaire qui était imposé au nom de la lutte contre le fascisme allemand.

La première réunion publique des trois partis communistes maghrébins (un parti communiste marocain venait d'être créé) se tint en août 1943. On y affirmait désormais : «C'est de l'union profonde des masses nord-africaines avec le peuple de France que dépend le sort des peuples maghrébins.» Lors de la 2e réunion (novembre 1943), les communistes soulignèrent même «la nécessité d'une politique d'union la plus large, de la France et de l'Empire, permettant d'accroître le rôle de la France dans le bloc des Nations unies». Allant plus loin encore en 1944, les partis communistes d'Afrique du Nord s'en prirent bientôt aux nationalistes marocains, algériens et tunisiens qui, gagnés à la charte de l'Atlantique, faisaient le jeu de «l'hégémonisme américain». Ainsi, de septembre 1944 à août 1945, menèrent-ils une véritable croisade contre les «pseudo-nationalistes» maghrébins. Dans ces conditions, la propagande communiste renonçant à la revendication indépendantiste pour se rapprocher de thèmes coloniaux, se coupa de ses militants autochtones, enfiévrés par l'espérance nationaliste. Les communistes le mesurèrent seulement à partir d'août 1945; ils esquissèrent alors un timide rapprochement avec les partis nationalistes qui devait les amener un an plus tard à leur proposer un Front national tunisien, un Front national démocratique algérien, un Front national marocain. Mais les nationalistes se gaussèrent pour la plupart des «zigzags du communisme, cette idéologie étrangère qui fait souvent cause commune avec les oppresseurs».

En Indochine le parti communiste, légal en Cochinchine depuis 1936, avait dû accepter de 1935 à 1939 la tactique du *Front commun démocratique* avec tous les éléments progressistes. Il se rallia au contraire avec satisfaction en 1939-1940 à la consigne de combattre à nouveau «l'impérialisme français pour recouvrer l'indépendance». Mais après l'échec du soulèvement armé de Cochinchine en novembre 1940, les dirigeants du P.C.I. (parti communiste indochinois) durent s'exiler en Chine.

Les nouvelles directives mondiales du *Komintern* les amenèrent en septembre 1941 à constituer un Front de l'indépendance du Viêt-nam (Viêt-nam Dôc-Lâp Dông Minh Hôi, en abrégé Viêt-minh), lequel se donnait pour but «la destruction du colonialisme et de l'impérialisme fasciste». Nguyên Aî Quôc, alias Hô Chi Minh (Celui qui éclaire) en fut le secrétaire général permanent, même pendant la période où les Chinois l'emprisonnèrent, avant de patronner les activités clandestines des partisans communistes au Tonkin. Le gouvernement nationaliste chinois rêvait, en effet, de constituer au Viêt-nam un État satellite, mais, grâce à son aide financière et militaire, le Viêt-minh réussit à s'implanter solidement dans le Nord du pays.

Dès le début de 1944, le Viêt-minh condamna la volonté du général de Gaulle de maintenir la souveraineté française en Indochine. Puis il passa à l'action militaire contre les postes français en novembre 1944. Cependant le 9 mars 1945 les occupants japonais annihilaient brusquement les autorités françaises. L'empereur Bao Daî déclarait aussitôt aboli le Protectorat français et constituait un gouvernement nationaliste du Viêt-nam.

Les Américains, le jugeant inféodé aux Japonais, décidèrent d'appuyer et d'armer le Viêt-minh. Celui-ci agit avec promptitude : quatre jours après l'explosion de la bombe d'Hiroshima et alors même que le Japon n'avait pas capitulé, Hô Chi Minh donnait l'ordre d'insurrection générale. Celle-ci se déroula presque pacifiquement : le gouvernement nationaliste s'effaça, l'empereur Bao Daî confia le pouvoir au Viêt-minh, puis abdiqua le 25 août. À cette date les communistes étaient maîtres de tout le Viêt-nam. Le 2 septembre, le gouvernement Hô Chi Minh proclamait l'indépendance et l'avènement de la République démocratique : «Nous déclarons n'avoir plus désormais aucun rapport avec la France impérialiste, annuler tous les traités que la France a signés au sujet du Viêt-nam, abolir tous les privilèges que les Français se sont arrogés sur notre territoire.» La proclamation ne comportait pas la moindre référence à l'U.R.S.S.

L'ONU ET LA DÉCOLONISATION FRANÇAISE : UN TRIBUNAL INTERNATIONAL OU UNE TRIBUNE DE L'ANTICOLONIALISME ?

L'Organisation des Nations unies, conçue par les États-Unis comme une nouvelle SDN, fut naturellement marquée, dès sa création, par l'anticolonialisme américain. La charte des Nations unies (25 juin 1945) consacra de ce fait de nombreux articles aux questions coloniales. En faisant référence au principe de l'égalité des droits des peuples et à leurs droits de disposer d'eux-mêmes, en posant le principe d'un contrôle sur «les territoires non autonomes», la Charte innovait : elle plaçait en fait l'ensemble du monde colonial dans le domaine de la responsabilité internationale. Pratiquement, elle définit aussi un régime de tutelle pour les anciens mandats de la SDN en créant un *Conseil de tutelle* chargé de la surveillance des autorités de la puissance administrante. Dominé d'abord par les représentants des États colonisateurs, et dénoncé comme «un aréopage tout puissant de gouverneurs généraux en retraite», le Conseil de tutelle dut ensuite se plier aux volontés de l'Assemblée générale des Nations unies. Celle-ci, par l'intermédiaire de sa 4e commission, conduisit une politique visant à précipiter la fin du régime des «territoires sous tutelle». Ce fut cette politique de plus en plus interventionniste, mise d'abord en action dans le Togo, que la France essaya en vain de freiner. Pour l'Assemblée, les territoires sous tutelle devaient être conduits à l'indépendance dans un délai rapproché.

Concernant les colonies proprement dites, «les territoires non autonomes», la Charte faisait obligation aux États coloniaux de développer la capacité des populations qu'ils administraient à une vie politique autonome. Ils devaient «assurer, en respectant leur culture, leur progrès politique, économique et social, ainsi que le développement de leur instruction». La création, le 16 décembre 1946, d'un modeste comité des statistiques, devenu le 2 décembre 1949, le Comité spécial pour l'examen des renseignements sur les territoires non autonomes, permit à ce dernier de se calquer sur le modèle du Conseil de tutelle. Il entendait obtenir un droit de regard sur tous les territoires d'outre-mer, en réclamant des informations d'ordre économique ou social mais aussi politiques.

L'anticolonialisme de l'ONU, d'abord modéré, devint de plus en plus violent et parfois inadapté aux réalités. L'ONU refusa par exemple d'accepter la départementalisation des Antilles françaises, plébiscitée par les populations, parce qu'elle-même n'avait pas été consultée. Elle suspecta la France d'étendre le suffrage politique dans ses territoires africains pour mettre en difficultés les partis séparatistes.

L'influence de l'ONU sur la décolonisation est le plus souvent fort exagérée. Elle ne parvint pas à se faire reconnaître comme un tribunal international. Même sur le plan politique, on remarquera que la fameuse Déclaration dite «historique» de l'ONU qui proclamait «solennellement la nécessité de mettre fin au colonialisme sous toutes ses formes et dans toutes ses manifestations» date seulement du 14 décembre 1960. Réclamer l'octroi de l'indépendance aux pays et aux peuples coloniaux après qu'eussent été reconnues les indépendances de tous les territoires asiatiques, et de la majeure partie des territoires africains, signifiait seulement prendre acte d'un processus historique. La décolonisation française, sauf celle des États sous tutelle, ne doit rien, on le verra, aux jugements et aux votes de l'Assemblée des Nations unies. Impuissante comme tribunal international, l'ONU s'affirma au contraire comme une influente tribune de propagande politique et développa peu à peu un mythe agissant. Les représentants des États qui se disaient anticolonialistes, tout en étant parfois totalitaires ou arriérés, exprimaient dans leurs discours, tout ce qu'attendaient les nationalistes maghrébins, togolais ou camerounais. Ils dénonçaient l'Union française comme un piège juridique, annonçaient «les proches funérailles du colonialisme français», s'élevaient contre l'envoi de représentants des territoires colonisés dans les Chambres françaises ou dans la délégation française à l'ONU. Ainsi leurs interventions constantes eurent-elles du moins le mérite de faire comprendre à la classe politique française et aux journalistes intéressés que la France n'était plus libre de diriger les affaires d'outre-mer à sa guise. Il n'est que de lire les rapports des chefs de la délégation française à l'ONU pour mesurer leurs inquiétudes. La France devrait bientôt, disaient-ils, «sauf à consentir la dislocation de ce qui fut l'Empire, se retirer des instances des Nations unies chargées des problèmes d'outre-mer» ou «consentir les réformes que nous jugeons opportunes ou nécessaires». Ainsi l'ONU posait-elle, sans aider à les résoudre, les questions relatives à la décolonisation française.

LA MONTÉE DES NATIONALISMES COLONIAUX DURANT LA GUERRE ET L'IMMÉDIAT APRÈS-GUERRE (1940-1947)

Le peuple français, qui mettait en partie ses espoirs de libération dans les ressources de son Empire, fut conforté dans sa vision par le loyalisme apparemment sans faille de ses sujets. Peu informé de ce qui se passait en profondeur dans les territoires de souveraineté française, il ne prit pas garde à la montée des nationalismes et fut stupéfait d'en découvrir la force et la violence à la fin de la guerre : alors seulement il jugea l'Empire menacé.

LA FIN DU MANDAT FRANÇAIS SUR LES ÉTATS DU LEVANT

Dans les États du Levant (Liban et Syrie), les nationalistes, bien que tenacement combattus par les autorités françaises, avaient affirmé leur puissance croissante durant l'entre-deux-guerres. Ils avaient même cru obtenir la levée du mandat français, grâce aux accords signés avec le gouvernement Léon Blum, en septembre et novembre 1936. Mais ces traités n'ayant pas été ratifiés par la France, les nationalistes arabes attendirent l'heure de leur revanche. Beaucoup d'entre eux mirent alors leurs espérances dans la victoire de l'Allemagne hitlérienne. Après la défaite et l'occupation de la France, ceux-ci s'affirmèrent ouvertement germanophiles. Les agents allemands faisaient projeter des films soulignant l'ampleur de la déroute française, multipliaient les promesses d'aide et proclamaient leur foi dans la constitution d'un empire arabe.

Les autorités françaises du Levant s'inquiétaient surtout de voir «les jeunes impressionnés par la puissance allemande se lancer dans la lutte et donner une vigueur nouvelle au mouvement nationaliste». Après un mois de grèves d'étudiants et de lycéens, en Syrie puis au Liban, qui dégénérèrent en affrontements, la démission des autorités mises en place par le haut-commissaire français, le général Dentz, représentant le gouvernement de Vichy, sentit la nécessité en avril 1941 de faire quelques concessions. Il réinstalla des gouvernements syrien et libanais modérés et créa des assemblées consultatives. Le chef du gouvernement syrien affectait de s'en contenter : «Les événements actuels font différer pour le moment nos aspirations politiques [nationales]».

Lorsque les nationalistes arabes d'Iraq se furent emparés du pouvoir par le coup d'État du général Rachid 'Alî al-Qaîlanî, les Britanniques intervinrent aussitôt; le gouvernement allemand qui souhaitait aider les nationalistes obtint du gouvernement de Vichy l'autorisation d'utiliser les ports et aérodromes du Liban et de Syrie, et de disposer des dépôts d'armes français. Winston Churchill décida alors d'envoyer une armée britannique dans ces États pour qu'ils ne devinssent pas une base stratégique allemande. Les «Français libres» s'y associèrent. Du 8 juin au 11 juillet 1941, de violents combats opposèrent les troupes françaises du Levant (35 000 hommes) et le corps d'armée anglo-australien (35 000 hommes), renforcé de la première division française libre. Bien que les forces de Vichy aient été indirectement aidées par l'aviation allemande, elles durent s'incliner. Le représentant du général Dentz signa un armistice qui remettait complètement le Levant à l'autorité britannique. Dès lors, malgré la proclamation de l'indépendance par le général Catroux, la France parut avoir été vaincue, et le prestige de la puissance mandataire s'effondra. Les nationalistes arabes se réjouirent que Churchill déclarât aux Communes le 9 septembre 1941 : «Il n'est pas question que la France conserve la position qu'elle avait en Syrie avant la guerre, ni même que, pendant la durée des hostilités, les intérêts des Français libres se substituent à ceux des Français de Vichy. La Syrie doit être rendue aux Syriens.»

Pour les Britanniques, il était plus important de «satisfaire les aspirations et de ménager les susceptibilités des Arabes» que celles des Français libres. Les Syriens dès lors refusèrent de négocier avec la France libre tout traité qui lui aurait reconnu le maintien de certaines positions, et le général anglais Spears les conforta dans leur souhait d'une indépendance totale. Le général Catroux, délégué de la France libre au Levant, annonça finalement le 24 janvier 1943 sa décision de rétablir en pleine guerre, la vie constitutionnelle au Levant et d'y organiser des élections. Celles-ci assurèrent en Syrie le triomphe des nationalistes et le retour dans le Parlement de bon nombre des élus de 1936. Réunis le 17 août 1943, les parlementaires syriens désignèrent comme président de la République, Choukry al-Quwatly, la personnalité la plus en vue du mouvement national, et l'un des signataires du traité franco-syrien de 1936.

Au Liban, les candidats francophiles furent battus et le général Spears fit désigner comme président de la République, Bechara al-Khoury, un chrétien maronite; ce dernier choisit comme chef du gouvernement un avocat musulman nationaliste arabe, Ryad al-Solh. Dès le 7 octobre, celui-ci annonça une réforme constitutionnelle qui effacerait «toute disposition inconciliable avec l'indépendance du pays». Le président du Conseil syrien en fit autant de manière à ce que fût unilatéralement aboli tout vestige du mandat français. Le nouveau délégué français, Jean Helleu, crut pouvoir mâter ces nationalistes, comme il l'avait vu faire à Meknès en mai 1934. Mais les temps avaient changé et le Comité d'Alger n'avait plus les moyens d'une politique de force. Cependant, le 10 novembre 1943, le président de la République du Liban et plusieurs membres du gouvernement furent arrêtés sur ordre de l'ambassadeur Helleu et la Chambre dissoute. Ainsi provoquée la nation libanaise, chrétiens et musulmans pour une fois d'accord, se révolta. Un gouvernement libanais libre se forma dans le Chouf, tandis qu'aucun notable pressenti par J. Helleu n'accepta de former un cabinet.

Le 13 novembre, de Gaulle avait décidé d'envoyer sur place le général Catroux avec pleins pouvoirs pour régler le conflit. Celui-ci s'y employa avec décision en rétablissant les ministres prisonniers dans leurs fonctions et en préparant le transfert aux gouvernements libanais et syrien des divers services communs. La signature d'un accord conforme le 22 décembre 1943 consacrait l'indépendance totale des États du Levant.

Une question pourtant demeurait réservée : celles des «troupes spéciales» syriennes qui, restées aux ordres des Français, pouvaient intervenir dans le maintien de l'ordre aux côtés de quelques unités françaises. C'est pourquoi le gouvernement syrien demanda en 1944, avec une insistance croissante, la cession à son autorité du commandement des «troupes spéciales» et l'évacuation des derniers soldats français.

Brusquement dans les premières semaines de 1945, la tension s'accrut. Depuis un an le nationalisme arabe flambait dans le Proche-Orient tout entier : les États arabes pensaient que l'heure était venue de ressusciter un grand empire arabe qui irait de l'océan Atlantique à «l'Océan arabe» (celui que les géographes appellent l'océan Indien). Le 7 octobre 1944, l'Iraq, la Syrie, le Liban, la Transjordanie et l'Égypte avaient signé un protocole d'accord qui esquissait le plan d'une ligue. L'Arabie saoudienne et le Yémen y adhérèrent au début de 1945. Enfin le 22 mars 1945 fut constitué le pacte de la ligue des nations arabes. On crut y voir l'annonce d'un empire unitaire.

Depuis janvier 1945, les populations du Levant multipliaient les manifestations antifrançaises, provoquant les réactions des troupes sous commandement français. Simultanément les Britanniques annonçaient qu'une division nouvelle allait renforcer leur 9e armée stationnée en Syrie, cependant que la France envoyait trois bataillons (2500 hommes) dont deux destinés à la relève. Le gouvernement syrien voulut y voir l'annonce de la reconquête alliée; des troubles éclatèrent à Beyrouth et ne cessèrent plus au Liban et en Syrie jusqu'à la fin du mois. Le 29 mai de véritables combats opposèrent à Damas les troupes françaises aux gendarmes et civils arabes qui réclamaient la constitution «d'une armée de libération nationale» contre «les oppresseurs français». Le général français donna l'ordre de réduire les centres de l'insurrection, utilisant deux canons et un avion. Ce «bombardement de Damas», comme l'appelèrent les Syriens aurait fait, selon eux, au moins un millier de morts (en fait 510 civils et 86 gendarmes syriens pendant toute la période).

Le gouvernement français ordonna le cessez-le-feu pour le 31 mai et le fit avant que Churchill n'eût envoyé à la France un menaçant ultimatum, préalablement lu à la Chambre des Communes car, disait-il : «le monde arabe ne doit pas avoir l'impression que le gouvernement britannique n'a rien fait pour soutenir la Syrie et le Liban contre l'agression française». Le «bombardement de Damas» devait provoquer de violentes réactions antifrançaises dans toutes les capitales arabes. Les gouvernements syrien et libanais en appelèrent à l'ONU, saisirent le Conseil de sécurité, demandèrent que les deux généraux français fussent mis en accusation devant un tribunal international. C'était la première fois que ces procédures furent imaginées; ce ne devait pas être la dernière. Français et Anglais négocièrent et aboutirent le 4 mars 1946 à un accord de retrait simultané de leurs troupes. Les derniers soldats français et britanniques évacuèrent la Syrie le 30 avril, le Liban le 31 décembre. Les États du Levant avaient obtenu, comme ils le désiraient, une indépendance qui ne fût assortie d'aucun traité. Pour la France c'était le début de la décolonisation. Cette phase s'était déroulée pour elle de manière souvent humiliante et le général Catroux était fondé à dire : «La France qui avait compris en 1936 la nécessité de mettre fin aux mandats a laissé passer l'heure des compromis acceptables. Pour avoir trop voulu retenir, elle avait tout perdu.»

L'AFFIRMATION DU NATIONALISME ALGÉRIEN

Politiquement l'Algérie devait sortir de la Deuxième Guerre mondiale complètement transformée. En 1940, la défaite militaire y avait ruiné le prestige de la puissance française et le régime de Vichy se complaisait dans le masochisme. Même si la figure du maréchal Pétain réalisa au début l'unanimité, les musulmans n'espérèrent pas longtemps de la «Révolution nationale» une amélioration de leur situation. Ferhat Abbas fit une ultime tentative le 10 avril 1941 pour inviter le gouvernement à réaliser un programme réformateur capable de donner à «six millions d'Orientaux qui vivent dans une position amoindrie» le désir de vivre ensemble avec les Français d'Algérie. Aucune réforme ne fut entreprise et le courant nationaliste antifrançais se renforça, attisé par les propagandes étrangères. Simultanément, la situation économique et sociale se détériorait tandis que se propageait une grave épidémie de typhus.

En novembre 1942, le débarquement anglo-américain apparut aux Algériens comme une victoire américaine, suivie d'une occupation par les troupes alliées. La France, qui n'avait pas pu s'y opposer, n'était décidément plus pour eux une grande puissance : l'heure était venue d'en secouer la domination. Dès le 20 décembre 1942, douze personnalités algériennes adressèrent «aux autorités responsables» un «Message des représentants des musulmans algériens» pour demander l'élaboration d'un nouveau statut politique assurant leur affranchissement politique. Les dirigeants français n'y répondirent pas. Alors en février 1943, Ferhat Abbas rédigea un *Manifeste du peuple algérien*, plus combatif qui réclamait pour l'Algérie l'application du droit des peuples à disposer d'eux-mêmes (cf. extrait du *Manifeste*, p. 58). Ce texte fut suivi d'un *Additif* le 26 mai, encore plus révolutionnaire. Ce dernier *Projet de réformes faisant suite au Manifeste* réclamait la résurrection du peuple algérien, la reconnaissance de la nation algérienne souveraine et la formation d'un État algérien «démocratique et libéral» : «À la fin des hostilités, l'Algérie sera érigée en État algérien doté d'une constitution propre qui sera élaborée par une Assemblée algérienne constituante, élue au suffrage universel par tous les habitants du pays». À titre immédiat l'*Additif* demandait la formation d'un gouvernement algérien dont les ministres seraient, à parité, français et musulmans, et l'égalité totale entre Français et musulmans. S'il prévoyait l'organisation avec le Maroc et la Tunisie d'une fédération d'États nord-africains ou *Union nord-africaine*, l'*Additif* ignorait toute possibilité d'un lien fédéral avec la France à laquelle n'était concédé qu'un «droit de regard».

De Gaulle et le nouveau gouverneur de l'Afrique, le général Catroux, ne pouvaient accepter une semblable perspective. En revanche ils décidèrent un premier train de réformes en août 1943, puis préparèrent d'importantes innovations que de Gaulle annonça dans son discours de Constantine le 12 décembre. Passant outre à l'opposition des Français d'Algérie, qui déclarèrent ne pas reconnaître ces «abandons», le président du C.F.L.N. annonça l'attribution de la citoyenneté française dans le maintien du statut personnel à plusieurs dizaines de milliers de musulmans algériens. L'ordonnance du 4 mars 1944 précisa les catégories concernées : environ 65000 personnes entraient dans le collège électoral français. Tous les autres musulmans étaient appelés à jouir de la citoyenneté selon les modalités que déciderait la future Assemblée constituante française. L'ordonnance abolit définitivement l'indigénat, établit le principe de l'égalité civile et augmenta la représentation des musulmans dans toutes les assemblées locales algériennes, portée du tiers au 2/5e. C'était réaliser enfin les promesses de la politique d'assimilation, mais à une date où les Algériens nationalistes la rejetaient comme contraire à leur idéal. Ils le firent savoir notamment en se regroupant dans un nouveau parti créé par Ferhat Abbas, l'*Association des amis du manifeste et de la liberté* (A.M.L.). Les membres du *parti du peuple algérien* dirigé par Messali Hadj, parti dissous en 1939 mais reconstitué dans la clandestinité, en prirent pratiquement le contrôle. Par l'intermédiaire des A.M.L. qui connaissaient un immense succès populaire, ils répandirent des mots d'ordre préinsurrectionnels.

À la fin d'avril 1945, la population s'attendait à voir la Conférence des Nations unies réunie à San Francisco, proclamer l'indépendance de l'Algérie et la Ligue arabe lui ouvrir une place dans la Fédération des États arabes. C'est dans ce climat que, quelques jours après la déportation de Messali à Brazzaville et à l'occasion de la célébration de l'armistice du 8 mai, éclatèrent de dures émeutes notamment à Bône, Guelma et Sétif où 29 Européens furent massacrés. Bientôt autour de Sétif et de Guelma, toutes les campagnes s'insurgèrent spontanément. Les révoltés attaquaient les gardes forestiers isolés, les fermes européennes, certains villages de colonisation (à Périgotville 12 colons furent assassinés). Le 12 mai, l'insurrection avait été écrasée par l'armée française, mais les «rebelles» se réfugièrent dans les montagnes et la lutte continua jusqu'à la mi-juin. La direction du P.P.A., surprise, ordonna la généralisation de l'insurrection, puis se ravisa devant la violence de la réaction française. Au total, 88 civils européens et 14 militaires avaient été tués; du côté musulman, la répression aurait fait officiellement de 1000 à 1500 victimes. Mais les nationalistes algériens ont avancé des chiffres beaucoup plus élevés : 20000 selon Ferhat Abbas, 40000 selon le P.P.A., 80000 selon les *'ulamâ'*. Finalement le P.P.A.-M.T.L.D. accrédita le chiffre de «45000 martyrs» qui correspond à peu près à l'ensemble de la population insurgée. Ainsi fut expliquée l'accusation de «génocide» portée par les Algériens contre la France. L'insurrection du Nord-Constantinois entraîna aussi une sévère répression judiciaire : 3630 arrestations et jugements, 1868 condamnations à des peines de prison et 157 condamnations à mort, dont 33 furent exécutées.

Après ces tragiques événements et malgré une large amnistie accordée en mars 1946, il fut difficile aux habitants de l'Algérie de reprendre une vie commune : deux peuples s'affrontaient irrémédiablement.

En apparence la vie politique se réorganisa sur des bases nouvelles. Une ordonnance du 17 août 1945 créait, pour les musulmans algériens, un second collège électoral qui désignerait 13 députés à l'Assemblée constituante française, le même nombre que le premier collège où s'étaient finalement inscrits 32000 Français musulmans. Ferhat Abbas, à peine libéré, se prononçait désormais pour une Algérie fédérée à la France et créait un nouveau parti pour défendre ce programme adouci : *l'Union démocratique du manifeste algérien* (U.D.M.A.). Vainqueur aux élections du 2 juin 1946, Abbas échoua à Paris où il ne put faire accepter son projet. Mais en novembre Messali, plus tardivement libéré, reconstitua à son tour son parti, le P.P.A., sous le sigle du *Mouvement pour le triomphe des libertés démocratiques* (M.T.L.D.). Recherchant un plébiscite, Messali présenta des candidats aux élections de novembre 1946, qu'Abbas boycotta; agissant ainsi Messali dérouta ses partisans et n'obtint qu'un tiers des voix du second collège.

Le Parlement français prépara alors ce qui devint le 20 septembre 1947, *le Statut de l'Algérie*. Toutes les propositions émanant des Algériens furent écartées au profit d'un texte assez conservateur préparé par le gouvernement. La principale caractéristique en était la création d'une Assemblée algérienne de 120 membres, chacun des deux collèges disposait de la moitié des sièges. D'autre part le statut prévoyait une série de réformes : il proclamait l'indépendance du culte musulman, le principe de l'enseignement de la langue arabe à tous les degrés, la réorganisation des territoires du Sud. Les Algériens ne prirent pas au sérieux ces promesses qui ne furent d'ailleurs pas tenues. Ils ne virent que le refus d'une autonomie algérienne.

EXTRAITS DU *MANIFESTE DU PEUPLE ALGÉRIEN*, FAIT À ALGER LE 10 FÉVRIER 1943; REMIS AUX AUTORITÉS FRANÇAISES LE 31 MARS 1943

... «Nous sommes en Afrique du Nord, aux portes de l'Europe et le monde civilisé assiste à ce spectacle anachronique : une colonisation s'exerçant sur une race blanche au passé de civilisation prestigieuse, apparentée aux races méditerranéennes, perfectible et ayant manifesté un sincère désir de progrès.

Politiquement et moralement cette colonisation ne peut avoir d'autre concept que celui de deux sociétés étrangères l'une à l'autre. Son refus systématique ou déguisé de donner accès dans la cité française aux Algériens musulmans a découragé tous les partisans de la politique d'assimilation étendue aux autochtones. Cette politique apparaît aujourd'hui aux yeux de tous comme une réalité inaccessible, une machine dangereuse mise au service de la colonisation.

L'heure est passée où un Musulman algérien demandera autre chose que d'être un Algérien musulman [...]

[...] Le Président Roosevelt dans sa déclaration faite au nom des Alliés, a donné l'assurance que dans l'organisation du monde nouveau, les droits de tous les peuples petits et grands seraient respectés. Fort de cette déclaration, le Peuple algérien demande : [...]

A) La condamnation et l'abolition de la colonisation, c'est-à-dire de l'annexion et de l'exploitation d'un peuple par un autre peuple...

B) L'application pour tous les pays petits et grands du droit des peuples à disposer d'eux-mêmes;

C) La dotation à l'Algérie d'une constitution propre, garantissant :

1° la liberté et l'égalité absolues de tous ses habitants, sans distinction de race et de religion;
2° la suppression de la propriété féodale par une grande réforme agraire et le droit au bien-être de l'immense prolétariat agricole;
3° la reconnaissance de la langue arabe comme langue officielle au même titre que la langue française;
4° la liberté de la presse et le droit d'association;
5° l'instruction gratuite et obligatoire pour les enfants des deux sexes;
6° la liberté du culte pour tous les habitants et l'application à toutes les religions du principe de la séparation de l'Église et de l'État;

D) La participation immédiate et effective des Musulmans algériens au gouvernement de leur pays.»

Les nationalistes du M.T.L.D. avaient refusé de participer au débat, déniant à une assemblée française le droit de statuer sur l'Algérie : «C'est au peuple algérien de se prononcer sur les institutions qu'il entend se donner», déclara le député Mézerna. Le parti s'en tenait à son programme : «Une assemblée algérienne constituante souveraine, la restitution des terres expropriées à leur légitime propriétaire (l'Algérie arabe), la restitution des médersas à la culture arabe et des mosquées à la religion musulmane.» Aux élections municipales d'octobre 1947, qui furent les dernières élections non truquées de la IVe République en Algérie, les partis nationalistes emportèrent près des deux tiers des suffrages. Le M.T.L.D. obtint même la quasi-totalité des sièges dans les grandes villes : «Le peuple algérien a voté pour l'idée de la nation algérienne représentée par le M.T.L.D.», écrivit le journal *Al-Maghrib al-'Arabî.*

LE DÉVELOPPEMENT DU NATIONALISME MAROCAIN

Pendant la guerre de 1939-1940, le sultan prit publiquement position en faveur de la France et quelque 6000 soldats marocains furent tués aux côtés des Français. Le loyalisme du Maroc faisait l'admiration des autorités françaises.

Le désastre de 1940 fut pour les Marocains une première atteinte grave au prestige du Protectorat. L'humiliation des Français renforça les espérances des nationalistes. Les propagandes étrangères anglaise et allemande, diffusées par radio en langue arabe, ne manquaient pas de célébrer les radieuses perspectives qui s'ouvriraient après la guerre aux États arabes dépendants. Toutefois, la plupart des nationalistes marocains, sauf ceux de la zone espagnole ouvertement germanophiles, ne se laissèrent pas abuser par les promesses allemandes. Quelques notables seulement, dont certains de l'entourage du sultan, auraient flirté avec les agents de l'Abwehr.

Lorsque survint le débarquement anglo-américain, les Marocains eurent le sentiment d'assister à une nouvelle défaite française. Le Protectorat leur apparut d'autant plus affaibli que les Américains se présentaient comme «des libérateurs» et ne cachaient pas leur volonté d'aider dans l'avenir le Maroc à s'émanciper. Les nationalistes marocains, qui suivaient de près les efforts des Libanais et des Syriens pour se libérer du mandat français, furent convaincus, après l'échec de l'épreuve de force de novembre 1943 au Liban, que l'heure était venue d'agir. «Après cet exemple et cet encouragement, avertissait le résident Puaux, une période difficile s'ouvre pour le Protectorat». En décembre 1943, les nationalistes jusque-là divisés, s'unirent et fondèrent un nouveau parti, le parti de l'indépendance, *Hizb al-Istiqlâl*. Pour eux il n'était plus question de réformer le Protectorat, mais d'obtenir l'indépendance. C'est ce qu'expliqua avec hauteur le manifeste du 11 janvier 1944, en le justifiant par une critique sévère du Protectorat et de la colonie française (cf. *le Manifeste*, p. 61). Cinquante-huit signatures de notables suivaient ce texte dont celle du secrétaire général du parti Ahmed Balafrej. Le sultan avait été tenu au courant et avait encouragé le mouvement.

Le commissaire du Comité de la libération nationale, René Massigli, opposa une fin de non-recevoir à ce rejet du protectorat et le résident Puaux exigea du sultan une condamnation de l'Istiqlâl. Abandonné par les Américains qui ne voulaient pas d'agitation en temps de guerre, le sultan désavoua le 20 janvier le manifeste nationaliste : «Le mot d'*Istiqlâl* doit disparaître des bouches et des cerveaux.» Les nationalistes expliquèrent qu'ils n'avaient pas l'intention de réaliser leur idéal par la violence et qu'ils ne rejetaient pas la collaboration avec les Français ni la sauvegarde de leurs intérêts. Mais alors que la Résidence croyait être parvenue à une «liquidation de l'incident», la crise rebondit le 29 janvier avec l'arrestation par la Sécurité militaire de quatre chefs de l'Istiqlâl, accusés d'intelligence avec l'ennemi allemand. Tout porte à croire qu'il s'agissait d'une provocation politique destinée à susciter une réaction marocaine et à justifier la «destruction de l'état-major d'un mouvement nationaliste qui s'avérait plein de menaces pour l'avenir», comme l'expliqua le chef de la Sécurité militaire. Or la réaction marocaine fut plus vive que prévu : du 29 janvier au 7 février, les principales villes du Maroc connurent de graves émeutes qui furent réprimées par l'armée. Ces opérations firent 30 ou 40 tués marocains, une centaine de blessés et entraînèrent 1843 arrestations. La répression judiciaire et administrative par son ampleur renforça la solidarité des Marocains et étendit la revendication nationaliste dans des milieux qui n'avaient pas été gagnés jusque-là. Bref, voulant crever un abcès, la Sécurité militaire avait propagé l'épidémie. De plus, le prétendu «complot hitlérien» s'avéra mensonger. De Gaulle, tardivement mis au courant, fit stopper la procédure et le procès des quatre nationalistes n'eut jamais lieu. La conclusion était claire : le mouvement de l'Istiqlâl ne devait rien aux intrigues nazies. Certains responsables proposèrent alors «une politique nouvelle de libéralisme calculé» et des réformes étendues. Mais le résident s'en tint à des réformes administratives et sociales et rejeta toutes les réformes politiques.

Révélées fin novembre 1944, ces réformes prévoyaient la séparation des pouvoirs administratifs et judiciaires dans les six villes principales, l'annonce d'un code pénal marocain, la création d'un Conseil supérieur du paysannat, l'institution d'un bien de famille insaisissable, enfin un plan décennal de développement scolaire. Ces nouveautés qui auraient donné satisfaction à quelques-unes des demandes des Marocains en 1934, leur parurent dérisoires. L'Istiqlâl y vit «un cautère sur une jambe de bois», les plus modérés parlant de «timide esquisse». Les nationalistes reprirent et développèrent leur action auprès des masses. L'Istiqlâl qui comptait quelque 3000 militants en 1944, disposait au début de 1947 de 10000 à 15000 fidèles. Un nouveau parti, le parti communiste du Maroc (P.C.M.) concurrençait désormais les «nationalistes bourgeois» : par sa critique des autorités françaises, une politique d'aide sociale et la revendication du droit syndical pour tous les Marocains, il s'attirait la sympathie du prolétariat naissant.

À partir de mars 1946, un nouveau résident imaginatif, Eirik Labonne, tenta de renverser le courant d'hostilité et de proposer des solutions neuves. Il fit libérer les deux leaders nationalistes de l'avant-guerre. Après onze ans d'exil, 'Allâl al-Fâsi et Mohammed Hassan Ouazzani purent reprendre leur militantisme. Ouazzani créa un parti dissident, le parti démocratique de l'indépendance, tandis que 'Allâl al-Fâsi devint le chef incontesté de l'Istiqlâl. Quant au programme ambitieux d'Eirik Labonne, qui prévoyait notamment l'industrialisation accélérée du Maroc, il se heurta à la double opposition des colons français et des nationalistes.

Le sultan tenu à l'écart se considérait comme «le prisonnier du Palais» et retrouva ainsi toute sa popularité. Dans un discours prononcé à Tanger le 10 avril 1947, le sultan parla des droits légitimes du Maroc, de son appartenance à la «nation arabe», de ses liens avec la Ligue arabe. Il remercia les États-Unis «pour les services rendus aux pays arabes», mais ne prononça pas la phrase que la résidence lui avait demandée, rendant également hommage aux Français «épris de cette liberté qui conduit le pays vers la prospérité et le

MANIFESTE DU PARTI DE L'ISTIQLÂL

Le parti de l'Istiqlâl (parti de l'Indépendance) qui englobe les membres de l'ex-parti national et des personnalités indépendantes;

Considérant que le Maroc a toujours constitué un État libre et souverain et qu'il a conservé son indépendance pendant treize siècles, jusqu'au moment où, dans des circonstances particulières, un régime de protectorat lui a été imposé;

Considérant que ce régime avait pour fin et pour raison d'être de doter le Maroc d'un ensemble de réformes administratives, judiciaires, culturelles, économiques, financières et militaires, sans toucher à la souveraineté traditionnelle du peuple marocain sous l'égide de son Roi;

Considérant qu'à ce régime les autorités du Protectorat ont substitué un régime d'administration directe et d'arbitraire au profit de la colonie française dont un fonctionnariat pléthorique et en grande partie superflu, et qu'elles n'ont pas tenté de concilier les divers intérêts en présence;

Considérant que c'est grâce à ce système que la colonie française a pu accaparer tous les pouvoirs et se rendre maîtresse des ressources vives du pays au détriment des autochtones;

Considérant que le régime ainsi établi a tenté de briser par des moyens divers l'unité du peuple marocain, a empêché les Marocains de participer de façon effective au gouvernement de leur pays, et les a privés de toutes les libertés publiques et individuelles;

Considérant que le monde traverse actuellement des circonstances autres que celles dans lesquelles le Protectorat a été institué;

Considérant que le Maroc a participé de façon effective aux guerres mondiales aux côtés des Alliés; que ses troupes viennent d'accomplir des exploits qui ont suscité l'admiration de tous, aussi bien en France qu'en Tunisie, en Corse, en Sicile et en Italie et qu'on attend d'elles une participation encore plus étendue sur d'autres champs de bataille, notamment pour aider à la libération de la France;

Considérant que les Alliés qui versent leur sang pour la cause de la liberté ont reconnu dans la Charte de l'Atlantique le droit des peuples à disposer d'eux-mêmes, et qu'ils ont récemment à la conférence de Téhéran proclamé leur réprobation de la doctrine qui prétend que le fort doit dominer le faible;

Considérant que les Alliés ont manifesté, à diverses reprises, leur sympathie à l'égard de peuples dont le patrimoine historique est moins riche que le nôtre et dont le degré de civilisation est d'un niveau inférieur à celui du Maroc;

Considérant enfin que le Maroc constitue une unité homogène qui, sous la haute direction de son souverain, prend conscience de ses droits et de ses devoirs, tant dans le domaine interne que dans le domaine international, et sait apprécier les bienfaits des libertés démocratiques qui sont conformes aux principes de notre religion et qui ont servi de fondement à la constitution de tous les pays musulmans;

Décide :

A) En ce qui concerne la politique générale :

1° De demander l'indépendance du Maroc dans son intégrité territoriale sous l'égide de Sa Majesté Sidi Mohammed Ben Youssef; que Dieu le glorifie!
2° De solliciter de Sa Majesté d'entreprendre avec les nations intéressées des négociations ayant pour objet la reconnaissance et la garantie de cette indépendance, ainsi que la détermination, dans le cadre de la souveraineté nationale, des intérêts légitimes des étrangers résidant au Maroc;
3° De demander l'adhésion du Maroc à la charte de l'Atlantique et sa participation à la conférence de la Paix.

B) En ce qui concerne la poltique intérieure :

De solliciter de Sa Majesté de prendre sous sa haute direction, le mouvement de réformes qui s'impose pour assurer la bonne marche du pays et laisse à Sa Majesté le soin d'établir un régime démocratique, comparable au régime de gouvernement adopté dans les pays musulmans d'Orient, garantissant les droits de tous les éléments et de toutes les classes de la société marocaine et définissant les devoirs de chacun.

Fait à Rabat, le 14 Moharrem 1363 (11 janvier 1944)

Source : cette version du «Manifeste du parti de l'Istiqlâl» a été publiée par le parti dans le recueil *Documents 1944-1946*, Paris, septembre 1946. Une version antérieure, peut-être conforme au texte original, présente de notables différences de forme mais non de fond.

progrès». Le résident Labonne fut aussitôt révoqué «pour avoir fait confiance à un homme hostile à la France» selon le ministre des Affaires étrangères, Georges Bidault. Celui-ci oubliait peut-être que le sultan avait été fait «compagnon de la Libération» par le général de Gaulle. Un nouveau résident fut nommé, le 14 mai, le général Juin. Il aurait reçu dans ses instructions, la consigne suivante : «En cas d'obstruction du Palais, envisager soit une abdication volontaire (du sultan), soit une déposition provoquée par l'autorité française.» Ce texte est d'autant plus vraisemblable que le président du Conseil Ramadier, avait dit en Conseil des ministres : «Il faut que le sultan sache qu'il peut être déposé par la France. Il faut donc envoyer à Rabat un militaire.»

LES PROGRÈS DU NATIONALISME TUNISIEN (1940-1948)

En Tunisie comme dans l'ensemble du Maghreb, la chute militaire de la France encouragea les nationalistes tunisiens à reprendre leur combat dans la clandestinité. Certains Destouriens mirent leurs espoirs dans l'Allemagne car ils redoutaient l'impérialisme italien. Mais leur leader, bien qu'emprisonné à Marseille, réclama de ses fidèles «un soutien inconditionnel aux Alliés». Cependant l'arrivée sur le trône d'un prince connu pour ses sentiments nationalistes et son courage, Moncef Bey, allait immédiatement poser au résident français de difficiles problèmes. À peine intronisé le 19 juin 1942, Moncef Bey réclama à Vichy, le 2 août, en 16 propositions, d'importantes réformes politiques et économiques. Il n'obtint pas satisfaction. Il se heurta aussi au résident, l'amiral Esteva, dont il demanda vainement le rappel.

Avec l'arrivée des troupes allemandes, le 11 novembre 1942, la Tunisie entrait dans la guerre; elle devint pour six mois un théâtre d'opérations militaires qui lui causèrent de graves destructions. Pendant cette période d'occupation germano-italienne, les Tunisiens se divisèrent : certains accueillirent très favorablement les Allemands dont ils obtinrent la libération des prisonniers politiques et des encouragements aux Néo-Destouriens; d'autres, dont le bey, pratiquèrent une politique d'attentisme. Les Tunisiens pouvaient librement bafouer la France et les Français. Dans les campagnes, les fermes des colons furent pillées, des policiers français attaqués.

Cependant, Moncef Bey constitua de sa propre autorité, sans en référer au résident réduit à l'impuissance, un ministère d'Union nationale et se garda bien de contrecarrer la renaissance de l'activité du Néo-Destour. Habib Bourguiba, libéré par les Allemands le 16 décembre 1942 et conduit à Rome, fut soumis aux pressions des Italiens, mais il se refusa à prendre les engagements qu'ils lui demandaient. Il ne put rentrer en Tunisie qu'après avoir prononcé à la radio de Rome un discours ambigu où il remerciait les puissances de l'Axe, mais où il mettait en garde ses compatriotes contre « les convoitises de l'étranger ».

En mai 1943, les troupes alliées libéraient Tunis et les Français entreprirent aussitôt de restaurer le régime du Protectorat. Le général Giraud décida maladroitement de destituer le bey Moncef et de l'exiler à Laghouat. Ce bey, déjà très populaire, devint dès lors aux yeux de tous les Tunisiens le martyr de la cause nationale. Le nationalisme se cristallisa autour de sa personne : tous les partis réclamèrent son retour jusqu'à sa mort en exil. À Paris, en avril-mai 1944, les Néo-Destouriens proallemands qui s'étaient enfuis de Tunisie dénonçaient devant des auditoires d'étudiants musulmans « La France qui avait livré l'Afrique du Nord aux Anglo-Saxons »; ils les appelaient à s'unir en vue de « l'émancipation de leur race et de leur patrie ». Pourtant les revendications réaffirmées à Tunis dans le *Manifeste du Front tunisien*, en novembre 1944, se bornaient « vu les circonstances » à réclamer « l'autonomie intérieure de la nation tunisienne ». Le résident Mast se limita à quelques réformes que l'opinion jugea dérisoires. Alors Habib Bourguiba, qui avait repris son rôle de leader incontesté du Néo-Destour, tout en prêchant une politique loyaliste vis-à-vis de la France, jugea en mars 1945 qu'il fallait forcer la main du gouvernement français depuis l'étranger. Il gagna clandestinement le Caire où venait de se constituer la Ligue des États arabes. Il devait y fonder un Comité de libération du Maghreb arabe, présidé par le vieux leader rifain Ben 'Abd el-Krîm. Il tenta aussi de sensibiliser à la cause tunisienne les États-Unis et l'ONU.

En Tunisie, malgré son absence, les nationalistes allaient de l'avant, après s'être regroupés dans un Front national tunisien. Ils étaient désormais solidement appuyés par une centrale syndicale nationale, l'Union générale tunisienne du travail (U.G.T.T.) constituée le 20 janvier 1946, en réaction contre la subordination de la C.G.T. au parti communiste. Le 23 août 1946, un congrès des principaux chefs nationalistes, notables et professeurs de la grande mosquée Zitouna, proclama « la volonté du peuple tunisien de recouvrer son indépendance intégrale. »

L'agitation nationaliste permanente fut à l'origine en janvier 1947 du rappel du résident Mast et de la nomination d'un ancien chef du cabinet de Léon

Blum, le préfet Jean Mons. Celui-ci aurait voulu faire revenir en Tunisie le bey exilé, mais le président du Conseil socialiste s'y opposa. Il procéda néanmoins à un certain nombre de réformes et investit un Premier ministre autorisé à constituer lui-même son gouvernement. Mais il ne lui appartenait pas d'accorder à la Tunisie ce que Bourguiba demandait : « un statut d'État souverain lié à la France par un traité d'alliance librement négocié qui garantisse à cette dernière ses intérêts stratégiques, économiques et culturels. » Dès lors l'expérience Mons échoua. La lutte sociale menée par l'U.G.T.T. tournait à la guérilla contre le régime colonial. L'agitation des étudiants de la Grande Mosquée reprit, manifestant l'émergence d'un courant arabo-musulman original, qui devenait autonome en rompant avec le Néo-Destour.

Avec la mort de Moncef Bey à Pau, le 1er septembre 1948, une période de l'histoire tunisienne s'achevait, celle du moncéfisme où les Tunisiens signifièrent à la France la fin du Protectorat. La disparition du « bey destourien » allait laisser la place libre à Bourguiba que ses fidèles appelaient déjà « le combattant suprême ».

L'INDOCHINE FRANÇAISE SOUS OCCUPATION JAPONAISE (1940-1945)

La défaite militaire française ouvrait l'Indochine presque désarmée à l'occupation japonaise. En septembre 1940, les forces armées japonaises obtinrent d'abord la disposition d'un certain nombre d'aérodromes et un droit de libre circulation. Bientôt, elles furent autorisées à s'installer dans toute l'Indochine (accords Darlan-Kato du 29 juillet 1941). À ce prix, la souveraineté française fut maintenue, aussi longtemps qu'elle parut commode aux occupants japonais. Ceux-ci soutenaient d'ailleurs discrètement divers mouvements et partis nationalistes vietnamiens, voire cambodgiens. Quant aux communistes, ils avaient déclenché une insurrection limitée en Cochinchine, le 22 novembre 1940, que les autorités françaises purent écraser assez facilement. Dès lors les communistes s'efforcèrent, dans la clandestinité, de se préparer à une lutte anti-impérialiste dirigée à la fois contre « le colonialisme français et le fascisme nippon ». Ils mirent sur pied dès mai 1941, une Ligue révolutionnaire pour l'indépendance du Viêt-nam ou Viêt-minh qui prépara aussitôt pour l'avenir un soulèvement général alors parfaitement impossible.

Le gouverneur général de l'Indochine, l'amiral Decoux, pensa devoir lutter contre la propagande et l'action japonaises en développant une curieuse politique de contre-feu national et fédéral. Face au mythe japonais de la Grande Asie orientale, il tenta d'instaurer une mystique de la Fédération indochinoise, au-dessus des trois États protégés, annamite, laotien et khmer. Un conseil fédéral de vingt-cinq personnalités autochtones nommées fut mis en place. Les États fédérés virent leur personnalité renforcée, leurs souverains furent traités, au moins au début, avec des égards nouveaux. Ni le nom du Viêt-nam ni son histoire n'étaient plus proscrits. Le sentiment national vietnamien devenait légitime. L'administration s'ouvrit aux talents autochtones : le nombre des fonctionnaires vietnamiens moyens ou supérieurs doubla en cinq ans. Une économie indochinoise naissait de l'autarcie forcée et d'une volonté d'édifier de grands travaux d'intérêt général. Bref, sans instructions d'un gouvernement vichyssois impuissant, l'amiral Decoux tenta l'impossible pari de renouveler la politique française dans une Indochine occupée : il entendait réaliser une association des élites et pratiquer un authentique protectorat.

Le nationalisme vietnamien se coulait avec habileté dans toutes les manifestations du nouveau régime : le salut quotidien au drapeau français s'accompagnait du salut au drapeau vietnamien, le culte de Jeanne d'Arc popularisé par Vichy était associé à celui des sœurs Trung, héroïnes de la lutte contre les Chinois. Au total, ce furent les Vietnamiens qui profitèrent de la Révolution nationale. Cependant, pendant le même temps, la police de l'amiral Decoux, la terrible Sûreté fédérale, pourchassait tous les opposants, nationalistes révolutionnaires, communistes, «dissidents gaullistes», peuplant les bagnes et les camps spéciaux. Le «despotisme éclairé» de l'amiral vichyssois fut impuissant à renverser le cours d'une évoluon vers l'indépendance. Face à lui, le Comité français de la libération nationale qui avait déclaré la guerre au Japon le 8 décembre 1941, entendait libérer l'Indochine de l'occupant japonais et associer le pays à la lutte contre l'impérialisme nippon. Une déclaration du C.F.L.N. annonçait le 8 décembre 1943 ce que serait la politique française : «À ces peuples d'Indochine qui ont su affirmer leur sentiment national et leur sens de la responsabilité politique, la France entend donner, au sein de la communauté française, un statut politique nouveau où, dans le cadre de l'organisation fédérale, les libertés des divers pays de l'Union seront étendues et consacrées; où le caractère libéral des institutions sera, sans perdre la marque de la civilisation et des traditions indochinoises, accentué; où les Indochinois enfin auront accès à tous les emplois et fonctions de l'État. À cette réforme du statut politique correspondra une réforme du statut économique de l'Union qui, sur la base de l'autonomie douanière et fiscale, assurera sa prospérité et contribuera à celle des pays qui lui sont voisins [...]. Ainsi la France entend-elle poursuivre en association libre et intime avec les peuples indochinois la mission dont elle a la charge dans le Pacifique».

Le général de Gaulle, qui se disait persuadé que les Japonais, après la capitulation de l'Allemagne, seraient amenés à «s'emparer de l'Indochine», demandait en février 1944 au responsable de la résistance intérieure en Indochine de s'y préparer, notamment en y associant «les populations indochinoises». Il fut précisé que la politique future de la France «c'est que l'Indochine bénéficiera de la plus grande autonomie [...] dans le cadre d'une fédération française unissant entre eux tous les pays français sur un pied théorique d'égalité».

Cependant les Japonais après leur défaite aux Philippines craignaient la possibilité d'un débarquement allié en Indochine. Ils décidèrent de liquider l'Administration française et de jouer la carte de l'indépendance. Le 9 mars 1945, les 60000 hommes de l'armée japonaise surprirent la plupart des garnisons françaises qui leur opposèrent une résistance désespérée au prix de 1770 morts. Seuls 6000 militaires échappèrent au coup de force et après une retraite de 1000 km se réfugièrent au Yun-Nan chinois. Les Japonais décidèrent de maintenir les souverains des États d'Indochine, dès lors qu'ils eurent dénoncés tous les traités conclus avec la France. Des gouvernements nationalistes furent mis en place. Bref, la domination coloniale s'effondrait et les nouveaux pouvoirs s'efforçaient d'effacer la présence française.

Le royaume chrétien indépendant de Madagascar fut après la conquête française de 1895, soumis au Protectorat, puis annexé en août 1896. Mais la colonie malgré l'écrasement des insurrections n'avait jamais accepté la domination française. Elle connaissait un nationalisme tenace mais limité aux couches les plus élevées du peuple merina. En 1915 la police avait démantelé une organisation nationaliste, la V.V.S., qui aspirait à recouvrer l'indépendance par la force. Parmi les personnes arrêtées figuraient le Dr Ravoahangy et le pasteur Ravelojaona qui s'affirmèrent ensuite comme des leaders nationalistes.

Durant l'entre-deux-guerres, malgré l'action communiste favorable à l'indépendance jusqu'en 1935, les nationalistes ne progressèrent guère. Les socialistes plaidaient pour l'égalité et l'assimilation que de nombreux Malgaches revendiquaient dans les années 1920. En 1937 le gouverneur Cayla fit adopter un décret autorisant l'accès à la citoyenneté française de certaines catégories de notables. Un décret du 7 avril 1938 accorda *de facto* la citoyenneté à certains diplômés. En 1939 il y avait moins de 8000 citoyens français d'origine malgache, 0,2 % de la population.

Pendant la guerre de 1939-1940 quelque 22000 soldats malgaches avaient été envoyés en France, dont 7080 combattants. Environ 10000 militaires ne purent être rapatriés et durent rester en France contre leur gré jusqu'en 1945. Les Malgaches, qui croyaient les Français invincibles depuis 1895 et 1918, furent très étonnés par la défaite de la France. Pour eux les Français étaient désacralisés. Les gens des hautes castes du peuple merina tournèrent d'abord leurs espérances du côté de l'Allemagne ; puis, après la signature de la charte de l'Atlantique, du côté des Américains et des Britanniques. Mais le gouvernement de Vichy dénonçait ces derniers comme responsables du blocus qui appauvrissait le pays. Il faisait appliquer dans la Grande Île, une politique de discipline et d'autorité, doublant les peines de l'indigénat et le nombre des journées de prestation. L'Administration réquisitionnait la main-d'œuvre pour l'envoyer travailler dans les plantations des colons ou les chantiers publics. Les 18000 Européens dont 8000 Réunionais et 3000 étrangers étaient satisfaits du régime de Vichy : les masses malgaches attendaient.

Il fallut les débarquements britanniques (à Diego Suarez en mai 1942, puis dans toute l'île en septembre 1942) pour troubler les populations. À leurs yeux c'étaient les troupes noires sud-africaines qui avaient vaincu les Français. La France combattante exigea un effort de production accru, instaura des cultures forcées, provoquant par les maladresses de l'administration des disettes et l'augmentation de la mortalité. La création d'un office du riz et la lourdeur des réquisitions paupérisèrent la paysannerie rizicole. Certains missionnaires redoutaient que « le mécontentement des populations ne dégénère en haine et en révolte. » Cependant les nationalistes excitaient les paysans à ne plus accepter les principes de subordination qui avaient jusque-là réglé les rapports entre Malgaches et *Vazaha* (étrangers, Français). Ils revendiquaient dès 1945 la restauration de l'indépendance de Madagascar et brandissaient leur drapeau national rouge et blanc, frappé de 18 étoiles (les 18 ethnies du pays). Ils rejetaient par avance toute intégration dans un ensemble français : « Cinquante ans de civilisation occidentale implantée dans un peuple foncièrement oriental en démontraient l'impossibilité ».

En février 1946, leurs deux premiers députés à la Constituante, Ravoahangy et Raseta, fondèrent à Paris un parti organisé à l'occidentale, le *Mouvement démocratique de la Rénovation malgache* (M.D.R.M.) dont le succès fut foudroyant (on a parlé de 200000 adhésions en un an). Le M.D.R.M. jouait double jeu : à Paris Ravoahangy célébrait les liens sentimentaux franco-malgaches et assurait que Madagascar avait la ferme volonté d'être un État associé à l'Union française. À Madagascar, les militants du M.D.R.M. avaient les yeux fixés sur le Viêt-nam et l'Indonésie; ils recherchaient l'appui des États-Unis, de l'Angleterre et de l'Afrique du Sud. Les missionnaires protestants étrangers leur prodiguaient encouragements et conseils. Le député Raseta était, lui, en relation avec les communistes qui lui donnaient, croit-on, de l'argent et des directives. Tous appelaient la jeunesse malgache à mourir pour la patrie (cf. texte, p. 70).

La vie politique devenait à Madagascar de plus en plus intense. De septembre 1945 à mars 1947, les Malgaches auxquels on avait accordé le droit de vote (263527 en 1947) furent appelés six fois aux urnes. Depuis les élections au Conseil représentatif, le 16 septembre 1945, les campagnes électorales étaient pratiquement continues. Vingt-deux journaux politiques, généralement bilingues, s'étaient créés. Ils exposaient presque tous, sans réticence, les aspirations autonomistes ou indépendantistes du peuple malgache. Environ 400000 lecteurs lisaient plus ou moins régulièrement une presse violente. Elle invoquait l'ancienneté de la nation malgache «constituée dès 1820, cinquante ans avant l'Italie», les principes de la charte de l'Atlantique et de celle de San Francisco; elle exaltait le courage des patriotes en dénonçant les souffrances de la patrie malgache et les crimes du colonialisme. En septembre 1946, certains journaux tonnaient contre le projet d'Union française qui entendait «constitutionnaliser le colonialisme.»

L'administration française débordée, tenue par les consignes du haut-commissaire socialiste, Marcel de Coppet, à une politique de tolérance libérale, devait laisser faire, quitte à tenter d'opposer au M.D.R.M. un parti loyaliste en faisant appel aux gens des basses castes, le *parti des déshérités de Madagascar* (P.A.D.E.S.M.). En janvier 1947, aux élections pour les assemblées provinciales, le M.D.R.M. remportait partout la majorité des sièges, sauf dans la province de Majunga (au total 64 M.D.R.M. et 28 P.A.D.E.S.M. pour l'ensemble des cinq assemblées). Pour la désignation en mars 1947 des membres de l'Assemblée représentative, le P.A.D.E.S.M. et les élus européens unirent leurs voix et obtinrent 12 sièges contre 9 au M.D.R.M.

En 1947, la situation devenait explosive : depuis plus d'une année les incidents se multipliaient, créés par l'action du M.D.R.M. Des Européens, des fonctionnaires français étaient lapidés ou assassinés, créant l'inquiétude générale chez les planteurs isolés. Des émeutes sporadiques, des mouvements de grève éclataient sur tout le territoire. Les autorités coloniales s'attendaient à une insurrection, mais ne disposaient que de forces dérisoires : 7000 policiers et soldats.

Dans la nuit du 29 au 30 mars 1947, toute une série d'opérations simultanées, furent déclenchées par des insurgés : trois réussirent (contre la ville et le camp militaire de Moramanga, contre un magasin d'armes à Diego Suarez et contre le poste de Sahasinaka). Ailleurs elles échouèrent ou furent décommandées (à Tananarive, à Fianarantsoa). Dans les jours qui suivirent, plusieurs villes furent attaquées, plusieurs chefs-lieux de district encerclés. Une zone rebelle fit progressivement tache d'huile sur l'ensemble de la côte est. Les insurgés, organisés en bandes mal armées, disposant parfois seulement de sagaies et de coupe-coupe, attaquaient les concessions des colons. Ils exécutaient certains d'entre-eux ainsi que les administrateurs français ou merinas fidèles. À Vohilava ils massacrèrent toute la garnison et le gouverneur malgache. Des combats furent livrés jusque dans les banlieues de Tananarive, Fianarantsoa et Tamatave. Au total, le 1/6e de l'île tombait entre les mains des révoltés. Ces régions étaient peuplées d'environ 1400000 habitants, dont 500000 environ auraient pris une certaine part à la révolte. Curieusement les hauts plateaux de population merina restèrent en dehors de la rébellion. Les renforts militaires français arrivèrent lentement par bateaux : six bataillons de tirailleurs sénégalais, nord-africains et un bataillon de la Légon, débarquèrent peu à peu, entre mai et juillet et passèrent à la contre-offensive à partir d'août 1947. En trois mois quelque 100000 Malgaches avaient fait leur soumission. Quand les insurgés se virent encerclés, ils se réfugièrent dans la grande forêt orientale, difficilement accessible, emmenant avec eux en otages des populations terrorisées. Interrompues à la saison des pluies, les opérations militaires reprirent en avril 1948. Les soumissions se firent peu à peu au cours de l'année. En décembre, le haut-commissaire de Chevigné annonça que la partie la plus inaccessible de la forêt, où s'étaient réfugiés les derniers rebelles, venait d'être occupée. L'insurrection était terminée.

Qui étaient les auteurs ou les inspirateurs de la rébellion? Les procès de six parlementaires du M.D.R.M. qui eurent lieu à Madagascar, de juillet à octobre 1948, ne firent pas toute la lumière. L'enquête avait été d'autant plus difficile que pour lever l'immunité des parlementaires, il fallut des débats houleux à la Chambre des députés et que toute l'affaire fut présentée selon une logique française. Le M.D.R.M. victorieux sur le plan parlementaire ne pouvait avoir intérêt à une rébellion : il n'en était donc pas l'auteur. La rébellion, ayant été mal organisée, était donc due à une machination colonialiste. À quoi les administrateurs français firent répondre que les sections locales du M.D.R.M. avaient été partout les centres moteurs de l'insurrection, que la désorganisation tenait avant tout à l'arrestation du «généralissime» Rakotondrabé. Au cours des procès, certains inculpés déclarèrent que les véritables organisateurs de l'insurrection avaient été les membres de deux sociétés secrètes mal connues, Jina et Pa-na-ma (cf. encadré p. 70), qui avaient infiltré le M.D.R.M. C'est aussi ce qu'affirmera Monja Jaona, leader de la Jina depuis 1943, et instigateur de la révolte du Sud de Madagascar en avril 1971.

Dans les zones que leurs «États-majors» contrôlaient, les insurgés déclarèrent relever d'un gouvernement malgache et combattre pour l'indépendance. Leur propagande répétait «Madagascar aux Malgaches! Vivent nos députés!» mais leur «généralissime» Samuel Rakatondrabé appartenait à la Jina. Dans une société paysanne très religieuse, l'insurrection revêtit aussi une nuance mystique de guerre sainte : tous les insurgés prêtaient des serments, marqués par des rites païens ou par la présence d'une Bible. Cela n'empêcha pas les Malgaches de s'en prendre aux églises catholiques qu'ils tenaient pour des symboles de l'occupation française. Ainsi fut accréditée en France l'idée d'une révolte païenne contre le christianisme menée par des sorciers.

Le bilan de la répression fut difficile à établir : dans un premier temps on parla d'environ 60000 à 80000 morts, chiffres aussitôt portés par le parti communiste français à 100000. Or un recensement précis effectué en 1949, aboutit au chiffre de 11505. En 1950 chaque district dressa la liste nominative de tous les disparus, ceux-ci représentant un allégement sur l'impôt à payer par les villages. Le total aboutit au chiffre de 11342; plus de la moitié des Malgaches disparus étaient morts en forêt, victimes de la faim et du froid, 1646 avaient été tués par les insurgés, 4126 par les militaires français. Du côté européen, 140 civils français avaient été massacrés et 148 militaires tués en opérations. Ces chiffres sont naturellement contestés par les Malgaches qui se prononcent pour des estimations évoluant entre 100000 et 200000 morts. Or ces disparitions massives, sur une population de 4100000 habitants, ne se retrouvent pas dans les courbes démographiques. Elles relèvent donc de la propagande.

Pourtant les Malgaches qui avaient cru devoir pendant longtemps désigner cette insurrection comme une «provocation (*fihantsiana*) colonialiste» ont finalement renoncé à cette thèse. Depuis 1967, le 29 mars est devenu la fête nationale en souvenir de «la glorieuse insurrection patriotique» (*fikomiana*). Les anciens dirigeants des sociétés secrètes sont depuis 1972 célébrés et honorés.

De même évite-t-on aujourd'hui de parler des milliers de condamnés à mort qui auraient été exécutés, car le bilan judiciaire est depuis longtemps établi : 5756 Malgaches furent condamnés par les tribunaux militaires et civils, parmi lesquels 169 furent condamnés à mort : 27 furent exécutés. La loi du 27 mars 1956 accorda l'amnistie aux condamnés à des peines égales ou inférieures à quinze ans de prison. En mai 1957, 600 détenus furent mis en état de libération conditionnelle. Le 18 mars 1958, l'Assemblée nationale accorda à tous les prisonniers l'amnistie sauf, sur amendement socialiste, aux chefs du M.D.R.M. qui devraient rester en France jusqu'en 1963. Ils revinrent à Madagascar en juillet 1960.

L'insurrection de Madagascar donna lieu en France et dans le monde communiste à de violentes campagnes d'opinion, à d'incroyables accusations de «génocide». En janvier 1950 le P.C.F. créa un Comité de solidarité de Madagascar, le COSOMA, chargé «d'agir pour faire connaître l'étendue des crimes commis par les impérialistes». Maurice Thorez assura de «sa solidarité fraternelle les familles des 90000 Malgaches massacrés, victimes de la monstrueuse machination colonialiste de mars 1947». Au 2e congrès universel de la Paix tenu à Varsovie en novembre 1950, un délégué malgache affirma aux 1396 délégués de 61 pays que «les colonialistes français ont mis à mort avec une préméditation digne de Himmler 80000 habitants de notre île». Le 20 juin 1951 une journaliste communiste française, Simone Gerlé, parla de «l'île aux 100000 morts», et des «victimes d'une provocation monstrueuse, la plus monstrueuse que l'histoire ait jamais connue». Pour toute une génération de colonisés, Madagascar, l'île rouge (couleur de la latérite) était devenue «l'île qui nage dans le sang».

D'autres conclusions s'imposaient aux hommes de réflexion : «Notre mainmise sur le pays ne peut se légitimer encore que si nous l'acheminons progressivement vers l'autoadministration pour aboutir à l'indépendance» écrivait courageusement le P. Dunan (S.J.) dans l'hebdomadaire malgache

HYMNE NATIONAL DU M.D.R.M. (TRADUCTION) (1946)

Madagascar notre patrie,
Chère et très sainte terre,
Précieux patrimoine que nous ont légué nos ancêtres,
Mourir pour vous c'est notre honneur!
Jeunes gens levez-vous!
N'ayez aucune crainte
Voici le moment et l'heure,
Tenez-vous debout, en hommes, avec audace.

Source : Cité par le haut-commissaire de Coppet à la Conférence des hauts-commissaires des colonies, le 24 février 1947.

DIRECTIVES ADRESSÉES PAR LE COMITÉ CENTRAL DU PA.NA.MA AUX CHEFS DES COMITÉS RÉGIONAUX (extrait, s.d., juillet 1946)

... Ce sont des directives brèves que nous fixons; ce sont celles que nous exécuterons ensemble. Elles ont pour but la rédemption de notre pays. C'est pour obtenir l'indépendance. C'est par les fusils et les canons que nous l'avons perdue. C'est par la FORCE qu'elle nous reviendra. C'est nous-mêmes et personne d'autre qui obtiendrons la résurrection de notre pays. Ce bien enlevé, nous l'obtiendrons par notre force et par notre courage, par notre union et, si c'est nécessaire, par notre sang [...] Nous prouverons que les jeunes Malgaches vivent par leur idéal et qu'ils sont prêts à mourir pour leur idéal. Les familles de ceux qui tombent seront l'objet de la sollicitude de la collectivité; quant aux blessés ils seront secourus pendant les jours qui leur resteront à vivre.

Nous et les partis politiques

... Peu importe que vous apparteniez à d'autres partis politiques [...]. Ce qui importe c'est de faire fonctionner notre mouvement d'une façon parfaite, car il a été le premier fondé [...] Ce que nous pouvons faire en pénétrant les partis politiques, c'est cacher le travail de notre propre mouvement (autrement dit nous pouvons appartenir à un autre parti, mais en gardant les directives de notre propre mouvement).

Source : Cité par J. Tronchon, *L'insurrection malgache de 1947*, p. 93.

Lumière (10 octobre 1947). Et le 31 mars 1948 le haut-commissaire de Chevigné reconnaissait «la légitimité de but du peuple malgache» : «celui d'un État librement associé avec tous les autres États membres de la grande communauté de l'Union française.»

LES RÉPONSES INSTITUTIONNELLES : L'UNION FRANÇAISE ET LE STATUT DE L'ALGÉRIE

VERS L'UNION FRANÇAISE

Face au défi des temps nouveaux, le Comité français de la libération nationale avait senti la nécessité de faire évoluer l'Empire sur les plans politique et constitutionnel. Dès 1943, un «statut politique nouveau au sein de la communauté française» avait été promis à l'Indochine; le 7 mars 1944, une ordonnance importante était accordée à l'Algérie. Quant au problème constitutionnel écarté par la conférence africaine de Brazzaville, le C.F.L.N. estima que l'étude devait en être amorcée à l'usage de la France libérée. De Gaulle avait expliqué : «Il appartient à la nation française et il n'appartient qu'à elle de procéder le moment venu aux réformes impériales de structure qu'elle décidera dans sa souveraineté». Pourtant, l'éventuelle transformation de l'Empire en Fédération suggérée par René Pleven fut discutée à Alger de mai à juillet 1944. La plupart des hommes politiques réunis dans une commission d'experts s'y montrèrent opposés. Ces résistants d'esprit jacobin se méfiaient des projets fédéraux. Les communistes craignaient qu'ils ne distendent les liens des colonies et de la France. Dans le concept de fédération, ils ne voyaient qu'un slogan utilisable seulement pour maintenir, voire renforcer, l'Empire : «Fédération ou pas, il faut souder.» Ils se prononçaient seulement pour l'institution d'une assemblée où les représentants des colonies seraient les plus nombreux; ils l'appelaient «la Chambre de la plus grande France». Les radicaux de leur côté entendaient aboutir à une «fusion plus complète des colonies et de la France, but suprême de nos efforts». Parmi les socialistes, P.O. Lapie se voulait le champion du fédéralisme, mais il était isolé. Face à lui, l'ancien ministre de Léon Blum, Jules Moch, déclarait : «Je suis hostile à donner les mêmes droits aux chefs nègres et aux représentants français [...]. Je ne veux pas que la reine Makoko [par allusion au Roi (= Makoko) Illo, souverain des Batéké qui signa avec Brazza le traité de protectorat du 10 septembre 1880] puisse renverser le gouvernement français.»

Le ministre des Colonies, Pleven, appuyé par le général de Gaulle, proposa cependant à Paris, en octobre 1944, de reconnaître à chaque territoire colonial la personnalité politique et d'organiser à la place du Sénat une grande assemblée représentative. En mars 1945, un bureau d'études constitutionnelles écarta à nouveau le principe d'une fédération et suggéra la création d'une Union française. Une troisième commission d'experts se prononça pour la représentation dans la future Constituante des citoyens et non-citoyens de l'Empire, élue au suffrage universel : elle proposait un nombre de 66 députés d'outre-mer sur 600 membres. Les États généraux de la Renaissance française, animés par les communistes, se prononcèrent aussitôt pour une représentation égale au «cinquième du Parlement de la France et aux quatre cinquièmes de l'Assemblée de l'outre-mer». Puis les communistes proposèrent d'accorder à tous les anciens sujets de l'Empire les droits de citoyens français. Le gouvernement, qui était favorable à la participation de toutes les populations d'outre-mer à la vie politique de la République, retint le chiffre de 64 députés (dont 31 pour l'Afrique du Nord et 33 pour les colonies). Ceux-ci seraient élus au double collège (collège des citoyens et collège des non-citoyens justifiant d'un certain nombre de conditions). C'était la première fois que des «colonisés» auraient la possibilité de participer à la préparation d'une Constitution de la République. On y vit alors la preuve des vertus assimilatrices de la France.

Dans *la première Constituante*, la commission constitutionnelle se prononça en avril 1946 pour un projet où aucun titre spécial n'était consacré à l'Union française. Le rapporteur Léopold Sédar Senghor, député du Sénégal, célébra les divers articles concernant les territoires d'outre-mer (on ne parlait plus de colonies) parce qu'ils étaient d'esprit assimilationniste et égalitariste. La France y était déclarée République indivisible, démocratique et sociale, formant avec les territoires d'outre-mer et les États associés (les États sous tutelle de l'ONU et éventuellement les Protectorats) «une Union librement consentie». Tous les nationaux et ressortissants de l'Union jouissaient des droits de citoyens, nonobstant les particularités des statuts personnels; mais il n'était pas précisé s'il s'agissait de la citoyenneté française ou de celle de l'Union française. Le projet prévoyait un Conseil de l'Union française, élu par les conseils généraux et les futures assemblées territoriales, dont les pouvoirs seraient seulement consultatifs.

Ce projet de constitution, qui devait, selon ses partisans, «donner 100 millions de citoyens à la République», fut adopté sans enthousiasme par 309 voix contre 249. Soumis à référendum le 5 mai 1946, il fut rejeté par une courte majorité de 53% de Non, alors même qu'il était accepté par les citoyens inscrits (français ou africains) de l'outre-mer (344623 Oui, 331773 Non et 501000 abstentions). Les métropolitains ne s'étaient dans l'ensemble pas intéressés aux articles concernant les «colonies», mais les députés d'outre-mer crurent, à tort, que le vote des métropolitains était dirigé contre eux. Devant leurs protestations, la Constituante reprit hâtivement, sous forme de lois, plusieurs articles du projet constitutionnel. Ainsi furent votées le 7 mai 1946 la loi Lamine-Gueye qui accordait à tous les ressortissants de l'Empire la citoyenneté française, puis trois lois organisant des assemblées locales outre-mer, élues au suffrage universel. Si l'on ajoute que les «vieilles colonies» des Antilles, de la Guyane et de la Réunion avaient été, à la demande de leurs représentants, transformées en départements français, on comprendra que l'opinion française se soit félicitée des résultats de «la généreuse politique d'assimilation républicaine».

Or dans *la deuxième Assemblée constituante*, les élus des peuples d'outremer manifestèrent des revendications bien différentes. Leur intergroupe parlementaire déposa un projet constitutionnel qui prévoyait que «la France renonçait à toute souveraineté unilatérale sur les peuples colonisés». Ceux-ci pourraient librement disposer d'eux-mêmes soit dans l'immédiat soit, pour les territoires ne jouissant pas encore du statut d'État, dans un délai maximum de vingt ans. La constitution de l'Union française serait rédigée par une assemblée composée d'élus des colonies, désignés par le suffrage universel. Simultanément les onze députés algériens nationalistes demandaient que l'Algérie devînt une République algérienne qui aurait le statut d'État associé dans l'Union française.

Devant les vives réactions de l'opinion française, le gouvernement proposa un projet de charte de l'Union française. Celui-ci, amendé, finit par être accepté à l'Assemblée le 29 septembre, par le peuple français le 13 octobre et promulgué le 27 octobre 1946. En France, un référendum avait approuvé la Constitution par 53 % cependant que le corps électoral de l'outre-mer l'avait rejetée (258438 Oui contre 335900 Non et 640000 abstentions).

L'UNION FRANÇAISE DANS LA CONSTITUTION D'OCTOBRE 1946

Les articles de la Constitution relatifs à l'Union française formèrent un titre spécial, le titre VIII (articles 60 à 82). On doit y rattacher trois paragraphes qui figuraient dans le préambule :

« La France forme avec les peuples d'outre-mer une Union fondée sur l'égalité des droits et des devoirs, sans distinction de race ni de religion.

L'Union française est composée de nations et de peuples qui mettent en commun ou coordonnent leurs ressources et leurs efforts pour développer leurs civilisations respectives, accroître leur bien-être et assurer leur sécurité.

Fidèle à sa mission traditionnelle, la France entend conduire les peuples dont elle a pris la charge à la liberté de s'administrer eux-mêmes et de gérer démocratiquement leurs propres affaires, écartant tout système de colonisation fondé sur l'arbitraire; elle garantit à tous l'égal accès aux fonctions publiques et l'exercice individuel ou collectif des droits et libertés proclamés et confirmés ci-dessus [c'est-à-dire au début du Préambule]».

Ces quelques lignes définissaient bien les principes ou les intentions des constituants. Ils entendaient d'abord remplacer l'ancien régime colonial fondé sur la subordination des sujets aux maîtres (les citoyens) par un nouveau système de relations défini par l'égalité des individus, quels que fussent leur race, leur religion ou leur statut social. À la traditionnelle subordination des colonies à une métropole était substitué ensuite un système d'association de peuples fondée sur une communauté d'intérêts. Enfin était annoncée une liberté de gestion administrative et politique. On pouvait y voir un engagement de décolonisation progressive et la promesse d'une inéluctable orientation vers l'autonomie.

L'organisation de l'Union française reposait sur trois éléments : 1°) un *président* qui était le président de la République française. Or celui-ci était élu par les deux Chambres du Parlement : Assemblée nationale et Conseil de la République dans lesquelles les États associés n'avaient nul élu. Le président «représentait» seulement «les intérêts permanents de l'Union»; il ne pouvait en assurer la conduite; 2°) un Haut-Conseil de l'Union française composé d'une délégation du gouvernement français et de la représentation des États associés; 3°) le gouvernement de la République qui assurait «la direction de la politique» et «la conduite générale de l'Union»; il pouvait être assisté par le Haut-Conseil.

D'autre part, avait été créée une *Assemblée de l'Union française*. Celle-ci était composée pour moitié de représentants de la France métropolitaine élus par le Parlement (en fait ils furent désignés par les groupes politiques) et de représentants élus des D.O.M. (départements d'outre-mer) et des T.O.M. (territoires d'outre-mer), de l'Algérie et des territoires associés (ils devaient être 240, mais la Tunisie et le Maroc n'ayant jamais adhéré à l'Union française, leur nombre fut ramené à 204, soit 102 pour chaque catégorie). Les pouvoirs de cette Assemblée étaient essentiellement consultatifs. Elle se prononçait sur les projets et propositions qui lui étaient soumis pour avis; son droit d'initiative se bornait à des propositions de résolutions sur des questions législatives, concernant les territoires d'outre-mer. On était loin du Grand Conseil souverain ou de la Chambre démocratique fédérale qu'avaient envisagés les novateurs.

Les départements et territoires d'outre-mer, mais aussi les États sous tutelle (Togo - Cameroun) étaient directement représentés à l'Assemblée nationale et au Conseil de la République. Tous les ressortissants de la République française, dont ceux des T.O.M. et des D.O.M., étaient citoyens français. Mais tous les ressortissants de l'Union française s'étaient également vu reconnaître la qualité de citoyen de l'Union française; comme le contenu de cette citoyenneté ne fut jamais défini, elle demeura sans objet. Enfin l'article 75 de la Constitution avait prévu que les statuts respectifs des membres de la République et de l'Union française étaient susceptibles d'évolution. Cet article permit à beaucoup d'élus d'outre-mer, bien que mécontents du titre VIII, d'adhérer à la Constitution. Certains estimèrent que, puisqu'aucun lien fédéral n'était prévu, la porte leur était ouverte vers la séparation. En fait l'article 75 ne fut utilisé qu'une fois, lorsque la Cochinchine, colonie française, fut rattachée à l'État associé du Viêt-nam.

Sur le plan juridique, l'Union française, fruit de laborieux compromis entre des principes opposés — assimilation et fédération — ne répondait à aucun modèle d'union de droit international. Son fédéralisme apparent n'était qu'un leurre; l'autorité demeurait entièrement entre les mains du gouvernement de la République. Sur le plan politique, l'Union française, œuvre du constituant français, ne fut pas proposée par référendum aux populations colonisées. Seuls furent consultés les membres du collège électoral des citoyens français, en majorité des colons, qui votèrent contre l'adoption de la Constitution. Les nationalistes algériens et malgaches eurent tôt fait de dénoncer «l'Union imposée» comme «une cage où personne ne voudrait entrer». De fait, les États marocain et tunisien refusèrent d'adhérer à l'Union, malgré les offres qui leur furent faites de devenir des États associés. Les États d'Indochine ne voulurent définir l'Union française que par des conventions bilatérales qui ignoraient la Constitution. Bref, le titre VIII de la Constitution se révéla immédiatement inadapté à la situation politique.

En France pourtant, les hommes politiques crurent avoir accompli un acte de portée révolutionnaire : l'égalité était désormais proclamée entre les races, le colonisateur permettait aux populations locales de choisir librement leurs représentants dans les assemblées locales et au Parlement (1/9 de députés d'outre-mer à l'Assemblée nationale, 1/5 au Conseil de la République, soit 73 députés et 58 «sénateurs»), le collège unique avait été instauré en A.O.F. et dans 5 autres territoires, tandis que le double collège subsistait seulement en A.E.F., au Cameroun et à Madagascar. Lorsque le président de la République, Vincent Auriol, se félicita en 1947 d'être le premier président à venir en Afrique noire et proclama que «de Toulon à Dakar, c'est le même peuple qui se retrouve», le maire de Dakar lui répondit : «Vous êtes la plus haute expression de l'Union française, de l'unité française et nous acclamons en vous le symbole de la Grande France aux cent dix millions d'habitants.» Mais il y avait loin du rêve assimilationniste aux réalités. Dans le même temps, l'Indochine et Madagascar étaient soulevées contre la domination française. Au Maghreb, les partis nationalistes et religieux tenaient l'Union française pour «une tour de Babel qui s'écroulerait au premier vent de l'histoire». Entre l'Union française et la Ligue des États arabes, leur choix était clair : ils se prononçaient pour «la Nation arabe».

LE STATUT DE L'ALGÉRIE

Le cas des départements algériens n'ayant pas été réglé par les Constituantes, il revint à l'Assemblée nationale, élue en novembre 1946, de définir le nouveau statut que beaucoup d'hommes politiques métropolitains et une partie de la population algérienne appelaient de leurs vœux.

La situation administrative de l'Algérie était devenue fort complexe; elle nécessitait à elle seule des réformes que justifiait plus encore la conjoncture politique. On rappellera seulement que l'Algérie était à la fois considérée comme *un prolongement de la France* avec ses départements dirigés par des préfets et des conseils généraux élus, avec des services administratifs «rattachés» à Paris (Défense nationale, Justice, Éducation nationale), avec des communes de plein exercice et des conseils élus, et comme *une colonie originale* avec ses immenses territoires du Sud (2 millions de km^2), ses 78 communes mixtes (peuplées de 3500000 habitants), ses centres municipaux, véritables communes issues des *douârs*. Toute une législation algérienne s'était créée, fort éloignée des règlements, décrets et lois en usage dans la métropole. En matière de régime foncier, de justice musulmane, de conditions juridiques des personnes, un droit algérien s'était peu à peu instauré, essentiellement adapté aux réalités du régime colonial traditionnel. Deux populations très différentes cohabitaient en s'ignorant sur un territoire qu'on déclarait assimilé. En fait, la rigidité de la situation coloniale opposait plus qu'elle ne les rapprochait quelque 900000 Français ou «Européens» en 1948 et 6800000 musulmans dans l'Algérie du Nord. Les «Européens» (appellation qui s'étendait aux juifs algériens, français depuis 1870) se considéraient encore volontiers comme «Algériens». Mais les musulmans revendiquaient désormais ce titre pour eux seuls.

L'autonomie algérienne, réclamée en vain par les colons français de 1870 à 1944, n'avait pas été accordée. Pourtant l'Algérie disposait depuis 1898-1900 d'une large décentralisation politique et de l'autonomie financière. Dotée de la personnalité civile et d'un budget spécial, l'Algérie était administrée par un gouverneur général et ses services, et par des assemblées délibérantes à attributions exclusivement financières et économiques. Ces assemblées, le Conseil supérieur de gouvernement (60 membres élus et nommés) et les Délégations financières (3 délégations de 24 membres : colons, non-colons et indigènes, tous élus par des collèges relativement restreints) exerçaient avec la représentation parlementaire (3 sénateurs et 10 députés élus par les seuls Européens) la réalité du pouvoir à la fin de la IIIe République.

Cette représentation exclusive des Français au Parlement fut condamnée après 1944 : les musulmans algériens, 1341978 inscrits, bien que non-citoyens, disposèrent de 13 députés en 1945 (dans le 2e collège), cependant qu'une élite d'entre-eux (environ 65000) était désormais intégrée dans le

1er collège électoral, celui des citoyens. Les Délégations financières furent supprimées en septembre 1945 et remplacées par une Assemblée financière de 37 membres (dont 15 musulmans). La citoyenneté française ayant été accordée à tous les ressortissants de l'Algérie en mai 1946, il fut question de fusionner les deux collèges électoraux. Mais devant les protestations des «Français de souche», la loi du 5 octobre 1946 maintint les deux collèges en attribuant à chacun d'eux 15 sièges de députés, et celle du 27 octobre, 7 sièges de sénateurs, soit au total 30 députés et 14 sénateurs pour les trois départements d'Algérie. Or les nationalistes algériens modérés réclamaient 106 députés dont 92 pour le 2e collège, cependant qu'ils proposaient simultanément la création d'une République algérienne autonome, État associé dans l'Union française, reposant sur le principe de la double nationalité. Ces exigences ayant été refusées, Ferhat Abbas et ses collègues de l'U.D.M.A. prônèrent l'abstention aux élections législatives de novembre 1946, ce qui permit au PPA-MTLD et aux communistes de remporter un succès électoral relatif, 7 députés sur 15. Aux élections pour le Conseil de la République, l'U.D.M.A. obtint 4 sièges sur 7. Ainsi furent confirmées la victoire des nationalistes et l'élimination des assimilationnistes. De leur côté, les électeurs du 1er collège, s'étaient prononcés très majoritairement contre l'assimilation égalitaire des musulmans et pour la «défense de l'Algérie française». Cette situation appelait une médiation de la métropole.

L'Assemblée nationale nouvelle fut bientôt saisie de six propositions de loi. En août 1947, le gouvernement Ramadier pressa la commission de l'Intérieur et l'Assemblée de se prononcer sur son projet de statut de l'Algérie. La discussion fut passionnée, entraînant des démissions et des menaces d'éclatement du gouvernement. Français d'Algérie et musulmans s'opposèrent avec vivacité. Lorsque le projet gouvernemental, assez conservateur, fut pris en compte contre celui de la commission, plus libéral, les députés musulmans quittèrent l'hémicycle et refusèrent désormais de participer à la discussion. Au Conseil de la République, un «sénateur» algérien, ami de Ferhat Abbas, récusa la citoyenneté française et révéla que les Algériens appartenaient au monde oriental et qu'ils auraient à préparer leur constitution en Algérie. Puis les quatre «sénateurs» de l'U.D.M.A. renoncèrent à leur mandat.

Dans ce climat, l'esprit de transaction ne pouvait prévaloir et les projets s'affrontèrent. Les députés algériens les plus modérés proposaient la création d'une République algérienne autonome, «État associé», dotée d'une présidence algérienne, d'un gouvernement algérien responsable devant une Assemblée algérienne, élue au suffrage universel avec collège unique. Un ministre délégué de la République française aurait voix consultative au gouvernement. Tous les habitants du pays seraient des citoyens algériens. Les communistes, bien qu'exclus du gouvernement Ramadier, ne réclamaient pas l'indépendance, mais voulaient faire de l'Algérie un territoire associé dans le cadre de l'Union française. Ils demandaient une Assemblée algérienne légiférant souverainement et un Conseil de gouvernement, tous deux à représentation paritaire, au moins pendant les cinq premières années. Les socialistes souhaitaient une assemblée algérienne de 120 membres élus par deux collèges électoraux à titre provisoire et un ministre de l'Algérie responsable devant le gouvernement français et résidant à Alger. Le projet du gouvernement enfin avait pour traits essentiels le maintien de l'Algérie comme groupe de départements français et la création d'une Assemblée algérienne paritaire, élue par deux collèges où les décisions seraient prises à la majorité des deux tiers.

Ce fut ce projet à peine amendé qui l'emporta à l'Assemblée nationale le 27 août par 320 voix contre 88 (180 députés dont 153 communistes s'étant abstenus volontairement). Le statut de l'Algérie ne fut voté par aucun parlementaire algérien et ne fut accepté que par 4 députés français d'Algérie sur 15. Ces votes étaient de mauvais augure.

Le «statut organique» de l'Algérie n'apportait que peu de nouveautés. Le pouvoir exécutif demeurait, comme par le passé, aux mains d'un gouverneur général représentant le gouvernement français et responsable devant lui. Les six membres du Conseil de gouvernement étaient seulement «chargés de veiller à l'exécution des décisions de l'Assemblée algérienne». Celle-ci était composée de 120 membres répartis en deux sections numériquement égales. Ils étaient élus pour six ans par les deux collèges : le premier comprenant 464000 citoyens de statut civil français et 58000 musulmans inscrits ès qualité sur leur demande; le second devait s'étendre à 1400000 électeurs de statut local. L'Assemblée algérienne votait le budget de l'Algérie présenté par le gouverneur; elle pouvait modifier par voie réglementaire la législation métropolitaine applicable à l'Algérie, sous réserve d'une homologation du gouvernement. Quant aux votes ils pouvaient avoir lieu à la majorité des deux tiers, à la demande du gouverneur ou à celle du quart des membres de l'Assemblée. Le statut comprenait enfin un certain nombre de dispositions spéciales, comme l'abolition progressive des communes mixtes et du régime militaire des territoires du Sud, la séparation du culte musulman et de l'État; enfin l'Assemblée algérienne était chargée d'organiser l'enseignement de l'arabe et de prévoir le vote des femmes d'origine musulmane. Aucune de ces dispositions ne devait être appliquée jusqu'en 1954.

En Algérie, le statut fut très mal accueilli : Européens et musulmans rejetèrent avec mépris cet arbitrage métropolitain. Les Français d'Algérie s'estimèrent dupés, «jetés en pâture aux musulmans»; ils condamnèrent cette Assemblée où l'on ne voterait pas par collèges séparés. Ils regrettèrent les strictes limitations imposées au Conseil de gouvernement dans lequel certains avaient salué à l'avance «une amorce de gouvernement algérien». Du côté musulman, où l'on avait espéré malgré tout une solution fédéraliste, l'accueil réservé au «statut octroyé» fut encore plus hostile. Le premier congrès national du M.T.L.D. l'avait rejeté avant le vote définitif. Fehrat Abbas couvrit de sarcasmes cette «caricature de statut», ce «prétendu Conseil de gouvernement qui n'est qu'un conseil de famille où le gouverneur jouera le rôle de grand vizir et le président de l'Assemblée celui de mandarin». Le parti communiste algérien condamna le statut, mais attendit pourtant le 5 novembre 1952 pour demander «son abolition immédiate».

La classe politique française, après deux ans de débats sur la question algérienne, n'avait pas pu se résoudre à faire des départements d'outre-mer de l'Algérie, un territoire ou un État associé de l'Union française. «L'idée d'une nation algérienne est impossible à concevoir», titrait en novembre 1946 un organe M.R.P. *Forces nouvelles*, mais telle était l'opinion de la classe politique tout entière, à l'exception des seuls communistes. Peut-être eût-il été possible de faire voter par l'Assemblée constituante en 1946 un statut moins conservateur. Mais il serait faux de laisser croire qu'une «grande

L'ALGÉRIE DU DEMI-SIÈCLE VUE PAR LES AUTORITÉS LOCALES

(extraits d'une enquête administrative réalisée en 1953 dans les communes indigènes, mixtes et de plein exercice)

La situation évolue d'une façon très défavorable pour les Français. On s'abandonne trop à un optimisme facile. Clandestinement, prenant exemple sur la résistance métropolitaine de 1940-1945, les éléments séparatistes travaillent au noyautage systématique des masses, à l'abaissement du moral des populations européennes rurales. Cette œuvre n'est actuellement qu'à l'état d'embryon. Il est à craindre que ce libre laisser-aller soit pour tous une désagréable surprise le jour où, en masses submergeantes, les éléments soigneusement préparés et aguerris se démasqueront et s'emploieront à renverser le drapeau tricolore de ce territoire, à l'exemple des événements actuels d'Indochine dont l'évolution est ici suivie avec beaucoup d'intérêt ainsi que tous les événements qui touchent le Proche-Orient.

(Philippeville, commune de plein exercice.)

Les populations musulmanes savent que la souveraineté française en Afrique du Nord est discutée par certaines puissances. Les PPA[1] fanatisés ont déclenché une campagne de dissidence, brandissant l'étendard du nationalisme, campagne qui a fortement influencé les masses. Cette évolution a été activée par la mansuétude dont a fait preuve le Gouvernement à l'égard de ces agitateurs. La population musulmane est persuadée que l'avenir est à l'indépendance de l'Afrique du Nord dans un temps plus ou moins proche.

(Guyotville, commune de plein exercice.)

La question se pose de savoir si nous devons assister en spectateurs à cette évolution accélérée ou si nous devons l'inspirer, l'orienter. Il faut choisir entre la solution du cantonnement surveillé ou celle de l'assimilation. La théorie du juste milieu n'est pas applicable en l'occurrence. La conjoncture politique et la conjoncture économique s'accordent pour nous imposer une action aussi puissante que possible dans le sens de l'assimilation.

D'autres solutions sont-elles possibles? Celle du *statu quo*, soulevée par les milieux influents qui depuis 1900 ont orienté selon leurs intérêts la politique algérienne, impliquerait un développement considérable de l'appareil militaire et de police qui ne nous garantirait nullement contre les conséquences internationales de notre politique, ni même contre la nécessité d'avoir, en peu d'années, à reconquérir toute l'Algérie par les armes [...].

En résumé, ni un redoublement d'action policière, ni l'accord d'une indépendance totale ou partielle ne sont susceptibles de nous apporter le succès. Nous nous trouvons devant un mur qui ne se laissera pas tourner. Ou nous assimilerons l'Algérie en transformant le pays et en formant l'homme ou nous la perdrons. Le délai qui nous est encore accordé sera court. Il faut agir partout à la fois. Sinon notre cause est perdue.

(Commune mixte de la Soummam.)

---

1. Membres du parti du peuple algérien du Messali Hadj.

occasion avait été manquée». Les nationalistes algériens ne reconnaissaient plus à la France le droit de leur imposer une constitution.

Les hommes politiques français, qui avaient cru résoudre les problèmes coloniaux à la satisfaction de la métropole par des compromis et de timides innovations, n'avaient apporté aucune solution d'avenir. Faute d'avoir adopté une solution fédérale, l'Union française et le statut de l'Algérie allaient se révéler des constructions mort-nées.

3 *L'échec de l'Union française et la première vague de la décolonisation*

(Indochine et protectorats du Maghreb)

L'ÉCHEC DE L'UNION FRANÇAISE EST-IL LIÉ À L'ACTION DE FORCES EXTÉRIEURES?

La France de la IVe République, puissance affaiblie dont l'influence déclinait, pouvait-elle affirmer sa politique coloniale, construire l'Union française et la faire accepter sans tenir compte de l'environnement international? Elle n'était plus en mesure, dit-on, d'imposer librement ses choix politiques. Mais avant d'affirmer *a priori* que la politique coloniale française fût dictée ou influencée par des pressions venues de l'étranger, mieux vaut recenser ce que furent réellement ces interventions extérieures, en choisissant, pour faire bref, un secteur sensible, celui du Maghreb.

LE RÔLE DES ÉTATS-UNIS

Le rôle des États-Unis y furent particulièrement ambigu. Certes l'administration Truman rompit avec l'anticolonialisme actif de F.D. Roosevelt, mais sa position restait hostile au colonialisme français. Un mémorandum du 5 juin 1945 en définissait le principe : «Notre politique respectera l'intégrité de l'Empire français tout en offrant aux peuples colonisés l'opportunité d'accéder à l'autodétermination.» De fait les U.S.A. renoncèrent à leur croisade anticoloniale, tout en se désolidarisant bien haut du colonialisme français. Pendant la guerre froide, le département d'État s'efforça de décourager les nationalistes maghrébins les plus radicaux, tout en suggérant de plus en plus vivement aux gouvernements français la nécessité d'une évolution graduelle des protectorats nord-africains vers l'autonomie.

Cependant les Américains étaient eux-mêmes divisés : certains pensaient qu'à soutenir l'immobilisme des Français l'Amérique jouait perdant, car le seul antidote au communisme résidait dans le nationalisme. Mais d'autres leur répondaient que «lorsque le colonialisme est écarté, le communisme prend sa place». D'autre part, la Tunisie et le Maroc constituaient une zone stratégique essentielle : en cas d'indépendance, ces pays ne risquaient-ils pas d'échapper à l'orbite de la défense occidentale et de devenir une tête de pont pour le bloc soviétique? Face à ces dilemmes et à ces craintes, les Américains choisirent de ne pas choisir : ils jouèrent soit le juste milieu, soit un jeu double et leur influence décrut.

Les nationalistes tunisiens et marocains s'affirmaient farouchement anticommunistes, pour retrouver l'appui américain, tandis que la France répétait inlassablement, comme le président de la République Vincent Auriol : «Derrière Bourguiba, il y a les communistes, derrière *l'Istiqlâl* marocain, il y a les communistes.» En 1950, le Département d'État américain fit connaître nettement ses souhaits au gouvernement français : «Nous estimons que les populations des territoires dépendants doivent être acheminées vers la conduite de leurs propres affaires.» Il précisa qu'il s'intéressait de très près au programme français de réformes politiques. Pour parer à cette tentative d'immixtion, la France accorda aux U.S.A. le droit de construire cinq bases aériennes stratégiques au Maroc. Néanmoins, en 1951, Washington signifia sa totale désapprobation vis-à-vis de la politique marocaine du général Juin. Il en alla de même lors de la crise franco-tunisienne de 1952. Le département d'État intervint à plusieurs reprises auprès du ministre des Affaires étrangères français pour que «les satisfactions légitimes des Tunisiens fussent satisfaites». Ce qui n'empêcha pas le gouvernement français de renvoyer le ministère Chenik. Le secrétaire d'État Dean Acheson s'en offusqua et son représentant à l'O.N.U. fit savoir publiquement le 17 juin 1952 qu'il renoncerait désormais à s'abstenir dans les votes concernant la question tunisienne.

Pressé par la France d'élaborer un accord stipulant la non-ingérence américaine en Afrique du Nord, le président Eisenhower s'y refusa. Mais simultanément il rejeta une demande de médiation présentée par les nationalistes du Comité pour la liberté de l'Afrique du Nord. Les officiels américains étaient convaincus que «les Français ne pourraient maintenir la stabilité de ces pays.» Leurs services de renseignements étaient même persuadés qu'une rébellion ne manquerait pas d'éclater en Algérie et que les Français devraient alors s'en retirer. Mais, tenus de ménager leur allié français au sein de l'O.T.A.N., les U.S.A. ne se solidarisaient pas avec les nationalistes maghrébiens, qui parlèrent dès lors de «la trahison de Washington».

Convaincus en octobre 1952 qu'il leur fallait agir, les U.S.A. votèrent l'inscription de la question tunisienne à l'ordre du jour de l'O.N.U. Les Américains devinrent alors pour la presse française, l'ennemi public n° 1, mais la tempête s'apaisa lorsque l'O.N.U. eut voté une motion inoffensive. Au Maroc où la sécurité de leurs bases primait toute autre considération pour les Américains, la France put impunément déposer le Sultan. En 1953 et 1954, Washington usa même de son influence pour calmer l'O.N.U. On ne peut donc pas dire que les États-Unis aient imposé aux Français leurs souhaits en matière de décolonisation de l'Afrique du Nord.

Pourtant les nationalistes maghrébins ne désespérèrent jamais tout à fait de provoquer un recours américain en leur faveur. Ils y étaient en effet encouragés par la Confédération internationale des Syndicats libres (C.I.S.L.), laquelle dépendait largement des riches et puissants syndicats d'outre-Atlantique.

L'INFLUENCE DE LA C.I.S.L.

Le syndicat national tunisien, l'U.G.T.T. (*Union générale tunisienne du travail*) fondé en janvier 1946 contre la C.G.T., dut s'affirmer malgré l'opposition de *l'Union syndicale des travailleurs de Tunisie* (U.S.T.T.) contrôlée par les communistes. En mars 1951 l'U.G.T.T., «le syndicat des nationalistes», rejoignit la C.I.S.L. qui ne lui ménagea pas son appui financier et politique. En novembre 1952 la C.I.S.L. demanda à l'O.N.U. la création d'un Comité des bons offices ayant pouvoir de médiation et de réglementation dans le conflit franco-tunisien. Elle dénonça le crime de l'assassinat du leader de l'U.G.T.T., Ferhat Hached. En 1953 elle intervint même directement auprès du gouvernement français. Les syndicalistes tunisiens devaient plus tard souligner publiquement leur dette de reconnaissance vis-à-vis de la C.I.S.L. : «Celle-ci a fait beaucoup pour nous aider, préparer notre promotion et notre émancipation.»

Au Maroc, la C.I.S.L. collabora avec les nationalistes : elle dénonça les violations de la liberté syndicale par le gouvernement français et «l'impérialisme communiste de la C.G.T.». En mars 1955 les syndicalistes marocains parvinrent grâce à elle à créer une centrale syndicale indépendante, *l'Union marocaine du travail* (U.M.T.). La C.I.S.L. intervint dès lors plus vivement encore, condamnant «les méthodes de répression aveugle de la France, les punitions collectives, l'arrestation de syndicalistes». Elle protesta contre l'envoi en Afrique du Nord d'unités militaires de l'O.T.A.N. et tenta d'envoyer des délégations d'enquête au Maroc. Grâce à son soutien, l'U.M.T. s'imposa : dès la fin de 1955, les syndicalistes cégétistes, qui n'avaient pas cessé de dénoncer son inféodation aux U.S.A., se rallièrent pourtant à l'U.M.T.

La C.I.S.L. devait tenter de jouer un rôle semblable en Algérie. Pesant de tout son poids sur l'Internationale socialiste, la C.I.S.L. obtint de celle-ci des condamnations fort sévères de la politique algérienne des socialistes français; en février 1956 elle favorisa la création de l'U.G.T.A., *l'Union générale des travailleurs algériens*. Mais celle-ci, soumise au F.L.N., prit ses distances avec la C.I.S.L. jugeant son aide insuffisante. Le F.L.N. avait pourtant, grâce à elle, isolé *l'Union des syndicats des travailleurs algériens*, d'obédience messaliste, et développé sa propagande jusqu'à l'O.N.U.

LES INTERVENTIONS DE L'O.N.U.

Les interventions de l'Organisation des Nations unies dans les affaires coloniales et notamment maghrébines, furent les plus redoutées et les plus durement ressenties par les gouvernements français sous la IVe République. Aucun d'eux ne pouvait oublier que le poids de l'O.N.U. avait joué de manière décisive en faveur de l'indépendance de l'Indonésie et préparé directement la naissance d'une Libye autonome. De fait l'O.N.U. tenta bien de s'instaurer en tribunal international, notamment dans les affaires maghrébines. En octobre 1951 les délégations arabes saisirent l'Assemblée générale : elles accusaient la France de violer la charte des Nations unies au Maroc et d'y bafouer la Déclaration des droits de l'homme. Leur demande ne fut repoussée que de justesse. Mais le 15 octobre 1952, treize États obtinrent l'inscription des questions marocaine et tunisienne à l'ordre du jour de l'Assemblée. Les résolutions votées en décembre, recommandant le développement de libres institutions dans les deux protectorats, furent certes assez modérées. Mais l'échec diplomatique de la France fut salué par les nationalistes et durement ressenti à Paris. Une partie de la presse française dénonça «l'entreprise de démolition à laquelle l'O.N.U. se livrait» et certains journalistes demandèrent que «la France choisisse entre l'O.N.U. et la survie de son Empire».

En août 1953, après la déposition du sultan Mohammed ben Youssef, les quinze États du groupe afro-asiatique de l'O.N.U. tentèrent, en vain, de saisir d'urgence le Conseil de sécurité. Mais en commission, puis devant l'Assemblée générale, des projets de résolution fort hostiles à la France ne furent écartés que de justesse, ou n'obtinrent pas la majorité requise des deux tiers. En 1954, lors de la 9e session de l'O.N.U., la majorité des États membres, sensible à l'action de Mendès France, décida d'ajourner l'examen des propositions concernant la Tunisie et le Maroc. En 1955, la question tunisienne avait été résolue par les six conventions franco-tunisienne du 3 août. Cependant le groupe afro-asiatique, prenant prétexte de nouvelles émeutes à Casablanca, tenta une fois encore de provoquer l'intervention du Conseil de sécurité, mais y échoua. L'assemblée générale, siégeant après la déclaration conjointe de la Celle-Saint-Cloud (5 novembre 1955), qui prévoyait de faire accéder le Maroc au statut d'État indépendant, se borna à exprimer sa confiance.

Ni l'indépendance de la Tunisie ni celle du Maroc ne peuvent donc être expliquées par l'action de l'O.N.U. Les États arabes ne parvinrent pas à obtenir des votes condamnant la politique française ou imposant la création d'une délégation de médiation. Les résolutions votées par l'O.N.U. exprimaient au plus l'espoir que «les parties poursuivraient sans retard leurs négociations en vue de l'accession des Tunisiens ou des Marocains à la capacité de s'administrer eux-mêmes». Il demeure que les gouvernements français se sentirent désormais surveillés par un «pseudo-tribunal des peuples» et contraints de plaider constamment devant lui.

LE RÔLE DE LA LIGUE ARABE

Les États arabes et les autres États musulmans avaient été les plus décidés dans leur soutien aux États maghrébins, mais n'avaient pas abouti. La Ligue des États arabes (*Jam'iyyat al-duwwal al-'arabiyya*) qui poursuivait depuis 1945 l'objectif de constituer une *Nation arabe* unitaire, fut-elle plus efficace? À court terme et jusqu'en 1955, elle s'intéressa bien moins au Maghreb (le Couchant) qu'au Machrek (le Levant); elle ne reprit même pas à son compte les revendications des exilés maghrébins présents au Caire ni le mythe apparemment mobilisateur de l'Unité maghrébine. Quelques campagnes dans la presse arabe, surtout égyptienne, en 1951 et 1953, quelques menaces de boycott des produits français furent pratiquement les seuls soutiens apportés par la Ligue à la cause maghrébine jusqu'en 1954. Sur le plan diplomatique toutefois, la Ligue arabe se montra plus active. Le Conseil de la Ligue adopta diverses propositions d'intervention auprès de l'O.N.U. et quelques communiqués de protestation contre l'exil forcé du sultan marocain. Mais la Ligue visait moins à mobiliser les opinions publiques arabes qu'à mettre en marche la lourde machine de l'O.N.U. Tout au plus la Ligue arabe servit-elle de caisse de résonance au procès intenté par le monde arabe au colonialisme français.

LA CONFÉRENCE DE BANDOENG

La Ligue des États arabes n'était qu'une organisation essentiellement régionale. D'autres organisations, qui revendiquaient notamment l'indépendance pour tous les peuples sous tutelle, avaient une vocation plus large d'instrument de la politique anti-occidentale. Tels furent *l'Asian Relations Conference* de mars 1947, le groupe afro-asiatique de l'O.N.U. et les conférences de Colombo, de Bogor qui préparèrent la conférence afro-asiatique de Bandoeng (17-24 avril 1955). Vingt-quatre États — cinq africains et dix-neuf asiatiques — y débattirent largement de leur avenir. Cette conférence célèbre qui marque incontestablement un tournant dans les relations internationales mondiales, ne fut pourtant pas un festival anti-occidental ou une grand-messe de l'anticolonialisme. Elle se sépara sur des vœux et des résolutions, non sur des consignes d'action ou de révolution. Vis-à-vis du Maghreb, la conférence écarta la revendication de « la libération de l'Afrique du Nord » demandée essentiellement par l'Égypte. La résolution finale se bornait à appuyer les droits des peuples de cette région « à disposer d'eux-mêmes et à être indépendants ». La conférence pressait le gouvernement français « d'aboutir sans retard au règlement pacifique » de cette question. Elle réclamait pour leurs étudiants « auxquels les droits fondamentaux en matière d'éducation et de culture étaient déniés un libre accès dans les universités d'Afrique et d'Asie ».

Ce qui frappe, c'est la modération des résolutions. Plus tard, l'Afrique noire francophone salua dans la conférence, « la prise de conscience de leur éminente dignité par les peuples de couleur ». Sur l'heure les observateurs y virent « une prise de conscience d'une 3ᵉ force neutraliste et anticolonialiste », constituée en dehors de l'U.R.S.S. Quant aux nationalistes des pays colonisés, ils saluèrent l'encouragement international apporté à leur cause. Mais on ne peut pas dire que Bandoeng ait sonné le réveil des peuples colonisés.

L'ÉCHEC DE L'UNION FRANÇAISE : LA GUERRE D'INDOCHINE

LE DÉCLENCHEMENT (1945-1946)

Le coup de force japonais ne signifiait pas pour le général de Gaulle la fin de l'Indochine française. Le 24 mars 1945, le gouvernement français fixait même le statut nouveau de l'Indochine. Elle n'était plus une colonie et devenait un État : la Fédération indochinoise. Cette fédération de cinq pays, politiquement et économiquement autonome, prenait place dans l'Union française. Elle aurait un gouvernement, présidé par le gouverneur général et composé de ministres responsables devant lui, et serait dotée d'une assemblée élue.

Ce statut, qui niait l'unité du Viêt-nam, divisé en trois pays, ne pouvait être accepté par les patriotes vietnamiens. Avant de pouvoir l'imposer, la France devait reconquérir l'Indochine occupée. Or Roosevelt y était totalement opposé et la Chine nationaliste peu favorable. Cependant, après la capitulation du Japon, la reddition de son armée d'Indochine fut confiée par la conférence de Potsdam aux Chinois dans le Nord et aux Britanniques dans le Sud : ces derniers n'étaient pas opposés au rétablissement de la souveraineté française.

Profitant de la période d'incertitude, les forces armées du Viêt-minh s'emparèrent du pouvoir le 19 août à Hanoi, le 23 à Hué, le 25 à Saigon. Le 2 septembre il proclamait l'indépendance du Viêt-nam et l'avènement d'une République démocratique d'obédience communiste. Le 24 septembre, tandis que les Français réarmés par les Britanniques essayaient de reprendre les bâtiments administratifs de Saigon, les Viêtnamiens enlevaient 300 civils français dont la moitié furent massacrés. À Paris certains journaux comprirent qu'une guerre commençait en Indochine.

Le gouvernement avait préparé un corps expéditionnaire placé sous la direction du général Leclerc. Débarqué le 23 octobre à Saigon, Leclerc s'assurait le Cambodge. Puis il balayait avec 35 000 hommes la Cochinchine et le Sud-Annam et y détruisait les unités militaires du Viêt-minh. À Hanoi le gouvernement d'Hô Chi Minh, redoutant la reconquête totale du Viêt-nam, faisait désespérement appel aux Américains. Ceux-ci depuis la mort de F.D. Roosevelt se montraient moins décidés à empêcher le retour des Français en Indochine. Les Soviétiques mirent surtout Hanoi en garde contre le risque de tomber dans l'orbite d'un gouvernement chinois anticommuniste et proaméricain. Le Viêt-minh fut donc contraint de négocier avec la France. Hô Chi Minh jugeait moins dangereux de devoir « flairer un peu la crotte des Français que de manger toute notre vie celle des Chinois ». De son côté, le haut-commissaire français, l'amiral d'Argenlieu, jugeait nécessaire de traiter avec le gouvernement d'Hô Chi Minh. Le général Leclerc pensait même devoir aller jusqu'à prononcer le mot d'indépendance, si le Viêt-nam restait dans l'Union française (cf. texte p. 87). Ainsi s'expliquent les accords franco-vietnamiens du 6 mars 1946 : « Le gouvernement français reconnaissait la République du Viêt-nam comme un État libre ayant son gouvernement, son Parlement, son armée et ses finances, faisant partie de la Fédération indochinoise et de l'Union française ».

Dans le même temps, la France négociait le départ des 180 000 soldats chinois installés au Tonkin et l'ayant obtenu, au prix fort, le 28 février 1946, le corps expéditionnaire français put débarquer à Haïphong au matin du 6 mars. Le gouvernement d'Hô Chi Minh s'était engagé à ne pas s'y opposer; en contrepartie la France promettait d'entériner, en ce qui concernait l'avenir des trois *Ky* (Tonkin - Annam - Cochinchine), les décisions prises par la population consultée par référendum.

Les accords reposaient de part et d'autre sur des arrière-pensées. La France entendait surtout grâce à eux pouvoir se réinstaller au Tonkin (cf. « le rapport du général Leclerc du 27 mars 1946 »). Les Viêtnamiens jugeaient ces accords comme une « pause » tactique et provisoire : « Nous avons choisi de négocier pour créer les conditions favorables à la lutte pour l'indépendance complète [...], pour protéger et renforcer notre position politique, militaire et économique » (Vô Nguyên Giap). Le Viêt-minh, qui s'était engagé à limiter ses troupes à 10 000 hommes, en comptait quelque 50 000 fin 1946. Le parti communiste, officiellement dissous, s'imposait au sein du Front de l'indépendance viêt-minh et réussissait par la terreur à asseoir son pouvoir : les mili-

LE GÉNÉRAL LECLERC DÉFEND LES ACCORDS DU 6 MARS 1945

(extraits du rapport adressé de Saigon, le 27 mars 1946, au gouvernement français)

Pour pouvoir rentrer au Tonkin, il était indispensable de trouver un gouvernement annamite, si imparfait soit-il, en place en Hanoi et n'ayant pas pris la brousse. [...]

Si nous avions trouvé, outre les Chinois, un pays soulevé contre nous, ou simplement en désordre, nous pouvions évidemment débarquer à Haiphong, mais — je l'affirme catégoriquement — la reconquête du Tonkin, même en partie, était impossible. Ce n'est pas avec une petite division — et en 1946 — que l'on conquiert un pays surexcité, armé et grand comme les deux tiers de la France. En outre, le problème n'aurait pas tardé à prendre une ampleur internationale.

C'est pourquoi on ne soulignera jamais assez l'importance des accords qui ont été conclus [...] Quelles que soient leurs imperfections, leur signature dans les conditions où elle s'est produite constitue un véritable tour de force [...]

C'est d'ailleurs la raison pour laquelle j'avais, le 14 février, télégraphié à Paris qu'il fallait aller jusqu'au mot d'indépendance pour éviter d'aller à un échec trop grave.

tants trotskystes et divers leaders nationalistes étaient arrêtés et exécutés, les notables enlevés et intimidés. Enfin des forces armées du Viêt-minh menaient une guérilla en Cochinchine.

Du côté français, les positions se raidirent progressivement. Le ministre de la France d'outre-mer, le socialiste Marius Moutet, recommandait dès le 13 mars de commencer une propagande politique sur le thème «La Cochinchine aux Cochinchinois». Le 1er juin l'amiral d'Argenlieu constituait un gouvernement autonome à Saigon. C'est sur cette question de la Cochinchine, qui devait être selon M. Moutet le «pivot de notre politique» qu'achoppèrent les conférences franco-vietnamiennes de Dalat et de Fontainebleau. L'amiral d'Argenlieu s'opposait à des concessions que le gouvernement français, très divisé, était plutôt disposé à consentir. Après l'échec des négociations de Fontainebleau, le 14 septembre 1946, Hô Chi Minh et Marius Moutet signaient pourtant un *modus vivendi* qui pouvait inaugurer une période de détente. Hô Chi Minh escomptait alors reprendre les négociations en janvier 1947 avec un gouvernement français «amical», issu des élections de novembre 1946 (le P.C.F. y obtint de fait 28,8 % des suffrages, le meilleur score de son histoire).

Cependant sur place la guérilla viêt-minh ne cessait pas : «Dans la quinzaine qui suivit le *modus vivendi*, 80 % des notables de Cochinchine ont été enlevés, supprimés, ou contraints de se cacher», expliqua Marius Moutet qui tenta en vain de récupérer 800 otages. Le 20 novembre 1946 éclatait à Haiphong un incident entre soldats français et vietnamiens. Le commandement local, puis le général Valluy, haut-commissaire par intérim, en tirèrent parti pour obtenir par un bombardement l'évacuation du port le 28 novembre. Le général Leclerc s'inquiéta qu'on voulût «briser par la force, la résistance vietnamienne, reprenant les méthodes de la conquête».

Réagissant à l'occupation française de Langson et de Haiphong, les éléments les plus combatifs du Viêt-minh prirent alors des dispositions pour infliger aux Français civils et militaires de Hanoi «une bonne leçon». Les 1200 soldats français furent brusquement attaqués dans la nuit du 19 au 20 décembre 1946, mais ils réussirent à refouler les troupes du Viêt-minh qui emmenèrent avec elles quelques 200 Français et Eurasiens en otages. On retrouva les cadavres de 40 civils Français massacrés dans leurs appartements. Le gouvernement Hô Chi Minh en fuite avait lancé le 21 un ordre d'insurrection générale dans tout le Viêt-nam. Le président du Conseil Léon Blum ordonna l'envoi de renforts militaires en assurant à l'Assemblée nationale qu'il reprendrait bientôt «l'œuvre interrompue : l'organisation d'un Viêt-nam libre dans une Union indochinoise librement associée à l'Union française». Pourtant la guerre d'Indochine avait cette fois vraiment commencé. Elle allait durer sept ans et un peu plus de sept mois.

Les responsabilités de cette guerre sont toujours passionnément discutées. Pour les auteurs communistes, elle fut seulement une «guerre d'agression française». Pourtant, si quelques responsables civils et militaires français crurent pouvoir régler le problème par la force, cette confiance dans la lutte armée était partagée par la majorité des ministres et des cadres du Viêt-minh : elle seule permettrait d'arracher l'indépendance totale aux «impérialistes et colonialistes français». Quant à la modération prétendue d'Hô Chi Minh, on se souviendra pour l'apprécier qu'il se glorifia en août 1949 «d'avoir rusé sans cesse pour gagner du temps afin d'organiser le soulèvement».

LA GUERRE ET LES INCERTITUDES POLITIQUES FRANÇAISES

Selon les responsables français en Indochine, il n'était plus possible après «l'agression du 19 décembre» de traiter avec Hô Chi Minh. Seule une restauration de la monarchie annamite paraissait possible à l'amiral d'Argenlieu. Mais le président du Conseil, Ramadier, écarta cette suggestion. Comme Léon Blum, il croyait aux possibilités de négocier sur la base de la reconnaissance de l'indépendance. Il révoqua d'Argenlieu et le remplaça par un préfet, Emile Bollaert. Hô Chi Minh cependant refusa les conditions d'armistice proposées par ce dernier. Emile Bollaert fit alors appel à l'ancien empereur d'Annam, Bao-Dai, exilé volontaire à Hong-Kong, qui accepta en posant ses conditions : unité et indépendance du Viêt-nam. Les socialistes français et le ministre Marius Moutet lui auraient préféré le chef du gouvernement de la Cochinchine, le général Xuân, franc-maçon, partisan d'une République laïque et progressiste. Le haut-commissaire Bollaert dut attendre le départ de Moutet et son remplacement par un ministre M.R.P., Paul Coste-Floret, pour signer un protocole secret avec Bao-Dai (7 décembre 1947). Mais ce dernier se rétracta presque aussitôt; selon ses conseillers, l'indépendance accordée était assortie de trop de conditions et Bao-Dai refusa de revenir au Viêt-nam.

Après de laborieuses discussions, le gouvernement français acceptait en mai 1948 la solution proposée par Bao-Dai : celle d'un gouvernement central provisoire du Viêt-nam confié au général Xuân. Une déclaration commune fut signée en baie d'Along, le 5 juin 1948 : «La France reconnaît solennellement l'indépendance du Viêt-nam auquel il appartient de réaliser librement son unité. De son côté le Viêt-nam proclame son adhésion à l'Union française [...] Dès la constitution d'un gouvernement provisoire, les représentants du Viêt-nam passeront avec les représentants de la République française les divers arrangements particuliers convenables d'ordre culturel, diplomatique, militaire, économique, financier et technique.»

Cependant Bao-Dai maintenait son attitude réservée, justifiée par les interprétations restrictives du ministre Coste-Floret et il refusa d'aller prendre en mains les affaires aussi longtemps qu'il n'aurait pas obtenu des garanties sur la réalité de l'indépendance. Bollaert, découragé et amer, renonça à poursuivre sa mission et céda la place à Léon Pignon, l'ancien conseiller de l'amiral d'Argenlieu. Celui-ci parvint enfin à un accord. Le 8 mars 1949, un échange de lettres entre Vincent Auriol, agissant comme président de l'Union française, et l'ex-empereur Bao-Dai précisait notamment que la France acceptait de transférer au Viêt-nam la Cochinchine, colonie française depuis 1862. Alors seulement Bao-Dai revint en Indochine comme chef de «l'État du Viêt-nam», un État qui disposait de son armée, de sa diplomatie, et qui obtint bientôt le transfert des services administratifs français communs aux trois États de l'Union indochinoise. Mais cet État était faible et ne disposait d'aucun soutien populaire, d'aucune assemblée représentative, d'aucune ressource financière, à la différence des États voisins du Cambodge et du Laos. Le Viêt-minh avait beau jeu de dénoncer «l'État bao-daïste, État fantoche.»

La guerre continuait : le corps expéditionnaire français tenta d'abord d'écraser le «sanctuaire Viêt-minh» établi dans la haute région du Tonkin. Mais, au terme de l'offensive d'octobre-novembre 1947, les unités régulières du Viêt-minh affaiblies n'étaient pas détruites. La guérilla et le terrorisme permirent au Viêt-minh de reconstituer ses forces : en 1949 «l'armée populaire» comptait quelque 100000 hommes en y comprenant les formations paramilitaires. Les forces françaises furent également accrues : de 115000 hommes en septembre 1947, elles atteignirent 146000 hommes en 1950 dont 68000 Français ou Européens. Les opérations de ratissage, qui dressaient contre les Français les masses paysannes sans apporter de résultats décisifs, étaient relativement coûteuses en vies humaines. De 1945 au 31 août 1949, 17000 militaires et 770 officiers français avaient été tués; fin 1950 les pertes françaises s'élevaient à 24099 hommes, fin 1951 à 27562. Mais la France l'ignorait; la guerre était menée quasi honteusement : même les grands blessés rapatriés d'Indochine par paquebots étaient acheminés de nuit dans les hôpitaux pour ne pas montrer à la métropole «les horreurs de la sale guerre colonialiste», dénoncées sans trêve à partir de 1949 par le parti communiste. Si les communistes lancèrent dès mai 1949 les slogans «Plus un homme, plus un sou pour la guerre d'Indochine», «Traitez avec Hô Chi Minh! Les mamans l'exigent», les socialistes demandaient eux aussi en juillet, l'ouverture de négociations avec le Viêt-minh. La classe politique française tout entière était divisée. Comme l'écrivait le haut-commissaire Léon Pignon, le 7 juillet 1949 : «La moitié du Parlement entend bien que Bao-Dai prenne au plus vite contact avec le Viêt-minh pour rétablir la paix, alors que l'autre moitié lui interdit tout contact "suspect" et lui demanda seulement d'appuyer l'action de pacification de l'armée.» Aux divisions politiques des Français s'ajoutait le sentiment unanime que «l'expérience Bao-Dai» était un «leurre» (général Revers), vu l'incapacité de cet homme à convaincre ses compatriotes, sauf les catholiques et les membres des sectes.

LE TOURNANT DE LA GUERRE

Dans l'été 1949, toutes les données politiques et militaires du conflit changèrent : la Chine tout entière tombait aux mains des armées communistes de Mao-Zedong. Dès lors la guerre franco-vietnamienne, qui était généralement interprétée à l'étranger comme une reconquête coloniale, allait prendre place dans la guerre froide. Le Viêt-minh annonça aussitôt à ses cadres qu'il n'était plus nécessaire de parler de négociation avec les Français, mais de se préparer à la guerre de mouvement en regroupant les unités régulières. Celles-ci étaient désormais dotées de matériel moderne livré par les Chinois et leur puissance de feu obligeait dès la fin de 1949 le commandement français à évacuer certains postes.

Sur le plan diplomatique, le gouvernement d'Hô Chi Minh demanda à être reconnu comme la seule autorité légitime du Viêt-nam. Dès le 18 janvier 1950 la Chine, bientôt suivie de l'U.R.S.S. et des États socialistes satellites, reconnaissait «la République démocratique du Viêt-nam» en affirmant qu'elle représentait «la majorité écrasante de la population de ce pays». Les États-Unis et la Grande-Bretagne durent en réponse, le 7 février, accorder la même légitimité à l'État de Bao-Dai et aux États associés : Cambodge et Laos. Pour la France, cela signifiait que la guerre allait s'internationaliser : elle ne pourrait continuer seule la lutte ou devrait renoncer totalement à l'Indochine.

Aussitôt après le déclenchement de la guerre de Corée (juin 1950), l'affrontement avec la Chine communiste se précisa. «L'armée rouge vietnamienne», équipée et entraînée par Pékin, contraignit les Français à abandonner toutes les places du Haut-Tonkin : à Cao-Bang la retraite mal conduite tourna en octobre 1950 à la défaite pour les unités françaises, qui y perdirent 4.000 hommes. Pour reprendre en main l'armée et faire face à l'invasion attendue du delta tonkinois, le gouvernement français envoya avec pleins pouvoirs civils et militaires, le général de Lattre de Tassigny. Celui-ci parvint à galvaniser le moral de l'armée et à briser les trois offensives successives du général Giap (janvier-juin 1951). Non seulement le delta fut fortifié, mais de Lattre bloqua l'entrée du pays thaï. L'illusion dura peu : un mois après la mort du général de Lattre, le 11 janvier 1952, son successeur Salan dut abandonner la place d'Hoa-Binh et laisser le pays thaï aux forces de Giap; dès lors le Laos était menacé (novembre 1952).

L'ÉCHEC POLITIQUE ET LA DÉFAITE MILITAIRE

Sur le plan politique ce fut au lendemain de Cao-Bang que l'Assemblée nationale entendit, pour la première fois le 19 octobre 1950, Pierre Mendès France souhaiter que la France se désengageât de ce conflit. Le gouvernement français préféra intensifier la guerre, grâce à l'aide financière américaine et

L'Indochine en 1949.

Dans les zones contrôlées par les forces françaises circulent des bandes de guérilleros.

Source : *Le Monde*, 1949.

au renforcement de l'armée vietnamienne. La guerre coûtait, il est vrai, de plus en plus cher : les dépenses militaires atteignaient 812,6 milliards de F de 1945 à 1951, dont 509 pour 1950 et 1951. Les dépenses civiles d'équipement et de reconstruction s'élevaient à 576 milliards de 1945 à 1951. Le président de la République, Vincent Auriol, affirma même fin 1952 que « la défense de la liberté en Indochine nous a déjà coûté matériellement le double de ce que nous avons reçu au titre du plan Marshall, 1600 milliards contre 800 ». Le général de Lattre avait évoqué lui, en septembre 1951, la saignée indochinoise : « nos 38000 morts dont plus de 20000 jeunes citoyens français et 1000 officiers ». Tous les officiels français réclamaient dès lors un soutien sans défaillance des gouvernements de l'O.T.A.N. Les États-Unis, inquiets d'un possible retrait français, augmentèrent leurs livraisons d'armes et leur aide financière jusqu'à supporter en 1952 46 %, en 1954 près de 80 % du coût de la guerre. Simultanément la France poussait les États associés d'Indochine à développer leurs armées nationales. En 1953, l'ensemble de leurs forces représentait un effectif égal à celui du corps expéditionnaire français, soit près de 450000 hommes au total pour les forces dites de l'Union française (et 400000 pour celles du Viêt-minh dont l'armement fut renforcé par la Chine libérée de la guerre de Corée, fin juillet 1953).

« Vietnamiser la guerre », comme on disait alors, et l'américaniser, ne suffisaient pas pour obtenir la victoire sur le plan militaire, ni pour persuader les peuples d'Indochine que la France entendait seulement les défendre contre le communisme. Face à leurs réclamations et à celles des Américains qui incriminaient « les attitudes coloniales désuètes des Français », le gouvernement Laniel annonça le 3 juillet 1953 : « Il y a lieu de parfaire l'indépendance et la souveraineté des États d'Indochine, en assurant, d'accord avec les trois gouvernements intéressés, le transfert des compétences que la France avait conservées dans l'intérêt même des États, en raison des circonstances périlleuses nées de l'état de guerre. » Le Laos accepta de réaffirmer librement son appartenance à l'Union française, le Cambodge obtint au terme de négociations difficiles sa totale indépendance. Quant à l'État de Bao-Dai, il ne reconnut que le 4 juin 1954 son adhésion à l'Union française, définie comme « une association de peuples indépendants et souverains, libres et égaux en droits et en devoirs, développant leur libre coopération en Haut Conseil, sous la présidence du président de l'Union ». Le traité intervint après la défaite de Dîen Bîen Phu ; pour la France il était trop tard pour « trouver une sortie honorable ». La guerre d'Indochine avait porté un coup fatal à l'Union française.

La victoire de l'armée populaire vietnamienne fut acquise dans la cuvette de Dîen Bîen Phu où le commandement français avait installé à 300 km d'Hanoi, pour défendre le Laos, une base d'opérations et un camp retranché. Encerclés et assiégés durant plusieurs mois par les forces du général Giap, qui finirent par atteindre 51000 hommes, les troupes franco-vietnamiennes (11200 hommes) ne purent être secourues, sinon par 4000 parachutistes. Après une résistance héroïque, Dîen Bîen Phu tombait le 7 mai 1954 et le Laos fut envahi. Dans le même temps, une conférence internationale s'était ouverte à Genève où la Chine communiste allait jouer le rôle décisif. Pour éviter une intervention américaine, le ministre des affaires étrangères chinois, Chou En Lai, imposa au gouvernement d'Hô Chi Minh la solution du partage de l'Indochine à hauteur du 17e parallèle. Cette ligne de démarcation militaire était déclarée provisoire et des élections libres devraient permettre la réunification, mais le gouvernement sud-vietnamien déclara ne pas se sentir lié par les accords de Genève du 21 juillet 1954.

La guerre d'Indochine avait entraîné de lourdes pertes pour les troupes de l'Union française : 19000 Français, 11000 légionnaires, 15000 Africains et environ 46000 «Indochinois». Sur 3000 milliards d'A.F. dépensés, 2385 furent pris en charge par le budget français. Sur le plan politique, le bilan n'était pas moins catastrophique : la France renonçait à sa politique d'association. Elle tenta vainement de maintenir son influence au Sud-Viêt-nam, car les États-Unis s'y opposèrent. Elle se désintéressa en revanche totalement du Viêt-nam du Nord. En avril 1956 les dernières troupes françaises quittaient le Sud-Viêt-nam après quatre-vingt-dix-sept ans de présence militaire.

LA GUERRE D'INDOCHINE ET L'OPINION FRANÇAISE

Malgré les sacrifices qu'elle imposa à l'armée, la guerre d'Indochine ne fut pas considérée par l'ensemble du peuple français comme une guerre nationale. Les gouvernements français le savaient bien, qui n'osèrent jamais y envoyer les soldats du contingent et n'y engagèrent jamais plus de 70000 militaires français. Cependant les Français furent longtemps divisés sur ce qu'il convenait de faire en Indochine. En juillet 1947, un sondage d'opinion indiquait que les Français se partageaient exactement entre partisans du «rétablissement de l'ordre par l'envoi de renforts» (37 %) et partisans de la négociation et de la «reconnaissance de l'indépendance» (37 %). Deux ans plus tard cependant, ceux qui voulaient continuer la guerre n'étaient plus que 19 %, ceux qui voulaient l'arrêter 49 %. La majorité de l'opinion n'approuvait donc plus la politique gouvernementale : les Français étaient 50 % à le dire dans les sondages en octobre 1953 et 60 % en février 1954. Très significatif aussi fut le nombre des indifférents : les pourcentages oscillèrent de 20 à 30 %. En février 1954, alors que 29 % des opinions recensées ne se prononçaient pas sur la guerre, un tiers des Français déclarait ne «jamais prendre connaissance des nouvelles sur l'Indochine», et 45 % seulement «de temps en temps». Bien entendu les variations d'opinion étaient considérables selon les électorats : en avril 1953, par exemple, étaient partisans de négocier ou de retirer le corps expéditionnaire : 28 % des électeurs R.P.F., 38 % des électeurs «modérés», 41 % de ceux du M.R.P., 43 % de ceux du R.G.R. (radicaux), 61 % des électeurs socialistes et 100 % des électeurs communistes.

Les communistes en effet, dans le contexte de la guerre froide, menèrent de 1949 à 1952 une action déterminée pour «la paix en Indochine». Ce fut la plus intense campagne anticolonialiste que le P.C.F. ait animée depuis la guerre du Rif. Le parti lança des grèves de dockers, des actions de cheminots; il recommanda le sabotage des fabrications de guerre et des envois de matériel; il dénonça les «atrocités» du corps expéditionnaire. La répression gouvernementale contre ces «activités antinationales» se borna à 180 poursuites judiciaires, mais il y eut aussi de bien plus nombreux licenciements de militants cégétistes. L'appui des intellectuels de gauche, et notamment de Jean-Paul Sartre, permit le développement d'une campagne d'opinion, «l'affaire

Henri Martin» : ce second maître de la Marine nationale, militant communiste avait été condamné à cinq ans d'emprisonnement sous l'accusation de sabotage; il devait être grâcié au bout de deux ans à la suite de l'agitation communiste. D'autres opérations de propagande permirent au P.C.F., «le parti de la propreté», d'accréditer l'accusation de corruptions des milieux politiques (on parla des «chéquards» comme au temps de Panama). Les banques et les affairistes se seraient, disait-il, enrichis grâce au «trafic des piastres». Des catholiques progressistes se mobilisèrent contre la torture, puis contre la guerre, notamment grâce à l'hebdomadaire *Témoignage chrétien*. Mais ces activismes ne parvinrent pas à susciter de véritable engouement pour leur cause. Ce fut seulement lors de la défaite de Dîen Bîen Phu que les Français se laissèrent «envahir par un sentiment amer où se côtoient l'irritation, l'humiliation, la surprise, l'accumulation des rancœurs, en même temps qu'un certain remords» (général Catroux). Une large majorité n'en accueillit pas moins avec soulagement les conditions du cessez-le-feu (64 %), cependant que 11 % parlaient de «véritable capitulation» et que 10 % s'en déclaraient mécontents. L'amertume des officiers se traduisit par un engagement lourd de conséquences : «Plus jamais ça!»

Les Britanniques avaient refusé «toute entreprise en vue de fournir une aide militaire aux Français de Diên Bîen Phu» : «Je ne vois pas pourquoi nous nous battrions pour la France en Indochine alors que nous avons renoncé à l'Inde», avoua Churchill. Quant au secrétaire d'État américain John Foster Dulles, il vit dans Dîen Bîen Phu «un bienfait insoupçonné», puisqu'il donnerait aux États-Unis la chance de sauver quelque chose dans une Indochine «lavée de la souillure du colonialisme français».

Mais la guerre d'Indochine eut surtout des répercussions auprès des peuples colonisés. Dès août 1951, le général de Lattre avait annoncé à Christian Fouchet : «Vous savez, tout cela ne s'arrêtera pas en Indochine. Nous avons fait la folie de faire combattre sous notre commandement des Musulmans et des Noirs, contre des Jaunes, et même parfois de les faire battre par des Jaunes. L'Afrique française est foutue». On n'allait pas tarder à le mesurer. Dîen Biên Phu fut perçu dans toute l'Afrique comme le signal de la décolonisation.

LA FIN DES PROTECTORATS FRANÇAIS DU MAGHREB ET DES COMPTOIRS FRANÇAIS DE L'INDE

L'INDÉPENDANCE DU MAROC (1947-1956)

Débarqué en mai 1947 d'un navire de guerre, le général Juin voulut arriver au Maroc en proconsul botté, comme pour mieux signifier que son autorité ne souffrirait pas d'être humiliée. Il annonça que sa première tâche serait de rétablir l'ordre du Protectorat : «Le Maroc dont la France a fait l'unité doit être un pays occidental qui doit se détourner des combinaisons orientales.»

S'il adopta aussitôt une politique d'autorité vis-à-vis de l'Istiqlâl, il ne découragea pas les nationalistes modérés, travaillant de son mieux à les opposer entre eux. Surtout il entendit mettre le Sultan au pied du mur en lui imposant les réformes qu'il jugeait nécessaires. Celles-ci visaient, semble-t-il, à transformer le régime du Protectorat et à établir, au bénéfice des Européens du Maroc, un régime de cosouveraineté franco-marocaine.

Il commença par des réformes du *Makhzen* (gouvernement) chérifien; il institua auprès du grand vizir (Premier ministre) cinq délégués marocains, chargés de collaborer avec les administrations techniques françaises du Protectorat, dites néo-chérifiennes. L'ancien conseil des vizirs présidé par le sultan fut maintenu, mais un Conseil des vizirs et des directeurs fut créé où se réuniraient dix Marocains et dix Français. Peut-être Juin espérait-il ainsi diminuer les pouvoirs du sultan. En octobre 1947, fut réformée la Chambre consultative, dite Conseil de gouvernement. La section marocaine composée de membres désignés fut désormais en partie élue au suffrage restreint indirect; ce qui n'empêcha pas l'élection de membres de l'Istiqlâl.

Le sultan, qui avait accepté ces réformes ambiguës, s'opposa au contraire à une réforme des municipalités qui aurait donné aux Français installés au Maroc des droits politiques égaux à ceux des Marocains : «Comment 266000 Français pourraient-ils être représentés à parité avec 8180000 Marocains?» Les nationalistes dénoncèrent cette tentative d'établissement de la cosouveraineté française.

En refusant d'apposer son sceau sur les projets de dahîrs que le résident tentait de lui imposer, le sultan bloquait la politique du général Juin. Ce dernier, qui entendait notamment intégrer le Maroc dans l'Union française, contre la volonté du Sultan, envisageait dès octobre 1947 de l'écarter du trône. Dans l'attente d'une occasion favorable, le résident général s'efforçait d'amenuiser la souveraineté chérifienne, et d'imposer au sultan les hommes et les fonctionnaires de son choix. Il lui opposait un chef de confrérie, le chérif El-Kittani, et un puissant féodal du Sud, le pacha de Marrakech, Thami el-Glaoui. Le sultan disposait quant à lui de l'appui des nationalistes et de leurs conseillers élus. D'où des accrochages très vifs du résident avec ces derniers, voire avec le sultan. Le gouvernement français tenta de détendre les rapports en invitant le sultan à venir en France. Mais ce voyage d'octobre 1950 fut un échec, car le sultan réclama vainement au président de la République et aux ministres français une révision du régime du Protectorat. Le 21 décembre 1950 une altercation grave opposa le pacha de Marrakech à son souverain. El-Glaoui aurait dit à Sidi Mohammed ben Youssef : «Tu n'es pas le sultan du Maroc, tu es le sultan de l'Istiqlâl!». Brutalement congédié, le pacha rameuta ses fidèles, tandis que le général Juin le 26 janvier 1951 exigea du sultan qu'il se désolidarisât des nationalistes : «Ou vous désavouez le parti de l'Istiqlâl ou vous renoncez au trône. Autrement je vous déposerai moi-même.» Après plusieurs sommations, le général Juin rompit ses relations avec le Palais et fit sentir la menace de destitution par l'arrivée de plusieurs milliers de cavaliers berbères autour de Fès et de Rabat. Le sultan demanda l'arbitrage du président de la République qui se déclara solidaire de Juin. Dès lors le sultan dut le 25 février s'incliner devant l'ultimatum du résident : il promit d'éloigner du Makhzen les personnalités proches des nationalistes. Il autorisa son grand vizir à condamner, sans le nommer expressément, l'Istiqlâl et laissa sans protester la police française arrêter un certain nombre de nationalistes. Mais il fit peu après connaître au monde arabe et à l'opinion internationale qu'il n'avait agi que sous la contrainte. La crise n'était donc pas dénouée.

Les nationalistes marocains des deux zones, française et espagnole, réagirent en constituant avec l'Istiqlâl, le 9 avril 1951, un Front national marocain. Celui-ci s'engageait à lutter pour l'indépendance complète, à ne pas accepter l'adhésion à l'Union française et à refuser toute négociation avec « l'occupant français ». Même si ce Front se montra finalement peu efficace, il était révélateur de l'échec de la politique d'intimidation du général Juin. Sur le plan international, la position diplomatique de la France se détériorait : sa politique marocaine était dénoncée par la Ligue des nations arabes et contestée par les Anglo-saxons. Pour la première fois l'O.N.U. allait être saisie de la question marocaine.

Inquiet de cette situation, le gouvernement français avait décidé le 28 août 1951 de remplacer le général Juin. Mais le successeur qu'il lui donna, le général Guillaume, ancien officier d'Affaires indigènes, considérait lui aussi que les nationalistes marocains devaient être traités en ennemis. Or l'Istiqlâl devenait un grand parti national rassemblant à cette date 114000 militants, qu'il recrutait désormais dans les milieux populaires. Dès lors le parti échappait quelque peu à ses dirigeants dont la plupart appartenaient à la grande bourgeoisie traditionaliste et il était tenté par la violence. On le vit bien lors d'un simple boycott électoral, le 1er novembre 1951 : les militants de base déclenchèrent des bagarres qui firent des morts et de nombreux blessés. De son côté, le sultan exprima à nouveau le 14 novembre 1951 le souhait de négocier un « accord qui garantirait au Maroc sa pleine souveraineté et établirait ses relations avec la France sur de nouvelles bases ». Puis il fit connaître officiellement au président de la République, le 14 mars 1952, sa volonté de voir s'ouvrir des négociations sur le statut du Protectorat. Une nouvelle convention permettrait d'assurer la continuité des rapports franco-marocains dans le cadre de la souveraineté retrouvée et d'établir au Maroc un régime constitutionnel. Malgré la modération de ce mémorandum, le général Guillaume s'y déclara résolument hostile. Le Quai d'Orsay ne répondit au sultan que six mois après, en insistant sur le caractère mixte, c'est-à-dire franco-marocain, de l'Administration française au Maroc. C'était une fin de non-recevoir et le blocage était total.

Des émeutes graves éclatèrent les 7 et 8 décembre 1952 à Casablanca, à la suite d'une grève de protestation contre le meurtre du leader syndical tunisien, Ferhat Hached. Non seulement la police ouvrit le feu, mais les Européens se heurtèrent aux manifestants marocains, dont certains furent lynchés. On ne peut donner aucun chiffre fiable du nombre des victimes, le résident parla de 33 manifestants tués et de 4 Européens assassinés; les nationalistes de 1000 à 1200 morts, chiffres manifestement exagérés, mais retenus par la presse internationale. La résidence fit arrêter des centaines de militants nationalistes et syndicalistes qu'on dut relâcher deux ans plus tard faute de charges. Le parti Istiqlâl fut provisoirement interdit.

Les Européens exultaient : « une bonne répression, disaient-ils, c'est dix ans de paix assurée ». Tandis que l'O.N.U. retentissait de critiques et de conseils de solutions amiables, la Résidence se préparait à aller plus loin, jusqu'à la déposition du sultan. Dès le 1er février 1953, un journaliste influent, Raymond Cartier, publia dans *Paris Match* à son retour de Rabat, un article intitulé :

«Le sultan doit changer ou il faut changer de sultan» et sous-titré «Ou la France, ou le Sultan s'en ira». Un véritable complot s'ourdissait : tandis que les élus français du Conseil de gouvernement exigeaient la déposition du sultan, l'éloignement définitif du prince héritier Moulay Hassan, l'interdiction définitive de l'Istiqlâl et du parti communiste, les Marocains conservateurs se rassemblaient autour du chérif Kittani et du pacha de Marrakech El-Glaoui. Le premier réunissait à Fès un congrès des confréries musulmanes qui s'éleva contre la politique religieuse du sultan; le second faisait signer par 287 pachas, qaïds et notables une pétition demandant le remplacement du sultan. Les Français du Maroc s'organisaient en groupe de pression dans l'association *Présence française* à laquelle s'opposa *Conscience française* fondée par une poignée de libéraux. Enfin, la Résidence organisa le 11 mai 1953 un grand rassemblement d'une centaine de milliers de montagnards et de goumiers berbères présidé par le maréchal Juin.

Le 31 mai, El-Glaoui crut pouvoir proclamer que, «pour les représentants qualifiés du peuple», le sultan était déchu, mais aussitôt 287 personnalités marocaines adressaient au gouvernement français une contre-pétition favorable à son maintien. Les partisans d'El-Glaoui ripostèrent par une nouvelle pétition de 335 notables. En France aussi face à une étrange apathie du gouvernement, youssefistes et glaouistes s'opposaient; les premiers étaient animés par le comité France-Maghreb dont le président était l'écrivain catholique François Mauriac, les seconds par le Comité central de la France d'outre-mer et l'ambassadeur F. Charles-Roux.

Au mois d'août 1953, le pression de la Résidence et des partisans d'El-Glaoui s'accentua au Maroc de telle manière que le ministre des Affaires étrangères, Georges Bidault, mesurant qu'il allait être mis devant le fait accompli, ordonna à la Résidence de trouver «une solution rationnelle au conflit». Pour El-Glaoui «il était trop tard». Un prétendant qu'il avait suscité, un oncle du sultan, Moulay 'Arafa s'était déclaré prêt à accepter le trône. Le général Guillaume entendit imposer au sultan une capitulation écrite qui lui retirait l'essentiel de ses pouvoirs. Le sultan, se déclarant «contraint par la force», accepta ce projet de règlement. Paris crut à l'apaisement, mais les glaouistes n'acceptèrent qu'un compromis dépourvu de signification : ils proclamèrent «imâm de l'Islam» leur candidat, le sultan légitime restant en place comme chef politique. En réalité pour un Marocain, l'imâm, le chef religieux, était nécessairement le souverain. El-Glaoui menaça alors la France en termes clairs : «Si, contrairement à notre attente, le gouvernement français n'ose pas en cette conjoncture faire preuve de la fermeté qu'espère le peuple marocain, la France aura perdu sa place au Maroc. Demain nos amis peuvent devenir les ennemis de la France.»

Le président du Conseil Laniel en tira la conclusion qu'il n'était pas possible «de faire tirer sur nos amis pour conserver le trône et la vie à un prince qui ne nous aime pas». Tandis que le Conseil des ministres divisé discutait, l'arrestation du sultan s'opérait le 19 août, sur ordre de la Résidence. Le lendemain, le collège des *'ulamâ'* de Fès reconnaissait Moulay 'Arafa comme souverain du Maroc, désigné «en accord avec le gouvernement français». Comme les Marocains stupéfaits ne réagirent pas sur l'heure, Paris en tira hâtivement la conclusion que le sang ne coulerait pas.

Pendant deux ans le Maroc privé de son souverain légitime résista au pouvoir que les Français essayaient de lui imposer : l'espoir des patriotes se tournait vers celui que la France avait exilé à Madagascar. Ce n'était plus seulement le parti de l'Istiqlâl qui menait le combat pour le retour du sultan, mais la majeure partie de la population, femmes et ruraux compris. La lutte prit un aspect religieux sous l'impulsion de jeunes chefs improvisés qui désignaient les Français et leurs collaborateurs marocains comme ennemis de l'Islam.

De là le fait que la résistance prit spontanément la forme du terrorisme. De fin août 1953 au 1er décembre 1955, on dénombra 6813 attentats, agressions et explosions terroristes qui firent 102 morts et 493 blessés parmi les Français, 639 tués et 1541 blessés chez les Marocains. Il y eut des attentats manqués contre «le sultan des Français», contre El-Glaoui et le général Guillaume, mais d'autres entraînèrent la mort d'un certain nombre de personnalités françaises. Les Européens ripostèrent en enlevant comme otages des notables marocains ou en recourant au contre-terrorisme : environ 70 Marocains et Français «libéraux» en furent les victimes. Malgré la répression policière qui permit d'arrêter 1707 «terroristes» — dont 47 furent condamnés à mort — les activités terroristes ne diminuaient pas.

Pendant toute cette période d'anarchie, la Résidence fut impuissante à mettre en application les réformes dont on avait assuré que seul le sultan exilé les avait empêchées. On créa bien des municipalités avec une représentation paritaire dans les chefs-lieux de région, mais les circonstances n'en permirent pas la mise en route. Il en alla de même pour le Conseil de gouvernement. L'autorité du sultan Moulay 'Arafa était annihilée. Il délégua son pouvoir exécutif à un Conseil privé où les Français étaient les maîtres et son pouvoir législatif au Conseil des vizirs et directeurs, où les Français avaient la majorité. Dès lors il apparut aux yeux de tous comme un souverain fantoche. Mendès France demanda au résident Francis Lacoste des mesures d'apaisement et des discussions avec les nationalistes. Mais ceux-ci refusaient de s'y prêter aussi longtemps que le sultan légitime serait prisonnier. Quant à celui-ci, il refusait de renoncer au trône. Francis Lacoste se révélant impuissant à agir, le gouvernement Edgar Faure le remplaça en juin 1955 par un haut fonctionnaire, Gilbert Grandval, qui avait une réputation méritée de courage et d'énergie. À peine arrivé celui-ci se heurta à l'agitation des ultras qui lui reprochaient ses premières mesures d'autorité contre les hauts fonctionnaires indociles. Hué par les Européens, acclamé par les Marocains, Grandval craignit que la restauration du sultan Ben Youssef devînt inéluctable. Il envisageait le départ du sultan Moulay 'Arafa, la constitution d'un Conseil de régence qui formerait un ministère de négociations et le retour en France du sultan exilé. Mais Moulay 'Arafa s'y opposa et surtout le 20 août un mouvement insurrectionnel, décidé en commun avec le F.L.N. algérien, souleva plusieurs groupes berbères du Maroc central. Ceux-ci se livrèrent à Oued Zem au massacre de 49 Français, à Aït Amman à celui de 19 Français.

Le gouvernement français voulut résoudre d'urgence le problème marocain pour pouvoir tenir l'Algérie. Les représentants de tous les partis marocains furent entendus à Aix-les-Bains par un comité de cinq personnalités françaises. Celui-ci décida le retour en France du sultan Sidi Mohammed, la constitution d'un Conseil de régence après le départ du sultan Moulay 'Arafa.

Mais ce dernier ne céda que le 1er octobre. Dans la nuit suivante des commandos, venus du Maroc espagnol, attaquaient les postes français. L'Armée de libération marocaine annonça qu'elle ne déposerait pas les armes avant la reconnaissance de l'indépendance et la restauration du sultan. Le gouvernement français choisit de négocier avec le souverain marocain les conditions d'un accord. Le ministre des Affaires étrangères français, Antoine Pinay, signa avec le sultan, à la Celle-Saint-Cloud le 6 novembre 1955, un accord qui prévoyait «l'ouverture de négociations destinées à faire accéder le Maroc au statut d'État indépendant, uni à la France par les liens permanents d'une interdépendance librement définie et consentie.» Cet accord faisait du sultan «le souverain constitutionnel d'un État démocratique». D'où le titre qu'il prit plus tard, le 15 août 1957, de roi Mohammed V. Les négociations de Paris, ouvertes le 15 février 1956, aboutirent dès le 2 mars à une déclaration commune. La France confirmait solennellement la reconnaissance de l'indépendance du Maroc. Les «deux États souverains et égaux» remettaient à de futurs accords «l'interdépendance des deux pays»; ils ne furent jamais négociés.

La rapidité avec laquelle le gouvernement français reconnut l'indépendance, sans insister sur les liens d'interdépendance, s'explique seulement par la guerre d'Algérie. Le Parlement français se résigna pour la même raison à ratifier les accords du 2 mars par 271 voix contre 59 et 200 abstentions.

LA CRISE FRANCO-TUNISIENNE ET LA FIN DU PROTECTORAT (1949-1956)

Le 8 septembre 1949, après un exil volontaire de quatre ans et demi, Bourguiba revint en Tunisie. Il s'efforça d'abord de recréer l'unité des nationalistes et de mobiliser l'opinion derrière le Néo-Destour, notamment en invoquant l'éventualité d'une épreuve sanglante avec le régime colonial. Puis en avril 1950, il alla présenter à Paris le programme des revendications indépendantistes. Simultanément il soulignait devant l'opinion française son offre d'une amicale collaboration franco-tunisienne. Socialistes et communistes ainsi qu'une partie du M.R.P. se montrèrent favorables aux demandes tunisiennes, cependant que les partis modérés, confortés par les réactions des Français de Tunisie et d'Algérie, se déclaraient hostiles à «tout renoncement de la France».

Le ministère Georges Bidault parut vouloir engager la négociation en nommant à Tunis le 31 mars 1950 un préfet qui connaissait bien le Maghreb, Louis Périllier. Le ministre des Affaires étrangères, Robert Schuman, déclara même dans un discours à Thionville que «la mission de L. Périllier était d'amener la Tunisie vers l'indépendance». Cette phrase fit sensation; G. Bidault la fit rectifier et R. Schuman dut publier une mise au point embarrassée. À la radio de Tunis, le résident Périllier lut un texte plus diplomatique où il était seulement question de «modifications institutionnelles progressives vers une autonomie conforme à l'esprit des traités». Le résident constitua un ministère où figuraient plusieurs Destouriens, tel Salah ben Youssef, secrétaire général du Néo-Destour. Le président, Mhamed Chenik, n'était autre que l'ancien Premier ministre de Moncef Bey. Puis un protocole franco-tunisien fut rendu public le 17 août; il précisait que le ministère aurait pour mission de négocier les réformes institutionnelles qui, par étapes, mèneraient la Tunisie «vers l'autonomie interne». Les négociations, tardivement engagées dans un climat tendu, aboutirent le 8 février 1951 à la promulgation de cinq décrets beylicaux par lesquels des transformations profondes étaient apportées. Ainsi le Conseil des ministres, où figurait un nombre égal de Tunisiens et de Français, n'était plus présidé par le résident qui n'en faisait plus partie; de même le secrétaire général français du gouvernement n'avait plus le pouvoir de viser les arrêtés ministériels. En ce qui concernait les emplois publics, les Tunisiens disposaient désormais des 3/4 des emplois subalternes, des 2/3 des emplois moyens et de la moitié des postes supérieurs. L'opinion tunisienne qui attendait plus, fut déçue, tandis que le *Rassemblement français* ne tarda pas à s'élever contre les «inspirateurs et les exécutants d'une politique d'abandon».

Le bey Lamine annonça alors son intention de constituer une Assemblée représentative purement tunisienne. À quoi le résident répliqua en demandant la représentation des Français dans les conseils municipaux. Or les Tunisiens, depuis qu'ils avaient appris que le sultan marocain s'y refusait, s'y opposèrent en affirmant que cette réforme eût introduit le principe de la cosouveraineté. Devant ce blocage le résident était décidé à «mettre en cause la position personnelle du bey». Bourguiba, parce qu'il souhaitait des appuis extérieurs, alla expliquer dans une série de voyages sa politique de bonne volonté. Le secrétaire général de l'U.G.T.T., Ferhat Hached, l'accompagna aux États-Unis et sut convaincre les dirigeants syndicalistes américains de la modération et de l'anticommunisme des Tunisiens. Le Bureau exécutif de la Confédération internationale des syndicats libres vota une motion de soutien à l'adoption de mesures propres à réaliser l'indépendance de la Tunisie. Dans ce climat, le Premier ministre Chenik crut pouvoir venir à Paris en octobre 1951 et convaincre le gouvernement Pleven de «réaliser dans un temps minimum l'autonomie interne sur le triple plan gouvernemental, législatif et administratif». Il demandait notamment la constitution d'un Parlement tunisien homogène dans lequel les Français n'auraient droit à aucune représentation. Ces exigences radicales heurtèrent la majorité des ministres français et les représentants de la colonie française. Bien que Robert Schuman ait proposé une réponse conciliante, la lettre du 15 décembre 1951, que le Quai d'Orsay rédigea, était d'une tout autre encre. Elle disait l'impossibilité d'écarter la participation des 150000 Français de Tunisie aux institutions politiques, et notamment aux conseils municipaux; elle soulignait «le caractère définitif des liens qui unissent la France et la Tunisie» et n'envisageait que «la recherche d'amélioration dans le fonctionnement du Protectorat». Le terme d'autonomie interne n'était pas mentionné, pas plus que la reconnaissance de la souveraineté tunisienne.

Le soudain raidissement de la position française paraît s'expliquer par l'ampleur des interventions des Français de Tunisie, et la peur de la contagion que pouvait entraîner l'indépendance de la Libye proclamée le 24 décembre 1951. Robert Schuman enfin avait cédé aux pressions des parlementaires radicaux pour conserver leur appui dans les affaires européennes. Le résident Périllier, qui avait finalement conseillé au gouvernement de donner satisfaction à certaines des revendications tunisiennes, fut rappelé et remplacé par un diplomate à poigne, Jean de Hauteclocque. Celui-ci choisit d'arriver à Tunis sur un navire de guerre.

L'épreuve de force

Les Tunisiens n'entendaient pas se laisser imposer le principe de la cosouveraineté. Deux ministres tunisiens déposèrent devant l'O.N.U. une requête officielle de saisine du Conseil de Sécurité. Le résident demanda aussitôt au bey leur révocation; il interdit le congrès du Néo-Destour et fit arrêter préventivement 150 Destouriens. Quant à Habib Bourguiba, il fut placé en résidence surveillée à Tabarka. Aux manifestations populaires et à la grève générale déclenchée par l'U.G.T.T., le résident répliqua par l'état de siège et confia à l'Armée «le ratissage» de la presqu'île du Cap-Bon. Cette opération de police, menée par la Légion avec rudesse et maladresse, provoqua l'entrée en scène de quinze États africains et asiatiques à l'O.N.U. Le bref gouvernement Edgar Faure affecta de croire à un «malentendu» et, condamnant le principe de la cosouveraineté, il voulut reprendre le dialogue. Mais il n'en eut pas le temps. Renversé, il fut remplacé par un gouvernement Pinay qui croyait que le retour à l'ordre exigeait une politique d'autorité.

Le résident Hauteclocque exigea alors du bey le renvoi de tout le cabinet Chenik, puis devant son refus, il fit arrêter le Premier ministre et trois de ses ministres, sous l'accusation infondée de collusion avec les communistes. Le bey saisit le président de la République, Vincent Auriol, mais en vain. Celui-ci tenu à la neutralité n'en demanda pas moins à A. Pinay «si on est devenu fou» et fit connaître en Conseil des ministres sa désapprobation. Encore ignorait-il que l'avion de la présidence conduisait à Tunis un héritier présomptif de Lamine Bey. Ce dernier, ainsi menacé, capitula; il désavoua les fauteurs de troubles et se résigna à accepter le Premier ministre et le Cabinet que le résident lui imposa. Ce ministère Baccouche présenta alors un plan de réformes que le gouvernement français «améliora» un peu, sans convaincre ni les Tunisiens, ni les Français de Tunisie. Ce plan ne fut pas formellement approuvé, ni désapprouvé par l'Assemblée nationale en juin 1952. Celle-ci ne parvint pas à conclure, tous les projets d'ordre du jour étant successivement rejetés. Pourtant le résident présenta au bey le projet français qui prétendait vouloir acheminer la Tunisie «vers l'autonomie interne».

Le bey convoqua alors, en Conseil de la Couronne, une quarantaine de personnalités représentatives. Ce Conseil, salué comme les États généraux de la Tunisie, rejeta le projet gouvernemental français, qu'il jugea dérisoire et attentatoire à la souveraineté tunisienne. Bien que le bey ait fait connaître son refus au président de la République, le gouvernement n'osa pas lui imposer ses réformes et proposa la reprise des négociations. Cette ouverture fut rendue vaine par l'assassinat du leader syndicaliste Ferhat Hached qui aurait été condamné par une organisation d'extrémistes européens, la Main Rouge. Cet assassinat provocateur relança l'agitation, les attentats et les arrestations de Tunisiens.

L'O.N.U. se saisit de la question tunisienne malgré l'opposition de la France. Mais la décision qu'elle prit le 17 décembre 1952 se bornait à exprimer «l'espoir que les parties poursuivront sans retard leurs négociations en vue de l'accession des Tunisiens à la capacité de s'administrer eux-mêmes». Le bey découragé se décida le 20 décembre à sceller deux décrets sur les assemblées locales, dont l'un assurait la participation des Français aux conseils municipaux. Le résident se crut vainqueur, mais il dut constater son échec aux élections pour ces nouveaux conseils qui se déroulèrent au printemps 1953. Les électeurs s'abstinrent massivement surtout aux élections municipales : 8,8 % seulement votèrent à Tunis, dont une forte proportion d'Israélites. La période électorale avait été marquée par une recrudescence du nombre d'attentats. Paris dut en tirer la leçon.

Hauteclocque fut remplacé le 2 septembre 1953 par Pierre Voizard, sans que le gouvernement Laniel se fût décidé pour une politique. Tandis que le nouveau résident s'essayait à créer une détente, un des principaux leaders du Néo-Destour, Hedi Chaker, fut assassiné. Voizard agitait des projets, mais sur ordre du Quai d'Orsay, il tenait systématiquement à l'écart le Néo-Destour, dont le chef restait assigné à résidence dans la petite île de La Galite. Il choisit un nouveau Premier ministre, Salah Mzali, qui dut prendre à son compte les réformes Voizard et réussit à les faire accepter par le bey, le 4 mars 1954. Elles en revenaient pourtant au principe de la parité de représentation, expression de la cosouveraineté rejetée par les nationalistes. Depuis La Galite, Bourguiba proclama son opposition à «des pseudo-réformes qui maintiennent la cogestion et n'établissent pas un régime démocratique».

L'épreuve de force continuait : des groupes de *fellaga* armés, qui se considéraient comme une armée de libération, tenaient désormais la campagne, assassinant des colons français. Le Néo-Destour expliquait le terrorisme par le désespoir et invitait la France à ne pas s'en tenir à des mesures militaires. De leur côté les Français de Tunisie imputaient l'action des rebelles aux mesures de libéralisation et à la faiblesse de la répression et ils justifiaient le contre-terrorisme. Le ministère Mzali mesurant son impuissance démissionna le 17 juin. Le même jour Mendès France prononçait son discours d'investiture où il marquait sa volonté de «reprendre avec les Tunisiens le dialogue malheureusement interrompu».

L'autonomie interne

Dès le 30 juillet 1954, Pierre Mendès France faisait accepter par le Conseil des ministres, le retour à la politique d'autonomie interne. Pour rassurer les Français, il nommait comme résident le général Boyer de la Tour, alors commandant supérieur des troupes en Tunisie. Le lendemain il atterrissait à Tunis, flanqué du maréchal Juin, comme caution supplémentaire et déclara au bey : «L'autonomie interne de l'État tunisien est reconnue et proclamée sans arrière-pensée, par le gouvernement français [...]. Nous sommes prêts à transférer à des personnes et à des institutions tunisiennes l'exercice interne de la souveraineté.» Mendès France avait auparavant fait discrètement consulter Bourguiba. Celui-ci s'était déclaré favorable à la participation du Néo-Destour à un gouvernement de négociation. De fait le cabinet constitué par Tahar Ben 'Ammar comprit cinq nationalistes indépendants et quatre Destouriens.

Ce gouvernement eut pour première tâche de convaincre les *fellaga* de cesser leur combat. Il y réussit : environ 3000 «combattants de la foi», confiants dans la parole du gouvernement tunisien, déposèrent leurs armes et ne furent pas inquiétés. Dans le même temps, Mendès France avait entamé à Paris les négociations sur les modalités de l'autonomie interne. Celles-ci furent difficiles : les Tunisiens entendaient préparer leur indépendance et Mendès France ne l'envisageait pas, même à terme. Les différents ministères français insistaient pour garder leurs attributions. Le général Boyer de la Tour refusait de livrer la Tunisie au Néo-Destour, «ce parti totalitaire qui instaurerait une République et exalterait le séparatisme algérien». Mendès France aurait voulu aboutir pour que la réussite des négociations ait des répercussions favorables en Algérie et au Maroc. Fin janvier, un projet partiel était accepté par les deux parties; le maréchal Juin s'y opposa ainsi que le général Boyer de la Tour qui vint mener campagne contre Mendès France jusque dans les couloirs du Palais-Bourbon. Le 5 février, le ministère était renversé et les négociations n'avaient pas abouti.

Elles ne reprirent que deux mois plus tard, malgré les protestations et agitations du mouvement *Présence française* et les divisions entre Néo-Destouriens. Pour aboutir, le président du Conseil Edgar Faure s'entretint directement avec Bourguiba, toujours assigné à résidence, mais en France. Le 21 avril 1955, les deux délégations signèrent le protocole d'accord qui allait donner naissance aux conventions franco-tunisiennes. Il consacrait l'autonomie interne sans autres restrictions que celles définies par les six conventions signées le 5 juin. Si le mot protectorat disparaissait et avec lui le contrôle de la souveraineté intérieure et la tutelle des directeurs et contrôleurs civils français, la France conservait la Défense et les Affaires étrangères et, pour quelques années, les services de sécurité. La Tunisie restait rattachée à la zone franc, les Français de Tunisie étaient admis à participer à la gestion des municipalités avec des représentations aux proportions variables. La France accordait à la Tunisie un crédit de 3400 millions de F et un don de 2600 millions. La majorité des Tunisiens s'estima satisfaite et le manifesta à Bourguiba, lors de son retour à Tunis. Pourtant Salah ben Youssef protesta à Bandoeng : il voulait relancer l'action des *fellaga* pour arracher l'indépendance totale immédiate. Même s'il dut s'enfuir de Tunisie, Ben Youssef défenseur de l'arabisme avait de nombreux partisans et menaça le nouveau pouvoir. Bourguiba ne cessa de dire que l'indépendance totale serait obtenue en accord avec la France.

Or le retour d'exil du sultan du Maroc détermina le gouvernement français, le 6 novembre 1955, à promettre l'accession du Maroc au statut «d'indépendance dans l'interdépendance». La Tunisie ne pouvait être maintenue dans une situation inférieure. Elle demanda et obtint, le 20 mars 1956, l'abrogation du traité du Bardo (12 mai 1881) et l'indépendance assortie «des modalités d'une interdépendance librement réalisée».

On remarquera qu'après soixante-quinze ans de protectorat, le passage de l'autonomie interne à l'indépendance avait duré moins d'un an. Les modalités d'application suivirent non moins rapidement : dès juin 1956, les Tunisiens obtinrent le droit d'avoir leur diplomatie et leur armée nationale.

Avec le recul de l'Histoire, la politique française en Tunisie, caractérisée par ses hésitations, ses revirements et ses échecs, peut être retenue comme révélatrice de l'incapacité à résoudre les problèmes d'outre-mer qui a entraîné la chute de la IVe République.

LA FIN DES COMPTOIRS FRANÇAIS DE L'INDE (1946-1956)

La fin des comptoirs de l'Inde passa au contraire presque inaperçue de l'opinion. Seuls les lettrés férus d'histoire se rappelaient que la France était présente dans l'Inde, depuis la fondation de Pondichéry en 1674. Par-delà le rêve d'un empire indien de Dupleix, la présence française se borna pourtant à cinq comptoirs éparpillés sur les deux côtes de l'Inde : les villes de Pondichéry, Chandernagor, Karikal, Yanaon et le village de Mahé. Ceux-ci étaient sous la IIIe République représentés au Parlement, puisque depuis 1848 tous les habitants étaient citoyens français.

En juillet 1940, les comptoirs se rallièrent au général de Gaulle, mais durent acceptés d'être intégrés dans une union douanière avec l'Inde britannique. Alors que celle-ci se préparait à l'indépendance, les comptoirs français, peuplés au total de quelque 300000 habitants, devinrent le 27 octobre 1946 un territoire d'outre-mer à statut particulier, représenté par un député et deux conseillers de la République élus au collège unique. La nouvelle assemblée représentative locale ne tarda pas à s'élever contre les fonctionnaires métropolitains et à réclamer la fusion avec l'Inde nationale. Devenue indépendante le 15 août 1947, l'Union indienne demanda aussitôt le retour des comptoirs coloniaux français, rejetant leur transformation en villes libres.

Pour le ministre socialiste Marius Moutet «les Établissements de l'Inde étaient partie intégrante de la République et l'on ne pouvait admettre, même à échéance très lointaine, l'éventualité d'un rattachement à l'Inde.» Un parti socialiste local développa cette conception. Fort heureusement le ministre des Affaires étrangères, Georges Bidault, sensible à ce qu'il appelait «le mouvement général des choses» ou «la révolte générale de l'Asie», fit prévaloir la négociation : la France s'engagea le 28 juin 1948 à restituer les comptoirs à l'Inde par la procédure d'un référendum dans chacun d'entre eux. À Chandernagor, située dans la banlieue industrielle de Calcutta et à 2000 km de Pondichéry, l'assemblée municipale fixa elle-même la date du référendum et celui-ci aboutit à la cession de la ville aux autorités indiennes dès août 1949. Paris ne ratifia le rattachement qu'en 1951.

Dans les autres comptoirs, la situation fut compliquée du fait de l'établissement par le gouvernement indien d'un blocus douanier et policier, qui interdisait toute relation entre eux. Le référendum autorisé par le gouvernement français ne put avoir lieu. Bientôt l'Inde changea de politique : elle repoussa le principe du référendum, exigeant la cession pure et simple. De 1952 à 1954, la France s'y refusa : «Tout abandon de notre part, sur un point quelconque du continent asiatique rendrait plus difficile encore, aux yeux de l'opinion nationale, l'acceptation des sacrifices que la France consent en Indochine pour une cause qui intéresse le monde libre» (janvier 1954).

Cependant le nombre des élus fidèles à l'Union française s'amenuisait : le parti socialiste local se transformait en Congrès de la libération et constituait un gouvernement provisoire de l'Inde française libérée. Tandis que l'on négociait à Paris et à New-Delhi, les nationalistes «libéraient» Yanaon le 13 juin 1954 et Mahé le 16 juillet. Le gouvernement Laniel envoya 50 gardes mobiles à Pondichéry, ce qui provoqua une très vive protestation de l'Inde.

Le gouvernement Mendès France, après avoir songé à un transfert *de facto*, tenta de sauver la face : le référendum rejeté par l'Inde fut remplacé par une consultation des conseillers municipaux qui votèrent le rattachement à l'Inde par 170 voix contre 8. Le 21 octobre 1954, un accord franco-indien, non publié au *Journal officiel*, prévoyait la prise en charge de l'administration des comptoirs par le gouvernement indien. Il fut suivi d'un traité signé le 28 mai

1956, qui entérinait la cession de souveraineté. Le Conseil de l'Union française consulté refusa de le ratifier. Ainsi s'achevaient trois siècles de présence française. Les Établissements français, qui auraient pu constituer des plateformes naturelles d'expansion culturelle et commerciale, furent liquidés sans compensation, au terme d'un combat retardateur imposé par l'incapacité des gouvernements à tourner la page.

LA LENTE ÉVOLUTION DE L'OPINION FRANÇAISE : DU MYTHE IMPÉRIAL À LA DÉCOLONISATION

Lorsqu'on compare l'évolution de l'opinion française vis-à-vis de la question coloniale à celle d'autres nations impériales, essentiellement celle de la Grande-Bretagne, on est frappé par leur décalage. Alors que le public britannique se serait très vite résigné à décoloniser progressivement et pacifiquement son Empire, l'opinion française aurait longtemps refusé d'envisager les transformations rendues nécessaires. Le public français se serait laissé entraîner à de longues guerres pour le maintien de ses dominations coloniales; il ne serait entré qu'à reculons dans l'ère de la décolonisation. Sans doute convient-il de vérifier et d'expliquer cet attachement un peu inattendu à l'Empire et ce conservatisme colonial surprenant.

LE MAINTIEN DU MYTHE IMPÉRIAL

L'idée coloniale et le vocable même d'Empire, condamnés à l'issue de la Deuxième Guerre mondiale par les U.S.A., l'U.R.S.S. et la Chine et simultanément par l'Organisation des Nations Unies, ne disparurent pas en France. Il semble même que l'idée d'Empire n'ait jamais été plus populaire en 1944-1945, qu'à aucun autre moment de l'histoire française. Le rôle joué par les soldats de l'Empire dans la libération du territoire fut alors magnifié par toutes les voix officielles. Du ministre des colonies aux commentateurs de presse ou de radio, la France célébra les « 500 000 soldats venus de l'outre-mer pour libérer la Patrie ». Le peuple français attendait aussi de l'Empire qu'il aidât à la reconstruction d'une métropole appauvrie et dévastée et qu'il devînt « l'élément le plus tangible de la grandeur française ». Bref, le vieux mythe du parti colonial, *la puissance par l'Empire*, reprenait vie : la France libérée grâce à l'outre-mer ne redeviendrait une grande puissance que grâce à ses territoires d'outre-mer.

Cette affirmation ne souffrait alors nulle contradiction. La presse tut de son mieux, ou les minimisa, les informations qui auraient pu troubler cet acte de foi : les troubles du Sud-Constantinois, les incidents d'Afrique noire, les revendications séparatistes de Madagascar. Curieusement seules les organisations du parti colonial tentèrent dès 1945 de faire savoir que de graves menaces pesaient sur la cohésion et l'existence même de l'Empire.

Or le parti colonial, fort de 58 associations en 1944 et d'une centaine en 1939, avait naturellement souffert de la coupure de la métropole et des colonies. Pendant la période de Vichy, les trois organisations les plus représentatives, *l'Union coloniale, l'Institut colonial français* et *le Comité de l'Indochine* avaient fusionné sous le nom de *Comité de l'Empire français*. Ce comité de notables et d'hommes d'affaires se présenta en 1945 comme l'expression de la communauté impériale française. En réalité, il n'était même pas le représentant du parti colonial tout entier, lequel s'efforçait seulement de se reconstituer. Peu à peu les anciens comités tels *le Comité de l'Afrique française* ou *le Comité de l'Afrique du Nord*, d'autres associations telle *la Ligue maritime et coloniale*, reprirent leurs activités en concurrence avec des organisations nouvelles comme *la Communauté française* dont l'organe de presse *Climats* acquit vite une certaine autorité parmi les rares périodiques coloniaux. Un succès de tirage plus considérable encore revint à l'hebdomadaire *Marchés coloniaux* plus représentatif des milieux d'affaires coloniaux. *Le Comité de l'Empire français* s'imposa cependant comme le plus actif et le plus énergique; il avait dû en juin 1948 renoncer à sa dénomination jugée désuète par les pouvoirs publics et s'intitula *Comité central de la France d'outre-mer*. Environ 400 sociétés commerciales ou industrielles cotisaient à ce groupe de pression économique qui fut aussi et surtout un centre de propagande. Il s'attacha à démontrer aux pouvoirs publics et aux hommes politiques la gravité de la situation politique dans l'outre-mer et à dénoncer la nocivité de la propagande anticoloniale. Le ton de ses interventions était celui de l'amertume «face aux improvisations constitutionnelles qui risquaient de saper l'autorité de la France métropolitaine» et au laxisme des gouvernements «devant les campagnes d'injuste dénigrement contre l'œuvre admirable de la colonisation». Mais certains de ses manifestes claquaient : «Les colonies, élément vital pour la France», «L'Empire ne sera ni disloqué, ni désagrégé», «Pour une politique coloniale cohérente». Il est vrai que jusqu'en juillet 1946, le C.C.F.O.M. n'arrivait pas à faire passer ses messages dans ce qu'il appelait «la presse idéologue» : seuls *l'Époque, l'Ordre, la Dépêche de Paris* et *l'Aurore* lui faisaient écho.

En août 1946 se tinrent à Paris les «États généraux de la colonisation française» qui secouèrent la classe politique et les partis «fossoyeurs de l'Empire» et interpellèrent le gouvernement qui renonçait à défendre «le principe sacré de la souveraineté française». Ils laissèrent derrière eux le programme d'une Union française fédéraliste et un *Comité d'action de l'Union française*. Dès lors les associations coloniales eurent tendance à agir en commun et à diffuser sous leurs différentes signatures des manifestes politiques collectifs. Le tour en était vif : («un ébranlement des bases de l'Union française serait une catastrophe pour la patrie, un coup fatal pour le régime, une régression pour les autochtones et une perte sèche pour l'économie mondiale»), les affirmations péremptoires : («aucun des territoires d'outre-mer n'est actuellement en état de poursuivre son évolution propre par ses seuls moyens indépendamment de nous, sans notre assistance et notre direction.»)

Le parti colonial haussa encore le ton après «la reprise des hostilités par le Viêt-nam» et l'insurrection de Madagascar. Les organisations vouées à la défense de l'œuvre française en Indochine expliquaient tour à tour dans des communiqués de presse et des brochures : «L'avenir de l'Union française se joue en Indochine.» Récusant le qualificatif de colonialistes, les représentants des activités françaises dans l'Indochine du Nord se considéraient comme des «fabricants de prospérité» : «Nous étions suivant la propre expression des Annamites le père et la mère de 350000 ouvriers heureux.» Le président du *Comité de l'Indochine* demandait que «le gouvernement mette fin à cette légende décourageante et injuste qui éclabousse nos armes» et à celle du colonialisme capitaliste. *L'Association nationale pour l'Indochine française* démontrait que «la somme des investissements publics et privés avait profité singulièrement plus aux populations qu'à la métropole.» Le président du *Comité de l'Empire français* soulignait, pour s'en inquiéter, «l'écho que les affaires d'Indochine avaient déjà eu dans l'ensemble de nos territoires d'outre-mer, particulièrement dans toute l'Afrique du Nord.» Encore ignorait-il que le journal viêt-minh *Cuu Quôc* (salut national) célébrait déjà en avril 1947 l'insurrection de Madagascar «qui a suivi notre exemple» et prophétisait l'extension du mouvement à tous les peuples de l'ancien empire français : «La vérité est que l'Union française s'achemine à grand pas vers la ruine.»

À partir de 1948, le parti colonial se crut délivré de la contestation des bulletins et journaux «pro-viêt-minh» de Paris. Il diffusa la bonne parole de ceux qui disaient par exemple : «La Cochinchine veut rester française» (une brochure de William Bazé). Mais, dès la fin de 1949, le pessimisme l'emportait à nouveau et le parti colonial adjurait l'opinion sur le mode pathétique : «Français, vous résignez-vous à perdre l'Indochine?» «Ce serait l'éviction de la France, la ruine de l'Indochine; ce serait la civilisation occidentale évincée d'Indochine; ce serait l'anéantissement du christianisme en Indochine.» Puis vinrent les «appels au monde libre» qui disaient la nécessité de ne pas abandonner à l'impérialisme soviétique tout le Sud-Est asiatique. La dernière brochure de propagande parue en février 1954 s'appelait «Faut-il abandonner l'Indochine?» Sous une préface du maréchal Juin, elle répondait bien sûr par la négative, mais le désastre de Dîen-Bîen-Phu allait imposer cette solution d'abandon total.

Les associations du parti colonial polémiquèrent de leur mieux dans les années 1949 à 1956 contre «les interventions intempestives de l'O.N.U. dans les affaires coloniales françaises», contre «les dangers du racisme panarabe», contre les risques d'une indépendance octroyée à la Libye «ce brûlot attaché aux flancs de la Tunisie française». Elles dénoncèrent sans trêve les machinations de la Ligue arabe, l'agitation entretenue autour des relations franco-arabes. Lors des crises nord-africaines, le parti colonial se mobilisa tout entier si l'on en juge par le nombre de ses communiqués et de ses brochures et le volume de ses correspondances. Il mettait notamment en cause «le défaitisme métropolitain et l'étrange coalition qui s'est formée entre l'anticolonialisme systématique et le communisme, entre la Confédération internationale des syndicats libres et la Fédération syndicale mondiale d'obédience soviétique». Il assurait que «la force du Néo-Destour n'était faite que de notre indulgente passivité»; il dénonçait dès 1950 «l'abolition à la sauvette du Protectorat», et présentait Habib Bourguiba comme «un personnage hanté par le rêve d'une dictature totalitaire» : «le *Führer* tunisien».

La presse française de gauche dénonçait de son côté le C.C.F.O.M. comme l'inspirateur du *Rassemblement français de Tunisie* ou celui du «lobby marocain» hostile au Sultan. Mais elle lui prêtait, semble-t-il, plus d'efficacité qu'il n'en avait. Certes quelques grands leaders d'opinion défendaient les mêmes positions, mais sans liens visibles entre eux. Quelques journalistes influents allaient même plus loin : ainsi ces éditorialistes du *Figaro* : Thierry Maulnier et André Siegried, qui assuraient sans réflexion que «le début de la décolonisation signifierait la fin de la race blanche». Mais le *Comité central de la France d'outre-mer*, qui avait publié 62 manifestes politiques de 1946 à 1956, reconnaissait lui-même en 1955 qu'il ne pouvait plus agir directement sur l'opinion, faute de moyens; il se bornerait seulement à mener une politique défensive «contre les officines anticolonialistes qui disposent de maisons d'édition». C'était reconnaître son échec.

L'ensemble du parti colonial en y comprenant les parlementaires, les élus et les publicistes eut-il l'influence considérable qu'on lui accorde généralement? Il est difficile de répondre, car les parlementaires les plus acharnés dans la défense du statu quo colonial, tels Martinaud-Déplat, Durand-Réville, Paul Devinat, Marc Rucart, Henri Borgeaud, Antoine Colonna, Gabriel Puaux, ne se reconnaissaient pas comme appartenant à un parti colonial, fût-il informel. Plus rares encore furent ceux qui, à tort ou à raison, passaient pour être les porte-parole des milieux d'affaires coloniaux. Mais il existait incontestablement un groupe de pression parlementaire, non homogène et venu d'obédiences partisanes diverses, mais qu'on découvre fort solidaire dans l'action. Ce furent ces parlementaires, radicaux, indépendants, voire gaullistes, que l'on retrouve dans tous les coups d'arrêt imposés à la politique des réformes. Ils avaient les mêmes adversaires attitrés, dont ils fustigeaient «les invraisemblables abandons», des hommes politiques aussi différents que Marius Moutet, que «l'inamovible Robert Schuman, l'homme dont les projets prévoyaient l'éviction progressive ou immédiate des Français du Maghreb» et bien sûr que leurs bêtes noires : Mendès France ou Edgar Faure. Mais s'ils réussirent à abréger leur carrière politique, ils ne parvinrent pas à renverser durablement le cours de la politique française sous la IVe République. Comme l'écrivit Edgar Faure, après avoir fait ratifier par le Parlement les conventions franco-tunisiennes en 1955, les suffrages minoritaires des opposants montrèrent au moins que «malgré l'influence du *lobby* il n'y avait pas que des réactionnaires parmi les Français.»

Quant à l'influence des associations coloniales sur les pouvoirs publics et les administrations, elle est plus facile à apprécier. Dans l'ensemble elles se révélèrent impuissantes comme force de proposition et peu efficientes comme force de retardement. Elles parvinrent tout au plus à freiner certaines initiatives, non à inspirer des mesures politiques ou économiques. Leur seule réussite fut d'avoir bloqué le Code du travail d'outre-mer de 1947 à 1953. Mais celui-ci fut néanmoins promulgué.

Ces échecs s'expliquent facilement. Le parti colonial, qui n'était composé que de groupes de personnalités, s'intéressait plus aux élites du pays qu'au grand public. Il fonctionnait selon les règles non écrites de la IIIe République, la République des comités, et ne prit pas la mesure de la IVe République, la République des partis. D'autre part, les associations coloniales utilisèrent, peu et mal, la radio et le cinéma; faute de moyens elles ne développèrent pas une presse importante. Leurs organes les plus diffusés avaient des tirages faibles : *Climats* (50000 exemplaires), *Marchés coloniaux* (15000), le *Journal de la marine marchande* (15000). Leurs bulletins et revues étaient souvent quasi confidentiels : *La Nouvelle Revue Française* publiée par le C.C.F.O.M. tirait à 1800 exemplaires avec 559 abonnés. Il est vrai que les associations coloniales expédiaient régulièrement aux journaux de province des notes d'information, voire des articles gratuits, volontiers reproduits par les feuilles modestes. Le C.C.F.O.M. se félicitait de toucher ainsi plus de deux millions de lecteurs en 1952 et près de trois en 1955, sans convaincre ses bailleurs de fonds qui déploraient son impuissance.

L'OPINION PUBLIQUE FACE À L'UNION FRANÇAISE

L'opinion française n'était pourtant point défavorable au maintien de l'Empire sous son nouveau nom d'Union française. Lors d'un sondage national effectué à la fin de 1949, auprès de 4000 personnes, 81 % des Français interrogés pensaient que «la France avait intérêt à posséder des territoires d'outre-mer». Parmi eux les jeunes adultes de 25 à 34 ans étaient encore plus nombreux à le dire, 89 %, et le pourcentage atteignait 94 % chez les membres des professions libérales. Interrogés sur la valeur de l'œuvre coloniale, 62 % des gens qui formulaient un avis, pensaient que dans l'ensemble la France avait «bien travaillé», 28 % répondaient «Non ou pas assez», 10 % hésitaient «cela dépend». L'importance du nombre des gens satisfaits doit toutefois être relativisée, vu le degré d'ignorance et le désintérêt traditionnel des Français quant à ces questions coloniales. Un tiers d'entre eux avouait n'avoir aucune information sur celles-ci et 52 % s'y déclaraient «indifférents». Aussi bien 19 % des Français ne pouvaient citer le nom d'aucun territoire d'outre-mer; 28 % seulement pouvaient en nommer cinq ou plus. L'Afrique occidentale française n'était connue que de 12 % des gens interviewés, l'A.E.F. par 11 %. Ni l'école ni la propagande coloniale n'avaient eu raison de la traditionnelle ignorance des Français pour la géographie.

Les grands élèves étaient évidemment un peu mieux informés mais leurs sentiments ne différaient guère. En février 1950 on interrogea un millier d'élèves des classes terminales du secondaire : 84 % croyaient que la France avait «intérêt à maintenir l'Union française avec les territoires d'outre-mer». Plus encore que les adultes, ils pensaient que «la France pouvait être fière» de son œuvre coloniale : 73 % de Oui ferme et 12 % de Oui nuancé. Ils étaient en revanche moins nombreux à dire que les pays de l'outre-mer français avaient intérêt à rester unis avec la métropole.

L'opinion française restait donc dans son immense majorité beaucoup plus attachée à la colonisation qu'on ne l'a dit. Elle ne cessa pas pendant longtemps de le manifester. Même après la perte de l'Indochine, 45 % des Français jugeaient encore «très important» que les pays d'outre-mer restent associés à la France, 27 % «assez important», 11 % seulement «pas très important». En avril 1956, 45 % des gens interrogés croyaient que dans dix ans, Madagascar et l'Algérie seraient toujours associés à la France, et ils étaient 43 % à le croire pour l'Afrique noire. Les Français ne se résignaient pas facilement à voir s'éloigner d'eux les Protectorats du Maghreb. En juillet

1956, seuls 32 % des Français pensaient qu'on avait eu raison d'accorder l'indépendance à la Tunisie, 19 % qu'on avait eu tort, 40 % restant sans opinion. Les pourcentages étaient pratiquement les mêmes face à l'indépendance du Maroc : 33 % estimaient que la France avait eu raison, 18 % tort et 41 % ne savaient pas.

La bonne conscience vis-à-vis du phénomène colonial persistait, peut-être même se renforçait-elle. En 1957, on trouvait 70 % des Français pour affirmer que la France avait fait du «très bon» ou de «l'assez bon travail» dans ses colonies. Il est vrai que l'information ne progressait guère. A la fin de l'ère coloniale le niveau des connaissances géographiques restait toujours faible. Une enquête de 1962, concernant les quinze États d'Afrique noire d'expression française, montre que les Français métropolitains ne pouvaient pas en nommer plus de deux en moyenne. Un quart de la population était incapable d'en citer un seul avec précision. Faut-il révéler que vingt ans plus tard et s'agissant des départements et territoires d'outre-mer, les D.O.M.-T.O.M., 40 % seulement des métropolitains savaient où placer les Antilles françaises, 38 % la Nouvelle-Calédonie et la Polynésie et 28 % la Réunion. Il n'empêche que pour 46 % des gens interrogés, les D.O.M.-T.O.M. «c'était toujours la France», la France d'outre-mer, mais pour 36 % «les derniers vestiges du colonialisme».

L'INFLUENCE LIMITÉE DE L'ANTICOLONIALISME

Il est dès lors assez vain de s'interroger sur la faible résonance de l'anticolonialisme dans le milieu français. Tout au plus faut-il rectifier quelques légendes. Dans la société française ce n'était point le prolétariat ouvrier qui était le plus opposé au «colonialisme», mais les ruraux traditionnellement méfiants ou hostiles. 67 % des ouvriers qui avaient répondu au grand sondage de 1949 croyaient aux bienfaits de l'œuvre coloniale, 39 % seulement parmi les ruraux et 38 % parmi les cadres agricoles. En septembre 1947, alors que les électeurs communistes déclaraient en majorité que la France avait échoué outre-mer, 62 % des ouvriers de l'industrie croyaient toujours que la France avait fait du bon ou de l'assez bon travail outre-mer.

Les campagnes anticolonialistes avaient-elles pourtant préparé l'opinion au phénomène de la décolonisation, jugée comme une issue souhaitable, ou comme une évolution fatale? Les premières campagnes furent menées dès 1944-1945 par la Délégation générale des Indochinois en France et par les trotskystes, puis par l'association France-Viêt-nam (créée en juin 1946) et quelques journaux d'extrême gauche : *Franc-Tireur*, *Combat*. Ce fut seulement à la fin de 1946 que le Parti communiste français et les associations satellites du parti recommencèrent à dénoncer le colonialisme. Les parlementaires de l'intergroupe des députés d'outre-mer, ceux du P.C.F. et une partie de ceux de la S.F.I.O. multiplièrent les déclarations et les discours, entraînant de nombreux intellectuels, de nouveaux journalistes et de grandes revues. Des chroniques de presse écrite et de radio dénonçaient les «forbans de la colonisation», les «cent vautours de la forêt» (les planteurs), les «rapaces consortiums», les «menaces de la Réaction». On y demandait «la fin du pacte colonial et de toutes les formes de travail forcé», la «citoyenneté pour tous les sujets» ou le droit des peuples coloniaux à disposer d'eux-mêmes. Le conflit d'Indochine aurait été préparé par «les jauniers matamores qui hurlaient à la guerre dès 1945». Une poignée de libertaires, une armée de marxistes et quelques chrétiens progressistes, s'exprimant dans quelques feuilles de combat, mais aussi de sérieuses revues pour intellectuels, comme *les Temps modernes*, *Esprit*, ne pouvaient certes transformer les mentalités. Et d'ailleurs les anticolonialistes militants s'inquiétaient de «l'enthousiasme que soulève encore la projection des films coloniaux devant le grand public». Leur action s'inscrivait cependant jusque dans les sondages, puisqu'en 1949, 30 % des Français interrogés se disaient peu ou prou critiques vis-à-vis de l'œuvre coloniale. Mais de l'anticolonialisme réformateur au souhait d'une décolonisation radicale, la distance restait considérable. Les jeunes de 1950 étaient certes plus violents dans leurs condamnations, mais ils étaient très peu nombreux à les proférer : 9 % jugeaient que l'œuvre coloniale était fondée sur la violence, l'exploitation ou la volonté «d'imposer sa civilisation». Par ailleurs 7 % pensaient que la France n'avait pas intérêt à maintenir l'Union française contre 2 % pour les adultes. Mais les fils d'enseignants étaient 21 % à le dire, ce qui confirmait le jugement du parti colonial, selon lequel le corps des instituteurs et des professeurs était le milieu le plus contaminé par la propagande anticoloniale.

La conclusion paraît donc s'imposer que, jusque dans les années 1950, l'opinion française tout autant que la classe politique restèrent majoritairement attachées aux mythes coloniaux de la tradition républicaine. Elles ne surent pas comprendre à temps la force irrépressible des mouvements nationaux de libération, ni agir ou réagir en conséquence. Pourtant une lente évolution commençait à se dessiner qui allait peu à peu transformer les esprits. Les facteurs intérieurs de cette progressive mutation qui conduisit la majorité des Français à accepter la décolonisation sont plus faciles à énumérer qu'à analyser. On peut choisir, pour faire bref, d'apprécier ce que furent le rôle des intellectuels et celui des Églises chrétiennes.

LE RÔLE DES INTELLECTUELS

Les intellectuels français ont accrédité l'idée qu'ils furent les champions de la décolonisation en France. Les historiens, plus réservés sur leur rôle et leur influence, conviennent pourtant qu'on ne saurait négliger leur action, au moins auprès de l'intelligentsia. Encore faut-il ne pas l'antidater. Avant la guerre d'Algérie, rares furent les intellectuels qui militèrent vraiment pour ou contre l'indépendance des pays d'outre-mer. Le vocabulaire même en témoigne. Le mot de décolonisation traduit de l'anglais n'entre dans l'usage qu'en 1952, année pendant laquelle apparaît l'expression de tiers monde; mais cette dernière mettra dix ans à s'imposer.

L'hégémonie intellectuelle du P.C.F., qui se proclamait modestement «le parti de l'Intelligence», fut dans la décennie 1944-1954 assez incontestée pour faire accepter par les écrivains «engagés» et les publicistes de gauche, une dénonciation globale du «colonialisme». Celui-ci n'aurait été qu'une des formes de l'impérialisme «stade suprême du capitalisme» et devait disparaître avec lui. Ainsi le voulaient les lois de l'histoire confirmées par «la lutte des peuples coloniaux contre le joug de l'impérialisme». Presque tous les intellectuels de gauche furent alors fascinés par ces explications à prétention scientifique. Peu ou prou ils acceptèrent aussi l'argumentation du *Kominform*, selon lequel les guerres et la répression dans les pays coloniaux étaient faites non seulement au bénéfice des sociétés coloniales, mais aussi dans le but de «déclencher une troisième guerre mondiale contre les pays du socialisme». «Soutenir activement le droit du peuple vietnamien à la complète indépendance, c'est lutter contre la troisième guerre mondiale, méditée par les impérialistes américains.» (M. Thorez.) Les compagnons de route du P.C.F., les neutralistes, les intellectuels du Rassemblement démocratique révolutionnaire, tinrent tous un même discours colonial, fondé sur des présupposés léninistes et des considérants moraux. Parmi eux des militants comme Claude Bourdet, Jean Rous, Daniel Guérin, acquirent dans les milieux parisiens et chez les colonisés, une audience inattendue. Mais le «pape de l'anticolonialisme» fut à coup sûr Jean-Paul Sartre, plus connu d'abord comme «pape de l'existentialisme». Même les communistes, qui ne l'aimaient pas, finirent par l'enrôler dans les rangs des zélotes de l'affaire Henri Martin. Sur le terrain colonial qu'il ne connaissait pas, Sartre ne fut pas un maître à penser, mais un polémiste, seulement convaincu de la fin de l'Europe («l'Europe est foutue»), de la culpabilité des colonialistes français et de la victoire du tiers monde.

François Mauriac, qui se croyait un homme de droite, prit conscience en 1952 de la vocation des chrétiens à faire front contre «le racisme, né du lucre et de la peur». Il entra dès lors dans la bataille avec ses amis de *France-Maghreb*, persuadé que «la justice demeure en Afrique du Nord la seule politique ouverte à la France». Éditorialiste du *Figaro*, jusqu'en 1953, ses prises de position favorables aux nationalistes maghrébins choquèrent la majorité de ses lecteurs, mais contraignirent à la réflexion une partie d'entre eux. Passé à *l'Express*, il contribua à bâtir le mythe d'un Mendès France anticolonialiste de principe, ce qu'il n'était pas en 1954.

Enfin il faut réserver une place à part à Raymond Aron. Son exceptionnelle lucidité politique, à peine reconnue en France vers 1950, mais déjà saluée à l'étranger, permit cependant à beaucoup d'esprits attentifs de surmonter les modes et les passions parisiennes. Prompt à saisir «la décomposition des empires coloniaux», à dire la nécessité d'abandonner l'Indochine si la France voulait garder l'Afrique, il fut longtemps le seul parmi les libéraux à faire comprendre que la grandeur d'une nation démocratique ne se mesurait plus à la surface de ses colonies et qu'il fallait avoir «le courage d'innover». Jusqu'en 1955, toutefois, la décolonisation ne fut pas un enjeu de la dispute intellectuelle entre les maîtres à penser du pays. Les guerres coloniales elles-mêmes, souvent dénoncées par les intellectuels dits «progressistes», le furent moins que la guerre de Corée, et le colonialisme français moins que «l'impérialisme américain».

Le renversement de l'idéologie coloniale dominante prit aussi des détours plus inattendus que celui des querelles entre intellectuels engagés. Le mouvement des sciences humaines, leur ouverture progressive à la littérature scientifique américaine préparaient un tournant dans les esprits. Le relativisme culturel opposé à la croyance traditionnelle en la Civilisation occidentale, la remise en cause de l'ethnocentrisme culturel des Européens, l'affirmation à Paris même du mouvement de la négritude remettaient en cause les certitudes du public cultivé. «La connaissance de l'homme noir» (Marcel Griaule), la découverte de systèmes philosophiques africains bousculaient les distinctions reçues entre peuples civilisateurs et peuples à civiliser. Plus que les pamphlets d'Aimé Césaire (*Procès de la colonisation*) ou de Frantz Fanon, plus que la prédication de *Présence africaine*, les révélations de ceux qui s'appelaient encore ethnographes brouillaient jusqu'à la légitimité scientifique de la colonisation. Déjà apparaissait chez les jeunes intellectuels et dans le peuple étudiant un complexe de culpabilité face à ce que certains théologiens devaient appeler «le péché de colonialisme».

LES ÉGLISES CHRÉTIENNES ET LA DÉCOLONISATION FRANÇAISE

L'influence des Églises chrétiennes sur la décolonisation française a été et reste un objet de discussions. Pour certains auteurs, les Églises se seraient rendues «coupables de complicité dans l'opération qui devait priver la France de son Empire.» Pour d'autres, leurs attitudes furent si diverses, leurs engagements si modérés et si tardifs, qu'on doit en négliger l'impact. En se prononçant contre la France d'outre-mer, le Vatican aurait été le principal responsable selon les anticléricaux, qui surestimaient les effets psychologiques de certaines décisions pontificales, comme la nomination d'évêques africains. Les auteurs chrétiens en soulignant que les Églises sont intervenues plus sur le plan religieux que sur le plan politique ont peut-être, eux, sous-estimé la portée de leurs prises de position auprès des populations colonisées.

L'ÉGLISE CATHOLIQUE ET LA DÉCOLONISATION (1919-1955)

L'Église catholique s'était associée dans une certaine mesure à l'expansion coloniale, notamment en demandant le patronage de certaines puissances pour les missions (au XIXe siècle c'était la France). Mais depuis 1919, le Vatican avait défini une nouvelle politique missionnaire. En condamnant «comme une malédiction» le nationalisme des missionnaires qui faisaient passer les intérêts et la gloire de leur patrie européenne avant ceux du «Royaume de Dieu», le pape Benoît XV invitait dans l'encyclique *Maximum illud* (30 novembre 1919) les congrégations missionnaires à rompre avec la tradition coloniale. Parce qu'il prévoyait en mai 1923 l'indépendance des colonies, Pie XI allait plus loin le 26 février 1926 dans l'encyclique *Rerum ecclesiae* : il montrait que l'action missionnaire devrait prendre fin et être remplacée par celle de prêtres autochtones : «Supposons qu'une population indigène parvenue à un degré assez élevé de civilisation et à l'âge de sa majorité politique veuille son indépendance, qu'elle exige le départ des fonctionnaires, des troupes, des missionnaires de la puissance coloniale et qu'elle ne puisse l'obtenir qu'en employant la force. Dites-le Nous : quelle ruine ne menacerait pas l'Église dans cette nation, si on n'avait pas entièrement pourvu aux besoins des nouveaux Chrétiens en établissant comme un réseau de prêtres indigènes sur tout le territoire ? »

Mais le pape n'entendait pas seulement justifier le remplacement des missionnaires par un clergé indigène; il affirmait aussi les droits de celui-ci à exercer son ministère « dans un champ qui est le sien et qu'il lui est naturel de travailler, à savoir le gouvernement de sa propre nation ». En envisageant l'indépendance des colonies et en soulignant les droits naturels des colonisés au gouvernement de leur propre nation, Pie XI ne cachait pas son opinion sur l'avenir de la colonisation. Un journal de droite, *l'Ordre*, expliquait en 1930 : « le Vatican pense que dans quarante ans, l'Europe aura perdu toutes ses colonies. »

Les catholiques français, à l'exception de quelques intellectuels et des groupes démocrates-populaires, y furent d'abord peu sensibles. Mais des chaires de missiologie créées dans les instituts catholiques répandaient la nouvelle doctrine pontificale : l'évangélisation ne devait pas être liée à la colonisation. Bientôt on entendit en 1930 un parlementaire catholique affirmer à la Chambre des députés : « Coloniser c'est éduquer, mais éduquer c'est émanciper » cependant qu'aux Semaines sociales de Marseille, un professeur de Droit, le R.P. Delos, répétait qu'aux yeux des chrétiens « la liberté des peuples colonisés était le terme idéal de la colonisation éducatrice ».

La nouvelle orientation pontificale avait donc été entendue. Dès lors s'affirma un courant chrétien proche des internationalistes de la S.D.N.; il réclamait l'émancipation progressive des colonies à travers des revues comme *Politique* ou *Esprit*, des journaux comme *Sept* ou *l'Aube*, des bulletins catholiques et les *Annales de la jeunesse catholique française*. Ce courant resta cependant minoritaire : les catholiques conservateurs redoutaient que les clergés indigènes ne tombent aux mains des mouvements nationalistes et révolutionnaires.

Malgré leurs préventions et leurs oppositions, la doctrine romaine s'imposait peu à peu. D'une part la formule « christianiser n'est pas occidentaliser » était devenue l'impératif de toute missiologie, d'autre part Rome, qui appelait en 1948 l'attention des cardinaux et archevêque sur « la soif d'émancipation » des peuples coloniaux, remplaçait discrètement les religieux français en Indochine par des prêtres, voire des évêques, vietnamiens, notamment en 1950. En juin 1951, une nouvelle encyclique *Evangelii Praecones* prescrivait aux missionnaires non seulement de ne plus occidentaliser leurs fidèles, mais de « s'indigéniser » eux-mêmes pour les mieux comprendre. Ces orientations pontificales facilitèrent aussi à certains clercs ou laïcs français la dénonciation des abus du colonialisme. Toutefois dans son ensemble le clergé français demeurait à l'issue de la Deuxième Guerre mondiale, hésitant et divisé. Son attitude se modifia à partir de 1948, lorsque l'archevêque de Lyon eut formellement condamné « l'impérialisme dominateur », cependant que Mgr Chappoulie célébrait le combat des peuples colonisés comme une cause juste et noble.

De plus, nombreux prélats firent écho à ces prises de position à partir de 1953. À cette date les évêques français de Madagascar rédigèrent une Déclaration collective dans laquelle ils reconnaissaient « la légitimité de l'aspiration à l'indépendance, comme aussi de tout effort constructif pour y parvenir ». Le texte en fut lu en chaire, traduit en malgache et repris par la presse locale.

L'administration condamna «ces manœuvres qui visaient à soustraire de la communauté un territoire, partie intégrante de la République». Les protestations du haut-commissaire de la République et les démarches du gouvernement auprès du Saint-Siège furent vaines : les évêques de Madagascar ne furent pas désavoués par Rome. Le pape Pie XII devait dans son Message de Noël 1954 se prononcer en faveur du «processus d'évolution vers l'autonomie politique des peuples coloniaux».

La prise de position de Pie XII intervenait alors qu'une polémique révélatrice avait opposé le P. Michel, qui parlait du «péché de colonialisme» et du «devoir chrétien de décolonisation», à l'ambassadeur français Charles-Roux, président du Comité français pour l'outre-mer et défenseur de la colonisation. Dès lors la campagne en faveur de la décolonisation se développa en France, même dans la presse catholique jusque-là hostile aux demandes d'autonomie des colonisés.

En Afrique noire les missionnaires eux-mêmes osaient dire que l'Afrique était proche de sa majorité et qu'il fallait en accepter les conséquences politiques et religieuses. Depuis mai 1954, Rome s'était prononcée pour l'érection de la hiérarchie, c'est-à-dire la constitution d'un clergé local dirigé par des évêques africains ou malgaches. En avril 1955, une conférence plénière des chefs de missions pour l'A.O.F. et le Togo affirmait «la légitimité» des aspirations à l'autonomie politique. Le 14 septembre 1955, neuf mois avant la loi-cadre, onze provinces ecclésiastiques étaient créées et les premiers évêques résidentiels africains sacrés peu après.

Décolonisation religieuse et décolonisation politique allaient désormais de pair pour le clergé et la majorité des fidèles en France. Les théologiens expliquaient que la colonisation, simple service d'éducation à l'usage des peuples attardés, représentait un stade dépassé. Et Mgr Chappoulie conseillait le 2 octobre 1955 de généraliser dans toutes les colonies françaises une politique d'autonomie progressive, un apprentissage de la liberté qui conduirait à une indépendance profitable.

LES ÉGLISES PROTESTANTES

De façon analogue mais originale, les Églises protestantes s'étaient prononcées «contre toute exploitation d'un peuple par un autre», contre la tentation d'assimiler les populations évangélisées et, parfois dès 1946, pour la promotion des peuples coloniaux à l'indépendance.

Il n'était pas indifférent de rappeler à une conférence de la jeunesse chrétienne de septembre 1947 que «le but de toute politique coloniale est de développer l'aptitude à l'indépendance des peuples dont certaines nations ont déjà pris la responsabilité». En mars 1948, un synode national de l'Église réformée de France, partageant «l'angoisse des chrétiens en présence des conflits coloniaux», adjurait le gouvernement de «prendre les risques d'une politique généreuse». Et la presse de signaler que la commission des églises protestantes pour les affaires internationales se proposait de «coopérer par son action auprès de toutes les nations au bien-être des peuples dépendants et à leur promotion à l'indépendance, dans le jeu des libres institutions politiques».

Considérant leurs missions comme «des organismes étrangers et provisoires», les églises de France poursuivirent plus activement la constitution d'églises évangéliques locales, authentiquement africaines ou malgaches et pleinement autonomes. Ainsi serait coupé, disait en 1955 le directeur de la Société des missions évangéliques, tout lien de dépendance entre la mission française et les «jeunes églises» locales qu'elle avait engendrées, dirigées désormais par des comités élus, composés de laïcs et de pasteurs autochtones. C'est dans cette perspective que furent conduites à leur autonomie de 1957 à 1963 les sept Églises dont la *Société des missions évangéliques de Paris* étaient responsables en pays francophones.

Sur le plan politique, les responsables de cette société avaient expliqué dès 1951 que les peuples colonisés accéderaient comme les églises à l'autonomie : «Nous le voulons, nous le préparons pour eux et avec eux.» Quant à l'opinion du «peuple protestant» sur le problème colonial, elle avait évolué moins vite semble-t-il. Peu nombreux furent les protestants qui se déclaraient prêts à la décolonisation avant 1954, mais ceux qui le firent comptaient parmi les plus généreux et les plus lucides.

À suivre la réflexion de ces personnalités dans les grands organes protestants comme les hebdomadaires *Réforme* ou *Le christianisme au XXe siècle*, comme *le Semeur* ou *Christianisme social*, on voit qu'ils procédèrent le plus souvent à une remise en cause progressive de la colonisation, parce qu'elle «insultait à la dignité humaine du colonisé». Dénonçant le caractère tardif des réformes législatives outre-mer, les fausses prudences, la duplicité à courte vue, ils montrèrent très tôt par exemple que «la fiction Algérie – département français ne pourrait être maintenue longtemps» (*Réforme* 1945) que «ce qui se passe aux Indes, en Indochine, ce qui se passera demain encore à Madagascar, en Afrique du Nord, avant l'Afrique noire, est prévisible et normal» (*Foi et Vie*, janvier 1950). À ceux qui se bornaient à demander dans les Journées d'études protestantes nord-africaines de 1953 des réformes sociales, *Christianisme social* objectait qu'elles ne légitimeraient que provisoirement la souveraineté de la métropole et souhaitait «une émancipation progressive puis totale des peuples nord-africains devenus majeurs.»

Au total à la veille du conflit algérien, on doit noter chez les Chrétiens des diverses Églises, au minimum une résignation, plus rarement une adhésion enthousiaste à la «décolonisation», prévisible ou souhaitée, en Afrique noire et à Madagascar, voire au Maghreb. Les attitudes plus engagées des Églises avaient donc joué un rôle important dans la prise de conscience de beaucoup de Chrétiens français, jusque-là partisans du statu quo colonial. Mais la guerre d'Algérie allait remettre en cause l'acceptation tacite de la décolonisation et accentuer les divisions entre Chrétiens.

4 La deuxième vague de la décolonisation : la guerre d'Algérie et les indépendances africaines et malgache

L'ÉVOLUTION ÉCONOMIQUE ET FINANCIÈRE DE L'UNION FRANÇAISE EXPLIQUE-T-ELLE LA DÉCOLONISATION ?

VERS UNE NOUVELLE POLITIQUE COLONIALE

La « mise en valeur » économique de l'Empire fut une directive essentielle de la politique coloniale française, après la Première Guerre mondiale. Mais la perspective demeurait celle du « pacte colonial » : les colonies devaient avant tout procurer à la métropole des matières premières nécessaires à son industrie et servir de débouchés aux produits manufacturés des usines françaises. Les investissements, qui provenaient en majorité de capitaux privés, visaient à développer par priorité les domaines ou les produits les plus rentables : par exemple le cacao (au Cameroun), le café (en Côte-d'Ivoire), le coton (dans l'Oubangui-Chari), le caoutchouc de plantation (en Indochine), le nickel (en Nouvelle-Calédonie). Les investissements d'infrastructure reposaient sur des fonds publics locaux ou des emprunts garantis par l'État français.

La crise économique des années 1930, qui prend fin en Indochine en 1934, mais en Algérie en 1938, avait conduit les spécialistes à imaginer une modification totale de l'économie coloniale. Celle-ci devait être développée pour elle-même autant que pour la métropole ; elle devait être aidée par des investissements publics beaucoup plus considérables, protégée contre la concurrence étrangère et assurée de ses débouchés par une politique qui lui confirmât la prépondérance ou le monopole sur le marché français.

De grands emprunts émis par les administrations coloniales à partir de 1931 procurèrent à la plupart des territoires des capitaux importants. En 1939, la somme des emprunts obligataires représentait l'équivalent de 3 389 millions de francs-or. S'y ajoutèrent les subventions traditionnelles de la métropole aux budgets de colonies déficitaires et des subventions directes à l'équipement : respectivement 773 millions et 1 925 millions de francs-or, soit au total 6 087 millions de francs-or. Ce flux d'investissements publics relaya efficacement le relatif tarissement des capitaux privés (1 624 millions de francs-or de 1915 à 1929 et 800 millions de 1930 à 1939), jusque-là très majoritaires dans l'investissement total. Il permit d'achever de doter l'Empire d'une infrastructure de base, surtout dans les domaines ferroviaires, portuaires, routiers et dans l'hydraulique agricole. Encore que ces emprunts aient trop souvent servi à pallier l'effondrement des budgets de fonctionnement, il n'est pas douteux qu'ils furent bénéfiques aux économies locales et aux exportateurs métropolitains, atténuant, à tout le moins, les effets de la grande dépression.

Les idées nouvelles d'économie dirigée et de planification de l'économie impériale gagnaient du terrain chez les techniciens et les conduisaient à proposer des projets plus révolutionnaires encore : nationalisation des banques coloniales jugées trop parcimonieuses dans la distribution du crédit, industrialisation des colonies surpeuplées (comme l'Indochine), création de pôles de développement. Mais aucun plan d'industrialisation ne vit le jour avant 1939. Il avait été question aussi à l'imitation du *Colonial Development Fund* britannique créé en 1929, d'un Fonds colonial. Mais si l'on renonça au principe imposé depuis 1900 de l'autonomie financière des colonies, on ne parvint pas à réaliser ce Fonds colonial de développement qui eût émargé au budget français. On y renonça en 1937, mais l'idée allait être reprise dès 1944. Au total on a pu évaluer à quelque 15 milliards de francs-or le montant des investissements totaux réalisés dans l'Empire en 1939. Cela représentait environ trois fois le volume des capitaux investis en 1914 et 40 à 45 % des investissements français à l'étranger réalisés en 1939.

Dès avant la libération de la France, le gouvernement provisoire de la République française avait décidé de transformer les principes mêmes de l'économie de l'Empire. Eu égard aux impératifs internationaux, à la nécessité de revivifier les colonies affaiblies par l'effort de guerre et à la volonté d'améliorer le niveau de vie des populations, le G.P.R.F. entendait planifier le développement économique : «la France consacrera ses ressources et son crédit au succès du Plan avec le seul souci du bénéfice qu'en retirera la communauté». Dès février 1944, fut créée une *Caisse centrale de la France d'outre-mer* (C.C.F.O.M.) qui recevait la mission de mettre en œuvre une politique de crédit, comme moteur de la croissance dans les territoires d'outre-mer. Elle recevait le privilège de l'émission des billets de banque coloniaux, dirigeait les offices des changes et s'attacha à limiter l'autonomie des banques coloniales non encore nationalisées.

La nécessité d'un plan «d'équipement et de développement économique et social spécial à l'outre-mer» prévalut avec la loi du 30 avril 1946. Celle-ci créait le Fonds d'investissement et de développement économique et social de la France d'outre-mer, le F.I.D.E.S., qui allait se révéler aux côtés de la C.C.F.O.M. le grand dispensateur de fonds publics pour les territoires d'outre-mer. La loi posait aussi le principe de la planification des investissements en vue de concourir à l'exécution des programmes de reconstitution et de développement de l'économie de l'Union française.

DE L'ÉCONOMIE DE TRAITÉ À L'ÉCONOMIE DE DONS

Très vite les besoins se révélèrent énormes et disproportionnés à l'effort que la métropole entendait consentir. En 1946 on prévoyait d'y affecter 10 milliards par an, 2 % du budget. Il fallut y consacrer 62 milliards pour les seuls territoires d'outre-mer (T.O.M.) en 1949, soit 5,1 % du budget, et 90 milliards en 1952. En 1946 le projet de mise en valeur des T.O.M. avait été chiffré à 285 milliards à répartir sur dix ans; 155 devaient être investis en 5 ans dont les deux tiers proviendraient du secteur public. En fait le plan décennal primitif fut divisé en deux plans quadriennaux, 1949-1952 et 1954-1957 (1953 constituant une année de transition comprise dans le premier plan). Or le montant réel des dotations métropolitaines ouvertes pour la période 1947-1952 atteignit 326 ou 356 milliards, selon les sources (chiffres valables pour les T.O.M., l'Indochine exclue). Le deuxième plan de modernisation devait couvrir en réalité les années 1954 à 1958. Il prévoyait en principe un montant de 348 milliards de crédits publics d'équipement, mais tous les sondages indiquent que ces chiffres furent dépassés.

Aux investissements publics prévus par les plans d'équipement, s'ajoutaient : 1°) certaines dépenses de fonctionnement qui auraient dû être inscrites dans les budgets locaux, mais qui furent prises en charge par le budget métropolitain; 2°) des dons, prêts, avances et subventions qui se révélaient indispensables pour équilibrer la balance des comptes des T.O.M. Les services du ministère des Finances et celui de la France d'outre-mer ne fournissaient pas les mêmes chiffres aux parlementaires et à l'opinion informée, mais les renseignements statistiques allaient tout de même révéler une croissance continue. On prit ainsi peu à peu conscience que la France avait investi dans les T.O.M. de 1947 à 1956, quelque 550 milliards de capitaux publics auxquels s'ajoutait l'apport de capitaux privés, estimés par l'Administration entre 20 % et 25 % du montant des investissements publics. De 1947 à 1957 les investissements totaux auraient atteint en onze ans un total de 762 milliards, soit plus de 900 milliards en francs-1957. En 1959 le Conseil économique révéla que de 1947 à 1958, la France avait investi en Afrique noire seulement, et à valeur monétaire égale, «environ trois fois plus que dans les cinquante années qui avaient précédé la Deuxième Guerre mondiale».

Or très curieusement ces statistiques financières étaient à l'époque récusées par les hommes politiques africains, plus sensibles aux immenses besoins de leurs pays respectifs qu'à l'effort financier consenti par la métropole. Les plus démagogues d'entre-eux, qui étaient souvent aussi les moins avertis en sciences économique et financière, croyaient que la France se procurait ainsi des denrées coloniales à bon compte et vendait outre-mer des produits de médiocre qualité à des prix surévalués. C'était donc le maintien du pacte colonial que poursuivait la politique française. Or il était facile de constater que la France consentait aux produits de l'Union française des prix de soutien supérieurs à ceux du marché mondial. Quant aux surprix des produits français, ils n'atteignaient pas les proportions de 30 à 50 % que dénonçaient certains élus africains. Des leaders africains insistaient aussi sur le fait que les crédits octroyés par la France ne demeuraient pas intégralement dans leurs pays. Ils prétendaient que l'essentiel revenait en France, sous forme de profits des sociétés et de salaires de leurs employés; «15 % seulement des capitaux F.I.D.E.S. demeuraient en A.O.F.» prétendait M. Ki-Zerbo, tout le reste étant transféré en France. Or une étude chiffrée officieuse démontrait que 61 % de ces crédits restaient bien en Afrique et s'y matérialisaient sous forme de ponts, de barrages, d'hôpitaux et d'écoles. Il était toutefois exact que ces «cadeaux empoisonnés» imposaient aux territoires de lourdes charges d'entretien et le développement d'une administration peut-être pléthorique. Il était tout aussi vrai que les investissements métropolitains obligeaient à augmenter chaque année les dépenses budgétaires locales parfois de 10 %, parfois de plus de 50 %, en A.O.F. par exemple. Mais précisément la Caisse centrale C.C.F.O.M. consentait des avances de trésorerie pour pallier les déficits des budgets locaux. Et ces avances sans intérêts, en principe remboursables à long terme, ne l'étaient que par exception. Il en allait de même pour les subventions d'équilibre de plus en plus élevées après 1953. Le développement des équipements sociaux augmentait plus encore les charges des budgets. Les dépenses publiques d'enseignement en A.O.F. - Togo passèrent de 1 120 millions de F en 1947 à 22 milliards en 1960, ce qui signifiait en francs constants qu'elles avaient été multipliées par 3. Mais le secteur productif local progressait lui aussi, quoique moins vite. Rétrospectivement on a pu calculer que le produit national brut réel de l'A.O.F. avait de 1947 à 1956 augmenté au taux record de 8,5 % par an et celui de l'A.E.F. de 80 % de 1948 à 1955, soit 10 % par an.

Ces progrès se matérialisaient dans la plupart des secteurs économiques : la valeur des exportations de l'A.O.F. progressait d'environ 7 % par an (plus de 10 % en Côte-d'Ivoire, 5 % au Togo), la production d'arachides du Sénégal augmentait en moyenne de 3 % par an, celle du café dans l'ensemble de l'A.O.F. de plus de 13 %, celle des bananes de 15,8 %. La progression du cacao fut moins spectaculaire (de l'ordre de 5 % annuellement), ainsi que celle des produits du palmier à huile (3,4 %). Pour parvenir à ces résultats, la France avait dû créer des caisses de stabilisation des cours de certains produits; elles ne fonctionnèrent peut-être pas bien, du moins avant la création du Fonds national de régularisation. Cela signifiait que par exemple la France achetait les arachides à des prix supérieurs aux cours mondiaux pour protéger les planteurs; mais ceux-ci protestaient contre le fait qu'ils fussent stagnants. Et les politiciens sénégalais d'affirmer que «le niveau de vie des paysans noirs ne cesse de baisser» ou de déplorer «une baisse des revenus des producteurs et des niveaux de vie dans les milieux agricoles», affirmations contredites par tous les chiffres officiels.

Ainsi l'indice des prix payés au producteur sur la base 100 en 1949, atteignait, en 1957-1958, 147 pour l'arachide, 343 pour le cacao, 409 pour le café. En moyenne les prix à l'exportation avaient été multipliés par 3,65 de 1947 à 1958. Dans les villes, le taux du salaire horaire du manœuvre non qualifié était sur la base 100 en 1949, de 240 à Dakar en 1959, de 394 à Abidjan.

Les progrès de la consommation du moins étaient visibles aux yeux de tous. Si l'on compare les chiffres de 1954 à ceux de 1938, qui fut en A.O.F. une bonne année pour la production, on constate que l'A.O.F. importait en 1954 deux fois plus de cotonnades, trois fois plus de sucre, quatre fois plus de lait en conserve et de machines diverses, quatre fois et demi plus d'automobiles et de pièces détachées, cinq fois plus de farine de froment. Pour l'A.E.F. les proportions étaient : deux fois plus de cotonnades, sept fois plus de sucre, neuf fois plus de farine. Pour le Cameroun : quatre fois plus de cotonnades, six fois plus de sucre, treize fois plus de farine. Il était donc mensonger de parler de «régression des niveaux de vie».

Ainsi se creusait entre les experts français et les leaders politiques africains un fossé d'incompréhension. Dès avril 1954, le rapporteur général de la commission d'étude et de coordination des plans de Modernisation et d'Équipement s'étonnait avec quelque naïveté que «le premier plan n'ait pas rapporté à la métropole un bénéfice moral à la mesure des sacrifices consentis». Qu'eût-il dit lorsque M. Houphouët-Boigny, ministre d'un gouvernement français, reconnut le 15 mars 1958 que «la France avait dépensé en dix ans plus de 600 milliards pour les territoires d'outre-mer», avant d'ajouter : «Mais nous lui en demandons bien davantage». Le président du Grand Conseil d'A.O.F. était d'ailleurs venu à Paris pour obtenir une contribution financière exceptionnelle de la métropole et la possibilité de lancer des emprunts à long terme sur le marché mondial : «Le développement économique, expliquait-il, exige des flots de capitaux qui ne se chiffrent pas par dizaines, mais par centaines de milliards». Le député du Tchad, Gabriel Lisette, invitait plus courtoisement les Français «à prendre conscience de l'étendue et de l'urgence des nouveaux sacrifices que comportera pour le contribuable métropolitain l'accélération de la promotion économique et sociale des régions les plus déshéritées de la communauté française». En vérité, il n'était même plus question d'aide mais de prise en charge totale. La colonisation devenait «le fardeau financier de l'homme blanc» au moment même où celui-ci était fermement invité à renoncer à tout autre rôle que celui de bailleur de fonds.

LA PRISE DE CONSCIENCE DU «FARDEAU COLONIAL»

Fort heureusement pour l'Afrique, les Français ignorèrent longtemps l'ampleur du fardeau colonial. La plupart d'entre eux croyaient vers 1950 encore que les colonies rapportaient à la métropole et ne coûtaient rien aux contribuables. Et le ministère de la France d'outre-mer expliquait encore en 1955, statistiques à l'appui, que 500000 Français environ résidant en métropole tiraient leurs revenus du commerce entre la métropole et les pays d'outre-mer. «Un ménage sur 28 vit grâce à l'existence d'un ensemble français». Mais quel était le coût de l'ensemble français? D'aucuns commençaient à s'en effrayer : la colonisation n'était-elle pas devenue économiquement une mauvaise affaire? Il fallut attendre 1955-1957 pour que les experts se décident à révéler à tous ce qu'ils dissimulaient de leur mieux jusque-là, par crainte des réactions de rejet du contribuable français. Selon un groupe d'études du ministère de la France d'outre-mer, les investissements réalisés de 1948 à 1955 inclus, auraient été, sur la base des paiements effectués, de 505 milliards en Algérie, 436 dans les T.O.M. et 60 dans les D.O.M. (en milliards de francs 1955). Or pour augmenter de 4 % le niveau de vie individuel des populations, le montant de l'aide publique extérieure devait atteindre annuellement plus du double de ce qu'elle était en 1955 (366 milliards au lieu de 170). Dans les seuls T.O.M. elle devait passer de 72 milliards à 125 jusqu'en 1960 et 170 jusqu'en 1965.

Deux équipes d'économistes travaillant sous la direction respective de François Bloch-Lainé et de Pierre Moussa, aboutissaient pour le bilan de l'année 1955, à des constats voisins. La métropole avait consacré quelque 173 milliards de francs pour les dépenses civiles et militaires de l'outre-mer (non comprises celles entraînées par les opérations de guerre) et environ 361 milliards au total pour l'ensemble des investissements publics et des charges.

LES RÉVÉLATIONS DE LA COMPTABILITÉ NATIONALE AUX DÉBUTS DES ANNÉES 1950

Parce que nous établissions les comptes nationaux nous comprenons pour la première fois que l'empire colonial, loin d'être une richesse, était une charge très lourde. Les administrations coloniales, les entreprises coloniales — dont les profits résultaient à la fois du coût apparent très bas de la main-d'œuvre coloniale, de l'exploitation d'équipements financés par la métropole, parfois de subventions et de débouchés protégés — tout cela était finalement source de richesses pour un certain nombre de Français. Mais globalement l'empire colonial prélevait sur la métropole des ressources qui, après quelques réorientations, auraient été mieux employées dans la création d'une force économique en France même.

Claude Gruson, *Programmer l'espérance*, p. 74.

Le système du pacte colonial s'est presque inversé au bénéfice des pays d'outre-mer. Désormais ceux-ci importent beaucoup plus en provenance de la métropole qu'ils n'exportent vers elle. Tout se passe comme si la métropole fournissait les francs métropolitains qui permettent à ses correspondants d'avoir une balance profondément déséquilibrée : ainsi s'opère aux frais de la métropole le développement économique de tous les pays d'outre-mer.

François Bloch-Lainé, *La zone franc*, p. 44.

Comparée à un budget métropolitain de 3969 milliards, cette somme représentait un pourcentage de 9 %. «On peut donc dire, grosso modo, que 9 % des impôts payés par les contribuables français le sont en vue de dépenses effectuées outre-mer.» (Pierre Moussa.) Ces enquêtes concordantes démontraient de plus que l'aggravation des dépenses civiles courantes et l'alourdissement progressif des investissements étaient inscrits dans la logique des plans de développement africain et algérien. Et cela avant même que ne fût formulé et chiffré (2990 milliards) le grandiose plan de Constantine. Les experts les plus favorables au principe de l'aide métropolitaine commençaient à se demander si «le fardeau colonial» ne paraîtrait pas trop lourd à la nation française. Avec un revenu national huit fois inférieur, la France dépensait pour l'Union française la moitié de ce que les États-Unis fournissaient aux pays sous-développés sous forme d'aide publique.

Il est vrai que certains experts jugeaient au contraire que la France devait augmenter son effort. Telle était la conclusion de l'équipe de François Bloch-Lainé. Tout en reconnaissant que la France avait octroyé sous formes diverses de 1947 à 1955 «plus de 1000 milliards de francs», l'auteur indiquait : «Il n'est pas certain que l'équipement des pays d'outre-mer occupe dans le budget français la place que lui assigneraient leurs immenses besoins.» D'autres experts jugeaient même que l'heure était venue d'une redistribution plus équitable du revenu national français entre la métropole et l'Union française. Le ministre de la France d'outre-mer, Robert Buron, expliquait que «l'assistance aux territoires d'outre-mer s'imposait comme un devoir moral de solidarité».

Mais si quelques hommes généreux se félicitaient de ce que le système du pacte colonial se fût renversé au bénéfice des pays d'outre-mer, et que leur développement économique s'opérât aux frais de la métropole, d'autres bons esprits n'hésitaient pas à déclarer que «les milliards d'équipement dépensés pour le mieux-être de populations ingrates et devenues dangereuses, seraient mieux employés à valoriser la métropole et à rajeunir ses moyens de production». Ce mode de raisonnement s'affirma sous le nom de «complexe hollandais» ou cartiérisme.

LE CARTIÉRISME

La formule du «complexe hollandais» désignait la mentalité de ceux qui se demandaient si l'effort que la France s'imposait à elle-même en faveur des pays d'outre-mer n'était pas au-dessus de ses forces. Tirant argument de la prospérité récente de la Hollande depuis qu'elle avait abandonné, contre son gré, l'Indonésie, ils suggéraient que l'éviction de la France de ses colonies pourrait bien être une bénédiction. Délivrée de ses charges coloniales, la France pourrait consacrer ses ressources au développement de ses provinces, à la modernisation de son industrie, à la rationalisation de son économie.

Cette argumentation, que Raymond Aron et plusieurs économistes libéraux développèrent à partir de 1955, reçut le renfort inattendu d'un journaliste très influent, Raymond Cartier. Rédacteur en chef de *Paris Match*, Raymond Cartier, connu jusque-là comme fervent zélateur de la colonisation, fit volte-face au retour d'une longue enquête en Afrique noire. Il avait découvert en 1956 et révéla à ses lecteurs ce qu'il appelait «nos dépenses démagogiques, les bureaux de poste et hôpitaux déclamatoires, les milliards gaspillés du F.I.D.E.S.» et l'importance de «notre coûteuse philanthropie». Or ses interlocuteurs africains ne lui avaient pas caché que cette tardive générosité venait trop tard et ne changerait rien à leurs revendications d'indépendance. Dès lors, concluait R. Cartier, la France n'avait pas intérêt à se sacrifier pour des populations qui n'aspiraient qu'à la mettre dehors. Les temps avaient changé, les colonies n'étaient plus source de puissance et de richesses, elles étaient une charge : «les 1400 milliards investis outre-mer (Maghreb compris) depuis 1946 eussent peut-être suffi à moderniser l'économie française et à la rendre compétitive». Les experts et les hommes politiques prirent dès lors position sur le cartiérisme. La droite conservatrice rejeta avec indignation ces «suggestions d'abandon», soutenue par le M.R.P. et le syndicat Force ouvrière qui y virent surtout une manifestation déplaisante d'égoïsme national.

À gauche on dénonça «le chauvinisme rageur» de Cartier et son mercantilisme. Quant aux Africains, ils furent les premiers à fustiger «le métropolisme ou cartiérisme». Peu de voix autorisées, mais pourtant quelques anciens ministres, approuvèrent ouvertement les thèses de Cartier. L'un d'eux écrivait fin 1957 : «Ne sacrifions pas des dizaines de milliards de notre budget à combler le déficit de certains budgets africains et à entretenir des gens qui nous méprisent. J'enrage à la pensée que, pour les adductions d'eaux, le budget français ne peut mettre à la disposition de nos campagnes que 15 milliards, alors que généreusement nous en octroyons des vingtaines à la Tunisie et au Maroc, et bien plus encore à des territoires où sous peu sera exigé notre départ, après qu'on aura tiré de nous le maximum». Aucun sondage d'opinion ne permet de savoir quel était l'impact réel du cartiérisme dans le public en

1956-1957. Certes, par réflexe conservateur, les Français entendaient «garder l'Afrique noire». Mais la démonstration selon laquelle la France était elle-même un pays sous-développé (10700000 Français ne disposaient pas encore de l'eau courante en 1960 et la pénurie de logements était telle qu'il fallait en construire 350000 par an au minimum), paraît avoir été approuvée par une majorité du pays en 1960. «Charité bien ordonnée commence par soi-même», répétait-on. Maurice Schumann notait en décembre 1960 : «Si vous ne voulez pas passer pour être intellectuellement faible, vous ferez bien, dès que vous entendrez parler de l'Afrique noire, de vous écrier : “Il est temps de consacrer au Lot-et-Garonne et aux Basses-Alpes, les dizaines de milliards que nous gaspillons au Sénégal et à Madagascar.»

«L'AVENIR DE L'UNION FRANÇAISE EST DE DEVENIR EUROPÉENNE»

La discussion des thèses cartiéristes conduisit aussi les experts à poser de nouveau comme dans l'entre-deux-guerres une question difficile : l'espace africain français pouvait-il être mis en valeur par la France seule? Leur réponse était désormais presque unanime : la France, répétaient-ils à l'envi, est dans l'impossibilité technique et financière de réaliser seule le programme nécessaire. Et de suggérer l'appel à des capitaux étrangers pour réaliser la mise en valeur de ce que l'on commençait à appeler «l'ensemble eurafricain français». Un Fonds européen d'investissement soulagerait l'effort des Français, mais ne saperait-il pas définitivement une souveraineté française déjà fort menacée? Le public semblait le craindre qui rejetait d'instinct «le *trusteeship* européen» sur les territoires d'outre-mer. Mais les partisans de l'Europe communautaire y étaient très favorables, exigeant même l'intégration de l'Union française dans la Communauté économique européenne. La France devait faire partager aux Six un fardeau financier devenu insupportable. Le gouvernement socialiste de Guy Mollet, pour qui «faire l'Eurafrique» grâce à des investissements européens paraissait une tâche politique primordiale, partageait cette opinion. En posant comme préalable à la conclusion du Marché commun, l'association des futurs États africains et malgache, il obtint satisfaction au traité de Rome de mars 1957. L'assistance financière leur était promise par la création du Fonds européen de développement financé par les Six États de la C.E.E., mais le montant prévu n'atteignait pas 150 milliards de francs.

LES FINANCIERS ET LES HOMMES D'AFFAIRES ONT-ILS POUSSÉ À UNE POLITIQUE DE DÉCOLONISATION?

C'est surtout pendant et après la guerre d'Algérie qu'une hypothèse, vite présentée comme une certitude, a prétendu que les hommes d'affaires et de finance, voire les industriels des sociétés implantées outre-mer comme dans la métropole, auraient poussé à une politique précoce de décolonisation. «Les responsabilités des grandes dynasties bourgeoises» (E. Beau de Loménie) ou celles des «libéraux d'affaires» ou du «Grand Capital» sont ainsi curieusement incriminées et par une certaine droite nationaliste et par les économistes marxistes. Cette politique anticipée de «dégagement» s'expliquerait par une attitude cartiériste ou la volonté de reconvertir des intérêts menacés. L'Algérie comme l'Indochine auraient été «perdues par l'Argent». Le Capital aurait forcé la main de politiques hésitants sur la conduite à tenir. Certains financiers ou hommes d'affaires ou banques auraient au contraire joué la carte des indépendances et se seraient faits ensuite, comme disait Guy Mollet, «les larbins serviles des nouveaux pouvoirs». Mais existait-il une troisième voie entre le repli et «la coopération néocapitaliste»?

Cette présentation des faits s'appuie à l'origine sur le cas de l'Indochine et le rôle controversé de la Banque d'Indochine. Cette banque, dotée du privilège d'émission de la piastre (renouvelé en 1931), était également une grande banque d'affaires qui travaillait dans tout l'Extrême-Orient, cependant qu'elle menait comme banque commerciale des opérations de crédit à court terme, en Indochine essentiellement. Ses actifs y étaient en 1939 considérables, ses immobilisations également. Mais on l'accusait de n'avoir travaillé que comme dispensateur de crédits à l'usage des grandes sociétés françaises d'Indochine, en ne soutenant pas le crédit agricole. Cette banque «coloniale» aurait constitué un véritable État dans l'État, que le Front populaire aurait voulu briser. Considérée comme citadelle vichyssoise et se sachant menacée après 1945, elle offrit spontanément en juillet 1947 de renoncer à son privilège d'émission, neuf ans avant l'échéance et ne retrouva jamais son influence. Elle n'en fut pas moins accusée de n'avoir pas défendu jusqu'au bout les intérêts français.

Mais la situation économique de l'Indochine le permettait-il? Après la révolution vietnamienne, la France ne réussit pas à restaurer son autorité : la guerre continua et la situation des affaires s'en ressentit. Malgré une amélioration relative des exportations dans les années 1947 à 1950, l'économie indochinoise ne parvint pas à retrouver son niveau d'avant guerre. Dans ces conditions beaucoup de sociétés françaises d'Indochine périclitèrent : entre 1946 et 1953, les actifs des sociétés diminuèrent des deux tiers, tandis qu'ils doublaient en Afrique noire et à Madagascar. En Indochine il y eut donc désinvestissement à partir de 1950-1951. Quant à la Banque d'Indochine, dont les profits baissaient malgré sa participation au financement du corps expéditionnaire français, elle transféra bientôt la totalité de ses capitaux libres en tirant partie de la surévaluation de la piastre. Peut-on dire qu'elle anticipa ou précipita la décolonisation? En réalité la modification de ses investissements était antérieure à 1950. Ses prises de participation s'inscrivaient dès 1945 dans le cadre d'une volonté de diversification de ses activités (vers des industries, ou dans le crédit foncier). Elles visaient une politique de développement de la banque qui voyait se fermer peu à peu le marché chinois : d'où ses implantations dans l'Union française (au Maghreb et en Afrique noire à partir de 1947), mais aussi en Arabie saoudienne (1948) et en Afrique du Sud (1949). Sa mutation en banque d'affaires métropolitaine se fit progressivement depuis 1945. Ses adversaires lui reprochèrent cette reconversion réussie. Quant aux sociétés françaises qui travaillaient pour le marché indochinois, elles étaient tout naturellement favorables au maintien de la présence française. Les industriels du textile (les cotonniers essentiellement, pas les

STATISTIQUES FINANCIERES

Subventions et crédits accordés aux territoires relevant du ministre de la France d'outre-mer (T.O.M.) et aux départements d'outre-mer (D.O.M.) depuis la loi du 30 avril 1946 jusqu'au 30 juin 1951 (en millions de francs)

T.O.M.	Subventions du F.I.D.E.S. (en millions)	Crédits de la C.C.F.O.M. (en millions)	Contributions propres des territoires (en millions)
A.O.F.	30 441	28 005	2 169
Togo	1 465	1 377	
Cameroun	9 067	9 073	
A.E.F.	12 604	9 857	59
Madagascar	5 761	5 277	606
Comores	239	194	
Somalis	1 392	1 250	60
Comptoirs français de l'Inde	85	70	
Océanie	1 231		339
Nouvelle-Calédonie	1 453	1 312	
St-Pierre-et-Miquelon	406	158	
Total	64 149	56 777	3 234
D.O.M.			
Guadeloupe	3 083	640	10
Guyane	2 065	429	
Martinique	5 127	706	86
Réunion	2 112	441	5,6
Total	12 389	2 218	101,6
Total général T.O.M. + D.O.M.	76 538	58 795	3 336

lainiers) et certains exportateurs traditionnels restèrent d'ailleurs jusqu'au bout farouchement attachés aux marchés protégés de l'Union française.

Après 1954, le patronat français dans toutes ses publications ne cessait de dire l'importance de ces marchés pour l'économie française. «Sans l'Afrique plus de métropole prospère», répétaient la plupart des responsables. Et de montrer que, dès 1954, les exportations de textiles vers l'Indochine baissèrent de 23%, celles vers le Maroc de 20%, et vers la Tunisie de 5%. Certes le Centre national du patronat français ne commandait pas les attitudes concrètes des industriels ou des commerçants français, dont les stratégies variaient. Mais les associations qu'il soutenait défendirent jusqu'au bout la politique de l'Union française ou de l'Algérie française. Le président du C.N.P.F., Georges Villiers, se montra personnellement fort engagé en ce sens, célébrant en octobre 1960 encore le plan de Constantine, la durée et la prospérité de l'Algérie française.

Dépenses de fonctionnement des services publics du secteur civil prises en charge par la métropole dans les territoires d'outre-mer (Indochine exclue)
(calculs faits en francs constants 1955)

Moyenne	En millions
1929-1931	2 600
1937-1939	3 200
1950	6 587
1951	12 281
1952	20 745
1953	34 833
1954	34 738
1955	35 800

Sur un indice base 100 pour 1929-1931, on obtient :

1950	indice	253
1951	indice	472
1952	indice	798
1953	indice	1 342
1954	indice	1 336
1955	indice	1 377

L'ensemble des dépenses pour le budget de l'État (métropole) a été multiplié par 11,19 par rapport à 1937-1939 (indice 123).

AFRIQUE DU NORD

Répartition des investissements contrôlés par la puissance publique pour l'ensemble des programmes de 1949 - 1950 - 1951 (en milliards de francs)

	Algérie	Maroc	Tunisie	Total Afrique du Nord
I. Ressources locales				
Budget ordinaire et caisse de réserve	27,6	28	2,7	58,3
Emprunts et crédits locaux	24,9	32,1	3,1	60,1
Avances du trésor local	2,7			2,7
Autofinancement	7,9	9,5	4,3	21,7
Total des ressources locales	63,1	69,6	10,1	142,8
Pourcentage des ressources locales par rapport au total des ressources	43,2 %	57,8 %	15,7 %	43,2 %[1]

(suite)

II. Ressources de l'extérieur				
Fonds de modernisation et d'équipement	60,6	38,8	29,4	128,8
Avances du trésor métropolitain	2,8		8	10,8
Emprunts et crédits métropolitains	12	11,4	13,4	36,8
Subventions du budget métropolitain	0,5	0,2	9,3	10
Total des ressources de l'extérieur	75,9	50,4	60,1	186,4
Pourcentage par rapport au total des ressources	51,9 %	41,9 %	83,3 %	54,2 %
Ressources d'origines diverses	7,2 %	0,4	1,9	9,5
Total général des ressources	146,2	120,4	72,1	338,7

[1] La participation des ressources publiques locales n'a jamais dépassé 19 % dans les territoires d'outre-mer (en moyenne 15 %).

Répartition pour la période 1949-1953 des investissements publics en Afrique du Nord (en milliards de francs)

TOTAL	Algérie	Maroc	Tunisie	TOTAL
	283	222	87,6	592,6
Dont				
Équipement économique	204,1	159,7	61,9	425,8
Équipement culturel et social	69,3	54,8	12	136,1

Fonds d'Aide de la France à l'Afrique du Nord de 1947 à 1955

Aide totale (en millions de francs) : 400.535
dont 208.135 pour l'Algérie

STATISTIQUES COMMERCIALES

IMPORTATIONS TOTALES (Quantités en 1000 tonnes)

	Territoires d'outre-mer	Des territoires de l'Union françaises d'outre-mer
1938	1 166	3 146
1944	711	3 390
1948	1 538	3 142
1950	2 232	8 312
1952	2 949	
1954	3 021	
1956	3 280	
1957	3 695	

EXPORTATIONS TOTALES

	Territoires d'outre-mer	Des territoires de l'Union française d'outre-mer
1938	2 199	18 228
1944	1 099	4 453
1948	1 910	15 261
1950	2 077	17 953
1952	2 265	
1954	3 842	
1956	5 263	
1957	6 100	

PART DE LA MÉTROPOLE DANS

	LES EXPORTATIONS DES T.O.M.	LES IMPORTATIONS DES T.O.M.
1950	68,3 %	66,5 %
1952	68,1 %	64,6 %
1954	65,2 %	65,3 %
1956	64,3 %	62,6 %

COMMERCE DE L'AFRIQUE NOIRE FRANÇAISE

Indices du volume des exportations
(base 100 en 1949)

Années	A.O.F.	A.E.F.	Cameroun	Togo	Afrique noire française
1939	90	74	56	96	84
1944	40	63	59	86	51,2
1948	90	107	96	152	96,4
1950	102,5	98	98,3	135	101,9
1952	105	111	108	143	107,9
1954	136	158	125	224	140
1955	133	169	143	237	143,4

Indices du volume des importations
(base 100 en 1949)

Années	A.O.F.	A.E.F.	Cameroun	Togo	Afrique noire française
1939	63,8	31			59,8
1944	25,5	28,5			25,6
1948	86,3	72,4			82,8
1950	112,4	99,2			109,1
1952	126	123			125
1954	170	110			158

Le commerce extérieur de l'Afrique noire était passé
— en quantités de 1349637 tonnes aux exportations en 1939 à 3413700 tonnes en 1955;
— et de 787280 tonnes aux importations en 1939 à 2265600 tonnes en 1955.

ÉVALUATION DU REVENU NATIONAL
Total de l'A.O.F., de l'A.E.F. et du CAMEROUN
(en milliards de francs métropolitains 1957)

1946	434 milliards
1949	655 milliards
1952	875 milliards
1956	1033 milliards

Indices de la production industrielle en Algérie (base 100 en 1954)

ANNÉES	Indices sans le bâtiment et les Travaux publics	Indices avec le bâtiment et les Travaux publics
1955	110,3	107
1956	113,9	110,3
1957	120,6	116,3
1958	133,7	131,6
1959	136,4	141,2
1960	149,7	151

Source : *Annuaires statistiques de l'Algérie.*

Indices par branches industrielles (base 100 en 1954)

	1956	1958	1960	1961
Industries alimentaires	145,7	197,2	211,6	221,5
Industrie de transformation des métaux	117,1	146,3	152,9	124,4
Industrie électrique	115,5	132,3	159,8	167,7
Industrie du verre	115,5	156,7	152,1	175,7

N.B. : Cette poussée de l'industrialisation s'explique essentiellement par les investissements massifs de la métropole conformément au Plan de Constantine (investissements réalisés au 31 décembre 1961 : 1443384000 N.F.)

Le Comité central de la France d'outre-mer, fort représentatif des milieux d'affaires, ne cessa de dire que la France jouait son destin outre-mer : «Si elle devait être privée de ses prolongements d'outre-mer, source de sa prospérité, elle serait atteinte dans sa métropole même. Un Français sur trois vit de l'outre-mer et l'ordre social ne résisterait pas au chômage généralisé, si deux millions de Français se repliaient sur leur pays d'origine». Le président de la Société financière pour la France et les Pays d'outre-mer, suspecté d'avoir voulu sacrifier les liens politiques pour sauver les liens monétaires et financiers, déplorait, au contraire, «la désintégration générale de l'Union française à laquelle un certain nombre de dirigeants de la France métropolitaine se rallient avec une légèreté étonnante. L'Union française est une lourde charge pour notre économie, et nous l'alourdirons encore davantage en rendant la liberté à nos territoires d'outre-mer».

Que certains responsables de firmes coloniales ou de grandes entreprises spécialisées aient dû diversifier leurs activités outre-mer, voire les replier successivement au sein de la zone franc, parfois en métropole, est un fait, mais les entrepreneurs durent le plus souvent faire face aux conséquences de la décolonisation. Ils ne l'anticipèrent pas, ni ne la déclenchèrent. Incriminer une prétendue politique de repli des libéraux d'affaires pour expliquer la

DE GAULLE « L'HOMME DE BRAZZAVILLE »

(extraits du discours prononcé à l'ouverture de la Conférence africaine de Brazzaville, le 30 janvier 1944)

S'il est une puissance impériale que les événements conduisent à s'inspirer de leurs leçons et à choisir noblement, libéralement la route des temps nouveaux où elle entend diriger les soixante millions d'hommes qui se trouvent associés au sort de ses quarante deux millions d'enfants, cette puissance c'est la France [...].

Mais en Afrique française, comme dans tous les autres territoires où les hommes vivent sous notre drapeau, il n'y aurait aucun progrès qui soit un progrès si les hommes, sur leur terre natale, n'en profitaient pas moralement et matériellement, s'ils ne pouvaient s'élever peu à peu jusqu'au niveau où ils seront capables de participer chez eux à la gestion de leurs propres affaires. C'est le devoir de la France de faire en sorte qu'il en soit ainsi.

(extraits du discours prononcé à Brazzaville au stade Félix Eboué, le 24 août 1958)

On dit : « Nous avons droit à l'indépendance ». Mais certainement oui ! Un territoire déterminé pourra la prendre aussitôt s'il vote « non » au référendum du 28 septembre. Et cela signifiera qu'il ne veut pas faire partie de la Communauté proposée et qu'il fait en somme sécession. La métropole en tirera la conséquence et je garantis qu'elle ne s'y opposera pas.

Mais si le corps électoral, dans les territoires africains, vote « oui » au référendum, cela signifiera que, par libre détermination, les citoyens ont choisi de constituer la Communauté dont j'ai parlé. Alors cette Communauté sera instituée. On la fera fonctionner. Je suis sûr que ce sera pour le bien de tous.

Mieux même ; à l'intérieur de cette Communauté, si quelque territoire, au fur et à mesure des jours, se sent, au bout d'un certain temps que je ne précise pas, en mesure d'exercer toutes les charges, tous les devoirs de l'indépendance, eh bien ! il lui appartiendra d'en décider par son Assemblée élue et, si c'est nécessaire ensuite, par le référendum de ses habitants. Après quoi la Communauté prendra acte, et un accord réglera les conditions de transfert entre ce territoire, qui prendra son indépendance et suivra sa route, et la Communauté elle-même. Je garantis d'avance que, dans ce cas non plus, la métropole ne s'y opposera.

décolonisation apparaît comme une thèse aussi inexacte que celle qui prétend l'attribuer aux cartiéristes. Ni les hommes d'affaires, ni les industriels, ni les publicistes ne furent jamais unanimes sur l'avenir de la colonisation. Ils furent tout autant incapables de pousser à une stratégie commune et raisonnée face à une décolonisation qu'ils n'avaient pas prévue.

DE GAULLE ET LA DÉCOLONISATION

Le général de Gaulle qui fut l'homme d'État de la décolonisation a été présenté, selon les opinions contradictoires de ses biographes, soit comme un zélateur de la mission impériale, défenseur entêté de l'Empire tardivement reconverti, soit comme un décolonisateur résolu de longue date, voire comme le liquidateur hâtif des colonies françaises. Est-il si difficile d'admettre que de Gaulle, en politique réaliste qui entendait se situer au niveau de l'Histoire, ait cru un temps au devoir de colonisation et aux responsabilités impériales de la France? Et qu'il ait dû tenir compte de la marche accélérée de l'Histoire dans les années de la Deuxième Guerre mondiale et de l'immédiat après-guerre? Chacun comprend aujourd'hui que son action et son discours aient été différents, lorsqu'il mettait entre 1940 et 1944 tous les espoirs de la France combattante dans la puissance et les ressources de son Empire colonial, et lorsqu'en 1960 il déclarait le 14 juin : « Le génie du siècle [...] nous conduit à mettre un terme à la colonisation », avant de préciser le 5 septembre : « L'émancipation des peuples est conforme à la fois au génie de notre pays, au but que nos grands colonisateurs avaient en vue [...], conforme aussi au mouvement irrésistible qui s'est déclenché dans le monde à l'occasion de la guerre mondiale ». Ce ne fut pourtant pas chez lui, une conversion de la dernière heure à la marche du siècle, car il avait dit par exemple au président Truman, en 1945, que « l'époque nouvelle marquerait l'accession des pays colonisés à l'indépendance [...]. L'Occident devrait le comprendre et même le vouloir. »

LA DÉFENSE ET L'AVENIR DE L'EMPIRE (1930-1945)

De Gaulle était un officier métropolitain qui ne fit pas de véritable carrière coloniale. Il servit pourtant, assez brièvement il est vrai, outre-mer, suffisamment pour comprendre la nécessité d'une politique coloniale libérale et évolutive. De novembre 1929 à janvier 1932, le commandant de Gaulle s'initia à Beyrouth aux difficiles problèmes soulevés par le mandat français sur les États du Levant. Un seul officier lui parut avoir « bien compris » la Syrie : le colonel Catroux. Celui-ci, gagné aux conceptions de Lyautey, avait osé définir après la révolte des Druzes une politique respectueuse du contrat mandataire, « cette tutelle provisoire et légère ». Cela supposait que la France s'entendît bien avec les nationalistes arabes. De Gaulle lui aussi, en juillet 1930, invita les jeunes Libanais à une « tâche nationale » : « construire avec l'aide de la France, un État et une nation ». Ce langage n'était pas celui d'un colonial traditionnel : il se situait dans la ligne d'un Lyautey convaincu de la nécessité de faire évoluer le protectorat marocain vers l'indépendance.

Peut-on dire que le désastre de 1940 ait renforcé les conceptions impériales du général de Gaulle? Oui à coup sûr, lorsqu'il décidait en juin 1940 de continuer la guerre perdue sur le continent européen, car il proclamait que l'Empire seul pouvait donner à la France les moyens « de se refaire une armée et une souveraineté ». D'où ses efforts pour rallier l'Empire tout entier au combat de la France libre contre les visées de l'impérialisme germano-italien et les concessions vichyssoises aux Japonais et aux Allemands. Il n'hésita pas à associer les Forces françaises libres aux armées britanniques, lorsqu'elles occupèrent la Syrie et le Liban mis à la disposition de l'aviation allemande par le gouvernement de Vichy. Dans le même temps, il annonçait lui-même et faisait annoncer par le général Catroux, aux populations du Levant, que la France libre conformément aux accords de 1936, signés mais non ratifiés, reconnaissait leur indépendance et mettrait fin au mandat. Le statut des États syrien et libanais serait défini par un traité qui préciserait leurs rapports nouveaux avec la France. L'indépendance fut officiellement accordée à la Syrie le 26 septembre 1941 et au Liban le 26 novembre, sous la seule réserve de positions que la France conserverait pendant la période de guerre. Par là le général de Gaulle s'affirmait devant l'Histoire comme ayant le premier réalisé la décolonisation de deux territoires confiés à la France par la SDN. Cependant il n'entendait pas voir la Grande-Bretagne, en appuyant ostensiblement les éléments nationalistes les plus pressés, évincer à son profit l'influence séculaire de la France. Ce traditionnel antagonisme franco-anglais dans le Proche-Orient conduisit ainsi à la détérioration des rapports de la France avec les nouveaux États et même à l'épreuve de force en novembre 1943.

Lorsqu'en septembre 1942, les Britanniques occupèrent Tamatave, de Gaulle exhorta les Français à maintenir «face aux manœuvres des Alliés» l'unité nationale et l'intégrité de l'Empire. Mais si Madagascar fut finalement placé dès décembre 1942 sous l'autorité de la France combattante, l'Afrique du Nord et l'Afrique occidentale française ne purent l'être qu'en juin 1943. De Gaulle salua alors depuis Alger «le labeur et le dévouement des colons [...], le loyalisme de ses chères et braves populations indigènes que la France nouvelle voudra et saura associer plus largement et librement à son destin». Par ailleurs, aux trois proconsuls d'Afrique du Nord, il indiquait le 22 octobre 1943 : «La France ne maintiendra sa position dans les pays musulmans d'Afrique du Nord que si elle justifie sa présence par des résultats concrets et visibles, notamment en matière sociale.» Déjà il redoutait que ces pays «ne glissent entre nos doigts pendant que nous libérons la France». Le général Catroux, qu'il venait de nommer commissaire d'État aux affaires musulmanes, put affirmer sans être désavoué, le 10 novembre 1943, que l'ère des dominations coloniales était close et le temps à jamais révolu «où l'on pouvait parler de races éternellement inférieures incapables de se gouverner elles-mêmes».

Que devrait être l'avenir de l'Empire après la guerre? De Gaulle s'exprima clairement à ce sujet lors de la conférence africaine et malgache qu'il réunit à Brazzaville à la fin de janvier 1944. Même s'il ne trouva pas au sein de cette réunion de gouverneurs des colonies la «volonté ardente et pratique de renouveau» qu'il souhaitait lui-même, de Gaulle fit savoir que la colonisation française dans l'Afrique noire devrait s'orienter vers des voies nouvelles : «Tous les hommes vivant sous notre drapeau devaient être élevés peu à peu jusqu'au niveau où ils seront capables de participer chez eux à la gestion de leurs propres affaires.» On a beaucoup dit que cette conférence de Brazzaville fut un simple contre-feu à la charte de l'Atlantique et aux projets de *trusteeships* internationaux. À supposer qu'il en fût ainsi, le discours inaugural du général de Gaulle l'engageait bien dans la voie d'une évolution libérale et il tint à ce que le peuple français en fût informé. Les Africains eux ne manquèrent jamais de célébrer «*l'homme de Brazzaville*, celui qui a su comprendre à temps nos aspirations» (Houphouët-Boigny).

De Gaulle confirmait d'ailleurs peu après cette orientation politique. Le 10 juillet 1944 il se prononçait pour la substitution à l'Empire traditionnel d'un «système de forme fédérale dans lequel la métropole sera une partie et où les intérêts de chacun pourront se faire entendre». Malgré l'opposition que ces propos suscitèrent au sein des milieux coloniaux, de Gaulle répéta dans une conférence de presse à Paris le 25 octobre 1944 ce que serait sa politique vis-à-vis de l'Empire : «La politique française consiste à mener chacun de ces peuples à un développement qui lui permette de s'administrer et plus tard de se gouverner lui-même.» Cet engagement révolutionnaire ne fut pas pris au sérieux par les Américains qui y virent un moyen de faire échapper à la tutelle internationale toutes les colonies européennes. Pourtant de Gaulle décida par exemple d'associer les colonies à l'élection de la Constituante, permettant ainsi à leurs députés de participer à l'élaboration de la future Constitution de la IVe République et de l'Union française qui remplaça l'Empire.

Vis-à-vis de l'Indochine occupée par les Japonais et dont le gouverneur général, l'amiral Decoux, ne s'était point rallié au G.P.R.F., de Gaulle avait aussi promis dans une déclaration faite à Alger, le 8 décembre 1943, de libérer le pays et de remplacer le système colonial par un statut politique nouveau «au sein de la communauté, où dans le cadre de l'organisation fédérale, les libertés des divers pays de l'Union (indochinoise) seront étendues». C'est dans cette perspective que fut préparée dès la fin de 1944 la déclaration rendue publique le 24 mars 1945, qui traçait à grandes lignes le futur statut de la Fédération indochinoise. Mais à cette date, cette déclaration était déjà caduque, puisqu'elle paraissait après le coup de force japonais perpétré dans la nuit du 8 au 9 mars 1945. La souveraineté française abolie, le pouvoir fut remis à des gouvernements autochtones sous le protectorat japonais. De Gaulle n'en voulut pas moins envoyer «envers et contre tous dans le monde» un corps expéditionnaire français pour rétablir en Indochine la souveraineté française. Il espérait notamment pouvoir remplacer le souverain d'Annam, Bao-Dai, coupable de collaboration avec les Japonais, par l'ex-empereur Duy-Than, naguère exilé tout enfant de sa patrie en 1917, dès lors que celui-ci s'était engagé comme officier dans les Forces françaises libres. Mais ce prince nationaliste et profrançais mourut le 28 décembre 1945 dans un accident d'avion.

Face à la prise du pouvoir par le Viêt-minh, que pouvait être la politique du général de Gaulle? Sans doute estimait-il ne plus pouvoir espérer après la révolution d'août 1945 et la proclamation d'une République démocratique du Viêt-nam, que son chef, le leader communiste Hô Chi Minh, accepterait de reconnaître la communauté française. Mais il n'est pas possible de préjuger ce qui aurait été sa position s'il n'avait pas quitté le pouvoir en janvier 1946.

L'ÉVOLUTION DE LA PENSÉE DU GÉNÉRAL DE GAULLE (1946-1958)

Pendant toute la période où il fut éloigné des affaires et qui coïncide partiellement avec les plus dangereuses années de la guerre froide, de Gaulle maintint tout à la fois son projet de constitution fédérale pour l'Union française et sa volonté de défendre celle-ci : «Unie aux territoires d'outre-mer qu'elle a ouverts à la civilisation, la France est une grande puissance. Sans ces territoires elle risquerait de ne l'être plus» (27 août 1946). «Pour nous, perdre l'Union française, ce serait un abaissement qui pourrait nous coûter jusqu'à notre indépendance. La garder et la faire vivre, c'est rester grands et par conséquent rester libres.» (15 mai 1947.) Dans la situation de guerre internationale potentielle, de Gaulle souhaitait que la France pût garder — au moins «pendant dix ou quinze ans», confiait-il plus tard à André Ulver — le contrôle de l'Union française. Dès lors, il entendait rejeter tout ce qui pouvait mener les populations à l'agitation, à la dislocation et notamment le principe de libre disposition. À la veille du vote du statut de l'Algérie, de Gaulle déclara, le 18 août 1947 : «Nous ne devons laisser mettre en question sous aucune forme, ni au dedans, ni au dehors le fait que l'Algérie est notre domaine. [...] La France, dont l'Algérie fait partie intégrante, est au fond très résolue à assurer elle-même le progrès de tous ses enfants, tout en restant maîtresse chez elle.» Mais en même temps, il déclarait à ses compagnons R.P.F., le 17 avril 1948 : «Nous entendons réaliser ce que nous-mêmes avons commencé depuis les jours historiques de Brazzaville et d'Alger, faire en sorte que chaque État ou bien chaque territoire reçoive la possibilité soit de se gouverner soit de s'administrer lui-même [...] Mais nous tenons pour nécessaire que l'Union française forme un tout de nature fédérale constitué autour de la France et pour lequel la France assure, en tout cas, la représentation extérieure, la Défense, et les dispositions économiques communes.» Cela s'appliquait notamment à l'Indochine. Sans s'engager sur le statut des États d'Indochine, de Gaulle, tout en convenant qu'il serait approprié d'élargir pour eux la formule de l'Union française, soutint jusqu'au bout que la France devait persévérer dans son effort : «la présence française devait être maintenue en Indochine» (7 avril 1954).

Mais de Gaulle ne renonçait pas à son libéralisme. De 1953 à 1958, se jugeant condamné à la retraite, il livrait à des confidents le fruit de ses réflexions sur l'avenir des empires coloniaux et singulièrement de l'Union française. C'est ainsi qu'il déplora comme une faute grave la déposition du sultan du Maroc et souhaita son retour sur le trône ou qu'il confia à Louis Terrenoire : «Nous sommes en présence d'un mouvement général dans le monde, d'une vague qui emporte tous les peuples vers l'émancipation». C'est pourquoi il refusa de condamner les *fellaga* (guérilleros) tunisiens comme le lui demandait le R.P.F. de Tunisie, et ne se méprit pas sur la portée de l'insurrection déclenchée en Algérie en novembre 1954.

Dès le début de 1955, il avouait à son plus proche collaborateur, Geoffroy de Courcel, avoir la conviction que «l'affaire d'Algérie ne se réglerait que par l'indépendance». Il confia aussi son sentiment à l'écrivain algérien Jean Amrouche en avril 1955 : «L'Algérie sera émancipée. Ce sera long. Il y aura de la casse, beaucoup de casse. Vous aurez beaucoup à souffrir.» Le 3 octobre 1956, il disait au prince héritier du Maroc, Moulay Hassan : «L'Algérie sera indépendante, qu'on le veuille ou non. Alors le tout sera le comment. Le fait est inscrit dans l'histoire. Tout dépend du comment.» Mais de Gaulle interdisait à tous ses interlocuteurs de rendre publics ses propos. Lui-même, dans une conférence de presse tenue le 30 juin 1955, évoquait pour le Maroc et la

Tunisie une formule d'association de nature fédérale et pour l'Algérie « l'intégration d'un territoire ayant son caractère à lui dans une communauté plus large que la France », ce qui supposait la transformation de l'Algérie en État autonome. Toutes ces indications suffirent à éclairer ceux qui voulaient bien l'être. Ainsi le président Bourguiba : « Je suis persuadé que le général de Gaulle pourrait servir la France dans un moment crucial de notre histoire, en tournant le dos au colonialisme, et reconquérir l'Afrique en reconquérant le cœur des Africains ». De fait, de Gaulle était bien convaincu que « l'ère des empires coloniaux touchait à sa fin et que le maintien de notre domination sur des pays qui n'y consentaient plus devenait une gageure, où pour ne rien gagner nous avions tout à perdre ». En mai 1958, il confiait à André Malraux : « Les colonies, c'est fini ! Il faut faire autre chose. »

COMMUNAUTÉ ET DÉCOLONISATION (1958-1962)

On comprend dès lors que revenu au pouvoir de Gaulle ait voulu régler la question algérienne et tenter de faire accepter par les Africains avides d'indépendance immédiate, la formule d'une nouvelle Union française très libérale. C'est pourquoi il offrit aux peuples africains et malgache la possibilité de choisir librement par référendum leur avenir : selon leurs vœux ils pourraient entrer dans la Communauté de style fédéral créée par la France ou choisir l'indépendance. Le pari était risqué, mais il réussit au prix de la sécession de la seule Guinée, que de Gaulle reconnut sans broncher. Pourtant la vague indépendantiste s'enfla à nouveau et de Gaulle jugea préférable de lui donner satisfaction : en 1960, la France accorda l'indépendance aux quatorze États africains et malgache qui l'avaient demandée.

De Gaulle avait créé la Communauté, sans illusion sur sa durée, et surtout peut-être pour servir au règlement de l'affaire algérienne. Il entendait réserver à l'Algérie, au sein de la Communauté, «une place de choix», comme il le déclara dès le 13 juillet 1958, mais l'édifice communautaire se disloqua avant que le gouvernement provisoire de la République algérienne en ait vu les avantages. Certes il était politiquement impossible après mai 1958 et l'intervention de l'Armée dans la définition de l'avenir politique de l'Algérie, d'associer l'Algérie française à un référendum véritable d'autodétermination. «Immédiatement il n'y aurait plus eu de De Gaulle», expliqua-t-il lui-même; l'Armée l'eût aussitôt renversé. De Gaulle qui connaissait la force de l'opinion : «Rien n'est possible qu'au nom de cette souveraine!» (*Le Fil de l'épée*) s'efforça à la dominer pour être libre d'agir. Mais il fut obligé de louvoyer pour faire progresser dans l'opinion l'idée que l'intégration n'était pas une politique réaliste. L'Algérie française lui apparaissait comme une formule dépassée : «L'Algérie de papa était morte.» À un fidèle comme Léon Delbecque, de Gaulle expliquait en 1959 : «Il faut trouver une formule qui nous permette de garder l'Algérie dans un système communautaire» et d'ajouter «Il ne faut pas avoir peur de prononcer les mots "l'Algérie doit être indépendante".» Après la tournée d'inspection militaire de fin août 1959, de Gaulle estima qu'il pouvait enfin se prononcer : «La décision est prise, annonça-t-il le 16 septembre, je m'engage à demander d'une part aux Algériens

DE GAULLE ET LA DÉCOLONISATION

Allocution télévisée du 14 juin 1960

[...] Le génie du siècle, qui change notre pays, change aussi les conditions de son action outre-mer. Inutile d'énumérer les causes de l'évolution qui nous conduit à mettre un terme à la colonisation. Par le fait des progrès accomplis dans nos territoires, de la formation que nous donnons à leurs élites, du mouvement d'affranchissement qui emporte les peuples de toute la terre, nous avons reconnu à ceux qui dépendaient de nous le droit de disposer d'eux-mêmes. Le leur refuser, ç'eût été contredire notre idéal, entamer des luttes interminables, nous attirer la réprobation du monde, le tout pour une contrepartie qui se fût inévitablement effritée entre nos mains. Il est tout à fait naturel qu'on ressente la nostalgie de ce qu'était l'Empire, tout comme on peut regretter la douceur des lampes à huile, la splendeur de la marine à voile, le charme du temps des équipages. Mais quoi ? Il n'y a pas de politique qui vaille en dehors des réalités.

Conférence de presse du 5 septembre 1960

[...] Sur l'ensemble du mouvement de décolonisation qui existe d'un bout à l'autre du monde, je n'ai jamais cessé, depuis le jour même où la guerre mondiale m'a amené à parler, à agir, au nom de la France, je n'ai jamais cessé de suivre la même direction.

Considérant que l'émancipation des peuples, car c'est de cela qu'il s'agit, est conforme tout à la fois au génie de notre pays, au but que nos grands colonisateurs, par exemple, Gallieni, Lyautey, avaient en vue dans leur œuvre colonisatrice, conforme aussi au mouvement irrésistible qui s'est déclenché dans le monde à l'occasion de la guerre mondiale et de ce qui s'en est suivi, j'ai engagé naguère, dans cette voie-là, dans cette voie de l'émancipation des peuples, la politique de la France et depuis deux ans, je l'oriente dans le même sens.

Ce n'est pas, bien entendu, que je renie en quoi que ce soit l'œuvre colonisatrice qui a été accomplie par l'Occident européen et en particulier par la France [...].

Mais je n'en crois pas moins qu'il faut savoir quand le moment est venu — et il est venu — reconnaître à tous le droit de disposer d'eux-mêmes, leur faire en principe confiance, et même attendre d'eux qu'ils apportent, à leur tour, leur contribution au bien de notre humanité. C'est là, en somme, et ce n'est pas ailleurs, qu'est la politique de la France [...].

Autrement dit, est-ce que les nouvelles souverainetés, les jeunes souverainetés doivent être acquises et exercées contre l'ancien colonisateur, en le maudissant par surcroît, ou bien, au contraire, en accord amical avec lui et en usant de son concours ?

La réponse me paraît être commandée par le bon sens. Je répète qu'à quatorze Républiques africaines et à la République malgache qui sont venues de l'Union française et auxquelles a été reconnue la libre disposition d'elles-mêmes, la France a proposé sa coopération. Une seule l'a refusée, nous n'y avons fait aucun obstacle. Mais je ne vois réellement pas quel avantage elle en a tiré.

Conférence de presse du 11 avril 1961

Depuis Brazzaville, je n'ai jamais cessé d'affirmer que les populations qui dépendaient de nous devaient pouvoir disposer d'elles-mêmes. En 1941, j'ai accordé l'indépendance aux États sous mandat de la Syrie et du Liban. En 1945, j'ai donné le droit de vote à tous les Africains, Algériens musulmans compris. En 1947, j'ai approuvé le statut de l'Algérie qui, s'il avait été appliqué, aurait vraisemblablement conduit à l'institution progressive d'un État algérien associé à la France. J'ai à l'époque donné mon assentiment à ce qu'il fût mis un terme aux traités de protectorat concernant la Tunisie et le Maroc. En 1958, ayant repris les affaires en main, j'ai, avec mon gouvernement, créé la Communauté et, par la suite, reconnu et aidé l'indépendance des jeunes États d'Afrique noire et de Madagascar. N'étant pas revenu à temps pour prévenir l'insurrection algérienne, dès mon retour j'ai proposé à ses chefs de conclure la paix des braves et d'entamer des conversations politiques. En 1959, j'ai proclamé le droit des populations algériennes à l'autodétermination et la volonté de la France d'accepter la solution, quelle qu'elle soit, qui en serait l'aboutissement. En 1960, j'ai, à maintes reprises, affirmé que l'Algérie serait algérienne, évoqué la naissance de sa future République et renouvelé nos offres de pourparlers [...].

En somme qu'est-ce que cela : c'est la décolonisation. Mais, si je l'ai entreprise et poursuivie depuis longtemps, ce n'est pas seulement parce qu'on pouvait prévoir et parce qu'ensuite on constatait l'immense mouvement d'affranchissement que la guerre mondiale et ses conséquences déclenchaient d'un bout à l'autre du monde et que d'ailleurs les surenchères rivales de l'Union soviétique et de l'Amérique ne manquaient pas de dramatiser. Si je l'ai fait, c'est aussi, c'est surtout, parce qu'il m'apparaît contraire à l'intérêt actuel et à l'ambition nouvelle de la France de se tenir rivée à des obligations, à des charges, qui ne sont plus conformes à ce qu'exigent sa puissance et son rayonnement [...].

Voici que notre grande ambition nationale est devenue notre propre progrès, source réelle de la puissance et de l'influence. Voici que l'époque moderne nous permet, nous commande, un très vaste développement. Voici que, pour la mener à bien, il nous faut employer d'abord pour nous, chez nous, les moyens dont nous disposons [...].

C'est un fait : la décolonisation est notre intérêt et, par conséquent, notre politique. Pourquoi resterions-nous accrochés à des dominations coûteuses, sanglantes et sans issue, alors que notre pays est à renouveler de fond en comble, alors que tous les pays sous-développés, à commencer par ceux qui hier dépendaient de nous et qui sont aujourd'hui nos amis préférés, demandent notre aide et notre concours ? Mais cette aide et ce concours pourquoi les donnerions-nous si cela n'en vaut pas la peine, s'il n'y a pas coopération, si ce que nous apportons ne comporte aucune contrepartie ? Oui, il s'agit d'échanges à cause de ce qui nous est dû, nous aussi à cause de la dignité de ceux avec qui nous faisons affaire.

Voici la base de la politique de la France en ce qui concerne ses rapports futurs avec l'Algérie [...]. La France serait, sans nul doute, disposée à prêter son aide économique, administrative, financière, culturelle, militaire, technique, au jeune État méditerranéen, à condition que soient assurés et garantis, la coopération organique des communautés en Algérie, un régime préférentiel d'échanges économiques et culturels, enfin les bases et facilités utiles à notre défense [...]. Voilà de quoi la France tient à discuter avec les Algériens en vue de l'autodétermination.

ce qu'ils veulent être en définitive et d'autre part à tous les Français d'entériner ce que sera ce choix.»

Mais, on le verra, il fallut encore deux ans et demi pour que l'on pût passer de l'énoncé du principe de l'autodétermination à sa réalisation. De Gaulle dut préalablement affronter les fureurs et les complots des tenants de l'Algérie française. Or ceux-ci rassemblaient la quasi-totalité des Européens d'Algérie, une grande partie du corps des officiers d'active et une minorité agissante de la société française. Face à un G.P.R.A. méfiant et intransigeant, conforté par l'appui de l'opinion mondiale, de Gaulle ne put faire accepter sa formule d'État algérien bâti en association avec la France. Les électeurs algériens la rejetèrent nettement par leurs abstentions au référendum du 8 janvier 1961. Comme il le déclara lui-même : «l'association a été implicitement proposée à l'Algérie. Pas un centième des musulmans d'Alger et d'Oran, pas un cinquantième de ceux de Constantine qui aient trouvé cela intéressant». Face à ces refus et à l'impossibilité de faire admettre aux deux parties une coopération organique des communautés, de Gaulle se décida à désengager la France de l'Algérie en négociant seulement au moindre mal avec le G.P.R.A. Encore lui fallut-il promettre à l'Algérie devenue indépendante «avec notre accord et avec notre aide», une coopération amicale et féconde.

La décolonisation, quand bien même la majorité des Français la jugeait nécessaire en 1960, n'aurait probablement pas triomphé sans déclencher une guerre civile, si de Gaulle n'avait pas fermement tenu la barre dans cette direction contre vents et marées. De Gaulle s'est révélé le seul homme d'État français capable de faire admettre aux élites françaises et à l'Armée «l'impensable décolonisation des départements algériens». Le devoir de l'historien est de lui en reconnaître le mérite.

LA DÉCOLONISATION DE L'AFRIQUE NOIRE FRANÇAISE ET DE MADAGASCAR

L'ÉVOLUTION DE L'AFRIQUE NOIRE (JUSQU'EN 1945)

Si le nationalisme africain ne fut clairement formulé qu'après la Seconde Guerre mondiale, on peut parler d'un protonationalisme nègre dans l'entre-deux-guerres. Celui-ci naquit au confluent du panafricanisme des noirs américains, de l'anti-impérialisme des communistes et de la tradition humaniste antiraciste française.

Certes le slogan «Mettre les Blancs à la porte!» apparut au Sénégal dès les années 1919-1920, en même temps que l'appel à la SDN pour délivrer le pays du carcan administratif de l'A.O.F. Mais les intellectuels africains furent surtout séduits par les idées du Jamaïcain Marcus Garvey, le précurseur du panafricanisme, et par ses mots d'ordre : «L'Afrique aux Africains», «Réveille-toi Éthiopie!» Sa *National Association for the advancement of colored people* prétendait sonner le glas de la domination blanche : elle réclamait «l'éviction progressive de la race blanche sur le continent noir».

Les premiers congrès panafricains parlaient dès 1921 de réclamer le self-government et invitaient la SDN à prendre en main l'indépendance des Noirs colonisés.

Tandis que des sujets britanniques réunis à Accra élaboraient les *Cahiers de revendications de la race noire*, le mouvement communiste international lançait à l'usage des Africains une doctrine d'action et de propagande fondée sur des thèmes divers et confus : émancipation du peuple nègre, union des nègres du monde entier, solidarité des «parias» et des prolétaires. Pourtant la Ligue anti-impérialiste, une filiale du *Komintern*, pensa à réclamer en 1932 «l'indépendance nationale des peuples du Sénégal et du Soudan». Mais les communistes de la *Ligue de défense de la race nègre*, puis de *l'Union des travailleurs nègres*, agissant à Paris, n'avaient aucune implantation en Afrique, à la différence des communistes malgaches. Dans ces conditions, l'appel lancé par une prétendue Ligue de lutte pour la liberté des peuples du Sénégal et du Soudan, publié dans le *Cri des nègres* en 1933 et 1934, ne représente nullement le premier manifeste indépendantiste de l'Afrique noire francophone : il fut rédigé par des communistes français incapables d'orthographier correctement les noms africains.

Enfin la tradition humaniste et antiraciste de la France des droits de l'homme et la force du courant assimilationniste séduisirent les premiers militants africains, les retenant de la tentation du nationalisme racial. La réhabilitation du monde nègre, puis l'affirmation de la «négritude» après 1939, suffirent aux intellectuels de cette période qui ne parlaient pas d'indépendance politique mais de revendication culturelle. Les petites organisations politiques nées en France ne devaient pas essaimer en Afrique, où la contestation politique, celle des «Jeunes Dahoméens» surtout, revendiquait essentiellement le statut de citoyens que possédaient «les originaires des quatre communes du Sénégal» depuis 1916. Ce sont des partis nouveaux qui furent fondés après la Deuxième Guerre mondiale dans une Afrique en partie transformée.

L'Afrique noire française tout entière fut engagée dans la guerre en 1939 : elle y demeura selon les territoires, ou partiellement ou entièrement, jusqu'en 1945. Elle dut fournir un immense effort de production et accepter une mobilisation étendue. L'effort de guerre total est difficile à mesurer. On a donné le chiffre global de 175000 mobilisés de 1939 à 1945. Au moment de la campagne de France en 1939-1940, les troupes d'Afrique noire auraient rassemblé 80000 Africains, encadrés par 17000 Européens. De novembre 1942 à mai 1945, l'A.O.F. seule mobilisa, semble-t-il, 42320 hommes, le Cameroun et l'A.E.F. ensemble 22844. Le recrutement porta aussi sur les «travailleurs forcés» en A.O.F., provoquant des fuites de paysans dans les colonies britanniques voisines. Une bataille de la production fut engagée qui visait à doubler notamment les tonnages d'arachides ou de coton, à augmenter les collectes de caoutchouc naturel. Dans l'ensemble, l'effort de guerre et les prélèvements fiscaux furent excessifs : ils épuisèrent les populations excédées de ces diverses exigences. Cette situation appelait au moins la reconnaissance de la nation française et un régime colonial nouveau.

La conférence de Brazzaville (30 janvier-8 février 1944), où ne se réunirent que des hauts fonctionnaires coloniaux, avait suggéré des réformes diverses comme la suppression de l'indigénat ou du travail forcé. Elle avait refusé l'évolution des colonies vers le *self-government* mais accepté que les colonies africaines puissent être acheminées par étapes de la décentralisation vers la personnalité politique. L'application de ces recommandations, freinée par l'opposition des planteurs et des colons, ne fut pas immédiate et certains «évolués» africains jugèrent que l'administration coloniale retardait volontairement les réformes.

On désignait alors sous le nom «d'évolués» les Africains qui avaient fréquenté l'école et qui parlaient et écrivaient le français. Ils étaient fonctionnaires, employés de commerce ou commis de l'Administration. On évaluait leur nombre à 100000 en 1945 sur 16 millions d'Africains en A.O.F. La plupart d'entre eux étaient politisés et déjà quelques politiciens exposaient leurs doléances contre l'Administration, notamment au Sénégal et au Dahomey. Dans les deux pays sous tutelle, Togo et Cameroun, quelques-uns invoquaient la charte des Nations unies et notamment l'article 76 qui exigeait le progrès politique, économique, social et intellectuel des populations et leur évolution vers l'autonomie et l'indépendance.

Quelques grandes réformes d'avenir avaient été immédiatement prises par le gouvernement provisoire, comme la création de syndicats professionnels, ou de communes de plein exercice (1944). Puis vinrent la liberté de la presse (1945), la liberté d'association et de réunion, l'abolition du travail forcé et l'extension de la citoyenneté française (1946). La reconstruction de l'économie et la nécessité de l'équipement posaient à la France appauvrie des problèmes plus difficiles, insolubles dans l'immédiat. Difficile aussi fut la reconversion d'une administration coloniale, peu nombreuse pourtant : en A.O.F. 593 fonctionnaires français d'autorité, dont 406 commandants de cercle, régnaient par le prestige plus que par la force, grâce à la chefferie traditionnelle : 2200 chefs de canton africains et 48000 chefs de villages. Mais le prestige du colonisateur reculait, cependant que les difficultés, les récriminations et les impatiences s'accumulaient.

La société africaine évoluait très vite au détriment des chefferies et au profit de la couche montante des «notables évolués» et des jeunes détribalisés. Les problèmes religieux s'y multipliaient avec la création de sectes ou de religions par des prophètes (Kibangu et Matsoua), l'extension lente du christianisme et la montée rapide de l'islam. L'animisme traditionnel reculait surtout devant l'islamisme qui en Afrique noire est synonyme de commerce. Or le commerce y était une activité plus rentable et plus prestigieuse que l'agriculture. Huit millions de musulmans sur vingt-trois millions d'Africains représentaient un pourcentage important, 34,7%, qui inquiétait l'administration. Celle-ci parlait du péril musulman, tout en se félicitant que l'islam s'exprimât encore essentiellement dans des confréries assez dociles (sauf l'*Hamaouiya*, secte très antifrançaise et très violente : en août 1940 elle massacra quelque 400 membres d'une confrérie adverse la *Tijâniyya*). Pourtant apparut dès 1946, une tendance nouvelle de musulmans intégristes ou «réformés» qui allaient chercher leur inspiration au Proche-Orient. Les chrétiens formés dans les écoles des missionnaires français ne posaient pas trop de problèmes aux administrateurs, encore qu'ils fussent moins soumis que les paysans animistes. En A.O.F. les chrétiens formaient 2,5% de la population, au Togo 12,3%, au Cameroun 23%, en A.E.F. 25% peut-être.

LE DÉVELOPPEMENT DE LA VIE POLITIQUE EN AFRIQUE NOIRE (1944-1956)

La vie politique se développa activement en Afrique noire dès 1944. Le retour des tirailleurs africains démobilisés fut marqué par un incident grave, la mutinerie de Tiaroye en décembre 1944 où 35 tirailleurs révoltés furent tués. Mais ce fut surtout la violence de la nouvelle presse qui échauffa les esprits : *L'Afrique libre, Jeunesse et Démocratie* proclamaient à l'unisson : «Le colonialisme est terminé», «Le Toubab (le Blanc) a peur»; *La Communauté* annonçait : «Nous n'acceptons plus pour longtemps la domination européenne [...]. Nous espérons que l'Europe tombera en poussière devant l'Afrique ressuscitée.» Cette presse saluait les progrès de la Fédération panafricaine et les discours enflammés du futur leader ghanéen N'Krumah; ce dernier ne répétait-il pas que la libération et l'unité de l'Afrique devraient se faire contre les puissances impérialistes.

Au Sénégal, des partis politiques existaient déjà, comme le parti socialiste sénégalais, dont M. Lamine Gueye fit peu à peu son parti, *le Bloc africain*. D'autres se créèrent : la vie politique y était d'autant plus active que l'on comptait en 1945 quelque 93000 citoyens dont 57778 à Dakar. Au Dahomey «le quartier latin de l'Afrique», la presse politique était particulièrement nombreuse et violente. Elle réclamait l'établissement d'un *trusteeship* de l'ONU, voire l'indépendance. En juin 1946 fut créée l'Union progressiste dahoméenne, le premier d'innombrables partis à vocation électoraliste. En Guinée, où il n'y avait pas encore d'évolués mais seulement «quelques milliers d'évoluants», ceux-ci développaient un racisme noir. Le communisme y eut immédiatement un grand succès, grâce à ses assurances doctrinales et à ses promesses, et les violences commencèrent dès octobre 1945.

Le Parti communiste français implantait depuis la fin de 1943, dans les principales villes, des G.E.C., groupes d'études communistes. Ceux-ci travaillaient à la formation de militants syndicaux ou politiques. Ils avaient pour consigne de préparer la création dans chaque territoire d'un parti politique «démocratique» destiné à rassembler les Africains et les Européens progressistes. En Côte-d'Ivoire, l'action politique naquit spontanément chez les planteurs africains qui s'étaient regroupés dans un syndicat agricole africain, créé en juillet 1944. Celui-ci était dirigé par une puissante personnalité, le Dr Félix Houphouët-Boigny, chef coutumier et riche planteur. Élu député en 1945, il fonda en 1946 un *parti démocratique de la Côte-d'Ivoire* dont le programme était clair : «L'Afrique noire en marche». Au Cameroun où des incidents graves avaient éclaté en septembre 1945, une assemblée représentative fut mise en place en octobre 1946. Le mot magique d'indépendance y était souvent repris. Il en allait de même au Togo où les Ewés, partagés en 1919 entre les mandats britannique et français, ne cessèrent de faire appel à l'ONU et aux Américains. La création d'une assemblée représentative permit à son président, Sylvanus Olympio, d'utiliser cette tribune pour accroître l'influence de son parti.

Face à cette fermentation politique, la France avait tenté d'abord d'instaurer une politique très libérale. «Pour la première fois dans l'histoire, avait annoncé de Gaulle, les colonies vont être appelées à participer aux élections générales de l'Assemblée constituante.» L'Afrique noire eut droit à 14 députés élus au double collège; ceux-ci s'inscrivirent aux groupes parlementaires des partis français, et jouèrent un rôle essentiel dans l'élaboration de la Constitution d'avril 1946. Or celle-ci, rejetée par le peuple français au référendum du 5 mai, avait été plébiscitée par les Africains (85,4 % de Oui). Un semblable divorce fut constaté au référendum du 13 octobre. La France accepta la Constitution que les électeurs d'Afrique rejetaient. Forte désormais de 23 députés (13 pour l'A.O.F., 6 pour l'A.E.F., 3 pour le Cameroun, 1 pour le Togo), et de 32 conseillers de la République (19 pour l'A.O.F., 8 pour l'A.E.F., 3 pour le Cameroun, 2 pour le Togo), sans compter les 40 délégués à l'Assemblée de l'Union française, l'Afrique noire ne s'estimait pourtant pas assez justement représentée. Le double collège supprimé, puis partiellement rétabli en 1946, était considéré comme une humiliation intolérable. Le droit de suffrage n'était alors accordé qu'aux évolués et les Africains réclamaient le suffrage universel. La plupart de ces exigences furent satisfaites : le nombre des électeurs tripla en A.O.F. entre 1946 et 1951, d'un million à 3062000, et le nombre des députés africains passa à 26. Comme par ailleurs chaque territoire était doté d'assemblées élues, dites Conseils généraux, puis Assemblées territoriales et que l'A.O.F. et l'A.E.F. disposaient de Grands Conseils, la politisation devint extrême. Face à des électeurs novices, la démagogie et la corruption sévirent. Députés et sénateurs africains eurent tendance à se considérer comme les nouveaux souverains de l'Afrique, cependant qu'ils intervinrent parfois de manière décisive dans les affaires intérieures de la métropole. On put croire pendant quelques années que la France avait implanté le régime représentatif et le multipartisme libéral en Afrique.

Parmi ces partis quelques-uns furent des mouvements interterritoriaux, comme les partis socialistes regroupés plus tard dans le *Mouvement socialiste africain*, mais le principal de ces mouvements fut le *Rassemblement démocratique africain* (R.D.A.). Il fut créé en 1946 à l'instigation du Bloc démocratique de Côte-d'Ivoire et du P.C.F. : sept députés africains lancèrent à Paris un manifeste où l'inspiration marxiste était évidente. Rejetant le fédéralisme, «qui n'est qu'une chape de plomb pour l'originalité africaine», il prônait «l'émancipation du joug colonial», c'est-à-dire l'indépendance et «l'adhésion librement consentie à une Union française des peuples démocratiques». Au congrès de Bamako (19-21 octobre 1946) fut fondé un parti qui entendait rassembler tous les partis locaux : le R.D.A. ne reconnut donc qu'un parti par territoire. Ainsi s'affirmèrent, comme sections territoriales, le parti démocratique de Côte-d'Ivoire, le parti progressiste nigérien, le parti démocratique de Guinée, l'Union soudanaise, le parti démocratique voltaïque. Les parlementaires R.D.A. s'affilièrent au groupe des compagnons de route du parti communiste qui les considérait comme membres d'un parti-frère. En août 1948, les leaders du R.D.A. expliquaient que leur option «pour le camp anti-impérialiste» se justifiait «par la victoire prochaine de ce camp, qui seule assurera l'émancipation de l'Afrique noire». En janvier 1949, le 2e congrès du R.D.A. «exprima sa foi dans l'alliance des peuples d'Afrique et du grand peuple de France, qui, avec à sa tête sa classe ouvrière et son parti communiste, lutte avec courage et confiance contre l'impérialisme américain». Le vice-président, Gabriel d'Arboussier, salua «les maîtres de la pensée prolétarienne et leur continuateur génial Joseph Staline». Le R.D.A s'implanta dans les masses en africanisant avec habileté les thèmes des communistes français, mais en exigeant aussi des adhérents les serments et les rites d'initiation à la nouvelle foi, conformes à la tradition. Le R.D.A. organisa une véritable administration parallèle, des tribunaux clandestins et des milices. Il se dota d'une presse qui célébrait le passé prestigieux de l'Afrique précoloniale.

L'Administration française finit par réagir en suscitant des partis qui dénonçaient l'alignement du R.D.A. sur le P.C.F. Le R.D.A. riposta en multipliant les incidents, les grèves, les marches de protestation. Des heurts s'ensuivirent avec les forces de l'ordre qui firent 21 victimes parmi les Africains en un an. Le P.C.F. et les États du bloc communiste lancèrent un campagne internationale sur «les horreurs de la répression colonialiste» assurant que «des milliers de dirigeants et de militants pourrissaient dans les bagnes français». C'est alors que, mesurant qu'on les poussait à une action de force ou à une insurrection, quelques dirigeants du R.D.A. décidèrent de rompre avec les communistes. Le président du Conseil, Pleven, encouragea Houphouët-Boigny dans cette voie. Dès le 8 mai 1950, les élus du R.D.A. se désapparentèrent des groupes communistes, mais certains militants refusèrent cette volte-face dans laquelle l'administration coloniale elle-même ne vit qu'une ruse. Elle réussit à faire battre beaucoup de candidats du R.D.A. aux élections législatives de 1951. Peu à peu cependant la réconciliation se fit : les autorités françaises appuyèrent discrètement la remontée d'un parti assagi, qu'un autre groupe, *les Indépendants d'outre-mer* (I.O.M.), contestait avec succès.

Sous la direction de Léopold-Sédar Senghor, les I.O.M., mouvement de cadres, fort de treize députés en 1951, lancèrent l'idée d'une République fédérale africaine qui serait elle-même reliée à une République fédérale (française) «une et divisible». Sédar Senghor espérait que cela hâterait l'émancipation des territoires tout en maintenant le rôle éminent de Dakar. Mais ce programme compliqué ne séduisit pas les masses. Le congrès des I.O.M., tenu à Bobo-Dioulasso en février 1953, définit bien la création d'un parti, mais celui-ci ne parvint pas à s'enraciner. Tout au contraire le R.D.A. majoritaire en Côte-d'Ivoire se renforça au Soudan et surtout en Guinée où Sékou Touré en fit un parti totalitaire. Aux élections législatives de 1956, le R.D.A. prit sa revanche sur les I.O.M., remportant 9 sièges de députés contre 6 aux I.O.M. En 1957, lors des élections pour les assemblées territoriales d'A.O.F. qui eurent lieu au suffrage universel total, le R.D.A. obtint 234 sièges sur 474. Déjà le gouvernement Mendès France s'était associé trois leaders des I.O.M. dont Sédar Senghor. Après les élections de 1956, le gouvernement de Guy Mollet obtint la participation, comme ministre délégué, d'Houphouët-Boigny. Le R.D.A. prétendra dès lors que ce fut grâce à sa présence que furent préparés la loi-cadre et les décrets d'application.

LA LOI-CADRE (23 JUIN 1956) ET SON APPLICATION (JUSQU'EN MAI 1958)

Dix ans après les réformes de 1946, l'impatience des élites africaines conduisit la France à préparer l'acheminement des populations de l'Afrique et de Madagascar vers la libre disposition de leurs propres affaires. Des urgences politiques extérieures, et surtout la guerre d'Algérie, en faisaient aussi nécessité. Pourtant les propositions d'hommes politiques français qui envisageaient une réforme de la Constitution et une transformation de l'Union française jouèrent un rôle moins décisif dans la préparation de la loi-cadre, que les projets de réforme administratifs : le ministère de la France d'outre-mer suggérait depuis longtemps une large décentralisation, au profit des assemblées représentatives des territoires. Le ministre Pierre-Henri Teitgen prépara en 1954 un avant-projet de loi sur les institutions de l'A.O.F. et de l'A.E.F. ; il eut le temps d'imposer une nouvelle loi municipale et de faire voter par l'Assemblée nationale un projet de loi instituant le collège unique et le suffrage universel. Mais le gouvernement fut renversé.

Le dossier fut repris par le nouveau ministre de la France d'outre-mer, Gaston Defferre. « Sachant que les populations d'Afrique noire ont les yeux fixés sur ce qui se passe en Afrique du Nord », celui-ci obtint l'urgence pour faire adopter une loi-cadre définissant les principes d'une vaste réforme, tandis que les décrets d'exécution étaient laissés au gouvernement. La loi du 23 juin 1956 accordait d'abord le suffrage universel et le collège unique à tous les territoires d'Afrique noire et de Madagascar. Elle prévoyait la réorganisation des gouvernements généraux — c'est-à-dire l'amoindrissement de leurs pouvoirs —, la création de « conseils de gouvernement » élus et l'extension des compétences des assemblées territoriales élues. Bref la loi créait des exécutifs dans chaque territoire d'outre-mer et augmentait les pouvoirs du législatif local. Enfin la loi-cadre posait le principe de l'africanisation des cadres, sous couvert d'une réforme des services publics et de la création de « cadres territoriaux » gérés par les autorités locales; elle s'engageait aussi à favoriser le développement économique et le progrès social.

Autour des décrets d'application qui s'échelonnèrent sur 1956 et 1957, la bataille politique fit rage, surtout en Afrique occidentale. Sédar Senghor dénonça la « balkanisation de l'Afrique, prévue par cette charte octroyée », tandis qu'Houphouët-Boigny estimait que « le pas en avant était considérable ». En France le parti communiste, qui redoutait lui aussi la balkanisation de l'Afrique noire, aurait voulu que des pouvoirs nouveaux reviennent aux grandes fédérations d'A.O.F. et d'A.E.F. ; celles-ci auraient pu imposer leurs vues aux futurs États. Mais sa stratégie échoua. Les gouvernements généraux disparurent au profit de « groupes de territoires », les Grands conseils de fédérations furent maintenus, mais leur rôle ne serait pas essentiel. Inversement les membres des « Conseils de gouvernement », qui reçurent le titre de ministres, obtenaient des pouvoirs réels, à parité avec les représentants du pouvoir central. Les « Conseils de gouvernement » restaient présidés par les gouverneurs, devenus « chefs de territoires », ou en leur absence par le vice-président, le conseiller africain élu en tête. Les Assemblées territoriales avaient un pouvoir de contrôle étendu et pouvaient contraindre tel ministre ou le Conseil tout entier à la démission. Quant à l'africanisation de la fonction publique, non réglementée par les textes, elle fut aussitôt mise en application jusqu'au moment où les gouvernements territoriaux réclamèrent tout à la fois de nouveaux fonctionnaires français, des techniciens et des crédits de fonctionnement accrus.

Avec la loi-cadre, la France entrait dans une ère nouvelle : *de facto* le fédéralisme s'était introduit dans les institutions, même si Paris refusait ostensiblement que cette transformation devînt constitutionnelle. Quant aux Africains, divisés sur la loi-cadre, ils étaient pourtant unanimes à ne voir dans ces réformes de structure qu'une étape : l'autonomie des territoires devait déboucher sur l'indépendance ou la constitution d'un État fédéral.

Les Indépendants d'outre-mer, devenus depuis le Congrès de Dakar (janvier 1957) un parti africain à vocation unitaire : *la Convention africaine*, demandaient que l'autonomie de chaque territoire fût assurée dans le cadre de deux États fédéraux, en A.O.F. et A.E.F. Ceux-ci pourraient être membres d'une République fédérale constituée avec la France et d'une «union confédérale des États» avec d'autres États indépendants. Le R.D.A., surtout celui de Guinée, était favorable à la création d'un exécutif fédéral à l'échelle des huit territoires de l'A.O.F., mais le P.D.C.I.-R.D.A. de Côte-d'Ivoire y était hostile, ainsi que la Mauritanie. Par ailleurs, la Côte-d'Ivoire et le Gabon souhaitaient leur rattachement direct au pouvoir central d'une éventuelle République fédérale franco-africaine. Pourtant tous les partis africains, à l'exception d'un petit parti africain de l'Indépendance (P.A.I.) créé en septembre 1957, tentèrent de se regrouper. Mais le R.D.A. en exigeant que le futur parti unifié se fît sous sa direction et son sigle, fit tout échouer en mars 1958. Un parti du regroupement africain (P.R.A.) fut bien constitué, mais ne put faire céder le R.D.A.

Pendant toute cette période (1956-1958) les positions des Africains se radicalisaient : les partisans de l'indépendance immédiate ou à court terme gagnaient du terrain, tandis que renaissait le rêve panafricain de ceux qui voulaient fédérer toutes les anciennes colonies européennes dans les États-Unis d'Afrique. Les étudiants africains en France, encadrés par des nationalistes de tendance marxiste, se montraient les plus violents contre la France, bien qu'ils fussent tous boursiers. Les syndicalistes rompaient eux aussi avec les centrales syndicales françaises : C.G.T. ou C.F.T.C. En avril 1956, Sékou Touré lança une C.G.T. autonome à l'échelle de l'A.O.F. : la C.G.T.A.; en juillet 1956 les syndicats africains de la C.F.T.C. se regroupèrent dans une Confédération africaine des travailleurs croyants (C.A.T.C.) ouverte aux musulmans aussi bien qu'aux chrétiens. Mais les cégétistes orthodoxes parvinrent en 1957 à refaire l'unité avec l'Union générale des travailleurs d'Afrique noire (U.G.T.A.N.) en dénonçant la loi-cadre et la balkanisation, et en se présentant comme l'avant-garde du combat libérateur.

La loi-cadre fut bientôt présentée comme imposant un «carcan étroit»; elle devait être dépassée. «En vérité elle était dépassée avant qu'elle ne fût votée» affirmait Sédar Senghor, «tous les partis politiques africains réclament l'autonomie interne et une révision de la Constitution dans le sens fédéral». Le 27 février 1958 Modibo Keita, pourtant membre du gouvernement français, ne craignit pas de dire, à Bamako, à son collègue ministre de la France d'outre-mer : «La France hésite, le temps passe. Les chances de construire la communauté franco-africaine diminuent chaque jour. Les événements vont plus vite que la reconversion spirituelle de certains hommes politiques français [...]. Si la France laisse échapper l'occasion de réaliser la communauté franco-africaine, l'Afrique, inévitablement, s'engagera sur la seule voie libre compatible avec sa dignité : la voie de l'indépendance. Le peuple, le Parlement et le gouvernement l'auront voulu.»

La classe politique française ne savait comment répondre à ces exigences : le fédéralisme proposé par les leaders africains était-il «la dernière chance de sauver l'Afrique française», comme le pensait P. Mendès France, ou le plus sûr moyen de faire éclater ce qui pouvait demeurer de l'Union française ? On parlait de révision de la Constitution et les projets se multipliaient. Mais l'opinion française ne paraissait pas prête à faire entrer la France, vieil État unitaire, dans une République fédérale ou une confédération multinationale qu'elle devrait financer.

L'INDÉPENDANCE DES ÉTATS SOUS TUTELLE : TOGO ET CAMEROUN

L'évolution des États sous tutelle, Togo et Cameroun, semblait déjà indiquer ce que serait le choix de la France.

• *Le Togo.* Après avoir refusé pendant des années de céder aux revendications des Ewés et de consentir à la fusion du pays avec le Togo britannique, la France, sous la pression du Conseil de tutelle de l'ONU, annonça dès juillet 1951 d'importantes réformes. Or celles-ci, qui prévoyaient l'autonomie, furent bloquées par le ministre de la France d'outre-mer, François Mitterrand, qui en redoutait le pouvoir contagieux. Elles furent reprises lentement entre 1952 et 1955 par des ministres modérés. L'autonomie fut enfin décidée en 1956 par un ministre socialiste.

La loi du 16 avril 1955 élargissait les attributions de l'Assemblée territoriale et instaurait un «Conseil de gouvernement», amorce du futur Conseil des ministres. Mais ces réformes furent combattues par le parti nationaliste le plus radical, *le Comité de l'unité togolaise* (C.U.T.) de Sylvanus Olympio, surtout représentatif de l'ethnie éwé. Battu aux élections par le *parti togolais du progrès* (P.T.P.), parti modéré, et par l'Union des chefs et des populations du Nord (U.C.P.N.), le C.U.T. boycotta systématiquement les nouvelles institutions qu'il dénonça à l'ONU. Cependant un plébiscite avait été organisé en mai 1956 au Togo britannique, qui se prononça pour l'annexion à la Gold Coast, devenue Ghana lors de son indépendance reconnue le 6 mars 1957. Cela mettait fin aux chances de la revendication des Ewés du C.U.T.

Le parti togolais du progrès (P.T.P.) de Nicolas Grunitzky, majoritaire, demanda l'abolition de la tutelle de l'ONU et la transformation du Togo en République autonome «en association avec la France». Le gouvernement français fixa alors par le décret du 28 avril 1956 un nouveau statut qui avait été négocié avec l'Assemblée territoriale. Il prévoyait une République autonome non associée à l'Union française : ce statut devait être soumis à référendum. Mais le Conseil de tutelle de l'ONU refusa de l'accepter et de contrôler un référendum qui ne prévoyait pas l'option d'une indépendance totale. Le nouveau statut fut néanmoins appliqué. La République togolaise fut proclamée le 30 août 1956, l'Assemblée territoriale devint l'Assemblée législative et Grunitzky fut nommé Premier ministre. Le référendum du 28 octobre 1956 donna 75,5 % de Oui parmi les électeurs inscrits. Cependant le C.U.T. avait donné des consignes d'abstention qui furent suivies dans le Sud.

Le nouveau statut du Togo, d'ailleurs modifié en mars 1957, puis février 1958, par le gouvernement français qui consentit de nouveaux transferts de pouvoirs, faisait de cet État une République autonome où seules la Défense et les Relations extérieures restaient aux mains de la France. Mais la double nationalité avait été consentie aux quelques Français qui y résidaient, ce qui permit à Sylvanus Olympio de déclarer à l'ONU que «la France avait annexé le Togo» et que les Togolais refusaient de reconnaître cette autonomie «consentie par une assemblée de moutons» dociles. Le C.U.T. en appela au Conseil de tutelle qui préconisa une consultation électorale menée sous son égide. Le gouvernement français de Félix Gaillard accepta en avril 1958. Les Togolais votèrent alors à 60 % des suffrages exprimés pour le C.U.T. qui écrasa l'U.C.P.N. (17,8 % des voix) et le P.T.P. (12,7 %). La population célébra *l'ablodé* (l'indépendance), tandis que les militants du C.U.T. réglèrent leurs comptes avec leurs adversaires politiques. Avec la France la situation se clarifia très vite : dès septembre 1958, et après négociation, la France fixa au 27 avril 1960 la date de l'indépendance totale. Par fierté nationale, Sylvanus Olympio avait refusé de s'associer à la Communauté.

Le Togo était indépendant sans que le rêve de Sylvanus Olympio, la réunion des Ewés, se fût réalisé. Surtout la victoire momentanée des populations du Sud sur celles du Nord empêchait la naissance d'une nation. En janvier 1963, Sylvanus Olympio, l'homme du Sud, fut assassiné.

• *Le Cameroun*. L'évolution politique du Cameroun, État sous tutelle depuis décembre 1946, fut rendue difficile par le manque d'unité du pays, les oppositions ethniques (on y parlait 90 langues), la présence de religions concurrentes (islam, protestantisme, catholicisme) et la multiplicité des partis politiques (84 en 1955). En simplifiant, on peut dire qu'aux partis réformistes ou ethniques s'opposait un parti révolutionnaire communisant, l'*Union des populations camerounaises* (U.P.C.), créé le 10 avril 1948 à Douala. Ce fut le seul de toute l'Afrique noire française à mener une insurrection armée de longue durée. Il revendiquait dès l'origine la levée de la tutelle de l'ONU, l'indépendance totale et immédiate, la reconstitution de l'ex-Kamerun allemand par la réunification avec le Cameroun britannique. Issu des syndicats cégétistes U.S.C.C., Union des syndicats confédérés du Cameroun, ce parti avait surtout une implantation ethnique chez les Basaà et les Bamiléké. Son leader, Ruben Um Nyobé, un Basaà membre d'une église protestante, avait été formé par la C.G.T. C'était un idéologue visionnaire, mais aussi un habile tacticien révolutionnaire. Après avoir lancé en avril 1955 une proclamation où il réclamait l'installation d'une Assemblée nationale constituante et l'institution d'un gouvernement provisoire de l'État camerounais souverain, il déclencha de graves émeutes en mai 1955 et fit dénoncer ensuite les «hommes de la répression colonialiste». L'U.P.C. fut interdite, mais ses chefs avaient «pris le maquis». Boycottant les élections, l'U.P.C. recourut à l'action terroriste, d'abord dans la région de la Sanaga maritime (où 95 Africains opposants furent massacrés en décembre 1956), puis en pays basaà et bamiléké en 1957 et 1958. Um Nyobé fut tué en combattant en septembre 1958, mais la «rébellion bamiléké» continua jusqu'en décembre 1960.

Le gouvernement français avait proposé en janvier 1956 à l'Assemblée législative camerounaise, désormais élue au suffrage universel, un statut d'État autonome. Celle-ci l'accepta bien qu'une partie des compétences de cet État restât sous direction française. Cette charte d'autonomie promulguée le 16 avril 1957 prévoyait aussi une fédéralisation de fait du pays en accordant à chaque région une assemblée. L'application en fut faite dans la légalité, mais fut compliquée par les rivalités des leaders : le chef de file des élus musulmans du Nord, Ahmadou Ahidjo, réussit ainsi à renverser le premier président du gouvernement, L. M'bida, un catholique (il devait devenir le premier chef de l'État indépendant en 1960 et le rester jusqu'en 1983). À l'initiative de l'Assemblée législative, le gouvernement du général de Gaulle demanda, en octobre 1958, à l'ONU la levée de la tutelle et l'accession du Cameroun à l'indépendance. L'ONU ayant accepté après enquête dans le pays, le gouvernement camerounais, qui avait signé en octobre 1959 un accord de coopération avec la France, mais refusé de faire partie de la Communauté «rénovée», proclama son indépendance le 1er janvier 1960. La nouvelle République naquit cependant dans le sang, les commandos de l'U.P.C. ayant lancé un raid meurtrier contre la capitale Douala. La nouvelle constitution fut soumise démocratiquement à un référendum en février 1960, et acceptée par 60 % des votants. Quant à la réunification des deux Camerouns, elle ne se fit que partiellement. Après un plébiscite, inspiré par les Britanniques et organisé sous la direction de l'ONU, en février 1961, le Cameroun britannique du Nord vota seul son rattachement au Nigéria, tandis que celui du Sud décidait de s'unir à la partie occidentale de la République qui devint la République fédérale du Cameroun, le 1er octobre 1961.

DE LA COMMUNAUTÉ AUX INDÉPENDANCES (1958-1960)

L'Afrique noire, qui pensait devoir arracher par la violence son indépendance, fut surprise par l'institution de la Communauté. De Gaulle, en offrant aux Africains et aux Malgaches le choix entre une libre association et la sécession, obligea les leaders politiques à réfléchir aux inconvénients d'une indépendance immédiate. Pour ne pas perdre l'aide financière et technique de la France, ils firent presque tous voter Oui au référendum constitutionnel du 28 septembre 1958. Les résultats furent un immense succès pour la Communauté conçue comme un prolongement de la République française, reposant sur un idéal commun et la solidarité des peuples qui la constitueraient : 7471000 Oui et 1121000 Non, dont 636000 pour la Guinée. Celle-ci avait voté négativement à 95 % sur l'ordre de son chef Sékou Touré. Dans les quatre mois qui suivirent la promulgation de la Constitution, les territoires d'outre-mer qui le souhaitaient purent par simple délibération de leur Assemblée devenir États membres de la Communauté. Préférèrent demeurer territoires d'outre-mer la Côte française des Somalis, les Comores, la Nouvelle-Calédonie, la Polynésie française et Saint-Pierre-et-Miquelon.

La Communauté — terme qui fut préféré à celui de Fédération (voire de Confédération) — c'étaient à la fois la République française et douze États : sept en A.O.F. (puisque la Guinée devenue indépendante s'était exclue), quatre en A.E.F. et Madagascar. Les États jouissaient seulement de l'autonomie interne. Relevaient des compétences communes de la Communauté, la politique étrangère, la Défense, la monnaie, l'enseignement supérieur, le contrôle de la justice, les transports extérieurs et les télécommunications. Les institutions de cette organisation originale s'apparentaient dès lors à celles d'un État fédéral. De Gaulle fut élu président de la République et de la Communauté; il était entouré d'un *Conseil exécutif*, constitué par le Premier ministre français, les chefs de gouvernement de chacun des 12 États et les ministres chargés des Affaires communes. On pouvait considérer ce Conseil comme la préfiguration d'un gouvernement fédéral. Étaient également prévus un *Sénat de la Communauté* et une *cour arbitrale*. La Communauté était en principe ouverte aux États dits associés, en fait aux anciens protectorats (Tunisie, Maroc, Laos, Cambodge et Viêt-nam) et aux ex-États sous tutelle devenus indépendants (Togo, Cameroun).

Les débuts de la Communauté semblaient conduire les États membres à former une grande fédération de nationalité française, dotée d'un drapeau tricolore surmonté à sa hampe de deux mains serrées. En réalité les critiques fusèrent contre cette évolution. Les Africains s'élevèrent contre le fait que les six ministres chargés des affaires communes fussent Français. Le secrétaire général de la Communauté leur apparaissait moins comme l'organe administratif du Conseil exécutif que comme celui du président. La présence sur leur territoire de hauts-commissaires, en qualité de représentants du président, était ressentie comme un vestige du colonialisme. Bientôt certains chefs d'États africains revendiquèrent le droit à une nationalité distincte et se dotèrent de drapeaux nationaux; trois chefs de gouvernement devinrent des présidents de la République (à Madagascar, dès avril 1959, puis au Congo et en Haute-Volta). Peu de mois après la naissance de la Communauté, la personnalité des États membres tendait à s'affirmer aux dépens de celle de l'État fédéral. À la fin de 1959 tous avaient leur ambassadeur à Paris.

Plusieurs des «Républiques fraternelles», célébrées par le président du Sénat de la Communauté, songeaient moins à l'unité franco-africaine qu'à la conquête de leur indépendance autour de la France. Certes Houphouët-Boigny croyait à l'avenir d'une fédération d'États égaux en droit et bientôt dotés de tous les attributs de la souveraineté, mais Sédar Senghor, les dirigeants du Soudan et de Madagascar avouaient que la Communauté n'était pour eux «qu'un passage, le temps de se préparer à l'indépendance». Sédar Senghor y voyait plus : le moyen de «restaurer les deux fédérations d'Afrique», puis une «nation négro-africaine». Lors de son congrès constitutif, le *parti de la Fédération africaine* s'était prononcé «pour l'indépendance des États au sein de la Communauté confédérale et la réalisation de l'unité africaine sur une base nationale». Le Sénégal et le Soudan tentèrent les premiers de regrouper les États de l'ancienne Afrique occidentale; ils y échouèrent et se bornèrent à former en janvier 1959, une Fédération du *Mali*, du nom d'un ancien empire médiéval soudanais. Quatre autres États de l'ex-A.O.F. (Côte-d'Ivoire, Dahomey, Niger et Haute-Volta) se dotèrent d'un *Comité d'entente* dont les attributions furent essentiellement économiques et diplomatiques. De leur côté trois des États membres de l'ex-A.E.F. se regroupèrent dans une Union des Républiques de l'Afrique centrale qui ne constituait cependant pas un État (Congo, Oubangui-Chari devenu République centrafricaine, et Tchad). Le Gabon et la Mauritanie restèrent à l'écart de ces tentatives de regroupement.

Le premier, l'État du Mali, réclama son indépendance le 28 septembre 1959. De Gaulle, contre l'avis d'Houphouët-Boigny, ne jugea pas politique de s'y opposer. À son avis l'indépendance pouvait être obtenue sans référendum organisé par la Communauté, dès lors qu'elle l'était à l'amiable et s'accompagnait d'accords de coopération. La République française et le Mali pourraient donc continuer à coopérer au sein de la Communauté. Des négociations s'ouvrirent avec le Mali et avec Madagascar qui avait présenté la même demande. L'heureux aboutissement de ces discussions conduisit à une modification du titre XII de la Constitution qui ne prévoyait pas qu'un État indépendant pût rester dans la Communauté. Elle fut obtenue par un vote du Parlement et du Sénat de la Communauté en mai et juin 1960. On crut devoir parler à Paris de «*Communauté rénovée*»; en fait les accords de coopération avec le Mali prévoyaient une transformation significative des institutions à caractère fédéral, et annonçaient la dislocation de la Communauté constitutionnelle. L'indépendance du Mali fut solennellement proclamée le 20 juin 1960, celle de la République de Madagascar le 26 juin. Les dix accords de coopération étaient pratiquement semblables pour les deux pays. La France s'engageait à apporter son aide pour le développement, par l'octroi de concours financiers, la fourniture d'équipements, l'envoi d'experts et de techniciens. Il était prévu que le Mali coûterait plus cher à la France après son indépendance qu'avant celle-ci.

Les négociations engagées ultérieurement avec les États de l'ancienne Afrique équatoriale française se déroulèrent de façon analogue. Après la signature des accords de transfert des compétences communes et d'accords de coopération, les proclamations des indépendances eurent lieu le 11 août pour le Tchad, le 13 pour la République centrafricaine, le 15 pour le Congo, le 17 pour le Gabon. Ces quatre États continuaient à faire partie de la Communauté et trois d'entre eux consentaient à la France un accord de défense plus complet que ceux acceptés par le Mali et Madagascar.

Il en alla différemment avec les quatre pays de l'Entente. Leurs chefs d'État, mais surtout celui de la Côte-d'Ivoire, Houphouët-Boigny, qui avait cru à une Communauté franco-africaine durable, s'indignèrent publiquement que de Gaulle eût cédé à leurs adversaires sénégalais et soudanais, permettant à ceux-ci de faire figure, comme Sékou Touré, de héros de l'indépendance. Pour eux la négociation aurait dû être menée avec la Communauté tout entière. Par dépit ils vinrent annoncer au président de Gaulle, le 3 juin 1960, leur volonté de proclamer leur indépendance, sans négociation concomitante d'accords de coopération. Ils se considéraient comme sortis de la Communauté et fixèrent unilatéralement les dates et le cérémonial de la proclamation de leurs indépendances : le 1er août 1960 pour le Dahomey, le 3 pour le Niger, le 5 pour la Haute-Volta, le 7 pour la Côte-d'Ivoire. Ils attendirent d'avoir été admis à l'Organisation des Nations unies en septembre 1960 pour négocier lentement avec la France des accords de coopération qui n'aboutirent qu'en avril 1961. Ces accords ne mentionnaient aucune appartenance à la Communauté.

La République islamique de Mauritanie procéda un peu plus tard de la même façon : signature des accords de transfert avant toute négociation de conventions de coopération. Elle justifia sa démarche par la nécessité de se présenter libre de tout lien avec la France devant l'ONU, car son existence même était contestée par le Maroc. Elle proclama son indépendance le 28 novembre 1960, mais son admission par l'ONU fut retardée par un veto soviétique jusqu'au 27 octobre 1961. En juin 1961 elle s'était résolue à signer des accords de coopération.

Dès le 20 août 1960 la République fédérale du Mali avait éclaté. Le Sénégal, menacé de colonisation de ses services par les révolutionnaires soudanais, jugea plus opportun de se dissocier de Bamako. Les tentatives de conciliation menées par le président de la Communauté échouèrent et la France se résolut à reconnaître la République du Sénégal et son président élu, Sédar Senghor. L'éclatement du Mali, dont le Soudanais Modibo Keita voulut attribuer la responsabilité à la France, eut pour conséquence inattendue de porter le coup de grâce à la Communauté «rénovée». Le Soudan, qui garda le nom de République du Mali, se considéra comme «libre de tous engagements et liens politiques vis-à-vis de la France». Le Sénégal reprit à son compte les accords franco-maliens, mais ne fit plus allusion à la Communauté, «notion aujourd'hui dépassée», comme le déclara le chef du gouvernement sénégalais en mars 1961.

La Communauté avait fait place à un réseau de conventions bilatérales ou multilatérales entre les États qui y participaient. La France s'engageait à fournir à tous, dans des conditions adaptées à chacun, une assistance technique et financière, une aide militaire, judiciaire, éducative et monétaire. Tous les États unis à la France par des accords de coopération pouvaient faire appel au Fonds d'aide et de coopération, le F.A.C., obtenir des équipements économiques et sociaux, disposer de fonctionnaires et d'enseignants français, compter sur les appuis militaires nécessaires au respect de leurs frontières.

La décolonisation de l'Afrique noire et de Madagascar avait été pacifique et rapide. Elle avait débouché sur l'établissement d'une authentique solidarité entre la France et ses anciens territoires d'outre-mer. La Communauté, bien qu'éphémère, s'était révélée une utile institution de transition pour transformer les rapports coloniaux et les liens de dépendance imposés en pratiques d'amicale coopération. La Côte française des Somalis fut la seule à repousser, à deux reprises, l'émancipation qui lui avait été offerte par la France au référendum de septembre 1958 (malgré 25 % de Non) et en mars 1967 (39 % de Non); elle ne demanda et n'obtint son indépendance qu'en 1977 (deux ans après les Comores).

L'INDÉPENDANCE DE L'ALGÉRIE

LA GUERRE D'ALGÉRIE SOUS LA IVe RÉPUBLIQUE

Les Français furent surpris par le déclenchement, le 1er novembre 1954, d'un soulèvement en Algérie. La plupart d'entre eux n'avaient pas attaché d'importance aux émeutes du Constantinois de mai 1945, qui furent une tentative insurrectionnelle spontanée. Pourtant, de 1945 à 1954, les nationalistes algériens ne cessèrent pas d'envisager une guerre de libération. Ils mirent sur pied en 1947 une Organisation spéciale, l'O.S., forte d'un millier de militants clandestins armés. Liquidée par la police française en 1950, sa reconstitution fut tardivement décidée en avril 1953. Simultanément le parti nationaliste le plus radical, le parti du peuple algérien, connaissait de graves divisions intérieures nées de l'apparition d'un mouvement berbériste, qui revendiquait une Algérie algérienne, propriété commune des Arabes et des Berbères. Bien que

SUPERFICIES ET POPULATIONS

AFRIQUE OCCIDENTALE FRANÇAISE (1940-1955)

	Superficies (en km²)	Populations (évaluations)		
		1940	*1950*	*1955*
Sénégal	196 200	1 692 000		2 292 000
Mauritanie	850 000	347 000	525 000	573 000
Soudan (actuel Mali)	1 240 000	3 500 000	3 631 000	
Haute-Volta (Burkina-Faso)	274 000		3 100 000	3 322 000
Niger	1 267 000	1 903 000	2 100 000	2 326 000
Guinée	245 857	2 094 000		2 501 000
Côte d'Ivoire	322 500		2 400 000	2 450 000
Dahomey (actuel Bénin)	112 600	1 383 000		1 578 000
		Populations totales (évaluations)		
		1940	*1950*	*1955*
		15 336 000 (34 000 Européens)	17 000 000 (61 823 Européens)	18 735 000 (62 236 Européens)

AFRIQUE ÉQUATORIALE FRANÇAISE (1951)

	Superficies (en km²)	Populations	
		(évaluation 1951)	dont Européens et assimilés
Gabon	267 667	413 000	
Moyen-Congo (actuel Congo Brazzaville)	342 000	723 000	
Oubangui-Chari (actuelle Centrafrique)	623 000	1 098 000	
Tchad	1 284 000	2 248 000	

le Bureau politique en ait profité pour épurer le parti et renforcer son autoritarisme, le P.P.A. sortit au total affaibli de la dissolution de l'O.S. et de la crise berbériste. Ainsi s'expliquent la scission du parti en juillet 1954 et le retard relatif des Algériens à se lancer dans la lutte indépendantiste. Cependant la défaite française de Diên Biên Phu convainquit certains de la nécessité d'agir. Un petit nombre de militants issus de l'O.S., sous la direction des «9 chefs historiques», créèrent une nouvelle organisation, le *Front de libéra-*

Populations des territoires d'outre-mer (sans l'Indochine)

Estimations ou recensements 1951-1955

A.O.F.	Recensement 1951	17 361 700	dont 49 458 «Français de souche»
	Estimation 1955	18 735 000	
Togo	Recensement 1952	1 091 000	dont 961 Français
Cameroun	Recensement 1951	3 156 000	dont 10 249 Français
A.E.F.	Estimation 1955	4 767 000	dont 19 212 Français
Madagascar	Estimation 1955	4 740 000	dont 46 831 Français
Comores	Estimation 1954	169 000	
Somalis	Estimation	62 800	
Nouvelle-Calédonie	Estimation	62 900	
Nouvelles-Hébrides	Estimation	50 500	
Établissements français d'Océanie	Recensement 1951	62 700	
St-Pierre-et-Miquelon		23 000	
Total T.O.M. selon estimation officielle 1955 : 32 901 500 dont 157 483 «Français de souche».			

tion nationale, le F.L.N. Le 1er novembre 1954 celui-ci donna le signal de l'insurrection par une trentaine d'attentats et lança une proclamation par laquelle il réclamait «la restauration de l'État algérien, État souverain, démocratique et social dans le cadre des principes islamiques». Le vieux chef du P.P.A., Messali Hadj, refusa de reconnaître ce pouvoir illégal et fonda le *Mouvement national algérien* (M.N.A.) irréductible adversaire du F.L.N.

Le gouvernement français, dirigé alors par Pierre Mendès France, réagit en envoyant des troupes en Algérie et le ministre François Mitterrand annonça que «tous les moyens seraient réunis pour que la force de la Nation l'emporte, parce que l'Algérie c'est la France». Le gouvernement tenta aussi de bloquer l'insurrection par une politique de réformes qu'il chargea un nouveau gouverneur, Jacques Soustelle, de définir. Le ministre François Mitterrand se prononça pour une politique d'intégration que J. Soustelle reprit à son compte. Son programme était conforme à l'idéal républicain d'assimilation; il visait à réaliser «l'égalité complète des Français et des Algériens, à transformer les citoyens diminués de l'Algérie en citoyens à part entière d'une démocratie française». Mais les Français d'Algérie firent connaître par la voix de leurs élus qu'ils «fuyaient l'assimilation aussi bien que le séparatisme», et qu'ils refusaient le collège unique. Les réformes égalitaristes de la métropole ne leur apparaissaient que comme «le salaire du crime et de l'agitation inspirée et déclenchée par l'étranger». Cependant l'extension du terrorisme prit le 20 août 1955 un aspect dramatique avec les émeutes qui ensanglantèrent le Nord-Constantinois et provoquèrent la scission recherchée entre musulmans et Européens. Les élus musulmans impressionnés ou intimidés par le F.L.N. démissionnèrent en grand nombre, cependant qu'une soixantaine signèrent une motion célébrant «l'idée nationale algérienne».

En France, les élections législatives du 2 janvier 1956 ne donnèrent pas d'indication claire quant à la politique algérienne. Cependant la victoire des

Tableau chronologique de la décolonisation (Afrique noire - Madagascar)

	Dates de signature de l'accord bilatéral				
	Sur l'exercice des pouvoirs réservés, les transferts et la coopération gouvernementale	Portant transfert des compétences de la Communauté	Date de la proclamation de l'indépendance	Date des accords de coopération	Date de l'admission à l'O.N.U.
Cameroun	31 décembre 1958 31 décembre 1959		01.01.1960	13.11.1960	13.11.1960
Togo	25 février 1959		27.04.1960		20.08.1960
République Centrafricaine		12.07.1960 13.08.1960	13.08.1960	24.04.1961	20.09.1960
Congo		23.07.1959 12.07.1960	15.08.1960	15.08.1960	20.09.1960
Côte-d'Ivoire		30.06.1959 11.07.1960	07.08.1960	24.04.1961	28.09.1960
Dahomey		11.07.1960	02.08.1960	24.04.1961	20.09.1960
Gabon		18.11.1959 15.07.1960	15.07.1960	17.08.1960	20.09.1960
Haute-Volta		11.07.1960	05.08.1960	24.04.1961	20.09.1960
Madagascar		02.04.1960	26.06.1960	27.06.1960	20.09.1960
Mali (Soudan)		19.05.1960	20.06.1960	20.02.1962	28.09.1960
Mauritanie		20.07.1959 19.10.1960	28.11.1960	19.06.1961	27.10.1961
Niger		11.07.1960	03.08.1960	24.04.1961	20.09.1960
Sénégal		04.04.1960 22.06.1960	20.06.1960	22.06.1960	28.09.1960
Tchad		12.07.1960	11.08.1960	11.08.1960	20.09.1960
Guinée			30.09.1958		12.12.1958

socialistes qui avaient fait campagne contre «la guerre d'Algérie imbécile et sans issue» paraissait annoncer la reconnaissance de la «personnalité algérienne» et le rejet de la politique d'intégration. Leur leader, Guy Mollet, devenu président du Conseil voulut nommer ministre de l'Algérie le général Catroux, dont le nom était lié à la restauration du sultan marocain. Le 6 février à Alger, Guy Mollet dut capituler devant une manifestation hostile des Européens : il annonça que «les liens de la France et de l'Algérie étaient indissolubles». Le nouveau ministre «résidant à Alger», le socialiste Robert Lacoste, subordonna tout à sa volonté d'écraser le nationalisme algérien. Fort de pouvoirs spéciaux civils et militaires, disposant dès 1957 de 400000 hommes face aux 20000 *mujâhidîn* de l'armée du F.L.N., Lacoste crut pouvoir l'emporter par la force. Mais le F.L.N. obtenait d'incontestables succès politiques en se ralliant les hommes de religion (les *'ulamâ'*), les leaders nationalistes modérés, le parti communiste algérien clandestin et les étudiants algériens. Le président Guy Mollet, dont le programme s'énonçait en trois mots : cessez-le-feu, élections, négociations (avec les élus), discutait aussi secrètement avec le F.L.N. Mais les envoyés de Guy Mollet se heurtèrent de juillet à septembre 1956 à l'intransigeance du F.L.N. qui entendait obtenir le droit de l'Algérie à l'indépendance et la formation d'un gouvernement provisoire pour préparer des élections générales au collège unique. L'arraisonnement en zone internationale d'un avion marocain qui transportait cinq leaders F.L.N., interrompit les contacts.

Une semaine avant que fût inscrite la question algérienne à l'Assemblée des Nations unies, le gouvernement français présenta une loi-cadre le 13 septembre 1957. Ce projet, qui visait à morceler l'Algérie en territoires autonomes mais prévoyait le collège unique, fut condamné par les Français d'Algérie et repoussé par le Parlement. Le gouvernement Félix Gaillard s'employa à l'édulcorer par la création d'assemblées de communautés paritaires et réussit à faire adopter sa loi-cadre en janvier 1958. Le F.L.N. la rejeta dédaigneusement en la qualifiant de «prétention ridicule au démembrement de l'Algérie».

Le gouvernement tunisien avait proposé en vain, en novembre 1957, ses bons offices à la France en vue de «concrétiser la souveraineté algérienne». Le gouvernement français, exaspéré par l'action de commandos algériens venus de Tunisie, invita le gouvernement tunisien à pratiquer une politique de stricte neutralité. Ce dernier se saisissant d'un incident de frontière — le bombardement d'un camp de soldats algériens dans le village tunisien de Sakhiet Sidi Youssef — en appela au Conseil de sécurité de l'ONU. Pour éviter une condamnation prévisible, Félix Gaillard crut devoir accepter une mission anglo-américaine de «bons offices» qui travailla à internationaliser le problème algérien. Devant l'Assemblée, le gouvernement ne put justifier sa politique : accusé de «capituler devant les volontés des Anglo-Saxons», il fut renversé. C'était la vingtième crise ministérielle de la IVe République. Robert Lacoste annonça à Alger qu'on «allait à un Diên Biên Phu diplomatique» et abandonna son poste. Or l'armée écœurée par les politiciens craignit que le président du Conseil pressenti, Pierre Pflimlin, partisan de la négociation avec le F.L.N., ne s'apprêtât à lâcher l'Algérie. Cédant aux pressions des Européens activistes, qui réclamaient «l'armée au pouvoir» et s'emparaient le 13 mai des bâtiments du gouvernement général à Alger, le général Massu prit la tête d'un Comité de salut public insurrectionnel. Mais la révolution algéroise aboutissait à l'investiture de Pflimlin et à un sursaut de défense républicaine. C'est alors que, pour éviter une guerre civile, le général de Gaulle annonça le 15 mai, qu'il était prêt à assumer les pouvoirs de la République et le 27 qu'il entamait «le processus régulier nécessaire à l'établissement d'un gouvernement républicain capable d'assurer l'unité et l'indépendance du pays». Investi dans les formes constitutionnelles, de Gaulle fut accepté par la classe politique comme le recours nécessaire : 68 % des Français interrogés par sondage partageaient cet avis.

LA GUERRE D'ALGÉRIE SOUS LA Ve RÉPUBLIQUE

Les militaires et les Européens d'Algérie triomphaient; ils s'imaginèrent à tort que de Gaulle ferait leur politique. Or ce dernier leur signifia très vite par son refus du slogan d'intégration qu'il n'était pas leur prisonnier. De Gaulle promettait à l'Algérie le statut d'État associé et «une place de choix dans la Communauté» et lui traçait par le plan de Constantine, un avenir économique et social. Selon lui, le Oui massif au référendum de septembre 1958 (96,5 % de Oui) permettait «aux Algériens et aux Métropolitains de construire ensemble l'avenir». Mais le F.L.N. refusa la «paix des braves», car il redoutait que les négociations ne portent que sur le cessez-le-feu. Dès lors la guerre s'intensifia sous le commandement du général Challe. Celui-ci entreprit à l'intérieur d'un pays désormais étanche aux infiltrations d'armes et de commandos, la destruction des *Katibas* (compagnies) de l'A.L.N. Mené avec des forces opérationnelles considérables, successivement déplacées d'Ouest en Est, ce ratissage aboutit à l'éclatement du potentiel militaire algérien. Pour détruire l'encadrement politique des populations par le F.L.N., l'armée française procéda à de vastes regroupements des ruraux; des centaines de milliers de fellahs furent déplacés : plus de 2 millions entre 1959 et 1960.

Cependant s'était constitué fin 1958 un gouvernement provisoire de la République algérienne, le G.P.R.A., immédiatement reconnu par quinze États. Le G.P.R.A., conscient que la situation militaire de l'A.L.N. devenait critique, faisait porter tous ses efforts sur l'action diplomatique. Sa propagande rencontra une audience accrue, notamment auprès de l'ONU. Celle-ci, qui avait écarté de justesse en 1958 une résolution reconnaissant le droit du peuple algérien à l'indépendance, s'apprêtait à voter en ce sens à la session d'automne 1959. C'est en partie en raison de cette conjoncture que, après avoir éclairé l'armée sur ses intentions («l'ère de l'administration de l'Algérie par les Européens est révolue»), de Gaulle proclama le 16 septembre 1959 que les Algériens auraient droit à s'autodéterminer. C'était annoncer la fin de l'Algérie coloniale.

Tandis que la réponse du G.P.R.A. fut dilatoire, la réaction des Européens d'Alger se traduisit par la dramatique semaine des barricades (24 janvier-1er février 1960). Les émeutiers qui avaient tué quatorze gendarmes se retranchèrent dans des réduits symboliques pour obliger l'armée à se prononcer contre de Gaulle. Cette tentative fut un échec. De Gaulle s'efforça à nouveau dans «une tournée des popotes» en Algérie d'expliquer sa politique aux officiers hésitants : il entendait aboutir à «une Algérie algérienne liée à la

France». Le propos fut répété dans une allocution du 14 juin qui s'adressait surtout au G.P.R.A. Celui-ci, peut-être inquiet du moral des combattants — plusieurs officiers de la *Wilaya 4* avaient rencontré secrètement à l'Élysée le général de Gaulle pour préparer une trêve — dépêcha en France deux émissaires. Mais les pourparlers de Melun (25-19 juin 1960) tournèrent court; de Gaulle, sans doute pour rassurer les officiers, avait décidé qu'il ne fût question que du cessez-le-feu. L'armée put développer le thème : «La France offre la paix, le G.P.R.A. la repousse».

Cependant la voie des négociations directes semblait coupée. Pour faire pression sur le G.P.R.A., de Gaulle créait des commissions d'élus algériens et brandissait la menace d'appel à une troisième force; mais il parlait aussi à l'usage des Français d'une «Algérie algérienne qui aura avec la France une union étroite et féconde» et même de «la République algérienne qui existera un jour». Lorsqu'il annonça un référendum national pour briser les oppositions intérieures, le G.P.R.A. se méprit : il crut que de Gaulle entendait imposer un statut, en contradiction formelle avec le principe d'autodétermination. Or lorsque de Gaulle eut encore obtenu le 8 janvier 1961 «un Oui franc et massif» (75 % en France, 69 % en Algérie, mais en y comprenant les militaires et avec 41,2 % d'absentions), il fit reprendre des contacts officieux avec un G.P.R.A. renforcé par les manifestations pro-F.L.N. des Algériens. Envoyés à Lucerne le 20 février, puis à Neuchâtel les 5 et 23 mars, les émissaires français, dont Georges Pompidou, renoncèrent à exiger le préalable du cessez-le-feu. Les négociations officielles furent retardées par le déclenchement du «pronunciamento d'un quarteron de généraux» : Salan, Challe, Zeller et Jouhaud. Cette junte insurrectionnelle s'empara facilement du pouvoir à Alger, mais ne réussit pas à entraîner l'armée et s'effondra d'elle-même en quatre jours (21-24 avril).

Les négociations de paix ouvertes le 18 mai furent longues et difficiles. En Algérie l'O.A.S. soutenue par les Européens déchaîna un terrorisme systématique. En s'attaquant aux musulmans, elle voulait sans doute provoquer des représailles du F.L.N. et obliger cette fois l'armée à basculer tout entière de son côté. Simultanément elle essaya d'agir en France, soulevant la réprobation générale. À Évian, puis à Lugrin, les négociations achoppèrent sur la question du Sahara. Le désert brusquement valorisé par les découvertes de gaz et de pétrole était, selon les Algériens, partie intégrante de leur territoire national. Ils en firent le préalable de la négociation. Lorsque le général de Gaulle eut levé cette hypothèque, en reconnaissant la souveraineté de fait de l'Algérie sur le Sahara, le G.P.R.A. divisé ne parut pas pressé de reprendre la discussion. Il fallut la recrudescence des attentats O.A.S. et surtout les projets officieux de partage de l'Algérie pour que le G.P.R.A. passât des contacts secrets aux négociations officielles décisives. Celles-ci aboutirent enfin le 18 mars 1962 aux accords d'Évian et au cessez-le feu.

La France reconnaissait la souveraineté de l'État algérien sur l'Algérie et le Sahara. Les Algériens auraient à se prononcer par référendum sur l'indépendance dans la coopération avec la France. Les Français d'Algérie conserveraient leur nationalité avec un statut d'étranger ou deviendraient citoyens algériens : un délai de trois ans leur était donné pour exercer ce choix. La France maintiendrait en Algérie une armée de 80000 hommes pendant trois ans, conserverait des bases dans le Sahara pendant cinq ans, et à Mers-el-

Kebir pendant quinze ans. La France promettait d'accorder à l'Algérie une aide financière et technique privilégiée. Elle pourrait y poursuivre son œuvre culturelle. L'Algérie s'engageait de son côté à faire partie de la zone franc.

Refusant de reconnaître ces accords, l'O.A.S. intensifia encore ses violences. Poussant la population civile européenne contre les forces de l'ordre, elle provoqua notamment la fusillade de la rue d'Isly. Puis elle recourut à la politique nihiliste de «la terre brûlée», avant de négocier avec le F.L.N. une trêve des destructions et des attentats. Le seul résultat de ces violences, qui firent quelque 2200 morts et 6000 blessés en Algérie, fut de provoquer un exode massif des Européens. Redoutant la vengeance des Algériens, ils préférèrent fuir ce pays qui était leur patrie. Avant 1962, environ 150000 Français avaient quitté l'Algérie; 651000 partirent en 1962. À la fin de l'année ils n'étaient plus que 200000; en juin 1963, 150000 et en décembre 1964, 118000 y compris les coopérants venus de France.

LES PERTES HUMAINES PENDANT LA GUERRE D'ALGÉRIE

Il n'y aurait pas à épiloguer sur les pertes de cette guerre si elles n'étaient encore, trente ans après, l'objet de polémiques. Cette longue guérilla fut relativement peu meurtrière pour les combattants : les forces françaises perdirent du fait des engagements et des attentats 15583 tués et eurent 35165 blessés. S'y ajoutèrent 7917 morts par accidents et 1164 morts de maladies, soit un total de 24664 morts (dont 3500 environ étaient des soldats algériens musulmans). Quant aux Algériens de l'A.L.N., leurs pertes furent, selon les sources militaires françaises, de 141000 tués. Le G.P.R.A. fut dans l'impossibilité de les recenser, mais en 1974 le ministère algérien a dénombré 152863 combattants tués. Les populations civiles furent également atteintes. Les Européens victimes d'actes de terrorisme de toutes origines furent au nombre de 2788 tués, 7541 blessés et 875 disparus jusqu'au cessez-le-feu. Après le 19 mars 1962, 3018 disparitions d'Européens furent signalées. Au 1er janvier 1963, malgré 1245 libérés ou «retrouvés vivants», 1773 demeuraient « manquants », dont 609 avaient sûrement été assassinés. Fin 1964, le ministre de Broglie évaluait à 1165 le nombre des Européens tués du 19 mars au 31 décembre 1962. Du côté des Algériens les victimes d'actes de terrorisme commis par le F.L.N., le M.N.A. ou l'O.A.S., furent de 16378 tués, 13160 blessés et 13296 disparus avant le cessez-le-feu. Après mars 1962, on estime que plusieurs milliers de supplétifs furent exécutés par leurs compatriotes, de 10000 à 30000 (?) dit-on, mais on ignore les chiffres. La Croix-Rouge internationale recensa seulement le nombre des *harkis* prisonniers : 25000 en 1964. En fonction de ces chiffres le ministère français des Armées évaluait à environ 180000 le nombre des Algériens tués pendant la guerre, chiffre que de Gaulle arrondissait à 200000. De son côté, le ministre du G.P.R.A., Krîm Belqacem parlait de 300000 morts.

Pourtant la propagande algérienne a tenté d'accréditer, non sans succès, des chiffres très supérieurs : un million, voire 1500000 «martyrs du fait de la guerre d'extermination menée par l'impérialisme français». Ces affirmations ne reposent sur aucune donnée vérifiable et se heurtent à l'examen du recensement algérien de 1966 : qui peut croire que l'Algérie peuplée de 9 millions d'habitants musulmans en 1954 aurait perdu de 11 à 16% de sa population, sans que sa pyramide des âges en ait été entamée? On peut aussi noter que du recensement d'octobre 1954 : 8470000 Algériens musulmans «présents en Algérie» à celui d'avril 1966 : 11744000, l'accroissement de la population se fit au taux moyen annuel de 3,36%. En admettant que la population ait crû pendant la période de guerre à ce taux, elle aurait dû atteindre 10650000 en juillet 1962. Or le calcul effectué de manière régressive à partir du chiffre de 1966 aboutit à une population de 10416000 pour 1962. Le déficit des populations serait donc de 234000. Si l'on applique la même méthode au nombre total des Algériens, émigrés en Europe compris, le déficit de la période de guerre atteint 203000. Ces chiffres sont des ordres de grandeur fiables. Ils comprennent les 153000 «combattants civils ou militaires» du F.L.N. nommément recensés comme *chouhadâ* («martyrs», morts pour la patrie) et les victimes indirectes de la guerre. Ajoutons qu'un historien ne doit pas comptabiliser parmi les «pertes de la guerre», les 161200 Algériens qui installés en France choisirent la nationalité française. Mais le recensement algérien de 1966 les ignora légitimement.

LES FRANÇAIS FACE À LA GUERRE D'ALGÉRIE

La guerre d'Algérie ne fut pas ressentie comme un simple combat retardateur du processus historique mondial de décolonisation. Une partie de la population française, et d'abord les Français d'Algérie, vécurent cette guerre comme un drame national. Les partis politiques, les syndicats, les églises, l'armée, les intellectuels se divisèrent et souvent se déchirèrent en se combattant sur la question de l'Algérie. Certains Français, militaires et civils, tentèrent même par désespoir, de déchaîner une guerre civile contre leurs adversaires politiques : au nom de l'Algérie française, l'Organisation de l'armée secrète (O.A.S.) recourut aux assassinats, au terrorisme collectif et multiplia les attentats contre le président de la République.

La guerre d'Algérie fut dans toutes les formations politiques à l'origine d'affrontements internes et parfois de scissions plus ou moins durables. Les socialistes de la S.F.I.O. qui dirigèrent le gouvernement en 1956 se divisèrent d'autant plus profondément que leur parti, après avoir mené campagne pour la paix par la négociation, choisit de recourir à une solution militaire. Une partie des militants socialistes rejoignit l'Union de la gauche socialiste, ou créa un parti socialiste autonome. Le parti M.R.P. se déchira lui aussi. Si la majorité approuva, non sans réticences, la politique algérienne du général de Gaulle, une minorité influente défendit les thèses de l'Algérie française. Georges Bidault, ancien président du M.R.P., fonda un nouveau parti, la Démocratie chrétienne de France et plus tard tenta de dresser contre de Gaulle un conseil national de la Résistance, à l'imitation de celui qu'il avait dirigé contre l'occupant nazi. Le parti communiste connut également des tiraillements intérieurs : il entra en conflit avec l'Union des étudiants communistes et certains intellectuels, qui entendaient, disait-il, «s'aligner inconditionnellement sur les positions politiques et tactiques du F.L.N.» Il condamna ceux qui prônaient l'insoumission ou la désertion. Au total il parvint pourtant, au prix d'exclusions, à sauvegarder son unité, mais son influence en fut définitivement érodée. Au Centre, le parti radical-socialiste, déjà divisé sur la question tunisienne, éclata : les radicaux antimendésistes firent scission en octobre 1956 et constituèrent le Centre républicain. À droite, le Centre national des indépendants parvint à sauver son unité de façade, mais dut renoncer à donner des consignes de vote à ses électeurs pour le référendum de 1962. Sous la quatrième République les gaullistes dits républicains sociaux, exigeaient un gouvernement de salut public pour la sauvegarde de l'Algérie française. En 1959, leur nouveau parti, l'Union pour la nouvelle République (U.N.R.) fondé comme devant être «le parti de la fidélité absolue au général de Gaulle» connut ses premières défections, les «hommes du 13 mai» choisissant l'Algérie française plutôt que la fidélité gaulliste. En 1961, une trentaine de parlementaires U.N.R. avaient quitté leur parti. Pourtant les deux camps désunis qui s'affrontaient en France, n'étaient pas de la même force. Plus la guerre dura, plus s'affaiblit le camp des inconditionnels de l'Algérie française.

Les syndicats ouvriers éprouvèrent eux aussi des difficultés du fait de la question algérienne. Pour la C.G.T. la lutte contre la guerre d'Algérie fut surtout une occasion d'attaquer l'ensemble de la politique gaulliste, mais elle ne parvint pas à y rallier l'ensemble de ses adhérents ni les autres syndicats. Force ouvrière et la C.F.T.C. connurent eux des divisions internes et même la scission, avec le départ de leurs fédérations d'Algérie. Mais ce fut surtout le jeune syndicalisme étudiant qui souffrit des affrontements sur la question algérienne. L'Union nationale des étudiants de France (U.N.E.F.) en renonçant à l'apolitisme provoqua la création des deux fédérations d'étudiants modérés. Malgré son éclatement l'U.N.E.F. avait sans doute réussi à persuader une partie de la jeunesse que l'avenir du pays dépendait de la paix en Algérie.

La division des étudiants reproduisait celle des intellectuels engagés. La plupart des intellectuels de gauche, en réclamant la fin de la guerre d'Algérie, entendaient certes défendre le droit du peuple algérien à disposer de soi. Mais ils voulaient surtout en finir avec le colonialisme et «travailler en France à l'instauration d'une vraie démocratie» socialiste (J.-P. Sartre). En dénonçant les ultras d'Alger, les militaires qui usaient de la torture, les «fascistes de l'O.A.S.», ces intellectuels se sentaient les héritiers des dreyfusards et les défenseurs de la République. Dans le camp opposé d'autres intellectuels, qui n'étaient pas tous de droite, défendaient l'Algérie française, l'unité de la nation, le libéralisme qu'ils estimaient menacé par la subversion communiste et la civilisation occidentale et chrétienne agressée par le panislamisme.

La guerre des intellectuels fut une guerre de l'écrit, car ils ignoraient encore l'utilisation de la radio et de la télévision ou en furent écartés. Jamais autant de pétitions ou de manifestes ne parurent dans la presse, notamment dans les années 1956 et 1960. Le journal *Le Monde*, qui leur ouvrit largement ses colonnes dès 1956, publia à lui seul 67 manifestes de 1958 à 1962, dont 11 seulement étaient favorables au maintien de l'Algérie dans la République. Certains de ces textes firent date, moins par le nombre ou la qualité des signataires que par les réactions qu'ils provoquèrent. Le manifeste du 4 septembre 1960, dit des «121», qui célébrait l'insoumission, bien que très peu représentatif de l'opinion, souleva les passions. Il choqua profondément les milieux traditionalistes et l'Armée, tandis qu'il fut célébré par le F.L.N. comme «le réveil de l'intelligentsia française». Il suscita de nombreuses réponses, tel le «manifeste des intellectuels français» signé par quelque 340 personnalités dont le maréchal Juin, mais ce manifeste n'obtint pas, semble-t-il, une grande audience dans la presse. Bref, les intellectuels jouèrent leur partie dans cette guerre. Mais leur rôle fut sans doute moins important qu'ils n'eurent tendance à le croire.

L'ÉVOLUTION DE L'OPINION PUBLIQUE

En revanche dans ce conflit algérien qui fut d'abord une guerre politique, où la partie non militaire fut plus déterminante que les opérations militaires, l'évolution de l'opinion métropolitaine peut être tenue pour un facteur essentiel.

Pendant longtemps, jusqu'au printemps 1956, les «événements d'Algérie» furent peu ressentis en France. Le rappel des 70000 soldats disponibles et l'envoi de près de 100000 hommes en Algérie, réveilla l'opinion en avril 1956. Interrogés par sondage sur la solution politique du conflit, 40 % seulement des Français se prononçaient pour le statu quo, l'Algérie «ensemble de départements français», et 33 % pour l'établissement de «liens moins étroits». En juillet 1956, 45 % des Français se disaient prêts à négocier l'indépendance, tandis qu'ils n'étaient que 23 % à croire possible l'écrasement militaire de l'insurrection. Le mythe de l'Algérie française qui rassemblait encore en 1955 la quasi-unanimité de la classe politique à l'exclusion des communistes, n'était pas partagé aussi massivement par l'opinion. Le pourcentage des Français partisans de l'Algérie française, qui atteignait 49 % en février 1956, décrut assez régulièrement en une seule année, tombant à 34 % en mars 1957. Bientôt, en septembre 1957, ceux qui pensaient que l'Algérie ne devait plus être un ensemble de départements français, l'emportaient dans les sondages et, parmi eux, 23 % des gens interrogés se disaient partisans de l'indépendance totale. Simultanément les tenants de la politique d'intégration n'étaient plus que 17 %. Pour la majorité des Français, il fallait donc négocier avec ceux qu'on appelait encore les rebelles : 56 % y étaient favorables en janvier 1958. Ainsi, à la fin de la IVe République, les partisans de l'Algérie française étaient-ils singulièrement moins nombreux que l'Armée et la classe politique ne le pensaient.

Aux lendemains du 13 mai 1958, les Français d'Algérie et les officiers s'imaginaient volontiers avoir fait basculer l'opinion française métropolitaine en faveur de leur politique d'intégration. Or en août 1958, 20 % seulement des Français se prononçaient pour l'intégration, 24 % restaient partisans de l'indépendance et 41 % estimaient qu'on en viendrait nécessairement à cette solution.

Divisée, l'opinion l'était depuis longtemps selon des critères politiques et sociologiques. En juillet 1957 par exemple, se disaient favorables à l'indépendance, de préférence à l'écrasement par la force, 89 % des électeurs communistes, 43 % des électeurs radicaux, 35 % de ceux du M.R.P., 31 % de ceux de la S.F.I.O. et 19 % des électeurs de droite. Du point de vue des groupes sociaux, les opinions se répartissaient de manière prévisible. La tendance favorable à l'Algérie française s'accroissait au fur et à mesure qu'on s'élevait dans l'échelle sociale, mais les cadres et les membres des professions libérales étaient aussi proportionnellement les plus nombreux à reconnaître que l'intégration souhaitable était une solution impossible (36 %

contre 26 % de la moyenne nationale). De manière plus inattendue les sondages montrent qu'il n'y avait aucun conflit de générations sur la question.

Les Français avaient espéré que de Gaulle apporterait très vite une solution de paix ; ils ne tardèrent pas à s'impatienter. En mai 1959, près d'un Français sur cinq estimait, en dépit des progrès de la «pacification», que la situation avait empiré depuis un an et 71 % des Français se disaient favorables à des négociations avec le F.L.N. Ils approuvèrent dès lors de Gaulle d'avoir proclamé le droit des Algériens à l'autodétermination : ils n'étaient plus en décembre 1959 que 18 % à se déclarer opposés «à des négociations avec le F.L.N. sur le référendum d'autodétermination» et, en mars 1960, seuls 10 % d'entre eux rejetaient la solution d'une «Algérie algérienne» contre 64 % qui la trouvaient bonne. Le référendum du 8 janvier 1961 montra que 75,2 % des suffrages exprimés approuvaient la politique d'autodétermination.

L'opinion des Français d'Algérie qui ne peut être connue, faute de sondages, se manifesta assez clairement lors de ce référendum. Alors que le pourcentage de Non par rapport aux inscrits fut de 17,1 % pour l'Algérie, on en recensa 31 % dans le département d'Alger, 33 % dans celui d'Oran (les Européens constituaient environ 35 % de la population de ces deux départements). L'opinion métropolitaine manifesta ensuite dans un sondage d'avril 1961, qu'elle était favorable, à 78 %, à des négociations avec le G.P.R.A. Un mois après, 69 % des Français interrogés répondaient que l'Algérie serait à l'issue de la paix, un État indépendant et en août 1961, 4 % seulement s'affirmaient encore pour l'Algérie française.

Les Français de la métropole se félicitèrent donc des accords d'Évian : 82 % se disaient satisfaits, 8 % mécontents, 10 % indifférents. L'affirmation courante selon laquelle les Français étaient sortis de cette guerre comme ils y étaient entrés, avec indifférence, apparaît totalement erronée. Aussi bien au référendum d'avril 1962, 90,7 % des suffrages exprimés approuvèrent les accords d'Évian. Les sondages ont le mérite de démontrer ce qui passa inaperçu à la plupart des contemporains : la résignation présomptive des Français à la perte de l'Algérie. Dès 1957 la majorité des Français penchaient pour une solution d'autonomie, dès 1959 pour l'indépendance. On s'explique mieux dès lors l'échec des partisans de l'Algérie française. La grande force du général de Gaulle fut d'avoir su s'appuyer sur la majorité silencieuse du peuple français. Il put ainsi imposer sa politique de décolonisation malgré la critique constante des partis, les réticences des élites et l'opposition de l'Armée.

Prise dans son ensemble, la population métropolitaine n'eut pas le sentiment d'une défaite humiliante en reconnaissant l'indépendance de l'Algérie. L'armée française victorieuse sur le terrain n'avait pas été battue comme en Indochine. Les dirigeants français n'avaient pas été contraints de subir un scrutin d'autodétermination imposé par les grandes puissances et éventuellement contrôlé par l'ONU. L'économie française ne subit nul dommage, du moins jusqu'à la nationalisation des pétroles et gaz algériens, et tira au contraire profit de l'arrivée d'un million de rapatriés. Ces derniers seuls expriment encore aujourd'hui leur nostalgie et pour certains leur ressentiment contre les «bradeurs» de l'Algérie française. Pourtant quels qu'eussent été ses dirigeants, jamais la France n'aurait pu mener à terme la francisation de l'Algérie par une guerre engagée à l'âge de la décolonisation contre un nationalisme arabe.

5 *Après la décolonisation*

DE LA DÉCOLONISATION À LA COOPÉRATION

La décolonisation ne devait pas aux yeux du général de Gaulle être ressentie comme une fatalité du destin historique, moins encore comme un échec de la France. Pour lui la colonisation française, lumières et ombres confondues, se traduisait par un «solde largement positif». Encore fallait-il que le bilan de la décolonisation apparût aux Français comme aussi satisfaisant. C'est pourquoi, dès son retour aux affaires, il s'employa à faire déboucher la décolonisation sur «l'œuvre nouvelle de la coopération». Celle-ci était le legs du devoir ancien de colonisation : «Nous avons une certaine responsabilité devant l'Histoire». La France ne pouvait abandonner ses pupilles au milieu du gué; c'était une question d'honneur. La France devait donc continuer l'aide financière, économique, technique et culturelle qu'elle avait consentie à ses partenaires de l'Union française et de la Communauté. Ce serait désormais «la grande ambition de la France».

Tout naturellement le Secrétariat général de la Communauté et plus tard le ministère de la Coopération eurent à veiller sur l'aide apportée aux États africains, y compris un jour à ceux qui n'avaient pas appartenu à la France, mais relevaient de la mouvance francophone comme le Zaïre, le Burundi et le Ruanda. Car l'assistance offerte d'abord aux amis de la France pouvait en principe s'étendre à ceux qui, même anciens adversaires, la demandaient, dans la limite des ressources de la France. Aussi s'explique par exemple la coopération avec les États du Maghreb, privilégiée avec l'Algérie, subsidiaire avec le Maroc et la Tunisie. Mais il fallut toute l'autorité du général de Gaulle pour faire accepter de ses ministres eux-mêmes l'aide financière massive accordée à l'Algérie. De 1962 à 1969, l'Algérie reçut en moyenne par an 22 % des crédits alloués par la France aux pays du tiers monde, soit au total 2306,8 millions de dollars en 8 ans, selon les experts internationaux (aide publique et privée à l'Algérie).

Cette aide généreuse, qui semblait pourtant continuer celle de la fin de la période coloniale, devait se révéler coûteuse. De Gaulle le reconnaissait : «Les 7 milliards de N.F. que nous prélevons ainsi annuellement sur nos ressources équivalent à plus de 2 % de notre revenu national et à plus de 10 % du montant de nos investissements.» Ces chiffres furent contestés. Edouard Bonnefous dans *Les milliards qui s'envolent* évaluait à 3 % du revenu national ce que la France offrait en 1961 aux pays d'outre-mer. Mais le pourcentage exact était de 2,41 % selon la source utilisée par cet auteur ou de 2,16 % selon les calculs du rapport Jeanneney-Nora de 1963. La presse affirma même que 10 % des recettes fiscales du budget métropolitain étaient versés en 1963 au titre de la coopération aux États d'outre-mer. En fait l'aide se montait en 1963

L'EFFORT MILITAIRE DE LA FRANCE AU MAGHREB PENDANT LES ANNÉES 1952 À 1962

(étude officieuse et calculs du service historique de l'armée de terre)

– Total des militaires de l'armée active (officiers, sous-officiers et soldats engagés) ayant servi au Maghreb entre le 1er janvier 1952 et le 1er juillet 1962, estimation en moyenne annuelle : (durée moyenne de séjour 3 ans)	96 060
– Total des appelés et rappelés français ayant servi dans l'armée de terre au Maghreb (1952-1962) : (pourcentage d'erreur 5 %)	1 342 544
– Total des appelés algériens ayant servi dans l'armée de terre française de 1952 à 1962 :	123 000
– Estimation des effectifs de l'armée de terre ayant servi en Algérie de 1952 à 1962 : (pourcentage d'erreur 10 %)	1 447 200

PERTES

L'armée de terre (non compris la gendarmerie) estime avoir eu : 1°) 13 601 tués au combat ou par attentats en Algérie, 296 au Maroc et 188 en Tunisie; 2°) 4953 décédés par accidents en Algérie, 298 au Maroc et 173 en Tunisie. Avec les décès divers (suite à maladie, rixes, suicides...) le total des morts aurait été de 21 287 en Algérie, de 949 au Maroc et 515 en Tunisie, soit pour le Maghreb : 22 751. Le nombre des blessés au combat ou par attentats serait de 23 966.

Ces chiffres établis en 1983 d'après les archives militaires et le bureau de l'État civil militaire ont été donnés comme pouvant comporter un pourcentage d'erreur de 5 %.

à 4 265 millions de N.F. sur un budget recettes de 91 277 millions, soit un pourcentage de 4,67 % (mais il avait été de 6,7 % en 1959).

Malgré l'importance de cette aide, des campagnes se développèrent en Afrique et en France contre « la faiblesse de cette restitution en comparaison du pillage du tiers monde ». Au Maghreb on dénonça dans cette politique la continuité de « l'esprit de domination » et la volonté de « maintenir l'emprise culturelle » de la France. Les communistes voulurent voir dans l'aide et la coopération « une ruse du capitalisme aux abois » ou une forme nouvelle de l'impérialisme (au sens léniniste) et réussirent à en convaincre beaucoup d'intellectuels dans les pays décolonisés.

En sens inverse, et parfois en réaction, se développa en France un nouvel accès de cartiérisme, à partir de 1964 surtout. « Attention ! disait Raymond

Cartier, la France dilapide son argent... L'aide aux pays sous-développés compromet la France de l'an 2000», et la presse antigaulliste de brocarder «les beautés de la coopération» en démontrant qu'elle était «un tonneau des Danaïdes». «Ne fallait-il pas, disait-elle, mettre d'abord en valeur la Bretagne avant le Dahomey», cesser de subventionner «la démocratie populaire de Ben Bella qui exige des milliards de Paris tout en expulsant les petits colons d'Oranie, après avoir confisqué sans indemnités leurs terres?»

Malgré l'impact provisoire de cette campagne de presse, les Français ne crurent pas que la coopération était plus onéreuse que la domination. Avec la croissance de l'économie française, l'aide totale de la France par rapport à son P.N.B. ne représentait plus qu'un pourcentage de 1,46% en 1963, 1,22% en 1966, 1,24% en 1969. Et l'opinion française resta fidèle à l'idée de la coopération, comme le montrent les sondages : 73% des Français la jugeaient nécessaire en octobre 1962, 52% en septembre 1964, 67% en novembre 1967.

LES CONSÉQUENCES HUMAINES DE LA DÉCOLONISATION : LE «GRAND REPLI» DES FRANÇAIS D'OUTRE-MER

L'une des conséquences les plus prévisibles de la décolonisation fut le retour en France de la très grande majorité des Français d'outre-mer. Elle surprit pourtant par son ampleur. Il est vrai que peu de métropolitains connaissaient le nombre, même approché, des Français qui vivaient «dans les colonies». Non compris les citoyens français des départements d'outre-mer, on évaluait en général vers 1954 leur nombre à 1745000 environ. La plupart étaient installés au Maghreb : 1565000 Français de souche et naturalisés (dont 990000 en Algérie - 325000 au Maroc et 250000 en Tunisie); 80000 en Afrique noire, 47000 à Madagascar, 30000 en Indochine et 23000 en Nouvelle-Calédonie. Or, si l'on met à part l'Afrique noire francophone et Madagascar, où résideraient encore provisoirement et selon des statistiques il est vrai peu fiables, environ 140000 Français en majorité d'ailleurs coopérants ou expatriés récents, on peut noter que la presque totalité des Français de l'ancien empire colonial sont venus se réinstaller en France. C'est le plus vaste retour de populations françaises attesté dans l'histoire. Si l'on rapproche le nombre des «rapatriés» français de ceux des autres puissances coloniales européennes (Belgique : 23000 rapatriés, Italie : 200000, Pays-Bas : 250000, Portugal : 600000); on doit même parler du «grand repli». Mais celui-ci ne fut pas une catastrophe humaine. Le traumatisme de la décolonisation n'empêcha pas les rapatriés (qui se disent expatriés) de se recaser, avec plus ou moins de bonheur. Cela contribua à apaiser leur ressentiment.

Non seulement le peuplement colonial français installé outre-mer s'est considérablement amenuisé ou a disparu, mais par un retournement saisissant de l'Histoire, de nombreuses populations autochtones des territoires de l'Union française se sont fixées en France. Parce que le nombre des réfugiés vietnamiens n'est pas connu (mais 22280 avaient la nationalité française en 1982), on pense d'abord aux quelque 60000 réfugiés algériens (notamment aux harkis) qui firent reconnaître leur nationalité française de 1962 à 1967 : avec leurs enfants, ils représentaient 140000 personnes fin 1968 et environ 400000 en 1988. Mais l'immigration maghrébine s'est surtout gonflée après 1962 (50000 Marocains en 1962, 441000 en 1982; 5000 Tunisiens en 1954, 190000 en 1982). On comptait en 1985 autant d'immigrés nord-africains que de rapatriés de souche française venus du Maghreb (1500000 Nord-Africains de nationalité étrangère selon le ministre de l'Intérieur sur 4448000 étrangers).

Ainsi apparaît-il que le développement de l'immigration nord-africaine et africaine subsaharienne (115000 en 1981) pourrait être une conséquence imprévue de la décolonisation. Le même phénomène se retrouve en effet en Grande-Bretagne, qui comptait en 1981 environ un million d'immigrés indiens ou pakistanais et plus de 500000 Antillais. Dans un pays comme la France où la démographie était relativement stagnante et la main-d'œuvre insuffisante, le «grand repli» des Français d'outre-mer et la poussée de l'immigration contribuèrent à développer les effectifs de la population active : entre les recensements de 1959 et de 1975, cette population augmenta d'environ deux millions et demi de personnes. Ce fut un facteur essentiel de la croissance.

LES CONSÉQUENCES ÉCONOMIQUES DE LA DÉCOLONISATION

Il avait été annoncé par nombre de politiciens et de pseudo-économistes que la décolonisation, notamment celle de l'Algérie «le meilleur client de la France», déclencherait une crise économique et sociale grave : «20 % de notre économie serait arrêtée (*sic*); un ouvrier sur cinq en chômage : le pétrole du Sahara perdu; deux millions de réfugiés à reclasser; misère, chômage, agitation, problèmes insolubles posés par l'afflux des réfugiés sans toit et sans pain».

Rien de semblable ne fut constaté. La France malgré le retour des rapatriés ne connut ni chômage (moins de 200000 chômeurs en 1964) ni accroissement démesuré de la consommation. Tout au contraire, l'économie française, comme libérée d'un écrasant fardeau de dépenses militaires et disposant d'une main-d'œuvre accrue, connut un développement assez remarquable (taux de croissance annuel du P.I.B. de l'ordre de 5,5 % en moyenne).

Certains techniciens de l'économie et des finances avaient pronostiqué à plus juste titre que la France, privée de certaines facilités commerciales et industrielles sur des marchés impériaux protégés, devrait moderniser ses industries archaïques, développer de nouvelles pratiques commerciales et redéployer ses échanges extérieurs. Ils ne se trompaient point et les résultats de cette nouvelle politique économique apparurent vite. La balance commerciale, presque constamment déficitaire avant 1959, devint excédentaire jusqu'en 1973, à l'exception des années 1968-1970 (du fait de la crise de mai 1968). Le déficit chronique de la balance des paiements, lié en partie à celle des T.O.M., disparut de 1959 à 1967; les soldes cumulés devinrent excédentaires de 4300 milliards. Certes tous les progrès économiques et sociaux des années 60 ne sont pas liés à la décolonisation, mais l'ouverture au monde substituée au « fardeau colonial », le commerce avec des pays industrialisés performants remplaçant les échanges immuables du troc colonial, la Communauté économique européenne l'emportant sur la zone franc, furent autant de facteurs du développement.

LA FRANCE ET SES DERNIERS DOM-TOM

Malgré la décolonisation des années 1958 à 1962, toutes les responsabilités coloniales de la France n'avaient pas disparu en 1962. Le mouvement de décolonisation s'est donc poursuivi progressivement par l'indépendance de l'archipel des Comores, reconnue le 6 juillet 1975, par celle des territoires français des Afars et des 'Issas, devenus la république de Djibouti, le 26 juin 1977, enfin par la transformation du condominium anglo-français des Nouvelles-Hébrides en État du Vanuatu le 30 juillet 1980.

Demeurent en 1990 de souveraineté française, des territoires qui ne sont point dérisoires, même si certains auteurs parlent de «miettes» ou de «confettis de l'Empire». Il s'agit des D.O.M.-T.O.M. qui comprenaient : premièrement cinq départements d'outre-mer : la Guadeloupe (1780 km^2 - 387000 habitants avec dépendances), la Martinique (1106 km^2 - 360000 habitants), la Guyane (91000 km^2 - 115000 habitants), la Réunion (2511 km^2 - 630000 habitants) et Saint-Pierre-et-Miquelon (242 km^2 - 6041 habitants), devenu en 1985 collectivité territoriale à statut particulier; et deuxièmement autant de territoires d'outre-mer : Mayotte (374 km^2 - 52000 habitants), Wallis et Futuna (255 km^2 - 12400 habitants), Polynésie française (4200 km^2 - 167000 habitants), Terres australes et antarctiques (440000 km^2) et la Nouvelle-Calédonie (191000 km^2 - 145000 habitants). La France d'outre-mer compte donc aujourd'hui encore plus d'un million huit cent mille Français, la plupart vivant dans les «vieilles colonies», considérées depuis le XIXe siècle comme de vraies provinces du sol national.

Dans certains départements d'outre-mer (Guadeloupe surtout et Martinique) s'affirme pourtant depuis 1950 une revendication autonomiste. Mais « la décolonisation des Antilles », réclamée par les communistes locaux et les indépendantistes, ne paraît pas être le fait d'une majorité de la population. Celle-ci a obtenu par les décrets du 26 avril 1960 le principe de la « départementalisation adaptée », qui permet notamment aux conseils généraux une intervention efficace dans les fonds d'investissement de la métropole. Elle réclame surtout une solution mieux adaptée encore aux besoins sociaux et notamment aux besoins de dignité. Les Antilles souffrent d'être des départements assistés, mais elles y gagnent un niveau de vie plus élevé que celui de toutes les îles de la Caraïbe. (Le P.I.B. par habitant était de 30830 F en 1986 à la Martinique, de 22020 F à Porto-Rico, de 2440 F à Haïti.) Il en va un peu de même pour la Réunion (P.I.B. 26000 F par hab.) submergée par sa poussée démographique et qui aspire à une aide toujours accrue. Enfin, la France constitue pour les populations antillaise et réunionnaise, un lieu de libre immigration : quelque 185000 Antillais et 120000 Réunionnais se sont installés en France. La «colonie» martiniquaise en métropole représente quelque 30 % de la population de l'île, la «colonie» réunionnaise 20 %.

POPULATION DES D.O.M.-T.O.M.

Départements d'outre-mer (1990)	Habitants	Densité au km²
Guadeloupe	386987	227
Martinique	359572	319
Guyane	114678	1,2
Réunion	597823	239
Total des D.O.M.	1459060	

Territoires d'outre-mer	Habitants	
Nouvelle Calédonie (1989)	164173 dont	44,8% de Canaques 33,6% d'Européens 8,6% de Wallisiens et Futuniens
Polynésie française (1992) 132 îles, 5 archipels (Marquises, Tuamotou, Société, Tubaï, Gambier)	200000 dont	104000 autour de Papeete (Tahiti)

Collectivités et Territoires à statut spécial	Habitants	Densité au km²
Wallis et Futuna (1990)	13705	53,7
Mayotte (1991)	94410	251
St-Pierre-et-Miquelon (1990)	6342	26,2
Total général des D.O.M.-T.O.M. et territoires à statut spécial	**1937690**	

AIDE PUBLIQUE DE LA FRANCE MÉTROPOLITAINE AUX DÉPARTEMENTS ET TERRITOIRES D'OUTRE-MER (EN MILLIONS DE N.F.)

ANNÉES	
1962	660
1966	1294
1970	1945
1974	2917
1978	5315
1982	9247
1986	11038

Les dépenses du seul budget de l'État pour les D.O.M.-T.O.M. se seraient élevés à 34700 millions de F en 1993.

VERS LA DÉCOLONISATION DE LA NOUVELLE-CALÉDONIE

La Nouvelle-Calédonie (19100 km² - 145000 habitants au recensement de 1983) est le seul des territoires d'outre-mer à attendre une décolonisation totale que la métropole après quelques résistances est prête à lui accorder à l'échéance de 1998.

Cette «libre province française du Pacifique», qui fêta en 1953 son centenaire de colonie, était alors sous-peuplée, en partie du fait de la faiblesse des superficies utilisables (15 % seulement de la superficie totale) et des spoliations foncières. 33000 autochtones mélanésiens, les Canaques, et 23000 Européens, dont une grande majorité de Français installés depuis longtemps, les Caldoches, y cohabitaient difficilement. Quelque 5000 Indonésiens et 4000 Vietnamiens complétaient cette mosaïque de populations dans un pays pauvre, «le Caillou», où la seule richesse était le minerai de nickel. Trente ans plus tard, après le *boom* du nickel, on comptait 42,6 % de Canaques, 37,1 % d'Européens, 15,7 % d'Océaniens et Indonésiens et 4,4 % de Viêtnamiens.

L'évolution vers l'autonomie prévue par la loi-cadre de 1956 ne se fit pas dans l'union malgré les souhaits du parti, majoritaire pendant vingt ans, *l'Union calédonienne* dont la devise proclamait : «Deux couleurs, un seul peuple». Sous l'influence du parti conservateur local, le futur *Rassemblement pour la Calédonie dans la République* (R.C.P.R.), Paris en revint progressivement à un régime d'autorité de style colonial. Le souhait d'autonomie devint dès lors unanime. En 1970 apparut le premier parti politique canaque et l'indépendance «Kanak» fut réclamée par un comité de coordination depuis 1975. Dès lors le parti de la libération «kanak» (*Palika*) créé en 1976, puis le Front uni de libération kanak (*Fulk*) et l'Union calédonienne regroupés en 1979 dans le Front indépendantiste entendirent «contraindre la France à décoloniser». Celle-ci, qui alla jusqu'à favoriser une immigration de Tahitiens, Wallisiens et Futuniens, en vint aux concessions. Elle accorda en 1976 un statut de large autonomie de gestion, en 1979 un plan décennal de développement et en 1981 une vaste réforme foncière au profit des Canaques.

Mais de 1981 à 1985, des troubles graves fomentés par les indépendantistes alarmèrent les populations caldoches qui abandonnèrent des régions entières et se replièrent dans la région Sud. Le gouvernement français fit adopter par le Parlement, le 6 septembre 1984, un nouveau statut d'autonomie interne avec référendum d'autodétermination prévu au bout de cinq ans. Il ne convainquit pas le nouveau parti, le F.L.N.K.S., *Front de libération nationale kanak et socialiste*, qui mit bientôt sur pied un gouvernement provisoire de *Kanaky* et développa une situation insurrectionnelle. Le délégué général du gouvernement annonça des propositions susceptibles de rallier une majorité autour de la promesse d'une «indépendance-associée» à la France, prévue pour le 1er janvier 1986. Mais le plan en fut aménagé et son application retardée par le gouvernement Fabius. La droite revenue au pouvoir en mars 1986 mit en place un nouveau statut d'autonomie qui ne prévoyait plus l'indépendance. Soumis à référendum le 13 septembre 1987, le principe du statut obtint 98,3 % des suffrages «pour le maintien de la Nouvelle-Calédonie au sein de la République», mais l'absention recommandée par les indépendantistes avait porté sur 40,8 % des inscrits. L'avenir de la Nouvelle-Calédonie n'était pas résolu et ne le fut pas plus par la loi du 22 janvier 1988 qui ne fut jamais appliquée du fait du retour des socialistes au gouvernement.

Il parut l'être après l'accord signé à l'Hôtel de Matignon le 26 juin 1988 entre les représentants des deux principales communautés caldoche et canaque. Le leader du F.L.N.K.S., Jean-Marie Tjibaou, estimait que c'était «la première fois depuis un siècle que les deux communautés ont décidé de faire un bout de chemin ensemble». La signature des accords le 20 août au ministère des D.O.M.-T.O.M., rue Oudinot, concrétisait la promesse d'un scrutin d'autodétermination en 1998. Les Néo-Calédoniens demandèrent que la France s'y engageât par un référendum national.

Ce référendum du 6 novembre 1988 se traduisit en France par une ample victoire du *Oui*, 80 % contre 20 % de Non, mais le taux record des abstentions (63 % des inscrits) et le pourcentage de votes blancs (4,41 %) montraient le peu d'intérêt des métropolitains pour cette consultation. Il est vrai qu'en Nouvelle-Calédonie 57 % seulement des suffrages se portèrent sur le Oui, et 42,97 % sur le Non. Or le R.C.P.R. et le F.L.N.K.S. avaient recommandé le Oui. Quelques mois plus tard les deux principaux leaders du F.L.N.K.S. furent assassinés par un extrémiste canaque le 4 mai 1989. Cependant aux élections provinciales du 11 juin 1989, le R.C.P.R. obtint 27 des 54 sièges, le F.L.N.K.S. 19, mais ce dernier disposait de la majorité absolue dans deux des trois assemblées provinciales. Depuis lors le calme politique revint. Au prix d'un constant effort financier métropolitain, encore accru en 1989, l'économie de la Nouvelle-Calédonie a considérablement progressé, mais cette perfusion financière pourra-t-elle être maintenue jusqu'en 1998 ?

Conclusion

Il est de tradition de parler des drames et des guerres qui auraient précédé ou accompagné la décolonisation française et de les opposer au processus pacifique de la décolonisation britannique, qui se préoccupait moins «de ne pas perdre une colonie que de gagner un membre au *Commonwealth*». Pourtant, on l'aura noté, il y eut aussi une décolonisation française accordée à l'amiable, «raisonnée et organisée» comme le demandait Mendès France en 1958. Cette décolonisation sans violences s'accomplit de 1958 à 1960 dans douze «colonies» et deux États sous tutelle d'Afrique noire ainsi qu'à Madagascar. Les États du Levant et les deux protectorats d'Afrique du Nord avaient déjà obtenu leur indépendance, au terme certes d'une crise politique et de quelques heurts, mais sans guerre de libération nationale. Pourquoi faut-il que cette série de décolonisations réussies soit moins célébrée que les décolonisations «arrachées dans le sang après des années de combat?» Le qualificatif de «décolonisation tragique», utilisé encore aujourd'hui par les auteurs communistes, ne caractérise en réalité que l'Indochine et l'Algérie. Encore pourrait-on considérer que la reconnaissance dès 1949 du Laos, du Cambodge et du Viêt-nam comme États associés, amorçait déjà un processus de décolonisation, dont la guerre froide seule empêcha l'issue pacifique.

Ces remarques ne visent pas à faire du «temps de la décolonisation» (comme il y eut le «temps des colonies») une période idyllique ou une époque glorieuse. Mais la décolonisation ne fut pas plus une page honteuse de notre histoire. Certes il eût été souhaitable de la faire accepter par tous comme une politique raisonnable. Les stratèges enseignent qu'une retraite en bon ordre vaut mieux que d'inutiles combats retardateurs. Or ce sont ces combats qui ont laissé le souvenir traumatisant d'une défaite en Indochine et même en Algérie, où il n'y eut pas de défaite militaire. Les deux guerres de décolonisation ne sont d'ailleurs ressenties comme des guerres perdues que parce qu'elles furent des guerres inutiles au regard de l'Histoire. Elles reposaient l'une et l'autre, au départ, sur des comportements passéistes et sur des erreurs de prospective politique. Mais elles ne suffisent pas à caractériser l'attitude d'une nation qui simultanément libéra sans combats, après autodétermination de leurs populations, quinze pays d'outre-mer en leur consentant durablement aide et coopération.

L'histoire de la décolonisation française tout comme celle de la colonisation ne sont malheureusement pas encore détachées de toute arrière-pensée idéologique et politique. Pourtant elles ne devraient plus avoir pour mobiles, avoués ou non, soit de développer un complexe de culpabilité chez les anciens colonisateurs, soit de condamner rétrospectivement «les fossoyeurs de l'Union française». La tâche de l'histoire de la décolonisation doit se borner à expliquer impartialement les origines et les diverses faces d'un mouvement qui balaya une grande partie du monde et n'a pas fini de faire sentir son action dans les derniers empires supranationaux (ex-U.R.S.S., Chine).

Chronologie sommaire

1918	9 janvier	Les Quatorze points du président Woodrow Wilson.
	6 mars	Manifeste du 1er congrès de l'Internationale communiste.
1919	25 avril	Création des mandats par le pacte de la SDN.
1920	avril	La conférence de San Remo attribue à la France un mandat sur la Syrie.
	juillet	Thèses de Lénine sur les questions nationale et coloniale au 2e congrès de l'Internationale (*Komintern*).
Avril 1925 à mai 1926		Participation des Français à la guerre du Rif.
1925-1926		Guerre dite des Druzes (Syrie).
1927	février	Congrès anti-impérialiste de Bruxelles « contre l'oppression coloniale et pour la libération des peuples opprimés ».
1930	10 février	Mutinerie de Yen-Bay.
Mai 1930 à février 1931		Insurrection populaire du « Nghê-Tinh ».
1936	9 septembre 13 novembre	Traité franco-syrien. Traité franco-libanais prévoyant l'indépendance dans un délai de 3 ans, non ratifiés.
1941	8 juin	La « France libre » annonce qu'elle mettra fin au mandat de la SDN sur les États du Levant.
1941	14 août 25 décembre	Charte de l'Atlantique. Le général Catroux proclame l'indépendance de la Syrie et du Liban.
1944	30 janvier-8 février	Conférence de Brazzaville.
1945	24 mars	Déclaration du gouvernement provisoire français sur l'avenir de l'Indochine.
	8-13 mai	Émeutes du Constantinois (Sétif-Guelma).

	18 juin	Charte de San Francisco (ONU).
	juin	Fin des mandats français sur les États du Levant.
1945	20 août	Proclamation de la République du Viêt-nam.
1946	19 janvier	Le ministère des Colonies devient le ministère de la France d'outre-mer.
	6 mars	Convention préliminaire franco-viêtnamienne.
	12-14 mars	Martinique-Guadeloupe-Guyane-Réunion deviennent départements français.
	11 avril	Suppression du travail forcé dans les territoires d'outre-mer.
	7 mai	Loi proclamant citoyens tous les ressortissants des territoires d'outre-mer.
	1er juin	Création d'une République autonome de Cochinchine.
	14 septembre	*Modus vivendi* franco-viêtnamien.
	19 décembre	Début de la guerre d'Indochine au Tonkin.
	31 décembre	Les derniers soldats français évacuent le Liban.
1947	29 mars	Début de l'insurrection de Madagascar (fin 4 décembre 1948).
	10 avril	Discours du sultan marocain à Tanger.
	20 septembre	Vote du statut de l'Algérie.
1948	5 juin	Accord de la baie d'Along (Bollaert-général Van Xuan).
1949	8 mars	Accord de l'Elysée (échange de lettres Auriol-Bao Dai).
	2 juillet	Bao Bai chef de l'État du Viêt-nam.
1949	19 juillet	Convention franco-laotienne : le Laos devient un État indépendant associé.
	8 novembre	Le Cambodge devient un État indépendant associé.
	30 décembre	La France transfère ses pouvoirs à l'État du Viêt-nam.
1950	29 janvier	Émeutes à Dimbokro (Côte-d'Ivoire).
1951	31 octobre	Le Premier ministre tunisien demande l'autonomie interne.
	15 décembre	Refus de la France qui affirme « le caractère définitif du protectorat ».

1952	février	Émeutes en Tunisie : ratissage du Cap-Bon.
	7-8 décembre	Émeutes de Casablanca.
1953	20 août	Déposition du sultan marocain.
	22 août	Traité d'amitié et d'association franco-laotien.
	29 août 17 octobre	Transfert au Cambodge des pouvoirs de la France en matière de justice, de police, d'armée...
1954	13 mars-7 mai	Bataille de Diên Biên Phu.
	21 juillet	Accords de Genève - Déclaration finale sur le rétablissement de la paix en Indochine.
	20 août	L'autonomie interne est promise à la Tunisie.
	21 octobre	Cession des comptoirs français à l'Inde.
	1er novembre	Début de la révolution algérienne.
1955	18-24 avril	Conférence de Bandoeng.
	3 juin	La Tunisie reçoit l'autonomie interne.
	juillet	Création du T.O.M. des Terres Australes et Antarctiques.
1956	2 mars	Indépendance du Maroc.
	20 mars	Indépendance de la Tunisie.
	23 juin	Vote de la loi-cadre par l'Assemblée nationale.
1958	2 octobre	Indépendance de la Guinée.
	14 octobre-8 décembre	Création et mise en place de la Communauté.
1960	1er janvier	Indépendance du Cameroun.
	27 avril	Indépendance du Togo.
	4 juin	Révision de la Constitution : la Communauté « rénovée ».
	20 juin	Indépendance du Mali.
	26 juin	Indépendance de Madagascar.
	1er août	Indépendance du Dahomey.
	3 août	Indépendance du Niger.
	5 août	Indépendance de la Haute-Volta.
	7 août	Indépendance de la Côte-d'Ivoire.
	11 août	Indépendance du Tchad.
	13 août	Indépendance de la République centrafricaine.
	15 août	Indépendance du Congo (Brazzaville).
	17 août	Indépendance du Gabon.
	19 août	Éclatement de la Fédération du Mali.
	25 août	
	11 septembre	Indépendance du Sénégal.
	22 septembre	L'ex-Soudan français devient République du Mali (indépendante).
	28 novembre	Indépendance de la Mauritanie.

1962	19 mars	Cessez-le-feu en Algérie - Accords d'Évian.
	3 juillet	Indépendance de l'Algérie.
1975	6 juillet	Indépendance des Îles Comores (sauf Mayotte).
1977	8 mai	Indépendance du territoire des Afars et des 'Issa devenu République de Djibouti.
1980	30 juillet	Indépendance du condominium franco-britannique des Nouvelles-Hébrides, devenues État de Vanuatu.
1985	11 juin	Saint-Pierre-et-Miquelon, ex-département d'outre-mer (depuis 1976) devient une Collectivité territoriale à statut particulier de la République française.
1988	26 janvier	Accord Matignon-Oudinot : un scrutin d'autodétermination pour la Nouvelle-Calédonie est prévu pour 1998.
	6 novembre	Référendum sur cet accord : 80 % de Oui en France, 57 % en Nouvelle-Calédonie.

Bibliographie

I) Colonisation et décolonisation : ouvrages généraux (ordre chronologique)

LABOURET (Henri), *Colonisation, colonialisme, décolonisation*, Paris, Larose, 1952.

DESCHAMPS (Hubert), *Les Méthodes et les doctrines coloniales de la France du XVI*[e] *siècle à nos jours*, A. Colin, 1953.

EHRHARD (Jean), *Le Destin du colonialisme*, Calmann-Levy, 1958.

VIARD (René), *La Fin de l'empire colonial français*, Maisonneuve, 1963.

GRIMAL (Henri), *La Décolonisation (1919-1963)*, A. Colin, 1965.

ROUS (Jean), *Chronique de la décolonisation*, Présence africaine, 1965.

ALBERTINI (R. von), *Dekolonisation – Die Diskussion über Verwaltung und Zukunft der Kolonien* (1919-1960), Westdeustscher Verlag, 1966.

YACONO (Xavier), *Les Étapes de la décolonisation française*, P.U.F., Que sais-je ?, 1971.

GUÉRIN (Daniel), *Ci-gît le colonialisme*, Mouton La Haye, 1973.

PAILLAT (Claude), *Vingt ans qui déchirèrent la France*, vol. 1 *Le Guêpier* (1945-1953); vol. 2 *La Liquidation* (1954-1962), Laffont, 1972.

AGERON (Ch. R.) (sous la direction de), *Les chemins de la décolonisation de l'Empire français*, Colloque IHTP, CNRS, 1986.

RUSCIO (Alain), *La Décolonisation tragique (1945-1962)*, Ed. Sociales, 1987.

Brazzaville, Aux sources de la décolonisation, Colloque IHTP, Institut Charles de Gaulle, Plon, 1988.

Histoire de la France coloniale, ouvrage collectif de THOBIE (J.), MEYNIER (G.), COQUERY-VIDROVITCH (C.), AGERON (Ch.-R.), vol. 1 *Des origines à 1914*; vol. 2 *1914-1990*. A. Colin, 1991.

PERVILLÉ (Guy), *De l'Empire français à la décolonisation*, Hachette, 1991.

BOUCHE (Denise), *Histoire de la colonisation française*, t. II, *Flux et reflux (1815-1962)*, Fayard, 1992.

MICHEL (Marc), *Décolonisations et émergence du tiers monde*, Hachette, 1993.

II) L'Union française et la Communauté

DEVEZE (Michel), *La France d'outre-mer - De l'empire colonial à l'Union française*, Hachette, 1948.

ESPRIT, *Dernière chance de l'Union française*, n° spécial, juillet 1949.

Divers, *La France d'outre-mer - Sa situation actuelle* (conclusion A. Sarraut), Plon, 1953.

LA NEF, *Où va l'Union française ?*, Julliard, 1955.

MUS (Paul), *Le Destin de l'Union française - De l'Indochine à l'Afrique*, Seuil, 1954.

BORELLA (François), *L'Évolution politique et juridique de l'Union française*, Lib.gle. de droit et jurisp., 1958.

GONIDEC (P.F.), *Droit d'outre-mer - De l'Empire colonial de la France à la Communauté*, Montchrestien, 1959.

GUENA (Yves), *Historique de la Communauté*, Fayard, 1962.

III) Décolonisation de l'Indochine et guerre d'Indochine

Devillers (Philippe), *Histoire du Viêt-nam de 1940 à 1952*, Seuil, 1952.

Mus (Paul), *Viêt-nam : sociologie d'une guerre*, Seuil, 1952.

Fall (Bernard), *Le Viêt-minh - La République démocratique du Viêt-nam (1945-1960)*, Cahiers de la F.N.S.P., A. Colin, 1960.

Isoart (Paul), *Le Problème national vietnamien : de l'indépendance unitaire à l'indépendance fragmentaire*, 1961.

Hémery (Daniel), *Révolutionnaires vietnaniems et pouvoir colonial en Indochine*, Maspéro, 1975.

Gras (général Yves), *Histoire de la guerre d'Indochine*, Plon, 1979.

Isoart (Paul) (sous la direction de), *L'Indochine française 1940-1945*, P.U.F., 1982.

Ruscio (Alain), *Les Communistes français et la guerre d'Indochine*, L'Harmattan, 1985.

Dalloz (Jacques), *La Guerre d'Indochine (1945-1954)*, Seuil, 1987.

Devillers (Philippe), *Paris-Saigon-Hanoi - Les Archives de la guerre 1944-1947*, Coll. Archives, Gallimard, 1988.

Tønneson (Stein), *1946, Déclenchement de la guerre d'Indochine*, l'Harmattan, 1987.

Valette (Jacques), *La guerre d'Indochine*, Armand Colin, 1994.

Ruscio (Alain), *La guerre française d'Indochine*, Complexe, 1992.

IV) Décolonisation de l'Afrique noire et de Madagascar

Siriex (Paul-Henri), *Une Nouvelle Afrique - A.O.F. 1957*, P. Plon, 1957.

Blanchet (André), *L'Itinéraire des pays africains depuis Bamako*, Plon, 1958.

Deschamps (Hubert), *Histoire de Madagascar*, Berger-Levrault, 1960.

Delavignette (Robert), *L'Afrique noire française et son destin*, Gallimard, 1963.

Brunschwig (Henri), *L'Avènement de l'Afrique noire*, A. Colin, 1963.

Mabileau (A.) et Meyriat (J.) (sous la direction de), *Décolonisation et régimes politiques en Afrique noire*, Cahier F.N.S.P., A. Colin, 1967.

Deschamps (H.) *et alii, Histoire générale de l'Afrique noire*, t. 2 *De 1800 à nos jours*, P.U.F., 1971.

Cornevin (Robert), *Histoire de l'Afrique contemporaine de la Deuxième Guerre mondiale à nos jours*, Payot, 1972.

Tronchon (Jacques), *L'Insurrection malgache de 1947*, Maspéro, 1974.

Benoist (J. Roger de), *La Balkanisation de l'Afrique occidentale française*, Dakar - Nlles édit. africaines, 1979; *La politique du général de Gaulle (1958-1969)*, Pedone, 1980.

Benoist (J. Roger de), *L'Afrique occidentale française de 1944 à 1960*, Dakar - Nlles édit. africaines, 1982.

Gifford (P.) and Louis (W.R.), *The Transfer of Power in Africa. Decolonization (1940-1960)*, Yale University Press, 1982.

Lisette (Gabriel), *Le Combat du Rassemblement démocratique africain pour la décolonisation pacifique de l'Afrique noire*, Présence africaine, 1983; *La Décolonisation de l'Afrique vue par des Africains*, L'Harmattan, 1987.

Hargreaves (John D.), *Decolonization in Africa*, Longman, 1988.

Michel (Marc) et Ageron (Charles-Robert) (sous la direction de), *L'Afrique noire française : l'heure des indépendances*, CNRS, 1992.

D'Almeida-Topor (Hélène), *L'Afrique au XXe siècle*, Armand Colin, 1993.

D'Almeida-Topor (Hélène) et Lakroum (Monique), *L'Europe et l'Afrique, un siècle d'échanges économiques*, Armand Colin, 1994.

Coquery-Vidrovitch (Catherine) et Moniot (Henri), *L'Afrique noire de 1800 à nos jours*, P.U.F., 4e édition, 1994.

V) Décolonisation du Maghreb et guerre d'Algérie

MAGHREB

Julien (Ch. André), *L'Afrique du Nord en marche*, Julliard, 1952.

Berque (Jacques), *Le Maghreb entre deux guerres*, Seuil, 1962.

Le Tourneau (Roger), *Évolution politique de l'Afrique du Nord musulmane (1920-1961)*, Colin, 1962.

Ageron (Ch.-Robert), *Politiques coloniales au Maghreb*, P.U.F., 1973.

Lacroix-Riz (Annie), *Les Protectorats d'Afrique du Nord entre la France et Washington - Du débarquement à l'indépendance (1942-1956)*, L'Harmattan, 1988.

MAROC

Taillard (J.), *Le Nationalisme marocain*, Cerf, 1947.

Bernard (Stéphane), *Le conflit franco-marocain (1945-1956)*, Bruxelles, 3 vol., 1963.

Cerych (L.), *Européens et Marocains (1930-1956)*, Bruxelles, 1964.

Spillman (général Georges), *Du protectorat à l'indépendance du Maroc (1912-1955)*, Plon, 1967.

Julien (Ch. André), *Le Maroc face aux impérialismes*, Jeune Afrique, 1978.

Oved (Georges), *La Gauche française et le nationalisme marocain*, 2 volumes, L'Harmattan, 1984.

TUNISIE

Perillier (Louis), *La Conquête de l'indépendance tunisienne*, Paris, R. Laffont, 1979.

Julien (Ch. André), *Et la Tunisie devint indépendante (1951-1957)*, Jeune Afrique, 1985.

Histoire du mouvement national tunisien, 6 volumes de textes commentés, Tunis, 1974-1983.

El Mechat (Samya), *Tunisie. Les chemins vers l'indépendance (1945-1946)*, L'Harmattan, 1992.

ALGÉRIE

Elsenhans (Hartmut), *Frankreichs Algerienkrieg*, Carl Hansen Verlag, München, 1974.

Ageron (Ch.-R.), *Histoire de l'Algérie contemporaine*, tome II, P.U.F., 1979.

Kaddache (Mahfoud), *Histoire du nationalisme algérien*, 2 volumes, Alger, S.N.E.D., 1980.

Harbi (Mohammed), *Le F.L.N. : mirage et réalité - Des origines à la prise du pouvoir 1945-1962*, Jeune Afrique, 1980; *Les Archives de la Révolution algérienne*, Jeune Afrique, 1981.

Droz (B.) et Lever (E.), *Histoire de la guerre d'Algérie (1954-1962)*, Le Seuil, 1982.

Pervillé (G.), *Les Étudiants algériens de l'Université française (1880-1962)*, C.N.R.S., 1984.

Stora (B.), *Les Sources du nationalisme algérien*, L'Harmattan, 1989.

Haroun (Ali), *La 7e Wilaya, La guerre du F.L.N. en France*. Seuil, 1986.

Rioux (J.-Pierre) (sous la direction de), *La Guerre d'Algérie et les Français*, Fayard, 1990.

Ageron (Ch.-R.), *Histoire de l'Algérie contemporaine (1830-1994)*, P.U.F., Que sais-je?, 10e édition, 1994.

STORA (Benjamin), *La gangrène et l'oubli. La mémoire de la guerre d'Algérie*, La Découverte, 1991.

PERVILLÉ (Guy), *1962 : La paix en Algérie*. La Documentation française, 1992.

AGERON (Charles-Robert) *et alii*, *L'Algérie des Français*, Le Seuil, 1993.

VI) La décolonisation dans le débat politique et idéologique

MEJAN (François), *Le Vatican contre la France d'outre-mer*, Fischbacher, 1957.

Chronique sociale de France, *Colonisation - Décolonisation - Sous-développement*, Lyon, 1959.

ROUS (Jean), *Chronique de la décolonisation*. Présence africaine, 1965.

MERLE (Marcel) (sous la direction de), *Les Églises chrétiennes et la décolonisation*, Presses de la F.N.S.P., 1967.

MONETA (Jacob), *La Politique du parti communiste français et la question coloniale (1920-1963)*, Maspéro, 1971.

GIRARDET (Raoul), *L'idée coloniale en France (1871-1962)*. La Table Ronde, 1962.

SORUM (Paul, Clay), *Intellectuals and decolonization in France*, North Carolina Press, 1977.

MADJARIAN (Grégoire), *La question coloniale et la politique du P.C.F. (1944-1947)*, Maspéro, 1977.

Mendès France et le Mendésisme, Colloque IHTP, Fayard, 1985.

CHATENET (P.), *Décolonisation*. Buchet/Chastel, 1988.

RIOUX (J.P.) et SIRINELLI (J.F.), *La Guerre d'Algérie et les intellectuels français*, Complexe, 1991.

VII) Questions économiques

MOREUX (René), *Principes nouveaux d'économie coloniale*, 1951.

LEDUC (Gaston), *Le Développement économique de l'Afrique noire*, Cujas, 1955.

MOUSSA (Pierre), *Les Chances économiques de la Communauté franco-africaine*, A. Colin, 1957.

POQUIN (Jean), *Les Relations économiques extérieures des pays d'Afrique noire et de l'Union française (1925-1955)*, A. Colin, 1957.

MOUSSA (Pierre), *L'Économie de la zone franc*, P.U.F., 1960; *L'Afrique et la crise des années 1930*, Revue française d'histoire d'outre-mer, n°s 232 et 233, 1976.

MARSEILLE (Jacques), *Empire colonial et capitalisme français - Histoire d'un divorce*, A. Michel, 1984.

JEANNENEY (J.M.) et BARBIER-JEANNENEY (E.), *Les Économies occidentales du XIXe siècle à nos jours*, F.N.S.P., 1985.

BONIN (A.), *Histoire économique de la IVe République*, Economica, 1987.

VIII) Les D.O.M.-T.O.M.

GUILLEBAUD (J.C.), *Les Confettis de l'Empire*, Seuil, 1976.

CHRISTNACHT (A.), *La Nouvelle-Calédonie*, la Documentation française, 1987.

CENADDOM, *Les dossiers de l'outre-mer*, 1986.

MATHIEU (J.-L.), *Les D.O.M.-T.O.M.*, P.U.F., 1988.

MATHIEU (J.-L.), *La Nouvelle-Calédonie*, P.U.F, 1989.

Table des encadrés et des statistiques

Table des matières

Armand Colin Éditeur
103, Boulevard Saint-Michel, 75240 Paris Cedex 05
N° 101057
Dépôt légal : novembre 1994

SNEL S.A.
Rue Saint-Vincent 12 - 4020 Liège
octobre 1994